D0176833

The Origins of

BOLSHEVISM

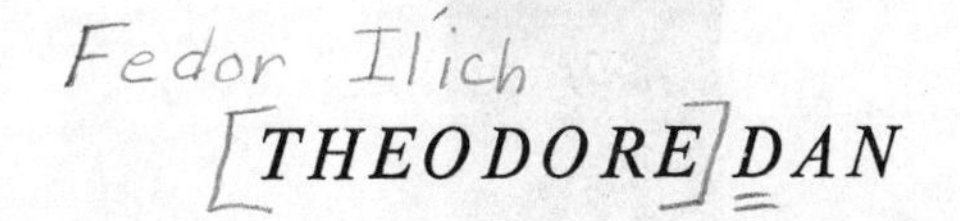

THEODORE DAN

The Origins of BOLSHEVISM

EDITED AND TRANSLATED FROM THE RUSSIAN BY

JOEL CARMICHAEL

PREFACE BY

Leonard Schapiro

SCHOCKEN BOOKS · NEW YORK

PROPERTY OF
CLACKAMAS COMMUNITY COLLEGE
LIBRARY

HX
312
.D333

First SCHOCKEN PAPERBACK edition 1970

English translation Copyright © 1964 by
Joel Carmichael
Library of Congress Catalog Card No. 70-123366
Published by arrangement with
Harper & Row, Publishers

Manufactured in the United States of America

Contents

23520

CONTENTS

A NOTE ON THEODORE DAN

THEODORE DAN (1871–1947) was one of the central figures in the Russian Revolution of 1917. A moderate Socialist who came into politics after being educated as a physician, his whole life was bound up with the Russian working-class movement from the time he moved to St Petersburg after his university education. Arrested after leading a weavers' strike, he was sentenced to one and a half years' imprisonment followed by three years of exile. After this he went abroad and became intimately involved in the affairs of *Iskra* ('The Spark') then being edited by Lenin, Martov, and others.

He was repelled by Bolshevism chiefly because of its amoralism, and after the split of the Russian Social-Democratic movement into Bolsheviks and Mensheviks Dan became and remained a Menshevik, playing a leading role in all Russian Socialist activities both as a writer and as an organizer. He was compelled to emigrate from Russia once again in 1907, and when he managed to return in 1912 he at once became the acknowledged leader of the Mensheviks, editing Menshevik newspapers and directing the Social-Democratic fraction of the State Duma. He was, however, arrested at the beginning of the World War and exiled to Siberia and then to Turkestan, where the 1917 revolution overtook him.

Dan hurried back to St Petersburg and at once occupied a guiding position (vice-chairman) in the most important revolutionary institution – the Soviet of Workers' and Peasants' Deputies; became the editor of the official *Izvestiya* and was a constant participant in the negotiations of the Soviet with the Provisional Government. He led the ruling bloc, made up of Mensheviks and Socialist-Revolutionaries, which sponsored the Provisional Government.

Even after the Bolshevik insurrection in October 1917 he still appeared a number of times in the Soviet Congress as representative of the Mensheviks. At the time of the Kronstadt uprising he was arrested and imprisoned for several months, and at the beginning of 1922 he was exiled permanently.

In Berlin and then in Paris he remained the acknowledged leader of the Mensheviks, especially after Martov's death. When the Germans took Paris in 1940 Dan came to the United States, where he continued his literary and organizational activities and wrote his opus, *The Origins of Bolshevism.*

TRANSLATOR'S NOTE

ALL dates are given in accordance with the Julian calendar, which is, for the nineteenth century, twelve days, and, for the twentieth century, thirteen days behind the Gregorian calendar now in general use. Exceptions are marked 'N.S.' (New style).

Pseudonyms were so common in the Russian revolutionary movement that Dan often gives them either in parentheses or as part of a hyphenated name.

The Arabic numerals scattered throughout the text indicate Bibliographical References, a list of which is to be found at the end of the volume.

The initials of various people mentioned will generally refer to the Russian form of their given names.

ACKNOWLEDGEMENTS

It gives me pleasure to acknowledge the invaluable assistance given me by the late Lydia Ossipovna Dan in checking the numerous details of her husband's work for which a library would have been inadequate.

J.C.

The publishers would like to thank Mr Boris Pasternak, his publishers – The Harvill Press, and William Collins Sons & Co. Ltd. for their kind permission to use an extract from DR ZHIVAGO for inclusion in the Preface.

Preface

BY PROFESSOR LEONARD SCHAPIRO

'This has happened several times in the course of history. A thing which has been conceived in a lofty ideal manner becomes common and material. Thus Rome came out of Greece and the Russian Revolution came out of the Russian enlightenment. Take that line of Blok's, "We, the children of Russia's terrible years". You can see the difference of period at once. In his time, when he said it, he meant it figuratively, metaphorically. The children were not children, but the sons, the heirs of the intelligentsia and the terrors were not terrible but apocalyptic; that's quite different. Now the figurative has become literal, children are children and the terrors are terrible. There you have the difference.'

DR. ZHIVAGO *by Boris Pasternak.*

I welcome as a privilege the opportunity of introducing this translation into English of the last work of the late Theodore Dan. Since its appearance in New York in Russian in 1946 this book has formed an important element in the education of those who have been trying to study and understand the political complexities of Russia as transformed by Lenin, and I, like many others, learned a great deal from it. If today, with the benefit of hindsight and armed with the results of the study and the publication of data in the past seventeen years, some of us may take a different view from Dan in this or that respect, it would be less than justice not to acknowledge the debt which we all owe him for having provided us with a framework and a point of departure for the study of Russian revolutionary thought.

What Dan set out to do, as he tells us, was to provide not a history of Bolshevism, but 'a history of its *origins* and *ideological* formation'. He has however done rather more than that. After all, Theodore Dan, though during the long years of his exile primarily active as a scholar, was throughout his earlier life a leading member of the Russian social democratic, or Menshevik, party. After Martov, whose sister, Lydia Osipovna, he married, and whose recent death has meant a tragic and irreparable loss to her many friends, Dan was for many vital years the leader of the Mensheviks. It was he who, on 25 October (7 November) 1917, presided over the Second All Russian Congress of Soviets which (after most of its socialist delegates had left) handed power over to the Bolsheviks. For five years thereafter, until he was permanently exiled in 1922, Dan was probably the most active among the Menshevik leaders in relentlessly opposing the methods of Bolshevik dictatorship – though always within the ever narrowing limits of semi-tolerated 'constitutional' opposition. It is natural that in writing about Bolshevism nearly thirty years later he should have posed the questions which every political exile must ask himself: Did we fight for the right cause? And why did we lose?

This book, therefore, is not only an important contribution to the history of political ideas. It is also a political judgement by a practical politician, reflecting in retrospect on the failure of the cause which he espoused – or perhaps one should say its temporary check. For Dan is above all concerned to argue that the ideals of Menshevism, though temporarily defeated, represented a permanent element in Russian social democracy which has only been temporarily eclipsed, and which is destined before long to reappear as an integral part of Soviet socialism.

It is Dan's main contention that Bolshevism was not an exceptional or accidental phenomenon in the history of the Russian revolutionary movement, but on the contrary, an 'historically inevitable stage' on the road to the consummation of the struggle for the liberation of the Russian people. Menshevism, as he sees it, was that element in the social democratic movement which looked primarily to the development of the working class as a revolutionary force. But Bolshevism with its organization and discipline, and its mobilization of peasant unrest, was the only force which could triumph, in Russian conditions, in 1917. It triumphed as a 'movement of emancipation' of an 'all-national' character. But this triumph was only feasible because of the preparatory work which the Mensheviks, not the Bolsheviks, had accomplished in developing the consciousness of the working class. Hence, Menshevism is, as it were, part of the blood-stream of Bolshevism, and from this Dan proceeds to draw certain conclusions for the future.

These conclusions are contained in a lengthy Epilogue. Viewing Europe in the immediately post-war setting of 1945 Dan sees socialism as destined to triumph in reaction to the defeat of Nazism and Fascism. In this process the Soviet example will provide the incentive. But the Soviet system in turn will undergo the influences of a Socialist Europe to become more truly democratic, more truly Menshevik, in a word. Thus the two elements of the Russian movement, like the thesis and antithesis of the dialectical process, will be resolved in a synthesis on a higher plane.

The Epilogue aroused considerable feeling among Dan's political colleagues at the time. Indeed, if read as an assessment of Stalin's régime of 1945–1946 it makes strange reading.

Its almost unqualified optimism on the nature of the Soviet régime, on collectivization, its reticence on facts which horrified the whole civilized world, may make some readers impatient. I would urge them to be more charitable. It was, after all, written at a time when optimism ran high among all kinds and conditions of men, both here and in the United States, that a new era was dawning in the Soviet Union. Many of the grim facts which have been disclosed about the Soviet régime have only been publicly admitted since the date when this Epilogue was written. The death of Stalin and the advent of Khrushchev have given us a new perspective both on Stalin's régime and on the potentialities of the régime of his successors for evolution in a more humane direction. Though it has not come about in the way in which Dan predicted, some humanization of the Soviet régime has, after all, taken place – though personally I should attribute that result to quite different causes, and not to the survival of Menshevik traditions in any more precise sense than the revulsion (sooner or later) of all normal human beings against terror, tyranny, injustice and intolerable conditions of living.

But the Epilogue is only a small, and not, for the reader, as essential a part of the book as it necessarily was to the author. Its main argument, together with that of the body of the book, on the inter-relation of Menshevism and Bolshevism is of interest and entitled to be heard, coming as it does from so prominent a Menshevik as Dan. To a non-Marxist it presents many serious objections. The victory of Bolshevism in 1917 was perhaps only 'inevitable' in the sense that, assuming all the actors in the drama, including the Mensheviks, behaved as they did, it became possible in October 1917 for Lenin to achieve his object of overthrowing the democratic régime which came into being in February 1917. The Mensheviks *could* after all, have followed the advice of Plekhanov and Potresov and have made it more possible for the Provisional Government to establish a stable régime, which *could* have taken Russia out of the war without the ensuing collapse. The Provisional Government, in turn, *could* have shown more foresight in realizing the importance of ending the war, establishing its own legitimacy, and disarming the Bolsheviks and their private army – and so on and so forth. There is nothing 'inevitable' in history except the fact that human beings behave in the manner which accords with their traditions, habits and preconceived prejudices. Or again it could be the case that the conception of a class dictatorship, which after all the Mensheviks accepted quite as much as the Bolsheviks, can only be exercised by some such means as Lenin and Stalin devised. The list of argument could be extended.

I advance these points not in order to sit in judgement on the Mensheviks – many of them fought and suffered for their ideals according to their lights – but in order to show how much is left out of an analysis of historical causes when it has to be forced into the conventional Marxist mould. If this book were merely an exercise in Marxist apologia for Menshevik policy it would be of some slight historical interest, but little more. But Dan's work is so very much more than that. It gives us a lively, intelligent, penetrating picture of the unfolding of Russian revolutionary thought. Unlike many histories of Russian revolutionary thought – and there are very few available in English – it presents this unfolding as a coherent whole. It gives it a pattern and a purpose. Both pattern and purpose may perhaps appear differently to different scholars. But without some pattern the study becomes an incoherent jumble of names, dates, and strange theories. It is precisely because it was one of the few coherent histories available that Dan's book found such a large response among those who could only read it in the original when it first appeared. I hope it will now serve to instruct and stimulate a wider circle of readers in English.

Revolution is pitiless, shapeless and nearly always seems to provide a cure which is worse than the disease. The aspirations for liberty out of which it grows have so often been trampled underfoot when, in Pasternak's words, 'the figurative becomes literal'. It devours not only its children, but as Stalin's régime showed – its parents. But those who have not lost all hope for mankind look forward to the ultimate triumph of the ideals which are no longer recognizable in the practice. It is the great service of books like this one by Dan that they remind us both of the ideals and of the transformation which they underwent.

L.S.

The London School of Economics and Political Science
February 1964.

Introduction

DEMOCRACY IN AMERICA AND RUSSIA

The advent of the '60s of the last century was signalized in Russia by the liberation of the peasants. It seemed that this liberation was bound to have the same significance for the further socio-economic and cultural development of Russia as the liquidation of slavery in the United States, which took place at about the same time.

Long before this, pecuniary relations had begun to penetrate the essentially feudal landholding economy of Russia and to break it up. Long before this there had begun appearing in Russia, too, together with the crafts, factories and workshops based on feudal and bonded labour, enterprises of a capitalist nature, which used voluntary hired labour. But it was only the liberation of the peasants, and the epoch of company promotion and the 'Great Reforms' bound up with it, that established all the conditions for the free and rapid development of capitalism. These were the vast reservoir of manpower that poured into the cities from the countryside, the newly established industrial centres, rail and water transport, a postal system that secured the accurate functioning of market relations and the mass circulation of people and freight, and a judical order that gave people and their property the elementary guarantees without which any widespread development of a system of production based on material interests, the spirit of enterprise, and the free competition of individuals, was altogether impossible.

Nevertheless Russian evolution took a course completely different from that of the United States, although Russia, even more than America, constitutes a whole continent with inexhaustible reserves of almost all kinds of raw materials essential for industry, and could use all the scientific, technical, organizational and ideological achievements of the capitalist countries of Europe that preceded her.

It is not the place here to linger over the conditions that governed the destiny of America. It is a fact that, during the half-century that passed between the abolition of slavery and the 1914–18 World War, American industry went through a process of gigantic development.

In many respects American capitalism outdistanced European capitalism. The organizer and leader of American capitalist economy – the rapidly growing bourgeoisie – actually became the ruling class in its own country. A firm, spacious and secure edifice of democracy was erected on a firm capitalist foundation.

During these fifty years the tempestuous evolution of Russia, interrupted by revolutionary explosions, took place quite differently.

In industry, despite some individual brilliant accomplishments, Russia remained a backward country up to the revolution of 1917 itself. To a high degree its capitalism was an imported, foreign capitalism. Its bourgeoisie never achieved the role of the ruling class – either in the sense of running the State or in the sense of influencing the masses of the people politically or intellectually. The 'Great Reforms' were not 'crowned' by a democratic constitution, as had been expected by their ardent sponsors, while the State Duma wrenched forth by the 1905 revolution was very quickly reduced to the role of a mock-parliament, scarcely masking the untouched autocracy.

But political democracy on a capitalist foundation proved to be equally decrepit and unviable in the 1917 revolution engendered by the First World War. In the course of some seven to eight months it perished – together with Russian capitalism and the Russian bourgeoisie. Only in the framework of Socialism – and a dictatorial Socialism at that – could the task be set, and partially even realized, of 'overtaking and passing' the advanced capitalist countries with respect to industry. In contradistinction to America, the 'americanization' of Russia is being realized not in a capitalist but a Socialist form. And there can be no doubt that if, as seems indicated, one of the consequences of the anti-Fascist victory proves to be the strengthening of political democracy, then in Russia, in any case, democracy can only be erected on a Socialist and not on a capitalist foundation.

The causes of the unviability of bourgeois democracy in Russia are contained, in the final analysis, in the historically belated entry of Russia on the path of capitalist evolution. This belatedness placed a stamp of singularity on the whole socio-economic, cultural, and political development of the country. This in its turn has predetermined the unique development of democratic ideas in Russia, to which this work of mine is devoted.

The study of this evolution has not only a theoretical, but a practical and political interest. It will help in the understanding of the situation that began to take shape in Russia during the war and whose results will make themselves felt during the next few years and decades. It is of vital interest for a judgement on the perspectives of post-war development of the European Continent, in the fate of which Russia will play a first-class role corresponding to the role it played in the military and political destruction of Hitler Fascism. Finally, this study may indirectly throw some light on the probable post-war evolution of political ideology in those countries, still more backward than the Russia of the past century, that the Second, really World and Total War brought out of relative age-old isolation and made into much more independent factors of future world development than they have been hitherto.

My work is not a history of the *struggle* for democracy in Russia, but a history of the Russian democratic *idea*. However, it goes without saying that an exposition of the history of an idea is impossible without linking it to the movement that it was born in, that it received its drive from, and that put it to a practical test. This is especially impossible if one keeps in mind the average Soviet reader (for whom I have deliberately intended this book and into whose hands, I hope, it will fall sooner or later), in whom, both because of the age of the Soviet reading public and because of all the circumstances of Soviet life, one must assume an imperfect acquaintance with the history of the Russian movement for revolution and emancipation. In many places, consequently, I give considerable space to the factual side of this movement too, while of course trying not to go beyond the bounds necessary for the understanding of the basic theme of the book.

I hope to enable the reader to understand 'Bolshevism' not as an accidental phenomenon that was summoned to life by a quite exceptional concatenation of circumstances and that interrupted the liberating struggle, which had been going on for decades, of the Russian intelligentsia, working-class and people as a whole, but, on the contrary, as a natural product of that struggle and an historically inevitable stage on the road to its consummation. For this reason any polemical intention is quite alien to this book. But neither have I set myself the task of giving a *history* of Bolshevism, which is more than forty years old, which for more than a quarter of a century now has been politically embodied in a dictatorial régime that has shaped the entire socio-economic and cultural profile of Russia, and that has been able to conduct the country victoriously through the most frightful of all the wars mankind has ever endured and secure for it the position of a first-class World Power. It is quite evident that any attempt to follow in any detail the process of evolution – and ramification – of the Bolshevik idea during this tempestuous and catastrophic period would have required at least two or three supplementary volumes and years of intense labour. Even in the concluding chapter I can note only in the most general terms the basic landmarks of this evolution, assess it, and comment on its prospects in the completely novel conditions of the post-war period.

I have set myself the much more limited, but for the assigned task quite adequate, goal of giving not a history of Bolshevism, but a history of its *origins* and *ideological* formation. The process of this formation was concluded in the 1905 revolution, which is also the concluding date for the investigatory part of my book; this opens with the emancipation of the peasantry, which for the first time made possible a 'European' setting for the question of political democracy in Russia. But I have considered it appropriate to devote the first, introductory portion of the book to a survey of the preceding period, that of the birth of the idea of modern democracy in Russia. It was just in this period that the foundations were laid of the entire subsequent development of Russian socio-political thought, without which even a brief characterization of this evolution would remain unintelligible.

New York City THEODORE DAN
December 1945

PART ONE

The Birth of the Democratic Idea in Russia

CHAPTER ONE

First Sprouts

1. PIONEERS OF RUSSIAN DEMOCRACY

Nineteenth-century democracy was born on the European Continent in the tempest of the great French Revolution, which marked the historical replacement of the feudal, absolutist *ancien régime* by a new bourgeois-liberal order. This contemporary democracy was far from achieving a complete and consistent realization in all civilized countries, but it maintained itself everywhere as a democracy of capitalist society – a society founded on the principles of 'free enterprise', on the right of the individual to dispose freely of his own property, and on free competition between individuals. It was purely political in content and parliamentary in form everywhere. It was also democratic and liberal – guaranteeing the equality of civil rights and the juridical 'opportunities' of individuals. But it disregarded the fact of the profound inequality of their socio-economic opportunities. Hence it was everywhere, in its basic concept, a democracy of property holders: '*Das Recht zum Leben . . . haben nur die, die etwas haben*' ('Only those who possess, possess the right to life') was the venomous expression Heinrich Heine gave this idea.

In accordance with this the political and ideological centre of gravity for the liberal and individualistic democracy of the nineteenth century was the same social force that was the prime mover of capitalist evolution: the bourgeoisie, or capitalist class. This class dominated society not only economically but ideologically. The social forces of the past – the Church, the monarchy, the landed aristocracy – adapted themselves to its demands. Its 'social laws' were obeyed by scholars, writers and artists. The petty-bourgeois masses of the city and countryside submitted to it. And its social antagonist, born of the same conditions of capitalist evolution – the working-class – also emerged from its ideology and for a long time used its ideas to formulate its own ideology. More than a few decades passed by before a *principled rupture* made itself felt between the ideology of the proletariat and the ideology of the bourgeoisie, and before the consciousness of the workers began to take form in special, 'class' ideological forms: before the proletariat, in the words of Marx, began to be 'not only a class in itself, but a class for itself', not the oppositional but the revolutionary class of capitalist society.

In Russia, too, rudiments of the idea of contemporary democracy appeared together with the beginning of the capitalist penetration of the old feudal society; they immediately found an echo in commercial and industrial circles. It is curious that as early as 1821 a police report to Alexander I, referring to a 'great deal of talk about a constitution' in the capital, considered it necessary to emphasize that it was 'especially energetic among the merchants of the Gostiny Dvor'[1] (a St Petersburg commercial district).

The progenitors of the Russian movement of 'emancipation' are of course considered to have been the 'Decembrists' – participants in a conspiracy that led to an unsuccessful attempt on 14 December 1825 at a military pronunciamento against Nicholas I, who had just ascended the throne, and that ended with the hanging of five of the conspirators (Bestuzhev-Ryumin, Kakhovsky, Ryleyev, Muraviev-Apostol, Pestel) and lengthy terms at hard labour for the rest.

This movement of youthful officers, however, lacked a clear and unified programme, either political or social. Dictatorial Jacobin tendencies, of which Pestel was the most extreme representative, were mingled in its ideology with extremely moderate and conservatively aristocratic dreams about the restriction of absolutism. Ever since the times of Peter I's successors this idea had not ceased haunting the Russian nobility, which, however, after almost a century-old experience of palace revolts and conspiracies, felt the hopelessness of the enterprise too clearly to give any support to its own youth.

Nevertheless a number of elements of the idea of contemporary democracy were inherent in the Decembrist movement. Rudiments of these ideas had been brought back by Russian officers from the anti-Napoleonic campaigns in Europe and the almost three-year sojourn of occupation troops in France, still suffused in the spirit of the revolution it had so recently lived through. But if these seeds could sprout on Russian soil it was because at this time the socio-economic terrain of Russia itself began to be 'europeanized' – largely through Russian participation in the European wars and the consequent strain imposed on the country's strength.

The old, patriarchal-feudal and preponderantly natural economy began to dissolve; the elements of a new economy, based on currency and capitalism, began to grow stronger and stronger. The economic ground began to slip out from under the feet of the old ruling class – the nobility – while at the same time, partially supplanting it, there began to appear a new ruling class – the bourgeoisie, recruited not only from the old mercantile stratum but also from individual feudal serfs who had grown rich enough to buy their freedom. In the beginning, to be sure, this process of the impoverishment of the nobility and of the socio-economic rise of the bourgeoisie was limited almost exclusively to Moscow and the central districts of Russia bordering it. But beginning in the '20s of the nineteenth century, it leaped so much to the eye towards the '30s and '40s and so changed the entire face of the old Russian capital that it was remarked on by all thoughtful observers.

Thus, travelling through Moscow in 1833, Pushkin remarks (in his *Thoughts en Route*) that Moscow had 'lost its aristocratic brilliance', but to make up for it was 'blossoming in other respects: industry, strongly sponsored, has revived there and developed with unusual energy'. The poet adds: 'The merchants are getting rich and settling in palaces abandoned by the nobility.' The same thing was noticed ten years after Pushkin by the well-known German traveller, Baron Haxthausen, who, as is well known, 'discovered' the Russian peasant commune. He writes: 'If you were to ask now whom this palace belongs to, you will be told: "To such and such a manufacturer, and before, to Prince A. or B." '[2] In the middle of the '40s Belinsky also noted that 'Moscow was predominantly a merchants' city' and exclaimed: 'How many ancient lordly houses have now become the property of merchants!'[3]

Pushkin's assertion that industry was 'strongly sponsored' was true only with qualifications. The awareness of the necessity for industrial development for the great power Russia had become was tempered by the awareness of the danger to the autocracy of the changes such a development was bound to introduce into the Russian socio-economic order. Hence the measures intended to accelerate industrial development were intermingled with measures intended to do the contrary, to slow down that development and more especially to forestall, as politically dangerous, the accumulation of large masses of factory workers in and around the capitals. Nicholas I's Minister of National Education, Count S. S. Uvarov, the author of the well-known triple slogan 'autocracy, orthodoxy, nationalism', said that he would 'die in peace' if he succeeded in 'holding back the development of Russia fifty years'.[4] And this tendency to 'congeal'* the economic development of Russia in order simultaneously to congeal its political and social development, remained the basic political idea of the monarchist reaction in Russia for a whole half-century.

Nevertheless it was in the reign of Nicholas I, during the '30s and '40s of the last century, that capitalist elements made a decisive entry into Russian economic life. And it was during these same years that the ideas of contemporary democracy decisively penetrated Russian political thought. Their champions were famous groups of writers, professors, and students, almost entirely aristocratic. From their midst there emerged the most brilliant exponent of Russian democratic thought in the '40s and '50s of the last century – Alexander Ivanovich Herzen (1812–70).

2. PECULIARITY OF RUSSIAN DEMOCRATIC THOUGHT

In the parallelism between the development of economic forms based on 'free enterprise' and the development of democratic thought, the political and intellectual history of Russia is similar to the history of other capitalist countries. But the profound peculiarity of Russian democratic thought lies in this, that from its very inception it never for a moment idealized capitalism and was not drawn to it, but, on the contrary, sharply criticized it. The nascent Russian bourgeoisie not only was in no way a hero for the Russian democracy that was seeing the light simultaneously with it, but, on the contrary, instantly became for it an object of hostility.

As early as 1844 Herzen, in his diary, characterized the 'mercantilism and contemporary industrialism' of Western Europe as a 'syphilitic chancre infecting the blood and bones of society'. It would be possible to quote endlessly remarks made by him and his friends against the 'middle-classness' that had become the 'final form of Western European civilization' and created a society in which 'on the one hand there were only middle-class property-holders, stubbornly refusing to surrender their monopolies, and on the other middle-class people without any means, who wanted to wrest away the others' property but were not strong enough'.[5] And in the arguments about the role of the bourgeoisie in general, especially its eventual role in the political evolution of Russia, which were being

* An expression of K. Leontyev, closest collaborator of a well-known reactionary journalist, M. N. Katkov.

carried on in the '40s and the very beginning of the '50s among the former members of these Moscow groups, V. P. Botkin was almost alone in coming to the conclusion: 'May God give us a bourgeoisie!' The overwhelming and almost general mood was a sharply negative attitude towards the bourgeoisie and the 'mercantile' spirit of the capitalist era in general.

It can be said that, from its birth on, Russian democratic thought was never liberal and purely political. A political protest against the autocracy was interwoven in it with the social protest against the principles of the capitalist economy that was supplanting the patriarchal, feudal economy. And the critique of capitalism led the youthful Russian democracy to the first steps on its historic path towards the embracing of Socialist ideas, in the form these ideas were then given in Western Europe as a direct effect of the social contradictions hidden beneath the wrappings of a social order in which the French Revolution had dreamed of finding the embodiment of 'liberty, equality and fraternity'.

For the most part the young Russian democrats drew the theoretical foundation of their political views from German philosophy: Fichte, Hegel, Schelling, and later Feuerbach. Robert Owen's teachings played only a secondary role in the theoretical grounding of their Socialism; for them the chief teachers and prophets of Socialism were the great French Utopians of that time: Cabet, Pierre Leroux and especially Fourier and Saint-Simon, later joined by Proudhon.* 'I revere the grandeur of Fourier's genius,' was the statement made before the Inquiry Commission by M. V. Butashevich-Petrashevsky.†

Thus the nascent Russian democratic movement drew its basic strength from the young Russian nobility. The process of its intellectual and political education is described very precisely in the poem *Confession of a Superfluous Man*, in which N. P. Ogaryov, himself (like Herzen) the son of an extremely wealthy landowner, speaks of three youths, i.e. really himself, his intimate friend Herzen and a third comrade of theirs, Vadim Passek:

* Louis Blanc was very influential. The novels of George Sand and Eugène Sue also played an important role in spreading Socialist ideas.

† Head of the society of so-called 'Petrashevskyites', destroyed in 1848, in which, together with other future famous writers (Saltykov-Shchedrin, Plesh-cheyev, Maikov, Grigoriev and others) there also took part F. M. Dostoevsky, who as a result was given a death sentence, changed to hard labour at the last moment.

'Whereupon all three of us – children of December
And disciples of a newborn world
Disciples of Fourier and Saint-Simon –
Did vow we would wholly dedicate our life
To the people and its liberation
And lay its foundations in Socialism. . . .'[6]

In assimilating the ideas of democracy the youth of the nobility, of course, made a decisive break with feudalism and with the caste pretensions of the nobility. 'We have no wish to extend our hand to the gentry and officialdom, indeed they look upon our sort as insane' was an entry in Herzen's diary for July 1842. Nevertheless the rejection of capitalism, which was dissolving the feudal landholding economy, and of the bourgeoisie, which was forcing the old aristocracy out of its Moscow palaces, undoubtedly reflected the mood of that rural nobility from whose ranks the youthful democrats were recruited and in whose traditions they had been brought up. A revulsion against capitalist 'mercantilism' and 'middle-classness' impregnated not only the democratic movement of 'Westernization', but perhaps too the 'Slavophil' movement.* This was even more characteristic of these same Moscow *milieux*, and during the succeeding decades it became the clearest expression of the political ideology of the nobility, which was compelled to live through the morbid process of the adaptation of its economy and way of life to the demands of the new era. It was only when the democratic anti-capitalism of the 'Westernizers' later became more and more Socialist and revolutionary that the liberal-conservative anti-capitalism of the 'Slavophils' took more and more of a turn towards the idealization of the 'original', patriarchal, hierarchical Russian past – towards social and political reaction.

Thus the aristocratic origin of the pioneers of Russian democracy undoubtedly played some role in its primordial anti-capitalist attitudes and ideas. Indeed, for a very long time the stamp of this social origin lay so clearly on the offspring of the nobility in the democratic movement at large that the well-known democratic journalist of the second half of the nineteenth century, N. K. Mikhailovsky, could even baptize this group of democrats with the name of 'conscience-stricken noblemen', a permanent addition to the Russian political lexicon. Even much later, in analysing the so-called 'populist' period of the

* The Aksakovs, Kireyevskys, Khomyakovs and others.

democratic movement, the same Mikhailovsky thought it possible to distinguish a special 'aristocratic form of Populism'.[7]

But it must be emphasized that the role of these 'aristocratic' impulses in laying down the 'anti-capitalist' character of Russian democracy was nevertheless extremely limited. The aristocratic origin of the pioneers of Russian democracy was, to be sure, a great help to them in rejecting capitalism and the bourgeoisie, but it cannot explain why their anti-capitalism failed to take on conservative and reactionary forms, and became Socialist and revolutionary. Moreover, as we shall see later on, the Socialist and revolutionary character of Russian democratic thought not only did not wane, but, on the contrary, it grew stronger precisely to the degree that the leading role in the democratic movement shifted from the scions of the nobility to the plebeian intellectuals who arose from the same social lower depths that gave rise to the Russian bourgeoisie.

The real causes of this singularity of Russian democratic thought must be looked for in the characteristics of Russian capitalism, on whose terrain Russian democracy was born and evolved. And the foundation of the peculiar development of Russian capitalism was its historical belatedness.

CHAPTER TWO

The Russian Bourgeoisie

1. THE BELATEDNESS OF RUSSIAN CAPITALISM

In Western Europe capitalist economy evolved on a socio-economic and cultural terrain prepared by the Middle Ages. Russia lacked both feudal-chivalrous traditions and traditions of 'free' autonomous cities and guild trades. She entered the capitalist phase of evolution as a country very far behind the states of Western Europe economically, socially, politically and culturally. Even slavery, the condition of the greater part of her basic peasant population, was liquidated only in 1861, i.e. three-quarters of a century after the beginning of the French revolution and almost half a century after the end of the Napoleonic Wars!

The emancipation of the peasantry from feudal serfdom created in Russia, for the first time, the rudiments of those juridical conditions without which the development of capitalist economic forms in any breadth is altogether unthinkable. At the same time the very penetration of these forms into Russia, towards the '30s and '40s of the nineteenth century, as we have seen, took place with a great historical lag. Capitalist economy began to make inroads into Russia at a time when European capitalist society had already undergone a rather lengthy and complicated evolution.

The consequences of this belatedness of Russian capitalism were extremely variegated. They made themselves felt with more and more force throughout the later development of the country – down to the revolution of 1917, which very quickly assumed a 'Bolshevik' character and put an end both to Russian capitalism and to Russian liberal democracy. Without an understanding of these consequences it is impossible to grasp the fate of the idea of democracy and Socialism in Russia. Accordingly it is necessary at this point to leap ahead and summarize in the most general terms the most essential of them.

Let us begin with the economics and sociology of Russian capitalism.

Capitalism did not come to Western Europe in a ready form. It was the natural product of its own preceding evolution and developed 'organically', gradually transforming the old industrial technique, the old economy, the old social relations and the old state of mind. And it was just as gradually, by a relatively slow process of expropriation of the only independent petty producers and a transition of the others from a natural economy to a money economy, that it created for itself a continually expanding reservoir of free 'working hands' and a corresponding 'internal market'.

In Russia this was different. Capitalist industry was 'implanted' there in a ready and indeed for the times a quite perfect form – in the sense of the technical equipment of the enterprises as well as their size. In this respect the development of heavy capitalist industry in Russia bore some resemblance to its development in colonial and semi-colonial countries.

This resemblance was also evident in the pre-eminent role played by foreigners in this 'implanting' of capitalist industry. First of all there were the foreign organizers and engineers. A foreign director speaking broken Russian – an Englishman, Belgian, German, more rarely a Frenchman – was a commonplace figure even in those businesses formed entirely with Russian funds. But an enormous role was also played by foreign capital. The designations of the big factories and workshops, mines, and oil installations are shot through with foreign names. Even the famous Yuzovka,* the metallurgical centre of the Don Basin, was named after an Englishman, Hughes. And as late as 1913, that is, towards the beginning of the First World War, out of a capital of 5.25 billion roubles invested in Russian industry about a third was foreign.

Another characteristic trait of this development was the relatively large size of the installations. In that same year, 1913, not less than four-fifths of all industrial workers worked in installations with 100 and more workers, and almost half of them in giant plants with 1,000 and more workers.

The swift filling-up of the reservoirs of 'hands' needed for such a development was achieved chiefly by the accelerated pauperization of the peasantry, which in being emancipated from serfdom had received inadequate allotments and because of the very conditions of the emancipation had been compelled to seek wages on the side in order to pay the heavy price of the land-owners' indemnification and the even heavier taxes to the state. The result was the impoverishment

* Later Stalino, now Dnieprovsk. (Translator's note.)

of the countryside, the extremely low level of its agricultural technique, and the negligible productivity of its labour. All this turned a crop failure of any consequence into a massive famine and made the formation of a sufficiently capacious internal market extremely difficult. But it was just this broad internal market that was particularly necessary for Russian industry, because its tardy birth greatly hampered its penetration of external markets that had been seized and divided up by its competitors. The idea of enlarging the internal market hence became the ruling idea of the economic policy of the Russian industrial bourgeoisie, especially its policy on the peasant question, which for Russia was crucial.

Thus the economic life of Russia was characterized by a sharp contrast. Russian industry, organized according to the *dernier cri* of science and technique, was a massive edifice that, though huge, was largely built on foreign models, and erected on a foundation of extreme socio-economic and cultural backwardness and on the extreme poverty and the primitive economy of its peasant masses. In the words of the famous song *Dubinushka*: the 'shrewd Englishman contrived one machine after another to help him work', whereas there was nothing for the Russian peasant to do in order to lighten work that was too much for him but sing his spirited song as before.

In these peculiar economic conditions the development of social relations was equally peculiar. With the emergence in Russia of capitalist heavy industry there also emerged a big bourgeoisie, in no way inferior culturally to its older European brethren. Feudal peasants of the day before and their sons became patrons of sciences and arts, investing vast funds in hospitals, institutes of good works, schools and universities, publishing houses, newspapers, theatres and museums. The wonderful university clinics in Moscow, built with means provided by the merchant class; the celebrated Moscow gallery of the Tretyakov brothers, who created a collection of Russian works of art unparalleled for value and rarity; the Moscow Art Theatre, created by Stanislavsky, the son of Alexeyev, the Moscow merchant – are a few examples, known all over the world, of the cultural activity of the youthful Russian bourgeoisie.

But politically and culturally this 'europeanized' bourgeoisie was, from the very beginning, divided by an abyss from the broad urban and even more the peasant masses it had itself only just emerged from. Between itself and the masses of the people there were no intermediate strata whose socio-economic and cultural gradation establishes a series of successive and almost imperceptible transitions in a normal bourgeois society from its capitalist summits to its popular depths and thus integrates it socio-ideologically. In Russia the thin stratum of the 'modern' bourgeoisie of the European and American type was separated by an abyss not only from the labouring masses, but also from the basic major and minor strata of its own class. Thus for a long time this class as a whole clung to that 'patriarchal' and uncultivated appearance everyone was familiar with through Ostrovsky's comedies.

Contrariwise, it was those same conditions of economic development of belated Russian capitalism that furthered the rapid growth and formation of the 'modern' proletariat, and its accumulating in large numbers in the decisive economic and political centres of the country. The rapid infusion of new workers from small towns and villages constantly kept bringing the advanced strata of the proletariat into contact with the offspring of the petty bourgeoisie and the peasantry, and in general through them with the remote Russian hinterland and provinces, which these offspring did not lose touch with for a long time.

This uninterrupted dilution of the Russian proletariat by elements that in terms of class were 'fresh' was unmistakably reflected throughout the further evolution of Russian Socialism. It also made itself felt in the course of both Russian revolutions – 1905 and 1917. But for the time being it enabled the advanced strata of the Russian working-class to influence the most backward strata of the nation and create for itself a mass support in the depths of the countryside.

Threads of mutual understanding knit together the Russian proletariat and peasantry all the more easily because the countryside, unfairly dealt with in the land allotments at the time of the emancipation, never stopped dreaming about 'total reapportionment', i.e. the expropriation of the land-holdings in its own favour. These expropriating tendencies, far more than the forms of communal landowning, which had outlived themselves and were already essentially degenerate, were the reason that the 'bourgeois' principle of the 'sacredness and inviolability' of private property in the means of production and especially in land, penetrated the consciousness of the Russian peasants with difficulty and not until after they themselves had become their own masters.

It is obvious that the proletariat for its part was that social force, and Socialism that political ideology, that could most fully meet these expropriating tendencies of the peasantry half-way. Thus conditions were created in which the Russian peasantry from the very beginning gravitated politically and intellectually not towards the bourgeoisie and its liberal-democratic interests, but towards the proletariat and its revolutionary Socialist tendencies. It was this circumstance, later to play a decisive role in the course of the Russian Revolution, that set its stamp on the entire evolution of political life and democratic thought in Russia.

2. THE POLITICAL WEAKNESS OF THE BOURGEOISIE

As a result of the situation described above the Russian bourgeoisie was extremely feeble politically.

To be sure, the impoverishment of the nobility and the growing economic and financial power of the bourgeoisie gave rise at times to the view, not only among outside observers but also among the leaders of the bourgeoisie itself and its ideologists, that in Russian political life it was destined to play the same role as it had in the advanced countries of Western Europe. During the epoch of industrial company-promotion and railway construction that started soon after the peasants' emancipation, the concessionaires and contractors seemed 'heroes and conquerors' to the poet Nekrasov. 'The merchant suddenly saw himself definitely in one of the loftiest places in society, the same as that which throughout Europe had long been officially and openly assigned to wealth,' wrote Dostoevsky in 1876 in the *Diary of a Writer*. 'Business can do anything!' was the greeting twenty years later of the newspaper *Volgar* to the All-Russian Industrial and Commercial Convention in 1896 and to the reception that was given for the Tsar at the same time by the merchants of the Nizhegorodsky Fair.

In fact, however, both in the conception of the 'lofty place' occupied by the bourgeoisie and in its own proud dreams there was more than a little aberration and illusion.

Deprived of mass support, the Russian liberal-democratic bourgeoisie was very quickly squeezed as in a vice between Tsarism and the swiftly growing working-class movement. Even by 1885, in speaking of the textile workers' strike in the Morozov factory in Nikolsky village, which played something of a role in the history of that movement, K. Skalkovsky, a well-known journalist and important functionary, was compelled to acknowledge: 'it is turning out that . . . revolutionary propaganda has already reached our factory stratum too, and the latter is formulating literally the same demands as workers in Western Europe. The idea of Marx and the International is now penetrating the factory-workers' *milieu*.'[8]

Up to 1861 Tsarism held in check, through serfdom, every emancipating effort of the nobility. And after the elimination of serfdom the fear of a peasant uprising, of a new 'Pugachov insurrection' and of 'total reapportionment', paralysed the political activity of the propertied classes for a long time. But now this peasant menace was joined by the menace of a working-class movement that politically paralysed the bourgeoisie itself. The exploitation of this threat against the liberal-democratic tendencies of the bourgeoisie became part of Tsarist policy.

Events demonstrated very quickly, it is true, that here the autocracy was playing with a fire that was even more dangerous for it than for the bourgeoisie. It was of course just this attempt to create a legend about the 'worker-Tsar', added to the long-established legend about the 'peasant-Tsar', that ended up with the firing on a workers' procession bringing the Tsar a petition (the 'Bloody Sunday' of 9 January 1905). It was this that finished off the legend once and for all and laid the beginnings of the 1905 revolution. Nevertheless Tsarism systematically applied this policy of frightening the bourgeoisie by the 'red spectre'. It was the objective situation itself of the Russian bourgeoisie that ensured a certain success for this policy. From the very outset it was forced to enter into a compromise with the monarchy and the remnants of the feudal past that the bourgeoisie of Western Europe had entered into only after lengthy historical experience.

This compromise assumed a political form when the 1905 revolution brought Russia for the first time the rudiments of representative institutions. The feelings of the big bourgeoisie were expressed in the Duma by parties, first the Party of Peaceful Reform, then the Octobrists (named after the 'constitutional' manifesto of 17 October 1905), that were seeking methods of combining the legislative functions of the Duma with the preservation of Tsarist autocracy. But even before this the compromise had in fact led to the rejection by the bourgeoisie of 'pure' politics in general, to its reconciliation with absolutism and to the attempt to defend its economic interests by backstage agreements with it. The Tsarist bureaucracy willingly met these attempts half-way. The Ministry of Finance on the one hand, and the Ministry of Trade and Industry on the other, became the government departments that worked in close contact with the economic organizations of the big entrepreneurs. S. Y. Witte was the clearest and most consistent sponsor of this idea of a *rapprochement* of the autocracy and the big bourgeoisie based on a so-called 'practical' policy. This also reinforced the blossoming of illusions concerning the 'all-powerful' merchant class.

As for those representatives of the bourgeoisie – on occasion the most substantial, independent, and enlightened capitalists in Russia – who were not satisfied with the purely material acquisitions that were possible via this accord with absolutism, but yearned for political freedom, even though only as a prerequisite for a foreign and domestic policy corresponding to the needs of large-scale capitalist evolution, there was nothing else for them to do but join the struggle of the Socialist parties. There was nothing exceptional in a scene depicted by a writer, S. Y. Yelpatyevsky,[9] in speaking of his stay in Ufa during the '70s of the last century: 'Merchants in Ufa used to hide terrorists being hunted throughout Russia, and did not stop their sons and daughters from entering the revolutionary movement. It was among these merchants' children that a group of revolutionary terrorists took form later on, and it was from this *milieu* that Sazonov, Prokofiev and others emerged.'*

In general it may be said that without the large-scale help that bourgeois groups gave the Socialist parties – in money, lodgings, conspiratorial rendezvous, accommodation addresses, etc. – these parties could never have been able to create the ramified illegal organization, the press, a system for transporting people and literature, and at times arms, across the borders, and the network of secret print-shops and secret stores that made up their strength. It is symbolic of Russian political evolution that during the years after 1905, which were most difficult for the illegal movement, it was only thanks to the generous monetary support of the biggest Russian capitalist, Sabbas Morozov,† that Lenin could maintain cadres of underground organizers (Stalin was one of the most prominent) who aided the Bolshevik Party to such an extent in its seizure of power in 1917.

Thus, together with the figure of the 'conscience-stricken noble'

* Eminent figures in the Socialist-Revolutionary Party. In 1904 Sazonov killed V. K. Plehve, one of the most reactionary Ministers of the Interior.

† A member of the same Morozov family in whose factory the above-mentioned strike had taken place some twenty years before this, and who were then given a Cossack detachment quartered in the surrounding villages in order to curb the rebellious workers. He committed suicide in 1910.

there also appeared in the Russian revolutionary movement the figure – inadequately studied, however – of what might be called the 'conscious-stricken bourgeois'!

3. ITS IDEOLOGICAL TRIVIALITY

The result of the socio-political feebleness of the bourgeoisie was that the liquidation of the autocracy was postponed until the working-class had become strong enough to turn into an independent force. But the result of this postponement was, in its turn, the most extreme intensification of all the socio-economic and political contradictions injected into the *ancien régime* by capitalist evolution but compressed under the leaden roof-top of the outlived autocracy, and hence – the inevitability of *revolutionary methods* of liquidating it.

In the circumstances of the revolutionary situation, however, which was becoming clearer and clearer, what made itself especially manifest was the ideological triviality of the Russian bourgeoisie. Its own position, as described above, clipped the wings of its socio-political thinking. But this thinking failed to receive any stimulus from outside either, for the political thinking of the bourgeoisie of the advanced capitalist countries had long since ceased being revolutionary.

The revolutionary quality of bourgeois-democratic thought had already been interrupted by the course of the great French Revolution and its Bonapartist outcome. It was struck a mortal blow by the revolutions of 1848, which led to the blood-stained 'June' slaughter of workers and the second Bonapartist finale in France, and to a capitulation to the monarchy and the feudal land-holders in Germany and Austria-Hungary. These revolutions demonstrated the extinction of the revolutionary potential of the bourgeoisie itself and its incapacity for leading revolutionary mass movements. They proved that in the course of a revolutionary crisis the masses, and especially the urban masses, slip away from the influence of the bourgeoisie and enter into conflict with it. Thus every revolution in the advanced capitalist countries would have the tendency in future to shatter the framework of bourgeois order and generate social-revolutionary mass movements. After 1848 the European bourgeoisie lost its taste for revolutions, and became more and more definitely counter-revolutionary. The reformist moods of its progressive strata also took on a more and more conservative character.

For the Russian bourgeoisie this bankruptcy of the European bourgeoisie with respect to revolution meant the disappearance of the last possibility of formulating a liberal-democratic ideology that would at all correspond to the vast revolutionary tasks history had set the country. The most prominent representatives of liberal thought, which were concentrated in the '80s and '90s in the *Vestnik Yevropy* (The European Courier)*, tried to prove in every way that their liberalism was 'not bourgeois'. Russia could have no 'bourgeois liberalism' at all, 'since we have no bourgeoisie in the Western European sense of the word'. On the other hand, there could also be no popular movement with a liberal programme in Russia, but that to make up for it 'liberal ideas were winning over more and more the advanced social force of our time – an enlightened bureaucracy'. 'A liberal reformist officialdom' – this was the force the ideologists of Russian liberalism were counting on. 'A harmonious alliance aiming at the reform of the government together with a society supporting and leading it – such was the solution of the problem given by liberalism', is the summing up by A. N. Potresov of the conclusions reached by his study of liberal journalism.[10] As we see, this 'solution of the problem' gives an exact reflection of the policy of business-like collaboration of the bourgeoisie with the government that meant its renunciation of any independent policy at all, and all the more so of any revolutionary policy.

The Socialist radicalism of the Russian democracy, on the other hand, was given a new and powerful thrust forward by the bankruptcy, as far as revolution was concerned, of the European bourgeoisie.

It was precisely after the revolutions of 1848 and under the influence of the class contradictions they revealed, that a working-class mass movement began to develop in the advanced countries of Western Europe. European Socialist thought, becoming class-conscious and revolutionary, left the realm of peaceful utopias and set itself the task of organizing this movement. Replacing Fourier and Saint-Simon, and then Proudhon, there came Karl Marx and Friedrich Engels, who on the eve of revolutionary events published the Communist Manifesto, which now, almost a hundred years later, still remains the gospel of revolutionary Socialism. Marx's ideas, particularly his virulent criticism of Proudhon in his *Poverty of Philosophy*, became known in Russia – via the young land-owners travelling abroad –

* Stasyulevich, Arsenyev, Slonimsky and others.

and some of the Petrashevskyites (Speshnev, Timkovsky), in contradistinction to the head of the society, who continued to 'venerate Fourier', declared themselves 'Communists'. But even later, for the next six or seven decades, right down to the 1914 war, the Russian democracy, coloured from its very birth, as we have seen, by Socialism, and confronted by revolutionary tasks, kept receiving new stimulus and support from Western Europe, where Socialism had become a massive political force in practice and the sole revolutionary doctrine in theory.

Thus democratic thought in Russia could develop only as Socialist thought. And if, as we have seen, there was no other way out for bourgeois circles at all radically inclined but support of the Socialist parties, a paradoxical situation was also created on the ideological front in which theoretically too these strata could only express their political ideas in a Socialist guise. Russian Socialist democrats found themselves acting as teachers of the Russian bourgeoisie. If as long ago as the '40s of the last century Belinsky's essays (see below) were 'eagerly read' by Siberian merchants,[11] then forty years later there also appeared in the provinces merchants who not only read radical newspapers but were also 'widely informed with respect to the Social-Democratic movement in Germany'.[9] They drew their information from, among other things, the Berlin reports of Yollos, which were very well known in their time and were printed in the liberal (not Socialist) Moscow newspaper *Russkiye Vedomosti* ('Russian Intelligencer'). *Apropos*, this also served the Russian Socialists as the chief 'legal' source of information concerning the ideas and policies of the German Social-Democrats.

It is no exaggeration to say that democratic thought and journalism were monopolized in Russia by the radical Socialist intelligentsia.

CHAPTER THREE

The Russian 'Intelligentsia'

1. THE EMERGENCE OF THE INTELLIGENTSIA

'Intelligentsia' is a specifically Russian word, and to express with precision in a foreign language the idea denoted by it can be done only by a mere transcription. The English word 'intellectuals', the French '*intellectuels*', the German '*Intellektuelle*', designate educated people whose principal occupation or the source of whose income is intellectual labour. The Russian word 'intelligentsia' does not mean a professional group of the population, but a special social group united by a certain political solidarity. Within its boundaries this group encompasses a rather broad gamut of world outlooks, philosophies, views, and parties. But what is common to all the educated people included in it is their political and social radicalism. Even the most learned and educated people, wholly preoccupied by intellectual work, stand outside this group, if they are temperamentally conservative or reactionary. In other languages there is no adequate expression for the Russian word 'intelligentsia' because outside Russia there was and is no such social phenomenon.

Ideas, including social and political ideas, have always and everywhere been formulated and spread by educated people, whose chief contingent has naturally been provided by the so-called 'upper' classes, who have the most leisure and the freest access to education. Educated people have remained allied with these classes not only socially but also spiritually: they have generalized the ideas of their class, moulded its ideals, and outdistanced it, but without cutting themselves off from it. They have been the vanguard of the class army. They have also swallowed up and intellectually assimilated into the ruling classes those relatively rare products of the 'lower' classes who have managed to acquire an education.

In pre-revolutionary and revolutionary times a considerable number of educated people who, by virtue of their intellectual development, were especially sensitive to the 'signs of the times', were able to break away from their class, whose dominance was nearing its historical end, but only in order to become the spokesman for the ideas and ideals of the class whose ascension had been prepared by historical conditions, and to join it in advance intellectually and socially. During the course of the preparation and development of the great French Revolution, which cleared the road for the ideas of modern democracy in Europe, it was possible to observe very clearly the replacement among the educated people of the time (Voltaire, the Encyclopaedists, Mirabeau, the Abbé Siéyès and others), of the aristocratic feudal landmarks with bourgeois liberal ones. This preceded the emergence of new cadres of educated people from the midst of the bourgeoisie itself.

In Russia, too, educated people maintained a close, and often even exclusive tie with the upper classes, from which, during the period of Russian culture that may be called aristocratic, the majority of them emerged. The great Russian critic V. Belinsky could say, quite rightly, of Pushkin, the greatest genius of Russian poetry of the '20s and '30s of the nineteenth century, that Pushkin's spiritual gaze 'saw a Russian land-owner everywhere', and that 'in this class he attacked everything that was contrary to humanity, but the class principle was for him an eternal truth'. Pushkin, as well as another great poet of the era, M. Y. Lermontov, was one of those 'for whom the word writer was, as it were, offensive', and who 'wished to be regarded primarily as men of the world, only occasionally deigning to busy themselves with literature'.[12]

The situation changed completely when together with the crisis of feudal society there also emerged the crisis of aristocratic culture.

Feudal economy was succeeded by capitalist economy, but the aristocratic culture was not succeeded by a bourgeois culture. By virtue of the political and ideological triviality noted above, the Russian bourgeoisie did not become a new social and intellectual centre of attraction for that educated stratum of the aristocracy from under whose feet the old economic and cultural ground was slipping. On the contrary, it instantly became an object of repulsion and hostility for this stratum. The relatively few representatives of moderate, liberal-democratic views in this stratum, such as the famous novelist I. S. Turgenev, Annenkov, Botkin, and others, either take as their standard not the Russian but the European bourgeoisie, and recommend it as a 'teacher', or else, as we have seen, painstakingly dissociate themselves from any suspicion of 'middle-classness'. But in one form or another – whether socialist, insurrectionary-anarchist, religious-anarchist, or reactionary-mystical – the majority, including the most talented, world-renowned Russian writers, plainly demonstrated their resolute 'unacceptance' of the bourgeois world, of bourgeois ideology, and of bourgeois ethics (Herzen, Bakunin, Leo Tolstoy, Dostoevsky and others). This 'unacceptance', by the way, contains one of the essential elements of the so-called 'Slavic soul'.

The aristocratic youths who emerged as the pioneers of Russian democracy laid the foundations of the formation of educated Russians as a special social group. For, by casting off from the aristocratic shore and not crossing over to the bourgeois, they also failed to find support among the popular masses, very largely still enserfed peasants to whose 'emancipation' they vowed to 'dedicate their whole lives'. For these masses, separated from them by a cultural abyss, the young democratic aristocrats remained 'masters'. This is why Herzen, the future publisher of the *Polyarnaya Zvezda* ('The Pole Star') and the *Kolokol* ('The Bell'), the first political organs of the Russian emigration, who insisted on a complete break with the 'lords and officials', was compelled to add, gloomily: 'The orthodox folk, if not openly at war with the educated people, are mistrustfully and enigmatically silent.' He speaks of this social isolation of 'educated people' as the 'tragic side of our life' (*Diary*, 11 September 1842), and in his essay on 'Dilettantism in Science' (1843) explains it in this way: 'We are living on the boundary between two worlds – which makes life for thinking people especially oppressive and difficult.'

2. THE ADVENT OF THE PLEBEIANS

This oppressive feeling of social isolation of democratically-minded educated people began fusing with a proud consciousness of their great historical 'mission' when they began being infiltrated and soon dominated more and more by the so-called *raznochintsy*, i.e. plebeians – peasants, petty-bourgeois, merchants, members of the liberal professions, and a very strong admixture of the clergy.* The 'intelligentsia' then began forming rapidly.

The first plebeian who occupied a leading position in the nascent Russian intelligentsia was the well-known literary critic Vissarion

* In colloquial speech *raznochintsy* meant people who had been wrenched out of their *milieu* by education, away from the various (= *razny*) non-noble social categories.

Belinsky (1811–48), son of a provincial physician. Plekhanov[13] is probably right in thinking that Belinsky received the somewhat mocking nickname of the 'furious Vissarion' from his noble friends because while 'practically the sole plebeian in his group' he behaved with respect to the 'accursed questions' of the time 'with far less restraint than the enlightened representatives of the nobility'. And he is unquestionably right when he says that Belinsky's 'fury' was like a sort of prototype of the 'fury' in social and political questions that towards the end of the '50s brought about a profound cleavage between the plebeian core of the intelligentsia and the aristocratic pioneers of the Russian democracy, including Herzen himself.

As indicated, Belinsky was practically the first and practically the sole plebeian in an almost exclusively aristocratic *milieu.* The intellectual and political work of the last years of his short life (he died at the age of 37) ended largely in a struggle for the spiritual emancipation of the plebeians from specifically aristocratic influences. This labour prepared the victory in Russian democratic thinking of those politically and socially far more radical 'plebeian' tendencies whose heralds were two of Belinsky's successors, N. G. Chernyshevsky (1828–89) and N. A. Dobrolyubov (1836–61), both of them sons of clergymen. And it was this plebeian victory that at the same time marked the consolidation of the Russian intelligentsia as a special social grouping.

What proved decisive was the fact that in Russia's peculiar social and cultural conditions not only democratic aristocrats but also democratic plebeians, while incapable of leaning on the bourgeoisie, were also incapable of finding any support among the masses of the people. 'The people need potatoes, but not a constitution in the least; that is what is wanted by the educated urban classes, who are incapable of doing anything,' wrote Belinsky to his friends after a trip through Russia in 1846. Incapable of becoming 'bourgeois', the democracy of the plebeians was incapable of becoming peasant either. Still less could its Socialism become proletarian; the Russian working-class was still embryonic.

Doomed to decades of historical solitude, the thin stratum of educated Russians, chiefly young people, was obliged to hoist on to its own shoulders the entire burden of the political and cultural 'europeanization' of Russia. Whole generations of the most talented, energetic, and courageous Russian intellectual youth were consumed in this unbearable enterprise. Between 1825–30 they went to the grave, perished on the gallows, or were 'buried alive' (title of a pamphlet by Dolgushin; see below) in hard-labour prisons, in the dungeons of the Peter-Paul and Shlisselburg Fortresses, in the boundless wilderness of the Siberian taiga.

Such were the historical circumstances that led to the birth of the 'intelligentsia', and set their stamp on the subsequent development of the idea of democracy and Socialism in Russia. Because of an inevitable inertia the tendencies of this isolation were preserved even when the historical conditions that had given it birth began to disappear, when the emergence of the working-class into the political arena during the second half of the '90s made it possible for one (Marxist, Social-Democratic) part of the intelligentsia to begin breaking its links with the 'intelligentsia' as an isolated social group and to lean socially on the proletariat, and when a second (the Populist) part of it began finding a path towards a *rapprochement* with the burgeoning revolutionary agrarian movement of the peasantry.

The definitive extinction of the intelligentsia as a specific social group and its transformation in Russia too into a professional group was to take place under the Soviet régime. It is only in the emigration that its remnants are living out their lives, as a sort of 'spiritual order'. Their radicalism, however, has become deeply diluted, and they have become reconciled to 'bourgeois' social, political, and material culture with whose 'non-acceptance' the Russian intelligentsia had actually begun, and are becoming more and more densely fused in a common 'anti-Bolshevism' with those fragments – also cast out into the emigration – of conservative and reactionary elements of Russian society that they used to be separated from by an unbridgeable chasm.

3. FORERUNNERS OF POPULISM

The revolutions of 1848 that careered through Europe came to a halt at the borders of Russia. Nevertheless their influence on the course of Russian political and intellectual life was tremendous.

Nicholas I was so enraged and frightened by them that at first he seriously considered declaring war on all revolutionary Europe. To some extent he actually realized his intentions by sending Russian troops to help the Austrian Emperor suppress the Hungarian revolution. His domestic policy became still more reactionary. The censorship to which the press, especially the periodical press, was subject became quite unendurable. A genuine terror descended on all the seeds of free, philosophical, scientific and especially political thought. And if as late as the end of the '30s the Tsar had minced no words in calling the talented P. Y. Chaadayev 'crazy' for having developed some pessimistic views on the destiny of Russia in his *Philosophic Letters*, now it was only death (26 May 1848) that saved Belinsky from arrest, while it was forbidden to mention his very name in the press. All private societies and clubs were wiped out. I have already mentioned the prison-sentences of the Petrashevskyites. The famous Ukrainian poet Taras Shevchenko also fell victim to a savage repression, and was drafted into the army for life because of his participation in the so-called Cyril-Methodius Society,* founded by the historian N. Kostomarov, in whose programme the ideas of Pan-Slavism and federalism were combined with ideas of Christian Socialism taken from the Frenchman Lammens.

The repression by the police and the bureaucracy created such a stifling atmosphere that the war with the Anglo-French coalition that began in 1853, especially the landing of the Allies in the Crimea, was met by the broadest circles of society with hopes that the triumphant blows of the coalition would shatter the barracks régime of Nicholas I. It was not the radicals and Socialists, but such conservatively and patriotically-minded people as the famous Slavophils Alexander Koshelev and Ivan Aksakov who were the first Russian 'defeatists'. As Koshelev testified later,[14] 'the mood of society and even of the people, though partly unconscious, was along the same lines'.[15]

As a matter of fact the military defeats, the death (or suicide) of Nicholas I (18 February 1855), and then the fall of Sebastopol (27 August 1855) struck a fissure into the régime and laid the foundations for a new revival in scientific and political thought. A strict censorship continued to disfigure books and newspapers, compelling writers to resort to allegorical language (later known currently as 'Aesopian'), and to dress up political articles in the form of literary criticism. But even a slight weakening of the censorship proved sufficient, in the *Sovremennik* bereft of Belinsky, for the voice of his still more radically and Socialistically-minded successors, Chernyshevsky and Dobrolyubov, to ring out more and more resoundingly. In 1858 these became co-directors of the periodical together with the famous poet N. A. Nekrasov.

But it was not only in the radicalization of Russian democratic

* Sts Cyril and Methodius are considered the teachers of the ancient Slavs and the composers of the Slavic, i.e. 'Cyrillic' alphabet.

thought that the influence of the 1848 revolutions expressed itself. The Russian democrats, who greeted these revolutions with enthusiasm and high hopes, were all the more impressed by their collapse and by the acuteness of the social contradictions they disclosed. The thought expressed by Herzen as far back as 1843,[16] to the effect that 'political upheavals that are not social have become impossible', was not strange to any of them. Now, however, in an article addressed to the French sociologist Edgar Quinet criticizing the course of the revolutions of 1848, this same Herzen declared that the paths of Russia and of Western Europe had diverged: 'We shall be taking different paths – you to Socialism through the proletariat, we through Socialism to liberty.'[17] Thus for the first time in Russia a thought was expressed that was posed as the political idea of the Bolshevik revolution some sixty years and a bit later: liberty is indispensable, but in Russia Socialism must precede liberty.

Chernyshevsky went much further in this direction. Belinsky, referring to the July revolution of 1830 in France, had already expressed regret that the workers had intervened in the fight between the bourgeoisie and the king: 'In blind and senseless self-abnegation the people did not spare themselves, struggling for the destruction of laws that had not made it any happier and hence were no more of its business than the question of the Chinese emperor's health.'[18] Chernyshevsky now (1859) proclaimed that as long as economic inequality existed the masses of the people had no interest in freedom at all. Speaking about the difference between the 'democrats' and the 'liberals' he wrote:[19]

> The democrats intend as far as possible to eliminate the domination of the lower classes by the upper in the state structure, on the one hand, and on the other to diminish the power and the wealth of the upper strata – in order to give more weight and well-being to the lower strata. As against this, the liberals absolutely refuse to allow the lower strata any preponderance in society, for these strata, because of their poverty and lack of education, are indifferent to interests that for the liberal party are paramount – the right of free speech and the constitutional order. For a democrat our Siberia, in which our common people enjoy well-being, is far better than England, where the majority of the people endure want.

An authentic democrat is 'disposed to bring about reforms with the help of material force and for the sake of reforms is ready to sacrifice both freedom of speech and constitutional methods'.

We shall see what an essential role was played by thoughts of this kind, which were expressed in Russian literature for the first time by Chernyshevsky, in the Bakunin (anarchist) wing of the revolutionary movement of the '60s and '70s.

An even more essential role was played by another idea, also first formulated with precision during these years. This was the idea of the 'originality' of the socio-economic and political evolution of Russia, and of the significance, from this point of view, of the communal land ownership that had been preserved since ancient times and that was bound up with periodic reapportionments of land corresponding to changes in the family situation of members of the commune.*

Baron Haxthausen, the German scholar, whose trip to Russia in 1843 we have already mentioned, got out a book at the beginning of the '50s in which he was the first to draw attention to the Russian peasant commune as a factor of social order. He came to the conclusion, comforting from his own conservative point of view, that a revolution (which he conceived of only as Socialist) was impossible in Russia, since there was no proletariat there but a communal régime that assured everyone of the possession of his property. Disappointed by the revolutions of 1848, which had proved unable to settle the 'social question', Herzen took up these ideas of Haxthausen's, not in order to proclaim the Russian commune as the antithesis of Western European Socialism, but on the contrary, in order to declare it to be the foundation on which Socialism could be erected more easily and without any revolutionary upsets: 'Standing in the camp of the defeated, I pointed out to them a people whose way of life contained more factors tending towards an economic upheaval than definitively established Western nations.'[20] Even in 1861 he insisted: 'That which in the West can only be consummated by a series of catastrophes and upheavals can develop in Russia on the groundwork of something already in existence.'[21]

After some vacillations Chernyshevsky, in his famous essay, 'A Critique of Philosophical Prejudices against Communal Landownership', adopted essentially the same point of view, to be sure with one not unimportant addition. Like Herzen, Chernyshevsky

* The basic function of the peasant commune (the *mir*) was the assessment of the tax *per capita*, for the collection of which the government laid the responsibility on the commune as a whole, leaving it up to its discretion to distribute the assessment among individual members.

ascribed immense importance to the effect of the Western European 'experiment' on the future evolution of Russia. But for Herzen this 'experiment' amounted to the sum of those ideas that were being worked out in the West, but because of socio-economic conditions there could not be realized. These ideas, on the other hand, found a favourable terrain in the 'communal' order in Russia. From the same point of view Chernyshevsky ascribed equal importance to the producers' 'associations' to which among other things he devoted his novel, *What Is to Be Done?* Indeed, he valued the commune itself, as Plekhanov remarked,[22] primarily as an 'institution that forms the spirit of association'.

Such an approach of course made possible the further evolution of views on the commune. We shall still see traces of this evolution in the brief activity allotted Chernyshevsky after the Manifesto of 19 February 1861 proclaimed the emancipation of the peasants. But only guesses can be made about the possible evolution of the opinions of the editors of the *Sovremennik*. On 17 November 1861, at the age of twenty-five, Dobrolyubov went to his grave. Half a year later arrest, fourteen years of hard labour and subsequent isolation in one of the most remote corners of Siberia interrupted for almost a quarter of a century the journalistic activity of the thirty-four-year-old Chernyshevsky. In the second half of the '50s, in any case, an affirmative attitude towards the commune played such a decisive role in their views that on this ground points of contact appeared between them (as with Herzen) and conservative Slavophilism, just at the time the 'Westernizers' began repelling them more and more through their 'liberalism'. Their work laid the cornerstone of the 'Populist' ideology of the succeeding decades: a conviction that Russia could 'skip' the capitalist stage of evolution and move directly to Socialism, and also that it was the peasant commune that guaranteed this possibility.

4. THE EVE OF EMANCIPATION

The specific Russian ideology of Populism was born as the direct reaction of Russian democratic thought to the drying-up of the socio-political creative forces of Western European society, so clearly revealed by the revolutions of 1848. This reaction was the same in Herzen, the most eminent of the aristocratic pioneers of Russian democracy, as it was in such unquestionably plebeian leaders as

Chernyshevsky and Dobrolyubov: the two latter were simply carrying to their 'logical conclusion' the ideas expressed by the former. Thus, when Alexander II came to the throne and preparatory labours began for the emancipation of the peasants, their practical programme also proved to be the same.

As early as 1848, in his diary, Chernyshevsky had declared himself 'a partisan of Socialists and Communists and of the most extreme republicans'. In 1853, when about to get married, he still thought it his duty to warn his bride that 'there was soon going to be an uprising in Russia' and that he himself was 'certainly going to take part in it'; he 'was not frightened by filth, by drunken peasants with clubs, or by slaughter', he would not be stopped by gaol, hard labour, or death. This revolutionary mood, which had ripened during the gloomiest years of Nicholas's rule, did not leave Chernyshevsky for the rest of his life. But with the death of Nicholas his régime also seemed to be expiring. The peasant question was put on the order of the day. And from the point of view of both Herzen and Chernyshevsky now, all political problems retreated altogether to the background before this central question whose settlement was going to determine the future social development of the country. It was only necessary for the peasant question to be brought forward as quickly as possible. And the programme outlined by Chernyshevsky in 1856[23] is striking not only in its extreme modesty, but also in its complete identity with the programme formulated in three points by Herzen in 1855. 'The emancipation of the peasants from the landowners, the emancipation of the taxed classes of the population from corporal punishment and the emancipation of the press from the censorship.'[24] The paths by which these were to be realized also coincided.

Now, while the peasantry was gripped by the hope of the 'freedom' promised by the Tsar, it was out of place to count on an imminent 'uprising'. At the same time it was obvious that among the masses of the people there were no forces that could have been leaned on for an organized struggle for reform against both the landowners and the government. In Russia there was no bourgeoisie capable of heading a revolutionary movement. The young Russian intelligentsia, lacking any popular support, was also powerless. In the given historical conditions the only force that was able to and, in its own interests, ought to have carried out a reform was the throne ('It's better for us to give it from above than wait for it to be taken from below,' said Alexander II). To fight for the throne, to make it an ally of the people against the upper classes and the upper bureaucracy that was socially fused with it ('thirty thousand police superintendents', was what Nicholas I called the landowners), to transform the Russian autocracy into a unique 'social monarchy' – such was Herzen's idea. But Chernyshevsky had come to the same idea; his indifference as a 'democrat' to the 'constitutional methods' and to the means of realizing the 'reform' helped him adopt this position. 'Thou hast conquered, O Galilean!' Herzen had greeted the young Tsar. 'Only one thing is necessary: let our autocracy take to the path of economic improvements, let Alexander II finish the work begun by Alexander I and by Nicholas,'* Chernyshevsky repeated after him.

But even at this time, for all their apparent harmony, there was in fact a gap between Herzen's views on the one hand and those of the plebeian wing of the intelligentsia on the other. It was to grow broader and broader.

The hopes Herzen pinned to the throne were hopes that it would be possible to live through the critical period painlessly and create conditions that would make possible the equally painless and gradual transformation of the entire socio-economic life of the country. For Herzen too, of course, political questions were secondary in comparison with social questions. But in his view political progress had to be made parallel with social progress. This was why he had such a high opinion of those liberal elements in the nobility who without, of course, relinquishing any of their material interests had reconciled themselves to the liquidation of serfdom and even to meeting it halfway, and in whose position a visible place was taken by the aspiration towards 'constitutional methods'. It was in collaborating and compromising with these elements that Herzen saw the best way to create conditions in which the preaching of the socialist 'idea' would become possible, while the idea itself would be taken up by broader and broader masses prepared for its acceptance by their own communal way of life. The 'social monarchy' Herzen dreamt of was conceived by him as an enlightened and benevolent régime, leading the people gradually towards social progress and simultaneously towards political liberty as well.

Chernyshevsky and Dobrolyubov had a completely different conception of the 'social monarchy'. They imagined it as a 'Jacobin', perhaps despotic, monarchy, but one that would mercilessly crush the

* Secret committees to deal with the peasant question had been convoked more than once during these two reigns.

resistance of the possessing classes to the radical social reconstruction of which the emancipation of the peasants was only supposed to be the first step. Herzen's slogan, 'through Socialism to freedom', was understood by them in a way quite different from its author's meaning. For Herzen the modest three-point programme he had formulated in his letter of 1855 was the expression of his genuine aspiration towards a gradual transformation of Russian life, without any upheavals or catastrophes. For Chernyshevsky and Dobrolyubov the same programme was scarcely anything but the initial stage of a path that led to Socialism only through upheavals and catastrophes and to freedom only through Socialism.

During the subsequent course of the liquidation of serfdom both these conceptions – Herzen's 'liberal' one and Chernyshevsky's and Dobrolyubov's 'democratic' one – proved illusory. But for the time being it was just this attitude towards the liberal nobility that became the water-shed between them. It was precisely in 'liberalism' that the 'democrats' saw Enemy No. 1, which was striving to make the throne an ally of the possessing classes, to strip the cause of peasant emancipation of any Socialist character, and by the immoderate eulogizing of every variety of political progress to distract the attention of society from infinitely more important social tasks. The articles of the *Sovremennik* editors were aimed at the unmasking of this enemy. Dobrolyubov, with the full brilliance of his talent, ridiculed him in prose and verse (under the pseudonym of Konrad Lilienschwager) in the *Svistok*, a satirical supplement of the journal.

It was this attitude towards 'liberalism' that led to a departure from the *Sovremennik* of those aristocratic writers who since the days of Belinsky had become the chief contributors to the artistic department. Turgenev, Grigorovich, Goncharov and others were replaced by a pleiade of talented plebeian youths (Nicholas Uspensky, Naumov, Levitov, Pomyalovsky, Reshetnikov and others). The works of these latter breathed forth social radicalism and testified to a familiarity with the way of life and the hopes of the lowest popular strata that was completely inaccessible to the aristocratic writers. It was on the same point, the attitude towards aristocratic 'liberalism', that the definitive rupture of Herzen with the editors of the *Sovremennik* took place in 1859–60.

Thus, in the struggle of social forces that was waged around the reform in preparation, intellectual tendencies were stored up and delineated that only received their definitive shaping and practical application during the two succeeding decades. But the same struggle also saw the consolidation of the 'intelligentsia' as a special social group, with special tasks that differed from the tasks of all other groups. In this way still another question that acquired primary importance during these same decades arose of itself: the question of the place of this 'intelligentsia' itself in the process of social evolution, the question of the role of the 'thinking individual' (Dobrolyubov).

Dobrolyubov paid a great deal of attention to this question. In an essay called 'Then when will the real day come?', devoted to Turgenev's novel *On the Eve*, which served as the immediate occasion of Turgenev's rupture with the *Sovremennik*, he gave a critical appreciation of the fact that the only man in the book whose words do not diverge from his deeds turns out to be not a Russian but a Bulgarian revolutionary, Insarov. He predicted that people of deeds and not words would soon make their appearance in Russia too. His essay ends: 'The eve is not far from the day that follows, whatever the night that separates them!'

Dobrolyubov was not deceived by his foresight: 'the real day', when the Russian intelligentsia began producing 'men of action', was already knocking at the doors of history. These doors were opened for it by the Manifesto of 19 February 1861 freeing the peasants from serfdom.

PART TWO

Revolutionary Populism

CHAPTER FOUR

The Reform and Russian Society

1. THE PEASANTRY AND THE NOBILITY

Were the peasants to be freed with land or without land? In the preparation of the Reform this question seemed to be central in the disputes between the 'partisans of progress' and the 'serf-holders'. It was decided in the 'progressive' sense. The emancipated peasants received allotments of land. Nevertheless the decree of 19 February 1861 not only deeply disappointed the Russian democrats, as we shall see, but it completely deceived the hopes bound up with the promised 'freedom' by the peasants themselves.

In the course of the evolution of land relationships in Russia, the firm conviction had rooted itself in the peasant masses that the whole of the land belonged to them, and had become the property of the landholders only in so far as the person of the peasant was secured to them together with the land, as a reward for service to the state. 'We are yours, but the land is ours', this was the formula for serfdom in the minds of the peasants. Because of this feudal relations lost all justification in the eyes of the peasants the moment Catherine the Great's ukase on the 'freedom of the nobility' (1785) freed the landowners from any obligation to serve the state. This was the reason they were convinced that when serfdom was liquidated the whole of the land would return to the peasantry.

In practice even the substantial portion of the land that the peasants did in fact make use of under serfdom was stripped away in favour of the landowners (the 'strips'). The peasantry was supposed to pay an unduly high price for the plots of land allocated to it, and the 'redemption payments' became an annual addition to the heavy poll-tax paid to the state, which handed over to the landowners the entire redemptive sum all at once in the form of bonds, the so-called 'redemptive certificates'. Over a period of eight years the peasants were supposed to perform certain duties on behalf of the landowner; they remained 'temporarily obligated'. Finally, the whole business of agrarian reconstruction, with all the attendant questions about the character of the appendages to the land (forests, pastures, etc.), the quality of the land, the location of the plots allotted to the peasants and so on, was put into the hands of the so-called 'arbiters' from among the nobility. To put the emancipated peasantry in a position in which both the holdings of the big landlords and industry would be secured by cheap labour whatever happened – such was the basic economic idea behind the Reform. 'Instead of feudal chains they thought up a great many others', was how Nekrasov characterized this idea.

It is understandable why in a number of localities the peasants resisted the implementation of the 19 February decree. There was a widespread popular conviction that the landowners and functionaries were concealing from the people the 'real' freedom promised by the Tsar, to replace it with their own 'seignorial' freedom. The excitement that seized hold of broad masses of the peasantry overflowed in a genuine revolt in a number of Volga provinces. It was drowned in blood by the shooting of a peasant mob in the village of Bezdna in Kazan Province (12 April 1861).

Severe repressions put a halt to the spreading of the riots and broke peasant resistance to the 19 February decree. But the legend about the 'peasant Tsar' and the expectation of the 'gold charter', which finally, in the teeth of the 'masters', would proclaim the longed-for 'real' freedom, lived on for a long time among the peasants. The Tsarist government was even able to make use of it itself, not only in order to contend with the various aristocratic demands for the limitation of bureaucratic omnipotence, but even more in order to discredit the Socialist revolutionaries in the eyes of the peasants as agents of the nobility.* A mortal blow was dealt this legend by the Tsar himself when Alexander III told peasant representatives, who had convened in Moscow from all over the country for the coronation (1883), to 'listen to the leaders of the nobility'. In these words he announced the beginning of a policy that in the conflict between the peasantry and the nobility openly took the side of the nobility, and even gave its representatives – the 'Land Captains' (*Zemskiye Nachal'niki*) – administrative and judicial powers over the rural population.

But this stage in the evolution of the post-reform relations between the nobility and the autocracy still lay in the future. The nobility met

* In 1876 this same legend was exploited by revolutionaries too (Leo Deich, Jacob Stefanovich and others), not without some temporary success, for the organization of a peasant movement in the Chigirin district of Kiev Province.

the Reform itself with mixed feelings. Three basic tendencies may be noted: aristocratic reaction, class conservatism, and liberalism.

The aristocratically reactionary tendency had manifested itself even during the course of the discussions of the peasant reform in a famous 'Note' handed to the government by M. A. Bezobrazov. The Note demanded the 'curbing' of the bureaucracy and the convocation of deputies from the nobility, with which the state power was, indeed, supposed to act in accord. After the Reform was introduced the chief organ of this tendency became the newspaper, *Vest* (News) which had been founded in 1863 by Skaryatin. It was in the same spirit that an address to the Tsar was composed by M. Katkov in 1865 and accepted by the Moscow nobility; it referred to the 'crowning of the edifice of reform' by an elected institution of the nobility.

The idea of conserving 'primordial' Russian principles and the caste régime, but with the convocation of an all-class consultative 'National Assembly' ('To the Tsar the power of authority, to the land the power of opinion') was championed by the Slavophil wing of the Russian nobility, which later on supplemented these ideas with a request for active 'Pan-Slavic' foreign policy. In 1856 the review *Russkaya Beseda* (The Russian Colloquy) with a special supplement called 'Agricultural Welfare' devoted to the peasant question, was founded as the organ of the Slavophils. The newspaper *Parus* (The Sail), begun in 1859 by Ivan Aksakov, was closed by the second number. Subsequently the Slavophils were occasionally subjected to repression for their struggle against the bureaucracy, in which they saw a pernicious 'partition' between the Tsar and the people.*

The liberal tendency was represented in pre-reform years by the St Petersburg review *Otechestvennye Zapiski* (Notes from the Fatherland), published by Krayevsky and edited by Dudyshkin. But it was the Moscow review, *Russky Vestnik* (The Russian Courier) that was the chief organ of aristocratic liberalism during these years. At this time its editor was the same M. Katkov, a former Moscow radical, who, as we have seen, had by 1865 already turned into an exponent of the aristocratic opposition to the bureaucracy and as editor of the newspaper *Moskovskiye Vedomosti* (Moscow News) soon became, together with K. Leontyev, a spokesman for the most extreme bureaucratic reaction.

* Conservatism of a 'Western' shading, in the spirit of British constitutional Toryism, was represented in the review *Biblioteka dlya Chteniya*, under the editorship of Druzhinin. But this sort of conservatism was not very widespread.

After the Reform the role of liberal champion swiftly passed over to the *Vestnik Yevropy*, which had been founded in 1866 but had only become a monthly review under the editorship of M. Stasyulevich in 1868. In 1871 there began coming out in Petersburg a daily liberal newspaper *Golos* (The Voice), also published by the above-mentioned Krayevsky. But it was the 'professorial' Moscow newspaper *Russkiye Vedomosti** that became the leading liberal-democratic organ from the middle of the '70s on. All these shades of Russian post-reform liberalism were characterized, as noted by A. Potresov (loc. cit.), by an aristocratic-rural, and not bourgeois-capitalist colouration, as well as by a programme of 'support for the small producer, the communal peasant, and home-crafts', with an increasing admixture of ideas of a Populist character.

The clearest political response of aristocratic liberalism to the Reform was a petition to the Tsar in 1862 by the nobility of Tver Province. The petition spoke out for the rapid liquidation of the 'compulsory relations of the peasants to the landowners' and of the 'artificial division into classes', and for a unitary system of universal taxation. It demanded the convocation of a 'National Assembly'. The government's answer took the form of administrative sanctions against the composers of the petition, headed by Unkovsky, a Provincial Marshal of the Nobility.

2. THE INTELLIGENTSIA TURNS REVOLUTIONARY

As preparations for the Reform progressed it grew more and more clear how little it would realize the hopes pinned to it in the beginning by the democratic section of Russian society. For this reason the attitude towards it of the more moderate groups of the intelligentsia, which gravitated towards the *Kolokol*, as well as of the more extreme, whose spokesman was the *Sovremennik*, also became more and more critical. Thus, when the real conditions of peasant emancipation became known, the *Kolokol* expressed the deepest disappointment of all strata of the Russian democracy, 'With bitterness of heart and profound grief' it noted that in essence the 'old system of serfdom had been replaced by a new one'.[25] At the same time the protest, occasionally very tempestuous, with which the peasantry met the Reform gave some grounds for the resurrection of notions about

* Professors A. Chuprov and A. Posnikov.

the imminence of the popular 'uprising' that had almost faded away entirely during the preceding years.

The reaction of the democratic intelligentsia to the new situation was neither unified nor straightforward. After the inevitable confusion and vacillation, some time elapsed before the basic tendencies defined themselves. These, while complicating the divergence already noted between the 'liberals' and the 'democrats', reflected the whole contradictoriness of the position of the Russian democracy in the face of the tasks set for it by the new stage in Russian history, and laid the foundations for the evolution of political thought and struggle that filled the stormy '60s and '70s.

The *Kolokol*[26] reacted to the Reform by advising the peasants to sabotage its practical implementation, and to see to it that the 'Tsar was of the land, in harmony with the land and elected by the land'. Thus Herzen's answer to the unsatisfactoriness of the Reform from a social point of view was a return to 'politics'. But this politics was nothing but a continuation – in new conditions – of that appeal to the 'social' Tsar Herzen had already come to while the struggle for the reform was being carried on.

It is true that at that time this appeal had been indispensable, in view of the absence in Russian society and in the peasantry itself of those forces that might have been relied on in the struggle for the Socialist character of the future reform. Now the excitement of the peasants seemed to indicate that forces of this kind were springing up among the masses of the people. But Herzen was still very far from regarding the struggle for the 'social' Tsar as lost. The ripening conflict did not appear to him to be a conflict of the peasantry with the throne, which sided with the nobility, but a conflict between the peasantry and the nobility, in which the Tsar would still have a decisive word to say.

'A clash is unavoidable,' he wrote on 15 August 1862. 'Until now we see no chance of the people's being ready to give up the land, or of the nobility's relinquishing it cheaply. They are both turning to the general arbiter – the government.' The throne is regarded by the people as a kind of 'social republic covered by Monomakh's cap'.* If the throne meets the social demands of the people half-way no one will be able to resist it; a revision of the 19 February decree, in the

* 'Monomakh's cap', i.e. of Grand Duke St Vladimir (980–1015), under whom the christening of ancient Russia took place. It was used in the coronation of the Russian kings.

spirit of the interests of the peasantry and its Socialist tendencies, will be carried out peaceably. However, as Herzen says in the same article, written in answer to a reproach by *Molodaya Rossiya* (Young Russia – see below) that he had lost faith in the revolution: 'We have not lost our faith in violent overturns, but our love for them.' And he insists that if a revolution proves inevitable, there's nothing to be done about it, it would have to be joined. But everything must be done to make this unnecessary: 'The fateful day will come, and then you'll stand up and fight, but don't call it a day you had wished for.'

As we shall see in a moment the reaction of the 'democrats' among the intelligentsia, or at least this most important section, in their disappointment at the Reform, at first glance seemed quite similar to the reaction of the 'liberal' Herzen. But this identity was just the same aberration we have noted above and shall have to note further on: the formal identity of 'slogans' concealed the whole differentiation of opinion in fact with respect to socio-political reality. The tendencies of revolutionary radicalism were beginning to be counterposed in a more and more definite way to the tendencies of reformist 'gradualism'.

The revolutionary character of the response to 19 February, even of those 'democrats' whose reaction was regarded at the time as being the most 'moderate', was also expressed in a purely external fact – the emergence of an 'illegal', i.e. secretly printed and distributed literature. In June 1861, some five months after the announcement of the reform, the first number of a leaflet called *Velikoruss* (The Great Russian) was circulated in Petersburg and Moscow. As far as is known this was the first 'illegal' printed work of the '60s.[27] The three *Velikoruss* leaflets happen to be of special interest since there is reason to believe that Chernyshevsky played a part in writing them, together with a number of other contributors to *Sovremennik* (Nicholas Serno-Solovyevich and others).

The first leaflet begins by referring to the peasant turbulence and accuses the government of 'leading Russia into a Pugachov revolt'* by disregarding the demands of the peasantry. It summons the 'educated classes' 'to take the conduct of affairs into their own hands and out of the hands of the incompetent government' in order to 'eliminate arbitrary administration' and 'replace it by a régime based on law'.

If 'the educated classes consider themselves powerless' then 'the

* Emelian Pugachov – the leader of a peasant uprising in 1773–5 that seized the area around the lower Volga.

patriots will be forced to summon the people to action that the educated classes would refrain from'.

The second leaflet, published in the beginning of September 1861, continues the line laid down in the first. Demanding the elimination of purchase money for the plots of a land allocated to the peasants, it points out that two parties are contending with each other among the peasantry – an 'extremist' one, which demands all the land belonging to the landowners, and a 'moderate' one, which agrees to be satisfied with the land that had been cultivated by the peasants under serfdom (that is, demanding only the return of the 'strips'). The leaflet advises supporting the 'moderate' party before it is too late, but adds that if the spring disappoints the peasants' expectations then a peasant uprising, and at the same time the triumph of the 'extremist' party will be inevitable. Consequently it is up to the 'educated people' to hurry; the leaflet insists that 'what it is necessary to demand is not the granting of a constitution, but the convocation of deputies in order to write one freely'. This is the first formulation in the history of the Russian revolutionary movement of the demand for a 'Constituent Assembly' that in the 1900s played such a central role.

Finally, in the third and last leaflet, which came out a fortnight after the second, a further step in the same direction is taken. It is proposed to the 'educated classes' that they 'try peaceable means' and send the Tsar a petition. A draft of the petition, 'written in the most moderate spirit, so that all liberals could subscribe to it', was appended to the bulletin; it ended up with this appeal to the Tsar: 'Deign, Sire, to convoke the representatives of the Russian nation to one of the capitals of our Russian homeland, in order to create a constitution for Russia.'

A shift towards 'politics', a turn towards the 'liberals', and so on – all this was so poorly integrated with the idea of the 'democrat' as conceived by Chernyshevsky only a couple of years before that the first *Velikoruss* leaflet evoked more than a little confusion. Over the signature 'One of Many' the following open letter appeared in the *Kolokol*[28]: 'What is the [*Velikoruss*] association aiming at? A constitution, or something else? Probably the whole of the nobility would stand up for a constitution. Let those to whom it may be useful secure a constitution. It's not for us either to help or to hinder them now. Our goal is the complete emancipation of the peasants, the right of the people to land, its right to organize and govern itself.' What is needed is not an appeal to liberal society, which 'will never genuinely go against the government and will never voluntarily give the people what they need', but an appeal to the people themselves.

It is evident that the *Velikoruss* leaflets outlined a shift towards 'politics', and at that a shift that was far more extreme and consistent than Herzen's shift. But such a shift was dictated to the 'democrats' by the whole course of events. The real character of the Reform, as frozen in the decree of 19 February, left no further room for illusions about the ability of Russian Tsarism to evolve into a 'social monarchy' of a Jacobin type. It was too clear that Tsarism was making its choice, and that it preferred an alliance with the nobility to an alliance with the peasantry. But this was just the reason why the 'uprising', hopes for which were revived by the peasant excitement, began appearing to the democrats no longer as a revolution of the people allied with the throne against the possessing classes, which only a short while before they could still dream about and which – in its 'reformist' variant – Herzen did go on dreaming about, but a revolution of the masses of the people against the throne and the possessing classes combined.

However, the circumstances had so peremptorily turned the thought of the democrats towards 'politics' that the author of the open letter himself could not make up his mind, as we have just seen, to characterize the various kinds of petitions as pernicious, but stopped half-way – in a position of peculiar 'benevolent neutrality': 'not helping or hindering'. But his criticism completely missed its target: his attack on the appeal of the *Velikoruss* to the 'liberals' was based on an obvious misunderstanding. None of the three leaflets leaves the slightest doubt that the appeal to the liberals, the petition to the Tsar, the visible moderateness of the demands and so on, in a word everything that for Herzen was its real programme, was simply a tactical device for the *Velikoruss*, merely a means of compromising both the 'liberals' and the throne, and every form of moderation – in the expectation of the 'real day', the radical and merciless revolution whose imminent explosion seemed beyond question. The *Velikoruss* leaflets scarcely concealed this; the final number ended with an impressive warning:

> If we see that the liberals cannot make up their minds to act we shall have no choice: we shall no longer be able to speak in the same language or about the same things. It is impossible to dawdle much longer about making a decision: if the educated classes will not make up a peacable

> opposition that will compel the government to eliminate all causes of an uprising before the spring of 1863, then the people will rise up irresistibly in the summer of 1863.

As though to fulfil this promise to stop speaking 'the same language' there came a proclamation to privately owned serfs, who were called upon to ready themselves for the revolution in which political and social aims were indissolubly linked. The proclamation was written by Chernyshevsky in the beginning of 1862; though it was never printed it served as the principal ground for sentencing him to hard labour after his arrest in July of the same year.

Attempting to use simple, popular speech, the proclamation declared that the decree of 19 February had put the peasants in 'eternal bondage'. To liberate themselves they had to win the same 'freedom' that existed in France, Switzerland, England and America. But for this 'the peasants had to be in agreement with each other so that they would all be as one when the time came. When there is harmony among you, orders will be given to everyone to begin in unison.'

The same motifs as in the *Velikoruss* leaflets developed, though with different shadings, in the other illegal works of the period: in a proclamation 'To the younger generation', written by the gifted poet M. Mikhailov* and published in the autumn of 1861, and in the proclamation 'Young Russia', which came out about the same time in the form of the first number of a projected periodical (*Molodaya Rossiya*), whose author was the son of a general, P. Zaichnevsky, and who was also later sentenced to hard labour.

Mikhailov, too, called for an 'elective and limited government', but in his thinking the centre of gravity was transferred to the sphere of a struggle for Socialist reconstruction. To his mind the defeat of Socialism in the revolutions of 1848 'simply proved one thing – the failure of the attempt for Europe, but it said nothing against the possibility of other social systems for Russia'. For, in contradistinction to Europe, Russia had a peasant commune, and 'enough land to last us ten thousand years. We are a belated people, and that is our salvation. . . . [Europe's] hopeless situation is a lesson for us. We do not want her proletariat, her aristocratic ways, her state principles

* Sentenced to six years' hard labour, he soon died in prison, at the age of thirty-nine. Many have thought him the author of the above-mentioned letter signed 'One of many'.

and her imperial régime. . . . We believe ourselves called on to introduce a new principle into history.' And if in order to realize the 'social aspirations' indicated it would be necessary to sacrifice a 'hundred thousand landowners', it would be wrong to stop at this.

As for a 'Pugachovite' revolt, which the *Velikoruss* had cautiously prepared the reader for while clearly dissociating itself from it, and which Mikhailov merely hinted at, 'Young Russia' called for one openly. In essence the programme of this latter was identical with the programme of Chernyshevsky's proclamation to the privately owned serfs. It demanded the transfer of all power into the hands of National and local assemblies, conventions, an elected court, parity in taxation, the building of public factories and workshops, the public education of children, the abolition of marriage, the elimination of the monasteries, the replacement of the standing army with a national militia and so on. To achieve these political goals the proclamation considered all means admissible, including terror, and called for the annihilation of the whole Romanov dynasty.

But the proclamation did not call for a political overturn alone. It called for a 'revolution that should radically change all, all the foundations without exception of contemporary society'. And if reactionary and conservative elements resisted such a revolution by force, then, 'with full faith in ourselves, in our own forces, in the sympathy of the people, in the glorious future of Russia, whose lot it is to be the first to realize the great cause of Socialism, we shall utter one cry only: "to the axe!" And then – then smite . . . without pity, as they have no pity for us now, smite in the squares, smite in the houses, smite in the dense intersections of the cities, smite in the broad avenues of the capital, smite in the country and on the farms!' Herzen's condemnation of the 'Pugachovite' summons of the proclamation was all the sharper since he saw in its 'nakedness of rejection' and 'logical mercilessness' proof of an alienation from the people, and a dangerous incomprehension that 'the people had no faith in us and were ready to stone to death those giving their lives for it'. Herzen's apprehensions were shared by many democrats, especially since it happened to be about this time that a rumour was circulated among the masses of the people and trustfully accepted that the frequent fires that had begun in Petersburg and a number of provincial cities were the handiwork of students and revolutionaries. To contradict this rumour 'Young Russia' published another proclamation entitled 'A Warning', explaining that although 'a popular uprising was imminent' the people were being led to this by the government, whereas the revolutionaries were only expressing a readiness to stand together with the people. 'The revolutionary party could never be capable of accomplishing a *coup d'état* by itself.'

Michael Bakunin, later the celebrated leader of international anarchism, came out against 'Young Russia' in his capacity of mouthpiece for the 'orthodox' wing of the democratic intelligentsia. He was not, of course, shocked by the 'insurrectionary' language of 'Young Russia'; he himself soon became the intellectual inspirer of just this 'insurrectionary' wing of the revolutionary movement. But he sharply objected to the political character of the proclamation: in his words the 'popular party' ought to set as its 'sole aim the triumph of the people's cause'. Consequently it 'had no prejudices either for the Tsar or against the Tsar, and if the Tsar himself, after having begun the great work, did not later betray the people the party would never fall behind the Tsar'. And Bakunin added: 'Even now it would still not be too late.' This remark of his was historically outdated: in the democratic intelligentsia hopes for a 'Jacobin' Tsar no longer found any widespread echoes at all. To make up for this, as we shall see, his decisive rejection of politics met with a very broad response in the coming years. An echo of ideas developed by Chernyshevsky during the years of preparation of the Reform, this rejection was stimulated anew by the victory of the 'principles of state' that M. Mikhailov 'had not wanted'. This stimulus was given by the bureaucratic degeneration of the Tsarist régime; this was what turned out to be the direct result of the 'epoch of Great Reforms'.

3. THE VICTORY OF 'STATISM'

With the publication of the principles of the peasant reform there immediately began, as we have seen, an intellectual crystallization of the nascent revolutionary movement of the intelligentsia. But the time for its *organizational* crystallization had not yet arrived. The proclamation's hints to the privately owned serfs of some link that existed between 'their own people' scattered 'everywhere' expressed daydreams far more than realities. And what was completely mythical was that 'central revolutionary committee' in whose name 'Young Russia' had published its periodical.

In fact, aside from some small fractional groups linked to each other simply by a common mood, nothing at all existed down to the very middle of the '70s. An enormous obstacle to the fusion of these little groups in any kind of centralized organization was the severe repression that as early as 1862–3 had removed and sent to hard labour, gaol, and exile practically the entire leadership of the democratic intelligentsia. The government kept this up during the following years as well, in a systematic attempt to wipe out its most active elements. But the basic factor that for almost fifteen years held up the organizational consolidation of the revolutionary movement and made these repressions possible to begin with was the process of socio-political evolution for which Russia after the Reform was the arena.

What proved to be decisive in this respect was the fact that the peasant excitement did not develop into the popular revolution that the immense majority of the democratic intelligentsia considered inevitable. After a comparatively brief flare-up the peasant movement subsided. Having felt their powerlessness to attain 'real freedom' at one stroke the peasant masses, biting their lips, 'accepted' the Reform. Within the narrow limits assigned them, they began rebuilding their lives, for the time being pouring out their hidden dissatisfaction only in passive dreams of the coming 'total reapportionment'. Once again revolutionary thinking, which had just begun orienting itself towards a 'people's uprising', had to reorganize itself and look for new paths. This quest was all the more difficult since during these two or three years the mood of the 'educated classes' had also radically changed. Both their liberal and their reactionary basic elements had decisively reverted to the side of a reconciliation with the government, and it was just this 'reconciliation' that in the final analysis caused the collapse of the peasant movement, helpless in the face of an alliance of Tsarism with the summits of society.

In its turn, to be sure, this movement, which had frightened the possessing classes, played a certain role in this shift towards a *rapprochement* with the government. But positive reasons were also present for this shift in the massive economic revival that had been given a push by the liquidation of serfdom.

In these new conditions a continually growing role was being played by financial and mercantile relations; in accordance with these the landowners' economy was also forced to reconstruct itself. The nobility hastily began 'bourgeoisifying' itself. But it also began moving nearer to the bourgeoisie from the other side as well: the loans it had been receiving from the government as a pledge of the 'redemptive certificates' concentrated vast financial means in its hands. Those who were unable to adapt themselves to the new conditions quickly squandered these funds in foolish schemes, merrymaking, and pleasure trips abroad, where the insane extravagance of the Russian 'boyars' became proverbial. But others put their money to work, and together with merchants and industrialists began to busy themselves with government contracts, flung themselves into the building of railways, canals, and other means of communication, the establishment of banks, industrial and commercial joint-stock companies and so on. It was the beginning of a real promoters' fever. For its part the government spurred this on in every way possible. Concessions, subsidies, guarantees became the most current terms among the men of affairs who thronged to the capital from all over the country in the hope of finding a place in some lucrative undertaking or of slipping into the bureaucratic apparatus that had swiftly begun expanding. All this created a broad material basis for the 'holiday of reconciliation' of the summits of society with the government that signalized the first years of the Reform. All it needed was an 'ideological' rivet: this was provided by the Polish insurrection that began in January 1863.

Russian revolutionary thought, which had been born in direct connexion with the European revolutions of 1848, also accepted the traditions of national emancipation of these revolutions. The idea of national self-determination – from the demand for the reorganization of the Russian state on principles of national federation to the demand for permitting 'complete freedom to the population of Southern Russia to dispose of its own fate' – was uniformly put forward in the proclamations of Mikhailov, of Young Russia, and the leaflets of the *Velikoruss*, whose very name stressed its desire to speak only in the name of the Great Russian branch of the Russian people. This 'Great Russian' self-restriction was emphasized all the more willingly since it was, after all, the peasant commune, the foundation of all hopes for an 'original' evolution of Russia towards Socialism, that was a purely Great Russian phenomenon. It had no roots either in the Ukraine ('Little Russia' in government parlance) or in White Russia, and least of all in the 'alien' areas: Poland, the Baltic, Turkestan and the Caucasus.

The Polish question, however, was special. In 1815 Alexander I had bestowed a constitution on the newly-formed 'Polish Kingdom', which bound it to Russia only via a personal union. In his speech from the throne he said that in the future he meant to extend the constitutional régime to Russia proper as well. In fact the Polish constitution, too, very quickly – especially under Nicholas I – began turning into a 'scrap of paper', but to freedom-loving circles in Russia Polish freedom became a sort of symbol of the approaching freedom of Russia. The Polish revolt of 1830 against the despotic régime of Nicholas I was hailed with sympathy by great numbers of Russian oppositionists. The demand for the restoration of Polish independence, destroyed after the revolt was suppressed, also found a place in the leaflets of the *Velikoruss* and Young Russia. Including the *Kolokol*, the Russian democracy also sided with Poland in the uprising of 1863. But now the bulk of the possessing classes came out decisively against Poland and on the side of the government. Great Russian nationalism, whose champion was the Tsarist government, became the ideological banner that covered society's capitulation to the autocracy.

Warsaw was the 'revenge for the defeat of Sebastopol'.[29] Society, which in the epoch of the Crimean War had been 'defeatist', now became profoundly patriotic. It was under the cover of this patriotism that there took place the ferocious suppression of Poland, the definitive liquidation of her former liberties, the 'pacification' of the Caucasus after the repression of the revolt led by Shamil (1859), the consolidation of Turkestan followed by the conquest of Khiva (1873), etc. There began an era of 'russification' of the border-lands – Poland, Lithuania, Caucasus, and Central Asia – that is, the violent suppression of their national cultures, the squeezing of local people out of the state and economic apparatus, the division among Russian newcomers of estates confiscated from the insurgents, or of the 'free' lands taken from the indigenous population, and so on. To carry out this policy the government had at its disposal everywhere hundreds and thousands of medium or petty landowners who were ruined or had squandered their 'redemptive certificates', enterprising businessmen from among merchants or the urban petty-bourgeoisie, lovers of easy profits and adventurers ready for anything.

The clamorous 'patriotism' of this rapacious army of 'russifiers'* assumed such a threatening character that even Nekrasov, who was the only editor left on the *Sovremennik*, on which such a short time before the voices of Dobrolyubov and Chernyshevsky had rung out,

* The famous Russian satirist Saltykov-Shchedrin gave them the nickname of 'Tashkentites', after the capital of Turkestan, which used to be a major arena of their activities. The nickname became fixed in popular usage.

felt obliged to address a paean of praise to Muravyov, the pacifier of Poland, who had been given the nickname of 'hangman' for his ferocity. Nekrasov thought he would be able to save the review with this poem (a source of tormenting remorse to him until the end of his life), but he failed. The *Sovremennik*, which had been suspended for eight months in 1862 (after Chernyshevsky's arrest), was banned altogether in 1866, after Karakozov's abortive attempt on the Tsar's life. At the same time *Russkoye Slovo* (The Russian Word), another radical periodical of the time, was also shut down for good. Its chief contributor had been young Dmitri Pisaryov.

Even in the months that preceded the open flaring-up of the revolt, reactionary demagogy, charging the intelligentsia with incitement, as we have already mentioned, used to add that 'students and revolutionaries' were conspiring together with the 'Poles'. Now the government took advantage of the nationalist fervour aroused by the uprising, which had also seized on substantial masses of the urban population, in order to isolate and demoralize the democratic opposition completely and to terrorize the liberal opposition. To a considerable degree it succeeded. The putting out of illegal literature in Russia stopped, while the circulation of the *Kolokol*, which came out in London but had penetrated deeply into Russia, thanks to the sympathetic support of oppositionists in society and officialdom, suddenly fell from 2,500 to 3,000 copies to 500.

Freed from both the revolutionary threat and from opposition of a liberal or oligarchic character, the Tsarist government was able to proceed without fear to a series of basic reforms. Reforms of this kind were indispensable in order to enable the country's economy to evolve on new principles of finance and commerce. But this evolution in its turn was quite indispensable in order to restore the national prestige of Russia, shaken by the Crimean War, and bring her economic and military power into harmony with the rapid tempo of development of European and world capitalism, which had proved to be the basic result of the 1848 revolutions. In 1863–5 a judicial reform was introduced, the status of the universities was transformed, new rules for the press were issued, universal military conscription was introduced, a decree concerning rural institutions was published, etc.

The torrential flow of reforms was a clear contrast to the oppressive immutability of Nicholas I's régime. Afterwards, both in the following years and even more in the succeeding reign of Alexander III, when all the progressive aspects of the reforms began being subjected to distortion and annulment, the age of the Great Reforms retrospectively took on the appearance of an epoch of unalloyed triumph of the principles of humanism and liberty.[30]

In many respects the reforms of the '60s really did transform the entire structure of Russian life. They established the minimal guarantees of justice, defence of the rights of the individual, freedom of scientific investigation, freedom of the press, etc., without which the country's transition from a serf-holding system to a 'bourgeois' order based on the principles of personal initiative and interest, freely hired labour and financial-mercantile relationships, would have been altogether impossible. But guarantees of civil law and order were also the boundary at which the reforms stopped. They gave no one any guarantees of political rights or political liberty, and questions of politics were also very carefully excluded from the sphere of competence of the Zemstvo, the new organ of local autonomy. The reforms preserved the insulation of the classes and their hierarchic division into those subject to taxation and those exempt from it. But from now on all classes without exception were supposed to be subject to the interests of the 'State', embodied in the autocratic power, which disposed unchecked of all the new sources of technical and financial power created by the 'bourgeoisification' of the country's economy, and exploited these sources through the gigantically expanded military, police, and civil apparatus.

Thus the direct result of the 'liberal' reforms proved paradoxical. In fact the autocracy became even more independent of any public forces, even more unrestricted and even more bureaucratized than it had ever been before. It was just because of this, to be sure, that from now on it was condemned to be the 'balancer' between the clashing and often irreconcilable interests of the various classes[31] and so became far less stable. But for the time being conditions were highly unfavourable for the revolutionary wing of the intelligentsia, which had scarcely begun to stir.

It was impossible even to think of the creation of an organization with any degree of centralization or ramification. In 1862 Nicholas Serno-Solovyevich, one of the contributors to the *Velikoruss*, tried to set up the organization Land and Freedom. But after the arrest of its initiator the organization very quickly dissolved; no further attempt to restore it or create another organization was made.*

* The organization called by the same name that appeared in 1876 was not a successor of Serno-Solovyevich's organization, but was named in its honour.

But in these circumstances it was difficult to continue even on the path of a return to 'politics' that a substantial segment of the intelligentsia had been about to embark on when conditions seemed to justify the assumption of an imminent peasant uprising. The threads of Populist ideas, torn by the shutting down of the *Sovremennik*, were taken up again in 1868 by the new editorial board of the *Otechestvennye Zapiski* (Nekrasov, Yeliseyev, and Saltykov-Shchedrin), and during the first period this review 'rejected all political ideals in the imminent future: the real question of the time is only the amelioration of the condition of the masses of the people'.[32]

The revolutionary intelligentsia, which at its very inception had been subjected to a savage repression, isolated both from 'society' and from the masses of the people, once again found itself at a crossroads. Above all it had to occupy itself with the generalization and elaboration into a system of the fragmented and clashing ideas that had simply arisen empirically in its ranks during the preceding years. Compulsory political inactivity made a demand for theoretical self-definition all the more urgent. And the revolutionaries, the 'men of action', confronted the same basic question about the place of the intelligentsia itself in social life and the role of the 'thinking individual' that Dobrolyubov had posed as he went to his grave.

CHAPTER FIVE

The Elaboration of Theory

1. DMITRI PISARYOV

What Is to Be Done? This, the title of Chernyshevsky's famous novel, also became, almost half a century later, on the threshold of tempestuous mass movements that culminated in the revolution of 1905, the title of a pamphlet by Lenin, which in its own way became famous too. The coincidence was not merely accidental. It reflects the fact that these five words give a precise formulation to the question that throughout those fifty years never ceased tormenting the Russian intelligentsia. Deprived of any organic bond with the social summits, separated from the popular masses by an intellectual and cultural abyss, it was whirled about between these two poles of contemporary society. It lacked both a stable, secure position in its mechanism, or a cause that might have fully satisfied its intellectual and ethical demands. What was to be done?

Young Dobrolyubov died in 1861 at the age of twenty-five; full of faith in the imminence of the revolution, he had given the following answer to this question: To develop in oneself a character and willpower that would enable one, on the 'real day', to become a man 'not of words but of action'.

Four years after his death it was answered by Dmitri Pisaryov, also twenty-five years old, who at this time, in accordance with the circumstances described above, finally lost his faith in the revolution – though it is true that he had not believed in it very much even in 1861, when his brief but brilliant literary career was just beginning.*

Pisaryov's answer was that 'the life of the people does not need powerful characters, it has enough of them; all it needs is simply and exclusively *consciousness*'.

* Almost all Pisaryov's literary activity took place in the dungeons of the Peter-Paul Fortress in Petersburg. He was imprisoned there in the middle of 1862, at the age of twenty-two, in the so-called 'Ballod' affair, which was linked to the publication of the above-mentioned proclamation of 'Young Russia'. Released in 1866, Pisaryov wrote little; in 1868 he drowned while bathing.

It was this antithesis – Dobrolyubov/Pisaryov – that for the first time accurately formulated the contradiction between spontaneity and consciousness, feeling and reason, the masses and the individual, the mob and heroes, that drew a red line through the entire subsequent history of Russian democratic and Socialist thought and politics. It reflected the objective contradiction between the boundlessness of the ideals that history had made the Russian intelligentsia the bearer of from its very birth, and the meagreness of the means that Russian realities left at its disposition for the realization of those ideals.

Intellectualism and individualism – such was the banner raised by the twenty-year-old Pisaryov, scion of a substantial landowning family, when he entered the journalistic arena in Blagosvetlov's periodical *Russkoye Slovo*. Pisaryov found his model banner-bearer in Bazarov, the hero of Turgenev's novel, *Fathers and Sons*, who personified the generation of those 'denyers' and 'nihilists' (Turgenev's term) who, on the borderline between two epochs established by the emancipation of the peasants, flatly 'denied' everything immutable and 'sacrosanct' for the dying epoch and without a merciless critical examination accepted 'nothing' (in Latin, *nihil*) of its faiths, dogmas, customs, and conventions.

The 'thinking individual' was declared to be the demiurge of history. The natural sciences, which at this time were beginning their astonishing triumphal march, were a method of freeing him from a mystical reverence for the 'secrets' of nature or social relationships. The primitive materialism of Büchner and Moleschott was its 'realistic philosophy'. Armed with these weapons of rational interpretation of all seemingly irrational phenomena and emotions, including the emotions of art and love, the 'consistent realist' became one of those ideal persons whose numerical increase and whose elevating effect on the human masses, stagnating in ignorance, prejudice and superstition, actually constitutes the sole rational basis of human progress. The individual, if he is a realistically thinking individual, thus becomes his own goal. He has a right to 'pleasure' since his pleasure cannot help but be reduced to the reasonable satisfaction of his intellectual and ethical demands, which in their turn cannot help but be reasonable in the 'consistent realist'. This is why their satisfaction also cannot help but serve as the guarantee of an increase in the sum of human happiness.

This question, What is to be done? which so tormented the youthful intelligentsia of the '60s and the beginning of the '70s, was given a simple, clear and practical answer by Pisaryov: to work for the improvement of one's own intellect. Seek, not the 'kingdoms of God', remote and hazy ideals, but practical 'realistic' information. This was what Pisaryov said to the intelligentsia as it entered the epoch of the Great Reforms with the dream that it had inherited from Chernyshevsky and Dobrolyubov, the leaders of the preceding generation, of the imminence of the most radical of all revolutions ever seen by mankind and that it had seen shattered at the very outset.

This summons to work on one's own personality could not have responded more closely to the mood of the somewhat disoriented intelligentsia of those years. It is not surprising that, from her own personal experience, the famous Russian revolutionary Vera Zasulich (see below) had this to say: 'The Pisaryov of 1864–5 was practically the most complete representative and exponent of the youthful generation, especially in the provinces, that was only just waking up and readying itself.' Comparing Dobrolyubov and Pisaryov, she explained: 'As the first voice crying out Dobrolyubov could arouse only a confused longing for some far-off land . . . But what Pisaryov said was simple, understandable, and valiant, and he immediately set them to work.' This 'work' was either self-education, or the acquisition of knowledge, and above all – of applied, scientific, medical, technical knowledge, and so on – a longing for which seized on the youthful intelligentsia of those years and through which it calculated on preparing itself for an activity that would help the masses of the people.[33] The same unique influence of Pisaryov on the youth of those years is mentioned also by O. V. Aptekman, who was active in the Land and Freedom movement (see below): 'Pisaryov possessed me completely. He aroused thought and forced one to evolve. Circles of students continued what he had begun.'[34]

In his 1862 essay on Bazarov, to be sure, Pisaryov (to go on quoting Vera Zasulich) 'in praising Nietzsche, describes, under the name of Bazarov, some sort of "Blond Beast", and admires it'. Indeed, in Pisaryov's early works in general the characteristic trait of the 'nihilist' and his 'pleasure' is an extreme sensuality and egocentrism, and a coarse physiological primitivism. This kind of gospel was able to lighten, and in fact did lighten for young people the agonizing process of the rupture with the way of life and the mores of that intellectually and culturally backward, squirely, mercantile, petty-bourgeois and clerical background it was emerging from. This gospel played a quite unique role in the struggle for the 'emancipation of women' that precisely in Russia achieved such great success. But the sensuality and eudemonism were too flagrant a contradiction of those rather 'ascetic' and 'stoical' tendencies in the youth – which was seized with the thirst for 'serving the people' that found such a clear expression in the figure of Rakhmetov (one of the heroes of Chernyshevsky's novel, *What Is to Be Done?*) – to become the symbol of their faith.

But it was just because of this that Vera Zasulich made the point that Pisaryov became the exponent of these youthful moods not in 1861–2, but in 1864–5. For in 1864, reverting to Bazarov again in an essay, *The Realists*, Pisaryov is already speaking of the sensualist 'explosion of youthful independence' as merely 'a very customary, perhaps even inevitable', but ephemeral phenomenon 'in the life of every thinking individual'. This explosion 'is put an end to by the first sober glance at the economic prose of life'. In the light of this 'prose' every 'consistent realist' must say to himself: 'After all, I belong to the society that formed me. All the powers of my mind constitute the result of the labour of others, and if I dissipate these powers on various agreeable stupidities I shall prove to be an insolvent debtor and a malicious bankrupt . . . an enemy of the very society that I owe absolutely everything to.'

Approaching the problem of individuality from this angle, Pisaryov wrote: 'When you come to such serious conclusions, then an aimless enjoyment of life, science, art will prove to be impossible for you. Only one pleasure will be left – that arising out of the clear consciousness that you are being of some real use to people, that you are paying off to some slight extent the heaped-up mass of your debts.' Pisaryov came to the conclusion that the goal of 'all the reflection and all the activity of everyone' was summed up in 'solving once and for all the unavoidable question of hungry and unclothed people; outside this question there is absolutely nothing worth worrying, thinking, meditating, and fussing about'.

Placed in this way at 'the service of society', Pisaryov's rationalistic and individualistic radicalism proved to be psychologically wholly acceptable to the youthful intelligentsia. It could combine this all the more easily with its own general collectivistic and communistic sympathies since it was just in this second half of the '60s that Western European bourgeois-individualistic radicalism also rehabilitated itself to a certain extent from the point of view of its own 'social-reformist' and pro-worker tendencies. It was only the tragedy of the Paris Commune that stopped this mood by 'confronting radica republicanism and democratic free-thought with the necessity of making a decisive choice between the world of labour and the world of capital, which were facing each other in an open civil war' (Martov).[29] After the Commune, Pisaryov's influence began rapidly subsiding. But for the time being it may be said that it was this cast of mind that distinguished Pisaryov's radicalism from that of the other 'opinion-moulders' of this epoch.

It was not for nothing that Pisaryov once said that if he had ever had a chance to talk to Dobrolyubov for 'half an hour alone' then 'in all probability they would not agree on a single point'.[35] Counterposing his own criterion of 'consciousness' to Dobrolyubov's criterion of 'character', Pisaryov at bottom also overturned the Populist foundations of Dobrolyubov's views – the faith in the creative powers of the social renovation that were hidden in the masses of the people and that were only awaiting a favourable occasion to transform all Russian life and speak to Europe 'in its own voice'. In an essay, *Motifs in the Russian Drama*, written in the beginning of 1864, Pisaryov categorically declared: 'Russian life in its own depths contains absolutely no instincts of independent renewal, it presents only the raw materials, which have to be fructified and remade through the influence of the ideas of mankind at large.'

In another essay, to be sure, *Flowers of Innocent Humour*, which was written around this same time, Pisaryov, too, seemed to consider Russian backwardness a favourable factor from the point of view of the future evolution of Russia. Russian civilization was 'still in its mother's womb; it had no deeply rooted scholastic traditions; there was not a legion of philistines in every city; there was no fanatical routine of medieval science'. But at a time when the representatives of Populist tendencies – for instance, the above-mentioned Mikhailov – saw in Russian backwardness 'our salvation' and proudly sang its praises as a guarantee of 'our' ability 'to introduce a new principle into history', Pisaryov saw in the infantility of Russian civilization merely a condition that enabled Russia to take over from the mature civilization of Europe not its 'medieval' sweepings, but the best and most up-to-date of its creations: 'Before us lies all European science: translate, read, study! After all, we're not going to be such fools as to take something from others that they are abandoning because of its worthlessness.'

But contemporary European civilization was bourgeois and capitalist. And Pisaryov's 'consistent realism', hammered out in the solitude of gaol, did not halt at the conclusion that flowed from this. In the same essay on *Motifs in the Russian Drama*, he expressed the 'idyllic surmise' that the process of multiplying of the 'thinking individuals' will also involve the young Russian capitalists and land-owners, who will stop transferring their capital abroad in order to squander it on insane luxuries and begin to invest it in the production needed by the country. And, dreaming of a way of placing their knowledge 'in the service of the country', which psychologically was utterly alien to the intelligentsia of the time, Pisaryov added: 'A good farm and a good factory, when the labour is rationally organized, make up the best and the only possible school for the country, first of all because this school will feed its pupils and teachers, but secondly because it will spread knowledge not through books but by means of the phenomena of living reality. Books will come in their own time; building schools in the factories and on the farms will be so easy it will accomplish itself of its own accord.'

The Russia of the first few years after the emancipation of the peasants, years of a sharp switch from the feudal and predominantly natural economy to a money- and market-economy was, of course, also familiar with apologists for capitalist development. Like Pisaryov they too leaned on the natural sciences and sought confirmation in them of their own views of capitalism as an economic order that flowed directly from the laws of nature and the conditions of human life. In the '60s and the beginning of the '70s the most eminent representatives of this complex of views were the sociologists and economists Paul Lilienfeld-Toal, who formulated the 'social-embryological' law of social development, and Alexander Stronin, who advanced the theory of the 'pyramidal' structure of society, corresponding with the 'laws of mechanics'.

But in the whole cast of their thought both Lilienfeld and Stronin were partisans of the same moderate bourgeois liberalism that lacked any points of intellectual contact with the revolutionary-minded intelligentsia. Pisaryov, on the contrary, was unique, and at that an unusually brilliant representative of bourgeois radicalism.* This was the wholly exceptional meaning of the role he played.

To be sure, the very compounding of 'bourgeoisie' and 'radicalism'

* In the '70s Zaitsev and Khristophorov, Pisaryov's fellow-thinkers and counsellors on the Blagosvetlov periodical, who had emigrated, began publishing an organ of general-democratic outlook, *Obshcheye Delo* (Common Cause). It did not have much influence.

was so 'groundless' in actual Russian reality, as we have indicated more than once, that this combination could only arise as a purely logical construction. It was the brainwork of a young man who had genius, but was cut off from life by prison walls even before he had had time to come in any actual contact with it. It was because of this that in the broad revolutionary movement that began in the '70s the intellectual influence of Pisaryov seemed indiscernible, and had begun being looked down on to some extent. Nevertheless Pisaryov's activity did not pass by without trace. It is he who may be considered the spiritual father of that modest but immense army of rural physicians, nurses, statisticians, agriculturists, teachers, technicians and so on, that became famous for their self-sacrifice and disinterested 'service to the people'*, and who in the history of the Russian revolution too played a gigantic role as the link between the revolutionists and those progressive strata of Russian society without whose sympathy and support, as we have already noted, the broad-gauge work of the revolutionary organizations would have been impossible.

2. PETER LAVROV

The 'critically thinking individual' as the creative factor of human progress, and knowledge, as the source and instrument of this creative force: in these two concepts the doctrine of Peter Lavrovich Lavrov (1823–1900) directly continued Pisaryov's gospel.

Son of a rich landowner, a scholarly professor at the Artillery Academy, it was not until 1861–2 that Lavrov, already almost forty years old, began drawing close to the radicals that grouped themselves around Chernyshevsky. He even entered the organization, Land and Freedom, founded by N. Serno-Solovyevich, and after Karakozov's attempt on the Tsar's life (see below) was exiled to residence in the Vologodsk Province. But he did not really become the revolutionary intelligentsia's 'own' until 1869–70, when the famous *Historical Letters* he wrote in exile began appearing under the pseudonym of Mirtov, at first in the form of a series of articles in the periodical *Nedel* (The Week) and then in a separate edition.

* Later on reactionaries were to christen this army the 'Third Element', in order to emphasize their 'alienness' to the two 'indigenous' elements of the countryside – the nobility and the peasantry. As often happens, the mocking nickname was taken up by those it was aimed at, and entered Russian political language as a term for the broad stratum of intellectuals who served the Zemstvos.

The *Letters* were so much in harmony with the mood of the youthful intelligentsia of those years and answered its needs so well that they became a bedside book for it. All at once Lavrov became its 'teacher'. In order to enable him to continue his literary work without hindrance, Herman Lopatin, later on one of the famous Russian revolutionaries, organized his escape abroad at the beginning of 1870. From then on until his death, for thirty years, Lavrov lived in Paris almost without a break. In Paris he fell into the fever of the Commune, came close to its leading figures and was even commissioned by them to go to London in May of the same year to get help for it. There he met Marx and Engels, became a member of the Paris section of the International and thus entered into relations with the European workers and the Socialist movement of the time. This played a not unimportant role in the formation of his own socio-political views and through him in the evolution of the ideas of the Russian revolutionary intelligentsia.

In his *Historical Letters* Lavrov laid down the so-called 'subjective method' of interpreting history and intervening in its course. He admitted, of course, that everything both in nature and in human society had its objective orderliness. He also admitted that in the final analysis both an individual's intellectual and his moral profile might and ought to be explained scientifically – by anthropological methods.[36] But he insisted that a man would 'always and above all divide his actions and those of his fellows into conscious and unconscious actions, and would have a different attitude towards these two categories'. Now, history is a process of conscious activity. Therefore, it is impossible to proceed with respect to it, with respect to the assessment of events of the past, and with respect to an active intervention in the prospects of the future, except in terms of one's own 'moral ideal'.

'We – with our moral ideal, which determines the perspective of the historical process – are halted at the end of this process; everything that has gone before takes on with respect to our ideal the aspect of preparatory stages, which lead inevitably to the determined goal. Consequently, history appears to us as a struggle between beneficent and harmful principles, where the beneficent principle has finally attained a point at which for us it is the highest good of mankind.' And further: 'the approximation of historical facts to the material and ideal optimum we are conscious of, the evolution of our moral ideal in the passing life of mankind, constitutes for everyone the sole meaning of history, the sole law of the historical succession of events, the law of progress, whether we regard such progress as *de facto* without interruption or as subject to vacillations, whether we believe its material realization or only in its existence within our own consciousness.' In establishing the 'formula of progress' from the point of view of the 'moral ideal' of the Russian democratic intelligentsia represented by himself, Lavrov comes to this conclusion: 'The development of the personality in its physical, intellectual and moral aspects; the embodying of truth and justice in social forms – there we have a short formula that seems to me to embrace everything that can be considered progress.'

This 'short formula' sounded to the democratic intelligentsia like the sanction of its 'moral ideal', even though for the time being it existed only in its own 'consciousness'. It could not have been more to the point, in those years when in the real environment of this intelligentsia there were so few chances for 'material realization' of this 'ideal'. But at the same time the 'short formula' also sounded like a sanction of the unflagging struggle for the ideal, and above all the struggle for 'the physical, intellectual and moral development' of one's own personality, that is, for the elevation of one's own intellect, that Pisaryov too had called for. For in the course of social evolution it was just this 'small group' of people who were consciously aspiring to the development in themselves of human worth that was, indeed, the moving force of progress.

But – and here Lavrov moved on to a second theme, also touched on by Pisaryov – in order for such a 'small group' to be able to educate itself, 'it was necessary for there to be, amidst the majority struggling without let-up for its own existence, a minority that was secure from the most burdensome cares of life'. Thus, the minority owed a 'debt' to the majority that it had to 'pay off', in order really to secure uninterrupted progress.

'Society is threatened by the danger of stagnation, if it stifles within itself the critically thinking individual. Its civilization is threatened by destruction if it . . . is turned into the exclusive possession of a small minority. Consequently, however slow the progress of mankind is, whatever there is is based exclusively on the critically thinking individuals.'

The individual as creator of progress; the accumulation of knowledge; the debt to society; the moral obligation to pay off this debt – these were the slogans proclaimed by both Pisaryov and Lavrov. But this external identity concealed a profound inner difference, and a difference in the importance of the 'Pisaryovites' on the one hand and of the 'Lavrovites' on the other in the intellectual formation of the democratic intelligentsia.

For Pisaryov the 'thinking individual' was a self-sufficient value; by his very existence he served the cause of progress. Such individuals had to be multiplied. But in any circumstances they were condemned to remain a minority. This was why it was important, from the point of view of progress, for as many substantial and influential people as possible from the summits of society to go into this minority. The thinking individual could raise himself up to the heights of 'consistent realism' only by way of the acquisition of 'positive' knowledge, that is, knowledge of the natural sciences and of technique. It was precisely by the application of his professional knowledge that he could and ought to be of benefit to society, pay off his debt to it and help settle the question of 'hungry and unclothed people'. The problems of the social order as such did not confront the 'thinking individual' directly; their solution was simply an oblique result of his 'practical' professional activity.

From Lavrov's point of view, on the contrary, questions of the social order were also supposed to be the focus of attention of this 'thinking individual'; his professional activity was supposed to be subordinated to their solution; his feelings were supposed to be devoted to the study, not of the natural, but of the social sciences. Professional knowledge had to be acquired to enable one to occupy a stable, steady and useful position in society, so that one could have some effect on it. Consequently one had to give oneself a thorough education, one had to go to schools and universities, one had to prepare oneself seriously for social activity. But – 'neither talent nor knowledge in and for themselves make a man the motor of progress; in this respect it is possible to do more with less talent and knowledge, if you do everything you can'. A lofty 'moral ideal' had to be worked out within oneself, and then one had to strive to affect the future course of history in that spirit. But that meant that this 'ideal' had to be brought to 'the people'. For the thinking minority could only become the real moving force of progress in so far as it succeeded in infecting a popular majority with its own ideals. The thinking minority could only pay off its own debt to this majority by bringing its own 'ideal' not to the privileged summits of society, but to its deprived lower depths. But with this condition it was not necessary to be a 'superman'; 'Yes, I repeat,'

Lavrov insisted in his fifth *Letter*, 'every man who thinks critically and decides to realize his thought in life can be a moving force of progress.'

Thus, if Pisaryov can be regarded as the spiritual father of the army of intelligentsia that saw its fundamental task in the 'practical' service of the diverse needs of the people, Lavrov was the spiritual ancestor of the army of 'propagandists' (later on, 'professional revolutionaries', in Lenin's term), who set as the fundamental task of their lives the preaching of their 'moral ideal' among the masses of the people and who while conscientiously serving the everyday needs of these masses nevertheless regarded their 'practical' work above all as a method of drawing close to them, and of winning their confidence in order to make them more receptive to their preaching.*

As Martov rightly points out, 'Lavrov's whole book was a summons to the Russian democratic intelligentsia to form a party and conduct a systematic struggle against the historic order in the name of Socialism.'[29] The youth that Pisaryov 'had set to work' to educate themselves was turned to by Lavrov with the cry 'To the people!' And it was just this cry that was triumphantly snatched out of his book by broad circles of the intelligentsia, whose attitudes happened to ripen on the threshold of the '70s and soon fused into a tempestuous movement, known as 'going to the people'.

Lavrov's own activity also took on a more and more 'party' character when he moved abroad. In accord with the Petersburg group of 'Chaikovskyites' (see below) that had come into being under his influence, in July 1873 he set about publishing the *Vperyod* (Forwards) collections of articles – five volumes were published before 1877 – and from 1875 on a fortnightly under the same title. Thus there sprang up for the first time an *émigré* press that was directly

* In his biography of Bakunin M. P. Dragomanov calls him the ancestor of the Russian 'professional revolutionaries', saying that in the period 1840–7 Bakunin became 'the ancestor of those Russians who at the political trials of the '70s and '80s answered the question, "What is your business?" with the answer, "The business of revolution", and outside this business really were incapable of doing anything else.'

What is true here is that Bakunin personally was the first 'professional revolutionary' of Russian origin. But the 'revolutionary business' he was in during the '40s was not so much Russian as pan-European. His 'professional revolutionary' activity of those years had no direct echo or continuation in Russia. As we shall see below, it was only towards the '70s that Bakunin, who had become an anarchist by that time, acquired a discernible influence over the intelligentsia.

tied to organizations active in Russia. This bond was possible because of the numerous *émigré* colonies that sprang up in various cities of Europe (chiefly in Switzerland). These were made up of people who had fled the savage persecutions that, as we have already noted, descended on the intelligentsia from the beginning of the '60s on, and of the youth, chiefly young women, who were seeking abroad the university knowledge that was not free enough or was closed to them in Russia.* All these served as intermediate links that ensured the provision of the *émigré* press with material, an exchange of opinions, and intellectual communication.

In his literary work abroad Lavrov remained faithful, of course, to the basic ideas he had developed in his *Historical Letters* and to the Populist views that at this time were practically the general possession of the Russian intelligentsia. But in emigration his work went on under the very powerful influence of the European working-class movement, with which he had come into very close contact, and of Marxism, which at the time ideologically dominated the International, which he joined. Under this influence his philosophical and sociological views became still more eclectic; his Populist outlook changed and complicated itself through essentially alien Marxist elements; his political line lost its precision and consistency, and began vacillating. None of this was merely a personal trait of Lavrov's; it was the expression of the new factors that just at this time began bringing into the intellectual development of broad strata of the Russian intelligentsia the influence of the Western European working-class movement and proletarian Socialism. This influence was conveyed by Lavrov and the 'Lavrovites'.

Lavrov's journalistic work as an émigré played the role of a canal through which the ideas of Western European Socialism poured into the Russian revolutionary movement. On the other hand, it was thanks to his 'party' ties with this movement that his work also became a sensitive barometer of the recurrent phases it underwent under the pressure of Russian realities. During the three decades of Lavrov's

* An exceptional role in the Russian revolutionary movement of the '70s was played by the women students' circle of the Zurich University, from which there emerged the most famous Russian women revolutionaries: Bardina, the Lyubatovich sisters, the three Figner sisters, the oldest and most celebrated of whom, Vera, has left reminiscences of more than twenty years. She wrote these in the Shlisselburg Fortress; they have been translated into many languages. The members of this group were called 'Fritsches' – after the name of the woman in whose house most of them lived.

work abroad this movement, as we shall see, went through quite a number of vacillations and zigzags, splits and alliances, occasions of boom and depression, crises of the old ideology and the birth of the new. The characteristic eclecticism of Lavrov's thinking made it much easier for him to adapt himself to all these successive phases of the movement, but it made his political position still less systematic. Further on we shall briefly note the stages of Lavrov's political evolution during the '80s and '90s. But, after his *Historical Letters*, Lavrov's authentic historical activity lay in his providing the theoretical foundations for the practical activity that revolutionary Populism passed over to during the '70s. It was primarily this work that the *Vperyod* anthologies and the periodical were devoted to.

Vperyod had set itself the task of being the organ of the social revolution. The newspaper's programme proclaimed: 'For us the social question is of paramount importance. The political question is to our mind subordinate to the economic question.' This social revolution could and must be accomplished only by the people itself: 'the reconstruction of Russian society must be accomplished not only with the aim of the people's welfare, not only for the people, but also by the people'. But the masses of the people were still not ready for such a 'reconstruction'. Therefore 'the triumph of our objectives cannot be realized all at once, it needs preparation and a clear comprehension of what is possible at any given moment'. It was just this preparation that was the 'debt' that the 'educated minority', the intelligentsia, was obligated to pay back to the people.

The task of the intelligentsia consisted primarily in the creation among the actual masses of the people of cells of conscious Socialists: 'the initial condition for the preparation of the social revolution in Russia must be the organization of the revolutionary minority that understands the tasks of working-class Socialism, among the communal and artel centres of the Russian people'. In No. 4 the newspaper explains the role of this 'revolutionary minority': 'Throughout history there has never been a single completely conscious movement. Complete awareness of ends and means existed in small groups and in individual units . . . When the conscious, semi-conscious and sympathizing strata are united in a powerful organization the suffering masses will inevitably join them at the moment of the explosion.'

But in constructing this 'powerful organization' the intelligentsia must fuse in it with the 'revolutionary minority' that had come out of the same 'suffering masses', must itself become a participant in the 'communal and artel centres of the Russian people'. The propaganda of the intelligentsia had to 'proceed not outside the usual centres of popular solidarity but inside them'; 'the summons to the revolution', when the time came, had to emanate from those who 'belonged' to the people on the basis of 'long-established living solidarity'. The revolution lay in the future. And so 'at any given moment' the programme of *Vperyod* was a programme of the long-drawn-out, intimate 'settling down' of the intelligentsia among the masses of the people with the goal of systematically propagating Socialism, the 'moral ideal' the *Historical Letters* had spoken of, and of the creation of a 'powerful organization' for the carrying on of such propaganda.

Reversing the idea of the European working-class Socialism, Lavrov soon also assimilated its three basic 'Marxist' propositions: Socialism arises on the socio-economic terrain prepared by capitalism; the working-class is the demiurge of the Socialist revolution; the working-class of all countries is bound together by ties of international solidarity.

The commune, of course, remains as before the original social form capable of passing over directly into a higher, Socialist form. But while for the pioneers of Populism the path to Socialism via the commune was the antithesis of the path to it via capitalism, this antithesis kept being more and more levelled off. And by 1876 *Vperyod* (No. 27) was already categorically declaring: 'Thus, in Russia the capitalist system is rapidly and luxuriantly evolving with all its consequences. The social overturn is being prepared by itself, as throughout the 'civilized' world, by the very successes of the capitalist system.'

It was all the easier for Lavrov to come to such a conclusion since towards this time the gigantic economic achievements accomplished by capitalism in Russia, and its disintegrating influence on the archaic forms of the socio-economic order, including the commune, had already become excessively manifest facts, which both the Russian intelligentsia and Russian literature willy-nilly had to take into account. Further on we shall see how the harmonious edifice of the Populist world-view began showing yawning fissures that foretold its coming collapse and pulverized the theoretical work of its epigones.* Highly talented Populist belletristic writers† began making a sharp distinction between themselves and the peasant idylls of the

* Nicholas K. Mikhailovsky, Vasily P. Vorontsov, and others.

† Especially Gleb Uspensky.

commune depicted by their immediate predecessors* and mercilessly unmasked the power of money, the triumph of the 'kulak' and the village usurer in the countryside, and the progressive dissolution and degeneration of the commune. Under the influence of inexorable reality the revolutionary organizations, scarcely born, began dissolving, splitting up and fighting each other. Lavrov also tried to take up and systematize this chaos of contradictory and clashing ideas in his own peculiar amalgam of new 'Marxist' views and old 'Populist' views.

The amalgam was arrived at by stressing the original peculiarities of the Russian terrain that the seeds of capitalist evolution were falling upon. These peculiarities consisted of the 'living social unit of the petty rural commune and the living social unit of the mobile workers' artel'. Thanks to these the Russian people was *a priori* 'prepared for the development of Socialism in its collective life'. But it was thanks to them, too, that the social substance of the 'working-class' called upon to accomplish the Socialist revolution had changed. In Western Europe this working-class was in the factories and workshops; in Russia it consisted primarily of labourers in primitive, manual and craft labour (carpenters, stevedores, rural labourers, etc.), united in voluntary and 'mobile' artels that roved about throughout the country, and, still more – of the workers on the land, the peasants. They were scattered and fragmented throughout the country with no links between them. But it was just because of this that the socialistically-minded youthful intelligentsia took on exceptional importance. The cause of its 'social-revolutionary alliance' consisted of 'organizing links between the rural population that was suffering uniformly in various parts of Russia but lacked solidarity'.[37]

Lavrov had written in the first *Vperyod* anthology: 'For the Russian Socialist the terrain on which the future of the bulk of the Russian people is going to evolve, in a direction indicated by the common tasks of our era, is the peasantry with communal landownership.' A year later, in the second *Vperyod* volume, he said, still more categorically: 'Our social revolution must not come out of the cities, but out of the villages.' And he added, rejecting any assumptions of a 'bourgeois' revolution: 'Our bourgeoisie of rural landowners, merchants, and industrialists lacks any political tradition, it is not united in its exploitation of the people; it suffers itself from the oppression of the administration, and has not developed any historic forces of its own.'

* Zlatovratsky and others.

The Populist re-working of the Marxist ideas of European working-class Socialism gave them the only form in which in contemporary Russian conditions they could ever have been taken up at all by large numbers of the revolutionary intelligentsia. But Russian life still lacked the slightest elements for the emergence of anything resembling the national, mass and class Socialist parties of the proletariat, for which, after the Franco-Prussian war of 1870–1, the German Social-Democracy had become the pioneer and model.

Parties of this type were the natural product of the evolution of the advanced capitalist countries of Europe. They demanded new forms of international association, which could no longer be satisfied by the International Marx had founded. This was *de facto* liquidated by 1872–3, and it was only comparatively slowly that the foundations were laid of a new International, the Second, which was not definitively organized until 1899. But from the point of view of Lavrov during these years, the formation of national parties contradicted the ideal of an international union of workers, indifferent to national boundaries, which was the only way he could even imagine the realization of the principle of international proletarian solidarity. To his mind the formation of national parties removed to 'the background the agitation on behalf of an international union of the proletariat for a united struggle against its enemies everywhere'.[38]

But Lavrov was even more critical of the political activity that in fact became the real task of Socialist parties. Their struggle for national independence, for power in the state, for a majority in legislative institutions, for a general right to vote and so on, and even more the compromise and agreements they had to enter into with the parties of bourgeois radicalism in the interests of this struggle – all this was unacceptable to Lavrov, who stubbornly clung to the traditional denial of 'politics'. With respect to Russia the programme of *Vperyod* categorically declared: 'All political parties, with their constitutional ideals of more or less liberal character, every attempt to replace the centralized and bourgeois empire with a centralized and bourgeois republic, to replace the existing territorial divisions by other divisions with other centres and other laws – all that is harmful to us . . . In the Russian constitutional party on the European model we see in general our out-and-out enemies, whom we shall have to struggle against at the first possibility of a serious clash of parties in Russia.'

But Lavrov did not carry even this 'apolitical' line to its conclusion.

In No. 21 of the periodical, in an objection made to one of the 'constitutionalists', he continued to call for 'resistance with all our strength to any party claiming that by getting rid of the imperial autocracy the Russian people will rectify its own position'. But by now he justifies his position by saying that for the masses of the people what is unbearable is 'not only' the autocracy, but 'to an even greater degree the economic system', and that because of this 'we socialist-revolutionaries'* are going to have to strive for the destruction of 'both the political and the economic system in contemporary Russia simultaneously'.

Lavrov's position on the question of politics and the state became all the shakier when it came under the fire of the 'anti-state' anarchist Bakunin, on the one hand, and the passionate 'statist', the Jacobin Tkachov, on the other (for both of these see below). While adopting Bakunin's 'denial' of the state in general, Lavrov soon began making concessions to 'statism' too, by setting up a theory about an 'indispensable', though constantly diminishing 'minimum' of statehood that could be eliminated only after the total victory of the Socialist revolution. As Lavrov himself said about this later ('The Populist Propagandists of 1873–8'), 'in Russia the recognition at any given moment of a minimum of state power provoked dissatisfaction not only among the Bakuninites, but also among many supporters of *Vperyod*, who clung to the principles of anarchism.' This 'dissatisfaction' was one of the causes of Lavrov's withdrawal from the editorial board of *Vperyod* (1876), as well as of the shutting down of the periodical soon after.

Properly speaking, Lavrov's period of creativity ended with his work on *Vperyod*. In the future, too, until his death, he remained the revered 'teacher' of whole generations of the Russian intelligentsia; he never stopped his literary and political activity. But this activity was mere repetition rather than a blazing of new trails. Moreover, it was not distinguished for consistency; his emphasis would shift first to one, then to another contradictory element in his world-view.

We shall see further on how and in what forms these elements were transformed into revolutionary activity. Lavrov's own attitude varied.

* This compound, which later became the name of a party that did not arise until after Lavrov's death, is used here, as far as we know, for the first time. It is worth noting because the views of the future 'Socialist-Revolutionary Party' (see below) were grounded in just this Lavrovite interpretation of Populism.

When the all-Populist organization, Land and Freedom, which was about to be born, broke up into an apolitical Party of Total Reapportionment that gravitated towards anarchism and the markedly political, combative People's Freedom, Lavrov sided with Total Reapportionment. In 1880 he even joined the émigré Total Reapportionment partisan Plekhanov, the future founder of Russian Marxism, for the joint publication of the *Sotsial'no-Revolyutsionnaya Biblioteka* ('Social-Revolutionary Library'). But when the People's Freedom reached its zenith (the assassination of Alexander II on 1 March 1881), and began declining, Lavrov joined it. From 1883 to 1886 he published in Paris, together with Leo Tikhomirov, the People's Freedom *Vestnik* (Courier). In 1895 Lavrov attacked the Russian Marxist Social-Democrats, who had just emerged in the Russian political arena, and provoked a sharp retort from the youthful Lenin.

3. MICHAEL BAKUNIN

Lavrov's historical antagonist in the Populist movement was Michael Alexandrovich Bakunin (1814–76), though Lavrov's theoretical attitudes were too eclectic to establish a sharp line of demarcation between 'Lavrovism' and 'Bakuninism' in the '60s, when the movement was taking ideological shape. The division between them was expressed all the more distinctly in the '70s, when the movement passed over to practical revolutionary activity.

Bakunin was an eminent member of the Moscow political groups of the '30s, and belonged to the same group as Stankevich, which Belinsky was also a member of at the time.* It was to a considerable degree under his influence, in 1837–40, that Belinsky went in for that streak of enthusiasm for Hegel in his 'rightist' interpretation, his 'reconciliation with reality' and his apologetic attitude towards Russian Tsarism, that he was later to recall with disgust.

In 1840 Bakunin went abroad and immersed himself completely in European life. His revolutionary activity became seething and variegated, his personal life dramatic. But in the course of almost a quarter of a century he had no discernible direct influence in Russia at all.

* This is what Herzen wrote about this group later on: 'There was not much sympathy between our group and Stankevich's. They didn't like our almost exclusively political tendency, and we didn't like their almost exclusively speculative tendency. They regarded us as Frondeurs and Frenchmen, we considered them sentimentalists and Germans.'

Hence we shall do no more than touch on this period of his life in the most general terms.

While abroad, Bakunin very soon shifted from the 'right' wing of the Hegelians to the 'left'; in 1842, he placed an article in the *Deutsche Jahrbücher* of the 'Young Hegelian' Arnold Ruge. It was called *Reaction in Germany* (sub-titled *Notes of a Frenchman* and over the signature Jules Elizard) and it contained a celebrated phrase characteristic of Bakunin's whole future development: 'The passion for destruction is a creative passion.'

In the pre-revolutionary years of 1840–7, Bakunin established ties with the most variegated groups of radicals, revolutionaries, and conspirators in all the countries of Europe, but he became more and more captivated by the Polish question and, via the Polish, by the general Slavic question. In November 1847, on the anniversary of the Polish uprising of 1830, he made a speech in Paris calling on the Poles and Russians to unite in a general revolution against the régime of Nicholas I, and thus lay the groundwork for the emancipation of all the other Slavic peoples as well. In 1848 he participated in a Slavic congress in Prague and became one of the leaders of the so-called 'Holy Ghost' uprising (named after Holy Ghost Day, 12 June). In the *Appeal to the Slavs*, written by him, the Slavic revolution is treated merely as a part of a general European democratic revolution.

After the Prague uprising was crushed, Bakunin fled to Germany, where thanks to his revolutionary connexions he again turned up, to his own surprise, at the head of an uprising that flared up in Dresden on 4 May 1849. He was arrested and imprisoned in the Königstein Fortress; in April 1850 he was sentenced to death, with commutation to imprisonment for life. Then he was handed over to the Austrian government, where he was sentenced to death once again, only to have the sentence commuted again to life imprisonment. Finally, in 1851 he was handed over to Russia, on the insistent request of Nicholas I, who calculated on squeezing out of Bakunin some facts about the supposed new 'Polish plot'.

In gaol Bakunin wrote his *Confession*, an astonishing human document, which became known only half a century after his death. Its author's real ideas are skilfully mingled and masked by lies intended to fool the Tsar and secure his release. But since Bakunin could not give the concrete facts about the 'Polish plot' that they were trying to get from him, the Confession had no results, and Bakunin spent almost six years in solitary confinement – first in the Peter-Paul Fortress, then in the Shlisselburg. It was not until February 1857 that his petition for a pardon, addressed to Alexander II, brought him a commutation of his prison sentence to residence in Tomsk, in Western Siberia. Other petitions to the Tsar lightened his sentence still further, and he was allowed to enter the service of his uncle, N. N. Muravyov-Amursky, Governor General of Eastern Siberia.

Full of illusions about the possibilities of reformist work now opening up before him, Bakunin entered so much into his new role of state functionary that he evoked dissatisfaction and even suspicion among his former friends. But his illusions were soon succeeded by disappointment; in 1861 he fled abroad – to London, to Herzen and Ogaryov, whom he tried to collaborate with. The Polish insurrection of 1863 was regarded by him as a prologue to an all-Russian and all-Slavic revolution. He persistently tried to persuade Herzen and Ogaryov to defend the insurgent cause, while he himself plunged into it and busied himself with the organization of a volunteer corps to be sent to Poland. The collapse of this enterprise led him to leave England and move to Italy.

The years he spent in Italy (1864–7) proved decisive in Bakunin's thought. It was there that the views that made him one of the most eminent figures of European and world anarchism assumed their definitive form. There his revolutionary activity took a definite turn towards the labouring masses, and assumed a definitely international tinge. And it was there that those elements of his doctrine matured that gave him an extremely noteworthy, and at times preponderant influence on the ideology of the Russian revolutionary movement of the '70s.

While still living in Italy, he had drawn up plans and programmes for a 'World Association of International Brothers'. After moving to Switzerland he organized an 'International Alliance of Socialist Democracy' with an anarchist programme, and in the spirit of this programme got out the first number of the *Narodnoye Delo* (The People's Cause), which had been founded in Geneva in 1868 by N. I. Zhukovsky.* He declared this Alliance dissolved when this proved

* With its second number (No. 2–3) the editorship of the *Narodnoye Delo* passed into the hands of Nicholas Utin, who considered himself a Marxist, and in the third (No. 4–5) the periodical announced its solidarity with the International. The 'Russian section' headed by Utin assigned its vote in the General Council to Karl Marx himself, 'whose name is only too well known to all these Russians who follow the social movement at all'. Utin's 'Marxism' did not stop

necessary for him to enter the International (1863) through its Geneva section, but in fact he preserved his own special organization as a secret society within the International, and began the systematic struggle against the General Council headed by Marx and Engels that in 1872 led to the exclusion of him and the French anarchist Guillaume, but at the same time to the decline and *de facto* liquidation of the International itself.

In 1869 Bakunin drew near the émigré Nechayev (see below) and showed a fervent sympathy for his adventurist enterprises, but he soon broke with him. The year 1870 saw Bakunin taking part in an uprising of the Lyons workers. In 1871 he took part in the activity of the Paris Commune. In 1871–4 he wrote his two principal theoretical works, *The German Empire of the Knout* and *The State and Anarchy*; he took part in the Spanish (1873) and the Italian (1874) uprisings, suffered failures everywhere; tired and disappointed, he died on 1 July 1876 in a hospital bed in Berne.

As an anarchist too Bakunin was more of a figure in the international and European revolutionary movement (especially in the Latin countries) than in the Russian.* Anarchist influence was expressed more than once in the pre-revolutionary years in the two branches of the Russian Socialist movement – the Populist ('maximalist') and the Marxist (i.e. the Makhayev group). In these years and in the years of the 1905 and 1917 revolutions, purely anarchist organizations played a noteworthy part (especially in the peasant partisan movement during the civil war in Southern Russia: Makhno's organization and others). But in general, anarchism as a finished system was never more than a peripheral phenomenon; it never played a major role in the evolution of Russian democratic and

---

the *Narodnoye Delo*, under his editorship, from following, in questions of the Russian revolution, a line that scarcely differed from that of Populism of the Lavrov type.

* The same may be said about the other eminent Russian theoretician of anarchism, Prince Peter Kropotkin (1842–1921). Kropotkin was part of the Bakunin wing of the International in 1872, during his trip abroad. After a short stay at home he emigrated for good in 1876, and for more than forty years lived abroad, first in Paris, then in London. There he also wrote his massive works, the most important of which was entitled *Bread and Freedom* (in the French original *La Conquête du Pain*). When he went back to Russia in 1917 at the age of seventy-five, Kropotkin did not play an active role in the revolution, but in his humanitarian emancipatory sympathies he in fact inclined to its moderate liberal wing.

Socialist thought. But all the greater was the role played in this development – especially during the above-mentioned years – by individual elements of anarchist ideology, especially those elements of the doctrine on the state, which was the cornerstone of anarchist theory and whose elaboration was the primary object of Bakunin's literary activity during the last decade of his life.

The state is the force by which the governing and possessing classes keep the masses of the people docile and enslaved. The state must be destroyed in order to untie the creative forces slumbering in those masses and enable them to pass through statelessness and absence of authority, through the chaos of anarchy to a new free organization of society. 'We summon anarchy, persuaded that out of this anarchy, that is, out of the complete expression of the uncurbed life of the people, there must emerge freedom, equality, justice and a new order,' Bakunin wrote in the *Narodnoye Delo*.

The State and Anarchy proved that the road to the social revolution did not pass through the seizure of the state, but through its destruction: 'The state on the one hand and the social revolution on the other – these are the two poles whose antagonism constitutes the very essence of the real life of all European society.' And this is the concluding phrase of this passionately written book, which gives the quintessence of Bakunin's views on the social revolution:

> The Pan-German banner reads, The maintenance and strengthening of the state at all costs; but on our social-revolutionary banner, on the contrary, there is etched in bloody letters the destruction of all states, the annihilation of bourgeois civilization, and voluntary organization from the bottom up by means of voluntary associations – the organization of the unleashed unskilled workers' mob, of all liberated humanity, the creation of a new world for all mankind.

We shall pause later on to consider the side of Bakunin's outlook alluded to by the words 'the unleashed unskilled workers' mob'. But the phrase just cited emphasizes another extremely important element of the views of Bakunin as anarchist: the 'anti-Germanism' of this former 'sentimentalist and German', his conviction that it was the German nation that history had made the banner-bearer of the 'state' he found so odious (he devoted his book on the *German Empire of the Knout* to defending this conviction). The counterpart of this conviction, which had matured within the framework of the Prussian victory of 1870–1 that made the German Empire the dominant power in

Europe, was his other conviction – that history had, on the contrary, made the Slavs the flag-bearers of 'anti-statehood'.

We have seen that Bakunin had nursed an interest in the Slavic question for a long time. But in the '40s he saw in the Polish, Czech, and other Slav revolutions merely extremely important and necessary links in the chain of general democratic European revolutions. In 1863 the Polish uprising had seemed to him to be the precursor of an all-Russian revolution. Now he approached the Slavic question from a completely different angle – that of the 'anti-German' mission of Slavdom.

This mission was far from being summed-up in the counter-position of 'Pan-Slavism' to 'Pan-Germanism'. On the contrary, in sharply criticizing the idea of the creation of a great Slav kingdom under the power of the Russian Tsar, Bakunin categorically declared: 'We are just as much arch-enemies of Pan-Slavism as we are of Pan-Germanism.' In the attempts of the Austrian and other Slavs to counterpose 'to the Pan-Germanism they hate . . . another repulsive imbecility, another ideal no less hostile to freedom and no less murderous for the people: Pan-Slavism', he saw only a proof of the 'degree to which this accursed German civilization, bourgeois in its essence and consequently statebound, has managed to penetrate into the soul of even the Slav patriots'.

According to Bakunin the real 'anti-German' mission of Slavdom consisted of the introduction into Europe and all mankind of 'anti-state' principles: 'by everything in their essence the Slavs are absolutely not a political, that is, not a statebound race . . . The Slavs never, by themselves, set up a state. They never set up one because they were never a conquering race. It is only conquering peoples that create a state and they create it inevitably for profit, to the detriment of the subjugated people . . . The Slavs were primarily a peaceful and agricultural race.'

The last phrase recalls that Bakunin sought the sources of Slav virtues and Teutonic vices not in their racial difference, but in their social history. But this very phrase sheds light on the place occupied by the 'anti-state' theory in the world outlook of Bukharin, an anarchist who was also an active participant in the international movement of the working-class. This place is outlined by Martov[29] when he says: 'Bakuninism is an attempt to fuse the class movement of the contemporary proletariat with a different kind of protest, that of those strata of the peasantry that were being annihilated and in the final analysis were annihilated or completely transformed by capitalism in the nineteenth century – annihilated for the most part by the forces of the contemporary bourgeois-democratic state.'* It was just because of this, indeed, that in the conditions of Russian life already mentioned so often Bakuninism was actually so easily able to become the ideology of a substantial part of the intelligentsia that was on the threshold of active revolutionary work.

To be sure, even this part of the intelligentsia accepted 'anti-statism' not so much in the principled and universal sense it had for Bakunin himself and his Western European fellow-anarchists, as in the limited approval it gave those to assumptions of the Socialist potentialities of the Russian commune and to the apoliticism of the time. The philippics of *The State and Anarchy* against constitutionalism completely responded to its moods:

> You have to be a donkey, an ignoramus, a lunatic to imagine that any constitution, even the most liberal and the most democratic, could improve the relationship of the state to the people; perhaps it might worsen it, burden the people still more, ruin it . . . but to free the people, improve its condition – that's simply foolishness.

Bakunin the anarchist's expressions of opinion on the commune were less precise. After all, in accordance with the universal theory of 'anti-statism', it was the state bonds fettering the masses of the people that had to be snapped everywhere so that their liberated creative forces would slowly begin, from the bottom upwards, to construct a new order of 'freedom, equality, and justice'. In this respect the Russian communal peasantry was no exception. Nevertheless Bakunin indicated three 'positive' traits of the 'ideal' of the commune that made it easier for the Russian people to assimilate the idea of the Socialist revolution. Firstly, there was the conviction that all the land belonged to the people. Secondly, the conviction that the right to exploit the land did not belong to individuals but to the whole commune, the *Mir*. Finally, there was the 'quasi-absolute autonomy

* This, the real historical significance of the 'anti-state' gospel, explains why Bakuninism had its greatest success not at all in the Slavic countries, the bulk of which are the most backward and neglected by the great highway of capitalist development in Europe. In the following decades Bakuninism had its greatest victories in the Latin countries, where capitalism had had time to display all its destructive effects on the old peasant life and the life of the people as a whole, but had not had time as yet to demonstrate the immense productive possibilities inherent in it.

and consequently the absolutely hostile attitude of the commune towards the state'. To be sure, these 'positive' traits were distorted by 'negative' ones: the patriarchalism, the swallowing-up of the individual by the *Mir*, and the faith in the Tsar. But it was just the struggle against these negative traits that constituted the task of the revolutionaries.

As we see, with all Bakunin's characteristic nuances, his views on the commune, 'politics', and even the state were not different enough from Lavrov's to set a gulf between the 'Bakuninites' and the 'Lavrovites' in practical affairs. There was a more definite divergence between Bakunin and Lavrov on the question of the moving forces of the social revolution. Here, too, to be sure, while setting his hopes for the West on the 'workers' world', in Russia he, like Lavrov, set them primarily on the 'peasant world'.[39] But in the light of his anarchist world-view both these 'worlds' – the workers' and the peasants' – were described in a way that was quite different from Lavrov's.

Bakunin agreed with Marx's economic theories sufficiently to translate the first volume of *Capital* into Russian. He saw 'one of the chief scientific merits of Mr Marx' in his 'having proved', in contrast to Proudhon, 'the unquestionable truth . . . that an economic fact always has preceded and does precede juridical and political rights'. To be sure, as his doctrine of the state indicates, Bakunin understood this 'unquestionable truth' in a completely 'non-Marxist' way. On the point of the conquest of the state by the working-class he disagreed with Marx and his followers even more sharply and definitely than Lavrov: 'We have already expressed more than once our profound revulsion at the theory of Lassalle and Marx that recommends to the workers, if not as an ultimate ideal then at least as the most imminent and chief goal, the founding of a people's state,' he wrote in *The State and Anarchy*. 'If there is a state then there is also dominion, and consequently slavery as well.' And in accordance with his own general view of the peasantry and especially his 'anti-Teutonic' view of the Slavs, he asked whether in the 'people's state' the workers would not regard as an object of dominion the 'peasant rabble which, as is well-known, does not enjoy the favour of the Marxists' or 'let us say, as the Slavs would be for the Germans'? And in approaching from this angle the problem of the moving forces of the social revolution, he solved it in a way quite different from Lavrov's.

For Lavrov it was only in Russia that 'the working-class' took on a special social profile. In the West he saw the basic force of the social revolution in that same proletariat of heavy industry that Marx was also calculating on. Lavrov merely criticized the political, 'statist' character that the struggle of the Socialist parties was beginning to assume in these years, and not in Germany alone. Bakunin the anarchist did not stop there. From a criticism of tactics he immediately passed over to an assertion of principle – that the moving force of the social revolution was not the factory workers at all, but the social cast-offs that had been given the semi-contemptuous nickname of 'lumpen-proletariat'. Hence, venomously jeering at the 'bourgeoisness' and 'petty-bourgeois-ness' of the trained workers of heavy industry, Bakunin maintained that 'backward' Italy, for instance, was far closer to a social revolution than 'advanced' Germany, just because 'in Italy there predominated that impoverished proletariat that Messrs Marx and Engels, followed by the whole school of German Social-Democrats, speak of with the deepest contempt'.

But in the 'peasants' world' of Russia, too, Bakunin based his revolutionary calculations not so much on the rank-and-file peasantry as on the 'declassed' elements, both of the peasantry and of Russian society as a whole.

To be sure, in the *Revolutionary Catechism* he wrote as early as 1869 for the 'Society of the Axe', or 'the People's Tribunal', which was invented by Nechayev but in reality never existed, Bakunin spoke of the 'muzhiks' as the real guardians of Socialist principles. 'Of course, the muzhiks never undertook to devise forms for the future communal way of life, but none the less by eliminating everything in their way they will be able to arrange things far better and more intelligently than anything that can emerge from all the theories and projects written by the doctrinaires of Socialism, who impose themselves on the people as teachers, but primarily as directors.' But in order to 'eliminate everything in their way' what was necessary was a 'people's revolution . . . that will nip in the bud every kind of state organization and extirpate all the state traditions of Russia'.

But who then is going to accomplish this? The *Catechism* answered without equivocation:

> Our cause is one of frightful, complete, universal and merciless destruction. Hence, in drawing close to the people we must above all unite with those elements of popular life that, ever since the Moscow state power was established, have never ceased to protest both in words and in deeds against everything connected with the state either directly or indirectly: with the savage bandits' world, the authentic and sole revolutionary world in Russia. To weld this world into one invincible all-encompassing force – that is our whole organization, constitution, and task.

The importance of 'bandits' in the Russian 'people's revolution' was explained by Bakunin in the proclamation, *The Formulation of the Revolutionary Question*, which he wrote at about the same time as the *Catechism*:

> Whoever does not understand banditry will never understand anything about the Russian people's history . . . He belongs in the camp of our statist enemies . . . In Russia the bandit is the sole authentic revolutionary . . . During the heavy intervals when the whole peasant and worker's world is sleeping . . . oppressed by the whole weight of the state, the bandit world of the forests continues its own desperate struggle, and it will struggle until the Russian villages wake up once again. And when both insurrections, the bandits' and the peasants', fuse together, the people's revolution will be born.

Bakunin's fundamental theoretical work, *The State and Anarchy*, sums up: 'If in the Russian people there are any who dare to go counter to the world – they are the bandits. That is why banditry is an important historical phenomenon in Russia – the first revolutionaries, Pugachov and Stenka Razin, were bandits.'*

We see how far the 'elements of popular life' taken by Bakunin as a guide differed from those 'communal and artel centres of the Russian people' that Lavrov was counting on! But their approach to the revolutionary tasks of the Russian intelligentsia was also quite different.

For Lavrov this task consisted of the acquisition and transmission to the people of the social science that would help it realize, through the commune and the artel, the 'moral ideal of socialism'. For Bakunin such an ideal, which would have had to be 'imposed' on the people 'from above', did not exist at all. The 'ideal' was supposed to arise 'from below', out of the revolutionary creativity of the people itself. Hence the intelligentsia's task consisted only in unloosing and in fomenting the spontaneous revolutionary passions that were in the masses of the people, the anti-statist uprising that was maturing in its depths and whose forerunners were the 'bandits'.

Science was unnecessary: 'For us the road to the emancipation of

* In his reminiscences[40] Akselrod, at that time a Bakuninite and later on the 'patriarch of the Russian Social-Democracy', tells a tragi-comic anecdote of how in 1874 he and the future 'Grandmother of the Russian revolution', C. K. Breshkovskaya, went out searching for a bandit who was active in the forests of Southern Russia and according to newspaper accounts had plundered rich landowners and Jews in order to distribute the plunder to the poor peasants. The search was not crowned by success.

the people by means of science is barred,' Bakunin wrote in 1870: 'consequently only one road is left to us, the road of revolution.' The conclusion is:

'Thus, young friends, hurry to leave this world, doomed to destruction, these universities, academies and schools . . . which have always striven to divide us from the people. Go to the people! There is where your career is, your life, your science . . . Don't fuss about with science, in whose name you are supposed to be tied down and made powerless. This science must die together with the world it is the expression of. But a new and living science will undoubtedly be born after the people's victory, out of the liberated life of the people.'

Making the blind elemental surging of the masses the real demiurge of history, Bakunin (in the programme of the 'International Brothers') assigns the individual a very limited role:

> Revolutions are never made by individuals, or even by secret societies . . . All a well-organized society can do is . . . to organize not an army (the people must always be the army) but something like a revolutionary general staff, consisting of devoted, energetic, educated individuals . . . capable of acting as intermediaries between the revolutionary idea and the instincts of the people.*

But a basic correction is introduced into this formulation by the proclamation, *The Beginning of the Revolution*, which Bakunin wrote in 1870. Here, too, Bakunin insists that the revolution as a 'radical overturn', requires the destruction of all forms of contemporary life 'without exception' and their replacement by 'other, novel, completely opposed' forms that can 'only emerge from total amorphousness'. But – the 'generations preceding the overturn include individuals who are incapable of restraining their passion for destruction until the advent of the general struggle, who swiftly seek out their enemies and who brood on their annihilation'. And as though sanctioning these acts of individual terror that were becoming more and more frequent in Russia, Bakunin adds: 'The wiping out of highly placed persons who personify state institutions or institutions of economic corruption must begin with personal exploits. . . . In this struggle the revolution sanctifies everything equally . . . They will call it terrorism! . . . Let them: it's all the same to us . . . Let all healthy young

* The constitution of the International Brothers says: 'For the international organization throughout Europe a hundred revolutionaries, strongly welded together, are enough. Two or three hundred revolutionaries will be enough to organize a big country.'

heads take up at once the sacred cause of the extirpation of the evil, the cleansing of the Russian Land by fire and sword, uniting fraternally with those who are doing the same throughout Europe.'

'To the people!' this was the slogan proclaimed for the first time by Herzen in November 1861, when in connexion with the student riots Petersburg University was occupied by troops and shut down. Addressing the students 'whom science was locked away from' he had written, 'To the people! To the people – there is your place, exiles from science! Show them that from among you there will come not scribblers but warriors, and not rootless mercenaries, but warriors of the Russian people.' 'To the people!' Lavrov and Bakunin both cried out now. But their appeals were completely different, and, what was more important, they were taken up in completely different ways by those they were addressed to.

The Lavrovites went to the people to help them transform into self-conscious Socialist ideas the confused and indefinite collective moods and passions they thought were generated among the labouring masses by their communal and artel way of life. The conscious assimilation of Socialist ideas was supposed to become a weapon of the masses in their conscious struggle for the Socialist ideal. The Bakuninites, on the contrary, went to the people to appeal not to their consciousness but to their 'instincts', in order to try to 'foment' everywhere and mobilize for immediate transformation into action, into an 'insurrection', all the confused passions, despairs, wrath, hatred and vengeance slumbering in the masses – in the assurance that out of the chaos of passions the 'unleashed unskilled mob' of workers would of itself, 'from the bottom upwards' give birth to a new order, a new awareness and a new ideal of 'freedom, equality and justice'. This difference was not always formulated with theoretical precision, nor was it even always clearly present to consciousness, but it drew a completely clear line of demarcation between the attitudes of the Lavrovite 'propagandists' and the Bakuninite 'insurrectionists'.

Here once again there was expressed that contradiction between the criterion of spontaneity or rationalism, emotion or intellect, character or consciousness, in quest of which the thought of the democratic intelligentsia had been condemned to evolve and that found such clear expression in the counterposition of Dobrolyubov and Pisaryov. Almost all the same Pisaryov expressions, in the contrary sense, were used by an eminent 'insurrectionist', Serge Kravchinsky, who protested to Lavrov: 'It's not ideas the people lack. Anyone who has roamed about a lot among the people will tell you that in its head the foundations of "elementary" (of course, not scientific) Socialism are completely mature. The only thing the people do not have enough of is passion.'

4. PETER TKACHOV

The attempt to overcome this counterposition of 'ideas' and 'passion', and to merge Pisaryov's rationalism and Bakunin's dynamism, characterized the position of Tkachov. This was different equally from the 'propagandism' of the Lavrovites and the anarchic 'insurrectionism' of the Bakuninites: 'Anarchy as an imminent, direct goal of the revolution, and propaganda as the practical means of realizing it, and finally an organization without discipline, hierarchy and subordination – aren't these all fantastic utopias, infantile dreams?' Tkachov wrote in the programme of his review *Nabat* (The Alarm). And he proceeded to work out a programme that both in its clearly 'political', statist aims, and in the 'Jacobin' methods of struggle it recommended, came into sharp contradiction with the opinions and tendencies that hitherto had been generally accepted by the radical democratic intelligentsia.

Son of a small landowner, Peter Nikitich Tkachov (1844–85) had entered the political movement in his earliest youth. As early as 1861 he had been put into the Kronstadt fortress for several months because of his part in some student riots. In 1862 he was arrested together with Pisaryov in connexion with the afore-mentioned 'Ballod Affair', and again spent several months in gaol, in the Peter-Paul Fortress. In that same year of 1862 Tkachov, eighteen years old, printed his first article, on law. From 1865 on he was a colleague of Pisaryov's on the *Russkoye Slovo*; when that was shut down, on the *Delo* (The Cause) that replaced it at the end of 1867. He became its chief contributor after Pisaryov's death. In 1869 he was arrested in connexion with the 'Nechayev affair' (see below); in 1871 he was sentenced to sixteen months' imprisonment followed by banishment.

Tkachov soon escaped abroad, and without stopping his collaboration on the *Delo* began his own literary work as an *émigré* under various pseudonyms, until down to the very beginning of the '80s. After some abortive attempts to work together with Lavrov, in April 1874 he printed a programmatic pamphlet, 'Tasks of Revolutionary Propaganda in Russia'; from the end of 1875 to the end of 1876 he published in Geneva, in conjunction with a group of Polish *émigré* sympathizers (K. Tursky, K. Yanitsky and others), the periodical *Nabat*, subtitled 'Organ of the Russian Revolutionaries'. He succumbed to a mental illness in 1883, and in 1885 died in a Paris hospital at the age of forty-one.

In the *Russkoye Slovo* and the *Delo* Tkachov preached individualism and intellectualism in the spirit of Pisaryov, but in contradistinction to him he concentrated the attention of the 'people of the future' (a parallel to Pisaryov's 'consistent realists') not on the natural but on the social sciences. In accord on this point with Lavrov, he diverged from him in not acknowledging the absolute value of the 'moral ideal'. In an article *People of the Future and the Heroes of Philistinism*, written in 1868, he insisted on every man's right to 'bear himself towards the prescriptions of the moral law . . . not dogmatically but critically'. After the appearance of the *Historical Letters* he subjected the whole subjective theory of progress to acid criticism, drawing his arguments from Spencer's positivism.*

His attraction to Spencer shows how exaggerated is a statement made by one of Tkachov's competent biographers, Nicholas F. Annensky,[41] to the effect that in his sociological views Tkachov was an 'extreme and consistent economic materialist', that is, a Marxist. He was a 'Marxist' only in the sense of acknowledging the most general foundations of the analysis of capitalism given by Marx in his economic doctrine, that is, in the most restricted sense in which both Lavrov and Bakunin, and it may be said the whole of the Russian revolutionary intelligentsia, were also 'Marxists'. But his views of the socio-economic evolution of Russia were so 'Populist' that it was precisely in his polemic against Tkachov that Engels[42] gave that criticism of Populism that was made use of more than once later on by the Russian Marxist Social-Democracy in its struggle against Populism.

Not diverging in principle from Lavrov and Bakunin in their general views on the peasant commune, Tkachov also did not differ from them in acknowledging the increasingly disintegrating effect that contemporary Russian capitalism was beginning to exercise on it. But from this he drew different conclusions, which were characteristic of his whole position.

* This article ('What is the Party of Progress?'), written by Tkachov in gaol, never saw the light: it was confiscated by the state police, in whose archives the manuscript was found after the 1917 revolution.

In *Tasks of Revolutionary Propaganda in Russia,* he pointed out that 'the commune was already beginning to disintegrate', that among the peasantry a 'class of kulaks was beginning to take shape', and that in general the formation 'on the one hand of an extremely powerful conservative class of peasants, landowners, and on the other of a pecuniary, commercial, and industrial bourgeoisie' was taking place. Hence the conclusion: 'That is why we cannot wait... The revolution in Russia is urgently necessary and moreover necessary right now. Now or very slowly, and perhaps never! Now the conditions are in our favour, in ten, twenty years they will be against us.'

'Now or very slowly, and perhaps never!' – the conclusion of this slogan, which became celebrated, was that 'we cannot wait', either until the propaganda of the Lavrovites organized the masses of the people for a conscious struggle for the Socialist 'ideal', or until there arose out of the uninterrupted chain of Bakuninite 'insurrections' that chaos that would give rise to 'freedom, equality, and justice'. All that referred to the future; the revolution had to be made today. It had to be made in the name of those ends that were accessible today, and those forces that were available today.

The programme of the *Nabat* speaks of the same thing even more definitely:

> Take advantage of the minutes. Such minutes are rare in history. Letting them slip by means voluntarily postponing the possibility of social revolution for a long time – perhaps for ever. So don't dawdle!... Enough of this constant interpreting of the 'preparation!' . . . Preparing the revolution has nothing whatever to do with the revolutionist. It is being prepared by the exploiters, capitalists, landowners, priests, police, functionaries, progressivists and other such people... The revolutionary does not prepare, he 'makes' the revolution. So make it! Make it right away! That is why we say: don't get too far away from the given realities, stand firmly on the terrain of sober, rational realism. Don't dream, but make the revolution, make it, and make it as quickly as possible!'

The programme also fearlessly drew the final political conclusion. In contrast with Lavrov and Bakunin, with their decisive denial of the 'people's state', it declared: 'The most immediate, the direct aim of the revolution must consist of nothing but conquering the governmental power and turning the given conservative state into a revolutionary state.' The programme emphasizes that the activity of this state 'must be twofold: revolutionarily destructive and revolutionarily constructive'. It also gives the slogan – 'The People's Duma' – that the revolutionary struggle was supposed to be conducted under and that was to play a role later on in the revolution of 1905.

In No. 9 of the *Nabat* Tkachov carries his idea to its conclusion: 'Political reforms, constantly being removed to the background, are more necessary than ever in our time day . . . the republic must finally cease being an empty sound, a deceitful promise . . . the time has come to go back to the traditions of '89 and '93 [i.e. the traditions of the French National Assembly of 1789 and of the Convention of 1793].' Thus Russian 'Jacobinism' gave rise to Pisaryov's 'bourgeois' radicalism – but it gave rise to it not in the realm of psychology, economics, and sociology, where Pisaryov himself desperately tried to establish it, but in the realm of politics, which Pisaryov had disregarded, but in which this radicalism had every chance of becoming one of the fundamental elements of the complex and contradictory ideology of the Russian intelligentsia.

But this also gave rise to Pisaryov individualism, in a transmuted form. For the contradiction between the necessity of 'making' the revolution, and at that a political revolution, at once and the only too obvious unpreparedness of the masses of the people for such a revolution, was solved if the demiurge, if not of history then at least of its revolutionary occasions, was not the masses, but the individual, not the majority of the people but its thinking minority.

In the above-mentioned pamphlet, written in the form of an open letter to Lavrov, Tkachov says:

> Surely you must understand that the revolution (in the usual sense of the word) is distinguished from peaceful progress just by this, that the former is accomplished by a minority and the latter by the majority? . . . The people of a real revolution are simply the tempestuous elements, destroying and annihilating everything in their path, always acting heedlessly and unconsciously. The people of your revolution – are civilized people completely clear as to their own position, acting consciously and purposefully . . . But where have civilized people ever been seen making a revolution! Oh no, they always prefer the path of peaceful, tranquil progress, the path of bloodless protests, diplomatic compromises and reforms – to the path of violence, the path of blood, killing and plunder.

As a counterweight to Lavrov, who placed on the 'critically thinking individual' only the task of developing the consciousness of the popular mass, and to Bakunin, who laid on him only the task of 'unleashing' its passions, Tkachov said to the intelligentsia, this hopeless 'minority', that it was precisely itself alone and not the 'mass' at all that could and must 'make' the revolution. In general revolutions had to be made by the minority on behalf of the people, and not at all 'by means of' the people, which was what was being proclaimed, though in different senses, by both Lavrov and Bakunin. Tkachov's pamphlet went on with its appeal to Lavrov as follows:

> Surely you must understand that a revolutionary always regards himself and must regard himself as right to summon the people to an uprising; what distinguishes him from the philistine philosopher is just this, that without waiting until the current of historical events itself indicates the moment, he selects it himself.

Tkachov is the last in the series of those distinguished thinkers and journalists who as early as the '30s and '40s of the nineteenth century had been building up the arsenal of Russian Populism. It was from this arsenal that all the Populist tendencies and groups whose revolutionary struggle filled the '70s, especially the second half, drew their intellectual weapons. But from the point of view of that struggle Tkachov's contribution was different in principle from Lavrov's and Bakunin's.

In the concrete historical framework of those years, both Lavrovite 'propagandism' and Bakuninite 'insurrectionism' were essentially no more than a way of circumventing or postponing any approach to a solution of the basic task. It was a task that the Russian intelligentsia was being more and more inexorably confronted with, and that demanded of it almost superhuman exploits – the task of a direct struggle against the Tsarist régime. The Lavrovites were postponing this to that future 'real day' when the 'consciousness' of the people would have fully ripened, while the Bakuninites put it off to the complete unfolding of all its insurrectionist potency. Looked at in historical perspective both Lavrovism and Bakuninism were in their own way the Russian intelligentsia's prayer to 'let the cup pass from it' before it stepped on to the Golgotha of history. Tkachov, in sharp antagonism to both Lavrov and Bakunin, called upon the intelligentsia to hoist immediately on to its own shoulders the burden of the exploits prepared for it by history.

In the movement of the Russian revolutionary intelligentsia of the '70s, so charged with sacrifices, the name of Tkachov was bound up with a stage of that movement that was brief but most majestic in its legendary heroism: the stage of the 'People's Freedom' (*Narodnaya Volya*).

CHAPTER SIX

The Work of Revolution

1. FIRST STEPS

In the history of Populism the '60s were primarily a decade of the theoretical elaboration of ideology. The '70s, by contrast, were chiefly a decade of the application of this ideology to the practical work of the revolution.

It goes without saying that in fact there was no absolute boundary between these two decades. The process of the formation of the basic elements of Populist ideology took in, as we have seen (Lavrov, Bakunin) the beginning of the '70s, and was even extended (Tkachov) to the middle of the decade. In the course of the '60s, again, especially during the second half, when the intelligentsia had begun emerging from the state of paralysed torpor it had been all but thrown into by the disappointments of the peasant reforms, and by the savage repressions and the moral and political isolation in connexion with the Polish uprising, fragmented little groups or even energetic individuals tried without let-up to draw some practical conclusions from the very often still highly confused ideas bequeathed by the preceding decades. Practical work demanded the adaptation of abstract ideas to the concrete realities of Russia, subjected the ideas themselves to a corresponding elaboration, forced the search for new paths, pushed thinking on ahead and sharpened the demand for theoretical generalization and formulation. Hence it proved to be the most immediate influence on the labours of the Populist theoreticians, as we have seen by the example of the effect of the so-called 'Chaikovskyites' on the work of Lavrov or of Nechayev on the work of Bakunin.

Thus there existed an uninterrupted reciprocal interaction between theory and practice even at a time when the emigration had become the chief laboratory of theory.* The theoretical labour prepared the

* It is superficial and erroneous in the highest degree to imagine the Russian political emigration of the Tsarist period as something wrenched out of Russian realities and alien to them. The emigration of this period was not a broken-off chunk of the Russian revolutionary intelligentsia, but a vitally necessary con-

practical movement and laid down new paths for it. For their part the practical enterprises confronted theory with new problems, and not only demanded their solution, but often prompted it. But in the '60s theory was the centre of gravity of the work, and it was only in the '70s that it began to be carried over into practice. It was only from this time on that revolutionary activity stopped being the property of little groups with few people, few in number, fragmented, introverted and isolated from each other, revolving around one or another eminent individual, and the revolutionary movement became a 'mass' movement in the relative sense that it took hold of the basic 'mass' of the social stratum of the Russian intelligentsia, made by history the bearer of the democratic idea in Russia. Vera Figner rightly remarks that the 'Chaikovskyite' group founded at the end of the '60s was 'the last group that bore the name of an individual'.[43]

Pisaryov, Lavrov, Bakunin, Tkachov – these four names symbolize the four basic ideas that entered the spiritual arsenal of Russian Populism: the individualistic idea of personal self-perfection; the rationalistic idea of Socialist enlightenment; the emotional-mystical idea of plebeian insurrection; the Jacobin idea of settling the political problem by the forces of the thinking intellectual minority – for the people, but not by the people.

In the theoretical shaping of these ideas, out of which Populist doctrine was moulded, people clashed sharply with each other, often with irreconcilable enmity. But this theoretical irreconcilability merely reflected the insolubility of the contradictions in Russian socio-political, cultural and moral life. At the same time each one of them expressed one side of the intellectual agony of the same social group: the Russian intelligentsia.

It was just because of this that each of these basic ideas was conceived empirically even before a generalizing idea had given it a definite theoretical form. And it was just because of this that all these ideas, despite their theoretical irreconcilability, lived on harmoniously in the quaintest combinations, together and at the same time, in the practical Populist movement. Later phases of its development were

---

stituent element. It was only after the 1905 revolution, which made possible more or less large-scale 'legal possibilities' of political activity in the country itself, that a certain fissure began to form between the emigration and 'Russia'. And it was only after the 1917 revolution, paralleling the dying-out of the intelligentsia itself as a distinct social group, that the emigration lost its roots in Russian soil and has been dying out as a living force.

marked not so much by a theoretical rupture with some basic ideas or the acquisition of others, as by the greater vociferousness, first of one, then of another in the collective chorus. The distinction lay not so much in ideology as in psychology; not so much in theoretical views as in moods; not so much in programme as in tactics. It is appropriate, accordingly, to look for a key to an understanding of the peculiarities of these groups and tendencies that sprang up in the '60s and '70s, came together, separated, and replaced each other, but that were all uniformly links in the same Populist chain. It was not until the '80s that the emergence of Russian Marxism introduced into the hitherto unified Populist world-view of the revolutionary movement a fissure of principle.

We have already mentioned the organization Land and Freedom, founded in 1862 by the disciples of Chernyshevsky, who was convinced that the dissatisfaction of the peasants with the conditions of the emancipation would lead in the immediate future to an explosion of the peasant revolution. Reality shattered this faith, and the organization proved extremely short-lived. A whole series of disappointments now descended on the revolution. Its ideological expression was given by Pisaryov's individualism. This placed not the political or the social struggle at the root of social progress, but a many-sided emancipation of the individual (especially the most oppressed individual – the woman) and the 'reasonable' utilization of the individual's abilities. What characterized the moods of the intelligentsia during these disappointments was a striving towards the organization of labouring collectives and colonies, which on the one hand were supposed to ensure all members an independent existence, and on the other were a sort of demonstrative oasis of the 'reasonable' life of 'thinking individuals' capable of emancipating themselves from the oppression and prejudices of their environment.

The most famous of such colonies was one founded in Petersburg by an ardent champion of women's emancipation, the gifted young writer, Vasily Sleptsov, author of a novel *Trudnoye Vremya* (A Difficult Time), in whose hero, the educated plebeian Ryazanov, it was not difficult to recognize a blood-brother of Turgenev's Bazarov (in *Fathers and Sons*), who had served Pisaryov as the prototype of the 'consistent realist'. But the attempt to turn this colony, which was given the name of 'commune' and with the exception of its founder consisted exclusively of women, into a genuine communist labouring collective, which is what its architects dreamt of, did not succeed. Nor was it possible, in spite of the complete apoliticism of this 'commune', to protect it against governmental repression. Its participants were too intimately associated with all the other strata of the intelligentsia whose political interests were beginning, in the middle of the '60s, to revive again. Arrested in 1866 in connexion with the Karakozov affair (see below), Sleptsov was soon released, but he was forced to leave Petersburg. His departure accelerated the dissolution of the 'commune', which even before this had been disintegrated by internal dissension.*

Among the groups of the intelligentsia in which political thought began stirring once again towards the middle of the '60s, the Moscow group of Nicholas Andreyevich Ishutin (1840–79) is of particular importance in the history of Populism.

Beginning with a purely propagandistic elaboration of Chernyshevsky's communist ideas, the Ishutin group gradually became a sort of microcosm of trends that were later given a precise formulation in the works of Populist theoreticians and embodied in their revolutionary practice. In its intellectual arsenal there can be found simultaneously embryos of Lavrovism, Bakuninism, and Tkachov Jacobinism. But the ideas of all members of the group developed in the same direction and at the same tempo, which made its organizational evolution extremely peculiar. Within the group there took shape a special secret society, the 'Organization', which included only those members of the group that considered their basic task neither self-development nor theoretical propaganda, but the preparation for an active intervention in the expected people's revolution. But towards the beginning of 1866, within the Organization itself, an even narrower conspiratorial group began singling itself out; it was given the gloomily romantic name of 'Hell'. The basic idea behind Hell was not to wait passively for the advent of the 'social revolution' but to try actively to 'unleash' it by some kind of 'grandiose, terrifying facts', capable of 'shaking up the slumbering people'. The most powerful impression on the members of the group, especially its head, Ishutin, was made by Orsini's attempt on the life of the French Emperor Naploeon III;

* The gifted but politically extremely unstable Nicholas G. Leskov gave a polemically coloured description of Sleptsov's 'commune' in his novel *Nekuda* (Nowhere to Go) (1864). This novel, and even more Leskov's next novel *Na Nozhax* (At Daggers Drawn) provoked an outburst of indignation from the radical intelligentsia, which even before this had been deeply outraged by Leskov's articles on the Petersburg fires (see above).

regicide automatically began moving well up into first place among these 'facts'.

But even before Hell came to a definitive conclusion on this question, one of its members, Dmitri Vladimirovich Karakozov (1840–66), a cousin of Ishutin's, on his own responsibility and at his own risk, decided to assassinate the Tsar. The other members of Hell, who had accidentally learned of Karakozov's plans, vainly took steps to stop the assassination: on 4 April 1866, in the Petersburg Summer Gardens, Karakozov fired a revolver at Alexander II; he missed and was seized on the spot. His arrest led to the swift and total destruction of the Ishutin group. Thirty-four of its members, together with Karakozov and Ishutin, were tried and given very harsh sentences. Karakozov was hanged on 3 September of the same year. Ishutin's death sentence was commuted to life imprisonment at hard labour. But his group, with all its organizational ramifications, came to an end.

Another Moscow group, which was formed among the students at the Agricultural Academy in the autumn of 1869, had a far more unified character. But this was because it existed only a very short time and was dominated absolutely by its founder, the young teacher Serge Gennadyevich Nechayev (1847–82), a man of considerable intellectual power but infinitely greater will-power.

In 1868–9 Nechayev, together with Tkachov, took part in the student movement, but at the beginning of 1869 he left for Switzerland, where as mentioned above he drew close to Bakunin and in spite of his youth had the most powerful influence over him. Here from the very beginning he displayed that unscrupulousness not only in the struggle against enemies but also in influencing friends and co-thinkers that later made Marx and Engels unjustly regard him as a mere 'rogue', practically a Russian *agent provocateur*. In Russian political parlance his name became a synonym for the most thorough-going amorality.

Describing his escape from Russia in the most fantastic way, Nechayev passed himself off as an agent of a non-existent organization, the People's Tribunal (*Narodnaya Rasprava*); he immediately published a periodical under the same name. We have already spoken of Bakunin's *Revolutionary Catechism* and the proclamation, *Beginning of the Revolution*, which he was commissioned by Nechayev to write and which sanctioned individual terror. But it was he who prompted Bakunin to address an appeal 'To the officers of the Russian army' to enter the People's Tribunal; *en passant* this expounded Nechayev's organizational principles: in the words of this appeal the

People's Tribunal was 'powerful through the passive obedience to all the orders of a single committee, which knew everything and was known by no one . . . The organization could be entered freely, but leaving it was impossible.'

Now these organizational principles of Nechayev's were immediately applied to the founding of the above-mentioned group in Moscow, to which he returned in the autumn of 1869: only a few weeks later (21 November 1869) on Nechayev's initiative, the members of the group killed one of their number, a student, Ivanov, not so much because of suspicions that he had been in contact with the police, which he was accused of, as because of Nechayev's desire to weld together all the members of the group 'by blood' and to secure their 'passive obedience' to all his 'orders'. The members of the group were soon arrested, and in 1871 the trial of the 'Nechayevites' took place. For many of the sixty-four members tried it ended with sentences of hard labour. In December of the same year, 1869, Nechayev himself turned up again in Switzerland, where he proceeded to get out the second issue of the *Narodnaya Rasprava.*

In the summer of 1870 his rupture with Bakunin, whom he had not been averse to embroiling in a sordid blackmail affair – in the interests, of course, of the 'revolution' – prompted Nechayev to move to London, where he began publishing a leaflet called the *Obshchina* (The Commune). Handed over in 1872 to the Russian government as a criminal, Nechayev was sentenced to twenty years' hard labour (the Russian Penal Code of the time had no capital sentence for crimes) and was subjected to the strictest solitary confinement in the Peter-Paul Fortress, where he died in 1882. But even there he did not lose his self-control, his will-power, or his ability to influence those around him. He was so successful in winning over his guards that they not only got him newspapers clandestinely and generally kept him abreast of events, but in October 1880 they even transmitted a letter to the outside in which he proposed to the Executive Committee of the People's Freedom (see below) that they organize his escape from the fortress. The Executive Committee responded favourably, but Nechayev himself categorically refused to be set free when he learned that this would delay preparations for an attempt on the life of the Tsar.*

* This action of the guards was discovered by accident; they paid for it by heavy sentences of hard labour. None the less, according to political exiles who met them in Siberia, even there they retained a benevolent attitude towards their former prisoner.

The bulk of the intelligentsia met 'Nechayevism' with hostility. It was not only its amorality, however, that repelled the intelligentsia, but also its general political ideas. In contrast with the predominant mood of the era Nechayev and his fellow-thinkers oriented themselves towards a peasant insurrection, which they were expecting in the immediate future – by February 1870, when the 'temporary obligations' of the peasants to their former landowners were supposed to come to an end (see above). Hence the Nechayevite Bakuninites were calling on 'the people' for the immediate preparation of an uprising at a time when even the other Bakuninite groups intended to do no more than sustain an 'insurrectionist' spirit in the people by means of partial protests, while waiting for the more or less remote future when the time would come for a people's revolution. Of the Lavrovites there is nothing to say at all.*

The most determined adversary of the Nechayevites was the Lavrovite group of the 'Chaikovskyites', which took shape in Petersburg in the autumn of 1869. It was made up chiefly of students at the Academy of Medicine (Mark Andreyevich Natanson and others) and named after one of its most eminent members, Nicholas Vasilyevich Chaikovsky, who in 1918 became the head of the anti-Bolshevik 'Archangel Government' of Northern Russia.

According to one of its members, L. Shishko, the group began 'taking shape just about the time Nechayev appeared; its founders were just those people who in the spring of 1869 resisted Nechayev's agitation in favour of an immediate revolutionary uprising'.[44]

The real historical significance of the Chaikovskyite group is that it gave rise to the most massive revolutionary organization of the '70s: Land and Freedom (*Zemlya i Volya*). But the organization of this famous society was preceded by the legendary epic of the 'going to the people', about which even the head of the Tsarist political police, the General of Gendarmes Shebeko wrote in his official *Chronicle*: 'a whole legion of Socialists set to work with an energy and self-sacrifice the like of which is unknown in the history of a single secret society in Europe.'

* The Bakuninism of the Nechayevites impelled them to study the history of popular psychology and of popular movements. Among those who returned from hard labour and Siberian exile there emerged quite a number of eminent investigators in this field (Pryzhov, Shchapov, and others). Let us add that on the right wing of the intelligentsia this same Bakuninism gave rise to a characteristic reactionary and mystical tendency in Populism (Kablits-Yuzov, Prugavin and others).

2. 'GOING TO THE PEOPLE'

In the tidal wave of the 'going to the people' of the intelligentsia *en masse* it is possible to mark clearly two billows, essentially distinct in mood – the billow of 1874–5 and the billow of 1876–8. But they were both preceded by the attempt, made by the 'Dolgushinites', members of a small group organized by Alexander Vasilyevich Dolgushin (1848–85) a former 'Nechayevite' (acquitted in court after having spent a year and eight months in gaol waiting for a preliminary hearing). With a store of proclamations written in the 'Bakuninite' spirit and illegally printed, in the summer of 1873, the members of the group moved on 'to the people'. But after a very short time they were all arrested; out of the twelve people tried (1874) five paid for a few days of revolutionary activity by long terms of hard labour, including Dolgushin himself, who never was released at all and died in 1885 in the Shlisselburg Fortress.

The fiasco of this peculiar historical rehearsal of 'going to the people' and the savage reprisals that followed it did not stop the tempestuously growing movement. From the autumn of 1873 on, hundreds of young people came to the capital from all over the country. There, in dozens of little groups, ardent discussions were carried on about the problems of working among the 'people'. Preparations were made for the spring, which because of the peasants' way of life was considered to be the most favourable time for beginning this work. Some of them (who were primarily, of course, 'Lavrovites' in their general inclination, headed by 'Chaikovskyites') prepared themselves to work on the land chiefly in the semi-intelligentsia roles of teachers, nurses, village clerks, and so on, helping the people with their own knowledge and thus winning its confidence. Others, insurrectionally-minded in the Bakuninite manner, from the very first condemned themselves to heavy physical labour in order to come into the closest contact with the masses of the people. But both one and the other displayed infinite enthusiasm, faith in their cause, and self-sacrifice. Students left universities, higher institutions of learning and special schools. Graduating physicians refused to take their final examinations. Young men and women furtively left their parents' homes, often rejecting a secure and even opulent life in order to equip themselves with a false passport, dress in peasant costume, turn themselves into 'one of the people', and embark on an uncertain, dangerous life in the countryside, in a *milieu* of peasants and workers that was completely unknown to the vast majority of them.*

There was no central organization to lead the movement as a whole, and it developed rather chaotically. The furnishing of passports, clothes, money for the trip and so on to those leaving was taken care of by the so-called 'mutual aid funds', which usually consisted of local people and received money from their more prosperous sympathizers. But in each locality, with the help of 'sympathizers' from the wealthy and influential landowning, bourgeois, and even functionaries' circles, 'revolutionary dens' were organized. These were taverns kept by reliable people, where a newcomer might stay, workshops where he could learn some craft or other, settlements where he could live and have his meals together with his comrades. These same 'sympathizers' found teaching, nursing, and clerical posts for those who wanted them, and sometimes also suitable physical work. Finally, they also warned the propagandists as much as possible of any police suspicions, and helped them to hide in case of a threat of arrest.

In the spring of 1874 all this army of the intelligentsia started getting under way. Hundreds of youthful apostles of Socialism surged into the countryside. More than thirty provinces became an arena for their activities. But the main stream moved into the areas of the old peasant uprisings (the rebellions of Stenka Razin and Emelyan Pugachov, the Ukraine, etc.) where the terrain was considered readiest for propaganda. Special attention was also given to the areas where the various nonconformist peasant religious sects were spread (the Stundists and others), whose anti-statist and semi-communist character seemed to ensure their receptivity to Socialist propaganda. Most of these 'goers to the people' were concentrated in the Volga, Don and Dniepr districts.

It was this very preference for the 'insurrectionist' regions that expressed the predominance of Bakuninite tendencies among the

* Barannikov (later one of the most prominent organizers of the attempts on Alexander II's life) was a typical example of the lofty spiritual ardour that seized hold of the young people who 'went to the countryside'. He left the Military Academy and 'without any transition or preparation rushed from a rich, noble family straight to the people', and became a farm-hand. The situation he found himself in was so strange that when he found a louse in his underclothes, something he had never seen before, his workmates had to tell him what it was. But this did not prevent him, from the very first day on, from zealously performing the filthiest and most onerous chores, and submissively enduring the horrifying conditions of life of one of the worst paid categories of the Russian proletariat.[45]

youth. However, in the *preparation* of the movement the most eminent role was that of the Lavrovites, especially the Chaikovskyites, though before the movement could take any practical shape the Chaikovskyite organization was bled white by arrests. But beyond these external, police reasons, the predominance of the Bakuninites also had internal reasons, rooted in the very nature of Lavrovism on the one hand and of Bakuninism on the other.

The Lavrovites were setting out primarily to bring the people 'knowledge'. They oriented themselves along the lines of an 'intimate', systematic and protracted propaganda and the acquisition of a controlling influence over the whole course of country life through the occupation of its 'key' positions, as mentioned above. The Lavrovites thought it necessary to prepare themselves thoroughly both for these novel functions and for the work of propaganda itself. In general, consequently, they were far less fanatical and impulsive than the insurrectionist Bakuninites, who were rather heedless of 'knowledge' and who went into the countryside to carry on 'flying' propaganda that had as its principal object the seeking out and 'fomenting' of peasant discontent to the greatest degree possible.

In fact, however, these Bakuninites' ideas and moods evoked little response among the peasants. In summing-up the results of his own experience Aptekman[45] writes: 'I noticed that any sharp sallies against the Tsar or against religion made an extremely disagreeable impression on the peasants; they were just as deeply perplexed by energetic appeals for a rebellion or uprising.' In the final analysis the Bakuninites too had nothing left to do but carry on the peaceable 'academic' propaganda of Socialist ideas by way of conversations and the distribution of pamphlets. This was what the Lavrovites also had in mind in going to the people; Vera Figner, who later became famous in the People's Freedom movement but was at this time a Lavrovite, makes the point in detail:

> 'Seeing that in the West political liberty had not made the people any happier . . . we . . . shifted exclusively to the terrain of economic relations. We considered it impossible to summon the Russian people to a struggle for rights that would not give them bread; together with this, while intending to replace existing economic conditions, we were hoping, by undermining the idea of Tsarism among the people, to secure the democratization of the political order . . . We thought we would convey Socialist ideas to the people without any concessions to the people's world-view . . . In short, we intended to develop among the people conscious Socialists in the Western European sense.'[47]

Thus, in spite of the 'insurrectionist' attitude of the vast majority of those who 'went to the people', the leader of the People's Freedom (see below), Andrew Zhelyabov, in his famous speech at the trial of the 'First of March' assassins of the Tsar in 1881 (see below) could with perfect accuracy retrospectively characterize the movement of 1873–5, which he also participated in, as a movement 'whose objective was the peaceful propagandizing of Socialist ideas. [It] was completely bloodless; it rejected violence, and it was not revolutionary but pacific.'

The non-revolutionary, pacific character of the movement did not save it from savage repression. As early as late summer of 1874 arrests began; they netted several thousand people by the end of 1875. Initially it was proposed to try 770 of them. Later the number of those tried at the 'big' trial was reduced to 193. But the bulk of those arrested had to be taken into 'preliminary detention' for several years, so that the trial did not begin until the end of 1877 and came to an end at the beginning of 1878. During this time a few dozen prisoners died in gaol; many fell ill; some of them went out of their minds. The 'trial of the 193' ended in acquittal for some of those tried, but most of them were gaoled and exiled, and some of them were given hard labour. Among those sentenced to hard labour was the organizer of an illegal printing-press that printed propagandist pamphlets, Ippolit Myshkin; he made a brilliant speech at the trial. Myshkin ended his life in the Shlisselburg Fortress; he was hanged for boxing the commandant's ears.

The first wave of 'going to the people' was stopped by the ferocious repressions. But those who took part in the movement – not only the 'insurrectionists', but the 'pure' propagandists too – saw more and more clearly that it was not only a question of repression; as Vera Figner says,[43] 'in their practical activities among the people they had had a fiasco', not only because of the 'political conditions of the country', but also 'among the people themselves'. M. R. Popov,[48] a participant in the second wave that 'went to the people', or as he put it himself, the 'second call-up', explains what this fiasco 'among the people themselves' consisted of:

> 'The period of the end of 1875 and the beginning of '76 was a period of disappointment of the hopes with which the revolutionary youth had gone out among the people. The programme, which had been worked out theoretically, on the basis of Socialist principles, with no relationship to real life, had been destroyed. At best we had managed only to gain the sympathies of the countryside; but hopes that the propaganda would call

forth the country people to an active struggle or at least inspire the peasantry with the faith that such a struggle would bear fruit – these hopes were not vindicated. The peasant listened to the revolutionary just as he listened to his priest preaching to him about the Kingdom of Heaven: the moment he passed the threshold of the church he lived exactly as he had been living before the sermon.'

The conclusions drawn by the revolutionary youth from the 'fiasco' it had gone through are given in a letter written two to three years later to Vera Zasulich (1849–1918; see below) by Serge Mikhailovich Kravchinsky (1852–95) dated 24 July 1878:

> The painful experience of a number of years cannot help but convince every serious man that 'scientific Socialism', the Socialism of the West, bounces off the Russian masses like a pea off a wall. . . . Everyone felt it was no longer possible to take the path we were on any further. Everyone was aware of the need to adapt ourselves to local conditions, to listen to the voice of the masses, to enter into the circle of its outlook on the world.

So it happened that about the time the majority of those active in the 'first call-up' were languishing in gaol while waiting for the 'big trial', a critical assessment of their experience was preparing the 'second call-up', that still more powerful second wave of 'going to the people' that was to be organized by Land and Freedom. As Popov says: 'The pioneers who had come back from the people with such impressions began talking about a revision and change in the programme . . . For the first time they put on the order of the day in the revolutionary *milieu* of Petersburg questions whose answers resulted in the programme of Land and Freedom, which in 1876 was accepted by the majority of the youth of the time.'[49]

3. 'LAND AND FREEDOM'

The army of the intelligentsia came back beaten from its first advance into the countryside. It had lost a considerable number of its best leaders and it was disappointed in the old strategy and tactics. But it was not broken, and had not lost its spirits or faith in its cause. Its mood remained combative, and it was this that ensured a copious infusion of fresh blood into its ranks. M. R. Popov says of this:

> 'We saw our predecessors disappointed, but it was a healthy disappointment. They were disappointed in the means of struggle, but the necessity

of the struggle against the government that had enslaved the people was beyond any doubt. We who were preparing to go to the people in the footsteps of our predecessors went there not with cooling passions but, on the contrary, with revolutionary energy . . . Disregarding the preparation for the trial of the 193 at this time, and the imprisonment of practically the whole of the first call-up of those who were going to the people, we, the second call-up, hurled ourselves into the people with even greater energy.'[49]

In spite of the commune and its traditions, the peasant 'people' in Russia, too, proved to be incapable of becoming the bearer of working-class Socialism in the 'Western European sense': for such Socialism to find any kind of broad terrain what was indispensable in Russia, too, was the emergence of a proletariat that singled itself out as a 'class'. But for the time being, in order not to reject activity among the peasants, it was necessary to reject 'Western socialism', which Lavrov and his followers had at first considered it possible quite simply to transfer to Russia, only in a different social *milieu* – peasant, and not industrial working-class. This was vividly expressed – in terms reminiscent of Bakuninism's 'anti-German' tendencies – by this same Kravchinsky in an 1878 article: 'Five years ago we cast off our German costume and put on a drab peasant coat in order to be accepted by the people in their own *milieu.* Now we see that this was not enough: the time had come to throw off the German costume from Socialism and dress that too in a people's coat.'

This 'Russian' Socialism underlay the programme worked out in Petersburg after a long-drawn-out, lively debate towards the autumn of 1876; it became the programme of Land and Freedom, which was founded at the same time. This is what was said about it by Alexander Dmitriyevich Mikhailov, one of its initiators, a famous conspirator known as The Concierge, in a deposition he made after being arrested: 'The Russian Socialists have left collectivism, a harmonious scientific theory, and by way of bitter disappointments, sacrifices, and painful sufferings have come to Populism.'

According to Vera Figner, this was just when the word 'Populism' came into use. Though the Northern Revolutionary-Populist Group founded in the winter of 1876–7 by M. A. Natanson and A. D. Mikhailov was called 'Land and Freedom' at the very outset (in honour of the old organization of N. N. Serno-Solovyevich: see above) the members of Land and Freedom proper only began to be referred to by their organizational name after the appearance of a printed organ bearing the same name (1878). Before that their current name had been 'Populists' (Figner[50]).

When Land and Freedom was founded its basic leaders were Lavrovites and Chaikovskyites who had escaped arrest or managed, like M. A. Natanson himself, to come back from exile. But the founders of the society tried to unite all existing revolutionary groups. Hence, more than a few Bakuninite insurrectionaries also turned up in its ranks. It was only the Tkachovites, grouped around the *Nabat*, who were missing. This does not at all mean that Tkachov's ideas had no effect. On the contrary, as early as the years when the 'second call-up' took shape, according to Popov,[51] 'the appearance of Tkachov's pamphlet very much disconcerted revolutionary circles', and, as we shall see, it did not remain without influence even on the programme of Land and Freedom. His ideas had an even stronger and more obvious influence during the critical years of the shifting of Land and Freedom over to the political terrorism of the People's Freedom. But there were hardly any organized groups of Tkachovites in Russia: its logically rounded-off aspect made the openly 'bourgeois' Jacobinism of the *Nabat* psychologically not very acceptable to the 'populistically' minded intelligentsia, and only a few in its ranks risked calling themselves openly Jacobin Tkachovites.* Though not more than thirty to forty people took part in a discussion of the Land and Freedom society's programme, when it was set up it proved possible from the very beginning to attract as many as 120 members in Petersburg alone.

> In contrast to the South, where there was a preponderance of anarchistically-minded 'insurrectionists' who opposed every sort of centralization, including organizations, in the North, where the Lavrovites were strong, the organizational question was always one of the most serious. Its satisfactory solution was of immense service to the revolutionary cause, since it ensured the continuity, the accumulation of experience, and the gradual building-up of the highest type of organization. As a matter of fact the southerners disappeared without leaving behind any traditions; their family tree was snapped. As Karakozovites, Nechayevites, Dolgushinites, they were cut off at the root; the single, very few individuals

* Of these few the most famous was Maria Nikolayevna Olovennikova (Oshanina, by her married name), a member of the Executive Committee of the People's Freedom. Daughter of a rich landowner in Orlov, Olovennikova was a disciple of the old revolutionary and Jacobin Zaichnevsky, the author of the proclamation 'Young Russia' (see above), who after serving his term of hard labour lived in Oryol under police surveillance.

who survived, if any, joined new groups and were completely swallowed up by them. But in the north, thanks to the greater degree of organization, there was some continuity in the revolutionary groups: in 1879 the Chaikovskyites laid the foundations of the society Land and Freedom, and in 1879 this gave rise to the Party of the People's Freedom. (Figner[52]).

But in the north, too, Land and Freedom was a landmark in revolutionary history as the first strictly centralized, combat, conspiratorial revolutionary organization in Russia, as Lenin notes with praise in his *What Is to Be Done?* The discipline and the centralized character of the organization, already fixed in its constitution of 1876–7, accepted at the same time as its programme, were strengthened considerably further by corrections introduced into the constitution in 1878.* Finally, as Figner relates[53] the organization took on the aspect of a three-storied building: in one of the conspiratorial apartments sat the leaders of the movement† who would decide practical questions. In another, less conspiratorialized apartment, theoretical questions would be debated by a somewhat larger group of members. As for the mass of the membership, it did not know the addresses of these conspiratorial apartments; even eminent people like Klements or Ivanchin Pisaryov could only get to see the leaders of the organization with some difficulty.‡

Rejecting the 'harmonious theory' of collectivism in favour of an empirical 'Populism', the programme of Land and Freedom that was worked out in 1876–7 categorically stated: 'We shall narrow down our own demands to whatever is materially feasible in the immediate future, that is, down to the people's demands and desires, whatever they may be at any given moment.'

'The transfer of all land into the hands of the rural workers ("We are convinced," explained the programme, "that two-thirds of Russia will own it on a communal principle") and its equal distribution; the breaking up of the Russian Empire into portions in accordance with

* One of these corrections formulated for the first time the insistence on 'no testimony'; in the following decades this became a sort of moral code for revolutionaries during interrogation by the political police.

† Natanson, Kharizomenov, Tishchenko, Preobrazhensky, Plekhanov, A. D. Mikhailov and others.

‡ 'They were some kind of troglodytes hiding in inaccessible chinks and concealed caves,' Klements joked; this gave rise to the joking name that made some much later 'historians' speak seriously of the existence of a 'troglodyte organization'. As we shall see below, Popov speaks of the use of this same joking nickname in another connexion as well.

local wishes; the transfer of all public functions into the hands of the commune, that is, complete autonomy.' The authors of the programme regarded these as the three points that the desires of the people could be reduced to at the given moment. This was why their practical demands were exhausted by them. But even these demands 'could be realized only by means of a violent overturn'. And the means for the preparation of such an overturn were to be the following: '(1) agitation, chiefly by way of deeds as well as by words, directed at the organization of the revolutionary forces and at the development of revolutionary feelings (insurrections, strikes)', and '(2) the disorganization of the state, which will give us hope for victory in accordance with the strength of the organization to be created in the immediate future by agitation'.

Very soon, however, this 'initial' programme proved completely out of relation to its own objectives. It reflected too inadequately the specific traits of the various currents in the revolutionary *milieu* to be a platform for their fusion into the unified revolutionary organization that Land and Freedom was striving for. It reflected even more inadequately that atmosphere of public excitement that had been created by the Russo-Turkish War that had started in 1877 and by the economic crisis accompanying it. Turmoil and workers' strikes, on the one hand, and the revival of a liberal, especially Zemstvo opposition on the other, furthered the swift growth in the intelligentsia too of those combative tendencies Popov speaks of with such insistence, which were seeking an outlet in the most variegated directions. Under these conditions it was decided to submit the programme to a radical revision and to convene for this purpose the so-called 'Great Council' made up of all the more eminent members of all the organizations who were present in Petersburg. The labours of this Council resulted in a new and a substantially altered 'second programme' of Land and Freedom.

Meeting the traditional Socialist psychology of the vast majority of the intelligentsia half-way, the new programme begins by attempting to smooth over the open rupture with 'collectivism' that had almost been proclaimed: 'Our ultimate political and economic ideal is anarchy and collectivism', it declares. Populism is no longer proclaimed as an antithesis of 'Western' collectivism, but only as an historically laid down Russian road to it, a sort of tactical manœuvre. The admissibility of narrowing programmatic demands 'down to the people's demands, whatever they may be at any given moment,' is justified precisely by the claim that 'if the people's demands and aspirations were realized at any given moment, it would constitute a massive foundation for the future successful course of the social cause in Russia'; it was only the impossibility of 'grafting on to the people, in the present conditions, other, and perhaps from an abstract point of view better ideals,' that aroused 'the Russian Social-Revolutionary Party' to 'inscribe on its banner the historically elaborated formula of Land and Freedom. Theoretically this was a return to those 'classical' ideas of the Socialist (just in this 'Western' sense) tendencies of the Russian peasant commune, in which the Lavrovite views had the most points of contact with the Bakuninite and Tkachovite views.*

But having made this concession to the psychological traditions of the intelligentsia, further on the programme shows extremely little concern with any theoretical harmony and consistency. In a purely mechanical way it compounds mutually contradictory ideas of Lavrov, Bakunin, and Tkachov. For what was decisive for the programme was the attempt of the new organization at all costs to unite within its framework all the revolutionary currents, and more than that, also to make itself the focus of the liberal opposition that had begun stirring. Vera Figner was right in saying that 'in contrast to former programmes, the new one extended the sphere of activity of its partisans throughout all strata of society'.[58] It took as its criterion not only work among the peasants, but also 'the conduct of contacts and connexions in the great centres of industrial workers, in factories and workshops', the propaganda and agitation in the higher schools of learning and even the collaboration with the 'liberals' – of course, 'with the aim of exploiting them in our own favour'. Against the background of the spiritual crisis provoked by the failure of the first wave that 'had gone to the people' and in the atmosphere of public excitement generated by the war, the revolutionary intelligentsia –

* Wholly in the spirit of these classical ideas, the leading article of the first number of Land and Freedom's new periodical speaks of the 'factory question', which 'we are leaving in the shadow, not because we do not regard the expropriation of the factories as necessary, but because history, which in Western Europe has placed the factory question in the foreground, has not posed it among ourselves at all, having replaced it by the agrarian question. Nevertheless the revolutionary movement, which has arisen in the name of the land, is predestined immediately afterwards to move on to the awareness of the necessity of the expropriation of the factories and of the total annihilation of every kind of capitalist production, because if it retained this it would be digging its own grave.'

not for the first or the last time in its history – made desperate efforts to emerge from its solitude and get a firm social terrain beneath its feet. The second programme of Land and Freedom consequently proved to be one of the most eclectic and contradictory documents of the Russian revolutionary movement.

This contradictoriness leaps to the eye at once, in the introductory theoretical part of the programme. The party refuses to 'violate the economic and political ideal laid down by history', but it opens a door to completely different ideas as well when – in the Tkachov spirit – it declares that a 'violent overturn', which is the only way even the modest 'demands and aspirations' of the people can be realized, must take place 'as soon as possible', since the 'development of capitalism and the growing penetration into the people's life (thanks to the protection and efforts of the Russian government) of the various ulcers of bourgeois civilization threatens the destruction of the commune and a greater or lesser distortion of the people's outlook on the world'.

But the programme becomes still more eclectic when it passes over to the practical tasks, which – in the spirit of the first programme too – are divided into 'organizational' and 'disorganizational'.

First of the 'organizational' tasks, of course, is the creation of 'a tightly-knit and smoothly working organization of trained revolutionaries . . . from the *milieu* of the intelligentsia as well as from among the workers in direct contact with them'.* But this 'smoothly working organization', which, as mentioned, is supposed to form ties with the 'liberals' as well, that is, the possessing classes, chiefly landowners and state functionaries, is advised at the same time not only to draw near to the religious and revolutionary sectarians hostile to the government, but also to the 'bandit gangs of the type of the down-river outlaws!' As though to explain this point of the programme, the first number of the organization's periodical (November 1878) recalls that 'the seizure of the landowners' and boyars' lands, the expulsion and sometimes the individual extirpation of all the representatives of the state', which used to be the programme of the 'people's socialist revolutionaries – Pugachov, Razin and their fellow-champions', remains to this day the programme of 'the vast majority of the

* This special reference to workers, which occurs here for the first time, though only as an element secondary to the intelligentsia, is characteristic of the increasingly noticeable role eminent working-class individuals were beginning to play at this time. We shall speak of this later.

Russian people', and consequently is accepted in its entirety by the revolutionary Populists as well.

As for the 'disorganizing' activities, the short, rather vague formula in the first programme is replaced in the second by a detailed description of various such activities, including work among the troops, 'principally among the officers', the involvement of government functionaries, and the 'systematic extermination of the most dangerous or eminent members of the government'. In this broad interpretation the 'disorganizing' part of the programme not only supported individual acts of terror, which just at this time were becoming more and more frequent, and not only met half-way those 'individuals' who, as Bakunin insisted, 'could not restrain their passion for destruction', but could be understood, and as we shall see actually was understood, as a sanction of the political struggle in the spirit of Tkachov's appeal to 'do it now!'

The contradictions introduced into the practical activity of Land and Freedom by this spirit of 'disorganization' played a decisive role in its subsequent fate and were the immediate cause of its dissolution. But that lay in the future. For the time being the members of the organization turned a good deal of their attention to the contradictions of the programme, since they were united not so much by these or other programmatic propositions as by a mood, a spirit of combat that it tried to carry over into the activity of all its members, whatever their social origins or the aim of their work. And if in the countryside the new organization replaced the old 'preaching of the principles of Socialism' by a 'programme of protests based on the vital interests of the countryside',[54] it also tried to introduce this same tactic of 'incitement to protest' in its activity in the cities.[50] In the countryside the intention was to give this 'protest' the form of 'agrarian terror', too – the burning of the estates of the more hated landowners and personal beatings-up of individual representatives of the local authorities. In the cities, together with attempts on the lives of individuals in the central government apparatus who were particularly notorious for their arbitrariness and cruelty, all sorts of public demonstrations were to be staged. The new organization publicized its actual emergence by a small demonstration at the Kazan Cathedral in Petersburg (6 December 1876), at which Plekhanov made a short speech (the origin of his party nickname the 'Orator'), while the youthful worker Potapov unfurled the red flag of Land and Freedom. This was followed immediately by: the organization of a demonstrative funeral to mourn the political prisoner Podlevsky, who had died in gaol; the intervention in the strikes of the Petersburg textile workers and their organization in a procession towards the palace of the Heir Apparent in order to hand him a petition concerning the improvement of the workers' situation and their defence against the pressure of the entrepreneurs; the leadership of the student movement, and so on.

Popov correctly notes 1878–9 as crucial years, not so much in the ideological and programmatic sense as in the sense of a change of mood and revolutionary practice, when he says that in his own memory these years

> 'are preserved as an occasion of sharp turn-about, of swift growth of the revolutionary temper. The representatives of the movement of the '70s, the first call-up, in their revolutionary psychology were in sharp contrast to the representatives of the revolutionary situation of 1878–9, when there was a high upsurge in the revolution . . . In so far as it was a question not of the abstract idea of an overturn, but of the concrete programme of means, the situations at the beginning and at the end of the '70s were in sharp contrast with each other.[55]'

Popov also characterized this difference in mood between the two 'call-ups' very graphically when in underlining the difference in the opinions of the activity of those acquitted at the trial of the 193 (including the future political leader of the terrorist People's Freedom, Andrew Zhelyabov, and its future theoretician, Tikhomirov) and of the representatives of the new organization, he says:

> 'The Land and Freedom people and the acquitted revolutionaries of the first call-up . . . spoke different languages. Zhelyabov and Tikhomirov, for instance, were horrified by the practical programme of Land and Freedom. The latter seemed to them to be made up of people who believed in violent means, not people with a pacific doctrine who were calling the masses to a new life on Socialist principles. It was from this time on that "troglodytes" became a current name for Land and Freedom.'[56]

We have already noted that among those active in the 'first call-up', which 'went to the people' during the years of public quietude, an immense majority were Bakuninite insurrectionists; this did not prevent this whole first stage of the movement from being in fact an extreme expression of Lavrovite propagandism. And on the contrary: theoretically and programmatically the 'second call-up' was closer to Lavrovism, but in the atmosphere of public excitement in which it had to emerge into the revolutionary arena its temper and practice became more and more Bakuninite and insurrectionary. It even, as we shall see, overcame both Lavrovism and Bakuninism in order to become Jacobin and Tkachovite. This paradoxical fact is a superfluous proof of how much the change in tendencies and groupings within the framework of an eclectic, but within this eclecticism unitary movement of the Populist intelligentsia, was a change not so much in theories and ideas as in practice and temper. And it was not the theoretical contradictions of the Land and Freedom programme, but the contradictions inherent in its practice, which in their turn reflected the contradictions of Russian life, that determined the astonishing evolution undergone in some one-and-a-half to two years by the flower of the Russian intellectual youth gathered under its banner.

4. THE CRISIS OF APOLITICISM

The 'second call-up' went to the people in a different mood and with different plans from the first, but it met with the same failure.

The excitement that had seized on certain strata of the urban populace died down at the boundary of the villages. 'In the capitals all was hubbub, orators thundered, wars of words kept bubbling, but there, in the depths of Russia, there was an age-old stillness.' These verses of Nekrasov give an incomparably accurate description of the difference in mood between the city and the country at that time. The growing subjection of the villages to the laws of the market and money economy, accelerated still more by the war, condemned the basic masses of the peasantry, expropriated by the emancipation, to an extremely low and almost impoverished standard of living. This demoralized them and paralysed their social energies. But it was just this that furthered the springing up of a not very numerous but influential stratum of comparatively 'big' and well-to-do peasants, the so-called 'kulaks', who both economically and socially dominated the 'rural pauper' mass. The development of capitalist relations in the cities was echoed in the countryside by the rapid dissolution of the communal system and the communal temperament, which had been referred to by both Tkachov and the Land and Freedom programme, and which is what the Populists had been afraid of.*

* In contrast to the idyllic tones used about the social life and the moods of the peasantry by the 'classical' belletristic Populist writers of the type of N. N.

Its inner homogeneity lost, pulled apart by antagonisms, the peasant commune responded very slowly to appeals for collective protest. Only once (1877) did an energetic group of southern insurrectionists (Bokhanovsky, L. G. Deich, Y. Stefanovich) succeed in conjuring up a broad movement in the Chigirin district of Kiev Province. It ended with the arrest of a thousand peasants. But they had such success only because they had circulated a bogus 'Imperial Charter' proclaiming to the peasants the 'real freedom' that was supposed to have been hidden from them by the landowners and the local authorities, and summoning them to self-authorized seizure of the big estates. This method was far from greeted with unanimous approval in revolutionary circles.

Thus 'among the people itself' those active in the 'second call-up' generally suffered a fiasco that was no less bitter than that of their predecessors. But an even more decisive fiasco met them in the 'political conditions of the country' V. Figner also mentions in analysing the failure of the first wave of 'going to the people'. These conditions affected the revolutionaries all the more gravely because the tactics of unleashing conflicts between peasants and landowners and the preaching of 'agrarian' terror naturally weakened the sympathy of certain strata of affluent though liberal society that had so facilitated the rural sojourn, if not the activities, of the 'first call-up'.

The result was that the bulk of the Land and Freedom members who had settled down in the country were condemned to practically total inactivity. Their passivity was more and more sharply contrasted with the tempestuous activity that the Land and Freedom people in the cities started developing at just this time. 'Sleepy farmers' was the mocking sobriquet by which their own urban comrades began calling them more and more often. They never became clear about the reasons for it, but in this way the Populist revolutionaries themselves

---

Zlatovratsky, the process of this dissolution was described with merciless honesty by Gleb Ivanovich Uspensky (1840–1902). He was well aware of the destructive effect exercised by capital on the communal system, but in clinging to the general world-view of Populism he saw no other methods of combating this influence except through completely hopeless attempts to turn back the wheel of history. 'To conserve the Russian agricultural system . . . it is essential to counteract by all means the influences destroying its harmony,' he wrote in one of his most remarkable works, *Vlast' Zemli* (the Power of the Land). But in the given circumstances this would have meant demanding the destruction of all elements of contemporary culture, from railways and factories to pyjamas and kerosene lamps.

learned that in spite of their theories the centre of revolutionary activity was shifting from the country to the cities, because with all Russia's economic and cultural backwardness it was the capitalist city and not the pre-capitalist village that was becoming the determining factor of her further socio-political evolution.

But it was not only the place of application of the revolutionary energies that changed. Imperceptibly, for the Populist intelligentsia itself, the goal and character of its revolutionary activity also changed.

In accordance with the official theory, the basic attention of the party was supposed to be concentrated on the peasantry in the 'agrarian question'. Its central organ, as we have seen, openly proclaimed that it was deliberately 'leaving in the shade' the 'factory question'. But in fact it was just this 'agrarian question' that the most active urban units kept moving more and more into the 'shade', and on the contrary, more and more insistently strove to intervene in the conflicts between the entrepreneurs and the workers that just at this time had begun becoming more and more frequent, and that signalized the entry of the 'factory question' into socio-political life.

In this intervention in the 'factory question', to be sure, the Populist revolutionaries themselves saw no more than a method of extricating from the labouring masses especially aware individuals who could be involved immediately in their own organization. But their recruiting proved so successful, such eminent working-class revolutionaries (Stepan Khalturin, Victor Obnorsky and others) were drawn into the ranks of the organization, and in such numbers, that it soon became possible and necessary to form two branches of the special 'Workers' Union' a northern (December 1878) and a southern (1879). And a short time later Plekhanov, who at that time was still thinking, in accordance with Populist dogma, that the factory workers 'in the immense majority of cases were the same peasants there were in the countryside', and that 'for them the factory was merely one kind of seasonal work' that did not in the least destroy 'their rural ties and sympathies' – could write in the organ of Land and Freedom: 'the question of the city worker is one of those that it may be said will be moved forward automatically by life itself, to an appropriate place, in spite of the *a priori* theoretical decisions of the revolutionary leaders'.

But under the flag of the old theories, there began to take place in another and still more decisive respect a practice that completely contradicted them.

In principle, as we have seen, Land and Freedom narrowed down its demands to the 'demands of the people at any given moment'. Thinking that questions of political liberty did not enter into these popular demands in any way they refrained for their part from a broad political struggle. But in spite of the theories of the Populists, the 'political conditions' V. Figner speaks of were swept into their 'apolitical' movement by repressions that became harsher and harsher, struck the organization more and more painfully, and more and more often summoned up a need for resistance. Since the organization lacked any mass base, this resistance was possible only in the form of terrorist attacks on individual representatives of the administration, the most pernicious or the most hated. But having begun as individual acts of protest of the more hot-blooded revolutionaries, the terrorist attacks very soon turned into a systematically applied method of 'self-defence' of the organization, and further into a form of transition from defence to an onslaught on the Tsarist autocracy.

The spontaneous character of this process of development could not be better underlined than by the fact that its initiator was Vera Zasulich, who was to become a partisan of Total Reapportionment (see below), and one of the co-founders of the Marxist Social-Democracy in Russia. Until her death she was always opposed in principle to political terror. On 24 January 1878 she shot at Trepov, the Police Chief of Petersburg, as a protest against his monstrous treatment of political prisoners; he had ordered one of them, Emelyanov (known by the revolutionary alias of Bogolyubov, a member of the 'Kazan' demonstration), to be given corporal punishment for not having taken off his cap in front of him. But unexpectedly for Zasulich herself her shot, which she had thought of only as an act of moral protest, produced, in the atmosphere of public excitement, far broader political repercussions.

A chain of uninterrupted terrorist acts was the immediate reaction. On 23 February of the same year (1878) an attempt was made to assassinate Kotlyarevsky, a member of the Kiev Circuit Court; on 25 May the assassination of the Colonel of Gendarmes Geiking took place; on 1 June there was an attempt at the armed liberation of Voinaralsky, who had been arrested in connexion with this affair; on 4 August the assassination of the Chief of Gendarmes Mezentsev, etc., etc. Political terror had made a decisive entry into Russian life. The exonerative sentence given Vera Zasulich on 31 March of that same year by the Petersburg Circuit Court was followed by the withdrawal of political affairs from a jury's competence, but the triumphant response in great segments of liberal society that greeted this sentence graphically indicated to the revolutionaries how much more sympathy society had for political terror than for agrarian and factory terror. Thus, for the Populist revolutionaries the line of political terror proved to be not only a line of forced retreat before the stubbornness of the 'people itself' and the invincible 'political conditions', but also a line of least resistance with respect to their social surroundings, whose sympathy and support were indispensable.

It is true that for a long time the more and more clearly expressed political character of its labours eluded the consciousness of the revolutionary intelligentsia itself. Only the Socialist and Populist messianism that elevated it far beyond the low level of the semi-feudal, semi-bourgeois society surrounding it could sustain the immense moral tension without which the performance of the heroic mission laid on it by history would have been unthinkable. Populist Socialism became the same moral 'self-defence' for it as terror was its organizational defence. The instinct of self-preservation forced it to close its eyes to the political prose of its revolutionary activities.

There were only very few in its ranks who could make up their minds to look this prosaic truth in the eye. For instance, during the debates on the 'second programme' of the winter 1877–8, when Valerian Osinsky proposed that the need for political struggle be openly acknowledged, his proposal was rejected almost unanimously. Even in the pamphlet *A Death for a Death*, which commented on Mezentsev's assassination, the very perpetrator of this terrorist act, S. Kravchinsky, vigorously denied its political character. He called the 'bourgeoisie' the only real enemy of the revolutionaries and, addressing the government, asked it only 'to stand off to one side' and not interfere in the struggle against the bourgeoisie. Along the same lines the leading article in the first number of the Land and Freedom organ, also written by Kravchinsky, calls on the revolutionaries not to be fascinated by terror. He explains that 'terrorism has nothing in common with the struggle against the existing order', that 'only a class can arise against a class', and that terrorists are merely 'a holding unit' assigned to protect revolutionaries working among the 'people' from the 'treacherous blows of their enemies'.

But these old words about the priority of working 'among the people' were incapable of eliminating the novel fact that in reality this work was resulting more and more in nothing, and that on the contrary the 'disorganizing' terrorists were not a modest 'holding unit' but were becoming more and more the controlling force of the organization. A gulf not merely of reciprocal incomprehension but also of 'moral disintegration' began to form between them and the 'sleepy farmers'.

In this connexion V. Figner wrote that the

> Petersburg Land and Freedom, intoxicated by their successes, vexed by failures, in the heat of a struggle that demanded a constant tension but at the same time constituted an agitational medium of unprecedented strength, began looking with surprise and contempt at the stillness of the Saratov and Tambov countryside. The absence there of any signs of active struggle, the visible futility of the presence in the countryside of whole dozens of people made them indignant to the depths of their soul.

On the other hand, 'it seemed to the Populists, in the narrow sense of the word, that the urban Land and Freedom people were busy with fireworks whose brilliance diverted the youth from the real cause, the *milieu* of the people, that needed their energies so much. In their eyes the assassinations of generals and chiefs of gendarmerie were activities that were less productive and necessary than agrarian terror in the countryside. The terrorist acts (in the cities!) passed by unnoticed in the countryside, no one could see the effect they produced; without a prologue or an epilogue they did not even move the rural Land and Freedom people themselves; they did not live through the alarms, fears and joys of struggle; amidst the monotony of the endless steppes and the sea of peasant faces they did not mourn their comrades going off to execution.'[57]

This 'moral disintegration' became even greater when the very logic of the terrorist struggle directed the thinking of the revolutionaries from individuals in the government to the bearer of the paramount power in the state it was proposed to 'disorganize'. It made the organization of regicide their fundamental objective. Vera Figner relates how 'little by little the two sides of the programme of Land and Freedom' changed places in the ideas of the immense majority of the influential members. In 1876, when the society was founded, the centre of gravity had been placed on rural activity, on the organization of a people's uprising; the 'bull's eye' was what was happening among the masses. Now, in 1878–9, the 'bull's eye' was the cornerstone of the state. It was this and nothing else that was supposed to unleash the living forces of the people. And when Figner, who was active in

Saratov Province, came to Petersburg in December 1878, she was painfully struck by the hostility with which Plekhanov (together with Popov, one of the few violent adversaries of the new tactic) argued with such eminent comrades as A. Mikhailov and N. Morozov, the leaders of the terrorist tendency.[58]

This mutual irritation turned into an open contest of the two tendencies in the spring of 1879, when a teacher, Alexander Konstantinovich Solovyov (1846–79), arrived in Petersburg from Saratov Province with a declaration of his determination to assassinate the Tsar at all costs, even if only on his own responsibility, but with a request that the organization co-operate with him. The stormy debates on this question ended with a compromise: 'as an organization Land and Freedom refuses to assist in the assassination, but single members can do so individually as far as they think necessary'.

The attempt at assassination, which took place on 2 April 1879 with the co-operation of some 'single members', ended in a fiasco; on 29 May Solovyov was executed. But his action played a decisive role in the fate of Land and Freedom. It not only gave many 'farmers' (including Vera Figner herself) the final push into the ranks of the terrorists, but the compromise that had been reached on it hastened the dissolution of Land and Freedom, for it provided an occasion for the emergence within it of a 'special group the other members did not know about'. Plotting without the knowledge of their own comrades, this little group, which was joined by such eminent Land and Freedom members as Barannikov, Kvyatkovsky, Mikhailov, Morozov, Oshanina, Tikhomirov, and others, 'began secretly recruiting partisans'. It even formed a 'secondary' circle (Kibalchich, Yakimova, Sophia Ivanova, Isayev, Shiryayev, and others) with a terrorist programme that now had a purely political character, with the motto 'Liberty or Death!' At the same time, together with the official organ of Land and Freedom, which had been coming out under the collective editorship of N. A. Morozov, Plekhanov, and L. A. Tikhomirov, there also began coming out, under the editorship of Morozov alone, the official 'Leaflet of Land and Freedom'. Here the preaching of political terror was carried on quite openly, and for the first time there began appearing the signature 'Executive Committee' – a designation that corresponded to nothing in the Land and Freedom organization but that later became the official designation of the core of the People's Freedom.

Under these circumstances it was decided to convoke a congress of

Land and Freedom, which met (illegally, of course) in Voronyozh on 24 June 1879. But a few days before this the partisans of the new tactic gathered in secret at their own fractional congress in Lipetsk; they had also attracted some southern revolutionaries: Zhelyabov, Kolodkevich and Frolenko, who had not been in Land and Freedom before but had undergone the same evolution as the Petersburg terrorists. The programme composed at the Lipetsk congress of the fractional group 'set as its goal the organization of the overthrow of the autocratic order and the establishment of political liberties, by means of an armed struggle against the government'.

The acceptance of this 'Tkachovite' programme signalized an open and decisive rupture with the traditional 'apoliticism' of Populism.* It also meant the liquidation of Land and Freedom, since for certain members such a rupture was completely unacceptable. The Voronyozh congress signalized its breaking up into two groups – Total Reapportionment (of the Land) and the People's Freedom. The meaning of this split was expressed very well by Morozov: 'We divided up the very name of the former organization: Total Reapportionment took over the "Land" while we took over the "Freedom", and each fraction went its own way.'[59]

5. 'THE PEOPLE'S FREEDOM'

Of all those who attended the Voronyozh congress only Plekhanov left it with the words: 'There is nothing further for us to do here.' Very few even of the 'farmers' joined the organization Total Reapportionment, which he founded together with P. B. Akselrod, V. I. Zasulich, and L. G. Deich – Plekhanov's future companions-in-arms when he founded the Marxist group, Emancipation of Labour (1883).

In announcing the publication of a periodical of the same name, Total Reapportionment declared itself the preserver of the old

* Vera Figner, who vigorously denies any kind of influence exercised by Tkachov and the *Nabat* on the revolutionary movement in Russia, reduces Tkachov's 'Jacobinism' to the idea not only of the 'seizure' but of the protracted retention of power by an insignificant revolutionary minority. In fact Tkachov's basic idea was, as we have seen, not the 'seizure of power' by a revolutionary minority, but its shifting over to a political struggle as soon as possible, and the consummation of a revolutionary *coup d'état* with its own forces. This stubborn denial of Tkachov's influence is not merely an echo of old fractional quarrels, but also a desire to underline in a censored form the hostility of the People's Freedom to 'Jacobinism' as it was realized under the Bolshevik dictatorship.

traditions of Land and Freedom. Once more it proclaimed that 'political overturns never and nowhere could secure the people's economic and political liberty', and warned the People's Freedom of its degeneration into a 'party of reaction and stagnation'. 'The agitational motto of the Russian social-revolutionary party' was formulated by the periodical in the words: 'let the worker seize the factory, the peasant the land'. In fact Total Reapportionment was incapable of doing anything perceptible at all, and very soon, with the departure abroad of Deich, Zasulich and Plekhanov, it began to break up. Its members either completely abandoned revolutionary activity or went over to the People's Freedom, like Stefanovich. And the same evolution towards 'politics' was indicated in the draft programme of the new organization, which in 1880 P. B. Akselrod almost put together, under the name of 'Party of Socialist-Federalists', out of the remnants of the Total Reapportionment followers. Its central conspiratorial core was supposed to be called the 'Great Russian Society of Land and Freedom'.[60]

Thus the sole heir and continuator of Land and Freedom in fact proved to be the People's Freedom. But this does not at all mean that the core of Land and Freedom radically changed its general world-outlook, or drew any theoretical conclusions from its own new practice, with the same logical dispassionateness as their leaders of the future People's Freedom had tried to show at the Lipetsk Congress. Popov is right in saying that the difference between the future Total Reapportionment party and the future People's Freedom in this case too 'was expressed . . . not in theoretical views, but rather in the practical programme of activity'.[61] The rank-and-file of the revolutionary intelligentsia clung as before to its own Populist Socialism, sought moral and political sanctions in it, and by its new activity stubbornly tried, even at the price of logical contradictions, to squeeze into the framework of the old theories a new practice that shattered that framework.

Very characteristic in this connexion is what Vera Figner says of Zhelyabov's speech at the Voronyozh congress, in the debate on the question of 'agrarian terror'. 'Whom is the revolutionary party thinking of leaning on?' he asked. 'On the people or on the liberal bourgeoisie that sympathizes with the overthrow of absolutism and the installation of political liberty? If it is the first, then both factory and agrarian terror are in place. But if we want to seek the support of industrialists, landowners, and urban functionaries, then such a policy will drive these natural allies away from us. Zhelyabov's question was followed by a unanimous answer – we were going to lean on the masses of the people and build our theoretical and practical programme accordingly.' It 'was decided to continue our activities among the people, but to include agrarian terror; in conjunction with this it was resolved to continue the terrorist struggle in the cities too, including regicide'.[59]

Thus the programme of the People's Freedom went through the same history as that undergone in its time by Land and Freedom. The first (Lipetsk) programme written by N. A. Morozov, which formulated the political idea of the new direction in a nakedly logical form, proved psychologically inacceptable to the immense majority of its partisans. In Voronyozh, says V. Figner, it 'did not satisfy those present, and Tikhomirov was delegated to write another draft', which after careful debate actually became the programme of the People's Freedom. This definitive programme, entirely analogous to the second programme of Land and Freedom, began with the words: 'In our basic convictions we are Socialists and Populists' – words that this time were accepted without great doubts or hesitations but that were aimed at both underlining the continuity 'with our past' and proclaiming once again that on the one hand 'political liberty was not an end for us but a means', and on the other that 'we were not pursuing the abstract ultimate objectives of Socialist doctrine but those demands and needs in the popular mind that in their essence included the Socialist principles of liberty'.[62]

The programme attempted to formulate the actual tasks of the political struggle in terms descended psychologically from the apolitical, anarchist, Bakuninite 'past' with which the People's Freedom had in fact definitively broken. 'The bourgeois-statist excrescence' on the body politic, it said, 'was propped up on nothing but naked violence: by its military, police and bureaucratic organization'. Hence 'we had to pose as our immediate task the removal from the people of the crushing oppression of the contemporary state, and the execution of a political overturn with the aim of transferring power to the people. Through this overturn we would achieve: first of all, the autonomous development of the people from now on, in accordance with its own inclinations; secondly, the acceptance and support in Russian life of many purely Socialist principles common to ourselves and the people.'

It was only on this terrain, psychologically prepared in this way, that the programme put forth the political slogan that from then on down to the 1917 revolution was to remain the general political slogan of all parties and fractions of the Russian revolutionary democracy without exception: the convocation of a 'Constituent Assembly, freely elected by a universal vote'.

It was with this same psychological cautiousness that the programme also approached the fundamental political method of the party – terror. 'Terrorist activity', it declared, 'has as its goal the undermining of the fascination of governmental power, the constant demonstration of the possibilities of struggling against the government, the elevation in this way of the revolutionary spirit of the people and its faith in the success of the cause, and finally, the formation of forces fit for and accustomed to battle.' But further on, when it proceeds to indicate the conditions of a political overturn, the programme assigns 'the people' a merely secondary role in the accomplishment of such an overturn: 'With respect to the overturn, what is especially important is administration and troops.' Of course, 'the party must pay attention to the people not less seriously', but the 'primary task of the party among the people is to prepare its co-operation in the overturn' and to secure the 'possibility of a successful electoral struggle after the overturn'. It is only in one of the concluding paragraphs that the programme expresses more definitely the central political idea of the new party: 'In view of the oppression of the people, and since by means of special repressions the government will be able to restrain the general revolutionary movement for a very long time, the party must assume the preparation of the overturn itself, and not wait for a time when the people will be able to get along without it.' But the programme concludes, 'by whatever means the overturn takes place, as the result of an independent revolution or through a conspiracy – the obligation of the party is to further the immediate convocation of a Constituent Assembly and the transfer to it of the authority of a Provisional Government created by the revolution or by a conspiracy'. How infinitely remote this is from the haughty 'give a constitution or don't give it, summon electors or don't summon them', proclaimed by Kravchinsky a year before!

'The execution of an overturn' in fact became the fundamental and very soon one may say the sole objective of the party, at least of its centre, which was given the name of Executive Committee. As for the 'methods of executing the overturn', the programme declared them to be 'not subject to publication'. In reality all these 'methods' boiled down to the organization of political terror. In accordance with the programme, to be sure, the members of People's Freedom were supposed to and did indeed carry on agitation and propaganda among the people, the troops and students, and in affluent society. But aside from the fact that the activity among the 'people' kept being reduced more and more to activity among only the urban workers, and the activity among the 'troops' to activity among the officers, the work among the students, by its very aim as well, became more and more the recruitment of individuals fit for an active part in terrorist enterprises. Only the activity in 'society' was oriented towards the winning of the political sympathies of broader circles. But this orientation too, by inevitably setting a specific stamp on the very character of the propaganda, aimed primarily at the creation of the material and organized base (apartments, accommodation addresses, passports, etc.) without which the realization of any complicated enterprise at all of this kind would have been impossible. Such was the implacable logic of the total concentration of the Executive Committee on political terror.

To be sure, the letter of the programme and of the constitution laid far more variegated tasks on the Executive Committee. Formally V. Figner is correct in writing as follows:

> On the occasion of an uprising it disposed of all the available forces of the party and could demand their revolutionary deployment, but until then it would direct its attention primarily to the organization of a conspiracy, that organizational labour that alone ensured the possibility of an overturn. The party's forces were adequately addressed to this aim: it was all the stranger when it was later called terrorist . . . Terror in and for itself was never the aim of the party. It was a means of defence, self-defence, and was considered a powerful medium of agitation . . . Regicide entered this category as a detail . . . Organizational and propagandistic activity always went hand in hand with the work of destruction.[63]

But she is even more correct – now not formally, but in essence – when she says:

> As the struggle grew more heated, as time passed and one magnificent exploit after another was conceived and executed by us, the former activity among the people grew dimmer in our eyes; the countryside receded into the distance. That part of the programme of the People's Freedom that spoke of the activity in the countryside gradually took on a purely theoretical, rhetorical character.[64]

All the other kinds of activity of the Executive Committee also 'grew dimmer', except for the organization of assassinations, and even, what was more, the preparation of 'details' like regicide.

All the energies of the People's Freedom were directed even more exclusively at the 'bull's eye', at regicide, than the forces of Land and Freedom during the last period of its existence. The party organization accordingly also became even more strictly centralized. All general party functions and general Russian affairs were under the unchallengeable control of the self-authorized Executive Committee, whose core was made up of the participants in the Lipetsk congress. As for the Executive Committee itself, it became a kind of monastic order that demanded of its members the strictest discipline and the complete transformation of the individuals into a collective. Its constitution required (1) a promise to surrender all one's spiritual energies to the cause of the revolution, to forget for its sake all bonds of kinship and personal sympathies, love and friendship; (2) if necessary to give up one's life, too, without heed to anything and without pity for anyone or anything; (3) no private property, or anything of one's own that was not at the same time the property of the organization; (4) the rejection of one's own individual will, subjecting it to the will of the majority, etc.

'By their strictness and loftiness they raised the individual beyond anything humdrum; the person felt more vividly that it was in him that the idea lived and must live,' is what Vera Figner says about these demands of the society.[65] She herself was one of the members of this unique monastic order. In reality these mercilessly severe demands reflected the immense upsurge of morale and will-power indispensable for the 'magnificent exploits' that swiftly succeeded each other and gave the memory of everyone who took part in these 'exploits' an aureole of unrivalled heroism in the eyes of succeeding generations of Russian revolutionaries, however critical they may have been with respect to the theoretical principles and the political practice of the People's Freedom. A small episode shows how much the lofty moral posture of these 'regicides' impressed even those against whom their terror was directed, even their judges and gaolers: in sending Vera Figner off to life imprisonment in the Shlisselburg Fortress (from which she was released only twenty-two years later, in the amnesty that followed the 1905 revolution), the General of Gendarmes Sereda asked his prisoner's permission – to kiss her hand!

Such was the revolutionary *milieu* that day by day, with unflagging energy and self-sacrifice, prepared all the new attempts on the Tsar's life and threw aside all the plans that had miscarried, having paid for them with their blood and learned from bitter experience, in order to take up new ones, more perfected, and move closer to the target. A mine bomb along the railbed of the Moscow-Kursk railway – which failed only because the mine exploded (19 November 1879) not under the train carrying the Tsar but under a decoy car carrying his suite – and the explosion in the Imperial dining-room (5 February 1880) executed by the carpenter Stepan Khalturin, who had come to work in the Winter Palace – which accidentally misfired only by a few minutes – were the most dramatic stages in this enterprise. In the course of several months a small handful of revolutionaries were able not only to force the Russian government to consider them its most menacing and dangerous enemy, but also to make the impression throughout the world that the end of the Tsarist autocracy was at hand. Pisaryov was right: it was not in any shortage of 'powerful characters' that lay the misfortune of Russian democracy!

On 1 March 1881 the activities of the terrorists were finally crowned with success: after the failure of a first worker, Grinevetsky, who was blown up by his own bomb, a second bomb, thrown by a young student, Rysakov, mortally wounded Alexander II, who died the moment he got back to the palace. Only a few of the direct organizers and participants in this affair were arrested at once; only six people appeared before a court made up of a special session of the Senate (26–9 March): Sophia Lvovna Perovskaya, Nicholas Ivanovich Kibalchich, Timothy Mikhailovich Mikhailov, Gesya Mironovna Gelfman, Nicholas Ivanovich Rysakov, and Andrew Ivanovich Zhelyabov, who had been arrested even before 1 March but on his own initiative had declared himself to be the chief organizer of the attempted assassination, in order to elevate the trial to the appropriate political heights. All six were condemned to death; the execution of the sentence was postponed only because of Gelfman's pregnancy, though she died immediately after giving birth, in obscure circumstances, in the Peter-Paul Fortress. The majority of the other members of the Executive Committee were also soon arrested. At the 'Trial of the Twenty', at which there appeared in the dock A. D. Mikhailov, N. A. Morozov and others, ten of the prisoners were sentenced to death, a sentence that was, however, executed only in the case of the former naval officer N. Sukhanov; the other accused were finally sent to hard labour and imprisonment in the Peter-Paul or Shlisselburg Fortress.

March 1 was the day of the party's greatest triumph, but it proved to be a day that dealt it a mortal blow. The arrests shattered the old combat-trained Executive Committee. 'Now there was a wilderness – there were neither enough minds nor enough hands, neither dominant originators, nor skilful executors,' writes Vera Figner, one of the last members of this famous Committee.

> In 1879 the Executive Committee included all the accumulated revolutionary forces that had survived the destructions of this period. It flung them into the political struggle; it performed an enormous amount of work and squandered all its capital in two years . . . The Executive Committee, in essence, terminated its own existence; the core of the People's Freedom was no longer capable of playing its former role.[66]

Formally, of course, the party went on existing, and even in the second half of the '90s there were People's Freedom groups in Russia carrying on propaganda among the workers and students and circulating 'Flying Leaflets'. From 1883 to 1886 there was published abroad the People's Freedom *Vestnik* (Courier), edited by P. Lavrov and L. Tikhomirov, who had emigrated. Individual People's Freedom groups tried to organize terrorist attacks too, and after an unsuccessful attempt on the Tsar's life timed for 1 March 1887, five young students (P. Y. Shevyryov, V. S. Osipanov, V. F. Generalov, P. I. Andreyushkin and the brother of the future Lenin – Alexander Ilyich Ulyanov) paid for it with their lives, while two (M. V. Novorussky and I. D. Lukashevich) were imprisoned for many years in the Shlisselburg.

But all these were merely belated and pale glimmers of the bright revolutionary flame that the full-blooded, passionate and impetuous party of the People's Freedom, born at the Voronyozh congress, had been blazing with and, in some twenty months, had been consumed by. The People's Freedom went to its historic tomb, and was followed by its own epigones and those of Populism generally. For on 1 March 1881 it was not only the organizational apparatus of the party that was shattered; its political ideology, too, was mortally smitten.

The successful regicide did not 'unleash' a people's revolution, or even a discernible people's movement. As in the preceding 'killings of generals and chiefs of gendarmerie', the assassination of the Tsar too 'passed by in the countryside without a trace'. In some places it was even thought to be an act of 'seignorial' revenge on the 'Tsar-

Emancipator'. The Populist Socialist illusions by which the revolutionaries sanctified the terrorist struggle in their own eyes were suddenly dissipated. The prosaic truth of this struggle, as in the struggle for the most elementary 'bourgeois' liberty, for the most moderate 'Western European' parliamentarianism, was displayed in a flash with such undeniable clarity to the consciousness of the surviving combatants that, in a letter addressed to the new Tsar on 10 March by the remnants of the Executive Committee, only two demands were put forward as a condition for the cessation of revolutionary activities: a general political amnesty and the convocation of people's representatives.

Vera Figner writes concerning this historic document:

> The letter to Alexander III we wrote a few days later is sufficiently characteristic of the general mood of the Petersburg members of the party in the period that followed 1 March. It was composed with a moderation and tact that evoked sympathy throughout Russian society. When published in the West it produced a sensation in the whole of the European press; the most moderate and retrogade organs declared their approval of the demands of the Russian Nihilists, finding them reasonable and just, and largely incorporated long since in the everyday usages of Western European life.[67]

That this moderately liberal programme was not simply retrojected by Vera Figner into the post-March temper of the People's Freedom members, but was really taken account of at the time as a modest summing-up of their heroic struggle, is also proved by a speech she made herself at the court she appeared before in 1884. 'In the programme by which I acted,' this speech concludes, 'the most fundamental aspect, which for me had the greatest significance, was the destruction of the absolutist form of government. Actually I do not lend any practical significance to whether our programme referred to a republic or a constitutional monarchy . . . What I consider the most essential thing is that those conditions appear in which the individual will be able to develop his own powers in a many-sided way and give them over wholly for the benefit of society. It seems to me that under our present order such conditions do not exist.'

A struggle for a moderately liberal constitution – this was the objective meaning of the legendary revolutionary activity of the People's Freedom. This striking contradiction between the breadth of the programme and the narrowness of the real political objectives, between the magnitude of the means and the modesty of the material goals must, of course, not be pointed out in retrospect in order to criticize and expose them, but in order to underline once again the tragic conditions in which, for decades, history placed the Russian intelligentsia, which shouldered alone the entire burden of the struggle for Russian democracy and Socialism. Even in the heroic mould of the People's Freedom the revolutionary intelligentsia could not solve the insoluble problem of conducting this unendurable struggle to a successful conclusion. But in this struggle the People's Freedom was a landmark of enormous importance because together with it both Russian Populism and the Russian movement of the revolutionary intelligentsia in general broke for ever with apoliticism. 'Politics' became its central goal, the overthrow of the autocracy its general slogan. 'Down with the autocracy!' – it was this popular outcry of the Russian revolutionary movement that was the legacy of the People's Freedom.

PART THREE

Revolutionary Marxism

CHAPTER SEVEN

From Populism to Marxism

1. AFTER 1 MARCH

The 'moderation and tact' of the letter addressed to the new Tsar by the remnants of the shattered Executive Committee testifies to what a turning point 1 March 1881 was for the whole political psychology of the People's Freedom. The party whose 'heroic exploits' had been resounding throughout the world only the day before had now turned into a powerless handful of revolutionaries who felt as though they were on an uninhabited island. At the most decisive moment the 'masses of the people' had not supported them in any way. And the more acutely the destruction of Populist illusions was experienced the sharper the about-face it had to execute with respect to the 'liberal bourgeoisie' that, in spite of Zhelyabov's appeals, the Voronyozh congress had turned away from so proudly. Now it had to seek its 'natural allies' among 'industrialists, landowners and urban functionaries'. But here too a cruel disappointment awaited the revolutionaries.

The wave of terrorist attacks that welled up during 1879–80 was widely taken advantage of by liberal society and the liberal press to express its wishes – of course in a form more or less masked by censorship – for the 'crowning of the edifice of reforms' by the convocation of the 'representatives of the land'. The same was said by many Zemstvos in their petition to the government. 'Give us a constitution, or else they'll shoot,' was the ironical summing-up, in both radical and governmental circles, of the relationship of liberal society to the terrorist struggle of the People's Freedom.

This formulation correctly placed the stress on 'us', since what was almost invariably understood by the phrase 'representatives of the land' was only the representatives of the Zemstvos, Town Dumas, Assemblies of the Nobility and similar organized collectives of the more or less affluent summits of society. But the reference to the 'constitutional' character of these liberal desires did not at all correspond to reality, since the question of the scope of the rights and powers of these 'representatives of the land', and hence also of the degree of restriction of the autocracy, was systematically left in the dark by all the various petitions and declarations. In any case it could be maintained that at this time the liberal circles of affluent society, in their immense majority, were not thinking seriously of constitutional parliamentarianism. An incontrovertible proof of this was the reaction to a summons addressed to 'society' by a Count Loris-Melikov, whom the frightened Tsar after the explosion in the Winter Palace (5 February 1880) had invested with dictatorial powers for a 'struggle against sedition' and for the implication of 'society' in a real share of that struggle.

The 'dictatorship of the heart' as the Loris-Melikov régime was christened by its praisers, did not put a stop to or cut down on the ferocious repression of the revolutionaries. Executions, sentences of hard labour handed down by exceptional courts, and administrative punishments followed their normal course. But at the same time the dictator declared his intention of meeting 'society' half-way and enabling it to take part in the functioning of the state. An appropriate draft was completely ready and merely awaiting the Tsar's signature when the People's Freedom bomb snuffed out the life of Alexander II. This draft had been given the current name of 'Loris-Melikov's constitution'. But the name did not correspond to its actual contents, since essentially it dealt only with the engagement of a limited number of rural and urban figures in a share in the labours of the State Council, which itself was an institution of purely bureaucratic and consultative character under the autocratic Tsar.

Nor could the 'dictatorship of the heart' promise anything more in general. Nevertheless, at the appointment of Loris-Melikov, sensational for that epoch, only twenty-five 'notable Moscow citizens' reacted with a 'note' that could have been interpreted as a demand for representation that, even though only of the propertied bourgeoisie, demanded definitely constitutional full powers. Handed to the government on 25 March 1880, this note referred to the need for convoking 'an independent assembly of the representatives of the Zemstvos and offering this assembly a share in the governing and in the elaboration of the necessary guarantees for the rights of the individual and freedom of thought and speech'. But this note was an exception, and in characterizing this 'opinion of the Zemstvo assemblies' in response to Loris-Melikov's appeal, Y. Skalon, himself an eminent landowner, observed that 'relying on the wisdom and good intentions of the authorities, they did not declare any demands and refrained from any indications of the reforms desired. A deep faith in the stability of the established order forced them patiently to await measures to be taken by the government itself.'[68]

But the more modest the political demands of society became, the more noisily there began to resound in its statements a readiness to participate in 'the struggle against sedition', and to be compensated for the modesty of the 'crowning of the edifice' that it was getting. This idea runs like a red thread through all such declarations and petitions down to 1 March. Thus, even the petition written for the Chernigov Zemstvo assembly by I. I. Petrunkevich, one of two brothers celebrated in the history of Russian liberalism, fortified its liberal wishes by promising 'a struggle against destructive tendencies'. Zemstvos, like those in Poltava, Kharkov and others, even more clearly declared their readiness to 'pluck out the evil at the root and combat the propaganda undertaken by the enemies of the government and of society'. And it was only a small and uninfluential group of Zemstvo radicals, united in a secret 'Zemstvo League', that expressed its dissatisfaction, in a pamphlet ('Immediate Tasks of the Zemstvos') as follows: 'We think that the Poltava and Kharkov Zemstvos have taken a wrong path. What constitutional benefits can we promise the Russian people if we bind ourselves in advance to stifle and destroy people living by them?'[68] After 1 March the juxtaposition of wishes for the convocation of 'representatives of the land' and the promise of help to the government in rooting out 'sedition' became a rule.

The representatives of the Right wing of liberalism went even further. Such eminent liberals and scholars as Professors A. D. Gradovsky and B. N. Chicherin handed the government notes giving it a direct warning against the introduction of a constitution and against any kind of concessions at all to 'sedition'. A note from Chicherin (uncle of the future Bolshevik People's Commissar for Foreign Affairs) given by him on 11 March 1881 to the Supreme Procurator of the Holy Synod, K. P. Pobedonostsev, with a copy to the Tsar himself, is of pre-eminent interest for the understanding of the motives that prompted this extremist Right-wing attitude in liberal thought.[69]

Criticizing the extraordinarily rapid tempo with which the reforms of Alexander II were being carried out, Chicherin says that the transformations were being accomplished, 'towards a catastrophic climax', at a time when 'our mentor on the path of civic development, Western Europe', was itself undergoing a 'crisis in both the intellectual and the political domains'. In Europe 'a struggle was going on between capital and labour; materialist teachings were agitating people's minds, while savage passions, churning up the masses of the people, were striving for the overthrow of all the foundations that underlie collective human life'. Hence it was not surprising that in backward and ignorant Russia the periodical press 'reveals itself as an element of dissolution'. 'It has given birth to the Chernyshevskys, the Dobrolyubovs, the Pisaryovs and their numerous followers, whose name is now legion. Even now, when the press is far from enjoying complete liberty, anyone who can read sees Socialist aspirations bursting through the liberal mask everywhere.' If the press were given its freedom, 'the way would be completely thrown open to Socialist propaganda', and it was impossible to hope 'that it would meet with any resistance from the healthy elements of society'.

As for the 'intellectual proletariat that had been given birth by the changing situation of our social strata', that is, the so-called 'intelligentsia', to imagine that it was 'possible to turn it back to useful civic activity through softness . . . would mean being far too naïve a utopian. As long as a Socialist party working for the overthrow of the whole social order is in existence, extraordinary measures will be indispensable.'

'The menacing peasant question' that was supposed to be on the order of the day 'was nothing but a myth created by the imagination of Petersburg liberals, not without the considerable influence of the Socialists'. In fact the basic 'causes of poverty' were summed up in 'the peasant's bondage to the commune', as a consequence of which 'those who have an opportunity of getting rich are forcibly reduced to the paupers' level'. The way out lay in the abolition of the commune and a transition to individual ownership of land. 'But it is just this sole reasonable way out of the peasant affair that provokes a howl not only from the whole of the mock-liberal press, which is always ready to stand up strongly for anything approaching Socialism, but also by a substantial section of the conservatives who are attracted by Slavophil ideas or frightened by the spectre of the proletariat.'

Having outlined with such precision the social and spiritual roots of his own 'rightism', Chicherin equally definitely formulates his own position, derived from it, on the question of 'what it has become customary to call the crowning of the edifice'. He points out that 'after the emancipation of the peasants the nobility dreamt for a time of constitutional rights, by which it intended to reward itself for its lost privileges'. But 'the most reasonable part of society' understood that 'in an epoch of basic transformation it was impossible to think of restricting the supreme authority'. It was only when 'minds had settled down' that the reasonable part of society could think of this; at that time 'even those who were not swept away by contemporary passions might also desire constitutional guarantees'. But 'the era for the tranquil assimilation of the transformation had passed by like a fugitive shadow. The new forces that had appeared with terrifying energy had introduced a terrifying confusion into the society that was only just beginning to become conscious. At the present time only the followers of nihilism can speak of the crowning of the edifice, or those who have already lost any capacity to think or understand anything at all. Now any restriction on the authorities would be fatal.' Now 'the whole of the current liberal programme must be abolished. It is only leading to the strengthening of the destructive elements of society while what we need above all is to give the preponderance to the elements that rivet things together.' This leads to the final conclusion, in the spirit of the Loris-Melikov programme: 'Political liberty may be the Russian's remote ideal; but the present requirement is solely for the establishment of a living bond between the government and society, for a joint resistance to destructive elements and for the introduction of order into the Russian land. This goal can be achieved by amalgamating in the State Council elected representatives from both the nobility and the Zemstvos.'

After a very brief period of hesitation Alexander III did actually exploit the helplessness of the revolutionary organization and the renunciation by liberal society both of revolution and of its own constitutional banner, in order to proclaim the unshakability of the autocracy and inter not only all 'constitutional dreams' but also the far more modest dreams of Chicherin's 'Note'. Loris-Melikov was dismissed and his draft buried. The question of 'amalgamating in the State Council elected representatives from both the nobility and the Zemstvos' waited almost a quarter of a century to come to the surface, when it was then no longer Rightist 'society' but the autocracy itself that tried – also unsuccessfully! – to hide behind this rampart from the storms of the approaching revolution of 1905.

Thus, the policy of collaborating with the government in the 'struggle against sedition' did not bring liberal society even those small concessions from the autocracy it had calculated on. Reality had once again shown that in the specific conditions of Russian development we have referred to more than once, Russian liberalism, by tearing itself away from the camp of Socialism, which was socially hostile to it, became powerless in the face of the camp of the autocracy and its bureaucracy, which was politically hostile. But this policy brought about a considerable demoralization throughout the liberal and oppositional *milieu*, and furthered their dissolution. This was attended to by the so-called 'Holy Guard', which was founded immediately after 1 March 1881 by Count I. I. Vorontsov-Dashkov, Minister of the Court and future Vice-regent of the Caucasus, Count Shuvalov, future Russian ambassador in Berlin, and other aristocratic figures.

The 'Guard' had the façade of an independent organization that aimed at reconciling the government with 'society' on the ground of a liberal programme, on the one hand, and of a merciless struggle against the revolution on the other. In fact it was the creation and weapon of the political police, which used it with some success for penetrating into the most variegated liberal and oppositional circles and disintegrating them. Formally liquidated only towards the end of 1882, on Alexander III's orders, the 'Guard' was of considerable service to the autocracy during the most critical months. It hastened the process of the political castration of liberalism and its transition to that 'practical' apolitical collaboration with the bureaucracy that we have already referred to in its place and that was one of the principal bulwarks of the policy of stagnation and reaction that characterized the '80s and the whole reign of Alexander III in general.

It was only the above-mentioned Zemstvo League, which changed its name to 'Zemstvo Union', that seemed as before to try to raise the banner of bourgeois radicalism. In August 1881 Michael Petrovich Dragomanov (1841–95) began publishing in Geneva a periodical, *Vol'noye Slovo* (Free Speech) in the name of the Union. The periodical criticized the People's Freedom and carried on a campaign against terror, but for its part demanded a democratic constitution, on the basis of a general vote, and a federative reconstruction of the state. In May 1883, in its sixty-first number, *Vol'noye Slovo* was forced to close down for lack of funds, and in 1884 the Zemstvo Union itself vanished noiselessly from the scene. It was not until a quarter of a century later, on the basis of materials discovered by the revolution in the police archives, that it was established that this Union was a more or less mythical organization, and that the funds for the publication of

Vol'noye Slovo came from this same Holy Guard through its agent A. P. Malyshinsky and were given Dragomanov and his colleagues (including P. B. Akselrod) without their knowledge of their source.

The radical changes in the domestic and international position of Russia that came about with the conclusion of the Russo-Turkish War were the material basis of this general pacification of the liberal opposition.

The crisis provoked by the war was followed by a streak of comparative economic welfare and even prosperity. Industry and the railways developed. The conclusion of commercial treaties furthered the export of Russian (primarily, of course, landowners') grain to the European markets. The improvement of state finances paved the way to the devaluation of the rouble and the shift to a gold standard, and made possible concessions to industrialists who were demanding credit, and to landowners who were soliciting not only new loans but also the liquidation of their old indebtedness to the state. The reverse side of this prosperity was, as we have already noted, the accelerated socio-economic differentiation of the countryside, the pauperization of a substantial part of the peasantry, the lagging of the domestic market behind the growth of industry, the appearance on the market of a vast number of free and cheap 'working hands' and similar phenomena. All this prepared the revolutionary upheavals of the future. But for the time being an atmosphere of 'calm' was created in the country. It was oppressive for the masses of the people and stifling for the radical intelligentsia, but it seemed to be stable. The government of Alexander III could not only 'put a full stop to the reforms' but also carry on a persistent policy of reactionary revision of all the liberal reforms of the preceding reign (rural, peasant, juridical, university, censorship, etc.), without encountering any serious opposition from the propertied classes.

But a new era arrived in Russia's foreign policy too. The peace treaty signed with Turkey at San Stefano (February 1878) met, as is well known, with some resistance from the European powers and was in fact cancelled at the Berlin Congress (July 1878), which deprived Russia of practically all the fruits of victory. The road to the Balkans and to the Straits, which had been closed to Russia for a quarter of a century before the Crimean defeat, was not opened for her by her victories. The domestic foreign policy of the new régime not only accepted this fact, but made it a point of principle to reject any aggressive policies in Europe. Alexander III became the 'Peace-

Maker'. What he tried to make the foundation of his European policy was the 'Union of Three Emperors' (Russian, German, Austrian) as a bastion of the conservative 'order' in Europe and a bulwark against any revolutionary longings. It was not his fault, but the fault of invincible historical circumstances, that this new version of the Holy Alliance proved even less long-lived than its famous predecessor at the beginning of the nineteenth century, and that by 1893 Alexander III himself had to conclude an alliance with the French Republic he hated.

The aggressive colonizing energy of Russia was shifted from the west to the east: to Turkestan, to Siberia (construction of the great Siberian trunk line) to the Amur, to the Far East. Talk was still going on of 'planting the cross' on Santa Sophia in Constantinople – but this was by now no longer so much a slogan of foreign aggression as an exalted expression of Great Russian nationalism, directing its sword not so much against internal as against foreign enemies, against 'aliens' of every kind – first and foremost against the Poles, and especially the Jews. By the irony of fate the specifically Great Russian 'nationhood', with the purely Slavophil cultivation of 'ancient heritages' and old customs both at court and in the church, in the school and in the way of life – had become, together with 'autocracy and orthodoxy' the banner of the régime just at a time when the Pan-Slav-Balkan dreams of Slavophils were being surrendered to the archives for a long time, if not for ever!

Thus once again conditions were coming about that in many respects were analogous to those the country had lived through during the first years following the emancipation of the peasants and the crushing of the Polish uprising of 1863. Just as then, the blossoming of the promotion schemes and colonizing enterprises made the government a centre that throngs of entrepreneurial, energetic, rapacious seekers of profit and wealth were drawn towards. Just as then, nationalism was becoming an ideal element that riveted together the vast majority of affluent society into a solid conservative *bloc*, and an ideal weapon of that majority in the struggle against the isolated, enfeebled revolution. It was just in these years that anti-Semitism became not only the official doctrine of the autocracy (which indeed it was to remain down to the revolution of 1917 itself) but also spread very widely in society, even penetrating some of its 'Left' sectors. Even among the peripheral remnants of the People's Freedom there were some small groups that tried to exploit, in a 'revolutionary' way, the anti-Jewish pogroms instigated and organized by the political police. And it was just in these years that the nationalist, chauvinist, and anti-Semitic *Novoye Vremya* (New Times) of the gifted but thoroughly unscrupulous A. S. Suvorin became the most widespread and influential organ of 'society'. As was demonstrated by his posthumously published cynical *Diaries*, Suvorin was perfectly aware of the character of the lightning-like evolution from radical liberalism to reactionary conservatism he had gone through himself, parallel with this 'society'.

In these conditions it was only a comparatively small number of the 'bourgeoisified' and cultivated aristocratic landlords and the most 'europeanized' bourgeoisie and its socially dependent topmost strata of economic organizers and members of the 'liberal professions' – engineers, lawyers, physicians, statisticians, pedagogical personnel, etc. – that remained the guardians of liberal traditions in the cities and the countryside. But this liberalism of theirs, whose principal organs were now the Petersburg monthly *Vestnik Yevropy* and the Moscow newspaper *Russkiye Vedomosti* took on a special aspect.

We have already explained why the idea of the expansion of the domestic market had to become the guiding economic idea of the most 'europeanized' elements of the Russian bourgeoisie. These were oriented not towards the rapacious exploitation of Russian backwardness and the decomposition of the old economic forms, but towards the progressive development of the Russian economy. Now, the only possible basis for such an expansion was an increase in the welfare of the broad peasant masses. And it was this 'pro-peasant' attitude that became in the '80s the basic idea of the new liberalism, which with complete subjective sincerity denied its own 'bourgeois' nature. The liberal economic programme of the time revolved around the following economic points: the defence of the ordinary peasant against extraordinary exploitation – by the government screwing up the tax vice; by the feudal landowners, and the rapacious usurers, as well as by their own rural kulak money-lenders; the strengthening of the peasant commune as the principal weapon of that defence; the stimulation of small crafts and the support of the artels and other kinds of cooperation as the principal means of protecting the interests of the small producers. For the implementation of these points politically enfeebled liberalism was counting, as we have seen, on an 'enlightened bureaucracy'.

It was in this way that a peculiar 'Populist liberalism' (Potresov's expression) took shape. Its formation was stimulated to an extraordinary extent through its being met half-way by the rise of 'liberal Populism' in place of the revolutionary Populism that on 1 March 1881 had been given a mortal wound.

2. POPULIST EPIGONES

Understandably, the revolutionary organizations of Populism directly embraced only the most combative and thus comparatively small part of the Populist-minded intelligentsia. The immense majority of this intelligentsia did not and could not take any systematic or active part in the revolutionary struggle, but merely supported it with its sympathy, material and technical aid and sporadic collaboration with one 'illegal' enterprise or another. The mass of this intelligentsia made up that numerically preponderant 'legal', non-organized, sector of the broad Populist movement, whose principal organ in the 'legal' press towards the end of the '60s was the *Otechestvennye Zapiski.**

We have seen what phases revolutionary Populism went through for some ten to twelve years – from complete apoliticism and the attempt to dissolve itself in the peasant masses ('Going to the people') to its concentration on the political problem and its attempts to solve that by its own forces, the forces of the small 'thinking minority'. Parallel with the evolution of this 'illegal' sector of Populism, its 'legal' sector also evolved during these years. Thus, towards the second half of the '70s, this same *Otechestvennye Zapiski*, which as we have remarked upon in its place (Chap. 4) had begun with a resolute rejection of any such 'seignorial intrigue' as the dream of a constitution, was already making the 'crowning of the edifice' by a constitution the basic idea of its own political propaganda.

But in all this parallelism of development there was always a certain distinction between 'legal' and 'illegal' Populism that could not be explained only by censorship conditions, which the former had to cope with and which the underground and *émigré* press of the latter was free of. It was also a question of the character of the intelligentsia that legal Populism was aiming at. This audience was far broader; but it was also far less moulded politically. Moreover, it was bound by a series of intermediate links to the same liberal 'society' that

* N. A. Nekrasov, M. Y. Saltykov-Shchedrin, G. Z. Yeliseyev, N. K. Mikhailovsky and others.

revolutionary Populism had so often, even though purely theoretically, come into savage conflict with. While sympathetically accompanying 'illegal' Populism in all the stages of its revolutionary struggle, and also absorbing into its own arsenal all the heterogeneous and contradictory ideas that constituted its spiritual arms, 'legal' Populism re-worked these ideas in its own way. It eliminated their 'extremism', corrected their 'one-sidedness', blunted their 'sharpness', smoothed over their contradictions, and lopped off from Bakuninite anarchic apoliticism the insurrectionist element; from Lavrovite rationalism, its ties to the ideas of the European revolution; from Tkachovite politicism, its Jacobin calculations on the seizure of power. In their 'legal' elaboration, the 'illegal' Populist ideas little by little lost their social-revolutionary character and took on a social-reformist hue that made them acceptable to the broad circles, not only of the Populist-minded but revolutionarily inactive intelligentsia, but also of its 'sympathizers' in liberal society.

This disharmony between illegal and legal Populism had already found expression by the beginning of the '70s, when the revolutionary youth drew the moral stimulation it needed to plunge selflessly over 'to the people' from the fighting spirit of Bakuninite 'insurrectionism', and when the *Otechestvennye Zapiski*, in the struggle against the effort to 'place reason behind feeling', came out as the vehicle of frigid Lavrovite rationalism. Even more characteristically, the legal Populist press reacted to the outburst of the People's Freedom in 1879–80 in tones that sounded more like an echo of the intellectual and political processes that, as we have seen, were taking place at this time in liberal circles, than like an echo of the immense tension of emotions and will-power – the magnificent plans, hopes and illusions – that then seized on the revolutionary vanguard of Populism.

'All around we see hunger and the manifest necessity for a change in the direction of the state economy,' Mikhailovsky, for instance, wrote in the *Otechestvennye Zapiski* ('Literary Notes') for December 1880, 'a series of unprecedentedly savage political crimes and the absolute impossibility of any further practical application of the government's world-outlook.* It is around these two groups of vital facts and the conclusions suggested by life that the whole really terrifying evil of the day has crystallized. To be or not to be, not for some kind of utopia, not for an Arcady with eternally blue sky and eternal

* A censored way of referring to the impossibility of preserving a purely bureaucratic absolutism.

emerald green, but even for the least bit bearable, peaceful life in our Russia?' But it was not only the programmatic utterances of the chief publicist of the *Otechestvennye Zapiski* that resounded in harmony with the modest, moderate programmes, aiming at not more than a 'little bit bearable' state reform, that liberal thinkers, exploiting in their own way the terror of the People's Freedom, were beginning to put forth at this time. The same concord could also be observed concerning the forces that were supposed to carry out this reform. By October of the same year (1880) – in the fever of the desperate struggle of the People's Freedom against the government – Mikhailovsky declared that only the government could take upon itself 'the very great labour of saving the motherland a duplication of the European struggle' (i.e. the class struggle), since it alone 'possessed both the means needed for this and the no less needed dispassionateness and indifference to the triumph of falsehood'.[70]

As long as the revolutionary movement was going uphill this process of shaping legal Populism into a special social-reformist tendency took a relatively slow and imperceptible course, for the readers of the legal Populist press as well as for the writers. Revolutionary Populism, which was attracting the attention of the government and of society by its 'magnificent exploits' and striking the imaginations of the broadest circles of the youth of the intelligentsia, initially by the whole glamour of 'going to the people', and then by the terror of the People's Freedom, not only set the tone within the generally Populist movement, but morally conquered political outsiders too, and even, as we have noted, circles that were downright hostile to it. Not for nothing does Suvorin, editor of the *Novoye Vremya*, tell in his *Diaries* of a conversation he had with Dostoevsky, a convinced monarchist and author of *The Possessed*, in which both men acknowledge to each other that they would have been incapable of handing over a revolutionary terrorist to the police, even if they had accidentally learned in time of the explosion planned at the Winter Palace.[71] It was typical that in the works of people of emotion, poets and artists, of the legal Populist press (Nekrasov, Saltykov-Shchedrin, Gleb Uspensky and others) revolutionarily combative notes rang out far more distinctly and far longer than in the articles of its journalistic writers.

The position changed when revolutionary Populism, in the form of the People's Freedom, lost a decisive battle and passed from the historical scene. Legal Populism suddenly came to monopolize

Populist thought. The role of the 'opinion-moulders' passed over in conditions that in many respects recalled, as indicated above, a worsened version of conditions at the end of the '60s and beginning of the '70s, when a satirist could sum up the mood of 'society' in a short but expressive formula: 'Our epoch is not an epoch of broad objectives' – a formula taken directly from the leading article of the most influential liberal newspaper of the time.[72] Now a depression began seizing broad strata of the intelligentsia, too. A special tendency even appeared within the framework of Populism, 'Abramovism',[73] that openly called on the intelligentsia to 'retire to second, to third place all broad-gauge socio-political questions' and devote itself completely to 'small deeds'.

In its extremist and consistent expression 'Abramovism' was merely a minor current in the Populist intelligentsia. The immense majority of the legal Populist movement criticized the preaching of 'small deeds' in principle, and did not remove 'socio-political questions' from the order of the day. But both in its theoretical approach to these questions and in its practical answer it underwent an evolution that drew it closer in fact not only to the 'Abramovites' but also to the conservative liberals of that epoch. Martov gives an accurate description of the general aspect of legal Populism at this time when he writes: 'The fall of the revolutionary People's Freedom was at the same time the collapse of Populism as a whole. Broad circles of the democratic intelligentsia were profoundly demoralized and disappointed in "politics" and in their own heroic mission. A modest "cultivation" in the service of the liberal segment of the possessing classes – this was the sign under which the part of the intelligentsia that had remained loyal to Populism entered the grey epoch of the '80s.'[74] It should merely be noted that the reverse side of the spiritual depression had great progressive significance. This was the fruitful work in and around the Zemstvos (statistics, medicine, pedagogy, etc.); the disappointed intelligentsia plunged into this. It coincided, not by accident, with a revival of interest in Pisaryov.

The first definite spokesman of this new neo-Populism, 'cultural' and social-reformist, was V. P. Vorontsov (1847–1918), who wrote under the initials V. V. Vorontsov rejected all revolutionary objectives. He emphasized that the 'practical realization' of the desires of Populism 'as defined in the post-reform epoch', under Russian conditions demanded 'the intellectual advancement of the masses; therefore this is posed as the principal objective of the present day'.[75] But this book, which was published in 1893, sums up the results of Vorontsov's preceding activities; he was the first to give the socio-economic 'groundwork of Populism' as a new formation, having made the cornerstone of this groundwork, in Martov's expression, 'the fatalistic idea of the unthinkability of the capitalist evolution of Russia'.[76]

As we have seen, in the course of half a century all the stages and zigzags in the evolution of the Russian democratic movement, and the Populism that had arisen in its depths, were defined in one way or another by the idea of the necessity of struggling against the danger of capitalist development that was threatening Russia. To declare that this danger did not exist, to prove, in Mikhailovsky's expression, that 'all hopes and fears about this are uniformly futile'[77] meant taking the soul out of Populism. In any case it meant taking the revolutionary sting out of it, by convincing it that by virtue of the anti-capitalist automatics of the socio-economic development of Russia it could reckon with certainty on the gradual realization of its ideals, even within the framework of the existing political system, without the revolutionary 'overthrow of the autocracy' that the People's Freedom had been calling for more and more vociferously down to the climax of its struggle – 1 March 1881. It was just this that was the political meaning of V.V's socio-economic theories; in the foreword to his major opus he wrote: 'The party of the people would have gained a great deal in practical respects if the duality that split its view of the world had been eliminated, if its faith in the viability of popular principles had been united with a conviction of the historical impossibility of the development of capitalist production in Russia.'[78] It was, indeed, to the demonstration of this 'historical impossibility' that his book was devoted.

In his argument V.V. starts from the real peculiarities of the development of capitalism in Russia, bound up with its historical belatedness. But all the difficulties that flowed from this – above all the absence of foreign markets and of an adequate internal market – presented themselves, from V.V's point of view, as absolute and insurmountable. This was all the more so because capitalism in Russia collided with the fixed communal and artel traditions of the Russian peasantry, which drew its energies for a successful struggle against capitalism from just these conditions and from the miscarriage of nascent capitalism. This doomed it to an inevitable ultimate defeat. This absolutely pessimistic assessment of the possibilities of capitalist development is united in V.V. with an equally absolute optimistic assessment of the chances of victory of small-scale peasant agriculture propped up on the commune, and of small-scale industry based on the artel. The 'pleasing facts' of economic, technical, and cultural progress in the countryside are registered without taking into account their real specific weight in the general economic and cultural balance-sheet of the country as a whole and of the countryside itself. They are interpreted as a proof of the vitality of the commune and the artel, locked in a duel with capitalism – just at a time when rural statistics were beginning to register systematically the process of the socio-economic differentiation of the peasantry, the growing concentration of all elements of progress in the hands of the 'kulak' summit, the growing pauperization of its immense majority, the growing role of heavy industry, etc., which signalized the growing successes of the advance of 'still-born' capitalism both in the countryside and in the country as a whole.

In direct connexion with the new socio-economic conception the attitude towards the state also changed radically.

For classical Populism in all its currents, down to Tkachovite Jacobinism, the actual Russian state of bureaucratic absolutism, if not the State *per se*, was the primordial enemy of the masses of the people and of the communal tendencies embedded in them. This led to a revolutionary posture in Populism even at a time when it decisively rejected 'politics' and even when, as in its embryonic period, it could dream of a 'social' Tsar. It could not be shaken loose from this revolutionary position even by such facts as the emancipation of the peasants plus the bestowal of land, or by the governmental sponsorship of the commune. It understood that the source of this sponsorship was not sympathy for the Socialist 'ideal' of the people but considerations of an administrative and fiscal order. The commune, which fortified the insulation of the peasantry as the 'lowest' estate, and bound its members together through collective responsibility for taxes, was an incomparably convenient instrument for governing the peasantry and levying taxes on it. It was just this progressive dissolution of the commune by capitalism that prompted the government to take a series of measures making it more and more difficult for the peasants to leave the commune, to shift from communal landowning to private homesteading and so on. Such measures aimed at preserving the commune, but in fact changed it more and more from a form of peasant land cultivation and autonomy into a form of compulsory organization of the peasantry for administration and taxes.

V.V., too, of course, saw that more and more often 'the commune was decomposing as a voluntary alliance, and remaining a "society" in the administrative sense, a group of persons forcibly bound together by mutual responsibility, that is, the responsibility of each one for the restricted capacities of all the tax-payers and the inability of the fiscal authority to heed this'.[79] But these negative phenomena were not linked for him with the dynamics of the socio-economic and political development of the peasantry and the country as a whole. They appeared to him to be merely the consequence of the more or less accidental 'incomprehension' by the government of its own advantages. But the fact that the state had freed the peasants together with land and made the commune a lever of its policies was a proof for him that at bottom it had met the people's aspirations half-way and would be forced to meet them half-way in the future too.

Thus the state was changed from an enemy of the people's ideals into a vehicle of ideas elaborated by 'the people's consciousness'. Consequently the practical objectives of Populism boiled down to a struggle to make the government in future realize, more definitely and consistently, a socio-economic programme corresponding to the wishes of the people. Its principal points were the legislative fortification of the commune and the restriction of small-scale peasant agriculture, on the one hand, and the state sponsorship of the small-scale, home-craft industry and its organization in artels on the other.[80]

As we see, this programme coincided completely with the programme that Populist-minded liberalism had been working its way towards. In breaking with the ideas of economic individualism it too set as its central objective 'the support of small-scale producers, the communal peasant, and home-crafts'.[81] But it also coincided with calculations on 'the enlightened bureaucracy' as the sole force that could and sooner or later would wish to realize this programme, as the sole 'viable' programme for the economic development of Russia. And some aspects of the policy of the new régime seemed to reinforce these calculations. For with all its reactionary nature the régime of Alexander III, in spite of Chicherin's advice, systematically strengthened the communal forms of rural organization. Beyond the already mentioned considerations of an administrative and fiscal order, this strengthening was a constituent element of the general policy, characteristic of this régime, of cultivating the external forms of 'peoplehood' and of 'patriarchal' Russian traditions. To an eye that was inadequately critical it was easy not to notice that behind this 'folk' façade a process was taking place of unprecedented destruction of all socio-economic, cultural, and customary 'primordial foundations' of Russian life, especially the communal foundations of the Russian countryside, where the sole material achievement of 'patriarchalism' proved to be the restoration of the administrative and juridical power of the nobility over the peasantry (the institution of 'Land Captains').

Far more precise than V.V. and other neo-Populist and liberal economists was N. F. Danielson (pen-name: Nicholas——on), who saw and with great knowledge described this destruction of the 'foundations'.[82] But in recording the destruction of the old farming and social structure of Russia, as a consequence of the 'capitalization of agricultural revenues' and 'capitalization of crafts', which had been growing stronger and stronger ever since the emancipation of the peasants, Danielson does not see the emergence, on the basis of this capitalization, of any elements that could form a new system or any social forces capable of fighting for this new system. Because of this, like V.V., he regarded the cause of capitalism in Russia as hopeless. Like V.V., he thought that because of its historic belatedness capitalism in Russia would develop with tenfold force all its negative sides, without being able to develop a single positive one, and would have to expire because of the absence of any foreign markets and the shrinking of the domestic market. For in destroying small-scale peasant farming it turned the basic mass of the peasantry into paupers with no buying power, without which the development of heavy industry on a capitalist basis is impossible. This is also why the 'capitalization of the home-crafts' could only create in Russia a predatory capitalist, not an organizer of the national economy, on the one hand, and only a mass of paupers, not a 'working-class' in the European sense, on the other. If this process of 'capitalization' of agricultural and craft revenues, which had begun with the emancipation of the peasants, went on any further without hindrance, it would only result in the irremedial socio-economic degradation of the country.

However, while at one with V.V. in acknowledging the impossibility of the development of capitalism in Russia, Danielson, a learned economist and a translator of Marx's *Capital*, considered it impossible to fight against development on the basis of an eternalization of small-scale economy. He wrote:

> all efforts must be directed at a unification of agriculture and manufacturing industry in the hands of the direct producers, but a unification not on the ground of small-scale, fragmented productive units – which would be the equivalent of the 'eternalization of general mediocrity' [N.B. an expression of Marx's!] – but on the ground of the creation of a massive, generalized production based on the free development of social productive forces and the application of science and technology, with the aim of satisfying the genuine requirements and well-being of the whole population.[83]

Putting the question in this way meant that what was being counterposed to the programme of capitalism was not the 'petty-bourgeois' programme of liberal Populism and Populist-minded liberalism, but a Socialist programme. But this programmatic distinction lost all practical significance in so far as Danielson denied the presence or even the inception, in a Russia undergoing 'capitalization', of any mass forces capable of making a Socialist programme their banner and of fighting for it. Because of this it was only on the union of 'society' with the government that he too laid the task of forestalling the ruinous consequences of this process of 'capitalization'. Within the framework of such a union the question, practically speaking, of forestalling these consequences could only be answered by the same preservation of the 'small-scale producers' that V.V. also called for. Under these conditions Danielson's 'Socialist' programme took on a completely abstract character; as an inessential detail it slipped past the awareness of his readers to such an extent that in the foreword to *Nashi Napravlyeniya* (Our Trends) V.V. himself noted the comprehensive coincidence between his own views and Danielson's.

V.V. and Danielson laid the economic foundations of that liberal Populism 'whose very existence in a developed form supposed the destruction of the former ideology'.[84] But it found its most brilliant exponent, philosopher, sociologist, and popularizer in the gifted and many-sided Nicholas Konstantinovich Mikhailovsky (1842–1904), whose early sociological works now became the theoretical foundation of neo-Populism. These works continued the work of Lavrov, but introduced into his 'subjective method' some very basic corrections.

For Lavrov the 'moral ideal' of the individual was the sole standard by which a man could and ought to approach historical events, define his relationship to them, and intervene in their course. No matter how this 'moral ideal' arose, once it did it 'constituted for everyone the sole meaning of history . . . [and] the law of progress'. No objective conditions, no discrepancy between this ideal and reality could diminish its absolute value. Therefore the 'development of the individual in his physical, intellectual and moral aspects', and the 'embodiment in social forms' of what the individual considered to be 'truth and justice' – such was the authentic 'formula of progress'. It did not matter whether 'we believed in its material realization or merely in its existence in our own consciousness'.

This absolute subjectivism of Lavrov's, which dictated to the individual a revolutionary relationship to reality, if that reality made the 'material realization' of his 'moral ideal' impossible, was infused by Mikhailovsky with an opportunistic relativity that left the individual only a 'freedom of choice' between tendencies in objective reality, and that recognized the ideal itself as 'moral' only if it was, quite definitely, one of these tendencies. Starting out from the doctrine of the Spencerian 'organic' school about the processes of differentiation and integration and about progress as the passage from the homogeneous to the heterogeneous, from the simple to the complex, Mikhailovsky gives his own 'formula for progress' in one of his early essays: 'Progress is a gradual approach to the wholeness of the indivisible, towards the fullest possible and manifold division of labour between institutions and the least possible division of labour between people. Everything that holds up this movement is immoral, unjust, pernicious and unreasonable.'[85]

In the light of this formula it was precisely the independent peasant engaged in a natural economy, combining agriculture with a craft and satisfying all his needs by his own labour, that was supposed to represent, on principle, the 'highest type' of individual, just as a society that consisted of such 'whole' individuals was the 'highest type'. This 'formula' was criticized sharply by Lavrov, but it proved an appropriate theoretical justification for the support of independent small-scale producers, just as subjectivism, narrowed down to a 'freedom of choice' and proposing merely a 'gradual approach' to the ideal, justified the policy of adaptation to material reality, which did not lend adequate support to the struggle for the realization of 'broad-gauge objectives'.

From the start of his literary career, in the second half of the '60s, Mikhailovsky was intimately bound up with the Populist movement and experienced its whole spiritual evolution, which was far from straightforward. Even after becoming a permanent contributor to *Otechestvennye Zapiski* in 1868, then one of its editors, Mikhailovsky did not tear himself away from revolutionary circles. Towards the end of the '70s he became personally friendly with many members of the People's Freedom, wrote in its illegal periodical of the same name under the pen-name of Grognard, and edited the letter addressed to Alexander III by the surviving members of its Executive Committee.

Mikhailovsky's protracted and close bond with all sectors of the Populist movement made him its natural spiritual leader, after its 'illegal' sector was ruined and the guiding role passed to the 'legal' one. It was also this intimate bond that enabled Mikhailovsky to understand how psychologically unacceptable it found the naked preaching of the decisive rupture with its revolutionary past that resounded in the doctrine of the 'historical impossibility' in Russia of that evil, the 'hydra of capitalism'. For a long time, after all, the struggle against capitalism had been a source of lofty moral emotion for the intelligentsia and inspired it to feats of self-sacrifice and unsurpassed heroism. Consequently, even while taking the same line as V.V. at the beginning of the '80s on questions of socio-economic analysis and the practical political conclusions it led to, Mikhailovsky thought it necessary to separate himself from that 'sole, but evidently extraordinarily important difference' between V.V.'s views and the traditional views of Populism. This was 'defined by V.V.'s conviction of the impossibility of any capitalist development for Russia'.[77]

The positions that were finally settled on in the first half of the '80s by V.V. and many others were not the final stage in Mikhailovsky's political career. When the *Otechestvennye Zapiski* was shut down in 1884 he collaborated on the liberal periodicals *Russkaya Mysl* and *Russkiye Vedomosti*; he remained true to the socio-economic programme of 'liberal populism', but made the reverse turn towards the rehabilitation of the 'constitutional' idea through which the intelligentsia reacted to the reactionary régime in the second half of the '80s, and which also took in the left circles of liberal society. At this new stage of his political activity Mikhailovsky also took an active part in *Samoupravleniye* (Autonomy), which came out in Geneva in 1887–8 as the 'Organ of the Socialist-Revolutionaries'.*

But with all his literary brilliance and in spite of the important role

* The first number of the periodical printed five 'letters to the editor' by representatives of various tendencies in the Russian emigration, expressing approval of the basic idea of the new periodical: the necessity of giving priority to the demand for political liberty. One of these letters came from the Marxist group, 'The Emancipation of Labour'; it was signed by Akselrod, Zasulich, and Plekhanov.

he played in the Populist movement, Mikhailovsky's thinking, while characterized by acuteness and an ability for broad generalizations, was inadequately subordinated to methodical discipline, and his political character, while unshakeable in its humanitarian purposefulness, lacked a combative revolutionary temper.

As early as 1873 (let us recall that it was in these years that Populism rejected politics and thought the 'bourgeoisie' its principal enemy), in rejecting a suggestion that he contribute to *Vperyod*, Mikhailovsky wrote Lavrov: 'I am no revolutionary; everyone to his own taste. A struggle against the old gods (i.e. the autocracy) does not occupy me because their song is sung and their downfall is a matter of time. The new gods (i.e. the bourgeoisie) are far more dangerous and in this sense worse.' In just the same way, after having changed his basic attitude towards the gods, old and new, and become a contributor to the organ of the People's Freedom, in the heat of its struggle, Mikhailovsky wrote, in his *Political Letters of a Socialist* (No. 2): 'The revolutionaries are counting on a popular uprising. That is a question of faith. I don't have that.' He advises (No. 3), as an orientation, a union with the liberals, which 'is also not terrifying if you go into it honestly and without hypocrisy, and announce to them your sacred motto, Land and Freedom. They will join you, and not you them . . . I think that many liberals are far closer to us than it seems to you.'[86]

Such are Mikhailovsky's characteristic views; they run like a red thread through all his political life. They were summed up in the letter to Alexander III he edited after the destruction of the People's Freedom. They made him the acknowledged leader of 'liberal Populism'. They dictated his articles in *Samoupravleniye*, where in raising the banner of a struggle for a constitution he insisted that success was guaranteed not by a 'party struggle' but by a 'coalition' struggle, in the union of the 'youth' with 'a society reviled by all', which towards 1 March 1881 'had proved unprepared' but which now 'would fight' (No. 1, December 1887). In putting forward the letter to Alexander III as a maximal programme of 'our wishes', he says beforehand that he is ready to be reconciled to any desired 'concrete forms for the realization of political freedom in Russia' (No. 2, May 1888). These characteristic views on the part of Mikhailovsky also explain, finally, why from the beginning of the '90s, the time of the emergence of the Marxist movement in Russia itself, it was just he who led the struggle against this new current of Russian democratic thought and made the periodical *Russkoye Bogatstvo*

(Russian Wealth), whose editor he became in 1892, the principal organ of that struggle.

3. FIRST SHOOTS OF THE WORKERS' MOVEMENT

Russian Marxism, which broke in principle with all the foundations of Populist ideology, was at the same time and above all a new stage in the revolutionary thought of the intelligentsia. Hence on the socio-political plane it felt itself to be and was in reality the historical heir of revolutionary Populism, whose last and most heroic expression was the People's Freedom.

But in distinction to all the successive currents of Russian revolutionary thought, Marxism was the first to succeed in finding the points of contact with the 'people' that the revolutionary intelligentsia had been seeking so passionately and so futilely. Only, Marxism did not find the 'people' that Populism had been looking for, and it did not find it where Populism had been looking for it. Marxism found the 'people' not in the countryside, but in the cities, in the factories and workshops; not the peasant 'people' but the workers. This new 'people', born of the development of Russian capitalism, had long since begun advertising its existence more and more insistently. But its formation as a special social group and the development of its movement had to reach a certain height before Russian Marxism could emerge from the crisis of Populist ideology, and before it could make the Russian working-class the principal object of its own revolutionary activity and the principal bulwark of its political hopes.

The emancipation of the peasants laid the foundations for the relatively swift growth of large-scale enterprises (more than 100 men). In twenty-five years, from 1865 to 1890, the number of workers in such enterprises doubled: from 706,000 to 1,432,000. But another result of the emancipation was the rapid increase in the price of grain and other primary commodities, and the establishment of a labour market based on 'free' manpower. The result was that the growth of industry was accompanied by an improvement in the material situation of only a few categories of specially trained workers, chiefly metal-workers. For the immense majority, especially for the workers in the textile industry, there was a substantial lowering of real wages, already extraordinarily low as it was. Thus, real wages went down towards 1883 by forty-three per cent for spinners, forty-seven per cent for mechanical weavers, and by a full fifty-two per cent for manual weavers. These miserable wages were substantially cut down further by the widely practised system of 'fines' for breaking factory rules.* Other conditions were no better. Thus, in the '80s the average length of the working-day in Russian industry came to twelve and a half hours; in textile factories it went as high as fifteen hours.

In 1881 the situation grew still worse – once again especially in the textile factories, which were geared to mass consumption, at a time when the chief consumer of metal was the state (the army and the railway system controlled by the government) – and an industrial recession began that lasted almost until 1887. It is understandable that the brief period of considerable industrial revival from 1878 to 1880, which was connected with the Russo-Turkish war, was marked by a wave of rather big strikes (in the twenty-nine strikes recorded for these three years as many as 35,000 workers took part) and that the principal segment of the strikers came from the textile workers in this case too. Of the strikes that took place in these three years there were two that took on a special significance: in the Petersburg New Paper-mill (March 1878 and January 1879), which lent impetus to the development of legislation protecting labour in Russia,† as did a later strike, already mentioned, at the Nikolsk Factory of Sabbas Morozov in Orckhovo, Zuyevo (January 1885).

These strikes showed that the workers were a mass force capable of collective struggle in their own interests. We have seen (Chap. 2) the reaction to the Morozov strike of the eminent government functionary K. Skalkovsky. There was a similar reaction from the most eminent government journalistic spokesman, M. Katkov, editor of the *Moskovskiye Vedomosti* (Moscow News), when the jurors of the Vladimirsk Circuit Court acquitted, in May 1886, all thirty-three 'instigators' of this strike, rejecting all 101 points of the indictment: 'A 101-gun salute rang out in honour of the working-class question, which now showed itself in Mother Russia,' was Katkov's comment on this acquittal. But that something new had 'showed itself' in the

* Up to 1886, when as a direct result of the Morozov strike (see Chap. II and below) a law was enacted allocating these fines to workers' needs, the entrepreneurs had been appropriating them.

† The first factory law in Russia was that of 1 June 1882, prohibiting children below the age of twelve from working in factories, and limiting the working-day for children between twelve and fifteen to eight hours; the second was a law of 3 June 1885 prohibiting night work in certain branches of industry for women and young people below seventeen.

Russian political arena was something that the revolutionary intelligentsia could not have helped noticing even earlier.

With all their theoretical gravitating towards the 'countryside', the overwhelming majority of the Populist intelligentsia of all shades, especially students, was always concentrated in the cities, and naturally found in the workers' *milieu* the most favourable terrain for its own activity. But it was the Lavrovites who paid the greatest attention to propaganda among the workers, as we have already noted. As early as 1873–4 the Lavrovites and Chaikovskyites organized a number of workers' clubs in Petersburg, which gave a political education to many workers who later played a major role in the revolutionary movement.* In 1875 the Lavrovite E. O. Zaslavsky founded in Odessa the first major workers' organization – the 'South Russian Union of Workers', which numbered as many as 200 members, but which was soon destroyed, not to revive until 1879 through the initiative of P. B. Akselrod. And the Moscow group of Lavrovites, active in the central industrial area under the name of 'All-Russian Social-Revolutionary Organization', made propaganda among the workers its exclusive task. The female members themselves acted as workers in the factories – the 'factory' variety of 'going to the people', the only one in the history of Populism!†

The trial of this last group, the so-called Trial of the Fifty (21 February–14 March 1877), which ended with fifteen sentences of hard labour, was, in distinction to the Trial of the 193 (18 October 1877–28 January 1878), which took place a little later, not a 'country' but a 'city' trial, concerning propaganda not among the peasants, but among the workers. Its climax was a speech by the weaver, P. A. Alekseyev, which ended with the prophecy that the time would come when 'the muscular arm of the millions of working people would be raised, and the yoke of tyranny, hedged round about by soldiers' bayonets, would shatter to dust'.

In these words of a weaver for the first time there faintly rang forth the idea that, in a precise form and as a conclusion of Marxist analysis of Russian life, was proclaimed twelve years later at the International

* Victor Obnorsky, Alexis Peterson, Semyon Volkov and others.

† The group consisted of former Zurich 'Fritsches' (see Chap. 5) – Betty Kaminsky, the Figner sisters, the Subbotin sisters, and the Lyubatovich sisters, Sophia Bardin and others – and of some young Caucasians who had also studied in Zurich (Dzhabadari, Prince Tsitsianov and others). The group was liquidated by arrests in February 1875. Before its destruction it published abroad the organ *Rabotnik* (The Worker), which was smuggled into Russia.

Socialist Congress of 1889 in Paris by Plekhanov, who predicted that 'the Russian revolution would triumph as a workers' revolution'. But awareness of the real meaning of this idea was still a long way off at that time. Even after the strike at the New Paper-mill prompted one of its active organizers, this same Plekhanov, to acknowledge that 'the question of the urban workers is being brought up automatically in spite of any *a priori* theoretical decisions', he still kept stubbornly trying to convince himself and others, as we have seen (Chap. 6), that the factory workers 'in the immense majority of instances were the same peasants as in the countryside'.

Nevertheless the mass movement of strikes not only forced the revolutionary Populists to give priority to the workers in spite of 'theoretical decisions', but it also directed the activity itself into an equally unforeseen channel. In this activity nothing could be done with 'communal' and 'artel' traditions. It made it necessary to seek ways and means within the framework of capitalist relations that could lighten the oppressiveness of capitalist exploitation. Confronted by all the might of the bureaucratic and police apparatus that defended this exploitation and used repression to disorganize the collective struggle of those being exploited, it was obliged to pass from purely 'economic' to 'political' demands. One of the fruits of this transition was the petitions addressed by the striking workers to the Heir Apparent, the future Tsar Alexander III: 'We turn to you as to a father. If our just demands are not satisfied we shall know that we have no one to put our hopes on, that no one will come to our help, and that we must rely on ourselves and on our own hands' – these concluding words of the petition, which began the process of the rupture of the working-class with Tsarism, were repeated almost verbatim a little more than a quarter of a century later, in the petition of 9 January 1905 that marked the culmination of this process.

Activity in a mass working-class movement could not help but set a certain stamp, even though it was just below the threshold of consciousness, on the whole world-view of the Populist intellectuals who took part in it. In any case it had the most powerful effect on the spiritual evolution of the Populist workers. It not only developed such figures as Peter Anisimovich Moiseyenko (1852–1923) who displayed enormous organizational gifts and a great political flair in leading the famous Morozov strike, mentioned so often above, and in the defence of the strikers in court who later, in the 1917 revolution, joined the Bolsheviks. It not only fostered hundreds and thousands of individual

Socialist workers, who towards the middle of the '90s gave Social-Democracy its first organized leaders. It also gave a direct impetus to the formation of the first workers' organization that could be called Social-Democratic because of its basic programmatic principles – the 'Northern Union of Russian Workers'.[87]

The establishment of a completely autonomous workers' organization, whose members constitutionally could only be workers, marks a certain stage in the development of the reciprocal relationships between the advanced workers and the revolutionary intelligentsia that had trained them.

For the intelligentsia the working-class *milieu* was primarily the object of propagandistic work. It was, to be sure, an object that acquired such paramount importance as the hopes set on the countryside were destroyed that after the collapse of Land and Freedom, for instance, both the fractions it broke up into thought it vital to publish special organs for workers: the People's Freedom published the *Rabochaya Gazeta* (The Workers' News) and the Party for Total Reapportionment published *Zerno* (The Seed). But the Populist conception did not ascribe to the workers any independent role in the revolution.

The point appeared in a different light in the eyes of the small but politically highly-trained strata of the advanced workers. The conditions of their lives, labour, and collective struggle for specially 'workers' ' interests very soon began to nurture in them a feeling of a certain social (in later Marxist terminology, class) separateness. Together with this feeling ideas and tendencies began to spring up among them that could not be harmonized with the Populism of the intelligentsia even while they themselves, in their own consciousness, still thought themselves 'Populists'. Thus, at the very inception of the working-class movement a question was raised in an embryonic form: 'workers for revolution or revolution for workers?' which in later years played such a role in the polemic of Marxism with the Populist epigones. Together with this question, still another question, once again in embryonic form, acquired a primary importance in the internal discussions of the Marxist movement itself. This was the question of the mutual relationship between the working-class and the 'intelligentsia', which, as we have seen, had arisen in Russia as a separate social group and for a long time retained the traits of this social separateness.

Peter Alekseyev, in his famous speech, spoke with a feeling of ardent gratitude of the 'youthful intellectuals' as the single 'good friend who had stretched out a fraternal hand' to the workers. But he and his fellow-prisoners at the trial could scarcely have been clearly aware that he was turning upside down all the traditional Populist ideas about the revolution and the role of the proletariat in it, when he said that 'it only remained for the Russian workers to rely on themselves', and that it was just their 'muscular arm' that was going to shatter the 'yoke of tyranny'. In just the same way it could hardly have been clear to anyone that Alekseyev was turning upside down all ideas of the mutual relations between workers and intellectuals when instead of an expression of assurance that the workers would follow the intelligentsia up to the very triumph of the revolution he maintained that on the contrary the intelligentsia 'would march inseparably together with us', the workers.

For an advanced worker the Populist intellectual was not, of course, someone from a different world, one of the 'gentry', as he sometimes seemed to the grey peasant mass in spite of all his 'love for the people'. From the very beginning the advanced workers strove to place their relations with the intelligentsia on the basis of complete parity of rights. Plekhanov, in his reminiscences of 'the Russian Worker in the Revolutionary Movement'[89], relates that a worker as distinguished as Stepan Khalturin 'blazed up like a fire' when 'some intellectual made a reference to the workers that was not wholly flattering', and that the 'Kazan' demonstration too [see above] was the result of the desire of the workers to 'make their own demonstration' and by its 'sharply revolutionary character completely eclipse' the demonstration made by 'intellectuals' that same year of 1876 at the funeral of Chernyshev, a student who had died in prison (in the Trial of the 193). This same warily jealous relationship about parity of rights also echoes in the letter the Northern Union of Russian Workers sent in response to the criticism of its programme. This appeared in No. 4 of the organ of Land and Freedom (see below). Noting with gratitude the 'rather unexpected' comradely tone of the criticism, the authors of the letter speak with bitterness of the 'many' who did not believe that the programme had been drawn up by the workers themselves, but considered it the 'handiwork of the intellectuals': 'that is the extent to which they mistrust our own powers, that is the extent to which the habit of regarding us as incompetent cattle is engrained in many people'.

What made the authors of the letter particularly indignant was that in the criticism of the programme many 'had gone so far as to consider the demand made by us, the workers, for political freedom as simply absurd and irrelevant to the question of filling the stomach'. But 'the expression of such thoughts means sneering directly at our minds and ascribing our solution of the social question to our stomachs alone'. The authors of the letter added with pride that such an attitude would have been explicable 'if we had drawn up our programme somewhere in Podlip.* . . . But the great thing is that we have already left that life.'

A living proof of the degree to which the Petersburg workers, at meetings of 23 and 30 December 1878, which gave the Northern Union organizational shape and confirmed its programme, had really left far behind the primitive conditions of the overwhelming majority of the Russian peasantry of the time, was the identity of the initiators of the Union itself – the carpenter Stepan Khalturin, mentioned so often before, and the locksmith Victor Obnorsky. The latter, who had passed through Chaikovskyite workers' circles, had afterwards stayed a long time abroad. There he had become familiar with the Western European working-class movement and with various fractions of the Russian revolutionaries. He had come close to the Tkachovites, from whom he got a printing-press and type for an illegal printing-shop when he returned to Russia in 1878. His experience abroad set its stamp on the whole programme of the Union. The emotional appeal of Lassalle's speeches about the working class as the foundation of the 'church of the future' can be heard in those paragraphs of the programme that speak to the workers of the 'moral strength' they need, of their 'containing all the strength and importance of the country', of their being the 'flesh and blood of the state', of 'all other classes' existing through them. Adapting itself to the forms of thought of the working-class mass, the programme characterizes the Union as the 'apostle of gospel truth'. The programme uses an out-and-out paraphrase of the Communist Manifesto by Marx and Engels in response to the reproaches that the Socialist workers 'corrupt the world, destroy the family, trample on property, desecrate religion': 'On the contrary, we are going to renew the world, regenerate the family, establish property as it ought to be, and resurrect the great teaching of Christ about brotherhood and equality.' There is a manifest point of contact with Tkachov's ideas, finally, when the programme – for the first time within the framework of an organized Populist movement, and anticipating its evolution into the People's Freedom –

* The name of a remote Ural village, whose primitive inhabitants are the heroes of a novel by Reshetnikov, *Podlipovtsy* 'The Podlippians'.

includes political struggle among the Union's most important tasks.

To be sure, the intellectual link of the new organization to 'Tkachovism' is limited to this point of contact. It does not motivate the necessity of political struggle in a Tkachovite way when it says that 'the resolution of the social question is ensured above all by the political struggle'. It does not express its political tasks in a Tkachovite way when it formulates a series of fragmentary political demands – freedom of speech, press and assembly, abolition of caste rights and privileges, the introduction of a militia, etc. and supplements this political 'minimum programme' by an equally fragmentary programme of the defence of the socio-economic interests of the proletariat. And it is quite definitely not Tkachovite in the way it approaches the methods of struggle for political freedom when, in clarifying the meaning of the formation of the Union it says that its initiators had 'come to the idea of organizing an all-Russian union of workers that, by cementing together the scattered forces of the urban and rural labouring population and explaining to it its own interests, aims and aspirations, would serve as an adequate bulwark in the struggle against its lack of social rights and give it the inner organizational strength necessary for the successful conduct of the struggle'.

A working-class organization that made its central objective 'the interests, aims and aspirations' of the working-class and from this point of view carried on a mass economic and political struggle – such was the fundamental idea of the Union's programme. 'Through an untiring and active propaganda among its own brethren, the Northern Union hopes to attain results that will advance the workers' estate at home too and force it to start speaking of itself, of its own rights.' It is only too obvious that this idea was never borrowed from Tkachov. The programme itself, however, indicates its source when it says: 'Our western brothers have already raised the banner of the emancipation of the millions – it remains for us only to join them,' and declares that the Union 'by virtue of its objective is in close conjunction with the Social-Democratic Party of the West' – an expression that as Martov rightly says could refer only to the German Social-Democracy, which had an 'almost reactionary' reputation among the Bakuninite-minded Russian Socialists of that time.* The

* An obvious borrowing from the 'Lassalle' wing of the German Social-Democracy was the demand put forward in the Union's programme for free state credit for producers' associations. For obvious reasons this 'Lassalle' idea was the most acceptable for the Russian Socialists, with their then attitude. It

idea of a struggle for political freedom, and under the aegis of solidarity with the Western European Social-Democracy at that, was so unusual for the era that Land and Freedom immediately reacted to the programme of the Union with a critical essay written by Dmitri Klements,[88] which was published in the same No. 4 (20 February 1879) that printed the already quoted leading article by Plekhanov about the role of the urban workers 'in a combat Populist revolutionary organization'.

The article in the organ of Land and Freedom noted the 'significant fact' of the formation of the Union and the publication of its programme as a proof that 'Socialism had found in the Russian proletariat not only convinced partisans but also people who were capable, with no outside help, of organizing themselves into a fighting party'. The article went on to criticize the 'theoretical part of the programme' for lacking a 'consistently developed system of views', and having 'a mixture of the programmes of various Western socialist parties': the 'denial of the state and the demand for communal autonomy puts our comrades into the camp of the socialist-revolutionaries, such as we ourselves would have wanted our comrades the members of the Northern Union to be, while the following paragraphs of the programme are taken directly from the catechism of the German Social-Democrats'. The programme is reproached for devoting too much space to political freedom and being too categorical in deciding the question of its positive significance, while saying nothing of the significance of 'propaganda by facts'. Finally: 'the clauses of the programme referring to the urban workers are worked out in great detail (according to the programme of the German Social-Democrats) . . . while agrarian questions are left untouched'.

All this, however, can be remedied, in the opinion of the author of the article: the Union's programme is only an initial experiment; they will be able to correct these political errors in the future, if its authors 'don't fall asleep on their laurels but go forward'. 'What is far more serious are the mistakes in the organizational part of the programme.' The author of the article passes on to a criticism of this 'organizational part', which makes the point that while 'candidates are accepted for membership on the recommendation of two members, the conditions are not indicated under which a person can be recom-

---

later found a place in the first draft of the programme of the Marxist 'Emancipation of Labour' Group.

mended' . . . 'Is it enough for him to be known as a Socialist and a virtuous man, or should the candidate pass through a certain trial to prove, not in words but in deeds, his devotion to his organization and his ability to work on behalf of the cause? . . . In our opinion what is important for a young organization is not the number of members but . . . their solidarity.'

This concentration on the organizational question and this dependence not on quantity but on 'quality' was symptomatic of the transition that was taking place around this time, from Land and Freedom to the People's Freedom, from propaganda among the 'people' to the political terror of the 'revolutionary minority'. But it had far deeper significance as an indication of the acute contradictions in whose clutches the mass working-class movement in Russia had to struggle ever since its inception.

To a certain extent problems of the mutual relations between the 'vanguard' and the 'mass' arise before every mass working-class movement. But in Russia they arose with special acuteness from the very beginning – both because the cultural and political distance was already tremendous between the thin layer of advanced workers and the newcomers from the only recently feudal-minded countryside (the 'Podlippians'!), and because the conditions of the political régime forcibly drove the workers' 'vanguard' into the tight network of 'conspiratorial' organizations and made it very difficult for it to have any organizational, political, or cultural effect on the backward masses of its own class. It was on this question (see below) that the Russian Social-Democracy was to split up into Bolshevism and Menshevism. The disagreements on the organizational question were to become a red thread running through the entire history of Bolshevism and Menshevism, uninterruptedly interwoven with their differences on programmatic, political and tactical questions.

Hence it was highly characteristic that the 'organizational question' arose acutely on the very threshold of the mass workers' movement in Russia. For the People's Freedom of the morrow it was just this question that was the object of the most 'serious' disagreement with the first revolutionary cell. Nor was it less characteristic that in the Union's reply, which Martov rightly calls 'one of the most interesting documents in the history of the revolution of social thought in Russia', and which was printed in the fifth and last number of the Land and Freedom organ (8 April 1879), it was on just this question that its leaders proved to be most unyielding.

'Your apprehensions,' they wrote, 'are unfounded. It is true that with a substantial membership it is not so easy to get on close terms; for many the very goals it has been decided to strive for are not so clear, nor, finally, can decisions be executed in such harmony. But our views of organization are such that quantitative superiority is not supposed to hinder the quality of the energetic and active members. Our paramount aim is to organize the workers' forces; because of this the shadings of opinion, as well as the character and direction of Socialist activity, which in the last analysis incline towards exactly the same thing, should not have any special significance for us.' Their answer to the reproach of having forgotten 'the propaganda of the facts' is directly connected with this. 'With the weakness of organization that is still present, with the shortage of energetic combative forces, our activity will have the character of propaganda and peaceful agitation among the workers and peasants. But by this we do not at all mean that a more or less open struggle, such as active participation and agitation during strikes, is excluded for the time being from our programme of activity. On the contrary, we must take advantage of every appropriate occasion, every incident where we might be able openly to declare our strength, individually as well as collectively.'

Then the authors of this reply begin a very energetic defence of the political part of their programme as well. They vigorously protest against being reproached for an eclectic combination of views of 'different shadings of the revolutionary party of the West' and 'a mixture of Socialist demands and constitutionalist demands'. Such an amalgam would be inadmissible if it were contradictory, but 'for our part we see nothing illogical in it . . . We rally round, organize, and take up the banner of the social overturn, so close to our heart, and move on to the path of struggle. But we also know that political liberty can safeguard us and our organization against the highhandedness of the authorities. . . . So for the sake of husbanding our strength and for the speediest success we demand that liberty.'

But this position of the principled defence of the proposition embedded in the programme – 'it is political liberty above all that ensures the resolution of the social question' – is not sustained to the end. In referring to the preponderant mood of the revolutionary intelligentsia, the authors of the reply begin by minimizing the principled significance of the demand for political liberty, declaring that 'it is not so difficult to calculate on its realization', since it is 'according to the taste of the chatterboxes (that is, the bourgeois liberals) – those figures in the future all-Russian talk-fest (that is, parliament)'. And they conclusively abandon their principled position, though with obvious reluctance, when they continue: 'But let it not be thought that in fact political liberty has entered into our own plans and that we have given it as honourable a place as we have our basic demand. No, we merely say that it would be better that way, that this liberty would nevertheless be a very important condition for the speediest overturn and the more or less intelligent solution of the social question. Intelligence in the movement, as you know yourselves, is in its turn an extremely important condition for the desired issue of the revolution.'

But as an example of an inadequate grasp of principle the explanations given by the leaders of the Union, in response to the legitimate reproach of their having forgotten the agrarian question, are still more characteristic: 'We have really given very special study to a review of our urban situation, we have steeped ourselves extremely thoroughly in the spirit of the various programmes of the West, and now it has turned out that we have left only a very small place for our own countryside. But let us be excused for this blunder, all the more since forgetting the countryside is not the work of our minds and feelings. For us the peasant and his native woods are just as dear to us as the factory-worker, and the amelioration of the lives of the former is even more important.' How close this last phrase is to the idea that the workers are just the 'same peasants' for whom factory work is merely temporary 'seasonal labour', and how remote it is, on the contrary, from the contention of the programme that it is the workers who sustain 'all other classes' and from the grand objectives of 'renovating the world' with which it confronted the 'workers' estate' and called upon it to join 'our Western brothers!'

It is, of course, quite out of place to seek any explanation of the intellectual shakiness of such people as Stepan Khalturin or Victor Obnorsky, who in deeds proved both ability for independent political thought and stubbornness in striving for the goal, in inadequate strength of character. Nor is it possible to look for it only in the spiritual crisis that the Land and Freedom movement happened to be undergoing at just this time and that presaged its imminent collapse. This crisis, of course, could not help but affect the working-class initiators of the Northern Union who belonged to Land and Freedom. Nevertheless, what was decisive was that, in the very conditions of the cause they had taken up, occasions very soon began occurring that undermined their initial optimism and their faith in a swift success.

We have already noted that in the decades directly following the emancipation of the peasants, which were characterized by the rapid development of heavy industry, real wages and the general working conditions of the overwhelming majority of the workers, especially the textile factory workers, showed a basic tendency to deteriorate, and that it was only the position of the trained 'workshop' workers – metal-workers and others – that improved.* On the basis of this difference in material standards there arose a proportionately far stronger difference in cultural and political standards between the 'factory' and the 'workshop' workers.

The textile worker, too, of course, freed himself relatively quickly from the primitivism of rural life. 'The factory-worker,' says Plekhanov, 'who has worked in the city for several years feels ill at ease in the country and goes back to it reluctantly. . . . Rural customs and institutions become unendurable for a person whose personality has begun evolving even a little.'[89] But while the cultural level of the general mass of 'workshop' workers was substantially higher than that of those in the factories, the cultural development and erudition of that thin layer of specially trained workers who had been differentiated out of this 'workshop' mass might have been envied by many students, as Plekhanov testifies. Nothing depicts so clearly the cultural rupture between the workers' *élite* and the overwhelming mass of the Russian 'people' of the time – peasants and workers equally – as the account by Plekhanov of an attempt made in 1876 by Land and Freedom to involve a number of Petersburg workers, highly trained both in their craft and culturally, in 'going to the people', and to send them to Saratov Province: 'These were experienced people, sincerely devoted to and profoundly imbued with Populist views. But their attempts to set themselves up in the countryside led to nothing. After roving about the villages with the intention of looking for a suitable place to settle down (at which some of them were taken to be foreigners), they shrugged their shoulders at the whole business and finished by returning to Saratov, where they established contacts among the local workers. No matter how astounded we were by this alienation from the "people" of its urban children, the fact was

* In the twenty years between 1862 and 1883 the real wages of the miners rose by thirty per cent and of carpenters by thirty-one per cent, etc. Among locksmiths only was there an average drop of ten per cent.

evident, and we had to abandon the idea of involving workers in a purely peasant business.'

It was just this workers' *élite* that the founders of the Northern Union belonged to. It was almost exclusively from it that they managed to recruit the two hundred charter members at the very beginning, and the 150–200 candidates who were marked out for acceptance in the future. In the provinces, according to Plekhanov, workers' circles (in Rostov, Saratov, Kiev, Kharkov) were 'far more . . . mixed than the Petersburg workers. There were members who in their cultivation and the high standard of requirements did not fall behind the Petersburg workshop workers, but side by side there were also completely "grey" workers, sometimes illiterate.' Such a motley composition naturally made these provincial circles not very suited for the organized political actions that the Northern Union began its work with. In its turn the great cultural homogeneity of the Union that isolated it from the broad masses of workers led it to enter into more or less intimate contact with them only during their tempestuous 'movements'. The thin threads that extended from the *élite* during the wave of strikes that rolled through the Petersburg factories in 1878–9 were snapped off the moment the wave subsided. The result was that the growth of the Union stopped, and by the end of 1879, after being founded with such hopes, it had already collapsed.

The Northern Union collapsed not only because the arrests following provocations tore away from it such eminent figures as Obnorsky, Peterson and others. It collapsed primarily because in the conditions described above it proved to be still impossible to create that organic bond with the masses of the workers its founders had been dreaming of, when they had said, in addressing their programme to these masses: 'You have no organizations, no ideas you can be led by, and finally no moral support, so necessary for a concerted resistance to the enemy. But we, the workers who have organized the Northern Union, will give you this guiding idea, give you moral support in a fusion of our interests, and finally give you the organization you need.'

The fate of the Union was determined by the fact that for the time being the masses of the workers did not respond, nor could they have responded to this appeal. The objective of 'advancing the workers' estate in Russia too' as an independent political force closely linked to 'our Western brothers' proved to be as yet unrealizable.

There was an historical paradox involved here. Khalturin and other advanced workers had evolved to the level of an idea that meant struggling for political liberty, which they cherished above all else. It was they who rushed headlong into the People's Freedom movement of the intelligentsia that had been disappointed in the masses.* Meanwhile such Populist intellectuals as Plekhanov and Akselrod, who had learned to appreciate in the workers' movement precisely its collective power above all else, had to pass through the stillborn Party of Total Reapportionment in order to evolve a new understanding of the bond between Socialism and political struggle, in a formulation that made them the spiritual ancestors of the Russian Social-Democratic movement. The paradox was no accident.

Almost fifteen years had to go by, however, before the process of formation and cultural elevation of the working-class achieved a level that made it possible for a movement to emerge from the confines of small circles and make itself known as a practical and viable political force. Meanwhile, the Northern Union proved to be merely an historical rehearsal of this coming movement, but a rehearsal that was all the more important and noteworthy since, as we have remarked, there were signs in it in an embryonic form of all the basic problems this movement had to take into account in future. The Union also gave impetus to the vast theoretical work that, in the conditions of the stagnation described above, laid the intellectual foundations of the future Russian Social-Democracy and that constituted the historic task of the Emancipation of Labour Group.

4. THE EMANCIPATION OF LABOUR GROUP

The founders of the Emancipation of Labour Group were the same members of the Party for Total Reapportionment who were in Switzerland: Plekhanov, Akselrod, Zasulich, Deich, who were joined by the young V. Ignatov, the son of a landowner, who gave the group some material support but who soon died. Of the leaders of the crumbling Total Reapportionment only Stefanovich went over to the People's Freedom party.

* 'Alexander II must be killed by a worker' was Khalturin's reason for moving into the People's Freedom: 'Don't let the Russian Tsars think that the workers are fools who don't understand their own true importance for the people.' After the unsuccessful explosion in the Winter Palace Khalturin organized the assassination of the Procurator Strelnikov in Odessa, on 18 March 1882, and on 22 March of the same year was executed together with his accomplice Zhelvakov.

In an announcement of the publication of a 'Library of Contemporary Socialism', dated Geneva, 25 September 1883, the members of the Group declared that they 'were definitively breaking with the old anarchist tendencies' and recognized that 'the struggle against absolutism is an historical objective common to Russian Socialists and other progressive parties in Russia'. But this struggle, said the Announcement, 'will not bring the Socialists any possible influence in future if the fall of the absolute monarchy finds the Russian working-class in an undeveloped condition, indifferent to social questions and lacking any understanding of the correct solution of these questions in their own interests'. Hence 'Socialist propaganda amidst those strata of the labouring population of Russia that are most receptive to it' constitutes 'one of the most serious obligations of the Russian Socialist intelligentsia', and for such propaganda a popular 'workers' literature' must be created. 'But before setting about the creation of such a literature, our revolutionary intelligentsia must itself acquire a contemporary Socialist world-view after rejecting the old traditions that are out of harmony with that. Hence a criticism of programmes and doctrines prevalent in its midst must occupy an important place in our Socialist literature.' And the Library had to serve just these two objectives: the popularization of 'the idea of scientific Socialism through the translation into Russian of the most important works of Marx and Engels' and the publication of 'original compositions', on the one hand, and the criticism of the traditional views of the revolutionary intelligentsia and 'the working out of the most important questions of Russian social life from the point of view of scientific socialism and the interests of the labouring population of Russia', on the other.

But beyond these propagandistic and theoretical objectives, the Group at its very inception also set itself broader aims. The Announcement asserted that 'the destructive activity of our revolutionaries was not complemented by the creation of any elements for the future working-class Socialist party in Russia'. It was the organization of the Russian working-class into a special party with a definite socio-political programme that was the goal the Group set for itself. But, being aware of the actual composition of the Russian working-class movement of the time, at the given moment it demanded of the Socialist intelligentsia no more than work 'on the organization at least of the most eminent representatives' of the working-class, that is, the creation of propagandistic workers' circles and societies of the type of the Northern Union, as the first seeds of the future workers' party.

In direct contrast with the tendency of the Populists of the latest school to counterpose Russian Socialism to European, the first Russian Marxists strove to underline its unbreakable ties with European Socialism. In this respect they were returning to the traditions of the progenitors of Russian democratic and Socialist thought, beginning with Herzen and Chernyshevsky and ending with Lavrov and Bakunin. But in contrast to them, and for the first time in the history of that thought, they formulated the problem of Russian Socialism not as a problem of the destiny of the Russian peasant commune, but as the same problem of the ideology and movement of the industrial proletariat that Socialism was in Europe.

The basic idea of the new group could be characterized in one word – the 'europeanization' of Russian Socialism. It gave back to Russian Socialism that European, 'German' costume that Kravchinsky and his friends had tried to remove. Only, the model for this 'costume' was now no longer taken from the pseudo-German theory of Bakuninite anarchism, now sinking into decline, but from the practice of the most powerful, most 'Marxist' workers' party in Europe, which had undergone a process of tempestuous growth – the German. This circumstance had the most fundamental significance for the whole history of Russian Marxism and Russian Social-Democracy in all its fractions and ethnic groupings.

The German Social-Democracy had been treated by the Russian revolutionaries only a short while before with disdain;* now, illuminated by the aureole of its heroic struggle in the vice of an exceptional law against Socialists, it impressed them more and more by its moral feeling, intellectual depth, and organizational power. We have seen the influence it had on the workers who founded the Northern Union. It left a still more powerful imprint on the education of the Russian Marxists. And from then on, ever since its inception, Russian Social-Democracy for three decades developed in the most powerful spiritual and political dependence on it. It was only the voting of war credits by the German Social-Democrats in August 1914 and the 'patriotic' support they showed the government of the Kaiser that abruptly snapped off this dependence. The immense majority of Russian Socialists considered this conduct an unexpected and

* According to Akselrod the very name 'Emancipation of Labour' was taken by the Group because it could not make up its mind to call itself 'Social-Democratic' straight out for fear of being rejected by the intelligentsia.

inexplicable, but therefore all the more shameful, 'betrayal' by the German Social-Democracy, not only of the principles of international Socialism but also of all its own past.

But while Russian Marxism developed under the influence of German Social-Democracy and was the bearer of the idea of European working-class Socialism in Russia, that does not at all mean that it was an alien plant on Russian soil. On the contrary, it was a natural and indispensable product of the social and spiritual development of Russia. It was out of the interaction of two factors that Social-Democracy was born in backward Russia: the first factor was the initial sprouting of the class movement of the workers, and the second was the final phase of decades of spiritual development of the revolutionary intelligentsia. The personal and political traits of its two chief architects, Akselrod and Plekhanov, even at the very inception of Russian Marxism, may be thought to embody this dualism in its history; it made itself felt throughout its entire subsequent career.

Paul Borisovich Akselrod (1850–1928) was born into a poor, one might say pauper, Jewish family. As he relates in his reminiscences,[40] it was only his poverty that he was obligated to for having been able to be given a college (*Gimnaziya*) education: the Jews were obliged – in the interests of 'russification' – to send a certain number of Jewish children into Russian government schools, and the rich masters of the Orthodox Jewish communities preferred to lay this obligation on the children of the poor. The traits of the semi-proletarianized *milieu* Akselrod was born and grew up in, and remained tied to for many long years, also explain the path by which he came to a revolutionary *milieu* and through that to Marxism.

The starting-point of his quest was the physical and moral sufferings, the material and spiritual destitution of his surroundings. He took up Socialism primarily emotionally.

The speeches of Lassalle, whom he might have met in '70–'71, made a moving impression on him through their emotional side. In Lassalle's 'church of the future' he saw a promise of that happy social order in which all the evil that weighed on his kinsmen, the pauperized masses, would be overcome, and in which, as he later wrote Plekhanov, people, turned into a 'race of gods on earth', would 'enjoy consciousness and self-consciousness'. But these 'ideological' enjoyments were a thing of the future. Having grown up in the depths of the people, Akselrod knew by personal experience how cruel and inert social relations are, how hard it is for a pauper to struggle against them, and how high a price he must pay for every step forward. Hence his attention was absorbed immediately by the question of the paths leading to the cherished goal of liberation. The practise of the German Social-Democracy, which was so evidently elevating the labouring masses spiritually, infected him with enthusiasm far more quickly than the theory of Marxism this practice was based on.

The transition from concrete social struggle to theoretical generalization was the road that led Akselrod to Marxism. It was the working-class meetings in Berlin that made a most powerful impression on him – Akselrod himself described it as 'enthusiasm' – during his first trip abroad (1874). During his second trip abroad (1876–8) as an orthodox anarchist, he systematically visited German Social-Democratic workers' meetings in Geneva and fell into raptures over workers' holidays as a 'prototype of life in the future socialist society'. In 1878 he published, in the Bakuninite *Obshchina* a series of articles on 'The Lessons of the German Social-Democracy', in which he subjected it to an acute anarchist analysis. But even in the introduction to these articles he declared that for the given time, as long as a 'more revolutionary [i.e. anarchist] fraction' had not yet appeared on the historical arena in Germany, the German Social-Democracy was 'relatively' a socialist-revolutionary force; later on, in his reminiscences, he found himself forced to admit that 'even in the course of my work on these articles I was unconsciously infected by Social-Democratic heresies'.

This 'infection' made itself very noticeably felt in 1879, when Akselrod returned to Russia. The same political demands (universal, equal, direct and secret voting, freedom of assembly and speech etc.) were introduced into the programme of the South Russian Workers' Union he revived as had been introduced in their time into the programme of the Northern Union – only, 'in order to calm a Bakuninite conscience', these demands figured under the heading of 'grounds for agitation'. These same 'grounds for agitation', supplemented by a broad catalogue of demands concerning the protection of labour, were also introduced by Akselrod into the draft programme he wrote for the Party of Total Reapportionment, whose very name he proposed to change to 'Party of Socialist Federalists'.* This Social-

* The founders of Total Reapportionment, who were in Geneva at the time (Plekhanov, Zasulich, Deich, Stefanovich), were against Akselrod's plans. 'This is not Populism, but Social-Democracy' they told a woman delegate who had been sent to them to negotiate a new programme.

Democratic 'infection' was expressed even more obviously in a speech made by Akselrod at an international Socialist congress in Khur, where he appeared as a 'Russian guest', in June 1880, after he had to leave Russia again.

It was in this way, step by step, 'unconsciously', that Akselrod became a Social-Democrat. It was only in 1883, upon reading the Foreword to Marx's book, *A Critique of Political Economy*, that he definitely became a Marxist. It is typical of Akselrod's whole cast of mind that what made the greatest impression on him in this famous Foreword were those 'ideas about the magnificent consequences of the worldwide victory of socialism' evoked by 'Marx's concluding remark that with the termination of the capitalist phase of the evolution of human societies and the emergence of the socialist phase the prehistoric period of the existence of mankind will end and its completely conscious, really historical life will begin'.

These traits of Akselrod's early political career make it understandable why in the future his thought was primarily concentrated on questions of tactics and organization and why for succeeding generations of Russian Social-Democrats he became the guardian of the finest moral traditions of the revolutionary movement. But just then, while the theoretical grounding of Russian Marxism was in the foreground, the principal activity fell to Plekhanov's lot. His development into a Marxist took a completely different path from Akselrod's.

Akselrod had risen into the *milieu* of the revolutionary intelligentsia from the very depths of the semi-proletarianized masses. It might be said that George Valentinovich Plekhanov (1857–1918) was a native member of that *milieu*. Son of a small landowner in Tambov Province, and a student at the Petersburg Mining College, by 1875 he had already begun, at the age of eighteen, to take part in the revolutionary movement; thanks to his passionate temperament, intellectual acumen, and literary and oratorical gifts, he suddenly moved forward into one of the first places. His activity in Land and Freedom and the Party of Total Reapportionment has already been commented on several times, especially the leading part he played in their literary enterprises.

In contrast to Akselrod, a man of revolutionary practice, Plekhanov was from his earliest years a man of theory and of generalizing thought. The many-sidedness of his intellectual interests moved him to a constant broadening of his knowledge: political economy, sociology, history, philosophy, literature, art – everything became an object for him of zealous study. He became incontestably one of the most educated Russians of his time; he rightly takes the place of the final literary spokesman of the Russian intelligentsia in that brilliant progression initiated by Herzen and Belinsky. The methodical profundity of his generalizing thought enabled him to understand more clearly and earlier than others the significance of the new elements and new forms of social evolution: we have seen that, while still in Land and Freedom, he was the first to observe that 'in spite of *a priori* theoretical decisions' it was life itself that advanced the 'question of the worker in the cities'. But these same intellectual traits of his made him extremely demanding theoretically. They set the stamp of rationalism and a certain conservatism on all his political thinking, making him cling stubbornly to any system of views once taken up, until he managed to work himself up to another equally harmonious and rounded off system. At the Voronyozh congress it was he alone who did not enter into any compromise with the future People's Freedom Party. He left the congress alone, as an irreconcilable Populist anarchist. But he also stubbornly defended the Populist theories of the Total Reapportionment, as we have just noted, even when in fact they were already being definitely contradicted by the Total Reapportionment practices, which inclined towards 'Social-Democratism'. He came to Marxism with far more spiritual resistance and came to it in a completely different way, it might be said by the reverse of the way that Akselrod had 'unconsciously' come to it.

In Akselrod's intellectual development 'ideology' was a sunlit height beckoning to him, which he slowly climbed up to from out of the gloomy depths of ignorance his native *milieu* was stagnating in. For Plekhanov 'ideology' was a native element. Russian 'social thought' in its latest attainments was the starting-point of his creative activity, which ultimately led him to Marxism through an independent analysis of German and French philosophy, the history of the French revolution, the creations of the great utopians of Socialism, the works of classical political economy, and the works of Marx and Engels. The elaboration of a Marxist world-view was the beginning of Plekhanov as a Social-Democrat. It was only afterwards that this new world-view was applied to the study of Russian life, to questions of social and political struggle and of the Russian and international workers' movement. In distinction to Akselrod, Plekhanov's political thought did not work its way up to the top from the bottom – from practice to ideology – but from the top down – to questions of practice from an ideology that kept growing richer and more refined.

A basic familiarity with Marx's doctrine can already be seen in the articles by the twenty-two-year-old Plekhanov on *The Law of Economic Development of Society and the Tasks of Socialism in Russia* which appeared in Nos. 3 and 4 of the Land and Freedom organ for 1879; in No. 4 references are also made to the growing importance of the 'question of the city worker'. But his first unmistakably Marxist work was the foreword to the Russian translation of the *Communist Manifesto*, which was published in 1882. This was followed in 1883 by the pamphlet 'Socialism and the Political Struggle',[90] which appeared as the first issue of the Library of Contemporary Socialism. It subjected the theoretical principles of Populism to Marxist criticism and revision; it seemed to be, as it were, a manifesto of the Emancipation of Labour Group, which had only just been founded. In 1884, in a book, *Our Differences*,[91] Plekhanov gave a brilliant analysis of the socio-economic development of Russia; it struck at the very root of the Populist world-view and for the first time laid a firm scientific foundation underneath Russian Marxism. In 1895, finally, as the last link in this theoretical labour, he published a book under the pseudonym of N. Beltov called *On the Question of the Evolution of the Monist View of History*, which played a colossal role in the spiritual and political development of the Russian intelligentsia.* In this book Plekhanov gives a Marxist criticism of the philosophical subjectivism of Populist sociology, whose most luminous exponent of the time was Mikhailovsky. This crowned his labours on the theoretical groundwork of Russian Marxism not only as a political tendency but also as a harmonious and systematically rounded off world-view.

Our Differences was an answer to the criticism that the pamphlet *Socialism and the Political Struggle* had been subjected to in the pages of the *Vestnik* of the People's Freedom by L. Tikhomirov, one of the two members of the Executive Committee† who after 1 March 1881 had managed to flee abroad and were active in the name of this famous organization. Though polemical in its form, Plekhanov's book nevertheless ended with an expression of sympathy for the revolutionary activity of the People's Freedom Party, and an appeal to

* The book came out in Russia 'legally'. The censorship of the time explains both the pseudonym and the cumbersome title of the book.

† The other was M. N. Oshanina (Olovennikova).

the 'young members' to reflect on the fact that 'an unconditional rupture with its present [i.e. Populist] theories and a transition to Marxism were an indispensable condition for the success of that activity'. After the Party of Total Reapportionment had rejected any absolutely negative attitude towards political struggle, there vanished the impassable barrier that had previously divided them from the People's Freedom. The summons to the 'young members' of the People's Freedom Party was only a natural inference from the efforts that the Party of Total Reapportionment had been making for three or four years – first towards the reunification of all tendencies and fractions of Russian Socialism, then for the assembling under the banner of Marxism of the remnants of all the shattered organizations.

By 1880 negotiations with P. Lavrov and the People's Freedom Party had already led to the founding of the Russian Social-Revolutionary Library. L. G. Gartman, P. L. Lavrov, and N. A. Morozov were elected as temporary editors. But a voluminous 'announcement' of it was written by Plekhanov; and his translation of *The Communist Manifesto* was published by it with the aforementioned Marxist foreword. Plekhanov was put on the editorial board of the *Vestnik* of the People's Freedom, which Lavrov and Tikhomirov started publishing in the autumn of 1883. No. 1 of this periodical printed a completely 'Marxist' article of Akselrod's on 'Socialism and the Petty Bourgeoisie',[93] and an article by Plekhanov on the historian A. P. Shchapov, ending with a prediction that a new period was beginning for the 'social-revolutionary party' – a 'social-democratic period'. But even the article 'Socialism and the Political Struggle' originally meant by Plekhanov for this same number of the *Vestnik* of the People's Freedom, had appeared in the form of a pamphlet published by the newly-founded Emancipation of Labour Group. For it was at this time that all negotiations about unification were broken off.

Formally the possibility of unification had been broken off by the unexpected refusal of Tikhomirov and Oshanina to accept the Party of Total Reapportionment into the People's Freedom Party as a separate group. But, in fact, as quickly became clear, the causes of the rupture lay much deeper. *Emigré* Populism, which (in the person of L. Tikhomirov and M. Oshanina) had been about to come out in the wrappings of an extreme 'Jacobinism', very soon, especially after Tikhomirov's secession in 1887 (he turned into an apologist for extremist autocratic reaction) embarked on a path of the same liberal transformation that its 'legal' twin had taken. Populism died as a revolutionary doctrine, and it proved impossible to throw a bridge between it and the nascent ideology of the Russian revolution – Marxism.* Russian Marxism was destined to evolve not in reunion with Populism but in a bitter struggle against it. The appeal of *Our Differences* to the 'young members' of the People's Freedom proved to be the swan-song of the dreams of unification.[92] It was not until ten years later that the question of the practical unification with the Social-Democrats was once again brought up by the Petersburg group of young members of the People's Freedom, who had taken into their ranks the last epigones of the People's Freedom, the majority of whom had theoretically gone over to Social-Democracy a long time since, and who very quickly dissolved in it completely.

While acknowledging the historic services of the People's Freedom in having made the struggle against the autocracy the primary revolutionary objective, and following its example in this respect, the former Party of Total Reapportionment strove at the same time to put the political struggle itself on a completely new basis. The problem of combining the struggle for political liberty with the struggle for Socialism for almost half a century had been, as we have seen, the central but also the insoluble problem of the Russian revolutionary intelligentsia. Now the group found in the teachings of Marxism a new ideological weapon for its solution. For, as Plekhanov said in his foreword to the *Communist Manifesto*, this teaching 'could forewarn the Russian Socialists against two uniformly miserable extremes: a negative attitude towards political reality on the one hand, and the forgetting of the future interests of the party [i.e. Socialism] on the other.'

'Every class struggle is a political struggle' – this proposition of Marx, which Plekhanov took up as an epigraph to his 'Socialism and Political Struggle', was supposed to soothe the Socialist conscience of his comrades in the Party of Total Reapportionment. But within these confines the task was relatively easy: at the time the immense majority of the Populists had already bidden farewell to their former apoliticism, and the influence of the anarchist – anti-statist and anti-political – ideas of Bakuninism had in general begun sinking rapidly in the intelligentsia. What was far more difficult was the struggle against the

*Even in *Our Differences* (Chap. I) Plekhanov asserts: 'Bakuninism and Populism, as *revolutionary* doctrines, have outlived their time and now find a cordial welcome only in the *conservatively* democratic literary camp.'

second of these 'miserable extremes' – the forgetting of the Socialist objectives of the party, or their being shelved under the pretext that the 'communal' instincts of the Russian people would automatically convert the political overturn into the immediate prologue of a Socialist overturn. Hence a substantial part of *Socialism and Political Struggle* and *Our Differences* is devoted to the struggle against 'Jacobin' ideas of conspiracy and the seizure of power by a revolutionary minority.

History teaches us, Plekhanov argues, how dubious the chances of conspiracies are in general. But what is incontestable is that our revolutionary intellectual minority has no chance at all for the seizure of power. To be successful a conspiracy would have to involve the influential summits of society: 'the rich landowners, the capitalists, functionaries, officers'. But even if that succeeded, these circles of society would not, of course, take part in the conspiracy except in their own interests. Hence the 'results of the conspiracy of a Socialist intelligentsia aiming at the seizure of power in the imminent future would become all the more dubious the more sympathy it encountered in influential spheres, that is, the more likely its external success was'. Socialists could come to power, and in coming to it conduct a Socialist policy, only if they were to be propped up on the labouring masses imbued with Socialist consciousness. 'Every class struggle is a political struggle.' But every political struggle must also be a class struggle if it is to have Socialist results. In any case it must be a mass struggle, so that its chances of success can be erected on a more solid foundation than the deceptive hazards of playing at conspiracies.

The Emancipation of Labour Group, which was irreconcilable to the conspiratorial character of the People's Freedom, had a positive attitude towards its terrorism. As its 1884 programme says, it 'acknowledges the necessity of a terrorist struggle against the absolute government, and diverges from the People's Freedom Party only with respect to the objectives of the immediate activity of the Socialists among the working-class'. As Plekhanov explains, [91] the group objected only to the conversion of secret workers' organizations into 'secret seedbeds for the nursing of terrorists from a working-class *milieu*'. The workers' movement had broader tasks; it was it and it alone that was capable of 'felling and finishing off at the decisive moment the beast the terrorists had wounded'. But 'other strata of the population' could take on themselves the actual terrorist struggle 'with far greater convenience'.

In a note to the 1905 edition Plekhanov attempted to clarify this attitude of the Group towards terror by saying that 'expressing yourself against the terrorist struggle of the intelligentsia was at that time absolutely futile: the intelligentsia believed in "terror" as in a god'. As we see, this retrospective explanation jars with the just quoted formulations of the programme in *Our Differences*. Nor for that matter is it necessary. The then attitude of the Group towards terror is completely explained by the conditions of a time when the workers' movement that the Marxists set all their hopes on still lay far in the future. Against the background of the social stagnation the intelligentsia was still left as the sole group politically active at all, and it was still impossible to point to any other practical means of political struggle, the necessity of which was proclaimed so insistently by the Emancipation of Labour Group. This is just the kind of explanation given by *Our Differences*: 'We by no means deny the important role of terrorism in the contemporary movement of emancipation. It has grown naturally out of our socio-political conditions and must just as naturally aid in their change for the better.'

The helplessness of the intelligentsia itself, as an independent factor of political struggle, had to be displayed so that the draft of the second programme, written by Plekhanov in 1887, could pose the question of terror in a completely new framework, treating it as merely one of the means of political struggle of the future secret workers' organizations. These, after uniting with each other, 'would not be slow in passing over at the appropriate moment to a general, decisive onslaught on the government, in which they will not stop at any so-called terrorist actions if this seems necessary in the interests of the struggle'. Thus, from a specific combat weapon of the 'revolutionary minority', terror was to be turned into one of the possible weapons of the mass revolutionary movement.

Reliance on the masses and not on the individual, on the 'crowd' and not on 'heroes', was a basic tactical principle of the Party of Total Reapportionment. 'The emancipation of the people must be the affair of the people itself' – this initial commandment of Populism (paraphrased from the catechism of Marxism), was stubbornly counterposed by it to the Populist emphasis on the role of the 'revolutionary minority'. Now the same principle was applied by it to the political struggle too; this had to be a mass struggle for its results to be of any benefit to the people. But where could those masses be looked for that might serve as a fulcrum of the political struggle? That they could never be found in the peasantry was known equally well to both the

Party of Total Reapportionment and the People's Freedom: it was, after all, the indifference, and frequently the hostility, of the peasantry to 'politics' that had been the starting point of the apoliticism of the former and the conspiratorialism of the latter. Were there any other masses in Russia that the Socialist revolutionaries could count on? This question was fundamental for nascent Russian Marxism.

Hitherto Populism of all shades had known only one 'mass', one 'people' – the peasantry: for it the city worker was the same peasant who had simply happened to be accidentally and temporarily torn away from his village for 'seasonal' work in industry. For all shades of Populism it was just the same for the 'communal' traditions of the peasants; these made them the born banner-bearers of 'Socialism' even though that might be original Russian, Populist Socialism. It was this innate 'Socialism' of the peasantry that underlay the apoliticism, in the beginning of Populism as a whole and then of its Total Reapportionment fraction. It was just this that underlay the conviction of the People's Freedom that the emancipation of the people from the oppression of the autocracy, even though by way of a conspiracy of the 'revolutionary minority', would automatically ensure the triumph of Socialism in Russia; they were certain that in the 'future Russian Constituent Assembly ninety per cent of the deputies would be partisans of the social revolution'.*

Now, when the former Total Reapportionment members had gone over to Marxism from Populism just because they had lost faith in native Russian Socialism, and when it was just this faith that had become the principal argument of the People's Freedom 'Jacobins' in defence of conspiracy and the seizure of power by revolutionaries, a substantial part of Plekhanov's labour was devoted to the demonstration of the dissolution and withering away of the peasant commune under the influence of evolving capitalism, its gradual degeneration into a purely fiscal organization† and the thoroughgoing speciousness of any calculations on its Socialist potentialities. Looking back, he even maintained that the very presuppositions of the Populist pro-

* As is well known, this 'prophecy', which Plekhanov caustically jeered at,[90] was vindicated with precision in the actual Constituent Assembly that convened on 5 January 1918. It was vindicated, to be sure, in quite different circumstances and with quite different results from those the People's Freedom 'prophets' had been counting on.

† Later on some new investigations by Russian historians persuaded Plekhanov that the Russian commune in general had a purely 'fiscal origin', and 'had nothing in common with primitive Communism'.[91]

gramme were false: that the 'people' had never striven at all for 'complete economic emancipation', just as it had never striven for the complete annihilation of the 'state'. Of course, 'the agrarian question lay at the root of all or nearly all manifestations of popular discontent'. But the 'peasants, with tranquil assurance, were expecting a resolution of this question from above; they had "revolted" not in the name of a reapportionment of land, but against the persecution of the administration, against the immoderate burdensomeness of the tax system, against the Asiatic method of exacting arrears, etc., etc. The formula that generalized the greater part of the occasions of active protest was a "state of law" and not Land and Freedom, as it had seemed to all of us at that time.'[90]

Thus Plekhanov, in diametric opposition to Populism, now flatly denied the presence in the peasant movement of any revolutionary socio-economic tendencies hostile to the bourgeoisie; hence he also denied the presence of the contradiction on which, as it had seemed hitherto, the cause of 'bourgeois' democracy in Russia had foundered. The Russian bourgeoisie – in contrast with the Western European – was not too powerless to lead the struggle for political liberty because in the socio-economic conditions of Russia that struggle would instantly have called forth the 'red spectre' of Socialism, but only because the Russian peasantry, in its backwardness, was incapable of giving political shape to its discontent and its longing for a 'state of law'. As the draft of the second programme says, 'the principal support of absolutism consists of just this political apathy and intellectual backwardness of the peasantry. The necessary consequence of this is the helplessness and timidity of those educated strata of the upper classes whose material and intellectual interests are contradicted by the contemporary political system.' 'Such a state of affairs would be completely hopeless,' the programme goes on to say, 'if the indicated movement of Russian economic relations [towards capitalism. T.D.] did not create new opportunities for the defenders of the interests of the labouring class. The decomposition of the commune is creating a new class among us, that of the industrial proletariat. More receptive, zealous, and evolved, this class will respond more easily to the summons of the revolutionaries than the backward rural population.'

But the class of industrial workers could become an impressive mass force only if the economic development of Russia followed the same capitalist path as Western Europe. Hence the question of the 'fate of Russian capitalism' became the central question of Russian Marxism in its struggle against Populism. This question became the principal theme of the passionate debates in intellectual circles. In the course of the next ten to fifteen years a countless number of articles and studies was devoted to its elaboration by Marxist economists and statisticians. Of these the most famous were a book by V. Ilyin (the pen-name of Vladimir Ilyich Ulyanov, the future Lenin) published in 1895 called the *Development of Capitalism in Russia*,[94] and a book that came out in 1898 by M. I. Tugan-Baranovsky (at that time a 'legal' Marxist: see below) called *The Russian Factory Past and Present*.[2] But the basic results of the Marxist analysis of the real development and perspectives of Russian capitalism had already been formulated by Plekhanov in *Our Differences*: 'If we ask ourselves once more whether Russia will pass through the school of capitalism we can, without hesitation, answer with a new question: Why should she not finish a school she has already entered?'

Thus, the socio-economic development of Russia is analogous with that of Western Europe. Consequently, not only did the class foundations of Russian Socialism have to be analogous with those of Western Europe, but also its objectives. Analogous, but not identical. For, in contrast to the countries of developed capitalism, Russia – so the draft of the second programme said – was one of those countries 'where contemporary capitalist production was still only striving to become the ruler, and where the labouring masses were under the dual yoke of evolving capitalism and the obsolete patriarchal economy'. It is this historical belatedness of Russian capitalism that also determines the singularity of the position of the Russian working-class, and hence the singularity of the political objectives of Russian socialism.

In countries where the cycle of capitalist development is already consummated or is close to consummation, the working-class is directly confronted by the task of a 'radical economic revolution'; this is just why its 'political training and hegemony are essential'.* Matters

* The first programme still conceives of both the conquest of that hegemony and its realization exclusively within the framework of governmental democracy, for 'only a thoroughly democratic hegemony can consummate an economic overturn in conformity with the interests of the producers'. It is only the draft of the second programme that introduced into the political inventory of Russian Marxism the idea 'of the dictatorship of the proletariat' as the premise for the Socialist revolution (it is not until 1903 that the term itself is used for the first time in the programme of the Russian Social-Democracy) in stating that the 'inevitable precondition' of a radical social reconstruction 'is the seizure of political power by the working-class'.

stood differently in backward countries. Here 'the Social-Democrats had to assume intermediate stages of social structure as were already in existence in the advanced countries and were essential for the further development of the workers' party'. Here, as it says in *Our Differences*, 'the Socialists simultaneously had to support capitalism in its struggle against reaction and had to be its irreconcilable enemies in its struggle against the workers' party of the future'. In short, the 'bourgeois' political revolution had to precede in time the Socialist revolution, because, as it had been put even in *Socialism and Political Struggle*, to 'link together two such essentially different matters as the overthrow of absolutism and the Socialist revolution, to guide the revolutionary struggle on the calculation that these occasions of social development will coincide in the history of our fatherland – means to put off the emergence of both one and the other'. The political and ideological impotence of the bourgeoisie, which for the Russian revolutionaries had hitherto been a circumstance that was extremely favourable to the Socialist revolution, was now declared to be 'one of the most pernicious consequences' of the backwardness of the Russian economy. For the future promised Russia 'above all – the triumph of the bourgeoisie and the beginning of the political and economic emancipation of the working class'.[91]

Such was the logically harmonious scheme of the country's future socio-economic and political evolution laid down by Plekhanov at the very birth of Russian Marxism. 'Our Socialism will cease being "Russian" and will fuse together with world socialism,' as Plekhanov concluded, when its partisans 'elevated themselves' as far as Marxism and understood that:

'(1) The communist revolution of the working-class could by no means grow out of the petty-bourgeois peasant Socialism being preached at the present time by almost all our revolutionaries;

'(2) By the inner character of its organization the rural commune will strive above all to yield a place to bourgeois but not to communist forms of society;

'(3) In the transition, what is destined for the commune is *not an active but a passive* role; it is incapable of *moving* Russia on to the path of communism; it can only offer less *resistance* to such a movement than small-scale private landholding;

'(4) The initiative of the communist movement can be taken only by the working-class of our industrial centres, a class

'(5) Whose emancipation can be achieved only through its own conscious efforts.'[91]

These five propositions signalize with the penetration of genius and great depth of thought those tendencies in the social development of the country guided by which the Russian Social-Democracy was able to evolve in only a decade into the first Russian Socialist organization bound up with and propped up on the masses, and to become a decisive factor throughout the subsequent development of Russian democratic and Socialist ideology. These propositions formulated with acute precision the Marxist understanding of the potentialities and prospects of the Socialist development of Russia, as contrasted with the Populist understanding. But it is in vain that we would examine them for an equally precise formulation of the political prospects of the country.

Plekhanov, of course, gave a completely rounded off solution of the political problem too. In Russia, just as in Western Europe, political liberty moved forward on the groundwork of capitalist development. In Russia, too, the political revolution would be 'bourgeois', and it was only under conditions of the 'state of law' it had created that the working-class could and should wage a 'final and decisive battle' for Socialism. But it was only in Russia that the 'class of industrial workers' would consummate this 'bourgeois' revolution, and not those peasants and masses of petty city-dwellers, as yet undifferentiated with respect to class, on which the bourgeoisie was propping itself up in its struggle against absolutism in Western Europe. Such was the diagram of the future political development of Russia that Plekhanov outlined and that, in its basic features, later became, for three and a half decades, the general property of all tendencies and fractions of the Russian Social-Democracy. But with all its apparent logical harmony this diagram contained inner defects that at that time Plekhanov's sharp mind could not but have been aware of. And if in the conditions of the time Plekhanov could not find sufficient material for the theoretical conquest of the internal contradictoriness that the political constructions of nascent Russian Marxism suffered from, at least this contradictoriness prevented him from lending these constructions the same precise form he had given his doctrine of the prospects of Socialist development.

The basic contradiction in these constructions was that they regarded as the principal moving force of the bourgeois revolution the 'class of industrial workers' that is, the social stratum that was being engendered by capitalism but was becoming a 'class' precisely in so far as it was beginning to be aware of its antagonism to the bourgeoisie that exploited it. Such a paradoxical situation had come about, as we have seen, through the belatedness of Russia's capitalist development, and her belonging to those backward countries where the working-class and the Social-Democracy were facing the objective of a struggle for the 'advanced' forms of social organization that had long since existed in the 'advanced countries'. But it turned out to be this same belatedness that conditioned a series of other phenomena that had the same fundamental importance for the fate of capitalism in Russia, hence also for the formulation of the political problem there.

Thus, it made likely above all a short life for Russian capitalism:

> It is not only that the development of Russian capitalism cannot take place so slowly as it did, for instance, in England, but even its very existence cannot be so protracted as it had been destined to be in Western Europe. Our capitalism will wither before it has had time to blossom completely; this is guaranteed for us by the powerful influence of international relationships.'[91]

But this short-lived capitalism also makes likely a short life for the hegemony of the bourgeoisie:

> The contemporary position of bourgeois societies and the influence of international relationships on the social development of each civilized country make it legitimate to hope that the social emancipation of the Russian working-class will very quickly follow the fall of absolutism. If the German bourgeoisie 'had come too late', then the Russian was even later, and its domination could not be long-lived.[90]

Plekhanov says this in a polemic against the Populists, who were demanding the 'complete abolition' of the capitalist phase of development on the ground that this phase would otherwise last a 'whole century'. But when on this occasion he makes the accusation that it 'does not enter the minds of our intelligentsia' that the complete abolition of a given historical period is merely a particular case of its cessation, and that by demonstrating the possibility of the first, we, by the same token and moreover to a far greater degree, confirm the likelihood of the second,[92] then it is impossible not to see that this argument can also boomerang against the Marxist diagram he has given himself.

On the reverse side of this belatedness of Russian capitalism there is another fundamental phenomenon – the unique historical 'prematurity' of the emergence of Russian Socialism. 'We must not lose sight of the circumstance, of cardinal consequence, that the Socialist movement started among us while capitalism was still in embryo. This singularity of Russian history was not thought up by the Slavophils or the Slavophil-minded revolutionaries.' [91] From the point of view of the Emancipation of Labour Group, after all, it was just this 'singularity' that not only made it possible but obligatory for the Russian revolutionaries, still in the midst of a struggle for political liberty, to move on to the construction of a class party of workers. More than that, it was this that enabled nascent workers' Socialism to exercise a decisive influence on the formation of the socio-political ideology of the peasantry too.

The extremely widespread opinion, accepted even by Martov,[95] that the Emancipation of Labour Group believed that 'the terrain for social-revolutionary activity among the masses in the countryside could be created only to the extent that the peasant smallholders were converted into a rural proletariat whose interests would coincide with the interests of the urban proletarians', is wrong. On the contrary, as early as *Socialism and the Political Struggle*, Plekhanov says definitely: 'We do not hold the view that the Socialist movement cannot meet with any support in our peasant *milieu* until the peasants are converted into landless proletarians, and the rural commune is decomposed by the influence of capitalism.' He was convinced merely that the development of the commune (which, let us recall, he at that time considered a hangover of primitive communism) into a 'higher communist form' was only possible under the 'immediate influence of a powerful and well-organized workers' Socialist party'. It is the draft of the second programme that gives a definitive formulation of his views on this question at that time, when in referring to the economic demands that had been advanced he says: 'These demands are just as favourable to the interests of the peasants as they are to the interests of the industrial workers; hence, in ensuring their realization the workers' party is paving a highway to its *rapprochement* with the rural population. Cast out of his village as an impoverished member of the commune, the proletarian will return to it as a Social-Democratic agitator. His appearance in this role will change the fate of the commune, at present hopeless.'

This optimistic and, as the future was to prove, accurate estimate of the possibilities of the workers' ideological effect on the peasantry substantially brightened the prospects of the Socialist development of Russia. But while foreseeing the involvement of the peasantry, too, in the orbit of Socialism, this estimate introduced still more complications into the political problem of the execution by the Socialist working-class of a 'bourgeois' revolution.

'A Socialist government – even though it were provisional – that did not exploit its own power for the creation of a Socialist order would be ridiculous,' wrote Plekhanov,[91] arguing against Tikhomirov. But in that case wouldn't the idea of a Socialist workers' movement that didn't exploit its own strength for the creation of such an order be equally ridiculous? There was no need to frighten the bourgeoisie prematurely by the 'red spectre', Plekhanov reminded the 'Jacobins' of the People's Freedom dozens of times: 'West European history tells us extremely convincingly that wherever the "red spectre" takes on any menacing forms the "liberals" are ready to look for protection to the most arrant military dictatorship'; surely 'our Russian liberals will not constitute an exception to this general rule'?[91] But, in that case, why should the Emancipation of Labour Group strive to sharpen class contradictions when the struggle against the autocracy demands the union of all classes? This was the objection made to Plekhanov by the liberal Populist *Samoupravleniye* in its turn. As a matter of fact, the reality of a violent Socialist workers' movement could not, after all, help but 'frighten' the bourgeoisie far more than the 'chattering' of powerless intellectual circles about the 'red spectre' that Plekhanov was making such angry accusations about.

Plekhanov looked for the resolution of these contradictions in his own kind of Marxist 'enlightenment': in propaganda for the idea of scientific Socialism, in the elevation of the consciousness of the future workers' party to a level that would make it capable of the greatest self-restraint in the formulation of its immediate goals. But if this sort of methodical dosage of 'support for capitalism in its struggle against reaction' and at the same time of 'irreconcilable enmity' to it 'in its struggle against the workers' revolution', is possible for small groups of revolutionaries, it is far more difficult for a party of any breadth, and completely unthinkable for those politically unschooled, multi-millioned masses whose active intervention in the course of events is indissolubly linked to the very idea of a 'workers' revolution'. The rationalistic resolution of the contradiction between the characteristics of the workers' 'elemental outburst' called for by nascent Russian Marxism, and the level of 'consciousness' demanded by it, thus proved completely abstract and hence false. It proved particularly false precisely from the point of view of scientific Socialism, that materialist philosophy of Marxism that Plekhanov was unflaggingly propagating, which teaches that 'consciousness' cannot be introduced into any social *milieu* arbitrarily but 'is determined by the reality' of that *milieu*.

But if even the powerful, systematizing thought of Plekhanov failed to find a harmonious resolution of the Russian political problem, it was because this problem was at that time theoretically insoluble altogether. Driven through the Populist 'door', the same insoluble contradictions of Russian socio-economic and political life that we have spoken of so often, and that Russian democratic thought had been beating against so agonizingly and so fruitlessly from its very inception, now burst through the Marxist 'window'. As we shall see, the insolubility of these contradictions underlay the whole subsequent internal struggle and all the splits in the Russian Social-Democracy. It was a profound source of those warring fractions and parties about which it may be said, as Plekhanov said about the numerous Populist fractions of his own time, that they were 'right, each in its own way, because with all its one-sidedness each one of them expresses a certain urgent need of Russian social life'.[90]

At that time, around 1885, even the most gigantic intellectual effort could not have foreseen the chain of wars and revolutions by which history in reality has not so much 'solved' as slashed through, and has gone on slashing through the unloosable knot of these contradictions. At that time, after the paralysing illusions of obsolescent Populism had been shaken off, it was primarily a question of accurately feeling out the real direction of Russian socio-economic and political evolution, and thus giving the Russian revolutionary movement, which had dried up as a movement of the isolated intelligentsia, a powerful ideological weapon to convert it into a mass movement, and thus into a mighty political force. It was this weapon that was given it by Plekhanov's theoretical work. He summed up its basic conclusion himself when with an insight of genius, running on decades ahead, he finished his brief speech at the Paris International Socialist Congress in 1889 with the historic words: 'The revolutionary movement in Russia can only triumph as a revolutionary movement of the workers. For us there is no other way out, nor can there be.'

CHAPTER EIGHT

The Russian Social-Democracy

1. THE PERIOD OF PREPARATION

The extremely difficult material conditions of existence of the Emancipation of Labour Group did not prevent it from winning, step by step, a firm position on the ideological front of the Russian emigration. Towards 1890 the Group was even able to set about publishing a thick 'politico-literary' periodical entitled *Sotsial-Demokrat* (The Social-Democrat). This was supposed to come out every three months; in fact it managed to get out three numbers in 1890, while the fourth, which came out in 1892, after a long interval, proved to be the last. It carried among other things an article by Plekhanov on *All-Russian Ruin*,[96] which, as we shall see, marked the advent of a new period in the history of the Russian social movement, and at the same time the emergence of new prospects for Russian Marxism and the Emancipation of Labour Group itself.

The Group very quickly succeeded in establishing firm bonds with the international Socialist movement too. Articles by its members – Akselrod, Zasulich, Plekhanov – began appearing systematically in the German and French Socialist press. Its delegate Plekhanov spoke, as we know, at the very first international Socialist congress in Paris in 1889 (P. Lavrov also spoke at this congress, in the name of the People's Freedom). The group sent a *rapport* to the second congress in Brussels in 1891 (the text of which has not been found). By the time of the third congress in Zurich in 1893, Plekhanov's international reputation as a Marxist already stood so high that it was he who was commissioned, as a *rapporteur* of the Commission on the War Question, to defend the 'Marxist' resolution of the German Social-Democracy against the Dutch anarchist Domela Nieuwenhuis, who was demanding that the workers' parties everywhere respond to a declaration of war by the declaration of a general anti-war strike. In line with the German resolution, Plekhanov proved that while the principle of a struggle for peace and for the exploitation of every war in the interests of the socio-political emancipation of the workers must be common to all parties, the forms and methods of that struggle in any individual country must correspond to the peculiarities of its socio-political structure. In particular, with respect to Tsarist Russia, Plekhanov took the 'defeatist' point of view, declaring that 'a war against our government would be a war for the emancipation of our people'. This same polemic against Nieuwenhuis gave Plekhanov an occasion to write a pamphlet against anarchism, which was translated into various languages and became part of the basic propagandistic literature of international Socialism. The Emancipation of Labour Group, which to a considerable degree had borrowed its intellectual arsenal from Western European Marxism, in its turn paved the way for the reverse influence of Russian Marxism on the development of international Socialist thought, which from then on never stopped, even during the political defeats and organizational decline of the Russian Social-Democracy.

But while it won positions in the emigration and in international Socialism, the Emancipation of Labour Group sank its roots in Russian soil only slowly. Its works penetrated Russia only in very small numbers and were read by very few. In Russia, to be sure, numerous Marxist circles and propagandist groups soon began emerging independently. One of the first of such groups was the so-called 'Party of Russian Social-Democrats', which was organized in the winter of 1883–4 by Petersburg technology students on the initiative of Dmitri Nikolayevich Blagoyev (1855–1924), the future leader of the Bulgarian Socialist '*Tesnyaki*' and later the Bulgarian Communists. This group even entered into contact with the Emancipation of Labour Group, and the two numbers they printed of the illegal newspaper *Rabochii* (The Worker) published articles by Akselrod and Plekhanov. The 'Blagoyevites' drew up a draft programme that in many respects was similar to the first programme of the Emancipation of Labour Group. But after Blagoyev was deported, and after the arrests that followed, the 'Party' cut short its existence in 1886. The Marxist groups that replaced it in the second half of the '80s in the capital and provinces had practically no links with the Emancipation of Labour Group.

Among these groups, the 'Association of Petersburg Craftsmen', founded in 1886 by Paul Varfolomeyevich Tochisky assumed comparatively great importance in the succeeding history of the Russian Social-Democracy. Son of a colonel who was a Polish nobleman, Tochisky had broken with his family and become a worker. The characteristic feature of his programme was a strong distrust of the intelligentsia, which he considered a 'fellow-traveller' of the workers only 'until the first constitution', after which 'our paths would sharply diverge from each other'. His organization itself was divided into two separate parts – a workers' and an intellectuals', thanks to which at the destruction of the 'association' by the police in 1888 many workers survived to play a considerable role in the Social-Democratic movement, for instance, V. A. Shelgunov. Another homogeneous group that was of special importance in spreading Marxism along the Volga and in Central Russia was one organized in 1888 in Kazan by Nicholas Yevgrafovich Fyodoseyev (1870–98). V. I. Ulyanov, the future Lenin, also played a part in this group.

By the beginning of the '90s the Marxist groups in the various industrial centres of Russia could already be counted in the dozens. Not only did hundreds of workers receive a Marxist education in them, but the intellectual cadres of the future Russian Social-Democracy also began their political activity in them. These included many of the figures of the first ten to fifteen years of the Bolshevik régime, who later became famous abroad as well, such as L. B. Krasin, the future Soviet ambassador to London and Paris, L. M. Khinchuk, the future Soviet ambassador in London, D. B. Ryazanov (Goldendach), the organizer and long-time director of the Marx-Engels Institute in Moscow, Y. M. Steklov (Nakhamkes), who was editor of the government organ *Izvestia* during the first few years of the Soviet régime, and others.

A special place among these groups belongs to the so-called 'Social-Democratic Society', which was organized in 1889 by the technological student Michael Ivanovich Brusnyov and which for the most part consisted, like the 'Blagoyev' group in its time, of his comrades at the Technological Institute. This society, which took as model the German Social-Democracy and set itself the objective of developing 'future Russian Bebels' among the workers, succeeded in laying a network of groups throughout a series of Petersburg districts and creating a centralized leadership for the organization out of the representatives of the workers by district, plus one representative of the intelligentsia. This was the first Russian Marxist group that began shifting from clandestine propaganda to attempts to lead a mass working-class movement: the hand-written paper and multigraphed proclamations that it issued during the winter of 1890–1, at the time of the strikes at the Tornton textile factory and Petersburg Port, had a great success with the workers. It was also the first to begin organizing political demonstrations. These were, of course, extremely modest both in the number of participants and in form, but they had some importance for the political training of the advanced workers and also made some impression outside. One such demonstration presented an address to the sick writer N. V. Shelgunov, and later some 100 'Brusnyovite' workers attended his funeral, carrying a wreath with the inscription 'To our guide to freedom and brotherhood'.* Finally this group organized for the first time in Russia, also in 1891, a secret celebration of May Day, in which as many as 100 workers took part.

In its dimensions, in its organized structure, and in the character of its activity, the Brusnyov Society was already in transition to the organizations of the new type, which began forming in the second half of the '90s. Their prototype was the famous Petersburg 'Combat Union for the Emancipation of the Working-Class', which arose at the very end of 1895, and was linked to the Brusnyov organization in the person of one of the latter's members, the engineer Stepan Ivanovich Radchenko, one of the organizers of the 'Union'. But 'Combat Unions' were already part of another period. For the time being Russian Marxism scarcely went beyond the confines of an extremely narrow circle of intellectuals and of educational propaganda in small workers' circles. In legal literature it was also represented almost exclusively by activities of a purely scientific, apolitical nature. Here an eminent place was occupied by the books and articles of Professor N. Ziber, who accepted Marx's economic doctrine but ascribed no importance to his teachings of the class struggle, and in general interpreted Marxism in the spirit of a fatalistic automatism. The Russian translation of the first volume of *Capital*, which had been done by Herman Lopatin, a member of the People's Freedom, and had come out as early as 1872 in 3,000 copies, had long since vanished, and reprinting it was forbidden. Marxism was barred from legal journalism; for that matter, too, the narrowly propagandistic activity of its first followers among the intelligentsia necessarily concentrated their thinking more on questions of Marx's economic and sociological theory than on the application of that theory to the analysis and elucidation of current Russian life. Outside the confines of the clearly reactionary camp the whole of the periodical press was in the hands of various shades of Populist-minded liberalism and liberal Populism towards

* As far back as 1861 Shelgunov had given a detailed exposition of Engels's book on the *Condition of the Working-Class in England* in the *Sovremennik*; in general he devoted a great deal of attention in his articles to the working-class problem.

which, as we have already noted, the views of the overwhelming majority of the intelligentsia, and educated society in general, had gravitated after the destruction of the People's Freedom. This press had a relatively tolerant attitude towards Russian Marxism as long as it remained the property of tightly-knit and isolated student and workers' groups. But this position began changing towards the beginning of the '90s, as the social temper also began changing.

The line of demarcation was the savage famine that struck the east and south-east of European Russia in the winter of 1891–2. This famine and the dreadful cholera epidemic that followed it, which wiped out hundreds of thousands of lives, plainly demonstrated the horrifying socio-economic situation created for the Russian peasantry by the conditions of its emancipation in 1861. It turned out that the very first serious crop failure doomed to genuine starvation even the sections of the country that were richest in grain: the exploitation by the landowners, the former 'masters', and by their own kulaks, and the government's tax policy pumped out of the countryside such a large portion of the fruits of its labour that the immense majority of the peasants could not even think of laying anything by for a 'black day', still less of any 'hoarding'. It also turned out that the government too, which forced the export of grain in all sorts of ways in the interests of strengthening state finances ('we won't eat ourselves, but we'll export,' said Vishnegradsky, Alexander III's Minister of Finance) lacked the reserves to help out the districts that had a bad harvest. At the same time, fearful of new attempts at a *rapprochement* of the intelligentsia with the exasperated and discontented masses of the people, it also set as many obstacles as possible in the way of the special organizations that began springing up in great numbers in order to give medical aid and supplies to the hungry (Leo Tolstoy led one of these organizations).*

All this turned the attention of society once again to the grand questions of the development of the productive forces of the country, the socio-economic foundations of the Tsarist régime, and from there to a critique of this régime itself. There appeared a profound fissure in the moods of compromise and collaboration. The political problem as

* Among the student youth there arose a peculiar reincarnation of 'going to the people'. Martov wrote: 'Hundreds of young men and women broke off their studies and went to the countryside. Many of them came there with the confused expectation that the starving peasants would begin an insurrection, and with just as confused a hope of taking part in it.'[97]

a problem of the liquidation of the autocracy once again began moving to the fore. And Plekhanov only anticipated the ultimate conclusion of this new shift in social ideology when he ended his article, *All-Russian Ruin*, devoted to the famine of 1891–2, with the words: 'A total economic catastrophe for our country can only be forestalled by its total political emancipation.'

As the attention of society shifted to the struggle for political emancipation, it was confronted once again by the question of the moving forces of that emancipation. The terrorism of isolated revolutionary groups had been discredited by the fiascos, while the policy of 'small deeds' and reliance on the enlightened elements of the bureaucracy had been discredited by the lessons of the famine. Once again the countryside was demonstrating its total incapacity for any organized struggle even in the face of the most savage calamities. The profound lack of civilization was attested to by a wave of 'cholera' riots that swept through the port cities of the Volga, where mobs of unemployed rural refugees were demolishing hospitals and killing physicians, calling them 'poisoners'. The regeneration of any hopes of political initiative on the part of the peasantry was impossible. Under these conditions greater response was given to the voice of Marxism, which pointed to the birth in Russia of the new class of the industrial proletariat. This was capable of playing the role of a 'popular' bearer of the idea of political emancipation that the peasantry had proved unfit for.

This voice also began to receive more attention from the representatives of capital, especially textile capital, which the 'all-Russian ruin' was threatening with a still greater contraction of the domestic market, inadequate enough as it was. It was, of course, interested primarily by that aspect of the Marxist doctrine that proved not only the possibility but also the inevitability and the historically progressive nature of a broad development of capitalism in Russia. The voice of Marxism also began to be listened to by a broad stratum of the intelligentsia, among whom events were once again stimulating a longing for political liberty, but at the same time an oppressive awareness of its own political impotence as long as it lacked the possibility of finding support in the 'people'. In literary clubs, secret discussion meetings, and student soirées, the 'legal' Populists who until only a short while before had been the unquestioned 'opinion-moulders' of the youth, began to be subjected to progressively sharper and more frequent attacks from the youthful Marxists. And their own literary attack on young Russian Marxism, which had scarcely begun to emerge from the tightly-knit underground of propagandist groups, began to grow more and more sharply polemical.

The leading role in this attack naturally fell to N. K. Mikhailovsky and his closest collaborators on the *Russkoye Bogatstvo*: V. Vorontsov, S. N. Yuzhakov, S. Krivenko and others. The Marxist recognition of the inevitability of capitalism in Russia began to be interpreted by them as the 'desire' of the Marxists to 'install' capitalism there; they interpreted the Marxist point that Russia was suffering not only from the development of capitalism but also from the belatedness, slowness, and inadequacy of that development, as a summons to the intelligentsia to pass from 'service to the people' to 'service to capital'. The assertion that it was not in the peasantry but in the industrial working-class that forces were maturing that were capable of solving the problem of the political emancipation of the country and the social liberation of the masses of its people, was interpreted as a rejection of the defence of the interests of the peasantry and even as a direct preparation for taking its land away and proletarianizing it as quickly as possible, etc. V.V. expressed the 'hope' that the opinions of the Marxists were 'conditioned by defects that were primarily intellectual, and not of a moral order', but added at once that 'the moral bond with the above-mentioned opinions would testify that the material interest of the intelligentsia as a part of the privileged classes was outweighing feelings of a higher order'.[75]

For his part Mikhailovsky divided the Russian Marxists into 'three categories': The Marxist onlookers, the 'uncommitted observers of the process' of the ruin of the Russian peasantry, the passive Marxists, who 'had no interest in the people on the land, but turned their attention and hopes to those that were already cut off from the means of production; and the active Marxists who 'were directly insisting on the further ruin of the countryside'.[98]

In this struggle against Russian Marxism, just raising its head, liberal Populism entered on a new stage of its development. Having already managed, as we have seen, to establish powerful links with the liberal strata of affluent society, it too was undergoing a process of political activization. But in the struggle against the growing influence of Marxism on just those intellectual and plebeian circles that it had hitherto monopolized, it not only revolutionized itself politically; in its own consciousness it began more and more insistently interpreting its own social conservatism (based on the preservation and further evolution of the 'independent' communal and artel principles) as 'anti-bourgeois' and thus as authentically 'social-revolutionary'. It counterposed this to the alleged capitulation of Marxism to the triumphant procession of capitalism and the bourgeoisie. Such was the preparation of the 'revolutionary' transformation of liberal Populism. Almost ten years later it was to underlie the programme of the 'Party of Socialist-Revolutionaries' that arose in the stormy years before the revolution.

But, for the time, what served as the ideological foundation of the Populist struggle against nascent Marxism were the theories we are already familiar with, of the miscarriage of Russian capitalism and the optimistic assessment of the prospects that the peasant commune, in the domain of agriculture, the producing co-operative (artel), in the domain of industry, and the consumers' co-operative, in the domain of commerce, would have in a struggle against it. The destruction of this theoretical foundation is what the efforts of the first Russian Marxists were concentrated on. An entire generation of young intellectuals, ignorant of any analogies with any other country or any other epoch, flung itself passionately into the study of the socio-economic and cultural history of Russia and other countries. 'Surplus value', 'the theory of markets', 'rural restratification' – all were argued about whole nights at a time in little groups. Studies devoted to the peasant economy, to industry, to home crafts, co-operatives etc., were leafed through till ragged. The dry collections of statistics that had used to be the property of a few specialists were now studied with enthusiasm by hundreds of young people. And the Marxists were given an unexpected opportunity of carrying their arguments with Populism into a more open arena in the winter of 1893–4, when, in harmony with the general change in the atmosphere, they began to be invited to the public sessions of the Imperial Free Economic Society in Petersburg. This had been founded by Catherine the Great and had received certain privileges from her, such as the right not to allow the police on to their premises, as well as a freer printing of its 'Proceedings' and the reports of its meetings.

This wave of general enthusiasm for economic and social questions did not pass without trace. Not only did it heighten extraordinarily the intellectual level of the future founders of the Social-Democratic Party, but it also gave rise to a series of most valuable studies. It led to the transformation of the actual methods used in rural statistics. People were forced to stop studying 'average' figures, which concealed the concentration of socio-economic assets at one pole of the village (or artel) and debits at the other, and start studying individual homesteads. Such studies revealed the 'restratification' of the peasantry and its decomposition, under the influence of evolving capitalism, into antagonistic groups, and so cut the ground from under the feet of the Populist theory about the 'levelling' tendencies of the commune. A whole constellation of brilliant economists, statisticians, sociologists, and historians blazed forth, many of whom, who later left Marxism also, made a world reputation for themselves, such as P. B. Struve, M. I. Tugan-Baranovsky and others.

In its verbal and literary grapples with Populism, Russian Marxism more and more decisively passed from defence to attack. Its aggressive spirit was clearly expressed in a pamphlet that came out in 1894, called *Who Are the 'Friends of the People'? and How They Fight the Social-Democrats* (*a Reply to Articles against the Marxists in Russkoye Bogatstvo*). The pamphlet, which was mimeographed, consisted of three separate numbers, devoted to Mikhailovsky, Yuzhakov (which has still not been found), and Krivenko. In the issue devoted to Mikhailovsky, the anonymous author of the pamphlet – Ulyanov (Lenin) – said that peasant 'Russian' Socialism, which had once been revolutionary, had now 'completely dissolved and given birth to a vulgar philistine liberalism that found "encouraging impressions" in the progressive currents of peasant economy, forgetting that these were accompanied (and conditioned) by the mass expropriation of the peasantry'. The Mikhailovsky of the revolutionary '70s, who defended the 'optimist' (a censor's metaphor for a revolutionary) Marx against 'liberal critics' was counterposed by the pamphlet to the Mikhailovsky of the present, who 'clamoured and sputtered against Russian Marxists who refused to be satisfied with the "defence of the economically most feeble", with commodity reserves, and improvements in the villages, with museums and artels for home-crafts, and with well-intentioned philistine advances – and who wanted to remain "optimists", and partisans of the social revolution'.

Ulyanov's pamphlet still came out illegally. But Russian Marxism – to a considerable degree thanks to the Free Economic Society – had already begun paving the way for its return to legal literature too. In 1894 there appeared a legal book by P. Struve, *Critical Notes*,[99] in which he criticized the economic ideas of Populism. It ended with a challenging phrase: 'Let us admit our lack of culture and take lessons from capitalism.' This phrase was not only snatched up by the opponents of Marxism as a proof of its 'capitulation' to capitalism, but also evoked a critical response from the Marxists themselves, especially Plekhanov and Ulyanov. As it later turned out, this phrase did slip out of the author accidentally, but it was a hint of his future intellectual evolution, which we shall have to mention in connexion with the separation of the so-called 'legal Marxists' from revolutionary Social-Democratic Marxism. But this separation still lay ahead. For the time being Struve, together with Plekhanov, Ulyanov, and Potresov, took part in putting together a clearly revolutionary and anti-Populist collection of articles, *Materials on the Question of the Economic Situation of Russia*,[100] which came out in 1895. This anthology was confiscated and burnt; nevertheless copies of it managed to be distributed by the hundreds. In 1895 there also came out the above-mentioned book by Plekhanov under the pen-name of Beltov,[101] and the following year his *Defence of Populism in the Works of Mr Vorontsov*,[102] under another pen-name, A. Volgin. At the same time the Marxists succeeded in arranging for the publication of a daily newspaper, the *Samarsky Vestnik* (Samar Courier), on which Peter Maslov, later a well-known economist, N. Fyodoseyev, and R. Gvozdyov (Tsimmerman) among others, collaborated. In the spring of 1897, finally, there passed into Marxist hands the Petersburg monthly review *Novoye Slovo* (the New Word) in which side by side with articles by members of the Emancipation of Labour Group, Lenin, Struve, Tugan-Baranovsky and others, articles by Julius Osipovich Tsederbaum (L. Martov) started appearing for the first time, and in whose art section a prominent place was occupied by the young Maxim Gorky.

But by this time Russian Marxism had already managed to come out not merely as a literary but as a political force, and one, moreover, that was propped up on a mass workers' movement.

2. 'COMBAT UNIONS' AND THE FOUNDING OF A PARTY

The immediate economic consequences of the 1891–2 famine were: the lowering of the purchasing power of the countryside, limited enough as it was; the rise in the price of food; the flooding of cities and industrial centres with starving peasants, ready to sell their 'working hands' at any price. The catastrophe that had descended on the peasants now hit the workers. Only a thin layer of metal-workers was protected against the catastrophe, up to a point, by its high qualifications as well as by a boom due to the accelerated pace of railway construction at this time. With all the greater oppressiveness it descended on the untrained or not very trained workers, especially the workers in the textile industry, which was geared almost exclusively to the domestic market. The workers' answer was a wave of strikes, which began to billow up primarily in the west and centre of Russia, regions of concentration of the textile industry, and which for a while touched the metallurgical south relatively little.

Because of the economic conjuncture, the total disorganization, and the low cultural level of the masses drawn into the collective struggle for the first time, these strikes ended almost invariably with the defeat of the workers. Not infrequently they would lead to bloody clashes with the police and the troops, with whose help the authorities would harshly put down the 'riots'. Nevertheless the wave of strikes kept growing uninterruptedly. It was fed by the hopeless situation of the workers. But it also received certain impulses from outside – from the general political excitement evoked by the 1891–2 famine. This in its turn enveloped the incipient movement of the industrial workers in the 'sympathy' of educated and liberal society; the more mercilessly the government dealt with that movement the greater was the sympathy.

This political excitement was stimulated anew by the new reign. On 22 October 1894 Alexander III died, and the throne was mounted by the young Nicholas II, to whom, as is often the case, rumour attributed a political antagonism to his father, the personification of political and social reaction, and in whom 'society' hoped to see a restorer and continuer of the 'liberal' traditions of his grandfather. The press began striking an optimistic note, while a series of Zemstvos and cities once again began accepting petitions of the type we are already familiar with. These expressed feelings of loyalty but also, in a more or less masked way, desires that society be involved in the direction of the state.

All the greater was the disappointment and indignation evoked on 17 January 1895 by the harsh interjection with which the young Tsar met a delegation of people active in the Zemstvos and in the cities that appeared before him to congratulate him on mounting the throne. He called the 'constitutional' desires of the Zemstvos 'senseless dreams', and categorically declared that he would maintain the principles of autocracy just as unwaveringly as had his father. Against the background of this disappointment, a telegram the new Tsar sent the Fanagory Regiment in April 1895, expressing imperial gratitude to the 'brave lads' who had fired on the striking workers in the textile factories of Yaroslavl, was also met with disapproval beyond the confines of the working-class. On the very threshold of the new reign the autocracy turned with challenging hostility both against liberal society and against the working-class that was just beginning to stir; with its own hands it helped their *rapprochement* within the framework of a 'movement of liberation' that culminated in the revolution of 1905.

Such were the conditions that insistently confronted the Marxist intellectual groups with completely new tasks. Hitherto the activity of these groups in the workers' *milieu* had boiled down almost exclusively to the organization of the most developed workers into small clubs, in which lectures were given on economic, social, historical, etc., themes, and Marxist propaganda was carried on. Now it was a question of establishing firm links with the mass workers' movement, the inevitability of whose emergence had been forecast by Russian Marxism, and of turning this movement into an exponent of the Social-Democratic policy whose basic lines had been laid down by the Emancipation of Labour Group. But even before this objective confronted the Marxists of Russia proper, it loomed most imminently before the Marxists of her western border areas.

Economically, socially, culturally, and partly, also, politically, these border areas (which, by the way, knew nothing of the peasant commune) were far more closely bound up with Western European traditions than central Russia herself. Their working-class was also far more 'europeanized' from the very beginning. It had developed in this way within the framework of a comprehensive attitude of political opposition, which was the response of these areas to the ethnic oppression that had become a permanent element in the policy of the Russian autocracy. This situation gave an exceptional stimulus to the awakening and growth of the political awareness of the masses of workers, though, of course, it also united their incipient independent movement by bonds of 'national' (ethnic) solidarity to the movements of the other classes of border-area society in the struggle against Russian Tsarism.

Among these border areas it was Poland, which in the course of the nineteenth century had responded to the 'russifying' policy of Tsarism by two insurrections, that had the most developed industry, the most 'European' type of culture, and the most powerful national traditions. It is not surprising that it was the workers' movement of Poland that in its evolution was far ahead of the workers' movement in the other parts of the Empire. As early as the end of 1892, when even in such an advanced centre of Russia as Petersburg Marxism was only just beginning to emerge from the narrow framework of little groups of students, the numerous Socialist groups in Poland were able to unite in the Polish Socialist Party, still in existence today.* But the whole background of the Polish workers' movement was too special for it to be able to exercise any noticeable influence on the movement in central Russia. What turned out to be a far more significant and immediate influence at a certain stage of that movement was the influence of the Jewish workers' movement, concentrated on the territories of White Russia and Lithuania and with Vilna as its centre.

A series of circumstances furthered the creation and strengthening of firm ties between the Jewish movement and the general Russian movement. Of all the nationalities of the western borders of Russia the Jews were the most oppressed, but at the same time the ones for whom the problem of the struggle for 'separation from Russia' and state independence did not and could not exist at all. The Jews did not respond to the policy of ethnic oppression by separatist tendencies, but on the contrary, by a struggle for the annihilation of the 'Pale of Settlement' that forcibly tied them down to a definite territory and separated them from Russia proper. The immense majority of the Jewish intelligentsia was 'russified'; it attended Russian schools, was brought up on Russian literature, and went through the same spiritual evolution as the Russian intelligentsia. The membership lists of the Russian revolutionary organizations are shot through with Jewish names, and the part played by the Jewish, the most 'urban' intelligentsia of Russia in the Socialist movement, became more and more noticeable as that movement passed from 'rural' Populism to 'urban' Marxism. Finally, for the Jewish worker too, oppressed by an absence of rights, the possession of the Russian language, Russian education, and Russian culture became a treasured weapon of the struggle for existence in the infinitely oppressive conditions created by Tsarist anti-Semitism.

Because of the exceptional importance that the Russian language and the general rise in cultural standards had for the Jewish workers, it was precisely in the 'Pales of Settlement' that the inadequacy of the

* The next year it gave birth to the 'Social-Democracy of the Kingdom of Poland and Lithuania' on Rosa Luxemburg's initiative; this denied the necessity of a struggle for the restoration of the independence of the Polish state.

propaganda of small groups made itself felt with special acuteness the moment the masses began to come into the movement. The advanced workers who had passed through the Marxist groups proved to be culturally too far ahead of these masses to become their leaders in the first stages of the movement, so primitive in both goals and forms. Moreover, for the industrial apprentices that made up the majority of the Jewish workers, the little groups that raised their cultural qualifications so much often served only as a way out of the proletarian *milieu* and their transformation into independent smallholders. The propagandist groups thus proved worthless as a bond of union between the Social-Democratic intelligentsia and the masses. Other paths had to be sought for any *rapprochement* with the mass movement and for its control. These paths were found in the transition from the propaganda of small circles to mass agitation.

The fruit of the critical review of the activity of the little groups, writes Martov,*

> proved to be a conviction that the focus of our activity had to be transferred to the sphere of agitation, and all propagandistic and organizational activity subordinated to this basic objective. In this what was proposed was agitation on the basis of everyday economic needs that led to a clash between proletarian and employer. There was not even a mention of any agitation on the basis of other social interests – on grounds of political, civil, ethnic oppression, or cultural demands. Instinctively we were following the line of least resistance, taking the average worker as he was at the time, limited by his local and shop horizon and by what appeared to be the impassable abyss that separated him from the social life of other classes. But we were convinced that once drawn into the social struggle on the basis of these everyday craft interests the masses would in this process be prepared for the acquisition of broader socio-political aspirations and . . . that on this new path we would proceed to the training of a Social-Democratic workers' movement.[103]

From this point of view the propaganda of 'revolutionary political ideas' became a mere supplement to the principal activity, that of agitation. In accordance with this, both the character of the activity in the little groups had to be adapted to 'the objective of developing some workers into leaders of a mass movement', and these activities themselves, as well as all oral and written agitation and propaganda,

* For his part in a student Marxist circle Martov was exiled in 1892 from Petersburg to Vilna, where he was active locally.

were carried on as far as possible not in Russian but in a language that was understood by the most ignorant masses, that is, in Yiddish.

This makes it understandable why the reconstruction of the work in the new direction collided with the determined resistance of the majority of the workers in the little groups. It was branded as an intrigue of 'intellectuals' who were trying to 'confine the world-view of the workers within the narrow circle of those elementary questions that can be seized upon in agitational and popular literature'. The intelligentsia was even accused of wishing to 'dominate the proletariat by depending on the unintelligibility for the latter of the language of educated people'.

It was only with difficulty that they managed to combat this resistance, and a considerable time went by before the new methods of activity won the right of citizenship. A fruit of this internal struggle was a pamphlet *On Agitation*,[104] which expounded and defended these methods. Written by Arkady Kremer (Alexander) and edited by Martov, this pamphlet, which for a long time was circulated only in handwritten copies, echoed far beyond the confines of Vilna, because it answered questions that the Marxist groups were being confronted with by the mass movement, and not in Vilna alone. This pamphlet, one copy of which was taken by Martov to Petersburg, gave a decisive impetus to the transformation of the activities in Petersburg and to the unification of a series of Marxist little groups into the Petersburg 'Combat Union for the Emancipation of the Working-Class'. This was the first Russian Social-Democratic organization that made mass agitation the pivot of its activity; it became the prototype of similar organizations in all the industrial centres of Russia.

The core of the Union was formed in November 1895 out of two groups, one headed by Lenin, the other by Martov. But the tempestuous development of the strike movement in Petersburg compelled the new organization to begin its agitational work even before it had had time to take definitive shape. A leaflet to the striking workers in the Thornton wool factory, written by Lenin but unsigned, was its first public act. The mass arrests that followed on 8–9 December deprived the organization of nearly half its leading members, including Lenin. In order to prove that the police had 'caught the wrong men' and thus lighten the lot of the arrested comrades, the remainder, headed by Martov, decided to hasten the formation of the organization. On 15 December a proclamation was published that for the first time addressed the workers in the name of the Combat

Union for the Emancipation of the Working-Class and also gave the Union credit for the two or three anonymous leaflets, to the Thornton workers and others, that had been published before. A fortnight later new arrests (on 4 January 1896) snatched away Martov and a number of other members from the core of the organization. But by this time the popularity of the Social-Democracy among the intelligentsia was already so great that it was easy for the Union to staff its centre with new figures, who until then had been working on its periphery,* and to develop an activity whose scope and rapid success proved utterly unexpected to the participants themselves.

In its activities the new organization followed the line laid down in the pamphlet *On Agitation*, known as the 'Vilna programme'. There were more than a few advanced workers in the organized cadres of the Union, especially the highly trained metal-workers. But its attention was focused on the broad masses of the workers, the majority of whom were still largely uncivilized and politically untrained. Penetrating into one factory after another, the mimeographed leaflets of the Union took as the point of departure for their agitation the elementary questions of wages, working hours, factory regulations, mutual relations between the workers and the factory management, and the general living conditions in which the given category of workers had to live, carefully assessing the psychology of the backward, frightened strata of the workers unaccustomed to collective struggle. Thus, the very first leaflet addressed to the spinners and weavers of the Thornton factory emphasized that 'in defending our demands, comrades, we are not mutinying in the least degree'. Even in its very name the new organization, as Martov, who originated the name, bears witness, purposely avoided any use of the word 'Socialist' or 'Social-Democrat', since 'what was most important was for it to be read by the most ignorant workers', who could easily have been frightened away by the 'seditious' word.

In accord with the Vilna programme, the fundamental objective of the Union was to accustom the workers to the idea that the emancipation of the working-class could only be the business of the workers themselves, and that they could only secure their emancipation by means of a concerted struggle. The very first official proclamation of the Union, after having enumerated the strikes that had taken place and reported the arrests that followed them, concludes: 'The strikes

* Among those who entered the Union centre at this time was the author of these lines.

and the struggle will not stop until the complete emancipation of the workers from the oppression of capital is achieved.' It resembles the conclusion of the proclamation addressed by the Union 'To the Petersburg workers' of 27 June 1896, which sums up the stormy half-year that ended with the famous mass strike of the Petersburg textile-workers (see below): 'Let us as before, firmly and relentlessly fight for our own interests . . . Our whole life of toil has taught us that we have no friends apart from ourselves. No threats frighten us, no sacrifices terrify us. We shall fight until we achieve our great goal – the emancipation of the working-class'.

In accord with the Vilna programme the Union's agitation was carried on almost exclusively 'on the basis of everyday needs that led to a clash between proletarian and employer'. But it went beyond the confines of that programme in one respect: from the very beginning it tried to explain to the labouring masses the connexion between those 'needs' and the general political conditions of the country. The Union's leaflets did not speak about the general autocratic order and carefully avoided any mention of the Tsar personally, but they systematically drove home to the workers the idea that their lack of rights prevented the success of their struggle against the 'employers', and that in this struggle the 'government' was bound to be on the side of their enemies. The very first official proclamation of the Union speaks of the 'authorities true to their duty – of looking out for the interests of the rich people', and the same idea is repeated in every leaflet of the Union.* The 1 May leaflet of 1896, written by Lenin in gaol and circulated in hundreds of copies, merely generalizes the political sense of the Union's agitation when, after telling about the 1 May celebration of the West European workers, it sums up: 'Comrades, if we unite as one, the time is not far off when we too, having joined our forces in orderly ranks, will be able to join openly in this

* The Union's methods of political agitation at this time were expressed most precisely in the concluding lines of the pamphlet, *On Fines*, written by Lenin in gaol in 1896: the workers 'will understand that the government and its functionaries will take the side of the factory-owners, and write laws in such a way that it will be easier for the boss to squeeze the worker. . . . When they have understood this the workers will see that they have only one means of defence left – joining together for a struggle against the factory-owners and against the unjust regulations that have been established by law.' As we see the author is trying to bring his readers to the conclusion about the necessity of a struggle against the autocratic order, but refuses to formulate this conclusion openly himself.

general struggle of the workers of all countries with no distinction of blood, race or creed, against the capitalists of the whole world.'

The climax of the Union's feverish labours was the strike of spinners and weavers of the Petersburg factories, which broke out on 23 May 1896 and rapidly drew in some 35,000 workers. The fundamental cause of the strike was, of course, the oppressive living and working conditions: it is enough to say that the principal demand of the strikers was for a shortening of the working day – to ten and a half hours! Its mass character was prepared by the constantly growing excitement of the workers, a result of an uninterrupted chain of individual strikes, and was fed by the unflagging agitation of the Union, in whose stormy expansion a great role was played by its 1 May leaflet. But the strike was triggered by the refusal of the factory-owners to pay the workers for the days of enforced work-stoppage on the occasion of the coronation ceremonies that were taking place in the middle of May in Moscow: 'pay for the coronation days' had first priority in the demands that were in fact made by the strikers, though it stood last in the list of demands formulated by the Union through its deputies.

But though this circumstance was insignificant in itself, it had an effect on the course of the strike and its outcome. On the one hand, it seemed to bring the solemn ceremony of the 'anointing into kingship', and thus also the personality of the Tsar himself, down into the sphere of those sordid questions that the ferocious contest of material interests was revolving around. Thus it undermined the mystical feeling of reverence for the Tsar that was still rather powerful among the ignorant labouring masses. On the other hand it heightened the interest in and sympathy for the strike in the liberal circles in which, as has already been noted, the authority of the young Tsar had been rapidly sinking even before. As is well known, the coronation ceremonies were accompanied (18 May) by a calamity, due to the criminal carelessness of the authorities in arranging for a people's procession in the Khodyn field (in Moscow) that cost the lives of thousands of people. This calamity and the Tsar's striking indifference to it called forth universal indignation. The attitude of liberal society was all the more tolerant; it even had a feeling of gloating sympathy for the mass strike that seemed to be an answer of protest to the 'Khodyn affair' and forced the autocrat to keep putting off from one day to the next his return to the capital, where the workers' 'riots' made it quite impossible to organize 'a triumphal entry'. The Khodyn affair shook the masses' confidence in the solidity of the autocracy. In the eyes of the peasants it was an omen that the new reign would be 'unlucky'. For liberal society the ability of the labouring masses, so unexpected, and displayed so spectacularly, to use its own movement to nullify the plans of the autocratic power was an incontestable sign of the inner weakness of the Tsarist régime, and hence also a stimulus to opposition. The further course of the strike and its final results merely fortified the moods generated at its inception.

It proved impossible to crush the strike by administrative means. With rare discipline the strikers conformed with the Union's summons 'to act calmly and in concert, with no uproar or violence', and to give the police no occasion for intervention. For a long time the press was forbidden to mention the strike, but finally it proved impossible to keep silent. On 10 June the Governor of Petersburg addressed an appeal to the strikers in which he threatened the diehards with exile, but promised to review the 'complaints' of those who would go back to work immediately. Five days later Witte, the Minister of Finance, came out with a public appeal to the strikers. Warning the strikers against 'instigators', he said that 'the workers were just as precious to the government as the factory-owners', and promised that the question of the shortening of the working day would be reviewed by a special government commission.

At the same time the material situation of the strikers began deteriorating severely. The money they received from the metal-workers and from the Union, which made special collections on their behalf, was not enough to keep them from extreme want. Against the background of this want the moral victory that this promise of the government constituted for the workers made the liquidation of the strike easy. By 18 June, four weeks after the beginning of the strike, the Petersburg textile-workers went back to work, only to start a new and equally massive strike at the summons of the reconstituted Union (most of its initial leaders had been arrested in June–August) at the beginning of January 1897, because of the delay in keeping the above-mentioned promise.

This time it was only the categorical announcement by the board of factory inspection that a law shortening the working day would be issued by April, that made the strikers go back to work. The resistance of the factory-owners once again delayed the fulfilment of the promise, and reduced to a minimum the measures for the defence of labour projected by the government. Nevertheless a law was issued on 2 June

1897 that for the first time shortened the working day for men (to eleven and a half hours!), limited the amount of overtime, and greatly improved the organization of the board of factory inspection.

In the history of the Russian workers' movement and Social-Democracy this strike played a quite exceptional role. It brought all working-class Petersburg to its feet and welded it together; collections on behalf of the strikers were made in all business enterprises, and in the January 1897 strike the metal-workers also began to be drawn in. The banishment of 1,000 strikers from Petersburg only contributed to the popularization of the Petersburg movement in the provinces and gave cadres of prepared agitators and organizers to a homogeneous movement that began to take in one industrial centre after another: according to official statistics no fewer than 221,000 workers took part in strikes in 1895–9. The practical successes of the movement, the most luminous testimonial to which was the law of 2 June, were expressed not only in the shortening of the working day, but also in the raising of wages, the improvement of all the internal regulations, and most important of all in the more considerate attitude towards the personal dignity of the workers that for the first time began taking root in factory life. All this fortified in the labouring masses a proud awareness of their own strength and served as a new stimulus for organization and struggle.

The response of the workers of other countries was an immense help. The Union, which from its very inception had been linked to the Emancipation of Labour Group, tried on the one hand to maintain contact through it with foreign workers' organizations, and on the other to attract the attention of Russian workers to the international working-class movement. This goal among others was served by the 1 May leaflet of 1896, and the celebration of 1 May, which from then on was to become customary. But even before this, in March 1896, the Union got out a leaflet dedicated to the twenty-fifth anniversary of the Paris Commune, and sent a welcoming address (written by Potresov) to the French workers. At an international Socialist congress that took place in London in the summer of 1896, together with the members of the Emancipation of Labour Group who received mandates from the Union and from the group of Jewish Social-Democrats in Vilna, there also appeared two Union delegates – Potresov and P. B. Struve. From the very beginning of the strike the Union had taken steps to inform comrades abroad of it and reminded the strikers:

'Comrades, let us remember that the eyes of the workers of the whole world are now turned on us.' The greetings and the money they received from the German and English trade unions made the deepest impression on the strikers, as the first practical lesson in working-class internationalism.

Thus there were born among the broad masses of the workers the first elements of that 'class consciousness' whose development the Union regarded as its fundamental task. But the strike produced some essential results from the point of view of the workers' political education, too. The Union's agitational activity took on dimensions that were unheard of in Russian revolutionary history. During the four weeks of the strike it put out and circulated more than thirty leaflets of the most variegated content: formulations of strikers' demands, information for them on the course of the struggle in various enterprises, organizational instructions, the exposure of the authorities' actions and an answer to the announcements of the government, explanations to 'society' of the significance of the events taking place, an appeal for support of the strikers, etc. The most ignorant workers began growing accustomed to the reading of 'illegal' literature, which so short a time before had frightened them, and began to be infected by an altogether novel interest in political questions. The leaflet the Union put out in November 1896, in answer to two government communiqués about the strike, summed up the strike's political educational meaning for the workers as follows:

> No matter how much government ministers reason about the failure of the struggle, the workers see how the factory-owners everywhere have grown tame; they know that the government is already convoking factory inspectors to consult on the concessions that must be made to the workers, for they see that these concessions are necessary. The strikes in 1895–6 did not take place in vain. They performed an immense service for the Russian workers; they showed how they must carry on the struggle for their interests. They taught them to understand the political needs of the working-class.

One of the signs of faith in this growing 'understanding' was that this time, without changing the general tone of its political agitation, the Union nevertheless risked heading its leaflet 'To the Tsarist Government'.

The Union could take this risk because its leadership of the strike raised the workers' confidence in it to an extraordinary degree. For the first time in the history of the struggle for democracy and Socialism in Russia it was not advanced individuals, but rather broad circles of workers that regarded a revolutionary organization as 'their own'. The arrests enfeebled the Union very much organizationally, but they could not hold back the growth of the Social-Democracy, which, through it, was putting forth roots in the working-class that were already indestructible.

But the popularity of the Union with the intelligentsia and liberal society also grew very strongly. This popularity was merely heightened by the two 'government communiqués' published after the strike. Wishing to minimize the initiating role of the Union, about which the most fantastic rumours were beginning to circulate, the communiqués spoke of it no longer as a 'band of instigators' who had involved the peaceful masses in 'riots' through fraud, but of 'ill-intentioned persons' who were merely 'trying to exploit strikes that were already taking place with the aim of lending them a criminal political character'. The results achieved were the opposite of what the communiqués had calculated on. For they were tantamount to an admission that the Marxists had been right in saying that a mass working-class movement would be the inevitable result of the socio-economic development of Russia, and that this movement would take on a 'political character'. They had been right in predicting that, in the form of the industrial proletariat, a mass force would for the first time appear in Russia that was capable of becoming a bulwark in the struggle against the autocratic régime. This was enough to strengthen still further the sympathy for Marxism in the intelligentsia and liberal society that had been dictated by the whole background of the years following the famine of 1891–2, and to secure for the Social-Democracy a copious influx of people and funds. It was also enough to heighten very greatly the political self-confidence of the youthful Russian Social-Democracy.

The Petersburg strike marked an occasion that was decisive for the whole subsequent political and revolutionary history of Russia, as the Russian working-class started turning Social-Democratic and the Social-Democracy began being transformed into a massive political force. Organizations of the type of the Petersburg Union sprang up in a constantly growing number of cities and industrial centres. They entered into contact with each other – on the subject of receiving and distributing supplies of illegal literature from abroad, the publication and diffusion of their own illegal newspapers and pamphlets, the creation of illegal printing-shops, collections of funds, etc. The need emerged of giving this bond a permanent, organized character. The idea sprang up of convoking an all-Russian congress. All this was over a period of some one and a half to two years.

As we noted above, the Jewish workers' movement also gave to the Marxists of central Russia an impetus to pass from the propaganda of little groups to mass agitation. Now, on the contrary, the initiating role passed to the Russian workers' movement. As F. Kursky, one of the oldest figures and historian of the Bund, the Social-Democratic party of the Jewish workers, testifies, it was under the 'enormous impression' made by the Petersburg strike that there was worked out 'a plan for the fusion of the disunited Jewish Social-Democratic groups scattered through dozens of cities into a united, centralized organization, which was realized by the founding of the Bund in October 1897.[105] In its turn the Bund, which had only just emerged, took the most active role in the organization and activities of the illegal Congress that convened on 1–3 March 1898 in Minsk and at which the Russian Social-Democratic Workers' Party was founded – the ancestor of the future 'Mensheviks' and 'Bolsheviks'.

Because of the uninterrupted arrests the Congress was attended by few people. Aside from the representatives of the Bund and a group that had begun publishing the illegal *Rabochaya Gazeta* (Workers' Gazette) in Kiev in 1897 (two numbers in all came out) delegates of only five local organizations took part in the Congress: the Petersburg, Moscow, Yekaterinoslav, and Kiev 'Combat Unions', and the 'Workers' Committee', also from Kiev. A 'Manifesto', which P. B. Struve was delegated to draw up, announced the founding of the party and formulated the fundamental principles of its programme and tactics.

The Manifesto started off with a reminder of the 'revivifying storm of the revolutions of 1848' that had 'swept through Europe fifty years ago' and given birth to the contemporary workers' movement. The Manifesto then mentioned the 'whole series of recent strikes in Russia and Poland, especially the famous strikes of the Petersburg weavers and spinners in '96 and '97', the government concessions forced by these strikes and especially the law of June; then the Manifesto went on to point out that these concessions were a proof of the growing strength of the working-class and would spur it on to the struggle for further demands dictated by its urgent needs.

'And what does the Russian working-class not need?' continued the Manifesto. 'It is completely deprived of what its comrades abroad freely and peacefully benefit by: participation in the management of state, freedom of speech and press, freedom of assembly – in a word all the instruments and means by which the Western European and American proletariat is improving its situation and at the same time fighting for its own ultimate emancipation – against private property, for Socialism . . .

'But the Russian proletariat can only win the political freedom it needs by itself alone.

'The farther you go to the East of Europe the weaker, more cowardly, and baser the bourgeoisie becomes politically, and the greater the cultural and political tasks that fall to the lot of the proletariat. On its own strong shoulders the Russian working-class must and does bear the cause of winning political liberty. This is an indispensable, though only a first step towards the realization of the great historical mission of the proletariat, towards the creation of a social order in which there will be no room for the exploitation of man by man . . .

'The first steps of the Russian workers' movement and Social-Democracy could not help but be fragmentary, and in a certain sense accidental, devoid of unity or plan. Now the time has come to unite the local forces, groups, and organizations of the Russian Social-Democracy into a unified "Russian Social-Democratic Workers' Party". Aware of this, the representatives of the "Combat Unions for the Emancipation of the Working-Class", of the group that publishes the *Rabochaya Gazeta*, and of the "Jewish General Workers' Union in Russia and Poland" have set up a congress whose resolutions are given below.

'The local groups uniting in a Party are aware of the full importance of this step. By it they will definitively ensure the passage of the Russian revolutionary movement into a new epoch of conscious class struggle. As a Socialist movement the R.S.D.W.P. will carry on the cause and the traditions of the whole preceding revolutionary movement in Russia; setting as the most immediate task of the Party its total conquest of political liberty, the Social-Democracy is advancing towards a goal, already set forth clearly by the glorious figures of the old People's Freedom Party. But the ways and means chosen by the Social-Democracy are different. Their selection is determined by its conscious desire to be and remain a class movement of the organized labouring masses. It is firmly convinced that the emancipation of the working-class can be only its own handiwork and will unswervingly make all its actions conform with this fundamental principle of international Social-Democracy.'

3. 'ECONOMISM'

The Congress elected a Central Committee of the Party, announced that the *Rabochaya Gazeta* was its Central Organ, resolved to set about the publication of pamphlets, assigning their drafting to Lenin, who was in exile, and assigned the representation of the Party abroad to the Union of Russian Social-Democrats founded in 1895 by the Emancipation of Labour Group, which from time to time issued a collection of articles entitled *Rabotnik* (The Worker).

Of all these organizational resolutions only the last remained in effect. The Congress ended on 3 March 1898, and only a few weeks later mass arrests began that razed the edifice of the new centralized organization to its foundations. The just elected Central Committee of the Party, the Central Committee of the Jewish Bund, a number of local organizations, and the illegal printing-shop that was to print the *Rabochaya Gazeta* were all wiped out. The central institutions of the Party ceased existing even before they began functioning; it proved impossible to restore them. Of the 'Party' that had just been founded there remained only its 'Manifesto' and its title. This was snatched up by local organizations that were beginning to multiply and grow at just this time, and one after the other changed from a 'Combat Union' into a 'Committee of the R.S.D.W.P.'

The contrast between the uninterrupted growth of the local organizations of the 'Party' and the impossibility of restoring its central institutions showed that the principal reason for the expiration of these institutions was not the police terror. The reason lay far deeper – in the internal intellectual and political and, later, the organizational crisis that the young Russian Social-Democracy underwent on the very threshold of its existence as a party, in spite of its tempestuous growth or, more accurately, precisely as a result of that growth. This crisis had begun, as we shall see, even before the Congress came together; the Congress itself merely totted up the balance of the first, initial period in the development of the Russian Social-Democracy rather than reflected its real composition at the time of its nominal formation as a party.

This first period was one in which the Marxist intelligentsia began binding itself organizationally to a mass workers' movement in order to achieve the objectives laid down in the programme of the Emancipation of Labour Group. The 'ultimate' goal of this programme was the Socialist emancipation of labourers. We have seen what exceptional importance in the history of Russian revolutionary thought, which indissolubly linked together the struggle for democracy and the struggle for Socialism, was assumed by the idea that in Russia, as indeed throughout the world, only the class of industrial workers could be the bearer of Socialism. Hence Russia, too, could not come to Socialism through the peasant commune, but only through the development of capitalism. It is understandable why it was just this idea that became the cornerstone of the theoretical world-view of youthful Russian Marxism and its theoretical struggle against the Populist epigones.

But if the idea of the Socialist emancipation of labourers from the shackles of capitalism was the 'ultimate', theoretical goal of the Marxist wing of the Russian intelligentsia, its 'immediate' practical goal was, and in the given historical conditions had to be the emancipation of the country from the shackles of Tsarism. Akselrod charted altogether correctly the spiritual genealogy of the programme of the Emancipation of Labour Group when he wrote, in November 1897, that this programme 'came as an answer to the question: how can we emerge from this painful situation [created by the destruction of the People's Freedom]? Where can we get the forces to renew the struggle against the autocracy and how can we carry on that struggle with the greatest likelihood of victory?' He was also right in his contention that 'for this group the idea of organizing a workers' party in Russia was bound up in the most intimate way with the socio-political tasks that have inspired and still inspire all democratic elements in our intelligentsia'.[106]

Practically speaking, this was how the question stood for the Social-Democrats in Russia too. In the programme he drafted for the 'Russian Social-Democratic Party' in 1895–6 Lenin pointed out that the living conditions of the workers were pushing them into a struggle 'against the unrestricted power of the autocratic government'; he declared the task of the future party to be 'to help this struggle of the working-class by the development of the workers' class consciousness, by co-operating with their organizations, and by pointing out the real goal of the struggle'. The 'development of class consciousness' emerges here as a *means* for making the struggle for political liberty more successful – wholly in the spirit of the concluding lines of the

Manifesto, which characterized the practical-political position of the Russian Social-Democracy as identical in aim with the position of the 'old People's Freedom', even though it was distinct from it 'in ways and means'. The question was put in just the same way in two pamphlets written by Martov (*Contemporary Russia*) and by Lenin (*Objective Tasks of the Russian Social-Democrats*) in 1896–7 in gaol and published abroad in 1898 with the enthusiastic recommendation of Akselrod, who called the second one of them a direct 'commentary on the Manifesto'.[107] It is worth noting, for the understanding of Martov's subsequent evolution to 'Menshevism' and Lenin's to 'Bolshevism', that even at this time Lenin (partly under the influence of conversations he had during his trip abroad in 1895 with members of the Emancipation of Labour Group and with French Socialists) was so 'wholly swallowed-up' by the struggle for political liberty that Martov and the other 'Vilna-ites' even formed the impression that he 'had a chilly if not disdainful attitude towards any activity aimed at raising the class consciousness of the masses by way of direct economic agitation'.[108]

But this evolution was still in the future. For the time being the shadings in the opinions of the founders and leaders of the Petersburg Combat Union were only just beginning to outline themselves; they lacked firmness and did not introduce the slightest disharmony into their general activity. The subordination of political to Socialist objectives was their general *theoretical* conviction; the exploitation of the economic struggle of the labouring masses in order to involve them as quickly as possible in the political struggle – was their general *practical* activity. It was just this combination of theory and practice, indeed, that was expressed in the Manifesto of the first Congress.

To the labouring masses themselves, however, the correlation between 'economics' and 'politics' happened to appear in just the opposite light. In responding sympathetically to the political notes that rang out in the economic agitation of the Union, tens of thousands of workers, drawn into an active organizational struggle for the first time, nevertheless accepted political emancipation merely as a remote 'ultimate' goal of their movement. For them the 'immediate' practical objective was those economic demands in whose name they were ready to risk striking and a possible loss of wages. In this respect the temper of the new layer of advanced workers, the new 'workers' intelligentsia' that was beginning to take shape in the fire of the mass struggle, fundamentally diverged from the temper not only of the

Marxist intelligentsia but also of the first generation of Social-Democratic workers, which had come to Social-Democracy not by the 'practical' way of economic struggle but by the 'ideological' way of propaganda in small groups. To anticipate here too, it is worth noting that later on almost all the most eminent of the working-class Social-Democrats of this 'first call-up' who lived to see the 1905 and 1917 revolutions (Babushkin, Shelgunov, Shapoval, Poletayev and others), turned up in the ranks of the Bolsheviks, while out of the ranks of the 'workers' intelligentsia', baptized in the strike movement of the second half of the '90s, there emerged those future cadres of the legal and semi-legal trade unions, co-operative, cultural enlightenment, etc., workers' movement that for a long time were the chief support of Menshevism.

In the new conditions created by the successes of the strike movement and the Social-Democratic agitation, the organizational problem also began assuming a new form. The Combat Unions were essentially no more than organizations of the intellectuals who led the movement. They were enveloped in the constantly growing sympathies of the labouring masses, but very few workers, comparatively, entered their organizational system. When they did it was only as a connecting link between the centre and the unorganized masses and in the role of executors of technical functions bound up with the organization of little circles, the collecting of information, the circulation of agitational and propagandistic literature and so on. The politically active, decisive role belonged solely to the centre, which was organized and staffed from above and was strictly conspiratorial. By virtue of both the conditions of its emergence and the character of its activity this centre consisted solely of intellectuals. It was only intellectuals who made revolutionary activity their principal if not sole occupation ('professional revolutionaries', in later terminology) who had the ability to observe all the rules of conspiracy demanded by this activity. It was only they, with their links to the more substantial circles of society, who could secure the relatively large funds indispensable for the technical apparatus of an illegal organization to be able to function.

The organizational nature of the Combat Unions also determined the character of the party organization created by their Congress. The 'Party' could only be an amalgamation of the local Social-Democratic and intelligentsia centres with the aim of securing better co-ordination of their political-agitational activity and of meeting their financial and technical needs in a centralized way. The founding congress of the Party did not even take any note of the problems bound up with the organization of the labouring masses that came into the movement and that the newly created Party wanted to control, i.e. the problems that in the near future were destined to come to the centre of the Party's attention and even to split it. But even before this beginning they were urgently posed by life. With respect to organization the first Congress merely drew up the balance-sheet of a phase of development that had already been lived through.

This problem confronted the Petersburg Union, soon after the culminating cycle of textile strikes, in the form of a demand, put by the active working-class membership that had grown out of these strikes, to put its representatives in the centre of the organization. This demand was not merely formal and organizational. In the minds of the workers it also entailed a change in the very character of the Union's activity. The emphatically political and hence ultra-conspiratorial character of this activity began to be explained by the intellectuals' failure to understand the real needs and interests of the mass of workers. The oppositionist workers did not deny political objectives. But while the Unions, who devoted a good deal of attention to the workers' professional demands and even made them the starting-point of all their activity, had nevertheless hitherto given priority to the political objectives, and even set up the organization accordingly – for the oppositionist workers matters stood exactly in reverse. From their point of view the political agitation, and the organizational sectors that served it, had to play no more than a supplementary role for the fundamental activity – the defence of the professional economic interests of the working-class. Accordingly, it was not the strictly conspiratorial centres of the political people who were the leaders that had to be the pivot of the organization, but the local, factory and district offices of mutual aid and struggle, the circles of self-education and the workers' collectives. These demanded far less strict conspiratorial behaviour and thus left far more room for the 'initiative' not of the 'professional revolutionaries', but of the workers, who did not have to leave their accustomed work or break off professional and living ties with their own class. It was just this ideological generalizing of these tendencies and the subordination to them of the activity of the Social-Democracy that 'Economism' aimed at.

In new circumstances and in a new form Russian Social-Democratic thought once again underwent the crisis of 'apoliticism' that it had undergone in its time in the ideological envelope of Populism. Akselrod was right in speaking (in the article quoted above) of the 'point of view that narrowed the activity of the Social-Democracy to the organization of the workers for the struggle against the entrepreneurs and to an active part in strikes': 'it may be said to be in its own way a kind of reincarnation of insurrectionism, only on a new social base and on another theoretical foundation'. The social base and the theoretical foundation were unquestionably new, but in its roots the apoliticism of Marxist 'Economism' was rooted in the old contradictions of Russian socio-economic and political reality that the apoliticism of Bakuninite Populism had in its time grown out of.

These profound sources of Economism were not clear, nor could they be, to the leaders of the Combat Union, who had carried with them into exile the Marxist 'orthodoxy' of the first period of Social-Democratic activity among the masses. At this time Economism seemed to them no more than a 'narrow understanding of workers' Socialism', that is, a purely logical error of judgement, and at that merely an error of 'individuals'. But from an external point of view Lenin[107] draws an extremely precise picture of that 'singularity in the historical development of the Russian Social-Democracy that gave rise to and temporarily had to give rise to' this tendency when he wrote: 'The spread of agitation brought the Social-Democracy into contact with the lowest, least-developed layers of the proletariat; the involvement of these strata demanded of the agitators an ability to adapt themselves to the lowest understanding, trained them to give priority to the "interests of the given moment" and to push the broad ideals of Socialism and political struggle into the background. The fragmented, home-made character of Social-Democratic activity, the extremely feeble links between the little circles of different cities, between the Russian Social-Democrats and their comrades abroad, who had more solid knowledge, richer revolutionary experience, and broader political horizons, naturally led to the immoderate exaggeration of this (completely indispensable) side of Social-Democratic activity; in the consciousness of certain individuals this could lead to the forgetting of the remaining sides.'

The 'old ones' – i.e. the chiefs, the founders of the Petersburg Union – had already clashed with these 'certain individuals' in February 1897, when they had been allowed to spend a few days in the capital before being sent off to Siberian exile, and had had the opportunity to meet their 'young' successors. They were shown the 'statutes of a workers' fund', worked out in accordance with the demands of the workers, that were supposed to unite active elements of the proletariat and to form the autonomous body of the Union, subordinating its controlling centre to its own control. In so far as the 'everyday practice of the Union was reflected as before in the leadership of the professional struggle of the workers', this kind of organizational structure, in the opinion of the 'old ones', 'was bound to fetter this controlling nucleus in any attempt to expand its revolutionary activity by taking it out of the shell of a purely professional struggle'. Hence, as Martov writes, 'always regarding the concentration of Party forces on this latter as no more than a strategic device that led by the straightest path to an immediate struggle against the autocracy, we had a sceptical attitude towards the statutes of the abovementioned fund and supported Ulyanov [Lenin], who criticized it rather sharply.'[109]

For a number of reasons, of which the principal one was the incessant arrests, the outlined reorganization of the Union never materialized. But even after the arrests of August 1896 the representatives of the new, 'Economic' tendencies had already begun acquiring a more and more perceptible influence within the organization. From October of the following year on they even began, as a completely autonomous group, to publish a newspaper called '*Rabochaya Mysl* (Workers' Thought), Organ of the Petersburg Workers', which, however, became the official organ of the Union in December 1898. The objectives of the new publication* were defined as follows in the leading article of the first number: '*Rabochaya Mysl*, whose first number is now in the reader's hands, is going to appear in order to restore the bonds between the workers. It will reflect the life of the workers as it really is, will help arouse in them an interest in what is around them and express their needs.'[110] *Rabochaya Mysl*, which from June 1897 on had to be printed abroad, did indeed become the principal organ of the theoretical defence of Economism. In this defence a considerable role was played by elements of the pamphlet *On Agitation* that Akselrod had already referred to in a foreword to its foreign edition, and that later, in 1901, Plekhanov subjected to a detailed criticism in an article *Socialism and the Political Struggle Once Again*,[111] but that slipped past the attention of the 'old ones' when they were laying the foundation of the mass Social-Democracy.

* Its principal editors were K. M. Takhtaryov (Tar), N. Lokhov (Olkhin) and the Finnish citizen Kok, who soon left the movement.

A. Kremer's pamphlet, *On Agitation* – as edited by Martov – started out from the idea that 'no matter how broad the workers' movement is, its success will not be assured until the working-class stands solidly on the basis of political struggle', and that 'the attainment of political power is the principal task of the fighting proletariat'. The problem confronting the authors of the pamphlet boiled down to how to bring to the 'basis of political struggle' not eminent individuals of the working-class, but its entire mass, which was unorganized, still poorly fitted for a collective struggle and at the same time politically illiterate and culturally backward in its overwhelming majority. The problem was solved by the transition from propaganda to agitation and by transferring the centre of gravity to the sphere of the 'everyday economic needs of the labouring masses'. This solution was formulated in the concluding lines of the pamphlet as follows:

> Thus the task of the Social-Democrats consists of constant agitation among the factory workers on the basis of existing petty needs and demands. The struggle provoked by this agitation will train the workers to defend their own interests, heighten their courage, give them assurance of their own powers and an awareness of the necessity for union, and in the final analysis ultimately confront them with more important questions demanding a solution. Prepared in this way for a more serious struggle, the working-class will move on to the solution of its most pressing questions.[104]

This formula served the theoretical defence of Economism in two respects. Firstly, it said that before moving on to political agitation the Social-Democrats had to pass through at least two phases of purely economic agitation, that is, which did not go beyond the limits of the socio-economic relations between the workers and the entrepreneurs – at first on the small scale of individual enterprises, later on the large, 'class' scale. It was just this idea that underlay the so-called 'theory of stages' put forward later by the 'moderate' Economists of the Workers' Cause group (see below). But, secondly, this formulation created the concept that, in order to 'ripen' to the point of being able to accept political agitation, the working-class, without departing from the narrow sphere of its own mutual relations with the entrepreneurs and without paying any attention to questions of the general socio-economic and political development of the country, could isolate its own struggle from any contact, positive or negative, with the struggle of other social strata, and limit in advance its own political objectives, as it said, to a 'changing of prevalent conditions in favour of the working-class'. It was just this idea that underlay the theoretical constructions of that 'extreme' Economism whose organ the *Rabochaya Mysl* became.

In their practical activity both the Vilna pioneers of this transition from propaganda to agitation and the initiators of the Combat Unions tried to weaken or eliminate potentially dangerous consequences of the new tactic. The former supplemented 'economic' agitation by political propaganda and the latter transformed this very agitation into a 'strategic method' of involving the masses in the political struggle as quickly as possible. It was a method that was extremely successful practically. Hence Martov could speak retrospectively in this way of the 'doctrinaire' formulations of the pamphlet *On Agitation*:

> Theoretically this doctrinaire quality was a weakness, but practically it was our strong point, since it infected us with the faith that completely alone, working only in the tightly-knit sphere of the immediate mutual relations between capitalists and workers, we could ultimately find a point of support with whose help we would, by the lever of the class consciousness of the proletariat, overturn Tsarist Russia.[112]

But what had been a merely 'strategic method' for the 'old ones' was converted for the 'young' apostles of Economism into an immutable principle of proletarian class strategy; the programmatic article of the first number of the *Rabochaya Mysl* expounded its own view of the objectives and methods of the workers' movement as follows:

> As long as the movement was no more than a means to soothe the conscience-stricken intellectual it was alien to the worker himself . . . The economic base of the movement was obscured by the constant attempt to remember the political ideal . . . The average worker stood outside the movement . . . The struggle for economic interests was the most stubborn struggle, the most powerful in terms of the numbers of people it was understandable to, and in terms of the heroism with which the most ordinary person would defend his right to existence. Such is the law of nature. Politics always docilely follows economics, and as a general result political shackles are snapped *en route*. The struggle for economic status, the struggle against capital in the field of everyday vital interests and of strikes as a method of this struggle – such is the motto of the workers' movement.

Economism, born in Russia, was soon carried abroad by the new emigrants. We have seen that by the end of 1897 Akselrod had exposed the 'birth of insurrectionism' in a Social-Democratic shell. But the partisans of Economism* soon won a majority in the Union of Russian Social-Democrats, and at the very first congress in November 1898 the Emancipation of Labour Group found itself forced to refuse to edit its publications. The *Rabotnik*, which it had been editing, was replaced by the *Rabocheye Delo* (Workers' Cause), which was edited solely by Economists of various shades. In March 1900 the Emancipation of Labour Group got out a sharply polemical pamphlet by Plekhanov: *A Vademecum for the Editors of Rabocheye Delo*. In April of the same year, at the second congress of the Union, Plekhanov left it, and with comparatively few of its followers – B. A. Ginzburg (-Koltsov), L. I. Akselrod (Ortodoks) and others – formed the 'Revolutionary Group of Social Democrats', the first in the long line of splits in the later history of the Russian Social-Democracy.

In the emigration, however, only a few Social-Democrats, such as Ivanshin and a few others, carried their Economism to the extreme 'apoliticism' of *Rabochaya Mysl*. A 'moderating' influence was exercised in this respect too both by the theoretical criticism Economism was constantly subjected to by the Emancipation of Labour Group, and by the immediate intellectual influence of the European workers' movement. Later on, also, the political revival that from the end of the '90s on became more and more noticeable, as we shall see, clipped the wings of Economism in Russia, too. Hence *Rabocheye Delo*, as Lenin wrote in 1902 in the foreword to his *What Is to Be Done?* expressed 'not a consistent Economism, but the diffusion and vacillations that constituted a feature of a whole era in the history of the Social-Democracy'. Its official doctrine soon became the already-mentioned 'theory of stages' that the agitation of the Social-Democracy had to pass through before becoming definitely 'political'. Krichevsky, for instance, wrote: 'Political demands, which in their nature are common to all Russia, must correspond initially to the experience extracted from the economic struggle by a given stratum of workers. It is only on the grounds of this experience that it is possible and necessary to move on to political agitation.'[113]

The influence of the European, especially the German Social-Democracy was one of the factors that prevented the Economism of the *émigrés* from evolving into a consistent 'apoliticism'. But in

* Of these B. Krichevsky, V. Makhnovets (Akimov), V. Ivanshin, Z. Koppelson (Timothy), E. D. Kuskova, S. N. Prokopovich, P. Teplov (Sibiryak), A. S. Piker (Martynov) later became well known.

the heart of the German Social-Democracy around this time there arose a powerful current of 'revisionism'. Eduard Bernstein became its champion in his well-known book, *Premises of Socialism and the Tasks of the Social-Democracy*[114] (January 1899). 'The movement is everything, the final goal nothing' – this slogan was sympathetically seized on by the Russian Economists. 'Revisionism' not only sanctioned the 'theory of stages'; it also laid the theoretical foundation for the evolution of ideas about the political objectives of the Russian Social-Democracy that took place under the cover of this 'theory'. The German revisionists preached 'reformism' concerning the struggle of the working-class for Socialism in a developed bourgeois society with a certain degree of political liberty. Their Russian followers carried this 'reformism' into the working-class struggle for the establishment of political rights, too. In the political programme of the Russian Social-Democrats the revolutionary struggle against the whole of the autocracy had to yield to the reformist struggle for partial political rights (legalization of strikes, right of association, of assembly, etc.) in so far as a demand for these rights arose among the workers as a result of the 'experience extracted by them from the economic struggle'.

Thus, against the background of this clash between 'politics' and 'economics' flowing from the contradictions of Russian life that Populism in its time had foundered on, and that Marxism was now beating up against, the premises were laid down for the emergence of the trend that proved to be the final product – Economism. As Plekhanov said: 'The course of ideas is ultimately very far from what we meet in the pamphlet *On Agitation*. But in "principle" it coincides with it.'[111] This current was given consistent expression in a document that has entered the history of Russian Social-Democratic thought under the name of the *Credo* (1899).*

The *Credo* forthrightly declared Bernsteinian 'revisionism' to be its theoretical basis; this was understood to be not a partial correction of the policy of the German Social-Democratic Party, but a 'basic change' in its 'practical activity' and at the same time in the Marxist theory that activity was supported by. 'This change will be not only

* Formally this document was only a rough copy written quickly by E. D. Kuskova. But in essence it gave an ample formulation of the chain of ideas whose principal representatives in the Union of Russian Social-Democrats were Kuskova and Prokopovich and that soon led them to a total rupture with the R.S.D.W.P.

towards a more energetic carrying-on of the economic struggle and a strengthening of the economic organizations, but also – and this is the most essential thing – in the relationship to the remaining opposition parties. Intolerant Marxism, negative Marxism, primitive Marxism (which takes advantage of a too schematic conception of the class division of society) will yield to democratic Marxism.'

As for the Russian Social-Democracy, this was the *Credo*'s conclusion: 'Talk about an independent workers' political party is nothing but a product of the transfer of alien objectives and alien experiences to our own soil . . . For the Russian Marxist there is only one way out: participation in, that is, help for the economic struggle of the proletariat, and participation in liberal-oppositional activity.' 'We were Social-Democrats, we must stop being such,' was how Plekhanov summed-up this conclusion.

Thus the last word of Economism proved to be a 'liberal Marxism' *sui generis*. Parallel with 'liberal Populism', it was indissolubly bound-up with 'legal' Marxism and, like its Populist predecessor, proved to be, for substantial and constantly growing strata of the intelligentsia, an ideological tool for the liquidation of their own revolutionary-Socialist rejection of 'liberal-oppositional' society, and a channel for melting away in it. From this point of view 'liberal Marxism', like 'liberal Populism', proved to be a stage in the historical process of the dying-out of the 'intelligentsia' as a separate social category, in the process of its 'redistribution' between the various strata of nascent bourgeois society.

But in contrast with the background against which liberal Populism had arisen and had become a 'moulder of opinion', when liberal Marxism emerged Marxism, as a revolutionary Socialist ideology, had already had time to become linked to a mass movement. In one form or another it had become the ideology not only of the intelligentsia, but of a constantly growing segment of the working-class. Hence liberal Marxism did not kill revolutionary-Socialist Marxism. The Social-Democracy did not cease being a Social-Democracy. On the contrary, the social revival that had begun on the threshold of the twentieth century furthered its rebirth. And it was just this sharp protest against the *Credo*, whose initiators had been 'orthodox' Marxists, that was the first symptom of this rebirth and of the tempestuous upsurge in the offing.

4. *ISKRA* (THE SPARK)

The attempt to 'politicalize' the movement that was once undertaken by the small group of the Workers' Banner,* which had emerged in 1898, turned out to be a fiasco. From 1897 on, Economism of one variety or another dominated more and more strongly the minds of the Social-Democratic 'practicals' who were carrying on the work initiated by the Petersburg Combat Union in 1895. But even at the apogee of its victories Economism was beginning to lose ground because from the end of the '90s on the whole political situation was beginning to change rapidly.

Both in its practical objectives and in the 'ideology' of the mass of workers the strike movement of '96–'97 was purely Economist: the strikers set no political goals and proclaimed no political demands. None the less the political importance of this movement was immense. For the first time certain political ideas and attitudes filtered through not only into the thin layer of advanced workers, but also into the heart of the masses, preparing them for their active political role they were destined to play in the next decade. But beyond this, the strike movement of '96–'97 also proved to be a turning-point in the development of Russian political thought because it provoked a basic change in the temper of the affluent, educated strata of society.

It has been noted several times how important for the political evolution of Russia was the fact that for the first time on the social scene popular masses appeared that were capable of becoming a bulwark in the struggle for a political democracy. These were, to be sure, workers; they saw their immediate enemy not in the autocracy, but in the factory-owner, the entrepreneur; the weapon they used was the strike – all factors that might have forced the affluent strata of society to put themselves hostilely on guard. But the specific conditions of development of this society in Russia, which we have had occasion to emphasize more than once, substantially weakened its natural aversion to the goals, forms and methods of the workers' movement.

Down to the second half of the '90s the chief exponents of Russian liberalism, tinged around this time with 'Populist' colours, were certain landowning circles (chiefly agriculturally 'impoverished' ones of central Russia) and the intelligentsia bound up with the Zemstvos. For these circles the very fact that the centre of gravity of the revolutionary

* V. P. Nogin, S. O. Tsederbaum (Yezhov) and others.

organizations began shifting from the countryside to the cities and that the carrier of the mass movements proved to be not the peasantry but the industrial proletariat, was reassuring and encouraging. But the strikes of '96–'97 gave impetus to the formation and the growth of liberal-constitutional trends also in the *milieu* of the magnates of the textile industry, which had been the chief arena of these strikes. It was just from this time on that Moscow, the centre of the textile area, also became the centre of a *sui generis* 'merchants' liberalism'.

This phenomenon, paradoxical at first glance, is explained by the fact that both the strikes themselves, which passed through the police barriers easily, and the concessions made under their pressure to the workers (shortening of the working day, expansion of factory inspection, etc.) showed the bourgeoisie the internal weakness of the autocratic régime and the impossibility of relying on its ability to defend bourgeois interests purely by police measures. Moreover, the government's disarray before the steadfastness of the strikers and its attempts to flirt with the workers ('workers and factory-owners are equally precious to the government'), evoked a suspicion among the bourgeoisie that at the critical moment the autocracy might even launch a legend about the 'workers' Tsar' to replace that of the 'peasant Tsar'. It might meet the workers' economic demands halfway in order to make the workers' movement a battering-ram against the political claims of the bourgeoisie just as it had done for a long time, and not without success, with the threat of a peasant uprising against the political claims of the nobility.

The next few years showed that these bourgeois suspicions were far

* From the end of the '90s on, the political police, on the initiative of Zubatov, chief of the Moscow Security Department, began trying to create 'independent' workers' organizations. These were promised sponsorship in the defence of purely economic workers' interests on condition that they rejected any political objectives. The autocracy was supposed to be the defender of the labouring masses both against the 'self-interest' of the possessing classes and against the 'alien' revolutionary intelligentsia. According to the scheme of the political police, this was the demagogic – in present-day terminology one might say Fascist – political platform of the 'independent' workers' movement.

This Zubatov enterprise, which managed to attract some extremist Economists of the Social-Democracy (especially in the area of the Jewish workers' movement) had some success. Its reputation in government circles stood very high down to 1903, when the Economic strike initiated in Odessa by the Zubatov-inspired officials encompassed, unexpectedly for its initiators, the whole of the city and acquired a clearly political character. The Zubatov manœuvre was from unfounded.* In any case there were enough of them to lend impetus to a shift in its temper. An understanding of the necessity of protecting its own interests by way of economic and political reforms began penetrating increasingly broad business and industrial circles, especially circles linked to the textile industry, which was geared to the domestic market and to mass consumption. These circles became oppositionist.

The extreme modesty of the demands presented by the strikers in '96–'97; the relative calm that took place afterwards even though these modest demands were given merely partial satisfaction; the 'reformist' character of Economism, which had replaced the original revolutionary temper of the Social-Democracy directly after the climax of the cycle of strikes and which had deliberately emphasized its rejection of any claims to political primacy and leadership; the more and more definite passage of 'legal Marxism' from the idea of social revolution to the idea of social reform, and from the defence of the working-class to the defence of the bourgeoisie as the exponent of capitalism against both the autocracy and the reactionary land-holding system of the nobility; the more and more insistent assurances that the time of classical, 'intolerant and negative' Marxism had passed by in general, even in its German homeland, and that the time had come for classless, appeased, democratic Marxism, ready to consider itself an organic part of bourgeois society and to take up a suitably modest place in the framework of that society – all these tendencies made it exceptionally easy for broad circles of the business

---

liquidated after this, but that did not prevent the Police Department the very next year from collaborating, even though in a more veiled form, in the establishment in Petersburg, under the leadership of one Father Gapon, of a 'Congress of Russian Workers', a sort of legal workers' club. The parade organized by this 'Congress' to the Winter Palace in order to present a petition to the Tsar as the workers' defender, culminated, as is well known, in the horrifying massacre of 9 January 1905 ('Bloody Sunday'), which marked the beginning of the Russian revolution.

But even so the political police went on making such attempts. Its final major action of this kind was having a deputy elected to the Fourth Duma (1912). He was an agent by the name of Malinovsky, who had managed to become leader of the Bolshevik fraction. It was part of his duty first of all to force a split in the Social-Democracy, and secondly to frighten off the liberal bourgeoisie by extreme radicalism. Malinovsky's speeches were edited and also often written in the Police Department. In the spring of 1914 Malinovsky was unmasked, fled abroad, and later, after his return from German captivity, was shot by the Soviet government.

and industrial class to pass over from apoliticism to 'politics', from purely 'practical' co-operation with the government to oppositional liberalism, and heightened their political self-assurance extraordinarily. This change in the feelings of bourgeois society was expressed most clearly and definitely in the conduct of its most impulsive and combative part – the student youth.

The student upheaval, based on a protest against the restrictions introduced into university, scholarly and corporate life by the reactionary university regulations of 1884, had not stopped since the very beginning of the new reign. The strikes of '96–'97 lent it new force. The student movement became more tempestuous; attempts were made to shift over to the methods of street demonstrations. During one of these organized by Petersburg students on 8 February 1899, on a student holiday, the participants were savagely beaten-up by the police and Cossacks. In answer to the protests the government published, in July of the same year, some 'Provisional Rules' concerning the drafting of students into the army because of 'the collective perpetration of riots', and at the end of the following year took advantage of some small riots, first at Kiev, then at Moscow University, to send some 200 students off to barracks. This step merely poured oil on the fire. Karpovich, a former student, shot and killed Bogolepov, the reactionary Minister of National Education (February 1901). Student disorders grew more and more frequent and multitudinous. A new beating-up of demonstrating Petersburg students in March 1901 evoked a public protest of liberal writers. The movement overflowed the boundaries of youth and began to take in the 'fathers' as well.

Faced by all this constantly broadening public protest, the government decided on some concessions. The new Minister of National Education, General Vannovsky, released the students from the barracks and announced an era of 'heartfelt solicitude' for the student youth. But it was already too late. Society saw nothing but a sign of weakness in the government's concessions. Two liberal organizations emerged that definitely set themselves the goal of struggling for a constitution. One was more moderate, the 'Group of Zemstvo Constitutionalists', and one more radical, the 'Union of Emancipation'; they soon made up a coalition. It was in this movement that the future head of the liberal 'Constitutional Democratic Party' ('Kadet'), Paul Nikolayevich Miliukov, came to occupy a leading position. But the principal ideologues and organizers of the movement, which according to its programme was moderately liberal but turned more and more revolutionary in its tactics, proved to be the 'legal Marxists': S. Prokopovich, E. Kuskova, V. Bogucharsky, and others. In June 1902, when the organ of Russian liberalism, *Osvobozhdenie* (Liberation) began to come out in Stuttgart (Germany), its editor was P. B. Struve, the author of the Manifesto of the R.S.D.W.P. that had formerly unmasked the 'baseness' of the Russian bourgeoisie. At the same time 'liberal Populism' also revived, radically revolutionized. It was headed by the old Land and Freedom and People's Freedom partisans who were returning from hard labour and exile (M. Natanson, M. Gots, O. Minor, C. Breshkovskaya and others) and fortified by new elements (G. Gershuni, V. M. Chernov, and others). In 1901 there was organized the illegal 'group of Socialist Revolutionaries' from which the party of the same name was later to evolve; from the spring of 1902 on it published its organ *Revolyutsionnaya Rossiya* (Revolutionary Russia) abroad and soon revived on a large scale the practice of political terror.

In this excited chorus of protesting and demanding voices the voice of the Social-Democracy was not heard much. From the point of view of Economism both the student upheavals and the liberal movement, whether aristocratic or bourgeois, appeared to be a matter outside the working-class and hence did not demand the active intervention of the Social-Democracy. It might have appeared, as a matter of fact, that the situation foreseen by the authors of the *Credo* had come about. The initiating role was passing wholly into the hands of 'society' and a merely auxiliary role was falling to the working-class. This situation, however, proved extremely short-lived; the position soon began changing radically.

After 1899 the general European industrial crisis began spreading to Russia. In contrast to the crisis evoked by the famine of 1891–2, what suffered now most of all was not the textile but the metallurgical industry. In the movement of the second half of the '90s the metalworkers played, as we have seen, a rather passive and in any case a secondary role. Now it was just this detachment of the Russian working-class, which included its most cultivated and advanced strata, that moved into the foreground. At the same time the principal arena of the movement also became, together with Petersburg, which had large-scale metal-working factories (chiefly for machine-construction) the south of Russia, which now, with the substantial help of foreign capital, became the centre of Russian metallurgy.

Such were the conditions marking this new phase of the Russian workers' movement. It differed from the movement of '96–'97 not only in its substantially greater mass character, but also in its far greater combativeness and above all in its definitely political hue. The quite exceptional success of the First of May agitation of the Kharkov committee of the Party, which the Kharkov workers responded to on 1 May 1900 by a general strike with clearly political slogans, marked the advent of this phase.

The movement grew swiftly. From 1901 on the workers in a number of cities (Kharkov, Moscow, Tomsk and others) also began taking part in student demonstrations, giving them a more combative mass character. Bloody clashes with the troops and police grew more frequent. The celebration of 1 May became more and more widespread. Repressions called forth resistance, and an attempt to crush the 1 May strike of 1901 at the Obukhov army factory in Petersburg turned into a real military siege of the factory ('the defence of Obukhov') as a result of which as many as 800 workers were arrested; many of them were sentenced to hard labour by a military court. In 1902 there flared up in Rostov-on-Don a strike of the railway workers, which was joined by the workers of the Rostov factories. During the strike the Don Party committee arranged mass meetings outside the city at which tens of thousands of workers listened to its orators (I. P. Bragin, A. Brailovsky, I. D. Stavsky and others). The government succeeded in breaking the strike only with the help of the army.

But the movement kept growing, bouncing over into other cities of the Ukraine (Odessa, Kiev, Yekaterinoslav), the Caucasus (Baku, Tiflis, Batum), the Volga region (Sormovo, Nizhni-Novgorod, Saratov). Under its influence the peasantry too began fermenting; in the spring and summer of 1902 large-scale peasant 'disorders' took place in the Ukraine (Poltava and Kharkov Provinces) and along the Volga. The government crushed them with armed force and subjected the 'instigators' to corporal punishment. The whole country was moving away from that political dead-point on which the preceding reign had apparently impaled it so firmly. And one of the chief arms of the political struggle was an arm borrowed from the workers' arsenal – the strike; this was now not an economic but a political strike. It was not only the workers who struck. The students also used the arm of the strike: in the winter of 1901–2 the country witnessed a general strike of the highest institutions of learning that took in more than 30,000 students. And only two or three years later the representatives of the 'liberal professions' – engineers, teachers, lawyers, and even functionaries – also began reaching out for the strike as a weapon.

Thus the course of events cut the ground away from under the feet of Economism – in so far as it wished to be not an ideological bridge to the camp of bourgeois-constitutional liberalism, but the leader of the workers' movement and of the Social-Democratic Party. One can see why it happened to be the south where the process of the rapid liquidation of Economism in the committees of the R.S.D.W.P. began in 1900. The literary exponent of this return of the Social-Democracy to 'politics' was the newspaper *Yuzhny Rabochii* (the Southern Worker),* which was printed in an illegal printing-shop of its own. The more radical circles of affluent society materially supported this renascent 'political' current in the Social-Democracy, and in every way facilitated its organizational activity technically (accommodation addresses, storage of literature, check-in points, lodgings, etc.). The aroused student *milieu* not only served it as an immense reservoir of propagandists, agitators, and organizers, but represented the masses of students excluded from institutions of learning or sent into exile, as well as the inexhaustible cadres of those 'professional revolutionaries' destined soon to play such an outstanding role as *Iskra*'s tireless 'agents' in its victory over Economism.

In the conditions described above an energetic protest against the *Credo* and the whole spirit of Economism, which in the summer of 1899 made itself heard from Siberian exile, began evoking an increasingly clamorous echo in Social-Democratic circles. The initiators of the 'protest of the seventeen' (from the number of participants) were Lenin and those comrades closest to him because of their previous activity and present place of exile.† This protest was immediately supported by Martov, who was in far-off Turukhansk, by a group of exiled Social-Democrats in Vyatsk Province,‡ and by many others. Practically speaking, accordingly, this was a protest on the part of the first, orthodox, and revolutionary generation of Russian Marxist 'practicals', temporarily condemned to the inactivity of exile but already preparing for a return to the arena of political activity, against their second generation, revisionist and reformist, which for a short time had become the exponent of a definite phase in the development

* N. Ginzburg (Naumov), A. Kagan (Yermansky), V. Rozanov, B. Tseitlin (Batursky), and others.

† Krzhizhanovsky, Starkov, Lepeshinsky, and others.

‡ A. Potresov, T. I. Dan, V. Vorovsky, N. Bauman, and others.

of the Russian Social-Democracy, but which completely failed to correspond to the objectives that the new phase of the workers' movement had confronted it with. In fact the 'protest', through the heads of the Economists, laid down its own kind of ideological bridge from the old generations of the Russian Social-Democracy to its new and swiftly growing cadres, which were taking shape in an atmosphere of social movements that were becoming more and more massive, more and more tempestuous and more and more pointed politically.

In its principled criticism of the *Credo* the 'protest' written by Lenin took as its starting-point the two 'perspectives' Akselrod had noted at the end of 1897 as the two alternative but historically equally possible lines of political development in the Russian workers' movement and Social-Democracy. One perspective was: 'The workers' movement will not emerge from the narrow channel of purely economic clashes with the entrepreneurs, and by itself as a whole will have no political character; but in the struggle for political liberty the advanced strata of the proletariat will follow the revolutionary groups and fractions of the so-called intelligentsia.' The other perspective was: 'the Social-Democracy will organize the Russian proletariat as an independent political party fighting for liberty, partly side by side and in alliance with bourgeois revolutionary fractions (in so far as these will be present) and partly by drawing into its own ranks or carrying along with it the most revolutionary elements of the intelligentsia'.[115]

'The mere possibility of the appearance of programmes' similar to the *Credo* proves to what extent Akselrod's apprehensions were well-grounded, says the 'protest'; it summons Russian Social-Democrats 'to exert every effort' to ensure that not the first but the second perspective is realized. But beyond these 'programmes' the very course of events gave enough justification, as we have seen, to the fear that the Social-Democracy's self-elimination from the political struggle would help turn the mass workers' movement into a purely physical force, politically led but also exploited by the liberal elements of affluent society and the intelligentsia connected with them, or at least lead to the weakening of an initiatory political role on the part of the working-class in the composition of the social forces that opposed the Tsarist régime. This idea (also expressed in the Manifesto of the Party), that it was just this seminal role of the working-class in the political struggle that was indispensable for the radical liquidation of the autocracy was, however, the new feature that Akselrod, influenced by the experience of the '90s, brought into the original formulation of the political problems of the Social-Democratic movement as made by the Emancipation of Labour Group in its first programmatic activities. The appeal of the Economists for self-elimination from the political struggle was answered by Akselrod by an appeal to – lead it.

In this Akselrod, more than any other member of the Emancipation of Labour Group, agreed in these years with the pioneers of the Combat Unions. Essentially Lenin was developing the same 'Akselrod' ideas, only lending them still greater sharpness when he wrote: 'In the struggle against absolutism, the working-class must isolate itself, for it alone is the consistent and unconditional enemy of absolutism to the end, it is only between it and absolutism that no compromise is possible.'[116] Plekhanov, finally, in an article already mentioned (*Socialism and the Political Struggle Once Again*) draws the final conclusions from these two ideas: 'Our party will take on itself the initiation of a struggle against absolutism, and consequently the hegemony in that struggle . . . It will make itself a liberator *par excellence*, a centre that all democratic sympathies will gravitate towards and all the greatest revolutionary protests will start from.'[111]

The word 'hegemony' was only uttered in 1901. But the idea not only of an active role of the Social-Democracy in the political struggle, but also a leading role as representative of the working-class, was just the platform on which during the years of exile the 'triple alliance', aimed at the 'conquest of the Party', of the most gifted figures in the old Petersburg Combat Union – Lenin, Martov, and Potresov – was prepared in correspondence and realized when their exile came to an end in 1900. The instrument of this conquest was to be the big political periodical scheduled for publication abroad in conjunction with the Emancipation of Labour Group; it was to be transported illegally into Russia and there reprinted in the organization's own illegal printing-shops. In Lenin's expression, it organized a 'Socialist post-office' of its own, relying on a dense network of correspondents, propagandists and all sorts of 'agents'.

It goes without saying that the theoretical foundation of the periodical had to be orthodox Marxism. But the pre-eminence of the objective of political emancipation, as against the Socialist and specifically working-class objectives of the Social-Democracy, and its leading role in the attainment of this 'all-national' objective, were underlined as 'neutral', in the Socialist sense, by the name of the periodical

(The Spark) as well as by the epigraph this title was taken from: 'From the spark shall be kindled a flame.' This line (from a verse with which the Decembrists of 1825, sentenced to hard labour, answered Pushkin's message to them) was supposed to confirm the right of 'our Party' to be the direct heir and consummator of that revolutionary cause that had been launched by the uprising of the aristocratic democrats more than three-quarters of a century before, continued by the 'plebeians' of the '40s and '50s, by the Populists of the '60s and '70s, by the People's Freedom of the '80s, and that was now passing into the powerful hands of the working-class in the form of its party – the Social-Democracy.

After a series of consultations with some people from Russia and lengthy negotiations between Lenin and Potresov, who had gone abroad, and the Emancipation of Labour Group (Martov had stayed behind a while in Russia to arrange organizational matters), an agreement was reached towards the autumn of 1900 between the *Iskra* group, which preserved its separate existence, and the Emancipation of Labour Group for the joint publication of a political periodical, *Iskra*, and a theoretical review *Zarya* (The Dawn). The German Social-Democracy was very helpful; Munich was selected as headquarters for *Iskra*, and Lenin and Potresov moved there under false names, soon to be joined by Martov and Vera Zasulich, while the secret printing of the periodical, whose first number came out in December 1900, was done in Stuttgart, at the well-known Social-Democratic printing-shop of Dietz.

The periodical's platform included the same idea of the primacy of political objectives and the hegemony of the Social-Democracy in the struggle for political emancipation we have just spoken of. The conclusion of the Statement of the Editors (whose basic text was written by Lenin) read as follows:

> Whoever understands the Social-Democracy as an organization serving the spontaneous struggle of the proletariat exclusively can be satisfied by local agitation and 'purely workers'' literature alone. That is not what we mean by Social-Democracy: we understand it as being a revolutionary party directed against absolutism and indissolubly bound up with the workers' movement. It is only when the proletariat, the most revolutionary class in contemporary Russia, is organized into such a party that it will be able to perform the historic task incumbent on it: to unite under its own banner all the democratic elements of the country and to consummate the stubborn struggle of a whole series of past generations by the final triumph over the hated régime.

This platform also gave a special sense to the merciless struggle against the 'revision' of Marxism, to which a great deal of attention was paid by *Iskra* and even more by *Zarya*. 'Revisionism' was rejected theoretically, of course, because it broke with the idea of a social revolution and called on the working-class to replace the struggle for the liquidation of capitalism with a struggle for its social 'reform'. But in the specific conditions of Russia the struggle against the revisionist 'critique of Marxism' was stimulated not by its social but by its political reformism: not because it distracted the proletariat from accomplishing a social revolution against capitalism, but because it distracted it from concentrating all its forces on a political revolution against the autocracy. And the *Iskra* Statement brands the enthusiasm for 'Bernsteinianism' and 'Economism' as an 'attempt to hold back the movement at its lowest stage, an attempt to move to the background the task of educating the revolutionary party that was leading the struggle at the head of the people as a whole'.

After making the political hegemony of the Social-Democracy the basic idea of the platform, it remained to be explained how this hegemony was to be achieved. In the initial resolutions of the Emancipation of Labour Group the question of hegemony never arose at all, while the contradictory problem of accomplishing a political revolution in capitalist society through the forces of a Socialist working-class was solved by calling for a heightening of the consciousness of the labouring masses to a level that would enable them to combine rationally the indispensable 'critique' of capitalism in its struggle against the proletariat with the no less indispensable 'support' of capitalism in its struggle against the pre-capitalist forces of Tsarism and feudal servitude. There was a great deal of rationalism in this solution of the problem, but not enough realism. This became more and more evident as the mass working-class movement left off theoretical prophesying and became a more and more noticeable practical factor in Russian political life. It was just the practical insolubility of the contradictions engendered by the course of this development that provoked the dichotomy in Social-Democratic thought that in its expression abolished the problem itself, if not practically at least theoretically. It led to conclusions like: 'We were Social-Democrats, we must stop being so', as well as to diametrically opposite ones: 'All genuine and consistent democrats in Russia must become Social-Democrats' (Lenin[116]).

Put in such an extreme form, this last conclusion sounded, of course, like a paradox, and Lenin himself, as we shall see, used to pose this problem in a wholly different way long before the establishment of *Iskra*. But in its paradoxical form Lenin's aphorism faithfully reflected the train of ideas that soon led to the idea of 'hegemony' expressed by Plekhanov when he said that the Social-Democracy had to become the 'liberating party *par excellence*'. This paraphrase of Marx's well-known remark could not, however, answer the question. Marx had spoken of the proletariat as the 'liberating class *par excellence*' in the perspective of a social revolution in which the working-class, by virtue of its organized character and Socialist consciousness, had to become the natural leader of all those masses of the peasantry, petty urban bourgeoisie, people in the liberal professions, etc., pauperized and uprooted by the development of capitalism, in order to lead them in the storming of the capitalist fortress. But in what way could a *Socialist* party of the working-class dominate the struggle for the political emancipation of *capitalist* society?

As we shall see, it was just these differing answers to the questions that had arisen in direct connexion with this basic problem of the Social-Democracy of the time that led to an acute crisis in the 'left' political current of the Social-Democracy almost immediately after its victory over Economism. And even long before this crisis symptoms were evident of an approaching divergence on these questions. But for the time being the foreground was occupied by the struggle against Economism, and the whole 'political' front of the Social-Democracy was ready to agree on the answer given by Akselrod. Essentially this constituted a further development of the same rationalist approach to the solution of the problems of the political activity of the Russian Social-Democracy.

As Akselrod wrote:

> The problem of acquiring adherents and direct or indirect allies for the Russian Social-Democracy among the non-proletarian classes will be solved primarily and chiefly by the character of the agitational-propagandistic activity among the proletariat itself. Hitherto this activity has revolved almost entirely around the direct economic exploitation of the workers by the employers. But the indicated objective calls for the broadening of the scope of agitation and propaganda by questions that themselves constitute nodal points in which the interests of the proletariat as well as of the other classes oppressed or squeezed by absolutism and the capitalist bourgeoisie it sponsors will converge and become interwoven. But on close examination these questions prove to be the most important and fundamental for our proletariat at the present time.[117]

In complete accord with this, the editors of *Iskra* said in their Statement: 'To expand the framework and enlarge the content of our propagandistic, agitational, and organizational activity – these words of P. B. Akselrod's ought to become the slogan defining the activity of the Russian Social-Democrats in the near future. We accept this slogan in the programme of our organ.'

Side by side with the objective of 'politicalizing' the Social-Democratic movement *Iskra* also set itself the task of reorganizing it. As the editors' Statement put it: 'The principal feature of our movement is its fragmentation, its home-made character, as it were,' that is, the mutual independence of little local groups, the absence of any traditions or continuity. This 'home-made' quality was a consequence of the narrowing of Social-Democratic objectives to the level of Economism; but in the conditions of the 'rapid diffusion of Social-Democratic ideas among our intelligentsia' and the 'independently emerging movement of the industrial proletariat' that met it half-way, it became of itself a cause of the eternalization of spiritual confusion: 'the discord between this fragmentation and the demands called forth by the strength and breadth of the movement creates, in our opinion, a critical situation'. It was necessary to pass on 'to a higher form of the movement', and the necessity of this transition 'was felt everywhere'. This led to the 'practical conclusion: we Russian Social-Democrats must rally round and direct all our energies to the formation of a powerful party fighting under the unitary banner of the Social-Democracy'.

But how could 'the formation of a powerful party' be realized after the nullification of the attempts undertaken by the constituent congress of the party in the spring of 1898? This is the answer given by the editors' Statement:

> The usual reply to this consists of saying that a central institution must be elected once again and charged with the restoration of the Party organ. But in the period of dispersion we are living through such a simple path would scarcely correspond to the goal. To create and consolidate the Party means to create and consolidate the unification of all Russian Social-Democrats, and for the reasons indicated above such a unification cannot be decreed . . . It must be developed. What must be developed, first of all, is a firm intellectual unification, eliminating the disharmony and confusion that – let us be frank – now prevails among the Russian Social-Democrats. The intellectual unification of the Party must be confirmed by a Party programme. What must be developed, secondly, is an organization specially devoted to the relations between all centres

of the movement, to the securing of complete and timely information about the movement, and to the efficient supplying of the periodical press in all corners of Russia.

'Intellectual unification' was the prerequisite of an organizational unification; hence, 'before uniting, and in order to unite, we must first decisively and definitely mark out the boundaries between us'. This phrase was not at all a way of masking a disinclination to unite, or the expression of a secret desire to leave the Economists outside the reborn party. On the contrary. Conversations with the members of Party committees in Russia had given the founders of *Iskra* the conviction that under the influence of events an immense majority of the Economists would return to 'politics'. It was just because of this that they had no desire even abroad to bind themselves organizationally to the part of the split Social-Democratic organization that thought the same way. The foreign organization of *Iskra* preserved its separate existence; it was not until the end of 1901, after the failure of attempts to restore unity (the Zurich congress in August 1901) that it fused with the organization of the *Sotsial-Demokrat* and the Emancipation of Labour Group into an '*Emigré* League of Russian Social-Democrats'.

The explanation above makes it understandable why *Iskra* came out against the attempts of the Union of Russian Social-Democrats to create as quickly as possible a small illegal congress in Russia for the restoration of a 'Central Committee'. The *Iskra*-ites counterposed to this plan of the editors of the *Rabocheye Delo* a plan for composing, from among the most eminent figures of the Social-Democracy in Russia, an 'Organizational Committee', for more or less protracted political and organizational activity. From the point of view of *Iskra* only such activity could prepare the conditions for convoking a congress corresponding, because of both its composition and the nature of its activity, to the tasks confronting the Social-Democracy. Such a congress could only be convoked, not in the narrow Russian underground, but abroad.

The 'Congress' that came together nevertheless, in Belostok in March 1902, proved to be so poorly attended, because of the mass arrests that preceded it, that its participants, most of whom gravitated towards the *Rabocheye Delo* group, saw themselves forced to declare the convention, in accordance with *Iskra*'s insistence, a mere 'conference'. The conference limited itself to the adoption of an all-Russian 1 May leaflet (based on a draft presented by the *Iskra* editors) and the election of an Organizational Committee to prepare a second Congress. The Organizational Committee elected was immediately arrested, practically in its entirety. But by the end of this same year – in agreement with *Iskra*, the *Yuzhny Rabochii* group and the Petersburg committee (which the Economists left around this time) – it was replaced by a new one, which also included a representative of the Jewish Bund and in which the majority of the members were no longer from the *Rabocheye Delo* but were definitely '*Iskra*-ites'.

Thus *Iskra* won a total victory. But in the double bottom of the valises with which the *Iskra* delegate (the author of these lines) illegally came to the Belostok conference the first several dozens of Lenin's new book, *What Is to Be Done?*, were taken into Russia. The ideas developed in this book proved to be dynamite; a year or so later they exploded the unity of the victors.

CHAPTER NINE

Bolshevism and Menshevism

1. THE ORGANIZATIONAL QUESTION

The basic objective of *What Is to Be Done?* was the concretization of the organizational ideas formulated in the *Iskra* programme, and a more detailed grounding and development of the organizational 'plan' that had been outlined by Lenin as early as May 1901 in an article *What Shall We Start From?*[118]

Against the background of the stormy events of the beginning of 1900 the work of 'marking out boundaries', begun by *Iskra*, very quickly ended with the victory of the 'political' tendency. In essence the *Rabocheye Delo* surrendered the basic positions of Economism when, under the influence of the torrential student movement, which thanks to the workers' support had begun assuming a revolutionary character, it called on the Social-Democrats to 'storm the autocracy', referring, in justification of this 'historical turn-about' (the title of an article printed in No. 6 of the *Rabocheye Delo* Leaflet) to a well-known aphorism of the German Social-Democrat Wilhelm Liebknecht: 'tactics must be changed within twenty-four hours, whenever the circumstances change'. But it was just this, not 'historical', but 'hysterical' turn-about – as it was called ironically by *Iskra* – that provoked a sharp criticism from Lenin, who pointed out that in the given case what was at stake was not a question of 'tactics' but of the basic character and direction of Social-Democratic policy, and that, in the absence of a central organization and in view of the weakness of the local organizations, to call for an immediate 'storming' of the autocracy would mean to condemn oneself to a real and swift defeat: 'On the present occasion our slogan cannot be to "storm", but must be to "set up the correct siege of the enemy's fortress". In other words: the immediate objective of our Party could not be a summons to all available forces to attack here and now, but must be a summons to develop a revolutionary organization capable of uniting all forces and leading the movement not only in name, but in fact.' It was just because of this that it was necessary to realize, as quickly as possible, the programme 'put forth' in the first number of *Iskra* for the creation of a powerful organized party aimed at the conquest not only of individual concessions but of the very fortress of the autocracy.

In the realization of this programme the 'first practical step' had to be 'the establishment of a general all-Russian periodical'. By opening its columns 'to the all-national unmasking of the Tsarist government' and 'by infiltrating through the proletariat into the ranks of the urban petty-bourgeoisie, rural home-craftsmen, and peasants', the Social-Democratic periodical 'would become a real people's political periodical', and thus fortify the hegemony of the Social-Democracy in the struggle against the autocracy. But the periodical was to be not only a 'collective propagandist and a collective agitator, but also a collective organizer'. The 'agents' who transported and circulated it illegally, while also organizing its supply of 'unmasking' material, would transform the very character of the activity of the Social-Democratic committees and groups. They would take them out of the narrow framework of leading the economic struggle of the local workers and concentrate their attention on political problems on an all-national scale. At the same time they would structurally bind together the local organizations each to each and also to the editorial board of the periodical.

In such a form the organizational plan outlined by Lenin conformed completely with the organizational ideas of all the *Iskra*-ites, and it was wholly in the spirit of these ideas that Lenin, in his *What Is to Be Done?*, said: 'The Social-Democrat's ideal must be not the secretary of a trades-union, but a people's tribune'. He also expressed the general opinion when, in a polemic against the Economists' backing of a democratic electoral principle in Social-Democratic organizations, he wrote as follows of the difference between an organization of 'professional revolutionaries' and an organization of workers for economic struggle:

> An organization of workers must be, first of all, based on their crafts; secondly, it must be as unconspiratorial as possible . . . In contrast, an organization of revolutionaries must take in, primarily and above all, people whose profession consists of revolutionary activity . . . this organization necessarily must be not very large and it must be as conspiratorial as possible.

And Potresov expressed the general attitude to Lenin's work of all members of the editorial board and the closest contributors to *Iskra* when he wrote him (22 March 1902): 'I've read your little book twice running and straight through and I can only congratulate its author. The general impression . . . is superlative.'

In *A Letter to a Comrade on our Organizational Tasks*, written in September 1902, Lenin went further. On the one hand he proclaimed a monopoly of the leading role for the 'professional revolutionaries', and on the other the principle of 'homogeneity' in the composition of the leading centres.

> The movement must be led by as small a number as possible of groups as homogeneous as possible, which have been tested by the experience of professional revolutionaries. The movement must be participated in by as large a number as possible of groups as variegated and heterogeneous as possible, from the most variegated strata of the proletariat (and other classes of the population).[119]

There were supposed to be two controlling centres: an intellectual one, in the form of a Central Organ, which thanks to its location abroad was protected against 'the influence of the Russian gendarmes' and hence was able in its turn to ensure the 'seasoning and continuity' of the intellectual leadership, and a practical one, in the form of a Central Committee, which was 'free enough for the direct handling of the whole practical side of the movement' but was 'always in accord with the Central Organ in all essentials'. This 'accord' was supposed to be guaranteed once again 'not only by the Party programme, but also by the composition of both groups. Both groups, both the C.O. and the C.C., had to be made of people who got on together completely.' Speaking concretely, that is, only people who were in complete harmony with the editors of *Iskra* could be members of the C.C.

In its turn such an *Iskra* C.C. had to have the right to determine not only the character of the activity of the Party organizations, but also the personal composition of the local committees as well as of the network of 'variegated and heterogeneous groups' that enveloped them.

> For the centre to work efficiently the local committees had to become specialized and more 'businesslike' organizations that would attain a genuine 'perfection' in one practical function or another. In order that the centre might not only advise, counsel, persuade, debate (as has heretofore been the practice) but really conduct the orchestra, what is necessary is for it to be known with exactitude who would play just which

violin and where; how, where, and which instrument is to be taught, who plays false where and why . . . and so on.

This plan, which concentrated all political initiative and activity in an extremely narrow and 'homogeneous' summit of the Party (in this instance it had to be the editors of the Central Organ) and turned the whole Party organization into a severely centralized and disciplined hierarchy of 'businesslike' executive organs, is of exceptional interest not only because it was what was defended by Lenin at the Second Congress of the Party*, where a split took place, but also because it was according to this plan that first the Bolshevik fraction was organized within the Party, and then the Bolshevik (Communist) Party, and it was this that was made the basis of the organization of the Communist International and of the Communist Parties throughout the world. It was in accordance with the homogeneous plan, moreover, that the organization of the Soviet State was, in essence, also set up.

The majority of the Party did not share what Martov called this 'hypertrophy of centralism'[120] that was so clearly expressed in Lenin's *Letter*. But neither did it see in it any special cause for alarm. Tied to Lenin by the solidarity not only of the *Iskra* political line, but also of *Iskra* organizational ideas, it was convinced that in the process of further joint activity the 'excesses' of Lenin's organizational plan would be smoothed over. It saw in them only a more or less accidental 'overshooting of the mark'.

The majority of the editors also regarded as the same sort of more or less accidental 'deviation' the theoretical propositions concerning the relationship between 'spontaneity' and the 'self-conscious' workers' movement and the introduction of Socialist ideas into such a movement from 'without', by which Lenin justified, in *What Is to Be Done?*, the principles of organizational centralism common to all the *Iskra*-ites. This was all the more so since, as Lenin himself let slip out, he was 'purposely' selecting an 'angular formulation' and expressing himself 'with simplified sharpness'. Once again Potresov was expressing the general mood of this majority when he wrote, in his above-mentioned letter: 'Somewhere, in the struggle against

* Convoked by the *Iskra* Organizational Committee, the Congress opened on 17 June 1903, and at first sat in Brussels, then in London. It was attended by forty-three delegates from twenty-six organizations, with fifty-one having a deciding vote and fourteen having a consultative vote.

"spontaneity", the author has overshot the mark in the direction of "consciousness".'

Lenin formulated his theoretical propositions in an answer to the *Rabocheye Delo,* which was looking for the 'deeper roots' of the difference between the Russian Social-Democrats in a 'differing estimate of the comparative importance of the spontaneous and the consciously "planned" element in the Socialist movement', and was charging *Iskra* with 'exaggerating the importance of the objective or the spontaneous element of evolution'.

On the threshold of Social-Democratic activity in Russia it was the more or less general conviction of the practical Social-Democrats that it was precisely in this process of economic struggle, in the course of the constantly increasing and deepening collisions between workers and employers, that the Socialist class-consciousness of the proletariat would take shape 'spontaneously'. This was how the pamphlet *On Agitation* put the question, nor did Lenin at the time put it any differently, when, in proclaiming the Russian worker the 'sole and natural representative of the entire exploited, toiling population of Russia',[121] he explained this exclusive role of the proletariat by the fact that 'the exploitation of the mass of producers [i.e. the peasants, artisans and home-craft workers, etc. (T.D.)] is on a small-scale, fragmented, and undeveloped, while the exploitation of the factory and workshop proletariat is large-scale, socialized and concentrated'. His conclusion was: 'Hence the workers sees the class, bourgeois-capitalist essence of the régime that other toilers are prevented from seeing by the medieval forms of their exploitation.' The workers' struggle 'is inevitably transformed into a war not against an individual, but against a class, the same class that oppresses and exploits the toilers not in a few factories and workshops alone, but always and everywhere'. Under these conditions the role of the Social-Democracy is reduced to the mere generalization and organization of this 'spontaneously' emerging Socialist class-consciousness: 'The political activity of the Social-Democrats consists of furthering the development and organization of the workers' movement in Russia, and transforming it from its present condition of isolated attempts at protest "uprisings" and strikes devoid of any guiding idea into an organized struggle of the entire Russian working-class directed at the bourgeois régime.'

The development of Economism into a special, apolitical tendency, and the experiment of 'workers' oppositions' that had arisen in the course of the mass movements, demonstrated the extreme one-sidedness of these assumptions of the purely 'spontaneous' emergence of a Socialist class-consciousness in the Russian labouring masses. Lenin now answered the *Rabocheye Delo* group with just as one-sided a denial of the significance of the 'objective or spontaneous element of development'. Referring to the 'trades union but not Social-Democratic' character of the 1896-7 strikes, Lenin continued:

> We said that any Social-Democratic awareness on the part of the workers was out of the question. It could only be introduced from outside. The history of all countries testifies that through its own forces alone the working-class is capable of developing merely a trades-union mentality, that is, a conviction of the necessity of uniting in unions, carrying on a struggle against the bosses, getting the government to enact laws of one kind or another that are vital for the workers, etc. But the doctrine of Socialism grew up out of those philosophical, historical and economic theories that were elaborated by the educated representatives of the possessing classes, the intelligentsia. The founders of contemporary scientific socialism, Marx and Engels, themselves belonged to the bourgeois intelligentsia by virtue of their social position. In the same way, in Russia, too, the theoretical doctrine of the Social-Democracy arose quite independently of the spontaneous growth of the working-class movement; it arose as the natural and inevitable consequence of the evolution of thought of the revolutionary Socialist intelligentsia.

We have already had occasion to explain why the organizational problem, which in Russian conditions became the problem of the interrelationship between the workers and the revolutionary intelligentsia, had to acquire quite exceptional importance with the emergence of a working-class movement in Russia. It had confronted the revolutionaries in its full acuteness for the first time as far back as the embryonic phase of the working-class movement at the end of the '70s. At that time the Northern Union advanced the idea of as broad an organization as possible, which would admit various 'shades of opinion' and leave the most 'energetic and active' elements to achieve a 'decisive significance' in the organization through their 'educational' effect on its rank-and-file members, and the editors of the Land and Freedom organ decisively protested against any 'breadth' of this kind and insisted that the organization must admit only people who had undergone a 'certain probation' and demonstrated their 'ability to work for the cause', since 'what was important was not the number of members' but their quality – 'their firm unwavering mutual responsibility, their solidarity'. This problem arose with the same acuteness a second time when once again, in the wave of the 1896–7 strike movement, relatively important cadres of advanced workers began pushing forward for the first time, with claims to the role of leader of their own class, and when Economism attempted to settle this contest between the workers and the revolutionary intelligentsia in favour of the 'average worker' and against the 'conscience-stricken intellectual'.

Now too this same problem arose with extreme acuteness for the third time, when vast masses of people were coming into the movement and when this very movement of theirs had itself begun to take on a more and more political character. But now, in diametric opposition to Economism, Lenin was deciding the question entirely in favour of the revolutionary intelligentsia, while trying, through his analysis of the significance of 'spontaneity' and 'consciousness' in the working-class movement, to provide this decision with a theoretical foundation as well.

In the circumstances the 'elective principle' could only have the most limited application. Hence the paramount practical requirement of the movement was the creation, 'from the top downwards', of a centralized organization whose backbone was and could only be constituted by the 'professional revolutionaries', i.e. in their overwhelming majority revolutionary intellectuals. This was one thing all *Iskra*-ites were unanimous about. But just when Lenin, reverting to the organizational principles of such 'conspiratorial organizations' as Land and Freedom and the People's Freedom, was trying to strengthen the dominant role of the 'professional revolutionaries' in the Party through basic organizational measures, while restricting the number of leaders as far as possible by limiting it to people 'tested by experience' and politically in 'complete harmony', most *Iskra* editors imagined – in the spirit of the Northern Union's organizational ideas – that the 'professional revolutionaries' would win for themselves the dominant positions in the party, and appear ubiquitously as its most 'energetic and active' workers, through their political and organizational activity 'educating' broader and broader circles of the advanced workers for a dominant political role in the Party and so preparing the workers to succeed the revolutionary intelligentsia.

However clear the distinction was between this 'democratic' centralism of the majority of the *Iskra* editors and the 'bureaucratic' centralism of Lenin, it seemed altogether trivial in the face of the unity concerning those basic principles, both political and organizational, whose consistent application raised *Iskra*'s authority so high and within a very short period enabled it to become if not formally at any rate in fact the dominant centre of the Russian Social-Democracy. Consequently, not only before the Congress but practically down to its very end it could not even occur, either to the closest contributors of *Iskra* or to *Iskra*-people in general, that just these disagreements on the organizational question would become the wedge that, after splitting the editors of *Iskra*, would also split the Party that had only just barely managed to unite under its banner.

Right down to the twenty-second session of the Congress (there were thirty-seven sessions in all), when an organizational draft worked out by a commission was put up for debate, the *Iskra* editors came out in a solid bloc not only on programmatic but on organizational questions. Even in its concluding sessions the Congress, with rare unanimity, passed a series of political resolutions whose authors were almost exclusively the editors who had been in a minority on the organizational question. And it was only in one case (the question of relations with the liberals) that each segment of the editorial board, henceforth split asunder, presented the Congress with a special resolution of its own – and the Congress passed both one and the other. (We shall return below to the programmatic and political questions confronting the Congress, in another connexion.)

On two occasions, in the first half of its sessions, the Congress had to deal with organizational questions. One was in connexion with the question of the 'position of the Bund in the Party', and the second was in the course of the brief discussion preceding Lenin's submission of the draft of the party statutes to the commission. Both times it happened to be Martov who spoke for the entire *Iskra* group. Speaking as a co-*rapporteur* on the *rapport* of the representatives of the Jewish Bund, he, without denying the right of the Bund to a certain autonomy, decisively objected to its ultimatum that it be the organization of the Jewish proletariat, 'unrestricted in its activities by any district boundaries', and to consider itself the 'sole representative' of this proletariat in the Party. He saw in this a demand for a completely unacceptable introduction into the Party of a federative principle of organization, and introduced a resolution in this spirit.* In the

* The passage of this resolution by the Congress led to the Bundist delegation's leaving the Party, in whose foundation the Bund had played such an eminent role. The Bund did not return to the Party until the Stockholm Congress of 1906.

debate on Lenin's draft resolution Martov 'associated himself with Lenin's conclusions' and disagreed with him on only two particular questions – the composition of the Party council and the methods of co-opting new members into the Central Committee. Moreover, Martov insisted that after the confirmation by the Congress of the list of Party organizations 'any further change in their composition must be left to the Central Committee,* just as in his turn Trotsky (who joined the Mensheviks after the Congress) proclaimed the right of the Party to an 'organized lack of confidence' *vis-à-vis* all its sections, and hence also the right of the Central Committee to a 'control of all local, district, national and other organizations'. The conviction of intellectual and political solidarity that bound together the entire *Iskra* group, and the necessity of guarding its unity in the face of the outside world at all costs, was so great that Martov also spoke in defence of Lenin against those attacks directed at the considerations in *What Is to Be Done?* about the role of 'spontaneity' and 'consciousness' by the small number of Economists and partisans of *Rabocheye Delo* who participated in the Congress.

The mood began to change only after it became clear, during the protracted labours of the commissions and the special meetings of *Iskra*-people that proceeded parallel with them, that it was a question not of different 'shadings' of one kind or another in the common organizational plan that could be smoothed over by way of compromises, but of two tendencies of organizational thought and practice that were hard to reconcile. Most of the *Iskra* editors thought that the introduction into the centralized organization of the Party of as much 'democracy' as possible under the existing political conditions was an indispensable condition if the Social-Democracy was going to be able to further the development of Socialist class-consciousness in the working-class movement and gradually transform itself from an organization of the revolutionary intelligentsia into an authentic class party of the proletariat. But the 'authoritarian' centralism Lenin had formulated in his *Letter to a Comrade* seemed to them in its turn an indispensable condition for the Social-Democracy to prepare both the labouring masses and itself for that dominant role in the forthcoming 'all-national' attack on the 'fortress of the autocracy' that was the aim of all the *Iskra*-people. It was just in this

* The relevant clause in the statutes passed by the Congress is as follows: 'The Central Committee shall organize committees, unions of committees, and all other institutions of the Party.'

clash between these two organizational tendencies that the meaning was to be found of the open struggle – at first not a struggle of the *Iskra*-people against the Economists, but a struggle of the *Iskra*-people between themselves – that started up at the Congress over the very first paragraph of the constitution and culminated in a split.

Who could regard himself as a Party member? This question was answered in two drafts submitted to the Congress. Lenin's draft read: 'Anyone can regard himself as a member of the Russian Social-Democratic Workers' Party who accepts its programme and supports the Party by personal participation in one of the Party organizations.' Martov's draft: 'Anyone can regard himself as a member of the R.S.D.W.P. who accepts its programme, supports the Party by material means, and co-operates with it regularly under the direction of one of its organizations.' The tendencies of these two formulations are obvious. The first attempts to limit the circle of Party members, i.e., individuals with the right to influence its political line in one way or another, only to members of organizations that must perforce be conspiratorial, i.e., primarily to 'professional revolutionaries'; the second, on the contrary, attempts to broaden that circle, also turning into plenipotentiary members of the Party those active and advanced workers who, because of their way of life, were unable to become members of the conspiratorial organizations but, as the Georgian delegate Kostrov (Noah Zhordania) said,

> were pedlars of proclamations, collected money, demonstrated in the streets, went to prison and into exile, but did not go into any committee or into any other organizations. . . . Our Party is a party of the masses, and it is impossible to include the masses in an organization; in the contemporary conditions in Russia that is unthinkable.

Akselrod had once said it was 'necessary to distinguish between the concepts of Party and of organization'; Martov developed this idea and said, in defence of his draft: 'The Party organization is a fly-wheel that sets in motion the activity of the Party as we understand it.' In Russian conditions, of course, the revolutionary organization inevitably assumed a 'conspiratorial' character. But 'for me a conspiratorial organization only has sense in so far as it is enveloped by a broad Social-Democratic working-class party.' 'The more broadly the title of Party member is diffused the better. We can only rejoice if every striker and every demonstrator can call himself a Party member.' Martov then dealt with the fears of some delegates that by exploiting the formal rights of members of the Party some its peripheral elements would be able to distort its *Iskra* political line; he said: 'According to our draft one of the rights of a Party member will be to inform the centre of his own opinions and wishes. Another right will be to form public opinion, and the more "conspirators" take that opinion into account the less danger that any question of "rights" will arise.'

This was Lenin's reply to Martov: 'If hundreds and thousands of workers arrested for strikes and demonstrations proved not to be members of Party organizations, that would merely prove that our organizations are good, that we are accomplishing our task – of making conspiratorial a more or less narrow circle of leaders and bringing into the movement the broadest possible mass.' As for the formation of the 'public opinion' of the Party, 'our task is to place the *de facto* control in the hands of the Central Committee. Our task is to preserve the firmness, tenacity and purity of our Party'.*

The Congress expressed itself in principle in favour of Martov's formulation (twenty-eight votes against twenty-two, with one abstention), and finally passed it by thirty-five against one, with twelve abstentions. These results were only possible because Martov was supported in this by a number of delegates who were not in the *Iskra* organization: representatives of the *Yuzhny Rabochii*, the Jewish Bund, and the *Rabocheye Delo*, while the majority of the *Iskra* delegates were clearly drawn to the organizational views of Lenin.

Defeated on the first paragraph, Lenin began fighting with all the more energy not only for the other paragraphs of the constitution, but most of all for what from the point of view of his organizational plans was more important than the constitution – for the personal composition of the Party centre,† for the creation of a 'consistent, honest *Iskra* cabinet'. In this he was successful, since the 'unexpected departure of the Bund all at once changed the whole situation. . . . We

* It was considerations of this order that made Plekhanov, too, side with Lenin: 'Lenin's draft may serve as a bulwark against the entry into the Party of all sorts of opportunists, and if only because of this all those opposed to opportunism should vote for it.'

† The Party centre was supposed to consist of the Central Organ (which the Congress appointed *Iskra* to be), the Central Committee and the Council of the Party, to which the Central Organ and the Central Committee sent two representatives apiece and which was headed by a fifth member (Plekhanov) elected at the Congress. In the Central Committee the Congress elected, by a secret vote, three members who were given the right – provided they were unanimous – to add to their own number through co-opting.

found ourselves in the majority, and we put anyone we wanted to into the Central Committee' (Lenin[122]). But a prerequisite for the creation of such a 'cabinet' out of *Iskra* people who were 'in complete harmony' with each other turned out to be, in view of the disagreements displayed, not only a careful selection of the C.C. members, but the reorganization of the *Iskra* editorship too. By nineteen to seventeen, with three abstentions (the editors did not vote), the Congress rejected Trotsky's proposal – to confirm in office all the former editors – and ordered only three editors to be elected, leaving them the same right of co-opting as the three-member C.C. elected by the Congress had received.

This directive was answered by Martov, in his own name and in the names of Akselrod, Zasulich, and Potresov, with a statement in which they all declined to be candidates for the editorial 'triumvirate'. He said:

> It is no secret to anyone that in this reform what is at issue is not a question of 'abilities' [of the individual members of the former editorial board] but the struggle for influence over the C.C. The majority of the editors have shown that they do not wish the C.C. to be turned into an instrument of the editorial board. That is why it was necessary to curtail the number of editors.... I thought, together with the majority of the former editors, that the Congress would put a stop to the 'state of siege' within the Party and introduce normal order. In reality the state of siege, together with exceptional laws against individual groups, has been prolonged and even exacerbated.

Lenin answered this as follows:

> Up to now the entire activity of *Iskra*, as a separate group, has been a struggle for influence; by now the issue is one of a greater organizational strengthening of that influence. . . . Martov blames me for a desire to influence the C.C., while I regard it as a merit of mine that I attempted and shall go on attempting to fortify that influence through organizational means.... In relation to the unstable and wavering elements we not only can but are obliged to create a 'state of siege'.

Having declined to participate in the editorial 'triumvirate' (in its election twenty-three votes went to Plekhanov, twenty-two to Martov, and twenty to Lenin), the Mensheviks* also declined to participate in

* 'Minoritarians' – those who remained in a minority on the question of the personal composition of the centres, in contradistinction to the Bolsheviks, or 'Majoritarians'.

the election of the C.C., as well as to enter it through co-optation. The break-up of the *Iskra* organization into two hostile fractions had become an accomplished fact.

Beginning with No. 46 (August 1903) *Iskra* began coming out under a new editorial board, made up of two members, Lenin and Plekhanov. Their efforts to invite the members of the old group to collaborate with them were unsuccessful. In Russia the three-member C.C. elected by the Congress (Krzhizhanovsky, Lengnik, Noskov), was soon supplemented by other Bolsheviks (Krasin, Galperin and others); it attempted to apply a policy of 'a state of siege' – dissolving some committees, unilaterally changing the composition of others and so on. These attempts met with resistance, and led to splits and the formation of parallel local organizations. The internecine strife threatened to paralyse all the political activity of the Party, just at a time when tremendous workers' strikes were taking place one after the other, accompanied by demonstrations and clashes with the police and troops, when peasant disturbances were becoming more and more frequent, and when feverish excitement had begun taking hold of 'society' – no longer the student youth alone but also members of the liberal professions, Zemstvo functionaries, and certain strata of the industrial and commercial bourgeoisie.

An organizational practice like this, which by Plekhanov's own admission[123] was quite unexpected by him, induced him to break with Lenin – after one of the C.C. members tried to apply it abroad as well – by declaring that the Foreign League was dissolved because of its refusal to admit members appointed by him and to annul decisions just passed by its Congress. In its turn this break provoked Lenin to announce his leaving the editorial board. Having published one number as sole editor, Plekhanov made use of his right of co-opting: beginning with the 53rd number (25 November), three months after the end of the Congress, *Iskra* once again began to come out under the former board of editors, minus Lenin, but with the *de facto* collaboration on the editorial board of L. Trotsky, B. Ginzburg(-Koltsov) and the writer of these lines, as well as somewhat later the former *Rabocheye Delo* member, A. Piker(-Martynov). But now the Bolsheviks began to boycott the newspaper in their turn, and while it formally remained the 'Central Organ' of the Party, *Iskra* in fact became the organ of Menshevism. It was not until December 1904 that Lenin succeeded in establishing the newspaper *Vperyod* (Forwards), which became the organ of Bolshevism.

However, the destruction of the organizational edifice erected by the second Congress did not stop with this. In August 1904 the Bolshevik C.C. set itself the task of reconciling the contending fractions. On the basis of its renunciation of the practice of the 'state of siege' three Menshevik representatives (i.e. Alexandrova, V. Krokhmal, V. Rozanov) were taken into it. But this did not improve the position within the Party. Lenin and those who agreed with him in Russia called the activities of the C.C. destructive of the will of the Congress. As a counterweight to the United C.C. he formed the 'Bureau of the Committees of the Majority', which made its first task the convocation of a new congress. This Congress, which called itself the third Congress of the Party, met in May 1905. It changed the constitution of the Party, liquidating the very institution of the Council, divested *Iskra* of the title of Central Organ and elected a new C.C. headed by Lenin. He was also assigned the publication of a new Central Organ – *Proletarii* (the Proletarian). The Mensheviks refused to acknowledge the Congress convoked by the Bolsheviks as a Congress of the Party. But a conference they convened at the same time, which took into account the *de facto* situation, did not wish to counterpose a C.C. of its own to that of the Bolsheviks; they limited themselves to the election of an 'Organizational Committee'* which was ordered to enter into negotiations with the Bolshevik segment of the Party.† These negotiations were not crowned with success, and while remaining formally within the united Party in fact the Bolsheviks and Menshevik fractions led a completely independent existence for a whole year (down to the Stockholm 'unifying' Congress in May 1906). A split from top to bottom proved to be the only way of enabling each of the warring fractions to deflect its energies away from the intra-party strife into the political activity insistently demanded by events.

2. FROM ORGANIZATIONAL TO POLITICAL PROBLEMS

The creation of a powerful, centralized organization and the intellectual unification of the Party were two tasks neither of which could

* A. Tarasevich, V. Guvtosky(Mayevsky), A. Grintser, L. Khinchuk, M. Panin.

† Plekhanov regarded this decision as a sanction of the Party's disintegration, and left the *Iskra* editorial board in protest. He did not return to the Menshevik fraction until a year later.

be solved by the constituent Congress of 1898, and which also confronted the second Congress. This Congress was also incapable of securing the organizational unity of the Party. But it laid down an organizational system, adapted to Russian political conditions, in whose framework there began from this time on the rapid organizational consolidation and the unflagging growth of the two fractions that had emerged from it – the Bolsheviks and the Mensheviks. In this sense it may be said that the Congress did settle the purely organizational problem it had been confronted with and hence became an authentic historic milestone in the organizational development of the Russian Social-Democracy.

The problem of spiritual and political unification was a different matter. The Congress never succeeded in coping with this task, and today, with historical hindsight, it is scarcely necessary any longer to demonstrate that the organizational disagreements that, at the second Congress, divided the *Iskra*-people into Bolsheviks and Mensheviks were merely the cover for incipient intellectual and political divergences that were far more profound, and above all more persistent than the disagreements between the Economists and *Iskra* that had receded into the past and been conclusively liquidated by the Congress. It was not an organizational but a political divergence that very quickly split the Russian Social-Democracy into two fractions, which sometimes drew close and then clashed with each other, but basically remained independent parties that kept on fighting with each other even at a time when they were nominally within the framework of a unitary party.* And it was not the organizational but the political divergence that later on – though in completely different historical circumstances – also found its echo and sequel in the collapse of international Socialism into 'Communism' and 'Social-Democracy'.

But at that time, at the beginning of the century, the political character of the split was far from immediately apparent, not only to the spectators on the side lines but to the participants in the fractional struggle themselves. On the contrary, both the unanimity of the whole *Iskra* part of the Congress on programmatic questions, and the disappearance of Economism as a separate and theoretically systematized current of Social-Democratic thought, seemed to justify the view that on political questions the Congress was a complete victory for *Iskra*,

* It was, of course, only in 1917 that the Bolsheviks changed the name of their Party to 'Communist', holding over from the past no more than the supplementary designation of 'Bolsheviks'.

and that it was only organizational dissension that cast a shadow over its conclusion. And even here, however formidable the divergence in principle between the *Iskra*-people, it evoked no more than one paragraph in the organizational statutes – that about Party membership. But even in this case the few explanations given by Lenin during the debate on this paragraph prompted Akselrod to ask himself whether he was not 'knocking on an open door', once Lenin was willing to 'meet him half-way' to such a degree; to which Lenin in his turn answered by saying, 'I absolutely do not consider our disagreement so fundamental that the life or death of our Party depends on it.'

As a matter of fact, as we already know, from the point of view of the organizational views Lenin had worked his way through to at this time, what was far more 'fundamental' was the question of the rights and the composition of the central Party institutions. But the circumstance that what served as the direct occasion of the split was not even the question of Party membership but the question of the composition of the *Iskra* editorial board – and that the division of the votes on this far 'narrower' question determined not only the adherence of the Congress members to one fraction or another, but also the very names of these fractions – seemed to prove, superfluously, that the split was due merely to disagreements of an organizational and even, what was worse, a personal nature. This was just how Lenin put the question in two open letters he addressed to *Iskra* after he left the editorial board. Even much later, in 1904, when the fractional struggle was already in full blaze, Lenin wrote, in the foreword to his polemical book, *One Step Forward, Two Steps Back*, that the 'differences dividing one wing from another at the present time boil down primarily neither to programmatic nor tactical but merely to organizational questions'.[124] Hence, even while calling Bolshevism the revolutionary wing of the Party and Menshevism the opportunist wing, he accuses the 'new' *Iskra* only 'of opportunism in organizational questions'. But by then these same differences on the organizational question had already had time to shift over to another plane.

At the Congress this question was formulated by both sides only on the plane of the passionate struggle against Economism and every sort of 'opportunism' under whose aegis *Iskra* had prepared the Congress. Martov had justified his refusal to participate in the editorial 'triumvirate' by pointing out that the reason the number of editors had to be curtailed was that most of them were against 'turning the C.C. into an instrument of the editorial board' (see p. 247). In his reply Lenin had not denied Martov's assertion, but had defended his own position by referring to the necessity of the 'state of siege' because of 'unstable and wavering elements'. According to him the dictatorship of *Iskra* over the Party (hence, too, the complete political trustworthiness of its board) was necessary in order to free the Party completely and safeguard it in future from every variety of Economism and 'opportunism'. In championing this point of view Lenin was expressing the opinion not merely of most of the *Iskra* delegates to the Congress, but of a very considerable number of *Iskra*-people in Russia too.*

But very soon afterwards the quarrels on the organizational question began shifting from the plane of intraparty relations to the plane of relations between the Party and the labouring masses. This transition was inevitable, primarily because the very struggle against Economism had been becoming more and more empty. As already noted, after the Congress it quickly began falling apart, and with a few exceptions its adherents dissolved in the fractions that took shape after the Congress, most of them, naturally, joining the Mensheviks. This was not only because the Mensheviks were fighting against the continuation of the 'state of siege' in the Party, but also because on the question of the relations between the Party and the labouring masses the Mensheviks had gone a long way towards the organizational ideas of Economism. In the very first 'Menshevik' number of *Iskra*[125] Plekhanov, sharply distinguishing himself as before from the Economist theoreticians, could write, in full accord with the new editors, that between these theoreticians and the Economist practicals 'there lay, in the essence of their aspirations, a whole abyss': at a time when the theoreticians of Economism were preparing the intellectual and political capitulation of Socialism to the bourgeoisie, 'the assets of the practicals of Economism were enriched by their . . . attempt to transform Socialism from an affair of small groups to an affair of an entire class, an exceptionally impressive point for a Socialist.'

Nevertheless it was just this question of the relations between the Party and the labouring masses, especially between the advanced workers thrust forward by the mass movement and the professiona

* The writer, on going abroad again after the Congress was over, said, about the 'cell psychology' of many of the 'young *Iskra*-ites' he talked to, that they were '*Iskra*-ites only in so far as they had ceased being in many respects Social-Democrats'. (Cf. supplement to Martov's pamphlet on *The Struggle against the State of Siege in the R.S.D.W.P.*[120]

revolutionary intellectuals, that acquired particular importance in the stormy conditions of those years. It was still the same question that, as we have seen, had emerged at the very inception of the workers' working-class movement at the end of the '70s and assumed rather acute forms during and as a result of the strikes of '96–'97. This organizational question concealed the emergence of the same problems of the conjunction of economic impulses, which led the rank-and-file labouring masses directly into the movement, and the decisive role in the solution of the political problems that was imposed on the Russian working-class by all the conditions of its own struggle and for which the whole of the *Iskra* Social-Democracy wanted systematically to prepare it. But as soon as both this question and these problems confronted the Social-Democracy with particular acuteness, the revolutionary movement, having taken hold of millions of workers and poured over into the countryside, began to draw into its orbit the propertied classes of society as well. The centre of gravity of the working-class movement itself began shifting from the relatively backward textile industry to the advanced metallurgical industry, which had far more important cadres of highly trained and intellectual workers.

The drastic cleansing of the Party of the remnants of Economism by 'state of siege' methods by no means solved the problems flowing out of the very nature of the movement of the labouring masses. Their supposed incapacity to raise themselves by their own efforts above a 'trade union consciousness' (*What Is to Be Done?*) created a constant danger that they might be deflected from the revolutionary political tasks and struggle demanded at the given historical moment by their own class interests. The dictatorship of *Iskra* over the Party had to be supplemented by a dictatorship of the Party over the masses of the working-class itself, to forestall this danger. In a resolution of one of the Bolshevik committees, quoted by Akselrod[126] we read: 'recognizing that in the present conditions a violent overturn can be brought about in Russia only through the support of the working-class of the great industrial centres, prepared for obedience and for an open uprising, we shall make the organization of the working-class the focus of our activity'. These same ideas were even more clearly expressed in a letter from the representatives of three Ural committees that was printed in *Iskra*.[127] After sketching the difference between the political workers' movement and the trade union movement, in which the 'role of the revolutionary intelligentsia is passive', while 'the movement is run by local workers', and reproaching the Economists with 'looking condescendingly at the intelligentsia, that is, the revolutionary Social-Democracy', the letter goes on:

> The preparation of the proletariat for a dictatorship – such is the important organizational task to which all others must be subordinated. This preparation consists among other things of the creation of a mood favourable to a powerful, authoritative proletarian organization. . . . It may be objected that dictators have appeared and do appear of themselves. But this has not always been so, and it must not happen spontaneously, or opportunistically, in the proletarian party. Here the highest degree of awareness must be combined with unchallengeable obedience – one must summon forth the other (awareness of necessity is free will).

In this way the 'authoritarian' principle shifted from the sphere of intra-party relations to the sphere of relations between the Party and the working-class. Once again Lenin was merely giving a generalized expression to this new stage in Bolshevik organizational thought when in his book *One Step Forward, Two Steps Back* he counterposed 'bureaucratic' to 'democratic' centralism as the real organizational principle of the Social-Democracy, and proclaimed 'discipline' not merely the basic requirement of proletarian organization, but also the basic virtue of proletarian psychology. It was only the individualist intellectual who found it difficult to submit to discipline. The worker was trained to it by the very conditions of his hierarchically organized labour. If the intellectual offspring of the bourgeois *milieu* were bearers of revolutionary Socialist consciousness in the workers' movement, the workers were the bearers in it of the principle of discipline. The anti-revolutionary and anti-proletarian character of Menshevik 'opportunism on questions of organization', in fact, is contained in its 'hostility to the bureaucratic idea of constructing the Party from the top down', in its revulsion against proletarian discipline, and in its indulgence, on the other hand, towards the anarchist individualism of intellectuals with weak nerves. It was from now on that discipline became the fundamental organizational slogan of Bolshevism. Lenin's response to the reproach that his whole organizational system had a dictatorial, 'Jacobin' character was this: 'A Jacobin indissolubly linked to the organization of a proletariat aware of its own class interests – that is just what a Social-Democrat is.'[128]

This same problem of the relationship between the Party and the working-class was solved by Menshevism in a contrary direction. The Social-Democracy was not supposed to train the labouring masses for unquestioning obedience to the instructions of an authoritative Party centre, but for independent, free and organized activity. 'The task of developing class consciousness and political initiative must govern not merely the tactics but also the organization of the Social-Democratic Party,' said a resolution passed by the Menshevik majority of the Congress of the Foreign League (26–31 October 1903, Geneva). The dominance of authoritarian organizational methods within the Party 'would make it impossible for it to fulfil its most immediate historical mission – to prepare the Russian proletariat for an independent political role during the period of the revolutionary destruction of the autocratic order in Russia'. Hence it was essential, 'within the framework of the Party statutes, to wage a systematic struggle against any tendencies towards bureaucratic centralism in the name of an authentically Social-Democratic centralism, indispensable for the unification of the Russian proletariat in an independent political party.' From then on, in contrast to Bolshevik 'discipline', the basic organizational slogan of Menshevism became – workers' initiative.

But in shifting from intra-party relations to relations between the Party and the working-class, the fractional disputes happened to enter just that area where the organizational problems were directly fused with political problems. It was Akselrod who took upon himself the clarification of this connexion,[129] and thus the initiative of shunting on to political rails the organizational disagreements that had split the Party into two fractions.

The basic ideas of the *Iskra* platform were, as we have seen, the primacy of political tasks over the task of leading an economic struggle of the proletariat, and the originating, dominant role of the Social-Democracy, its 'hegemony' in the 'all-national' struggle for political liberation. 'To unite all democratic elements of the country under its own banner and to crown the tenacious struggle of a whole series of past generations by the ultimate triumph over the hated régime' – this was the ending of the Statement in which the *Iskra* editors explained their understanding of the historical tasks of the Russian Social-Democracy. It was in the name of this 'unification', too, that they opened the pages of the Social-Democratic organ 'for the exposure of all the vilenesses of the Russian autocracy' not only to the Socialists but 'to all those crushed and oppressed by the contemporary political order'. It was in its name, furthermore, that they called upon the Social-Democrats in their turn 'to go to all classes of the population', in order to preach the gospel of an implacable struggle against Tsarism.

There is no doubt that Bolshevism carried on this *Iskra* political tradition. It was precisely in order to make the Social-Democracy capable of concentrating all its energies on the struggle against the autocracy and of playing a dominant role in that struggle that Lenin, indeed, demanded a dictatorship of 'firm' *Iskra*-ites in the Party and a 'state of siege' against 'unstable and wavering elements'. As for the Bolshevik committees, they were to struggle against the 'trade union' narrowness of the labouring masses via their 'disciplining'.

As we have already emphasized more than once, Russian Marxism, too, had to take into account, from its very inception, those contradictions of the struggle for democracy in Russia that Populism had struggled with and been shattered by. These contradictions arose to confront it in the form of a dual but internally contradictory task – to combine the political emancipation of *bourgeois* society with the organization of the *Socialist* movement of the working-class. We have referred to the attempt made by the Emancipation of Labour Group to solve this fundamental contradiction of its programme theoretically, and to Akselrod as the author of the novel solution of this problem that was taken up by *Iskra* – the idea of the dominant role of the Social-Democracy in the 'all-national' struggle for political liberty, and its 'hegemony', for whose realization what was necessary was only the 'broadening of the scope of agitation and propaganda through questions constituting nodal points' in which the interests of the proletariat 'fuse and are intertwined' with the interests of other classes opposed to the autocracy. But at the very first clash with reality of the more and more tempestuously heaving mass workers' movement, which drew other classes of the population into the political maelstrom, the practical insubstantiality of this theoretically rounded-off formula also began to be revealed. Akselrod was the first to sound the alarm here too.

In the above-mentioned articles[129] he writes: 'The influence of the proletarian or Social-Democratic element in the contemporary revolutionary movement in Russia can only be expressed in the fact that the preparatory process of the bourgeois revolution will simultaneously constitute a process of political training and unification of the labouring masses into a party of revolutionary socialism.' This should be recalled particularly 'in such stormy moments' as Russia was living through, since 'elemental historical forces . . . are pushing our movement to the side of bourgeois revolutionism – in defiance of our desires and consciousness'. Accordingly, both Lenin and Akselrod agree that the 'elemental forces' of Russia's socio-political development are pushing the workers' movement towards 'bourgeois-ness'. But while Lenin saw the basic cause of this phenomenon in the incapacity of the working-class to cross over from a 'trade union' consciousness to a 'class' Socialist consciousness by its own powers, and set all his hopes on the revolutionary intelligentsia, which was to supplement the labouring masses' insufficient Socialist consciousness 'from without', Akselrod, while agreeing that because of the historical conditions of the development of the Russian proletariat 'there was no factor there capable of taking on itself the task of arousing it from its profound historical slumber and moving it into the arena of historical activity', saw the principal danger precisely in this, that 'this task was to be shouldered by a factor outside it (the proletariat) – the radical intelligentsia'.

Akselrod said a situation had been created in which the Russian Social-Democracy would 'only try to become the political organization of the labouring masses', and in fact 'for the time being was still primarily an organization of the principled backers of the proletariat among the revolutionary intelligentsia'. Nevertheless, the 'very gravitation of the radical intelligentsia towards Socialism and towards the proletariat objectively, historically, and in the final analysis is evoked and conditioned not by the class struggle of the latter, but by the general democratic need for all nations and classes to extricate themselves from the oppression of the hangovers of the serf-holding age'. The 'general democratic' hue of the intelligentsia's Socialism led to this.

> with a shift of the centre of our Party activity to the sphere of agitation on the terrain of the general democratic antagonism of the proletariat to the Tsarist autocracy, any revolutionizing of the labouring masses with the aim of 'involving them in the struggle' against it, has acquired among many Social-Democratics the same significance of a universal method of class education of those masses that the narrowly economic agitation used to have for them before. An equal sign has been placed between our political tasks and the pressing general democratic task of the struggle against the police-Tsarist régime, as long as the Social-Democracy leads the masses in this struggle.

The initiator in his time of the struggle against Economism, Akselrod now with equal energy turned his critical faculty against ultra-'politicism', seeing in it – in the changing conditions – the same tool of the political subjugation of the proletariat by the bourgeoisie as Economism had been before.

> If the last word of the Social-Democratic trade unionism was propaganda for the political tutelage of the proletariat by the liberal intelligentsia, the last word of the passion for 'politics' in the one-sided sense indicated would be the surrender of the labouring masses to the revolutionary elements of the bourgeoisie, even though because of circumstances of time and space these elements would also have to realize their mission under the banner of the Social-Democracy.*

Further developing the proposition formulated in the above-quoted resolution of the Foreign League (he was the principal author of the resolution) Akselrod's articles asserted that 'the development of the class consciousness and political initiative of the labouring masses, their unification as an independent revolutionary force under the banner of the Social-Democracy' was not only one of the sides of the dual task confronting the Russian Social-Democracy, but was the 'goal' that had also confronted the West European Socialist movement. It was a goal to which the political struggle had to be subordinated as a 'means' for the creation of the 'preliminary conditions' 'for the direct and immediate fulfilment' of this sole authentic and historic task of the Russian Social-Democracy. But history

> behind our backs has assigned the predominant role in our movement not to the end but to the means, not to our fundamental principled task, but to those historically more elementary tasks without whose at least partial realization there would be no objective possibility of pursuing the primary task consistently and many-sidedly. This alone has introduced into the development of the Russian Social-Democracy that contradiction that runs like a red thread throughout all its phases.†

But establishing this contradiction between the class-Socialist and the general political tasks of the Russian Social-Democracy meant

* After Akselrod many eminent 'Left' theoreticians of the German Social-Democracy – Karl Kautsky, Rosa Luxemburg, Parvus – expressed the same views on the political significance of Bolshevik 'bureaucratic' centralism.

† Akselrod ends his second article with the opinion that it was 'only now, after the Social-Democracy of the intellectuals has moved far enough ahead in its appointed task ['the revolutionizing of the proletariat'] . . . that its political leadership of the labouring masses is gradually becoming a synonym for the political independence of the proletariat'. But this optimistic prognosis, aimed at Akselrod's predominantly intellectual audience, was not only not justified by his analysis, but clashed sharply with the results of that analysis.

establishing its practical insolubility by the rationalist methods by which Russian Marxism had been attempting to overcome it theoretically during the twenty years of its existence. In the facts of Russian life and the Russian revolutionary movement there was no possibility of organically and harmoniously combining the two sides of the dual task that were emerging out of that life and movement. The Russian Social-Democracy could only realize its 'dual' task by being itself split into two fractions. These fought each other bitterly, but at the same time they were a kind of political 'Siamese twins'. Each one of them expressed (and, as is always the case in a fight, in a one-sided and often exaggerated form) one of the two equally vital and indispensable tendencies of the workers' movement in the conditions of the expanding revolutionary fight against the Tsarist autocracy. It was only in their conjunction that they responded fully to the dual task history had set this movement. In this sense what Plekhanov had said in his time (see above) about the fractions of revolutionary Populism, may be said about Bolshevism and Menshevism with even greater justification: in historical retrospect they were both 'right, each in its own way, because with all its one-sidedness each one of them was expressing a certain essential need of Russian political life'.

Theoretically and in principle, of course, both Menshevism and Bolshevism equally acknowledged the 'duality' of the tasks confronting the Russian Social-Democracy. The programme passed by the second Congress remained common to both fractions down to the final destruction of Tsarism in the 1917 revolution. They strove equally to embody in their activity both tendencies of the movement – the general-democratic and the Socialist. But in practice, in their political, tactical, and organizational constructions, they did not spread the emphasis equally between these two tendencies. Bolshevism took shape as the bearer of predominantly *general-democratic* and *political* tendencies of the movement, and Menshevism as the bearer predominantly of its class and *Socialist* tendencies.

This fundamental character of both fractions to a considerable degree defined their influence on the workers. The mainstay of Menshevism became the advanced metallurgical south and highly-trained professions like the printers; the mainstay of Bolshevism became the textile centre of the country and the backward metallurgical industry of the Urals. This same fundamental character of both fractions also determined, as we shall see, the specific role each of them played in the development of the Russian workers' movement and of the revolution. It is most characteristic of the contradictory conditions of this development that by a paradoxical irony of history the final point in the evolution of both of them proved to be diametrically opposite their starting point: Bolshevism and Menshevism seemed to have changed roles.

But this evolution still lay in the future. At this time, under an autocracy that was still maintaining inviolate a régime of bondage and that had a powerful apparatus of repression at its disposal, but that was being shaken by the increasingly powerful blows of the revolutionary movement, the specific cast of mind and the incipient polarization of political thought of both fractions found a characteristic expression in the political problems each one focused its attention on. What started more and more to become a central problem for Bolshevism was to secure for the Social-Democracy a dominant role in the preparation of the 'all-national armed uprising' that was supposed to be the final, culminating act of an all-national, general democratic onslaught on the fortress of the autocracy. For Menshevism it was the exploitation of all the possibilities created by the break-up of the autocracy in order to shape a politically highly-trained workers' vanguard that would be capable of taking the political leadership out of the hands of the 'revolutionary intelligentsia' and thus secure the workers' class interests in the course of the all-national final attack on Tsarism.

But by focusing their attention on so many different political problems both Bolshevism and Menshevism equally, though from different angles, once again returned the thought of the Social-Democracy to the same fundamental question – its role in the bourgeois-capitalist revolution, which both fractions continued to acknowledge as the pending Russian revolution. Once again, accordingly, a critical review had to be made of the 'hegemony' that seemed to have solved this burning question so fortuitously, and for whose realization there was needed only an enlargement of the content of Social-Democratic agitation by themes on a 'all-national' scale and the conveying of that agitation 'into all classes of the population'. Now this simple solution of the problem seemed inadequate. A new answer was required: what were the forms and content of 'hegemony'? Each of the fractions taking shape gave its answer in its own way, by that alone making the political water-shed between Bolshevism and Menshevism more definite.

Akselrod's article did not speak of 'enlarging the content of agitation' but about the 'active intervention in the socio-political life' of the workers' vanguard under the leadership of the Social-Democracy. Nor was this intervention recommended any longer as a way of turning it into a political leader of the 'all-national' movement of liberation, but as 'the best, not to say the only school for the development of the class consciousness of the proletariat'. 'Hegemony' was presented as the specific task of the Social-Democracy imposed on it, in contrast with the West European democracy, by the specific peculiarities of a backward country, where there were present, to be sure, the socio-economic premises for the development of the class struggle between the proletariat and the bourgeoisie, but where the 'preliminary' political conditions essential for the free evolution of that struggle did not yet exist. Now, by way of making an argument in favour of 'active intervention', Akselrod no longer referred to the specific peculiarities of the Russian Social-Democracy, but precisely to the practice of the 'Western' Social-Democracy. This, 'in developing the political independence of the proletariat by that alone also develops its class consciousness'. He went on: 'The Social-Democracy, by systematically involving the labouring masses in direct clashes and a direct struggle against the whole constellation of bourgeois ideologies and politicians concretely reveals to them the irreconcilable conflict of interests between the proletariat and the rule of the bourgeoisie.'

It is evident that the concentration of attention on the 'irreconcilable conflict' between the interests of the proletarian sector of the movement of emancipation and the interests of its bourgeois sector, had little in common with the assignment of priority to those 'nodal' points in which the interests of the working-class 'fused and intertwined' with the interests of all the other participants in this movement. Nevertheless, in Akselrod's tactical constructions, which underlay the whole future tactic of Menshevism, both these methods, so different and even opposed, were combined. This was because – and here the analogy with the West came to an end for Akselrod – in backward Russia the disclosure of the 'irreconcilable conflict' was of no use in mobilizing the working-class for a direct struggle against the 'rule of the bourgeoisie', as it did in the political practice of the West European Social-Democracies. In backward Russia this disclosure was supposed to be no more than a tool of the class 'education' of the proletariat, merely a 'school' for the development of its 'class consciousness', and hence a conscious reconciliation of it with the 'rule of the bourgeoisie', as an historically foreordained result of the revolution.

But concentrating the Party's tasks in the sphere of class political pedagogy and the preparation of the proletariat for the role it would have to play in the future, Socialist revolution meant in fact refraining from 'heading up' the revolution that was not in the future but in the *present*, and being satisfied – according to an expression that could scarcely have slipped Akselrod's pen accidentally – with a struggle for the 'influence of a proletarian or Social-Democratic element' over it. It meant leaving the dominant role in the solution of the 'all-national' task of the revolution – the task of replacing the Tsarist by a revolutionary government – to non-proletarian, bourgeois social forces that were trying to give the proletariat no more than the role of an influential opposition 'pushing' the bourgeoisie towards political radicalism and compelling it to make substantial socio-economic concessions to the working-class. It meant, essentially, liquidating the whole concept of 'hegemony'.

In theory Menshevism never abandoned this concept, and later on it appealed to it more than once, incorporating it in its political calculations. Fundamentally, in fact, twenty years later, it had returned to the original concept of the Emancipation of Labour Group – a concept that as we have seen was based on the 'triumph of the bourgeoisie' (Plekhanov[91]) and on the struggle for the 'possibility of an active and fruitful participation of the working-class in the future political life of Russia'.[130] The problem of the accomplishment of a bourgeois revolution by working-class forces was solved by means of rationalistic calculations on an upsurge of 'class consciousness' of the proletariat that would make it capable of administering rational doses of 'support to capitalism in the struggle against reaction' and of 'irreconcilable hostility to this same capitalism in its struggle against the workers' revolution of the future'.

It was not only Menshevism, however, that liquidated the concept of hegemony. Bolshevism, too, liquidated it in fact – but in a direction that was diametrically opposed to that of Menshevism. Bolshevism, too, was confronted by the question of the inadequacy of the 'enlarging of the content of agitation' and of introducing it 'into all classes of the population' in order to secure the Social-Democracy a dominant role in the bourgeois revolution. But, as we shall see, Lenin's response to the question that once again confronted the Social-Democracy was this: the dictatorship of Bolshevism over the Party and the dictatorship of the working-class, in the form of the Bolshevik Party, over all other social forces taking part in the revolutionary process.

The real liquidation of the concept of hegemony proceeded only gradually in the political constructions of both fractions of the Social-Democracy. For this liquidation itself was far from being the fruit of purely theoretical calculations alone. It was accomplished in the course of the practical contacts and collisions of the Social-Democracy with bourgeois liberalism and with revolutionized liberal Populism, reborn in the form of the Social-Revolutionary Party. It was the political shaping up of the social strata represented by these currents that transformed the revolutionary movement of the intelligentsia and workers into a 'movement of emancipation' that gave the revolution an 'all-national' character.

3. THE 'MOVEMENT OF EMANCIPATION'

'Striving to attain its most immediate goals, the R.S.D.W.P. supports every oppositional and revolutionary movement directed against the existing social and political order in Russia.'

This was the next to the last paragraph of the programme that was unanimously passed by the Congress. This paragraph was directly referred to in the resolution on relations with the liberals introduced by Potresov, supported by the whole Menshevik section of the *Iskra* editors, and passed by the Congress. But another resolution on the same question, introduced by Plekhanov and Lenin and also passed by the Congress, also begins with the observation that the 'Social-Democracy must support the bourgeoisie in so far as it is revolutionary or even only oppositionist in its struggle against Tsarism'. Hence it 'welcomes the awakening of political consciousness in the Russian bourgeoisie'. Nevertheless Yegorov (Levin), the delegate of the *Yuzhny Rabochii*, was right when he said: 'In the programme we say we must support every oppositionist and revolutionary movement. We have two such movements: the liberal and the revolutionary Socialist. Actually, we have a negative attitude towards both movements. The conclusion is: the moment a movement takes on concrete forms – down with it! What is the way out of this contradiction?'

Indeed, Potresov's resolution came out for the admissibility of 'provisional agreements' with 'liberal or liberal-democratic currents'; but as a condition of such agreements it required among other things 'a clear and unequivocal' statement by these tendencies that 'in their struggle against the autocracy they would decisively take the side of the Russian Social-Democracy' and 'would not put any demands in their programme that went counter to the interests of the working-class and the democracy generally'. I.e., in essence, this was a rejection by these tendencies of their own bourgeois and liberal nature. Hence the sole conclusion of the Plekhanov-Lenin resolution was an 'urgent recommendation' to all Party members 'in their propaganda to draw the attention of the workers to the anti-revolutionary and counter-proletarian character of the tendency expressed in Mr P. Struve's organ', that is, in *Osvobozhdeniye*, 'since there was no other (liberal) tendency', as Plekhanov himself emphasized in his speech.

Nor were matters different with the attitude towards the Social-Revolutionary Party. The resolution drafted by Akselrod and unanimously passed by the Congress declared its activity pernicious for the cause of Socialism, since it 'theoretically and practically counteracted the efforts of the Social-Democracy to concentrate the workers in an independent political party and, on the contrary, strove to preserve them in the state of a politically shapeless mass capable only of serving as a tool of the liberal bourgeoisie'. Hence the resolution refused to regard the Socialist-Revolutionaries as Socialists and 'laid it down that they were no more than a bourgeois democratic fraction'. But even as such a fraction the Socialist-Revolutionaries 'were completely worthless' – just because they 'were pursuing their bourgeois tendencies under the banner of Socialism'. Hence the 'Congress considered their activity pernicious not only for the political development of the proletariat but also for the general democratic struggle against absolutism'.

Martov tried to answer the question posed by Yegorov by saying that 'the contradiction here was merely apparent'. But to do this he had to appeal from the specific conditions of Russia to Western Europe, where 'the growth of the Social-Democracy was accompanied by a decline of bourgeois-democratic parties', and where the Social-Democracy was 'killing' these parties by 'revolutionizing the consciousness of their followers and attracting them into its own ranks'. Martov was not solving tnis problem of the interrelationship between the Social-Democracy and the liberal-democratic tendencies during the process of preparation of the bourgeois revolution that Russian Marxist thought was grappling with, but by-passing it. In identifying the operating conditions of the Russian and the Western European Social-Democracies and hence substituting for the task of 'supporting' the bourgeoisie the task of 'killing' it, he went on: 'This is just how the Russian Social-Democracy must also act. It will support every oppositionist and revolutionary movement in just this way, by confronting it with a dilemma – either go forward, or lose influence over the awakening social elements to whom the Social-Democracy is pointing out a place in its own ranks.'

But neither was any solution of the problem given by Akselrod's answer to the question of 'how to reconcile in practice our attitude of principled antagonism' to bourgeois movements 'with the tactical proposition of supporting them in the struggle against the reaction'. Concerning the liberals, this answer went as follows: 'Taking into account the political passivity of our liberal bourgeoisie, there can at present be no question of any real support for it in the literal sense from the Russian Social-Democracy. At the present moment, in order to "support" it in practice, we must systematically exploit the oppositionist and revolutionary mood of the upper classes in the interests of the development of the revolutionary initiative and political independence in the labouring masses.' 'At first glance this conclusion seems paradoxical', as Akselrod himself thought it necessary to add to his explanation. But none the less paradoxical must his conclusion also have seemed concerning the Socialist-Revolutionaries. 'At one and the same time the S.R. Party harms the cause of Socialism and the struggle of emancipation against the autocracy', Akselrod recalled once again in order to lead up to this conclusion: 'Hence, with the exception of some rare concrete instances, the Social-Democracy has no reason to discuss any practical support for the S.R. Party either, as a revolutionary-bourgeois party.'

As a matter of fact the 'paradoxicality' of the practical interpretation of what theoretically would have seemed to be a perfectly clear point in the programme bore witness not only to the contradictoriness of the task confronting the Russian Social-Democracy and formulated in this point, but also to the 'unclearness' in the relationship to this point that Akselrod himself had noticed in his correspondence with Plekhanov as far back as July 1901. This correspondence had arisen in connexion with Lenin's article, *Zemstvo Persecutors and the Hannibals of Liberalism*. Here Lenin sharply criticized Struve's foreword to the secret Note of S. Y. Witte on the Russian Zemstvo that had been given him by liberal Zemstvo circles and published by *Iskra* in agreement with them. Plekhanov (who at the Congress later acted in accord with Lenin concerning Struve, as we have seen) was at that time against placing this article in *Zarya*, for which it had been intended: 'We must, after all, behave towards the liberals as towards possible allies', he wrote to Lenin, 'while your tone, one must admit, is far from that of an ally.' Akselrod, on the contrary, while considering the article's 'criticism of Russian liberalism, and of the foreword in particular, essentially just', found it impossible to refuse to print the article 'because of its sharply polemical tone alone' . . . 'even though', he added, 'hitherto we have not clarified in our own minds or had any debates about a line of behaviour. The time is evidently ripe for that.'

And in fact the necessity of working out a practical 'line of behaviour' on this question had begun becoming more and more obvious as the liberal-democratic movements of the bourgeois strata of society themselves had begun being transformed from a theoretical prophecy into a practical factor of Russian public life. At the same time, as we have seen, the triviality of the more or less abstract and rationalistic formulas by which Russian Marxism had been trying in theory to solve the contradictory problem had begun revealing itself.

The intellectual and political formation and organizational consolidation of the liberal-democratic trends took place in an atmosphere, and as a direct result, of the revolutionary fermentation that was taking hold of the country with constantly growing force, and that had been begun in the second half of the '90s by the movement of the labouring masses, its focal point. But even before this an attempt had been made, in 1893, to form an organization of a definitely liberal-democratic type. This organization had been made up of intellectuals alone; it called itself the 'Party of the People's Right' (*Partiya Narodnogo Prava*). Its initiators were former adherents of the People's Freedom* who had come back from exile at around that time. These were joined by some old figures of legal Populism,† as well as by the younger elements of the radical intelligentsia.‡

The People's Right was not in the least a product of the mass movement. At that time this existed only in embryonic form, but it was destined in three to four years to mark the advent of a new pre-revolutionary period in Russian history. On the contrary, the members of the People's Right merely summed-up the results of that period of relative political calm we have referred to above, with its initial passion for 'cultivation' and 'petty affairs' and its subsequent disappointment, which had ensued after the destruction of the People's Freedom but had already receded into the past. And Martov was quite right in

* Natanson, Tyutchev, and others.

† Such as Mikhailovsky.

‡ A. Bogdanovich and V. M. Chernov, the future theoretician of the S.R. Party.

saying, about the People's Right, that its 'real base was the *rapprochement* between the Third Element, democratic in its composition, and the advanced segment of the Zemstvo officials that took place in the course of the '80s in joint cultural activities, under a hail of repressions from the reaction that came pouring down on both social groups.'[131] But because of this a 'fundamental premise for the success' of the programme of 'revolutionary constitutionalism' advanced by the People's Right (defended by A. Bogdanovich[132]) 'was a rejection of Socialism, and of slogans, demands and methods of work that assumed the sowing of social discord among the masses of the people'.

A belated reflection of a combination of social forces and ideas that had already receded into the past, the People's Right showed little capacity for life; it was unable to recover from the arrests that by 1894 had already broken its organization. It was not until five to six years later that its ideas were taken up by the 'Workers' Party for the Liberation of Russia', which G. A. Gershuni, the future organizer of the 'Combat Organization' of the S.R. Party, was close to. This Workers' Party, which had a restricted sphere of activity in the Western portion of Russia, was also short-lived. But having emerged on the very threshold of the twentieth century in conditions of growing revolutionary excitement it did not vanish without a trace, like the People's Right, but together with a number of other groups became a constituent element of the social conglomerate that gave birth to the S.R. Party.*

In contrast to the Social-Democratic Party, the S.R. Party, did not take shape through the unification of local organizations and the centralization of their activities. It arose 'from above', from the fusion of small groups in Russia and abroad that had sprung up or revived under the influence of the events of the end of the '90s. Though uniformly 'Populist' in their general trend, these groups were distinguished by great political and intellectual diversity. If, as we have seen, the West Russian group inclined towards the People's Right, the programme (1899) of the north-east group, which took the name 'Union of Socialist-Revolutionaries', was based on a connexion with the mass movement. At the same time it insisted, in contrast to the Marxists, on the parity of the peasant and the workers' movements. A 'Manifesto', on the contrary, that was issued in 1901 in the name of the 'Party of Socialist-Revolutionaries' by a group that had sprung up

* The initiator of the People's Right, M. Natanson, did not enter the S.R. Party until 1905.

in the south, the locale of immense workers' strikes during these years, lay special emphasis on precisely the workers' movement, preserving a sceptical attitude towards the revolutionary potentialities of the countryside and preparing its own general directives. These, as Martov remarks, were 'very similar to the views of the *Iskra* wing of the Social-Democracy'. Still greater was the difference in the views of the two groups of the old Populist emigration that entered the new party. Thus, the 'Group of the Old People's Freedom'*, which in the summer of 1901 published the first number of a review, *Vestnik Russkoy Revolutsii*, (Russian Revolutionary Courier) 'propagandizes for the formation of a party on the model of the People's Freedom, combining the leadership of the workers' movement with terrorist struggle . . . while at the same time rejecting all hopes for a fighting role on the part of the peasantry'. Contrariwise, the Agrarian Socialist League† 'gave first priority to the peasant movement . . . and in the programmatic pamphlet *The Current Question* laid down the foundations of a specifically agrarian Socialism that combined elements of Russian Populism and West European revisionism' (Martov).

It was out of the organizational *rapprochement* and unification of these heterogeneous groups that the Party of the Socialist Revolutionaries was formed towards the end of 1901. Gershuni became its practical leader, while Chernov (Gardenin) became its theoretician. The overthrow of the autocracy was made the focus of the Party's tasks. But in the circumstances in which it emerged neither its theoretical views nor its political line could distinguish themselves by any great clarity. It was only towards the middle of 1904 that the editors of *Revolyutsionnaya Rossiya* (Revolutionary Russia), whose publication was shifted abroad and which became the Central Organ of the Party (the *Vestnik Russkoy Revolyutsii* was also declared a Party organ) succeeded in elaborating the draft of a programme that in its fundamental traits was later sanctioned by the Party (at the first Party Congress, in December 1905). But in the very first period the cement that bound together the heterogeneous elements in the new Party was, together with a general sympathy for Populism and an aversion to Marxism, not so much its political programme as its 'combat' tactic.

This tactic was based primarily on political terror, which under Gershuni's leadership chalked up some substantial successes. A string of terrorist acts started in 1901 with the attempt of an official,

* Rusanov (Tarasov), M. Gots, Rubanovich.

† Zhitlovsky, Shishko, Volkhovskoy, Chaikovsky.

Lagovsky, to assassinate Pobedonostsev, and with the assassination of the Minister of National Education Bogolepov (by a student, Karpovich); on 2 April 1902 a student, Stepan Balmashov, killed the Minister of the Interior, Sipyagin; that same year a Jewish worker, Hirsch Leckert, made an attempt on the life of the Vilna Governor-General Von Wahl, who had ordered corporal punishment for some striking workers, while a worker, Thomas Kachura, tried to kill the Kharkov Governor Obolensky, who had suppressed a peasant uprising; in May of the following year Bogdanovich, the Governor of Ufa, who had dealt ferociously with the metal-workers of the Zlatoust, fell victim to the terror, and so on.

The participation of workers in the performance of terroristic acts shows that terrorist propaganda met with some sympathy in the working-class, too. As a matter of fact some individual groups of workers organized by the Social-Democrats began going over to the Socialist Revolutionaries. Even more noticeable was the gravitation towards the S.R.s of certain intellectual circles connected with the Social-Democracy; Karpovich, Balmashov, Ivan Kalyayev (who killed Grand Duke Sergius Alexandrovich), Yegor Sazonov (who killed Minister of the Interior Plehve), Boris Savinkov, and other terrorists who later became famous, all came from the ranks of the Social-Democracy.

This fear that the practice of terror would break up the mass workers' movement that the Social-Democracy was setting its hopes on was also the reason why *Iskra*, which in the beginning was rather sympathetic towards the S.R.s, as comrades-in-arms in the struggle against the autocracy, very soon came out sharply against them. *Revolyutsionnaya Rossiya*,[133] to be sure, explained that S.R. terror was distinct from the terror of the People's Freedom just because it did not replace the mass struggle, but supplemented and stimulated it as a means of 'excitation'. In practice, however, during the first few years of the S.R. Party's existence, terror occupied such an exclusive position in its activities that to carry it on a special 'Combat Organization' was created that formally was part of the Party's general organization but in fact enjoyed the broadest autonomy.*

But the Party tried to lend a 'combat' character to the mass

* After the arrest of Gershuni, who was informed on in 1903 by Thomas Kachura, the head of the 'Combat Organization' was Yevno Azef, who was later exposed as an *agent provocateur*. His exposure dealt a blow to the tactic of political terror that it never recovered from.

movement itself – to strikes, demonstrations, etc., by propagandizing for the necessity of armed resistance to the troops and police, and creating with this end in view special 'combat companies'. From the point of view of the Social-Democracy this meant hindering the process that was taking place in those years of involving ever broadening backward masses in the movement, and provoking premature collision of that movement with the government apparatus in conditions in which the forces of the movement were far from ripe, while the apparatus itself was still not sufficiently shaken up. Hence the tactic of 'armed demonstrations' met even stronger opposition in the ranks of the Social-Democrats than the tactic of individual terror.

However, it soon became clear that the fears of the Social-Democracy were exaggerated: the workers' sympathetic response to terror and to the 'combat' tactic in general proved to be too limited and transitory to introduce any noticeable disorganization into the mass movement. Sympathies for the terror were more extensive and lasted longer among the liberal and radical intelligentsia that Marxism in both its variants, Bolshevism and Menshevism, repelled by its 'class' exclusiveness, and in those circles of the liberal possessing classes in whose eyes the terrorist struggle, in contrast to the mass movement of the workers and peasants, was devoid of any social tinge hostile to them, and who, moreover, were calculating on plucking the political fruits of that terror themselves, as in the time of the People's Freedom.

In these circumstances the attitude of the Social-Democrats to the S.R. terror began to lose its sharpness. The assassination of Plehve (15 July 1904) prompted even the Menshevik *Iskra*, both in articles and in a proclamation specially published on this occasion (written by the author of these lines) to note the positive significance of eliminating from the political arena the Minister of the Interior who had harshly crushed the 'constitutional' movement, just beginning in these years, of Zemstvo and municipal functionaries, and whose name had therefore become hateful even to the most moderate elements of liberal society.* This positive assessment was reinforced by the appointment as Minister of the Interior of Prince Svyatopolk-Mirsky, who proclaimed a policy of 'confidence in society' in conditions in which the

* After negotiations with M. Natanson, Plekhanov went even further and introduced a proposal into the Party Council that an agreement be concluded with the S.R.s on the basis of recognizing the appropriateness of terror in the given political situation. It was only the categorical ultimatum of Akselrod and Martov that forced him to withdraw this proposal.

'constitutional' movement of the affluent strata very soon assumed such breadth that the government was no longer capable of coping with it by police measures alone.

The peasant disorders that began in the spring of 1902 revived the hopes of the S.R.s in the possibility of finding a mass base in the peasantry, and stimulated the development of Party activity in the countryside. The demands for 'egalitarian use of the land' that were put forth during the peasant movement were a proof to *Revolyutsionnaya Rossiya* that 'the peasantry was even now already coming out with a semi-Socialist programme' and was Socialist in its 'principles', and that hence 'we [the S.R.s] must merely give a rational, scientific formulation to these completely sound principles in order to extract from them the pure idea of Socialism'.[134] As for the appeal published by the Peasant Union of the S.R. Party, it declared the slogans of the peasant movement to be a 'socialization of the land' understood in the form of communal property in land with systematic 'egalitarian' reapportionments, and the 'evolution in the peasantry of every possible kind of co-operation'.

These slogans were laid down in the foundations of the S.R. programme and in accordance with the traditional views of Populism were linked to the proclamation of the peasantry as a mass bearer of the struggle for Socialism in Russia. Just as legitimate and just as valuable as the industrial proletariat, it formed, together with it as well as with the idealistically minded intelligentsia, a united 'working-class'. Distinct from the Social-Democracy in their understanding of 'working-class', as well as of the trinity of 'industrial proletariat, labouring peasantry and revolutionary intelligentsia', the S.R.s were also distinct from classical Populism in that they did not start out from the struggle for a Socialist forestalling of the bourgeois transformation of socio-economic relations in Russia, nor from the denial of the very possibility of such a transformation because of the specific conditions of Russian development. What they did was remove from the order of the day the very problem of the bourgeois revolution in Russia on the grounds that such a transformation had already been consummated: 'There was no purely bourgeois revolution in Russia – a revolution from below – because it was forestalled by a revolution from above. The so-called epoch of Great Reforms was also a metamorphosis of the feudal autocracy into an aristocratic-bourgeois bureaucracy'; since then the bourgeoisie and the government have been 'united by firm bonds'.[131]

But this was just the reason no 'purely bourgeois revolution' could take place in Russia in future either. On the one hand, 'all attempts to implicate the bourgeoisie as a class in the political struggle have proven futile. . . . Political emancipation is the cause of the Russian intelligentsia and the Russian labouring masses; it is time to understand that no one else is going to take an active part in it' (Novobrantsev[135]). On the other hand, by virtue of just this make-up of the revolutionary forces, the approaching revolution, even if not wholly Socialist, will at least effect a substantial redistribution of property, which is just the side of it that the S.R.s must concentrate on:

> The whole weight of the struggle against the autocracy, [runs the draft programme] despite the presence of a liberal-democratic opposition, which is taking hold primarily of elements of 'educated society' that from a class point of view are interstitial, is falling on the proletariat, the labouring peasantry and the revolutionary-Socialist intelligentsia. Hence the indispensable task of a Socialist Party to which the dominant role in this struggle is passing over, is a broadening and deepening into a revolutionary situation of those social and proprietary changes that the overthrow of the autocracy must be bound up with.[136]

But towards 1903 the upsurge of peasant riots subsided, and the rural agitation began yielding extremely modest results. Together with the terrorist activity, which naturally was concentrated in the cities, the centre of gravity of the propagandist activity of the S.R.s also began shifting to the cities. Here, however, in spite of individual, partial successes, the competition with the Social-Democracy among the workers proved beyond the capacity of the S.R.s. It was more and more the intelligentsia that became the S.R. sphere of influence in the cities; on this terrain they drew near to the intellectual wing of the liberal movement, which in 1903–4 happened to be undergoing a process of radicalization. After organizing in a separate Union of Emancipation it had begun separating from the more moderate Zemstvo and land-owning wing of the movement (see below). In autumn of 1904 the S.R.s, together with the Union of Emancipation and different ethnic groupings, convoked abroad a 'Conference of Revolutionary and Oppositionist Parties', whose participants agreed on the general validity of the most immediate democratic objectives of all those gathered together, merely stipulating a difference of tactic (both Social-Democratic fractions declined to attend the conference).

This *rapprochement* with non-Socialist radical movements and organizations was made easier for the S.R.s by their general view of the character of the coming Russian revolution. This enabled them to regard the liberal movement itself as 'non-bourgeois', and to reduce the entire distinction between it and the Socialist movement to a difference of generations and temperaments, to a difference between 'fathers' and 'sons'. The same Novobrantsev whose article we quoted above wrote (on the occasion of a polemic of *Iskra* against the Union of Emancipation): 'There is no doubt that the "fathers" differ from us in the moderation of their tactics and demands, but that is not an antithesis of principle.'

And in fact the 'antithesis of principle' soon began being smoothed over just as the S.R.s' political passion began being concentrated not so much on the 'broadening and deepening of those social and proprietary changes into a revolutionary situation' as on those 'most immediate democratic objectives' that they had in common with their bourgeois-radical allies. Because of this they did in fact dissolve in the joint 'movement of emancipation' as its 'Left' ultra-democratic wing, but without playing the independent role in this movement that was played by both Social-Democratic fractions, each in its own style, which had set themselves, together with general-democratic objectives, their own special, 'class' objectives as well, and thus brought into the 'movement of emancipation' itself an element that distinguished them in principle from the other members of this movement and even led to hostile collisions more than once.

It was only the semi-parliamentarianism created by the revolution of 1905, which at first evoked a hostile boycott from the S.R.s (as well as from the Bolsheviks), that paved the way for the steady growth of the S.R. Party and its political formation as a party whose specific objective was the parliamentary representation of the middle strata of the peasantry. What served the S.R.s as the drive-shaft of these middle strata was the Third Element, which in the person of the teaching and medical personnel, statisticians and every possible kind of Zemstvo functionary was the real prop of the Party and, in close contact with the countryside, injected S.R. slogans and ideas into it.

The twenty-two million votes received by the S.R.s in 1917 in the elections to the Constituent Assembly showed how broad the sympathy for these ideas was among the peasant masses. However, the absence of any violent reaction to the dispersal of the Constituent Assembly by the Bolsheviks and the swift collapse of the 'Constituent Assembly front' in the civil war incontrovertibly demonstrated one thing: at a time when the organized cadres of the Party were investing all their passion in the struggle for political democracy, the peasant masses once again showed that for them, on the contrary, what was basic in the S.R. ideas were 'those social, proprietary changes' that the S.R. Party programme had promised 'to link to the overthrow of the autocracy', but whose realization had been postponed by the Party's political practice in the name of the maintenance of the democratic order.

The formation of the Russian liberal democracy proved to be even more complicated and contradictory than had the formation of the Populist democracy.

Towards the beginning of the new century, as we have seen, 'legal Marxism' proved to be the ideological bridge by which a substantial part of the Russian intelligentsia for the first time passed over to a democracy that was not Socialist. Like the Social-Democracy, it too had decisively broken with all forms of Populism and was definitely counting on the capitalist path in the evolution of Russia. But in contrast with the Social-Democracy, which was oriented towards the working-class, it was depending on the 'bourgeois' forces certain to be engendered by that development.

These forces did, in fact, come into being – not only in the form of the intelligentsia's 'Third Element', which served the growing heavy industry and was bound up in one way or another with its fate, but also in the form of the progressive segment of the capitalists themselves – primarily in the textile industry – who were naturally concentrated in Moscow. However, for the reasons already noted at the very beginning of this work (Part I, Chap. 2) this progressive stratum of the Russian bourgeoisie lacked those social, political, and ideological resources that would have been indispensable to enable it to emerge as an independent political force, openly laying claim to the leadership of an 'all-national' movement against the autocracy. Because of the experience of the developed revolutionary movement, of the 1905 revolution itself and the concentration of all conservative forces called forth by this experience, a considerable portion of this bourgeois stratum came to lean on the liberal Zemstvo movement. One of the most eminent architects of this *rapprochement* was A. I. Guchkov, future leader of the October 17th Party (Octobrists). This movement had age-old aristocratic-cum-landholder oppositionist traditions, but the mass of mercantile Russia was repelled by just these aristocratic traditions. During the first few years of the emancipation movement the oppositional activity of this progressive Russian bourgeoisie was primarily expressed – aside from the remarkable cultural activity we have already commented on – in the broad material support individual representatives of it gave the revolutionary Socialist parties – expecially the Social-Democracy, which impressed them not only by its ability to draw the broadest masses into a struggle for political liberty, but also by its 'realism', which had opportunely brought the coming revolution within the socio-economic framework of the capitalist system.

Thus, an outspoken 'bourgeois' liberal democracy made its appearance not so much as an organization of even the most advanced elements of the bourgeoisie itself, but as a group of 'ideologues' who 'represented' it only theoretically. Free of the limiting influence of practical interests, they were able in a form that was all the more 'pure' to express the 'ultimate' interests of the class they were gravitating towards. In the given historical setting these interests reduced themselves on the one hand to the elimination of all the socio-economic, cultural and other survivals of the past that hindered the free development of capitalism in Russia, and on the other to the winning of democracy as the political system that in principle most corresponded to the requirements of that development.

Leaving the 'working-class question' entirely to the Social-Democracy, this ideological group, whose most eminent representatives were P. Struve, M. Tugan-Baranovsky, and V. Bogucharsky, towards the beginning of the century embodied just this kind of liberalism. It was consistently democratic, free of the reactionary socio-economic illusions of Populism, and did not disguise its authentic image by a more or less 'Socialist' mask. As we shall see, this was just what Lenin was seeking in these years, as a longed-for and indispensable comrade-in-arms for the Social-Democracy in its political struggle. Hence, in spite of the sharp polemics against the 'Bernsteinian' reformist theories of 'legal Marxism', it turned out to be Lenin himself who at this time was the most zealous partisan of a political *rapprochement* with its representatives. In May 1900 Struve and Tugan-Baranovsky were invited to a small conference in Pskov (Lenin, Martov, Potresov, S. and L. Radchenko), at which it was decided to found *Iskra* and support was promised for the new organ. Struve had secured a secret memorandum about the Zemstvos written by Witte, and he gave it to the *Iskra* group to be printed. He also published two articles on the theme of the Autocracy and the Zemstvo, in the first few numbers of *Iskra*. There even arose (against Martov's opposition) a plan to publish a joint organ with an extensive discussion section, and it was only Struve's arrest in March 1901, in connexion with a demonstration of Petersburg students, that broke off the negotiations, which had almost been concluded.

However, that same year of 1901 the situation began changing radically. Revolutionary excitement, which was spreading more and more definitely to the working-class and students, and was already beginning to overflow into the countryside, forced the liberals in the Zemstvos to bestir themselves. Making use of all the advantages of the Zemstvo apparatus, as early as 1901 Zemstvo functionaries had begun systematically assembling in private conferences and congresses, debating the situation, working out a programme, and creating a political organization. But liberalism, which was emerging in Russia for the first time in the shape of a formed political organization of the possessing strata of society, though only of the Zemstvo segment of that society, could not, of course, fail to exercise an immense magnetic power over the ideologues of 'bourgeois' liberalism, too.

Some new overtones could already be detected in the foreword written by Struve to Witte's Note in the second half of 1901. Struve insisted on the necessity of forming a 'moderate' party. Of course, he argued, 'the creation of a clear-cut political movement... is the task of the Social-Democratic Party'. But a liberal party was destined to play a 'major political role': 'by skilful tactics the moderate parties will benefit by the sharpening of the struggle between social extremes'. It was just this orientation, based on the exploitation of the revolutionary conflict between the working-class and the autocracy in the interests of moderate liberalism, that also became fundamental for the *bloc* of bourgeois-intellectual liberalism and Zemstvo liberalism that took shape towards the middle of 1902 and whose fruit was the review *Osvobozhdenie*.* Developing his own previous ideas, Struve tried to prove as early as 1903 that the principles of the Social-Democracy 'coincided with the ideas of liberalism as a political system of freedom and equality', and that because of this Russian liberals ought to take up a position 'not against the Social-Democracy, but together with it and in an alliance with it'.[137] But the fundamental tone of the review was already completely different.

* The first number came out 1 July 1902 (N.S.), published by the Stuttgart Social-Democratic printer Dietz. P. Struve was the editor, with the agreement of the Zemstvo people.

The programmatic article in the first number was signed by 'Russian constitutionalists'; in the text they underlined their close links with the 'Zemstvo group'. The article reads: 'The difference between our organ and other periodicals published abroad is that we propose to unite those groups of Russian society that cannot find a vent for their feeling of indignation in either the class or the revolutionary struggle.' The first task of the organ was 'to work out a political programme . . . in whose framework the Zemstvo might be able to act jointly with other social groups without at the same time rejecting those advantages that can lend its activity a special importance during the transition to a new political régime'. This programme was supposed to include the conferring on the Supreme Power of broad liberties, equality of citizens before the law and 'national representation independently of social classification' as granted by the legislative power. The elaboration of a constitution was to be entrusted to an assembly of Zemstvo representatives, since any other arrangement would be a 'leap into the unknown'. The draft programme is silent about social reforms of any kind just as it is about the general application of an electoral law in the future legislative assembly.

Printed in this same number was a welcoming 'open letter from a group of Zemstvo people who told of their efforts to create an organization charged with 'abolishing anarchy in the government and among the people'. This expressed itself even more definitely, to the accompaniment of direct attacks on the revolutionary and especially the peasant movement. The letter recalled the 'common class and personal interests that were mounting like a menacing volcano, which at any moment might wreak the most frightful havoc'; it speaks indignantly of peasant riots brought about by the 'revolutionary propaganda' that had fallen on the soil of the 'people's poverty, ignorance, and incomprehension of the most elementary principles of civil law'.

Martov correctly summed up the political sense of all these programmatic expressions: 'The general tone of all the articles in this number with any programmatic significance clearly indicates that the founders of *Osvobozhdenie* have set themselves the goal primarily of organizing a rural party propped up on the mass of landowners and benefiting from all the advantages of being situated between the government and those elements of the people contending with it.'[138] It was, however, just this revolutionary struggle of 'people's elements' that very rapidly drove a wedge into the only just consolidated bloc of the liberalism of the bourgeois intelligentsia and the liberalism of Zemstvos and land-owners.

In Zemstvo liberalism itself, the revolutionary events of 1902–3 were echoed at first by a sharpening of the antagonism between its 'constitutional' wing and the 'Slavophil' wing (led by D. N. Shipov). The latter also desired certain reforms but insisted above all on the inviolability of the autocracy and of the so-called 'immemorial principles', whose essence boiled down to the maintenance by the landed nobility of its ruling position. But the war with Japan began on 26–27 January 1904; for Russia it turned into an endless series of the most severe defeats on land and at sea. It put a stop to the process of differentiation within Zemstvo liberalism, and by moving its general line 'leftward' brought both wings to a new *rapprochement*. Among the ninety-eight participants in a congress that took place on 6–8 November 1904 there were also some 'Shipovites', and 'constitutionalists'. Shipov himself was voted chairman of the Congress and made a member of the delegation it elected to see the Tsar.

The general 'leftward' movement of Zemstvo liberalism was a natural response to the almost improbable feebleness and triviality of the autocratic régime, so pitilessly exposed by the war. But this leftward movement and *rapprochement* of both wings of Zemstvo liberalism were also helped considerably by the inconsistent policy of the government itself, which testified to extreme perplexity. At first its liberal minister, Prince Svyatopolk-Mirsky, permitted the Congress to be called, then he forbade it, without, however, deciding on any measures against those who disregarded the prohibition, while at the same time he forbade the press to print anything about the Congress everyone was talking about. The result was that the Congress formulated eleven theses demanding freedom of conscience, press, assembly, and organization, equality of citizens before the law, the inviolability of the individual, equal rights to the peasantry as to the other estates, rural and municipal reform, a political amnesty, the abolition of exceptional decrees, and, finally, the convocation of an elected organ to represent the people. On the question of the functions of this organ once again a watershed made itself felt between the 'constitutionalists' and the 'Shipovites': seventy-one votes were cast for a legislative organ and twenty-seven for a consultative organ.

The response to the November demands of the Zemstvo people was a ukase of 12 December 1904 'on the means for the improvement of state order'. The ukase did not meet with any sympathy even in moderate Zemstvo circles. It is true that it proposed the broadening of the authority of the Zemstvos, toleration and a number of other liberties, a peasant reform, a revision of the exceptional laws, etc., but its silence on the main demand – the convocation of a people's representative institution – evoked doubt in the sincerity of these promises. These doubts were turned into certainty when a government communiqué was published the very next day defaming the 'emancipation movement' and calling upon the 'right-thinking portion of society' to combat this 'sedition' mercilessly. Meanwhile, the uninterrupted military defeats continued to stimulate oppositionist moods in all strata of society, and the inglorious capitulation of Port Arthur (24 December 1904) considerably facilitated the creation of an atmosphere in which the economic strike of the Putilov factory workers was transformed in a few days into a massive political movement of the whole of the Petersburg proletariat. On 9 January 1905 this culminated in the shooting down, with many thousands of victims, of the workers who were going to the Winter Palace with their celebrated petition to the Tsar.

We shall speak further on the significance of this day, which has gone down in history as the opening day of the 1905 revolution. After 9 January the 'emancipation movement' began taking giant strides forward. Under its pressure the government tried to make another concession to 'society'. On 18 February an order in the name of the new Minister of the Interior, A. G. Bulygin (Svyatpolk-Mirsky had been dismissed into retirement after 9 January) announced the Tsar's intention to 'invite to the preliminary elaboration and assessment of legislative proposals the worthiest individuals chosen from the people and enjoying the confidence of the nation', but with 'absolute maintenance of the inviolability of the fundamental laws of the Empire'. A ukase the Senate published the same day charged the Council of Ministers 'with the review and assessment of views and proposals proceeding in Our Name from private persons and institutions, touching on the improvement of the public welfare and the amelioration of the welfare of the people'.

It is true that the test of the order left no doubt that what was intended was merely a consultative organ, very restricted both in composition and in scope – in other words a belated realization of the Loris-Melikov proposals that had been interred by Alexander III more than two decades before. But the simultaneous publication, on this same 18 February, of a Manifesto that once again called on 'right-thinking people of all estates and conditions' to 'extirpate the sedition in our land' and did not mention a word about the promise made in the order to invite those 'chosen from the people' to some kind of participation in the legislative activity, once again underlined the autocracy's insincerity. The Manifesto was interpreted as a new attempt by it to stimulate demagogically the people's 'infernal' instincts against the 'seditious' propertied educated strata of society.*

But regardless of all this, for the first time in the history of the Russian imperial autocracy a decisive word was spoken about the convocation of elected representatives of the people; in this sense the 'emancipation movement' was able to record its first success in principle. It spurred it on considerably.

The ukase to the Senate, however, proved to be even more important for the further development of this movement. The Senate immediately made use of the ukase – naturally in spite of the real intentions of its authors – as a legalization of the 'right of petition' – the right of both private bodies and such 'institutions' as the Zemstvos and Municipal Councils to assemble for the passing of political resolutions directly to the Tsar.

In April 1905 a new congress of Zemstvo people convened. In essence it duplicated the programme of the November demands, but it supplemented it by a demand for a one-chamber system in the future national representative body and for a general, equal, and direct electoral law with a secret ballot. But this time the thirty-seven delegates who voted against direct elections (seventy-one voted for the resolution) were no longer led by a 'Shipovite', but by one of the celebrated constitutionalist brothers, P. I. Petrunkevich. His attitude expressed that mistrust of the popular masses, especially the peasants, and even more that fear of their movement that had been growing in the Zemstvo *milieu*, at first parallel with its leftward swing, then outdistancing it and turning the general line of Zemstvo liberalism rightward. It forced even the most consistent constitutionalists to gaze upon the imperial power with growing trustfulness, in the hope of finding in it an ally that by timely concessions would save it both from itself and from an elemental outburst of the people.

This was the same mood that had been expressed just before the November Zemstvo Congress of 1904 by one of the other famous

* By Russian law the Imperial manifestos were made public in the churches, and hence became known to the widest masses of the people, while orders and ukases were accessible only to the stratum of newspaper readers, which in pre-revolutionary Russia was extremely thin.

liberal brothers, Prince Eugene Trubetskoy, in an article that made a considerable stir at the time.[139] Having observed with sorrow that 'the extremist parties have taken into their own hands a monopoly of organization . . . a monopoly of free speech also belongs to them at the present time . . . their influence . . . is growing hour by hour', the author addressed an appeal to the Supreme Power to curb the 'bureaucracy', which must be 'not a ruler over a voiceless herd, but an instrument of the throne supported by society'.

Such attitudes, which marked a new turn in the general line of Zemstvo liberalism, by now definitely 'rightist', were very clearly reflected in the activities of the May 1905 congress. This was the first congress at which there assembled, utilizing the ukase to the Senate of 18 February, not the representatives of the individual Zemstvo groups, but the elected delegates of all the provincial Zemstvos of Russia. The congress did not reject, of course, the previously formulated political programme. But as far as the Tsar was concerned it clearly expressed its readiness to be satisfied with the promised consultative organ, emphasizing that questions of 'war and peace' and questions of the 'renovation of the state system' equally were to be decided by the elected delegates only 'in accord with You' – i.e., the Tsar. It expressed its desire for the soonest possible convocation of popular representatives in a form that emphasized the role of the Tsar as the country's saviour from 'anarchy'.

A speech along the same lines was made by Prince S. N. Trubetskoy, who spoke in the name of the twelve-member deputation of the congress that was received by the Tsar on 6 June. 'Cast aside your doubts. My will – the Imperial will – to convoke the people's elected representatives – is unshakeable,' said the Tsar in order to soothe the delegation. Two weeks later he received a delegation of the most reactionary rural nobility (Count Bobrinsky, Naryshkin, and others), and dismissed them with the same soothing words, insisting on the maintenance of the autocracy in all its inviolability, as a counterweight to the Zemstvo congresses.

But by now nothing could restrain the development of revolutionary events, spurred on by the fiascos of the war. It could not be restrained by the Manifesto of 6 August, relating to the forthcoming convocation of a legislative consultative State Duma (the so-called 'Bulygin Duma'), with a very complicated system of representation according to districts that was based on social estates but that completely excluded the workers. Nor could it be restrained by the peace negotiations with Japan, which had been begun on the initiative of President Theodore Roosevelt on 11 August 1905 and finished by the signing of a peace treaty on 23 August. Least of all could it be restrained by the cancellation of the ukase of 18 February, which was simultaneous with the publication of the Manifesto of 6 August.

The whole country was in a ferment. In the cities the populace was appropriating its own freedom of assembly by simply assembling, and the students, who had been striking now for several weeks, took advantage of the ukase of 27 August about the granting of autonomy to the higher institutions of learning to go back to the universities, in accordance with a slogan put out by *Iskra*, and turn the halls and auditoriums into places for mass-meetings and assemblies that went on from morning till late at night without a stop. Workers' strikes took place one after the other in an uninterrupted chain until, finally, the railway workers' strike, which began on 7 October and was supported by a general strike of practically all the workers in the country, dealt the shaken autocracy a final blow. The Manifesto of 17 October 1905 proclaimed to the populace the granting of full constitutional liberties and the transformation of the State Duma from a consultative into a legislative organ, with electoral rights for the workers, too.

But the share of Zemstvo liberalism in all these events kept growing less and less noticeable, and the August congress of 1905* evoked only a very limited response. The duality of attitude already noted, which made it more and more necessary to consider the Tsarist autocracy not so much an 'enemy' as a possible ally in the struggle against the revolutionary movements, and this movement, on the other hand, not so much an ally as an 'internal enemy', coloured the politics of all wings of Zemstvo liberalism more and more and paralysed its political activity. It was only the semi-parliamentarianism created by the 1905 revolution, though that too was only in the mutilated and distorted form in which it emerged from the insurrection of 3 June 1907 (see below), that created the conditions enabling the conservative elements of Zemstvo liberalism to return to the political arena as a tangible political force.

It was in a directly contrary direction that the bourgeois intelligentsia allied with Zemstvo liberalism evolved during these feverish

* Among other things, this congress saw a split in Zemstvo liberalism along a new axis: on the question of the autonomy of the ethnic regions, primarily Poland. A. I. Guchkov led the most decisive opponents of autonomy.

pre-revolutionary months and years. During the time when stormy mass movements were stimulating the growth of elements of conservatism and even of political, social, and nationalist reaction in the Zemstvo *milieu*, the great mass of the urban intelligentsia reacted to these movements with a rapid 'radicalization'. Engineers, technicians, teachers, physicians, lawyers, writers, and so on, including even government functionaries, especially Post Office and Railway Department officials – all the intellectual cadres of the socio-economic and state apparatus of the country entered the movement one after the other, grouped themselves in professional congresses and made use of them not only for the creation of corporate organizations but also for the assertion of sharper and sharper and increasingly insistent political demands, formulated by now no longer as a 'petition' to the government, but as an anti-governmental platform for the country. Borrowing from the proletariat the idea of 'professional political unions', they also borrowed from it, in the last analysis, the idea of the 'strike', as an instrument of struggle for political demands. They appropriated the slogan, 'Not against the Social-Democracy, but side by side with it,' which Struve had tried in vain to make the general slogan of Russian liberalism.

But the growing movement of the urban intelligentsia also changed the political position of Struve himself. The small group of intellectuals he led, which had entered into a *bloc* with Zemstvo liberalism, as the representative of 'bourgeois' liberalism, received the same mass support in this movement as the S.R.s were receiving at the time among the Zemstvo intellectuals – but only with all these advantages in the sense of organization, fighting ability, and energy that are given the urban intelligentsia in comparison with the rural, by its concentration in the vital centres of the country and the place it occupies in the social and state apparatus. The 'radicalization' in its attitude was reflected in the 'radicalization of the political line of *Osvobozhdenie*. Struve began[140] by pointing out the indispensability of a decisive rupture between 'constitutionalists' and 'Slavophils', i.e., Shipov's group. But he was soon[141] demanding that the 'constitutional' party itself became 'democratic': he included in his programme the universal right to vote and social and also agrarian reforms, rejected the slogan of a Zemstvo Assembly, just as he did any claims of the Zemstvo people to a monopoly in working out the future constitution. Continuing along this line, *Osvobozhdenie*[142] published a draft agrarian programme, which for the first time in the history of Russian liberalism acknowledged the principle of forcible alienation of landholders' property in favour of the peasantry – a principle that was later of course made part of the foundation of the agrarian programme of the Kadet Party.

Some hesitations and even some reverse tendencies were introduced into this evolution of the *Osvobozhdenie* political line by the Russo-Japanese war. Counting on the possibility of a new *rapprochement* with Zemstvo liberalism on the basis of the 'patriotic fervour' evoked by the war, and on the assumed development of 'socio-civic elements' within the framework of this fervour, Struve preached extreme wariness both in political slogans and in the criticism of the government's conduct of the war, in so far as they might offend the patriotic feelings of 'society'. 'We need a common ground with those who still do not understand us.'[143] He also recommended the same wariness to the student youth, which had been about to demonstrate against the patriotic monarchist street processions with ikons and portraits of the Tsar, arranged by the authorities themselves. He advised that these processions be met by the shout of 'Long live the army!' but that 'sharper slogans' be refrained from.[144]

This new zigzag in Struve's political line had no future, in so far as the shamefully inept conduct of the war excluded any possibility of the development of any kind of progressive 'socio-civic' movement within the framework of a martial patriotism. Even after Plehve's assassination, as a counterweight to the 'confidence' in the autocratic régime demanded by Prince Svyatopolk-Mirsky in response to the 'confidence' it promised to have in 'society', Struve once again stated decisively: 'the choice can only be between democracy and autocracy'.[145]

Nevertheless, this 'military' zigzag was no accident. Based on supposed Zemstvo attitudes, it attested the firmness of the political and ideological bonds by which the 1901–2 *bloc* had bound Struve to Zemstvo-aristocratic liberalism, and that he was no longer capable of bursting. As a matter of fact, in demanding the 'democratization' of the 'constitutional' party, he conceived of this party as before as one that 'united in its ranks the progressive nobleman with the plebeian and peasant'. In calling for a choice to be made 'between the democracy and the autocracy' he left no doubt as to which social spheres this appeal of his was addressed to, when on behalf of democracy he argued that 'only the democracy would lead the working-class and the peasantry into the channel of a legal struggle for rights'. Even during the sharpest divergence between himself and Zemstvo liberalism, even its 'constitutional' wing, Struve dealt with this divergence merely as an accidental one, a transitory and vexing episode. His entire subsequent political career bears witness to the firmness with which elements of political and even more of social conservatism entered into his political and ideological stock-in-trade.

Hence it is not surprising that as the revolutionary crisis grew more acute Struve's 'radicalism' began more and more obviously to lag behind the 'radicalism' of the mass of urban intellectuals whose spokesman he wanted to be. In the near future, after the culmination of the revolutionary cycle, the overwhelming majority of this motley intelligentsia were also fated to find themselves bolt-holes in one conservative-liberal grouping or another. But at this historical juncture almost all of them were living through a period of extreme and constantly growing revolutionary fervour, and the last thing they thought of was an imminent shunting of the 'all-national' onslaught on the autocracy 'into the channel of a legal struggle'. On the contrary, freed of the paralysing fear of the workers' and especially of the peasants' movement, which was no immediate threat, it attempted as quickly and completely as it could to include itself in this movement, which was dealing the autocratic régime of bondage such mighty blows. In this stage of its development it was decisively alienated from Zemstvo liberalism by its watchful and even hostile attitude towards the movement. This was dictated by socio-economic considerations that even in Struve's periods of maximal 'radicalism', on the contrary, evoked a sympathetic response from him.

For all these reasons Struve proved unfit to become the authentic political leader and ideological champion of the movement of the urban intelligentsia in preparing and realizing the revolution. This movement produced its own political leaders on the spot, out of its own matrix, while in its ideological leadership the role of others, the offspring of 'legal Marxism' who had not left Russia, like E. Kuskova, S. Prokopovich, and others, proved far more substantial than that of the *émigré* Struve. It was just these who were the intellectual inspirers of the Union of Liberation in which the urban intelligentsia for the first time created its own political organization, 'bourgeois' in its principles. This was completely independent of Zemstvo liberalism, and its first public act was to take part in the above-mentioned 'Conference of revolutionary and oppositionist parties' of autumn 1904, to which the Social-Democracy, on principle, refused to send its own delegates, but at which not a single Zemstvo liberal trend was represented either.

Supported by the professional-political Union of Unions on the one hand, and by the Union of Liberation, on the other, the urban intelligentsia developed a noisy campaign of its own, parallel with the Zemstvo movement and partially exploiting it. It organized a series of 'banquets', at which progressively sharper political speeches were made, and a peculiar political 'fraternizing' took place with the representatives of the Socialist parties, the workers, and every other kind of 'deputation'. In addition to the 'banquets' it sent its own speakers to popular meetings in the universities and by means of all this it established political contact for the first time with the mass of small urban bourgeoisie that later on produced the cadres of city voters for the Kadet Party. A whole series of unions of the professional intelligentsia took an active part in the October general strike that dealt the autocracy a final blow. It joined the 'Soviet of Workers' Deputies' that was created by the Petersburg proletariat and that immediately generated imitations throughout the country.

In the 1905 revolution the bourgeois-democratic sector of liberalism moved forward 'side by side with the Social-Democracy and in alliance with it'. It was to leave the revolution in another mood, but we shall speak of that below.

4. ON THE THRESHOLD OF THE REVOLUTION

As the 'emancipation movement' took shape, the problem that was fundamental for the Russian Social-Democracy – the combination of Socialist-proletarian and bourgeois-democratic tendencies in the process of the bourgeois revolution – naturally began to assume a concrete form. It became the problem of the attitude of the Social-Democracy towards the liberalism – Zemstvo and bourgeois-intellectual – that in this movement, for the first time, had begun moving into the political arena as an independently organized force. But at the same time the practical contradictoriness and uselessness of those mellifluous theoretical formulae that the Social-Democracy had been using to solve this vital problem began to find a more and more insistent expression. It became necessary to accept the factual unrealizability of the 'support' promised by the Party programme 'to every oppositionist and revolutionary movement', and to admit that in reality 'there could not even be any question of serious support' from authentic Russian liberalism. It became necessary, as a matter of fact, to renounce even the idea of 'hegemony', and any calculations based on the possibility that the Social-Democracy would become the focus of attraction for 'all classes of the population', and hence be acknowledged as the leader of the bourgeois sector of the 'emancipation movement' too. Thus a new solution had to be sought for the same old problem.

As we have seen, the new solution offered by Menshevism was essentially a return to the original theoretical constructions of the Emancipation of Labour Group. Having renounced in advance any competition with the bourgeoisie in the struggle for power, Menshevism made its focal task the exploitation of the decisive role of the Russian proletariat in the bourgeois revolution with the aim of giving an upsurge to its class consciousness, independence, and organization that would, while reconciling it to the historically inevitable phase of the political rule of the bourgeoisie, enable it at the same time to secure the realization of that rule in extreme democratic forms, and with the most perfected social legislation. This alone would give it a chance, immediately after the 'bourgeois' revolutionary transformation, to begin a systematic struggle – now against the bourgeoisie directly – for its own Socialist goals.

Bolshevism too gave the old problem a new solution. We shall speak of this below in greater detail, but in principle it boiled down to a struggle, as has been mentioned before, not only for the elimination of the bourgeoisie from the revolutionary régime, but also for its subjugation to the revolutionary dictatorship itself. In this new solution Lenin, too, was essentially returning to an idea he had expressed as far back as 1899, when in objecting to Akselrod's idea of 'supporting' the bourgeois opposition and of an 'alliance' with it,[146] he wrote to Potresov: 'In my opinion we must use a far firmer and more appropriate word than "support" and "alliance". The latter indicates an equality of rights between the allies, whereas they must bring up the rear, sometimes even grinding their teeth. They have absolutely not grown up to the idea of equality of rights, and with their cowardice, isolation, lack of cohesion, etc. they never will.' It was this old idea of 'teeth-grinding' that Lenin now returned to, after undergoing an evolution on the question of the relationship to the non-Socialist opposition that was still more zigzag in form and contradictory than that undergone by the original fathers and future leaders of Menshevism. The objective contradictions, already emphasized often, of the dual task set the Russian Social-Democracy by history, are enough to explain the contradictoriness of this evolution. For the

Mensheviks the idea that constituted the unifying principle of Menshevism through all its zigzags was the idea of the primacy of the class-proletarian, Socialist elements of this task: for Bolshevism the corresponding idea was the primacy of its general democratic, political elements.

The same idea already colours Lenin's first works, too – *Friends of the People* and the articles on Struve's book in the Marxist *Sbornik*.[147] These were written when, in the struggle against Populism and for self-affirmation, Russian Marxism emphasized with special insistence the capitalist, 'bourgeois' character of Russian economic evolution, the 'class struggle' as a motor force of social evolution, and the special role of the industrial proletariat in the struggle for Socialism. It was just its disregard for class contradictions that Lenin at that time considered the basic methodological vice of Struve's book. He characterized this as a 'narrow objectivism, restricted to the demonstration of the inevitability and necessity of the process and making no effort to reveal at every concrete stage of this process the form of class antagonism inherent in it – an objectivism that characterized the process in general, but not those antagonistic classes and units whose struggle the process is composed of'. For Lenin it was just this that gave rise to the 'necessity for another formulation of the question . . . for a more consistent carrying out of the theory of class contradictions'.

As Martov noted,[148] Lenin had built up his polemic against the Populists during these years primarily on 'the parallel between the classically consistent democracy and radicalism of the Populists of the '70s and their epigones' of the *Russkoye Bogatstvo*. But if this was so Struve's 'objectivism' seemed to Lenin particularly dangerous just because it led to the belittling and even the disregard of those revolutionary-democratic tasks that the Social-Democracy had set itself and that enabled it to regard itself as the heir of the People's Freedom. And in that case Lenin thought it indispensable to shield Populism too against the attacks of the Marxist Struve. Because of this Lenin made an extremely critical assessment of Struve's 'references to the "rationalism", the "progressivism", the "reasonableness" etc. of liberal, that is, bourgeois policy in comparison with the policies of Populism', and especially Struve's staking everything on the peasant, 'economically powerful and adapted to commodity production'.

This is what Lenin wrote about Populism:

> Philosophizing about the possibility of 'other paths for the fatherland' is only the external trappings of Populism. But its content is the representation of the interests of the Russian small producer, the petty-bourgeois. . . . It would be absolutely incorrect to reject the entire Populist programme in its entirety, without discrimination. Its reactionary and its progressive sides must be strictly distinguished. Populism is reactionary in so far as it proposes measures binding the peasant to the land and to old methods of production. . . . But there are also other points concerning self-government, the free and large-scale access of the 'people' to knowledge, the expansion of 'national' [e.g. small-scale] farming by means of cheap credits, improvement of technique, the regulation of marketing, etc., etc. Mr Struve, of course, also entirely admits that such generally democratic measures are progressive. . . . Populists have an incomparably more correct . . . understanding of, and in this respect represent the interests of, the small producers, and the Marxists must, while rejecting all the reactionary traits of their programme, not only accept the general-democratic points, but also develop them more precisely, more profoundly, and further.*

Lenin's conversations with the members of the Emancipation of Labour Group during his trip abroad in 1895 immediately revealed a fundamental divergence between him and the Group on the question of the relationship of Russian Social-Democracy to bourgeois liberalism. Akselrod, even more than twenty years later, in the full blaze of his irreconcilable hostility to Bolshevism, recalled these conversations as a 'genuine holiday', 'one of the happiest, most radiant moments in the life of the Group', and with great praise referred to the 'real revolutionary Social-Democratic thought' that 'had finally awoken' in Russia, and especially Lenin's articles in the *Sbornik*. But he severely criticized Lenin's 'abstract' attitude towards the 'liberals': 'You are identifying our attitude toward the liberals with the attitude of the Socialists towards the liberals of the West. But . . . at the given historical moment the immediate interests of the proletariat in Russia coincide with the fundamental interests of other progressive strata of society'. To this Lenin replied that Plekhanov too had made 'exactly the same remarks' to him, saying: 'What you [Lenin] turn to the liberals is your back, while we [the Group] turn our faces'.

As a result of repeated conversations Lenin, in Akselrod's words,

* The 'Aesopian' language of the article is due to its having been written for an anthology subject to censorship.

'stated that he acknowledged the correctness of the Group's point of view on this question'. This was undoubtedly so, judging by his utterances on this theme during the next few years: he not only refrained from extolling the superiority of Populism to bourgeois liberalism but, on the contrary, he proclaimed the basic condition of the progressive nature of this liberalism to be its utter lack of any admixture of Populist attitudes or a 'conciliationist' relationship to it. He even reproached Akselrod, in the above-quoted letter about the 'grinding of teeth', with his 'indulgence' not so much to liberalism in general as to 'the agrarianizing Fronde'.*

Lenin's change of position had been expressed very obviously as far back as 1896, when the question of grain prices, which had been brought up by the 'agrarians', was being stormily debated in the press and at meetings. In the arguments on this subject Struve and Tugan-Baranovsky – in accord with the big land-owners – spoke out for high grain prices, taking as their starting-point the proposition 'concerning progressivism and the inevitability of a capitalist development in agriculture', and taking the view that the 'high price of bread was a factor of such a development, whereas low prices would further the maintenance of the stubbornly surviving forms of servitude in the countryside'.[149] In the dispute between them and the Populists (who were defending low grain prices in the interests of the great mass of impoverished peasants as well as of the urban population), and the 'Samarsky' Marxists who were supporting the Populists on this question and were headed by P. P. Maslov, an economist who was to become well known later, Lenin was entirely on the side of Struve and Tugan-Baranovsky. He completely disregarded the 'objectivism' of their position and the 'staking everything on the economically powerful peasant, adapted to commodity production' that he had so sharply exposed in the *Sbornik*.

In his article *What Heritage Are We Rejecting?*[150] Lenin even tried to link the ideological lineage of Russian Marxism to the ideas not of the revolutionary Populists of the '60s and '70s, but to Skaldin,† one of the few openly 'bourgeois' journalistic economists of the time. This was his explanation: 'Yes, of course, Skaldin is a bourgeois,

* By this clumsy expression Lenin meant not only the Zemstvo-aristocratic opposition, but in general a Populist orientation based on the social forces not of the evolving Russian cities but of the backward Russian countryside.

† This was a pseudonym for Yelenev, who later became an extreme reactionary and was one of the most ferocious of the censors.

but he is the representative of a progressive bourgeois ideology, instead of which the Populists have a petty-bourgeois ideology, which on a whole series of points is reactionary'. In answer to Potresov's reproaches with respect to this article Lenin excused himself by saying that in general 'we ought not, perhaps, take up historical-literary themes'. In a personal letter he said: 'That we must inherit something from other people is incontestable. . . . But the essence of the article, after all, is that it says bourgeois liberalism must be purged of Populism'.

Freedom from any admixture of Populism and 'agrarianism', an orientation based not on the semi-peasant countryside but on the 'bourgeois' non-proletarian classes of the city, a rejection of political competition with the Social-Democracy among the workers, and later an openly bourgeois character in ideology and politics that did not hide itself behind a Socialist mask – such were the criteria of 'progressive' liberalism for the Lenin of those years. Nothing could be more indicative in this respect than the assessment he gave in 1896–7, in a pamphlet,[116] of the Party of the People's Right (see above), which incidentally was leading a rather shadowy existence at this time.

Lenin considered the virtue of the People's Right to be that 'it was ashamed of the primitiveness of Populist doctrines and openly entered into a polemic against . . . the most repellent reactionaries of Populism'. All that was needed was 'for the followers of the People's Right to abandon their false shame, which hindered a *rapprochement* with the bourgeois strata of the people, that is, for them not only to talk about the programme of the non-Socialist politicians but to act in accordance with this programme, stimulating and developing the class-consciousness of those social groups and classes that do not find Socialism in the least necessary, but that are feeling more and more the oppression of absolutism and the indispensability of political freedom'. If the adherents of People's Right were guilty of anything it was just this – that they had not yet definitely freed themselves of this 'false shame': they had 'expressed a desire to free the tasks of the democracy from their connexion with the obsolete forms of "Russian Socialism", but they have far from liberated themselves from the old prejudices, and were far from consistent when they named their own party a 'Social-(??!)revolutionary' party . . . and stated in their 'Manifesto' that 'the People's Right accept the idea of the organization of national production' . . . thus surreptitiously introducing the same prejudices of the Populists. . . . But if in this party there are not masquerading [Lavrov's expression – T.D.] but genuine non-Socialist politicians, non-Socialist democrats – then this party can do more than a little good by trying to make a *rapprochement* with the politically oppositionist elements of our bourgeoisie and by arousing the class-consciousness of the class of our petty-bourgeoisie, petty merchants, petty artisans, etc.'

This recommendation to the People's Right – to mobilize the petty bourgeoisie as a counterweight to industrial and finance capital – is in obvious contradiction with the statement made a little earlier in the pamphlet, that the 'Social-Democrats support the progressive social classes against the reactionary social classes, the bourgeoisie against the representatives of the privileged, hereditary land-owners, and against officialdom, and the big bourgeoisie against the reactionary longings of the petty-bourgeoisie.'

This was the same contradiction that, as we have seen above, prompted Lenin to praise the Populists in one article[147] as representing the interests of the 'Russian small producer, the petty-bourgeois', as a counterweight to Struve and other apologists of the big bourgeoisie, and in another article[150] to give his preference to the 'bourgeois ideology' of Skaldin as against the 'petty-bourgeois' ideology of the Populists.

What was even more contradictory, of course, was his readiness to recognize the People's Right as consistent and thus useful democrats only in so far as they freed themselves from their 'false shame' and became open 'non-Socialist democrats'. This was in even greater contradiction to the proposition, formulated once again in the same pamphlet and already cited above, that 'all true and consistent democrats in Russia must become Social-Democrats'.

These theoretical contradictions, which reflected the contradictions of objective reality and gave rise to that 'unclarity' so clearly expressed in the debates and resolutions of the party Congress on the question of the 'support' to be given the non-proletarian opposition, were characteristic, as we have seen, not only of Lenin but of the entire Russian Social-Democracy. But what characterized Lenin's own attitude towards the problem of 'support' in those years was just this decisive rejection of 'agrarianism' and an equally decisive orientation based on the non-proletarian elements of the city and not the country-side. His virulent polemic against Struve's foreword to Witte's Note was largely called forth by the Zemstvo leaning Struve's liberalism had shown in it. But we have already seen how readily Lenin moved on towards a *rapprochement* with Struve, Tugan-Baranovsky and other 'legal Marxists' when he saw in them the representatives of a purely 'bourgeois' liberalism. Indeed, he even hailed the very appearance of *Osvobozhdenie* as an organ of the non-Socialist opposition in these words: 'We have had and still have so much diffuse, liberal-Populist, quasi-Socialism that in comparison with it a new liberal trend is a clear step forward.'[151]

As the peasant movement grew stronger and the Zemstvo opposition grew more radical politically, Lenin's wariness with respect to every form of 'agrarianism' and one-sided 'urban' orientation grew fundamentally weaker. He was now prepared on occasion to 'stretch out his hand' even 'to Messrs the Marshals of the Nobility'. As we have seen, he even accepted the conception of the 'hegemony' of the proletariat in the 'all-national' struggle against Tsarism by which Akselrod had tried to solve the contradictions of the bourgeois revolution. But from the very beginning – and more and more definitely afterwards – Lenin introduced into the concept of 'hegemony' the organizational-cum-technical approach that was typical of his political methodology. It was this, as we have seen, that brought him to the idea of overcoming 'opportunism' in the Social-Democracy through a dictatorship of the *Iskra* group within the Party, and of the 'trade unionist' trends of the working-class mass movement through a dictatorship of the Party over this movement, and that had long since also set its stamp on his conception not so much of the 'support' of the liberal opposition as its 'utilization'.

For Lenin the feebleness, inconsistency, and political worthlessness of this opposition with respect to the autocracy were not so much an inevitable consequence of the socio-economic and other conditions in which classes were set that had only just begun to be able to be a social foundation of this opposition in Russia as in the West, as they were the result of the personal, moral and organizational vices of its political exponents ('cowardice, isolation, fragmentedness', etc.) These vices also gave the Social-Democracy grounds for counting on the possibility of forcing them 'to bring up the rear, sometimes grinding their teeth'. And this same approach was prominently expressed in the explanation of why an openly bourgeois liberal was preferable to a Populist, from a Marxist point of view, that was given by Lenin – again in 'Aesopian' language – in an already quoted article:[150] 'The enlightener [i.e. the bourgeois liberal – T.D.] believes in the given social development [i.e. the capitalist development of Russia with all its political consequences – T.D.] since he fails to notice the contradictions peculiar to it. The Populist is afraid of the given social development since he has already noticed these contradictions.' It was clear why a Marxist 'who believes in given social development because he sees a warrant for a better future only in the complete development of these contradictions', has greater chances of politically 'utilizing' the bourgeois liberal who 'fails to notice' these social contradictions than a Populist representative of the petty-bourgeoisie who is frightened by these contradictions.

For Akselrod, who fathered the idea of 'hegemony', the objective of this 'hegemony', as we have seen, was the equivalent of the 'objective of the Social-Democracy winning over adherents and direct or indirect allies among the non-proletarian classes.' But this objective was to be attained 'primarily and above all by the character of the agitational-propagandistic activity among the proletariat itself.' The attention of the working-class was to be focused on 'questions constituting nodal points in which there converged and intertwined the interests of the proletariat as well as of other classes oppressed by absolutism and the capitalist bourgeoisie sponsored by it.'[152] The Social-Democratic proletariat had to win the sympathy of the non-proletarian opposition in order to make it its ally and thus become the 'hegemon' in the all-national struggle against Tsarism. Such was the view of Akselrod and the majority of the *Iskra* editors.

While accepting in their entirety Akselrod's formulae, which had become the programmatic formulae of *Iskra*, Lenin from the very beginning gave them a basically distinct content of his own, whose meaning did not become clear until considerably later, not only to the majority of the editorial board of *Iskra* but to himself. The very idea of 'hegemony' was interpreted by him not so much as the task of winning over 'allies' in the non-proletarian classes as the task of 'utilizing' these classes by the Social-Democracy. In Lenin's mind, accordingly, the means for solving these problems were also basically different. He supplemented (in *What Is to be Done?*) Akselrod's formula about activity 'among the proletariat itself' by a formula about the obligation of the Social-Democracy 'to go into all classes of the population'. To be sure, he justified the necessity of this 'going into all classes' by saying that a 'political class consciousness' that could be introduced into the working-class movement 'only from without' could be found only in the 'domain of the attitude of all classes and strata towards the government, the domain of the interrelationships between all classes'.

With this justification, the new formula proved acceptable to everyone. An atmosphere of combat solidarity united the *Iskra* editors in a passionate struggle against Economism and for the 'politicalization' of the party, and those articles of Lenin in which he more and more definitely interpreted this 'going into all classes' not as a method of 'bringing' political class-consciousness to the working-class movement but as a formula for 'accommodating' the liberal opposition with the organization of an 'illegal apparatus' that was indispensable for it under an autocracy seemed merely like an overshooting of the mark. With its 'cowardice and fragmentariness' the liberal opposition was incapable of constructing this itself, but, without 'noticing' this it would pay for it through submission to the political leadership of the Social-Democracy.

In this version, to be sure, 'hegemony' presupposed the presence of a liberalism that did not merely 'fail to notice' the social contradictions of capitalism, but openly proclaimed its own 'bourgeois-ness' and consciously restricted its own tasks to 'exclusively political transformations'. But as we have seen, in Akselrod's and Potresov's interpretation too the idea of hegemony led in the final analysis to a quest for some such liberalism that had renounced in advance those 'demands that clashed with the interests of the working-class and the democracy in general, or obfuscated their consciousness', and that obligated itself 'to come out decisively on the side of the Social-Democracy'. A liberalism, that is, that had never and nowhere existed in Russia, nor could have existed. It was just because of this that the idea of 'hegemony' was destroyed only just before the Social-Democracy – not theoretically but practically – was confronted by the problem of concrete 'support' for a concrete 'non-proletarian opposition' in autocratic Russia.

The idea of hegemony was destroyed in both its interpretations – Menshevik and Bolshevik. It was never realized either by way of the winning of the sympathy of the non-proletarian classes through Social-Democratic agitational and propagandistic activity 'among the working-class itself', nor by way of drawing the non-proletarian opposition into the channel of Social-Democratic politics through 'accommodating' its 'illegal' needs. But the entire preceding history of the development and bifurcation of *Iskra* thought makes it understandable why, in tacitly recognizing this destruction, Menshevism refrained from any claims to the 'leadership' of bourgeois policy and reverted to the task that had already been put forward by the

Emancipation of Labour Group – the maximal 'influence' over that policy by the Socialist proletariat. Bolshevism, in the person of Lenin, went back in its turn to its own initial idea – to impose on the bourgeoisie *by force* that 'leadership' of the Social-Democracy it had refused to accept voluntarily, and *to force it* to 'bring up the rear' behind the Social-Democracy, even though 'grinding its teeth'.

The war and its fiascos, which from the Bolshevik point of view presaged the imminence of an 'all-national uprising', (when the 'military collapse' took place) accelerated this evolution. The leading article of the first number of the Bolshevik organ *Vperyod*,[152] while not rejecting the task of 'sending detachments of our forces among all classes of the population', at the same time insisted that 'the nearer the decisive struggle the more the focus of our activity must be shifted to the preparation of the proletarians and semi-proletarians themselves for a direct struggle for freedom'. We have seen how while insisting on the victory of proletarian 'discipline' over the 'sloppiness' and 'individualism' of the intelligentsia, Lenin turned against the Mensheviks such a 'Menshevik' slogan as the 'disengagement' of the Party from the political command of the revolutionary intelligentsia and its conversion into the political organization of the working-class itself. Nothing could be more characteristic of the contradictory development in the political thinking of both fractions of the Russian Social-Democracy than the opportunity given the Bolsheviks to turn polemically against the Mensheviks, especially against Akselrod, the 'Akselrodian' appeal to shift the 'focus' of the Party's attention to activity not 'among all classes' but 'among the proletariat itself'. This opportunity was given by the so-called 'Zemstvo campaign' worked out by the *Iskra* editors.

This plan, which made an attempt to give some practical application to the ideas developed by Akselrod in the above-mentioned articles on the *Unification of the Russian Social-Democracy*,[129] was proposed by the *Iskra* editors in a letter they sent the Party organizations in November 1904, in connexion with the constantly broadening activity of liberal, especially Zemstvo circles that we have spoken of. Starting from the conviction that 'Russia had never before been so close to a constitution', the letter proposed to exploit the constantly growing numbers of legal and semi-legal assemblies and congresses of these groups in order to organize the 'active intervention in the social and political life' of the workers' vanguard under the leadership of the Social-Democracy referred to in Akselrod's articles. This 'intervention' was supposed to be realized through carefully prepared actions of the workers' delegation. This is how the letter spoke of their tasks:

> In the person of the liberal Zemstvos and Dumas we have to deal with enemies of our enemy, who are not, however, willing or able to go as far in the struggle against him as is required by the interests of the proletariat. But in coming out officially against absolutism and confronting it with demands aimed at its annihilation, by that alone they show themselves to be our allies (in of course a very relative sense), even though they are not resolute enough in their actions or democratic enough in their aims. The facts and manifestations of this irresoluteness and half-heartedness produce concrete material for a graphic description of the social realities and the socio-political tendencies of the bourgeois fractions, and as an illustration of the hostile counterposition of the interests of the classes they represent, on the one hand, and of proletarian interests on the other. And we, of course, are obliged to exploit this material to the utmost, in accordance with the principled requirements of our programme. But within the limits of the struggle against absolutism, and particularly in its present phase, our attitude towards the liberal bourgeoisie is defined by the task of imbuing it with more courage and impelling it to join in those demands being put forward by the proletariat led by the Social-Democracy. But we should be falling into a fateful blunder if we set as our goal the forcing at this very moment of the Zemstvos or other organs of the bourgeois opposition, by means of energetic measures of intimidation, to make a formal promise, under the influence of panic, to present our demands to the government. Such a tactic would compromise the Social-Democracy, since it would transform our entire political campaign into a lever for the reaction.

The duality and the contradictoriness of the tasks – practical and political, on the one hand, and class and pedagogical, on the other – set by the 'Zemstvo campaign' are reflected in this letter just as unmistakably as they were in Akselrod's articles. The old idea of 'hegemony' essentially took as its premise the proposition of a 'qualitative' identity between the political line of the bourgeois opposition, 'in the present phase' of the struggle against the autocracy, and the proletarian line ('the annihilation of absolutism'). There was only a 'quantitative' difference between them ('not enough', 'half-heartedness'); hence there was a possibility of 'imbuing it with more courage', after winning its sympathy, and impelling it to 'join in' the political demands of the 'proletariat led by the Social-Democracy'. This old idea contended with the idea of exploiting the 'Zemstvo campaign' for the inculcation in the minds of the workers of the idea of the 'hostile counterposition' of the interests of the bourgeoisie and the interests of the proletariat. But just as in these articles, this contest was decided 'in the present phase' by the reduction of the practical and political tasks of the 'campaign' to the attempt to 'influence' the policy of the bourgeoisie, on the basis of a tacit acceptance of its claims to revolutionary authority, and by the emphasis laid on class and pedagogical tasks objectives:

> Not only the labouring masses but the members of our Party as well have not as yet gone through a school of political struggle such as would have prepared them for the kind of political campaign now being demanded of us by the present occasion. . . . We must not forget that we are only taking the first step on the new path, that we are, so to speak, exercising the proletariat and our Party itself with the aim of preparing them both for the forthcoming engagements with the parties of the exploiting classes and of the state power.

And it was just because the political demonstrations of the workers' vanguard in the 'Zemstvo campaign' were aimed at this enrichment of its class consciousness via these engagements, not of today but of tomorrow, that *Iskra* declared them to be 'demonstrations of the highest type' – in comparison with those mass demonstrations in which tens and hundreds of thousands of workers took part and whose revolutionary significance it did not, of course, either deny or belittle, but whose political content never passed beyond the confines of a 'general democratic antagonism between the proletariat and the Tsarist autocracy', and hence was exhausted by the 'all-national' slogan, undifferentiated in terms of class, of 'Down with the autocracy!'

Lenin answered this in a special pamphlet devoted to a critique of the *Iskra* plan:

> We, the party of the proletariat must, of course, 'go among all classes of the population', openly and energetically championing our programme and our most immediate demands before the entire nation; we must strive to state these demands to Messrs the Zemstvo gentry too, but for us the central focus and the guiding thread must be its effect not on the Zemstvo people but on the government. . . . It would be unreasonable to disregard this ally [described in the pamphlet as beforehand in terms identical with those used in the *Iskra* letter, i.e., 'known in advance . . . to be conditional, problematical, unreliable and half-hearted' – T.D.] it would be absurd to set oneself the goal of intimidating and frightening it. . . . But the central focus and the guiding thread of our agitation must be, I repeat, not its effect on this ally, but the preparation of a decisive set-to with the enemy.' In other words: the emphasis of the Social-

Democracy had to be just on this 'all-national' slogan of 'Down with the autocracy!'

This relatively guarded and gentle critique of the 'Zemstvo campaign' took a sharper turn to the extent that against a background of more and more serious military defeats the Bolsheviks grew more and more convinced of the imminence of an all-national uprising, which they were going to synchronize precisely with the 'military collapse'. It was this that led to the 'defeatist' position of the Bolsheviks with respect to the war, in contrast with the Mensheviks, whose position was expressed in the formula of 'peace and freedom', and whose slogan was the convocation of the All-National Constituent Assembly with the dual task of making peace and working out a constitution. It was this that led to the constantly increasing concentration of the tactical thinking of Bolshevism on the tasks of preparing an insurrection and securing for the Social-Democracy, as the party of the working-class, a leading role in that insurrection. And it was, finally, this that led to the increasingly virulent and irreconcilable attitude towards Menshevik plans as diverting the thought of the Party from these primary tasks.

'The proletariat must support the bourgeois constitutional movement', said the afore-mentioned leading article in the first number of *Vperyod.* 'It must stir up and rally to itself the broadest possible strata of the exploited masses, gather together all its forces and raise an insurrection when the desperation of the government is greatest and when the excitement of the people is greatest.' The leading article ends up: 'We must prepare ourselves with all our energy for this event [the "military collapse"]. When that happens the proletariat will rise to the leadership of the insurrection in order to conquer freedom for the whole nation, and to secure for the working-class the possibility of an open struggle for Socialism enriched by the entire experience of Europe.'

This perspective of the leadership of an 'all-national armed uprising' was to become overriding and all-determining in the tactics of Bolshevism, while at the same time its antagonism to Menshevism was also to achieve its apogee after the 'Bloody Sunday' of 9 January 1905, which both fractions of the Social-Democracy interpreted as the 'beginning of the revolution'.

At the end of December 1904 a movement of an economic character began at the Putilov factory in Petersburg; on 3 January 1905 it brimmed over into a strike. No one could have expected that this strike, which at first set itself such a modest goal as the reinstatement of four workers dismissed by the factory management, would in the course of a week or so seize hold of the entire capital, be transformed into a gigantic political movement of the Petersburg proletariat, and give the last push to the precipitation of the Russian revolutionary avalanche that some nine months later would force the autocracy to capitulate, via the 'constitutional' manifesto of 17 October. Still less could anyone have expected that it would be the 'Assembly of Russian Factory and Workshop Workers', legalized by the authorities, which had sections throughout the industrial districts of the capital but whose activity was limited to the organization of mutual aid and tasks of a cultural-educational, and religious-ethical character, that would cast the spark into the powder-keg the revolutionary movement had set beneath the foundation of the autocracy, and that it would cast it by the hands of the Orthodox priest, George Gapon. Least of all, of course, could such a turn of events have been expected by the Police Department which – full of 'Zubatovite' calculations on deflecting the workers away from 'politics' – had subsidized and was co-operating with the organization of the Assembly and whose organizer and leader, Gapon, had been in close contact with it. But in the atmosphere of revolutionary excitement of those days the events had overturned all the Zubatovite plans even more rapidly and thoroughly than had been the case with the 'Zubatovite' organizations in Odessa in 1903.*

Without discrediting themselves and the very idea of the favourable disposition of the Tsarist government to the workers' economic needs, the organizers of the Assembly could not prevent it from coming to the defence of its four members, by whose dismissal the factory management had emphasized among other things the general hostile attitude of the entrepreneurs towards the demagogic tendencies of 'Zubatovism'. They were unable to counteract either its turning for support to the workers of other districts as well, or the transformation of the district sections of the Assembly into places for mass meetings and passionate discussions. These very quickly passed from the individual incident at the Putilov factory to the theme of the extremely oppressive material situation and the complete absence of rights of the Russian worker in general.

The movement developed with dizzying rapidity, drawing into its orbit the most backward strata of the labouring masses and not giving

* See Note p. 222.

the 'leaders' any time to think things over. Under these conditions the idea occurred to the leaders of the Assembly, especially Gapon, to have the workers turn for their defence to the Tsar himself. At first this idea met with no opposition in the Police Department either, which in its turn was somewhat flabbergasted by the unexpectedness of the role that had fallen to the lot of the 'reliable' organization it itself had been pampering. It also seemed to the higher government circles that a few benevolent words from the heights of the throne, accompanied, perhaps, by some insignificant measures for the benefit of the workers, would be enough not only to turn back into its channel the workers' elemental outburst that was overflowing its banks, but also to reinforce the tottering faith in the legend of the Tsar as the 'workers' defender'. Thus the idea was born of a 'petition', and a solemn procession to the Winter Palace with ikons and sacred images, portraits of the Tsar and the chanting of prayers and hymns, to entrust it to the Tsar on bended knees.

This procession, in which between 150–200,000 workers took part, actually took place on Sunday, 9 January. But in blatant contrast with its archaic forms, calculated on the basis of the religious-monarchical sentimentality of the most backward strata of the populace, there emerged political demands that were included in the petition under the influence of the Social-Democrats – beginning with the eight-hour working day, freedom of assembly for the workers and land for the peasants, and ending with freedom of speech and press, separation of church and state, the stopping of the war and the convocation of a Constituent Assembly.

The Social-Democratic organization of Petersburg, which at that time had broken up into a Bolshevik 'Committee' and a Menshevik 'Group', was also caught unawares by the events. For it too the role played in these events by the Gapon Assembly was completely unexpected. But the moment it began to be clear that it was becoming the organizing centre of a workers' mass movement, the Social-Democrats energetically intervened in the course of the movement. They sent speakers to the district meetings of the Assembly, introduced emendations and additions into the original text of the petition, and so on. The description given above of the development in the thinking of the fractions makes it understandable why it happened to be the Menshevik Group* that displayed the maximum of initiative and zeal

* Among others M. Berdichevskaya and K. Arkhangelsky were killed in the street clashes with the police and troops.

on this occasion.[154] Heedful of the composition of their audience, the Social-Democrats carried on this agitational work with extreme wariness, avoiding any open actions in the name of the Party. But, supported by the advanced workers, their emendations and additions were finally accepted by the rank-and-file as well, step by step forcing the leaders of the Assembly too, who originally had behaved towards the Social-Democrats' actions with extreme hostility, to retreat and seek compromises with them.

The procession of workers moving from the various districts of the capital towards the Winter Palace were, as is well known, stopped by salvoes from the troops. That day cost the demonstrators more than a thousand killed and as many as two thousand wounded. 'We no longer have a Tsar,' Gapon said that same night in an address to the workers; he simultaneously called on the soldiers to consider themselves freed of their oath 'to the traitor, the Tsar, who had ordered innocent blood to be spilt.' It was in these words that the authentic political lesson of this 'Bloody Sunday' rang forth.*During the strikes at the end of the '90s and beginning of the 1900s the vanguard of the working-class began liberating itself from monarchistic sentimentality. The shots on 9 January had killed 'faith in the Tsar' even in the most backward strata of the proletariat. Moreover, they had dealt an irremediable blow to this faith both in the non-proletarian urban populace and in the peasantry, and had shaken it profoundly in the rank-and-file soldiery too, and thus also in the mainstay of discipline, the Tsarist army and fleet. These political consequences of 9 January made themselves equally felt in the strikes that swept Russia at the beginning of 1905, called forth chiefly by economic factors, and even more in the wave of gigantic demonstrative strikes (Georgia, Baku, Odessa, Ivanovo-Voznesensk, Lodz, Nizhni-Novgorod, Sormovo, etc.) and military demonstrations that filled the spring, summer, and autumn of 1905, and whose 'Sunday punch', indeed, was actually the all-Russian strike of the railway workers in October, which dealt the autocracy a final blow.

* Gapon was saved from death on 9 January by an S.R., P. M. Rutenberg, a young engineer from the Putilov factory (later a well-known Zionist) who had become friendly with him during the course of events and helped him escape abroad. There Gapon joined the S.R. Party but soon left it, and at the end of 1905 returned to Petersburg. Here he tried to establish connexions among the workers through the former members of the Assembly, but he got tangled up in the police network and when he was unmasked as an agent of the Police Department Rutenberg killed him.

As indicated before, both fractions of the Social-Democracy regarded 9 January as the 'beginning of the revolution'. In their first reaction to the January events they uniformly interpreted them as the harbinger of an imminent 'all-Russian armed uprising'; the Menshevik *Iskra* printed articles illustrated by diagrams concerning the 'tactics of street fighting', just as did the Bolshevik *Vperyod.* Nevertheless, their approach to the question of the role of the Social-Democracy in the preparation and conduct of an 'all-national uprising' from the very beginning was dissimilar and soon became, it may be said, diametrically opposed.

As early as March 1904, in a polemic against the Bolshevik *Vperyod*, Martov had written in a leading article[155] that the

> Social-Democracy can 'prepare the uprising' in only one sense – by preparing its own forces for an eventual uprising of the masses. The technical side of this preparation, however important it is, must definitely be subordinated to the political side of the matter. And the political preparation of our Party and of the whole conscious proletariat for this entirely feasible uprising must, once again, be included in the deepening and broadening of the agitation, in the consolidation and development of the organization of all revolutionary elements of the proletariat.

This primacy of political over technical problems in the question of the uprising too is extremely accurately reflected in another leading article of Martov's,[156] which was *Iskra*'s first reaction to 'Bloody Sunday'. It goes without saying that the leading article formulated and decided the political problems too, in the perspective of the self-limitation of the struggle for the maximal political 'influence' of the Social-Democracy. It was in this, as has been noted more than once, that Menshevism at this time was seeking a way out of the insoluble contradictions of Social-Democratic activity in the objective conditions of Russian life; it also lent the old word 'hegemony' a completely new sense in the political lexicon of Menshevism.

> The ninth of January has shown everyone,' said Martov's article, 'that not only is the revolutionary attitude of the people not an invention of Social-Democracy, but that a people's uprising is also no mere delusion of it.... We, the party of the class-conscious proletariat, shall accomplish the revolutionary mobilization of the masses by means of the rallying and organization of the proletariat into an independent proletarian party.... When the voice of this collective agitator – the workers' party – begins to be heard in all corners of Russia; when its political slogans are

accepted by all Russia-in-arms, as they were accepted on 9 January by working-class Petersburg; when the links of a Social-Democratic, proletarian organization, strengthened by hourly exercise in manœuvres, skirmishes and serious battles, begin to encompass all the fighting revolutionary elements in the core of the people – at that time the Russian Social-Democracy will be assured of the political leadership of the all-national uprising against Tsarism that is inevitable and is rapidly approaching realization.

We are told that in going into this work we are leaving to one side the 'most important' of the tasks of the moment – work on the arming of the proletariat, on the systematic preparation of the organization that would secure us the military-technical leadership of the masses at the moment of the decisive struggle. Our reply to this is: as the most organized and conscious political force we cannot, of course, disregard technical tasks either. Like all revolutionaries, we must concern ourselves with the arming of the masses moving towards the uprising, but we must not forget that underground organizations can do very little in this respect. None of their efforts will have much meaning if they are incapable of arming the people with the one irreplaceable weapon – the burning necessity of attacking the autocracy and of arming itself for that. That is where we must direct our energies – towards a propaganda among the masses of self-arming for the aims of the uprising. And such propaganda can be fruitful at all only in connexion with a tactic that will revolutionize the consciousness of the masses of the people in a many-sided way. Equally, we can hope to ensure the adaptation of our conspiratorial organization to the tasks of the technical leadership of the uprising only in so far . . . as we succeed in forging an organizational link welding together all the living forces of the Russian proletariat. And that in its turn is possible for the Social-Democracy only through an incessant and intelligent political agitation, only by methods that will develop proletarian independence, initiative and zeal.

The leading article then made this point:

It would be absurd and harmful to dream of a monopoly for the Russian Social-Democracy of an active role in the coming uprising. But what it can and must rightfully 'dream' of is the political hegemony of its own class. . . . And that role cannot be obtained for us by our succeeding in taking in our own hands the total technical organization and execution of the uprising. . . . We shall be only too glad if, in the wake of the priest who popularized among the masses our demand for a rupture between the state and the church, in the wake of the monarchist workers' association that organized the people's march on the Winter Palace, the Russian revolution will enrich itself by a general who will be first in leading the masses of the people into a victorious battle against Tsarist troops, or a functionary who will be the first to proclaim the official overthrow of the Tsarist power.

Martov concludes: 'Hence our task at the given moment is not so much the "organization" of the people's revolution, as its "unloosing".'

This conclusion, which stressed the basic element of Menshevik tactics during the revolutionary months that preceded the victory in October, was formulated somewhat one-sidedly. As we shall see, this tactic of 'unloosing' the revolution was indissolubly combined with an effort to 'organize' it politically – primarily by the creation of constantly renewed forms of the class organization of the proletariat. Martov's formulation proved to be one-sided; it was polemically aimed at an article, *Results and Prospects*, printed in the same number with a note from the editors. The author of the article was Parvus (Helphand), who had been extremely critical of the 'Zemstvo campaign' before and now, like Trotsky too, had a basic divergence of views with *Iskra* on the political conclusions to be drawn from the situation created by 9 January. Trotsky wrote that after 9 January the working-class movement 'slipped into an uprising'. Hence the Constituent Assembly in and for itself could no longer be the fundamental and generalizing slogan of the Party. After 9 January it was necessary to prepare for an armed uprising and the replacement of the Tsarist government by a revolutionary Provisional Government that alone could convoke a Constituent Assembly. Hence the Party slogan had to become 'Long Live the Provisional Government!', and the Social-Democracy could and must orient itself towards a participation in that government. Parvus, from the very beginning, went further: he put forward the slogan of a 'Social-Democratic Provisional Government', and headed one of his proclamations, published by *Iskra*: 'No Tsar, but a workers' government!'

But with all their political divergence from Menshevism and their aiming at an 'armed uprising', Parvus, and Trotsky still more definitely, nevertheless understood the 'organization' of the uprising and of the revolution not so much in a military-technical as in a political sense, in terms of masses and classes. This was the common ground that made collaboration with both of them possible for the Mensheviks during the October days of 1905, and with Trotsky even much later (the so-called 'August *bloc*' of 1912). Hence the leading article in the next number of *Iskra* (written by the author of these lines) expressed the thought common to all its writers, including Parvus and Trotsky, when it said, in rebuttal of Lenin's attacks:

A movement of hundreds of thousands of people, even though indirectly led, not by ourselves, but bearing our political slogans, is incomparably more valuable than the secret operations of the most orthodox 'subtle' groups of conspirators. Because we believe in the revolutionary mood of the labouring masses and believe that the logic of the political situation will in the final analysis push these masses into our Party organization too. And, on the contrary, we do not believe in the dubiously orthodox alchemy of a 'staff of trained and prepared leaders', which, by leaning solely on the blind 'faith' of the masses will conduct them into the kingdom of national liberty.[157]

Lenin's reply to Martov was: 'The separation of the 'technical' side of the revolution from the political side of the revolution is the greatest twaddle.'[158] The politics of the uprising is determined by whoever has the technical control – such was in essence the conclusion drawn by Bolshevism from 9 January, in diametrical opposition to the conclusion drawn by Menshevism. It was completely in the spirit of the general political methodology of Bolshevism that *Vperyod* declared the 'chief instrument' of such a leadership to be the 'staff of trained and prepared leaders in every industrial centre', insisting that 'all committees must now, without of course neglecting for a moment their customary task of rallying the class-conscious proletariat through their Social-Democratic propaganda and agitation, carefully think through the question of the instruments of direct proletarian struggle'.[159]

However, the fall of Port Arthur had so obviously brought nearer the moment of the 'military collapse' that the 'armed uprising' was being synchronized with at this time, while 9 January, it seemed, had made just this form of resolution of the revolutionary crisis so inevitable and so incontestable, that the military-technical tasks of the moment, in the political framework of Bolshevism, began taking priority over the 'customary task' of the Social-Democracy to just the same degree that in the minds of the Mensheviks, on the contrary, such military-technical tasks had been completely shelved in favour of their own political tasks. It was just this Bolshevik position that Lenin formulated when he wrote, in the same leading article that had been his first reaction to 'Bloody Sunday':

The immediate arming of the workers and of all citizens in general, the preparation and organization of the revolutionary forces for the annihilation of governmental authorities and institutions – such is the practical basis on which all revolutionists can and must unite for a general blow.

The proletariat must always go its own independent way, without weakening its links with the Socialist party and remembering its great ultimate aims of the freeing of all mankind from all exploitation. But this independence of the Social-Democratic proletarian party will never force us to forget the importance of a general revolutionary onslaught on the occasion of a real revolution. We Social-Democrats can and must go forward independently of the revolutionaries of bourgeois democracy while preserving the class independence of the proletariat, but we must go forward hand-in-hand during the uprising, in dealing direct blows to Tsarism, in resisting the troops, in attacking the Bastille of the accursed enemy of the whole Russian people.[160]

A favourable terrain for such propaganda was created by the broad-gauge movement of 'self-defence' of the workers, which was a response to the anti-Socialist, anti-Semitic and anti-intelligentsia pogroms that were becoming a more and more important factor in the arsenal of the government's 'struggle against the revolution', and by the activity among the troops that was stimulated by the disorders and mutinies in the army and fleet. In this effort of self-defence and propaganda among the troops the Mensheviks were also active. The political leaders of the Potyomkin mutiny, for instance, were two members of the Odessa Menshevik group, Kirill and K. Feldman, just as the author of the uprising in New Alexandria also joined the Mensheviks – Second Lieutenant Antonov-Ovseyenko, who went over to the Bolsheviks only just before the 1917 revolution. Nevertheless, in work of this kind the Mensheviks invested far fewer forces and ascribed to it far less significance than the Bolsheviks. In complete contrast with the Bolsheviks they had a very watchful attitude from the very beginning towards those 'combat companies' that a great many organizations of self-defence turned into, and that during the years immediately following the 1905 revolution began to concentrate their activities not so much on tasks of workers' defence as on so-called 'expropriations' and similar enterprises of a 'guerrilla' character.

As against this, it was just on this terrain of the organization of armed self-defence that there took place a *rapprochement* of Bolshevism with the 'national' Social-Democratic organizations of Western Russia (the Bund, the Baltic countries, Poland) for whom questions of self-defence assumed special significance at this time. Because of this they accepted certain elements of Bolshevik tactics even when they did not share, or not fully, the fundamental revision to which Bolshevism was obliged to subject its previous political orientation –

in so far as the military-technical preparation of an armed uprising from now on became for it the 'practical foundation' of the interrelationships of the Social-Democracy with other participants of the 'movement of emancipation'.

It was primarily the old question of 'allies' that had to be radically revised once again. The 'cowardice and fragmentedness' of the liberals, who were incapable of constructing by their own efforts an illegal apparatus that was useful even to themselves, evidently made them the least fitting allies in the cause of 'the annihilation of governmental authorities and institutions', 'resistance to the troops' and an 'attack on the Bastille', and still less suitable candidates for the staff of 'trained and prepared leaders' of an armed uprising. On the contrary, in this connexion it was the S.R. terrorists who could not have seemed more suitable. It was from this point of view, indeed, that there took place a new and this time a fundamentally definitive turn of Lenin with respect to 'bourgeois' liberalism, on the one hand, and 'Populist' democracy, in the form in which it had been resurrected in the S.R. Party, on the other. This turn, which, as we shall see, had a more profound, and it might be said a decisive, significance for the whole subsequent political orientation of Bolshevism, was established in a special leaflet of the official Bolshevik centre, the 'Bureau of the Committees of the Majority', entitled *The Attitude of the R.S.D.W.P. towards the Liberals*.[161]

The leaflet distinguished two constituent elements in the 'bourgeois-liberal opposition' – the 'Zemstvo constitutionalists', who represented the 'group of enlightened landowners and capitalists', and the 'Union of Emancipation', or the 'Democrats', whose support 'for the most part consisted of the intellectual bourgeoisie (professors, writers, lawyers, engineers, etc.)'. But with neither one part or another of this 'opposition' could the Social-Democracy find common ground: 'For us an alliance either with the "Zemstvo constitutionalists" or with the "Democrats" is impossible; formal agreements are useless – they would be broken in their own good time anyhow. We must fight against introducing the confusion of liberal ideas among the workers.' The programme, to be sure, said that the 'Social-Democracy will support every kind of oppositionist movement'. And the Bureau of the Committees of the Majority would not go back on this programmatic demand. But it would give it its own kind of, one might say, caricatural character in substituting for the support of the 'oppositionist movement' the 'support' of individual liberals who were being pursued by the government or who needed some 'illegal' accommodation: 'The Social-Democracy will support both the Zemstvo liberals and the "Democrats", but with no obligations. The Social-Democracy will protest against any violence *vis-à-vis* the bourgeois liberal if it takes place; it will shelter the fleeing liberal "Democrat" ... but there will be no formal connexion.'* But the most important thing was that our so-called bourgeois democrats were also 'in essence not democrats'. 'The bourgeois intelligentsia has appropriated only the name "democrats", and it was convenient for it to do that because we still have no real democratic party at all; the best of the real democrats are hiding in the S.R. Party, where they have become intermingled with the vaguer Socialist elements.'

The starting-point of this kind of rehabilitation of the S.R.s, who so recently were still being called 'harmful' both for democracy and for Socialism, at the expense of the 'liberals', was the quest for suitable 'allies' for the Social-Democracy in the light of the perspective of an armed uprising with it playing the leading role in its military-technical preparation and execution. But in the conditions of the 'movement for emancipation', when not only party-ideological groups were beginning to move into the arena of the struggle but also the social layers these groups were supported by, or hoped to be, a re-assessment of the revolutionary significance of the groups could not help being linked to a re-assessment of the revolutionary potential of the social forces backing them. For the Bolsheviks this was a novel, and, as it seemed, this time a definitive shift of the political perspective from the non-proletarian sector of the cities to the countryside – a shift that presupposed a radical re-assessment of the significance and role of the peasantry.

For Populism the peasantry, as the special, specifically Russian socio-economic category, was the fundamental force of the Russian revolution. The differences, divergences, and splits in Populist ranks were prompted by questions of methods of struggle (insurrectionism and propagandism) and of the place to be taken in this struggle by

* Here, to be sure, the Bureau was in essence merely repeating an idea Lenin had had in 1901, when he wrote that if the liberals were 'unable to organize themselves in an illegal party', then, 'in that (more probable case) we would not "turn our backs" on the liberals, but would try to strengthen our ties with individuals, acquaint them with our movement, support them by unmasking among the workers all the various vilenesses of the government and the tricks of the local authorities, and draw them into supporting the revolutionaries'.[162]

objectives of a purely political character. But what was axiomatic for all its trends was the conviction (also reflected in the names of the Populist parties: 'Land and Freedom' and 'Total Re-apportionment'), that the fundamental lever, motor, and content of the coming Russian revolution would be an agrarian revolution of the peasantry, presupposing the annihilation of all types of large private landholding and the passage of all land into peasant hands.

This focus of the Populist system of formulations also became the central target of the attack launched against Populism by nascent Russian Marxism. This proclaimed the fundamental factor of the preparation of the Russian revolution to be the development of capitalism, which was to liquidate all survivals of serfdom, and at the same time also the specific socio-economic peculiarities of the Russian peasantry. The fundamental content of this revolution was the annihilation of the autocracy and its replacement by the political order of bourgeois democracy; the fundamental motor of the revolution was to be the working-class.

From this point of view the agrarian revolution of the peasantry not only ceased being the pre-condition of the Russian revolution, but, as we have seen from Plekhanov's utterances of the period, it became possible itself only under the influence of the industrial proletariat, and as a constituent element of the future social revolution that was to become its objective after the victory it had had in the 'bourgeois' revolution. But in this same bourgeois revolution there could be no place for an independent political role of the peasantry. Its proletarianized portion, the 'agrarian paupers', had to lean on the urban proletariat, its small-farmer mass on the urban bourgeoisie. In so far as a 'minimum programme' of the Social-Democracy could be spoken of, that is, a programme tailored to the bourgeois revolution, it would meet the small farmers' interest half-way through its general democratic demands. In the socio-economic domain its tasks with respect to the peasantry would be summed-up by the struggle for the annihilation of 'survivals' of serfdom that perpetuated the forms of bondage of peasant exploitation by landowners and by usurious capital and that hindered the free development of bourgeois-capitalist relations in the countryside. It was these ideas that underlay the agrarian programme adopted by the second Congress, which in economic matters limited itself to the demand for the return to the peasants of (1) the purchase payments they had made to the landowners for the plots of land left to the peasants; and (2) the 'strips', i.e. the appendages of landed property (forests, pastures, etc.) cut off at the emancipation of the serfs – again in favour of the landowners – from the lands that had been under peasant cultivation during serfdom.

The real author of this agrarian programme, and especially of the idea of the return of the 'strips' as its central demand, was Lenin. In Martov's words,[163] in the Moscow deportation prison as far back as the beginning of 1897 Lenin's closest friends were talking about the 'strips' as 'Ilyich's invention', during his Petersburg imprisonment. But nothing was said about the 'strips' in the draft programme written by Lenin during his imprisonment (1895–6). It is mentioned for the first time in the second draft of the programme he wrote in 1899. Demanding the 'annihilation of all remnants of the peasants' enserfment by the landowners', this draft paid special attention to those cases in which these 'remnants' would have arisen 'from the fact that the cutting-off of the peasants' land by the landowners would place the peasants in fact in the hopeless situation of the previous enserfed peasants'.

The idea of limiting the agrarian programme of the Social-Democracy to the demand for the 'restoration of the strips' flowed logically from the general theoretical approach of the Social-Democracy of that epoch to the peasant question. As Martov says, this happened to be 'a political demand in the realm of agrarian policy that, while satisfying the land hunger of the peasants and thus giving the Social-Democracy a chance to find some support in the peasant movements, at the same time, if it was realized, did not risk any slowing down of the course of economic development'. To be sure, as Martov admits:

> at times doubts arose within me whether it might not be more correct for the Party not to be confused by the temporary and partial retrogression of the productive forces that would be the result of realizing the 'total reapportionment' envisaged by the peasant programme, that is, the seizure of all the big estates, but to back such a reapportionment in the hope that a powerful jolt would be given by this reapportionment to the whole of the national economy and would rapidly smooth away the traces of this retrogression.

But the logical harmony of the scheme overcame these doubts; the 'invention' not only 'in the final analysis pleased' the Social-Democrats who were debating it in the Moscow prison, but later on was accepted by the entire editorial body of *Iskra*, and was included in the draft of the programme presented by them to the second Congress.*

This draft met objections of principle at the Congress, for the most part from the Economists and the *Rabocheye Delo* people, who attacked the 'paltriness of the demands' made by the agrarian programme at a time when in 'other parts of the programme we are demanding maximums' (Lieber). But the general position of *Iskra* was expressed by Lenin in replying to Lieber: 'Comrade Lieber has forgotten the distinction between the democratic and the Socialist part of our programme . . . He has failed to notice that the Socialist part of our programme is to be found in another place, namely, in the working-class section, which deals with agriculture, too. Only S.R.s, with their characteristic unscrupulousness, can confuse and do constantly confuse democratic and Socialist demands.'

Trotsky put the question in the same way: 'We are bringing the peasantry the general-democratic part of our programme: we are going towards the rural paupers with the propaganda of Socialism.' He came to the conclusion that in general the Social-Democracy did not need an 'agrarian programme adapted to a capitalist régime'. Finally, Plekhanov expressed himself in the same way: 'The demand for the restoration of the strips . . . has one peculiarity. It has the objective of modernizing our society. Indeed, our agrarian programme contains only such demands. When the question arises of the most modern bourgeois society, we hold the view of Kautsky, and we do not consider it necessary to work out a special agrarian programme.'

But what would be the relationship of the Social-Democracy to the peasant movement if it was going to jump out of the framework of the 'modernization' of society, the 'elimination' laid down by the Social-Democratic programme of the 'remnants of the serf-holding system' and the 'free development of the class struggle in the countryside'? Plekhanov responded as follows to this question of a possible 'total reapportionment':

* The traditions of the 'agrarian revolution' were so strong in the Russian revolutionary *milieu*, however, that it was just this part of the *Iskra* platform that was assimilated with the greatest difficulty by the local functionaries of the Party, especially after the peasant rioting that began at the beginning of the 1900s. The writer of these lines had the opportunity to convince himself of this during a tour of the local Party organizations which he made on behalf of *Iskra* in March 1902.

> We are told that in putting forward the demand for the restoration of the strips we ought to remember that the peasants will go beyond this demand. That does not frighten us in the least... A movement like that in favour of the reapportionment would be a movement in favour of the bourgeoisie. We are not, of course, obliged actively to put forward a programme for the bourgeoisie, but if in the struggle against the remnants of serf-holding relations the peasantry were to take this path, we would not hold back this progressive movement. Our role, in contrast with our S.R. opponents, who see in it the beginning of socialization, would consist only in our directing all our efforts to removing any illusions from the proletariat about the results of this movement, and to unmasking its bourgeois character.

However, this policy of 'friendly neutrality' *vis-à-vis* the agrarian revolution of the peasantry, accompanied by the propagandistic 'unmasking' of its bourgeois character, also called forth a sharp protest from some of the *Iskra*-ites: Makhov, a delegate from Nikolayev, answered Plekhanov as follows:

> This revolution, if it can be called that, will not be a revolution, but a reactionary movement. It would fling us backwards, and it would be another twenty years before we returned to the present position ... The distribution of the land and the restoration of the purchase and other payments would have the same influence as would the confiscation of the factories and workshops and their distribution among the proletariat, or, what would be even worse, among the whole people.

Makhov also returned to this question in the debates on the 'support for oppositionist and revolutionary movements', and formulated the proposition that the 'peasant wars at the time of the Reformation had a reactionary character, even though they were an oppositionist movement, just as are our peasant riots'. Makhov was seconded by Lyadov (Mandelshtamm), a future eminent Bolshevik and the first Bolshevik historian of the Russian Social-Democracy: 'The only revolutionary class is the proletariat; the peasant wars were not revolutionary.'

This estimate of the peasant wars and the peasant revolution sounded too paradoxical to be taken up by the other delegates. But it was hardly accidental that it met with no decisive resistance on the part of the theoretical and political leaders of the Congress either – the *Iskra* editors. For in essence it was merely a consequence, carried to its 'logical conclusion', of the premises that underlay the *Iskra* programme of 'restoration of the strips'. But if the agrarian revolution of the Russian peasantry was not a 'reactionary' but a 'progressive movement', as Plekhanov maintained, then it was incomprehensible why this revolution had not found a place for itself in the programme of the party that was leading the revolution – the Social-Democracy. It was also incomprehensible why the Party whose programme proclaimed its determination to 'support' *every* 'progressive movement' had to restrict itself, precisely in relationship to *this* peasant movement, by a promise 'not to hold it back'. Plekhanov indicated, to be sure, that the agrarian revolution of the peasantry would be a 'movement in favour of the bourgeoisie'. But this line of argument loses persuasiveness when it is recalled that the realization of the programme of the 'restoration of the strips' would also go 'in favour of the bourgeoisie', and, moreover, that the formulation of such a limited programme also happened to be motivated by the attempt to 'create freedom of bourgeois relations' in the countryside (Lenin).

This inner contradictoriness of a logically harmonious theoretical construction once again reflected the contradictoriness of the objective tasks confronting the Russian Social-Democracy. But it was just because of this that in this case too the schema began to lose its harmoniousness and was quickly overthrown by the collision with the realities of the peasant movement, which had almost subsided towards 1903 but began to revive once again in the revolutionary ferment that seized the entire country after 9 January 1905. This movement only too obviously justified the prediction of Lange, a delegate to the Congress from the Northern Union, that the agrarian programme proposed by *Iskra* 'would of course be propagated in [Party] circles, but in the sense of mass propaganda among the peasants its role would be negligible'. But what became only too obvious was also that out of all the possible decisions of the peasant question 'in favour of the bourgeoisie' the revolutionary seizure by the peasantry of estates happened to be the decision that aroused the maximum resistance, not only of the liberal Zemstvo aristocrats, but also of the liberal urban bourgeoisie, and, on the contrary, the maximum sympathy of the intermediate peasantry, the 'rural paupers', and the urban proletariat. Both fractions of the Social-Democracy had to draw the appropriate conclusions from this fact.

The conclusions drawn by Menshevism were formulated in a resolution passed in May 1905 by the Geneva Conference of Menshevik representatives.*

* 'The First All-Russian Conference of Party Workers. Special Supplement

The resolution primarily called for an 'exploitation of the circumstances in order to intensify agitation among agricultural workers, to organize a strike movement and to rally the workers into unions for a struggle for their professional interests'. Further, it insisted on the necessity of 'establishing as close an interrelationship as possible between the revolutionary movement in the cities and in the countryside'. The second half of the resolution reads: 'But aside from the struggle of wage labour against capital, an emancipatory movement of the peasantry as a class is also taking place in the contemporary countryside.' In relation to this class movement of the peasantry the first task of the Social-Democracy is to agitate 'on the basis of its agrarian programme', that is, the programme of the 'restoration of the strips'. However, the

> Social-Democracy supports, at the same time, all attempts of the peasants aimed at the violent seizure of the land, while explaining to the peasants that its conquests in the struggle against the landowners can be firmly secured only by a freely elected Constituent Assembly, which must be presented with a demand for the formation, on a democratic basis, of special committees for the definitive elimination of the old rural regulations that were so oppressive for the peasantry (the peasant committees).

As we can see, the resolution officially sanctioned the attitude towards the agrarian revolution of the peasantry that had been formulated by Plekhanov at the second Congress as the position of the Social-Democracy in case the peasants were to 'go beyond' the demand for the 'restoration of the strips'. The resolution, to be sure, recommended that this agrarian revolution be 'supported', while Plekhanov had merely spoken of 'not holding it back'. But essentially this was a mere terminological distinction. The Menshevik Social-Democracy as before was counterposing to the programme of the agrarian revolution of the peasantry its own programme – of the class

---

to *Iskra*, No. 100, Geneva, 1905.' At the same time there took place a conference of the other section of the Party too, called the 'Bureau of the Committees of the Majority', in agreement with the Central Committee, which once again had changed its position on the organizational question. In contrast to the Menshevik conference, this conference called itself the third consecutive Congress of the Party, elected a Central Committee, and charged Lenin to publish a new central organ of the Party, *Proletarii* (the Proletarian) instead of *Iskra*. The fraction organ of Bolshevism, *Vperyod*, was suspended with its eighteenth issue, and on 14 May the first number of *Proletarii* came out, to be suspended in its turn with its twenty-sixth issue, dated 12 November 1905.

organization of the rural proletariat in the name of the struggle for Socialism and of 'general democratic demands' on behalf of the small-farmer mass of the peasantry. And by promising to support 'attempts at a violent seizure of the land', in so far as such attempts would play a role, it was not even then promising to make 'seizure' its own programmatic demand. It was promising only to introduce into the agrarian-revolutionary movement of the peasantry the democratic idea of the Constituent Assembly and the liquidation of the 'rural regulations' that had outlived themselves – not by the revolutionary organs of the peasantry itself, but by 'special committees' elected on a 'democratic basis' and called 'peasant' not so much by virtue of their origin and composition as by virtue of the object of their activity having to be the 'peasant' cause. As is indicated by the very name of the resolution – 'On Our Work among the Peasants' – what was at issue was not a new relationship in principle towards the agrarian-revolutionary movement of the peasantry, but only the adaptation to this movement of the Party's propagandistic-agitational activities.

It can be shown that this was contradicted by the third part of the resolution (its fourth and final part speaks of the 'convocation of a special conference of rural agitators'), which rejects 'agrarian terror as an instrument of a systematic struggle', but calls for agitation for 'the arming of each person for self-defence against governmental violence . . . refusal to pay taxes . . . supplying of recruits . . . free election of officials, and – as a result – the revolutionary self-government of the countryside and the revolutionary unions of self-governing agricultural communes as an organization of the peasant uprising against Tsarism'.

But this part of the resolution and these appeals had no connexion with the specifically agrarian revolution of the peasantry. As we shall see, they merely expressed, with respect to the peasantry, Menshevik ideas about the forms of preparation and execution of 'an all-national uprising' that were organically bound up with the general conception, already described, of the interrelationship of social forces and tasks of the Socialist proletariat in the 'bourgeois' revolution. Around this time Menshevism had been working its way towards this general idea, and logically it led to a reconciliation, with the passage of key political positions in the course of this struggle into the hands of the bourgeoisie, the denial of any independent political role for the peasants 'as a class' and the self-limitation of the Social-Democracy to a role of the opposition, pushing the 'bourgeois' revolution on ahead and utilizing both all its stages and its ultimate results for the preparation of the labouring masses for the future, Socialist revolution. Fixed in the resolution was a positive attitude towards a possible agrarian revolution of the peasantry, but it did not introduce any changes of principle into the general conception of Menshevism. As we shall see below once again, a resolution adopted by the same conference, concerning 'the conquest of power and the participation of a provisional government', categorically states that the 'Social-Democracy must remain the party of the extreme revolutionary opposition'.

In a foreword to an anthology that came out in 1908, Lenin wrote as follows about the agrarian programme of the second Congress, i.e. of his own programme about the 'strips': 'Events have shown that our then programme was inordinately narrow and underestimated the forces of the revolutionary peasant movement.'[164] These lines were written in September 1907, but the resolution of the Bolshevik Congress, 'On the Attitude towards the Peasant Movement', bears witness that as far back as May 1905 Lenin had succeeded not only in radically revising his own estimate of the peasant movement, but also in drawing along with him in such a revision his own followers in the Party.

The resolution – whose very title is characteristically different from the title of the corresponding resolution of the Menshevik Conference – lays it down categorically that with all its 'elemental spontaneity and political unconsciousness', the 'peasant movement that was now expanding . . . would infallibly turn against the existing order and against the remnants of serfdom altogether'. To be sure, it obscurely mentions the necessity of 'purifying the revolutionary-democratic content of the peasant movement of various reactionary admixtures', but it says nothing about what these 'admixtures' consist of. It simply explains that the task of 'purifying' must be performed by the Social-Democracy, 'by developing the revolutionary self-consciousness of the peasants and leading their democratic demands to a conclusion'. In any case, there is not even a word in the resolution about any possible 'reactionary admixtures' in the socio-economic demands of the peasantry, about any restrictions on these demands in the name of 'freedom of bourgeois relations' in the countryside, or about the counterposition of its own agrarian programme to the programme of the agrarian revolution of the peasantry. The resolution does not even mention the agrarian programme of the second Congress. On the contrary, it states that the 'task' of the Social-Democracy is 'the most energetic support of all revolutionary measures taken by the peasantry . . . including the confiscation of landowners', government, church, monasteries' and appanage lands'. Thus it tacitly liquidates the programme of 'strips', and at the same time the sociological conception underlying it. In accordance with this, the 'revolutionary peasant committees' put forward by the Congress resolution 'as a practical slogan of agitation among the peasantry and as a means of introducing maximum consciousness into the peasant movement', also turn out to be, in their conception, not state organs for the revolutionary land-management of the peasantry, as they are in the resolution of the Menshevik Conference, but peasant organs of the agrarian revolution, directed simultaneously against both the autocracy and the large estates. Their goal is said to be the 'implementation of all revolutionary-democratic transformations in the interests of extricating the peasantry from the oppression of the police, the officials, and the landowners', and their generally peasant 'caste' character is underlined by a directive – 'to strive for the introduction into the peasant committees of representatives of the rural agricultural proletariat', while striving towards 'the independent organization of that proletariat' and 'towards its fusion with the proletariat of the cities under the banner of the Social-Democratic Party.'

This resolution accurately reflected the new orientation, which sought support for the proletariat in its struggle against the autocracy not in the consciously democratic movement of the liberal urban bourgeoisie, 'purified of Populism and agrarianism', but in the 'spontaneous and politically unconscious' movement of the peasant caste, which was radical in terms of its socio-economic demands. But the new orientation, which was naturally bound up with that revision of the question of 'allies' prompted, as already noted, by the Bolshevik formulation of the problem of the 'armed uprising', was also expressed in the resolutions passed by the Congress 'on the practical agreements with the S.R.s' and 'on the attitude towards the liberals'.

The resolution about the S.R.s begins, of course, with a 'confirmation of the attitude of the R.S.D.W.P. towards the S.R. Party as determined by the resolution of the second Congress', just as the resolution on the liberals begins with a reminder that 'the Social-Democracy must support the bourgeoisie in so far as it is revolutionary or merely oppositionist in its struggle against Tsarism', and so must 'welcome the awakening of the political consciousness of the Russian bourgeoisie'. But while the concrete political conclusion of the resolution on the S.R.s is the Congress's 'authorization' to the Central Committee and to local committees 'to enter in case of need into temporary combat agreements with the S.R. organization', the concrete political 'directive' of the resolution on the liberals is simply 'an urgent recommendation to the comrades . . . to explain to the workers the anti-revolutionary and counter-proletarian character of the bourgeois-democratic tendency in *all* its shadings, beginning with the moderate-liberal, represented by the broad strata of the landowners and factory-owners, and ending with the radical, represented by the Union of Emancipation and by the numerous groups in the liberal professions'. This directive was made even more categorical by the removal of Potresov's resolution, passed by the second Congress, in other words, the forbidding of even 'practical agreements' with any parties or groups at all of a 'bourgeois-democratic', i.e. non-Socialist tendency.

The concept of the 'hegemony of the proletariat in the bourgeois revolution' had been the sociological idea underlying the *Iskra* tendency, unifying all its shadings. The practical worthlessness of this idea, which had become clear in the course of events, prompted the Menshevik wing of the *Iskra* group, as we have seen, to return to the concept of the Russian revolution and the proletarian role in it that had been formulated in the first works of the Emancipation of Labour Group. The above-quoted resolutions of the Bolshevik Congress show that Bolshevik thought was moving in a completely different direction during the process of revision of the idea of 'hegemony'. However, these resolutions, as indeed all other official decisions of the Congress, gave only very feeble expression to that completely novel sociological concept of the revolution that Lenin had moved very close to at this time, but that, because of its acute contrast with the traditional concept of Russian Marxism, was still incapable of being completely absorbed even by its Bolshevik wing. It was only over the next few years, gradually, with inevitable halts, reversals, disagreements, and contradictions, that another concept entered into Bolshevik ideology and became decisive in Bolshevik practice. The chief elements of this concept had been carefully marked out by Lenin in the *Vperyod* articles that laid the foundations of the Congress. These were justified by him in detail in a pamphlet published immediately after the Congress, *Two Tactics for the Social-Democracy in the Democratic Revolution.*[165] In a little more than ten years this was to become the ideological mainstay of the 'Communism' that germinated in the matrix of the Russian Social-Democracy.

For Lenin at this time the 'bourgeois' character of the incipient revolution remained, as before, incontestable:

> Only the greatest ignoramuses can disregard the bourgeois character of the democratic overturn now taking place; only the most naïve optimists can forget how little the labouring masses still know of the aims of Socialism or the methods of realizing it . . . Anyone who wishes to travel towards Socialism by any road but that of political democracy, will infallibly arrive at absurd and reactionary conclusions, both economic and political. If any workers ask us why we are not realizing our maximum programme we shall answer by indicating how alien to Socialism the democratically inclined masses of the people still are, how undeveloped the class contradictions still are, how unorganized the proletarians still are.

But – within the confines of 'bourgeois-ness' – both the character of the 'democratic overturn now taking place' and its results can be basically distinct, depending on the social forces leading it:

> It is advantageous to the bourgeoisie if the bourgeois revolution does not decisively sweep away all remnants of the past, but leaves a few of them, i.e. if the revolution is not wholly consistent, does not finish conclusively, is not resolute and merciless . . . It is advantageous to the working-class, on the other hand, if the indispensable transformations in a bourgeois-democratic direction take place precisely by way not of reform but of revolution, for the path of reform is the path of procrastination, of delay. of a tormentingly slow dying-out of putrefying parts of the national organism. And it is primarily and above all the proletariat and peasantry that suffer from their rotting away.

Here Lenin essentially was returning to the idea that had occurred to him as far back as 1896–7, of a 'democratic overturn' accomplished by the proletariat in alliance with the petty bourgeoisie and aimed at the big bourgeoisie. But if at that time (in the pamphlet *Tasks of the Russian Social-Democrats*) he had been counting, as we have seen, on the petty urban bourgeoisie – the 'merchants, petty artisans, etc.' – now he was seeking a prop and an ally for the proletariat in the petty rural bourgeoisie.

> 'Our tactical slogans coincide with the slogans of the democratic-revolutionary and republican bourgeoisie', he wrote. 'To be sure, this bourgeoisie and petty bourgeoisie have not yet formed into a powerful

people's party in Russia.* But the existence of its elements can only be doubted by someone with no understanding of what is going on now in Russia. . . . There are such elements among the peasantry above all. In dividing up the most important social groups according to their political tendencies, we can, without erring too much, *identify the revolutionary republican democracy with the masses of the peasantry* . . . [My italics: T.D.]. If we are destined to undergo a really great revolution, if, this time, history will not allow any "miscarriages", if we are able to carry the revolution to its conclusion, to a definitive victory . . . it will be a revolution with a preponderance of peasant and proletarian elements.'

The proletariat, the peasantry, and the revolutionary-Socialist intelligentsia (the professional revolutionaries), as the three basic motor forces of the Russian revolution – this sociological concept, novel for Russian Marxism, was also in its own way a 'going backwards', except that in distinction to the Mensheviks, it was not towards the original concept of the Emancipation of Labour Group, but towards the fundamental features of that concept that had been the ideological foundation of revolutionary Populism, but now, as we have seen, had been resurrected in a liberal transformation in the doctrine of the S.R.s. But this general similarity of Lenin's new concept to the S.R. concept could not mask the profound difference that from the very beginning had existed between them, and had foreordained a most profound difference throughout the further development of the S.R.s on the one hand and of Bolshevism on the other.

What was different, primarily, was something embedded in their foundation, the idea of the social character of the Russian revolution. For the S.R.s of 1905 the 'bourgeois' revolution was already in the background. It had been accomplished more than four decades before in the abortive form of the emancipation of the serfs and of the 'Great Reforms'. Hence the revolution that was beginning now, on the threshold of the twentieth century, was not bourgeois nor could it be. The overthrow of the autocracy would inevitably be bound up with 'social, proprietary changes', and the basic task of the Socialist party on the 'revolutionary occasion' was summed-up in the 'broadening and deepening' of these changes. For the Lenin of this epoch, on the other hand, the bourgeois character of the incipient revolution was an axiom that 'only the greatest ignoramuses' could not understand. He

* In a characteristic note on this passage Lenin says, about the S.R.s, that they are 'a terrorist group of the intelligentsia rather than the embryo of such a party, even though the objective significance of this group boils down to just this realization of the tasks of the revolutionary and republican bourgeoisie'.

was far from denying the connexion between the 'overthrow of the autocracy' and the 'social proprietary relations': his attitude towards the agrarian revolution of the peasantry bespeaks this convincingly enough. It was only that in view of the bourgeois character of the revolution the rôle of these changes had to be subordinate: the social demands and hopes – and, as we shall see, not of the peasantry alone, but of the proletariat, too – should and must be transformed into levers for the 'radicalization' of the political revolution, but under no circumstances could they become the fundamental task of the Socialist party on the 'revolutionary occasion'. What had to be the focus of attention at the given time of all those who 'wanted to move towards Socialism' and save it from 'absurd and reactionary conclusions' was 'political democracy'. Lenin also reproached the Mensheviks directly both because in its resolution on the revolutionary government their Conference had 'forgotten to mention the republic', and because they were 'now giving priority to the trade unions'.

Directly connected with the difference in the S.R.s' conception of the social nature of the Russian revolution on the one hand and Lenin's on the other, was their attitude towards the liberal bourgeoisie. Here they were diametrically opposed. For the S.R.s it might be said that no such social category existed at all. We have seen how the *Revolyutsionnaya Rossiya* taunted *Iskra*, which 'found the bourgeoisie' where the S.R.s saw merely 'fathers' who were distinguished from their Socialist 'sons' not by any principles, but merely by the 'moderation of their tactics and demands'. For the S.R.s there was no 'principled counterposition' between the trinitarian *bloc* of the proletariat, the peasantry, and the Socialist intelligentsia and the liberal elements of educated and affluent society. In the struggle for the overthrow of the autocracy as understood by the S.R.s these elements were not competitors and not opponents, but merely insufficiently consistent and decisive allies. In Lenin's concept, on the contrary, the alliance of the proletariat, the peasantry and the Socialist intelligentsia was directed precisely at the 'liberal bourgeoisie', which was the adversary against whom a bitter struggle was indispensable if the political revolution against the autocracy was not to turn into a reformist 'miscarriage' but culminate in a 'decisive victory' over Tsarism. The destruction of the 'liberal bourgeoisie' by a revolutionary-republican alliance of the proletariat, the peasantry and the Socialist intelligentsia while still in the midst of the 'bourgeois-democratic overturn' was the fundamental condition of the political radicalization of that overturn. For Lenin the liberal bourgeois became, on the threshold of the 'bourgeois' revolution, just the same 'Enemy No. 1' that the liberal nobleman had been for Dobrolyubov and Chernyshevsky, as we have seen, on the threshold of the emancipation of the serfs.

There was, finally, a third and politically decisive difference. For the S.R.s the industrial proletariat, the peasantry and the Socialist intelligentsia were fused together into a single social category that was homogeneous both in its interests and in the foundations of its ideology, and scarcely differentiated internally by more than shadings and degrees of Socialist consciousness. It was only the trinity of these elements that embodied the 'working-class', which the S.R. Party regarded itself as the intellectual and political leader of. For the Marxist Lenin, on the contrary, even in his new concept, it was only the proletariat, both urban and rural, deprived of the tools of production, that remained the 'working-class', while the proletariat of heavy industry was the central pivot of that class. In declaring that the chief instrument of the anti-Tsarist revolution was the closest possible union between the working-class and the peasantry 'identified' with the revolutionary-republican petty bourgeoisie, he did not forget that the petty-bourgeoisie was a class that differed from the working-class. Hence, even in the framework of this union there was no question of the disappearance of those contradictions of interest between the proletariat and the peasantry as a 'caste' that had prompted the Bolshevik Congress, at the same time it sanctioned the agrarian revolution of the peasantry, to emphasize with intentional sharpness that 'the Social-Democracy as the party of the proletariat had in any and all circumstances to strive towards an independent organization of the rural proletariat and to make clear to it the irreconcilable opposition of its interests to the interests of the peasant bourgeoisie'. In direct opposition to the S.R. concept, 'the proletariat and the peasantry' in Lenin's conception were not a unitary social force with unitary interests and a unitary programme, but an *alliance* of two different social forces, and at that an alliance in which the leading role had to belong to the proletariat.

'The outcome of the revolution depends on whether the working-class plays the role of a helpmate of the bourgeoisie, powerful by virtue of its onslaught on the autocracy but politically powerless, or the role of a leader of the people's revolution' (*Two Tactics*). Identifying Bolshevism in this case with the embodiment of the authentic interests of the working-class, he also demanded for it, in this alliance with the revolutionary-republican bourgeoisie, i.e. the peasantry, that was indispensable for a 'decisive victory' over Tsarism, the same leading role that, as we have seen, he was demanding for it within the proletarian movement itself: 'We intend (in case of a successful outcome of the great Russian revolution) to lead not only the proletariat, organized by the Social-Democratic Party, but also the (revolutionary-republican) petty bourgeoisie, which is capable of marching with it side by side.' Here it was just this novel conception, which merged with the general line of the political and organizational development of Bolshevism, that carried it from the idea of a dictatorship of the Bolsheviks – of the 'professional revolutionaries' – over the Party, to the idea of a dictatorship of the Party over the working-class, and further – to the dictatorship of the working-class over the whole of the 'movement of emancipation'. For the worker-peasant government, which in accordance with the new conception was going to be the outcome of the revolution against the autocracy accomplished by the alliance of the proletariat and peasantry in the struggle against the reformist bourgeoisie, could only be a dictatorship: 'The decisive victory of the revolution over Tsarism will be the *revolutionary-democratic dictatorship of the proletariat and peasantry*' – Lenin italicized this as the basic political conclusion of the new conception as it was defended in the pamphlet *Two Tactics*.

The new conception Lenin had arrived at as a result of the revision of the old 'general-*Iskra*' idea of the 'hegemony of the proletariat' was the direct antithesis of the conception that the Mensheviks were arriving at during this same revision. As a counterweight to the *de facto* refusal of Menshevism to struggle for the 'seizure' of the revolutionary power, Lenin not only referred to the fact that the 'party that sets itself the goal of overturning the government must inevitably think of what government to substitute for the old government it has overthrown', but also insisted that the problem of the struggle of the proletarian-peasant alliance against the liberal bourgeoisie for the conquest of power was the fundamental problem of the Russian Social-Democracy: moreover, that the government of the workers and peasants that emerged from the revolution could only be a *dictatorial* government.

We have already had occasion to recall that the R.S.D.W.P. was the first of the Social-Democratic parties to introduce into its programme the term 'dictatorship of the proletariat'. But this slogan was not on the agenda of the 'bourgeois' revolution, but of the future Socialist revolution. It is true that in appealing to the 'social revolution' as the 'ultimate goal' of the Russian Social-Democracy as well, one of the Siberian delegates to the second Congress, Posadovsky (pseudonym for Dr Mandelberg, a Menshevik) formulated the question of whether the Party should consider itself bound by 'democratic principles' in the forthcoming bourgeois revolution too: 'Must we subordinate our future policy to these or other basic democratic principles, recognizing their absolute value, or ought all democratic principles to be subordinated exclusively to the interests of our party?' For his part Posadovsky answered:

> I absolutely support the latter. There is not one democratic principle we should not subordinate to the interests of our Party (Interjection: 'What about the inviolability of the individual?') Yes, the inviolability of the individual too! As a revolutionary party striving towards its ultimate goal we must conduct ourselves with relation to our democratic principles exclusively from the point of view of the swiftest possible attainment of that goal, from the point of view of our Party interests. If one demand or another is not advantageous to us we will not include it.

Plekhanov was the only one to support Posadovsky: 'The success of the revolution is the highest law. And if it were necessary for the sake of revolutionary success to demand a temporary restriction of one democratic principle or another it would be criminal to hesitate.' In giving an affirmative answer to the question whether this applied equally to the principle of the universal right to vote, Plekhanov continued:

> The revolutionary proletariat might limit the political rights of the upper classes, just as the upper classes at one time have limited its rights . . . If in an outburst of revolutionary enthusiasm the people were to elect a particularly good parliament . . . we should have to try to turn it into a long parliament; but if the elections proved unsuccessful we should have to try to disperse it, not two years later but if possible two weeks later.*

And it was typical of the general intellectual mood of 'Menshevism', only just beginning to become a distinct entity, that it was precisely two future Mensheviks who championed the idea concerning the

* It may be worth mentioning in this connexion that the entire congress, against ten votes, voted down a proposal of the extreme Economists to introduce into the programme a demand for the abolition of the death penalty.

absolute subordination of the Party's politico-democratic objectives to its proletarian-socialist objectives that twelve to thirteen years later became the fundamental dogma of 'Bolshevism in power', which it began to fulfil by dispersing the Constituent Assembly.

But in spite of all Plekhanov's authority, his and Posadovsky's position did not find the slightest support at the Congress. Indeed, the whole question seems to have appeared to him too to be so abstract and 'academic' that upon encountering firm resistance at the Congress he (as well as Posadovsky) never even once returned to it. The 'absolute value' of democratic principles was at that time such an unchallengeable article of faith of all tendencies of the Social-Democracy, including and even particularly its future Bolshevik wing, that Trotsky was unquestionably expressing the general view of the Party when, in protesting against the apprehensions of an extreme Economist, V. Makhnovets (Akimov), concerning the 'dictatorship of the proletariat' in the future Socialist revolution, he said soothingly: 'He is frightened by the dictatorship of the proletariat as by a Jacobin act. He forgets that that dictatorship would be possible only when the Social-Democratic Party and the working-class – whose mutual opposition disturbs him so – will be closest to identification. The dictatorship of the proletariat will be not a conspiratorial "seizure of power" but the political dominion of an organized working-class constituting a majority of the nation.'

In proclaiming a dictatorship, and at that a dictatorship led by the Social-Democratic Party as representative of the working-class, a stage and an instrument no longer of the future Socialist revolution of the proletariat against the bourgeoisie, but of an 'all-national', 'bourgeois' revolution against the autocracy, Lenin broke sharply with the quarter-of-a-century-old traditions of Russian Marxism. It was with all the greater insistence that he emphasized that 'it would of course be not a Socialist but a democratic dictatorship' (*Two Tactics*). And it was with all the greater energy that he spoke out against all attempts (this was his chief difference at the time with Parvus and Trotsky) to impose any Socialist objectives on the revolution headed by this dictatorship. 'In trying to set a Socialist overturn as its immediate goal the Social-Democracy would really only disgrace itself,' he said in *Vperyod*.[166]

It was precisely such confused and unclear ideas of our S.R.s that the Social-Democracy has always fought. It was just because of this that it

> always insisted on the bourgeois character of the revolution looming up in Russia, just because of this that it always demanded a strict distinction between the democratic minimum-programme and the Socialist maximum-programme. All this can be forgotten during an overturn by individual Social-Democrats, inclined to throw in their hands before an elemental upheaval, but not by the Party as a whole.

Thus the goal of the dictatorship of the proletariat and peasantry was supposed to be only the conduct of 'political democracy' as far as possible – the conquest of the republic, about which, however, 'to avoid misunderstandings' Lenin immediately said by way of 'qualification' that 'by republic we mean not only and not even so much a form of government as the entire conjunction of the democratic transformations of our minimum-programme'. The minimum-programme of the R.S.D.W.P., that is, the materialization of the broadest political liberties and all the socio-economic reforms located within the framework of a 'democratic overturn' – which in the words of a resolution of the Bolshevik Congress concerning Provisional Government (see below) 'will not weaken but strengthen the rule of the bourgeoisie' – such are the limits the dictatorship must not go beyond if it does not want to arrive at 'absurd and reactionary' conclusions.

As the revolution evolved the watershed between Menshevism and Bolshevism was established with growing distinctness in their methods of solving the classic dual problem – political democracy and/or Socialism.

Menshevism tried to make the cornerstone of its policy the struggle for the realization of its class, Socialist objectives. The conquest by the proletariat of more and more political positions in a society hostile to it for class reasons, the reinforcement of its class organization, and the development of its class-consciousness in the process of the bourgeois revolution, were supposed to prepare the working-class for a more successful struggle on behalf of Socialism in the future Russia, politically free, though bourgeois. The leadership of the purely political overturn was *de facto* left by Menshevism to the bourgeoisie itself. It based its assumption of the radical character of this overturn primarily on the 'pressure of the proletariat' and on the ability of this 'pressure' to elevate bourgeois political antagonism to the autocracy to an acuteness reminiscent of the great French Revolution. This assumption proved erroneous, nor could it have been otherwise. The contradiction in the dual task confronting the Russian Social-Democracy made and had to make the Menshevik position on this question internally contradictory. It was, after all, just this growth of class isolation and class combativeness of the Russian proletariat, which Menshevism had made its fundamental task, that drove and had to drive the political oppositionism of the Russian bourgeoisie into a narrow framework for which not only the gigantic dimensions of the great French Revolution dreamt of by the Mensheviks, but also the modest scale of the abortive revolutions of 1848, proved too great. Having become primarily the exponent of the primacy of the class, Socialist objectives of the proletariat in the bourgeois revolution, Menshevism fell into insoluble contradictions in the face of the problem of political democracy.

The concept of the 'dictatorship of the proletariat and peasantry' that crowned the thought of Bolshevism, as exponent of the primacy of political-democratic radicalism in the Russian revolution, incontestably resolved the contradictions of the political problem in which Menshevism was floundering. But all the sharper and more insoluble were the contradictions it created for the problem of the class, Socialist objectives of the Russian proletariat in the bourgeois revolution. If the revolutionary Social-Democracy, which was organizing the urban working-class and mobilizing the rural proletariat under the banner of Socialism, was also going to be able to subjugate the peasantry as a 'caste' and lead it in an assault not only on Tsarism but also on the bourgeoisie, and make it its partner in a dictatorship that leant on 'a military force, on the armed masses, on an uprising' – and hence be capable of smashing the 'desperate resistance' once again not only of Tsarism but of the bourgeoisie too, in order to realize the whole of the Social-Democratic maximum-programme – why should the revolutionary proletariat stop there? Why could the Social-Democracy that was 'leading' the worker-peasant dictatorship not move on to the realization of its maximum-programme? And why should only the 'greatest ignoramuses' dream about moving on to such a realization?

But, Lenin answered in the above-cited article,[161] 'the course of events in a democratic overturn will bind us to such a mass of allies from the petty bourgeoisie and the peasantry . . . that the fears of too swift a transition to the maximum-programme are simply ridiculous': these 'allies' would not allow 'us' to pass over to a maximum-programme because their 'material needs will require the execution of a minimum-programme'. In other words, the petty-bourgeoisie and the peasantry would not allow the working-class to cross the line dividing the bourgeois from the Socialist revolution. Moreover, Lenin added (*Two Tactics*), the 'labouring masses themselves still know very little about the aims of Socialism or the methods of realizing them'; the 'class contradictions are not yet developed', 'the proletarians are still not organized', the 'democratically inclined masses are still alien to Socialism'. But in that case – how could a proletariat that was unorganized and knew so little of Socialism be capable of heading the peasantry and leading it in a battle against Tsarism and the bourgeoisie simultaneously? And how would 'allies from the petty bourgeoisie and the peasantry' that were so clearly adverse to the 'maximum-programme' and were able to stop any attempts to move on to it, assume the political leadership of the Social-Democracy, that is, of a party that happened to be proclaiming just this maximum-programme, which distinguished it in principle from all other, bourgeois parties, and which in addition was now obligating itself to 'make clear to the agricultural proletariat the irreconcilable opposition of its interests to the interests of the peasant bourgeoisie'?

Lenin himself could not help sensing the contradictoriness and unconvincingness of this line of argument. Only two months after *Two Tactics* appeared he tried, in an article on 'The Attitude of the Social-Democracy towards the Peasant Movement'[167] to give a completely new reply to this question. 'We are at this very moment beginning to move away from the democratic revolution, and to the limit of our strength, the strength of a conscious and organized proletariat, we are beginning to pass over to the Socialist revolution. We stand for an uninterrupted revolution. We shall not halt half-way.' But this appeal to an 'uninterrupted' (in the terminology associated with Trotsky's name, 'permanent') revolution, which stood in such manifest contrast with all the preceding arguments, seemed a mere accidental zigzag, and Lenin never went back to it. And in the last analysis the sole guarantee of the non-Socialist character of the worker-peasant dictatorship headed by the Social-Democracy and the revolution that proceeded under its leadership, proved to be, in his arguments, merely the ideological tenacity of the 'Party as a whole'. This in its turn was guaranteed, as we know, in accordance with the general conception of Bolshevism, only by the ideological 'self-restraint' of the kernel of professional revolutionaries led by the Party, on the one hand, and by the strict discipline of the masses on the other.

This kind of argumentation fitted quite consistently within the framework of those fundamental ideas of Bolshevism whose development we have been following. But in essence what it meant was that Lenin had to look for a way out of the contradiction in the new concept of the 'democratic dictatorship of the proletariat and peasantry' by appealing to 'consciousness' in the same old way as the Emancipation of Labour Group, just as Menshevism in its turn was also doing in its attempts to solve the problem of the 'Socialist tasks of the proletariat in the bourgeois revolution'. The sole difference was that in accordance with the general ideas of Bolshevism Lenin was appealing to the 'consciousness' not of the masses, but of the leaders. But, as we have already had more than one occasion to note, this purely rationalistic and hence illusory appeal to 'consciousness' was a continually renewed testimony to the insolubility, within the framework of Russian realities, of the contradiction in the basic problem – democracy-Socialism – with which these realities kept constantly confronting the Russian Social-Democracy.

We know how paradoxically life was to solve, later on, not the basic contradiction of the problem – which history has carried inviolate down to our own days – but those contradictions that Menshevism and Bolshevism were beating up against in their attempts to solve this problem, which forced them as it were to change roles. More and more Menshevism began to turn the struggle for 'bourgeois' political democracy and its preservation into its own paramount task, reformistically subordinating to it the 'class' Socialist objectives of the proletariat. Bolshevism, on the other hand, stressed the 'construction of Socialism'; it cast aside and attacked the very idea of a 'consistent democracy' that from the very birth of Bolshevism had been its fundamental fraction slogan in the general ranks of the Social-Democracy.

This paradoxical finale to the development of the two fractions had, of course, been prepared by the whole preceding course of events and by the special role played by each fraction. But it was only in the course of the 1917 revolution and under its direct influence that it received a precise form. In 1905 neither of the fractions would have recognized in it its own future visage. Not only would the Bolshevik Congress have sharply recoiled from the idea of Socialism without democracy, but, as has already been noted, even the idea of a 'democratic dictatorship of the proletariat and peasantry' seemed so difficult for it to accept that it was not formulated in any one of its resolutions. And it was only the resolutions of the Menshevik Conference and of the Bolshevik Congress concerning the Provisional Government that expressed in any careful, even though far from consistent way, the above-mentioned divergences between Menshevism and Bolshevism on the basic problems of the revolution that threw both fractions into a virulent and passionate polemic.

The Menshevik resolution on the Provisional Government begins with the statement that 'the decisive victory of the revolution over Tsarism' might be signalized '*either* by the institution of a Provisional Government emerging from the victorious people's uprising, *or* by the revolutionary initiative of one or another representative institution, which, under the direct revolutionary pressure of the people, would decide to organize an All-National Constituent Assembly'. This second half of the dilemma referred to the self-appointed 'representative institution' the idea of which had arisen in *Iskra* circles in connexion with the 'Zemstvo Campaign' but also, of course, the State Duma, drafts of which were being worked out at the time in the government. In any case it was also oriented towards the possibility of a further development of the Russian revolutionary process in the forms of the great French Revolution, in which the General Estates were directly replaced by the National (Constituent) Assembly, and then by the plenipotentiary Convention, and in which, for this reason, there had been no place for any 'Provisional Government'.

But whatever the forms to be assumed by the 'decisive victory', it was in any case going to be merely the 'beginning of a new phase in the revolutionary epoch' – a phase in which the 'definitive liquidation of the whole monarchical régime of social estates' would be consummated 'in the process of mutual struggle between elements of the politically emancipated bourgeois society for the realization of their own social interests and for the direct conquest of power'. It was in terms of this phase of the class struggle within the already 'emancipated bourgeois society' that the Russian Social-Democracy had to ground its tactics even now, if it wanted to defend the interests of the proletariat in the revolution, and not in terms of one form or another of its 'definitive victory' over Tsarism. Hence it had to 'aim at preserving throughout the breadth of the revolution a position that would ensure for it better than anything else the possibility of moving the revolution forward, would not tie its hands in the struggle against the inconsistent and self-interested policy of the bourgeois parties and would preserve it from dissolving within the bourgeois democracy'.

The Provisional Government that was to arise on the crest of the 'victorious people's uprising' could change nothing in this situation.

In so far as 'our revolution' was 'bourgeois' by its historic character, the Provisional Government too 'would have not only to advance the revolutionary development by regulating the mutual struggle between the opposed classes of the nation *en route* to self-emancipation, but also to struggle against factors threatening the foundations of the capitalist system'. Hence, the 'Social-Democracy did not have to set itself the goal of seizing or sharing the power in the Provisional Government', but had 'to found its tactics on the calculation of maintaining for the Social-Democratic Party a position of extreme revolutionary opposition *vis-à-vis* all the governments that would succeed each other in the course of the revolution'.

The basic elements of the Menshevik line, already described more than once, were expressed in the resolution with consistency. Only a small, though characteristic discord was introduced into the harmonious tactical schema it had outlined by a paragraph stating that the general negative attitude towards the 'seizure or division of power did not exclude the appropriateness of a partial, episodic seizure of power and the formation of revolutionary communes . . . in the exclusive interests of furthering the spread of the uprising and the disorganization of the government'. This paragraph fails to indicate either the dimensions of this 'partialness' or the duration of the allowed 'episodes'; it by-passes in silence the question of the appropriateness of 'furthering the spread of the uprising', and of a more focal participation in the 'seizure of power', as well as the question of when, under what conditions, and in what form the Party was supposed to stop taking part in the 'revolutionary communes' organized with its collaboration. Hence in essence it opens a breach in the logic of the resolution. But once again this breach testifies only to the contradictoriness of the conditions in which the Russian revolution was destined to proceed, and in which the Russian Social-Democracy was to perform its task of politically mobilizing and organizing the Russian working-class.

The resolution of the Bolshevik Congress is considerably less precise and consistent, not in individual paragraphs but in its entire construction. It is another testimonial to the difficulty with which even the Bolshevik wing of the Party accepted the ideas, novel for the Social-Democracy, that Lenin had developed: not merely the idea of a worker-peasant dictatorship, but also the far more modest idea of the participation of the Social-Democracy in a Provisional Government.

The Bolshevik resolution did not pose the question of the 'decisive victory' in alternatives. The democratic republic was, of course, a programmatic demand of Mensheviks and Bolsheviks equally. But for the Mensheviks, before whose political vision there constantly loomed up the historical prototype of the great French Revolution, the definitive forms of the state could also be no more than the product of a 'mutual struggle' between the classes of the 'politically emancipated bourgeois society'. From this it followed that a democratic republic would still have to be fought for in that 'new phase of the revolutionary epoch' that would be opened up by the 'decisive victory'. This, indeed, was the reason the resolution had 'forgotten' to mention the republic. For the Bolsheviks, on the contrary, the 'decisive victory' itself was a synonym for the 'replacement of the autocracy by a democratic republic', because such a replacement was demanded 'just as much by the direct interests of the proletariat as by its struggle for the ultimate goals of Socialism'. Hence Lenin used the silence about the democratic republic in the Mensheviks' resolution as a direct reproach to them. There was only *one* road to the winning of a democratic republic:

> the realization of a democratic republic in Russia is possible only as a result of a victorious people's uprising, the organ of which will be the Provisional Government, which alone is capable of ensuring complete freedom for pre-electoral agitation and of convoking, on the basis of a universal, equal, direct and secret ballot, a Constituent Assembly that will really express the will of the people.

Further on in the resolution, however, we shall seek in vain for any indications that this 'victorious people's uprising' must be led by the Social-Democracy; that in the process of this leadership it is supposed to rally, around the working-class, the peasantry that had only just become the embodiment of 'revolutionary and republican democracy' in Russia; that aside from the proletariat and peasantry in general 'there is no one else to win a decisive victory over Tsarism' that would be at the same time a victory over the 'liberal bourgeoisie' too; that, in leading the uprising the Social-Democracy not only had to enter into its 'organ' – the Provisional Government – but also to occupy a leading position in that organ; that, by virtue of all this, by the democratic republic 'we mean not only and even not so much the form of government as the entire conjuncture of democratic transformations of our minimum-programme'; and so forth and so on.

None of these basic elements in Lenin's new conception, systematized in *Two Tactics*, found a place in the analytic part of the resolution, and still less in its directive part. On the contrary, the resolution lays it down that 'the democratic overturn in Russia, given its socio-economic system, will not weaken but strengthen the rule of the bourgeoisie, which, stopping at nothing, will infallibly attempt to take away from the Russian proletariat as large a part as possible of the conquests of the revolutionary people'. Thus, the republic that will emerge from the victorious uprising is presumed to have little in common with the implementation of the 'entire conjunction of the democratic transformations of our minimum-programme'. The working-class will simply have to 'demand' of the Provisional Government the 'realization of all the most immediate political and economic demands of our programme [minimum-programme]'. Such was the wording of the resolution's first directive point.

The very formulation of this first point is already very remote from the demand that the Provisional Government be headed by the Social-Democracy, or even from the demand that the Social-Democracy participate in that government. But the Congress's reluctance to make such a demand the political directive of the Party becomes completely evident in the formulation of the second point of the directive section. This merely speaks of the 'inadmissibility' of participating in the Provisional Government under specific conditions, and even participating in it not with the revolutionary-aggressive aims as in Lenin's conception, but with aims of a class-defensive character. 'Depending on the correlationship of forces and other factors not susceptible of a precise preliminary definition, participation in the Provisional Revolutionary Government is admissible for our Party plenipotentiaries with the aim of a merciless struggle against all counter-revolutionary attempts and in order to champion the independent interests of the working-class.' It is impossible to assess the point immediately following except as an expression of the inner disquiet with which the Congress sanctioned the participation of the Social-Democracy in the Provisional Government even in this extremely weakened form: 'An indispensable condition for such participation is a strict control of the Party over its plenipotentiaries and an undeviating maintenance of the independence of the Social-Democracy, which is striving for a complete Socialist overturn and to that extent is irreconcilably hostile to all bourgeois parties.'

Finally, parallel with the breach knocked into Menshevik conceptions by the point about the 'partial and episodic' participation of the Social-Democracy in governmental organs created by the revolution, a still greater breach was made in the conceptions of Bolshevism by the concluding point of the resolution:

> Independently of whether it will be possible for the Social-Democracy to take part in the Provisional Government, propaganda must be carried on in the broadest strata of the proletariat for the idea of the necessity of a constant pressure on the Provisional Government on the part of the armed proletariat, led by the Social-Democracy, with the aim of preserving, reinforcing, and broadening the conquests of the revolution.

Here the action of the Social-Democracy, from above, through a Provisional Government supported by 'armed force, the armed masses, an uprising', gives way to 'pressure' on the Provisional Government from below, by the armed proletarian masses led by the Social-Democrats. This scarcely differed from the Menshevik conception of the time except by the emphasis on 'armed'.

As is known, the 1917 revolution forced Menshevism and Bolshevism to change roles with respect to the question of the Provisional Government too. Menshevism proclaimed the necessity of taking part in the Provisional Government and in fact put this participation into effect. Bolshevism not only declared participation in the Provisional Government to be inadmissible, but also set itself the goal of overthrowing it, in which the slogan of the uprising led by the Bolsheviks was not the formation of another Provisional Government, but the transfer of 'all power' to the Soviet of Workers', Peasants' and Soldiers' Deputies. In other words, the 'decisive victory' of the armed uprising was marked by the transformation, foreseen in the Menshevik resolution, of the 'self-appointed representative institution', which was what the Soviets were, into a fully empowered Convention. But that was a matter of the relatively remote future. For the time being, in the face of the problems confronting the Social-Democracy of the 1905 revolution, the disagreements, inconsistencies, vacillations, and contradictions in the political position of *both* fractions testified to the insolubility of these problems under Russian conditions. In the final analysis they *both* appealed from these conditions to those of international life, in order to find a solution, though for the time being a merely theoretical one, of the contradiction of the Russian revolution.

'There is only one case,' reads the Menshevik Conference resolution, 'in which the Social-Democracy on its own initiative would have to direct its efforts towards the conquest of power and keep it in its own hands as long as possible. It would be precisely in case the revolution shifted into the advanced countries of Western Europe where conditions for the realization of Socialism have already attained a certain maturity. In that case the restricted historical limitations of the Russian revolution may be substantially expanded, and the possibility of advancing on the road of Socialist transformations would appear.' But Lenin too saw in this appeal to internationalism a final solution of the contradiction of his own conception of a worker-peasant dictatorship. In *Two Tactics*, in speaking of there coming into being 'not, of course, a Socialist but a democratic dictatorship', he emphasizes that this dictatorship 'may carry the revolutionary flame to Europe'.

Underlying this appeal of both fractions to the 'flame in Europe' was the growing comprehension in them both of the fact that the contradictions of the Russian revolution, Russian democracy, and Russian Socialism could be given an authentic solution only within the framework of an international Socialist revolution. This forecast was justified by the forty years of subsequent socio-political development in Russia and confirmed beyond question by all the realities of our catastrophic epoch, consumed by wars and revolutions.

5. THE BAPTISM OF REVOLUTION

The Menshevik Conference and the Bolshevik Congress (more precisely the ideological foundation with which Lenin had provided its decisions) consummated the intellectual and political formation of the two fractions of the Russian Social-Democracy. They not only fortified the preponderant gravitation of one of them towards the proletarian-class objectives of the Party, and of the other towards its revolutionary-democratic objectives, but also made each one of them the exponent of a special conception of the Russian revolution, of special ideas concerning the correlationship of social forces in it, and of the place and tasks of the working-class in the system of those forces.

But it must be remarked that at that time, on the eve of the October victory of the 1905 revolution, this process of the self-definition of the fractions succeeded in taking far more definite and subjectively conscious forms among the Mensheviks than among the Bolsheviks. We have seen how in spite of all Lenin's prestige, which even at that time stood matchlessly high among the Bolsheviks, it was only with obvious resistance, and partially, that the Bolshevik Congress agreed to lend the official sanction of the fraction to Lenin's innovational ideas. To what extent the essence and the depth of the fraction differences were at that time obscure even to the pinnacle of the Bolshevik leadership is evident if only from the text of the 'Open Letter' with which the Central Committee, just elected by the Congress, addressed the Menshevik Organizational Committee, proposing to enter into discussions with it at once concerning the restoration of unity.

'Disunity oppresses you, we are convinced, no less than it does us,' says the Letter, printed at a time when the negotiations were already under way.[167] 'Surely it is not impossible to have done with it?

'What is dividing us? Tactical differences? But surely these are not so serious that for their sake it is worth splitting the Social-Democracy into two parties? The differences between the tactical resolutions of the third Congress and your first Conference are so insignificant that to a bystander it would even be difficult to notice them at once.'*

But whatever the degree of ideological formation of the fractions around October 1905, neither one of them, of course, was clear in its own mind at the time concerning the 'ultimate' conclusions to be drawn from its own ideas. The bulk of the then Mensheviks would never have recognized themselves as the apostles of political-democratic reformism who only within that framework were capable of conceiving of the class struggle of the proletariat for Socialism. Similarly, the Bolsheviks would not have recognized themselves as the future liquidators of the Constituent Assembly and the pioneers of 'Socialist construction', not only leaving behind the 'path of political

* The negotiations, which went on for the whole month of July 1905, had no positive results. But immediately after 17 October the Bolshevik Central Committee renewed its campaign for the restoration of unity. In an address 'To All Party Organizations and to all Working-Class Social-Democrats'[169] it proposed that in agreement with the Menshevik Organizational Committee a 'Fourth Congress' for unification be convoked, to be preceded by the introduction of the electoral principle into the whole system of party organization. At the Congress itself 'each side would receive an equal number of deciding votes' but 'would first take on itself the firm and indestructible obligation to submit to all the rulings of the majority of this general congress'. At the November conferences of both fractions the question of convoking an amalgamated congress was decided affirmatively; the six-member 'Unifying Central Committee' (three representatives per fraction) was charged with preparing it. The unifying congress, based not on equal but on proportional representation, assembled in Stockholm in the spring of 1906.

democracy' but also overthrowing the very principle of 'mangy' (Bukharin's expression) political democracy. In the beginning of April 1917, when Lenin appeared in Petersburg, his famous *Theses*, which took only an initial and extremely wary step towards bringing to a 'logical conclusion' the conception he had expounded twelve years before in *Two Tactics*, evoked among the 'Old Bolsheviks' an even more unanimous and violent rejection than was evoked among the 'Old Mensheviks' by the international Socialist position of Martov, who returned from abroad soon after him. In its turn this too was only an embryonic form of that system of opinions Martov was to expound afterwards in his own 'April' theses of 1920, which became the platform of the so-called 'Martov' trend in Menshevism.*

But the war that began in 1914, and more definitively the revolution of 1917, once again turned the attention of the Party to great ideological problems. The intervening ten to twelve years are characterized by the stagnation and even, in a certain sense, the retrogression of its theoretical thought. Throughout this time the basic ideas of Menshevism and Bolshevism remained in the same 'unfinished' and hence, as we have seen, clearly contradictory form in which they had condensed towards the beginning of the 1905 revolution.

Even the narrow, police-controlled freedom that was brought by the 1905 revolution was enough to confront the Party with a multitude of completely novel practical problems. Party thought was concentrated on their solution during the period between the two revolutions. In the discussions and disputes on the more or less elementary questions of tactics, and the organizational questions bound up with them, the internal connexion would often be lost between the tactical and organizational dispositions of each of the contending fractions and the grand conceptions they had begun finishing off during the process of their divergence. In any case these large-scale conceptions almost disappeared from the field of vision of the rank-and-file Social-Democrats. And while this political-organizational 'practicalism' created during the course of this whole period constantly renewed oppor-

* The following episode is characteristic of the mood of the Party Bolsheviks in March–April 1917: At the very first appearance of the author of this book at the Petersburg Soviet (9–10 March) he was approached by a woman representing the Petersburg Committee of Bolsheviks, with a request to permit the Committee to reprint a popular pamphlet the author had written as far back as 1905 on the 'All-National Constituent Assembly'. Permission was not given, for fraction considerations.

tunities for co-operation, *rapprochement*, and even 'unification' between fractions that would have appeared to be hopelessly divergent, there was, on the other side, an elaboration in each of them of 'fraction-spirit', for which transient, tactical and organizational rulings of one's own fraction were to become the unchallengeable dogma and banner of 'proletarian Socialism', and which strove to carry each divergence to an extreme even in personal, peripheral, and private questions. Thus even in the 'united' Party a mutual distrust and psychological alienation kept growing between its two parts that laid the groundwork for its definitive split. This was formally proclaimed by the Bolsheviks as early as 1912, but it was realized practically only in the 1917 revolution – in the form of the transformation of the Bolsheviks from 'Social-Democrats' into 'Communists'.

In spite of the polemics, which at times were extremely virulent, this wall of mutual alienation did not yet exist, in any case, when the Manifesto of 17 October 1905 and the incomplete though rather broad political amnesty that followed it a few days later allowed the leaders of both fractions to stop being *émigrés* and return to Russia. The Petersburg Bolsheviks succeeded at once in taking over the editorship of a newspaper, *Novaya Zhizn* (New Life) just founded by the poet Minsky; on 27 October this actually began appearing under the new editorship, replacing the Geneva *Proletarii*, which was soon put a stop to. (Lenin came to Petersburg a little later; his first article did not appear in the *Novaya Zhizn* until 10 November.) By 13 November the Mensheviks in their turn managed to organize their own paper, *Nachalo* (The Beginning). Parvus and Trotsky also became editors of this, on coalition terms, together with the old, *de facto* editors of *Iskra* (which now came to an end) – Martov, Potresov, Martynov and Dan. The conditions of the short-lived but stormy 'days of freedom' were such that the first few weeks of activity of both fractions on Russian terrain not only did not envenom their mutual relations, but on the contrary led to a certain *rapprochement* that even made possible the publication of a joint newspaper, *Severny Golos* (Northern Voice) after both *Nachalo* and *Novaya Zhizn* were shut down by the government, on 2–3 December. But the revolutionary movement was already beginning to decline. The government was even able to arrest a general assembly of the Petersburg Soviet of Workers' Deputies without provoking any decisive resistance on the part of the labouring masses of the capital. Under such conditions *Severny Golos*, which had only begun to come out on 6 December, proved even shorter-lived than had been its fraction predecessors: by the third number it was shut down. The first number of *Nash Golos* (Our Voice) managed to come out in replacement on 18 December, but the type of the second number was broken up by the police, and the official editor, D. M. Gertzenstein (who had played the same role on *Nachalo*) was arrested. The longing at that time of both fractions for a *rapprochement* was shown by an attempt to create a joint organ, this time under the expressive title of *Sliyanie* (Fusion) but this final attempt was also disrupted by the refusal of the printers to print a Social-Democratic newspaper unfavourable to the government.*

This *rapprochement* was possible because contact with revolutionary realities immediately shook the positions of both fractions, which in any case were still inadequately consolidated. These realities lacked any essential elements to which the ideas each of the fractions had succeeded in working out up to this time could be applied.

The Menshevik conception of the 'pressure' of the working-class on the bourgeoisie with the aim of 'revolutionizing' it and pushing it into power, while simultaneously strengthening and organizationally reinforcing the class positions of the proletariat, proved to be unfeasible – primarily because the presumed object of the 'pressure' was simply not there. The tempestuous inundation of the revolutionary movement, whose chief force was the working-class, whose chief weapon was the strike, and whose organizational centre was the Soviet of Workers' Deputies, not only did not provoke the political activization of the bourgeoisie, but in fact made it eliminate itself temporarily as a political factor. It was only after the destruction of the Soviet in December 1905 and the *de facto* decline of the workers' revolutionary movement that the bourgeoisie began to emerge as an organized force. When it did even its left wing, by the character of its critique of the stormy stage of the revolution it had only just undergone as much as

* Later the legal Social-Democratic newspapers, no longer unified but fractional, were able to come out in fact only during the session of the State Duma, but even then only by submitting to frequent prohibitions and hence uninterruptedly changing their names and using 'dummy' editors. On the eve of the war of 1914 the daily Social-Democratic press was destroyed for good, not to reappear until after the 1917 revolution. But reviews and weeklies, political and professional, were able to appear throughout this time – also, of course, with frequent forced interruptions. At the beginning of 1908 the majority of the intellectual leaders of both fractions were once again in the emigration (from which a few – Martov, Dan, Kamenev and others – were able to return to Russia in 1913), where they resumed the publication of fraction organs.

by the very name of the party it founded (Kadets = Constitutional Democrats), demonstrated its remoteness from that 'revolutionariness' the Menshevik conception had been oriented towards.

Nor were there any more elements in revolutionary reality for the practical realization of the Bolshevik conception either, for the 'democratic dictatorship of the proletariat and peasantry', as the instrument for the execution of the 'bourgeois-democratic overturn' in its most radical forms. The workers' October strike movement, which swept the country, called forth a new and tempestuous upsurge of the agrarian movement in the countryside. But in that movement the peasantry least of all showed itself to be the petty-bourgeois 'revolutionary-republican democracy' capable of becoming the partner of the proletariat in a dictatorship that would set itself the primary task of materializing a radical political democracy and consequently direct its fire at bourgeois liberalism. In the peasant movement of that period political ideas and slogans played a minimal role; it was wholly concentrated on economic questions, primarily, of course, the question of land. It was highly characteristic that the S.R. Party, also oriented towards the peasantry, owed its own rather considerable successes at this time, not only among the peasants but partly also among the workers, primarily to its agitation in favour of 'proprietary changes', that is, its own socialistically tinted economic agitation, not at all to its political radicalism. In the sphere of 'politics', on the contrary, it was just at this time that there began the already mentioned intellectual development of the S.R. Party towards a *rapprochement* with the far from 'radical' democratic liberalism represented by the Kadet Party. This process, by the way, also laid the intellectual foundation for the S.R.s' participation in the 'democratic' coalition that signalized the first period of the 1917 revolution, and also the so-called 'Constituent Assembly front' in the epoch of the civil war.

Thus, in spite of all theorizing, it was the working-class that proved to be the sole active political force of the 'movement of emancipation' during the October revolution of 1905. Not only politically undeveloped groups of employees, salesmen, petty officials, rank-and-file city government and Zemstvo intelligentsia had to lean upon the organization created by the proletariat, the Soviet of Workers' Deputies (in whose system the Petersburg Soviet played not only a local role but also that of an all-Russian centre), but also, as has already been pointed out, the trained and at this time extremely radically-minded 'bourgeois' intelligentsia that grouped itself into professionally centred unions united in a general Union of Unions.

But it would be a mistake to exaggerate, not so much the political 'radicalism' as the degree of genuine political interest of the working-class itself in this period. Both in the Petersburg Soviet originated by the Mensheviks and in the provincial Soviets the leading role of course belonged to the Social Democracy,* and the radical democratic slogans and proclamations dictated by it were enthusiastically and without protest accepted by all workers' mass-meetings. As a matter of fact, however, under this deceptive cover a fundamental shift in the real mood of the labouring masses themselves very quickly began making itself felt. The opportunity they had achieved of a free and organized struggle began turning their attention from the problems of the liquidation of the autocracy, and the radicalization of the democratic system replacing it, to more immediate and intelligible problems of their own economic and juridical situation. This was attested by the wave of more and more frequent economic strikes that kept surging through the country. These drew irresistibly into their wake every category of labourer without exception, including the most backward, each one of which hastened to set up its own trade union. The pressure of the labouring masses was invincible; in yielding to it the Petersburg Soviet found itself forced, towards the middle of November, to declare a new general strike. This was, to be sure, given a 'political' hue by the protest against the introduction of martial law in Poland, but its real objective was an attempt to introduce by 'physical action' the eight-hour working day in all industrial and commercial businesses.

Whatever had been the ideas of the Mensheviks and Bolsheviks, they both had to take into account the irrefragable fact that in the first stage of the revolution the working-class had proved to be the sole active political force, hence also as it were the sole and unrivalled pretender to the revolutionary power that had been created. In order not to tear themselves away from this power and to fall foul of it they willy-nilly had to take into account, also, the equally irrefragable fact that the interests of the broad strata of the labouring masses, including the advance detachments of the industrial proletariat, had begun to shift away from political to economic problems. As they saw, moreover, the labouring masses naturally tried to carry on their economic

* The only known exception was the Belostok Soviet of Workers' Deputies, which was under the influence of the S.R.s and anarchists.

struggle by the very methods of 'physical' implementation and 'seizure' that on the initiative of the Social-Democracy itself they had only just been applying with such success in the political struggle. Because of this the economic struggle itself began taking on the 'anarcho-syndicalist' character of 'direct action'. From the Menshevik point of view this masked the danger of the total 'isolation' of the proletariat from all the other forces in the 'movement of emancipation', thus also of its defeat. From the Bolshevik point of view there was the danger of 'apoliticism', the divorce of the labouring masses from the struggle for the 'revolutionary-republican' democracy.

Thus both Menshevism and Bolshevism had to introduce into their theoretical conceptions some practical corrections, which not only shattered the integrity of these conceptions but also threatened to explode them altogether. Traditionally Menshevism was oriented towards the 'elemental spontaneity' of the working-class movement and the organized independence of the proletariat; it stressed 'class' Socialist objectives and was convinced that if ever the course of events imposed, however prematurely, a revolutionary régime on the proletariat by force, that régime would in any case be utilized for the *Socialist* transformation of social relations. It is quite understandable why Menshevism at this time was psychologically so much more flexible than Bolshevism in relation to such corrections, which generally tended towards the views of Parvus-Trotsky about a 'workers' régime' as the historically fore-ordained grave-digger and heir of the Tsarist power, and about the 'permanent revolution' as a process of the direct transformation of the bourgeois Russian revolution into a Socialist revolution.

This flexibility was shown by the very fact of the coalition of the editorial board of *Iskra* with Parvus and Trotsky for the joint publication of a newspaper that began coming out in the middle of November, that is, at a time when the peculiarities of the political situation indicated above had already become completely definite. But this flexibility was expressed still more precisely in the 'Trotskyite' themes that began echoing more and more loudly in the utterances and articles of eminent members of the *Iskra* editorial board (first and foremost Martynov and the author of these lines) with the manifest approval of a substantial segment of the Mensheviks, especially of the Menshevik workers. The general editorial line of *Nachalo* also began becoming more and more 'Trotskyite'. *Nachalo* was clearly treating the constantly growing isolation of the proletariat not so much as a source and harbinger of its defeat, as a heaven-sent opportunity to accelerate its Socialist liberation.*

The 'Trotskyite' trends introduced elements of blatant contradiction into the general Menshevik conception. They would inevitably have pushed a substantial segment of the Mensheviks to a principled revision of it if the failure of the November strike and the following defeats in December of the workers' movement led by the Soviets had not spectacularly demonstrated the illusoriness of any calculations on the 'brilliant isolation' of the proletariat as a condition favouring the struggle of the working-class for power and for Socialism. But in the 'post-December' process of the return of Menshevism as a whole to its fundamental conceptions certain contradictions also continued for some time, as we shall see. These had been stimulated by the 'days of liberty' but they also found renewed sustenance in the events of the succeeding months and years. In any case, in responding to the taunting by some bourgeois-democratic circles of the discord in the ranks of the Social-Democracy, Lenin (in an attempt, characteristic of the time, to belittle fraction differences) was able with some justice to write:

> In the *Severny Golos* the Mensheviks together with the Bolsheviks called for a strike and an uprising, called on the workers not to curtail the struggle until the power was in their hands. The revolutionary background in and for itself suggested the practical slogans. Disputes seemed to be mere details in the assessment of the events; *Nachalo*, for instance, regarded the Soviets of Workers' Deputies as organs of revolutionary self-government, *Novaya Zhizn* as embryonic organs of revolutionary power that united the proletariat and the revolutionary democracy. *Nachalo* was inclined towards a dictatorship of the proletariat, *Novaya Zhizn* held the viewpoint of the democratic dictatorship of the proletariat

* Martov (as well as Akselrod and Plekhanov) stubbornly opposed the growth of 'Trotskyite' trends in Menshevism; they tried to stand firmly on the terrain of the Menshevik conception of the bourgeois character of the revolution, of the bourgeoisie as the only possible recipient of power, and the fateful significance of the 'isolation' of the proletariat for itself as well as for the fate of the revolution. The discord between his own views at the time and the tendencies of a substantial segment of the Mensheviks was sensed by Martov so painfully that it deprived him of any desire to take part in the Stockholm congress and in general substantially curtailed his party activity. In May 1906 he was arrested and deported abroad; he was unable to return until 1913. This was also the reason why in 1906–7 it was not Martov but the author of these lines who appeared to the outside world as the official representative, so to speak, of Menshevism.

and peasantry. But surely such and similar differences within the Social-Democracy would be shown by any period at all in the development of any Socialist party at all?[170]

But the fact that *Novaya Zhizn*, *in principle*, 'held the viewpoint of the democratic dictatorship of the proletariat and peasantry' had just as little effect in preventing the appearance in its columns of articles of a 'Trotskyite' deviation as the appearance of such articles in the pages of *Nachalo* was prevented by the circumstance that *in principle* all the Menshevik members of its editorial board without exception held as before the same viewpoint that had been expressed in the resolutions of the May conference of 1905. Still less did it prevent the constantly growing colouring of the political agitation of both fractions by this 'deviation'. It was not a mere slip of the tongue for Lenin himself to indicate in the passage just quoted that the united Bolshevik-Menshevik editorial board of the *Severny Golos* called on the *workers* 'not to curtail the struggle until power was in *their* hands'. For whatever might have been the theoretical views of each of the fractions, the 'practical slogans', as Lenin correctly said, were 'suggested' to them both by the 'revolutionary background'. But this background of the 'days of liberty' was such, as we have seen, that practically speaking both Mensheviks and Bolsheviks were pushed towards 'Trotskyism'.* For a short time 'Trotskyism' (which at that time, to be sure, still lacked a name), for the first and last time in the history of the Russian Social-Democracy, became its unifying platform. Hence it was no accident also that after the arrest (in November) of Khrustalyov, the chairman of the Petersburg Soviet of Workers' Deputies, it was precisely Trotsky – who at this time had *de facto* left *Nachalo* and was independently editing the cheap, popular *Russkaya Gazeta* (the Russian Gazette) – who became his natural heir, challenged by no one – for the few short days the Soviet itself still had to live.†

* 'For a time we Mensheviks forgot the leitmotif of our tactics: to elude a premature isolation of the proletariat.'[171] In these words an eminent 'practical' of the Menshevik Social-Democracy of the time recalls the fundamental political zigzag undergone by the Mensheviks during the 'days of freedom' of 1905. It is only in retrospect, forty years later, that he explains this – through the shortcomings of Menshevik memory – as due to 'forgetting'.

† After the arrest of the plenary assembly of the Soviet and of Trotsky himself, Parvus became chairman of the Petersburg Soviet. But at this time the Soviet itself was losing its previous character and significance; it was turning into an illegal organization forced to assemble in secret and with extremely few members.

But the *rapprochement* between the fractions took place not only on the terrain of the great political problems of the revolution, but also on the terrain of the vast organizational, agitational, and propagandistic work that the Social-Democracy had begun during the pre-revolutionary days and carried on with tenfold zeal during the 'days of liberty'.

As noted before, after 9 January both fractions of the Social-Democracy oriented themselves towards an 'armed uprising', as an inevitable phase of the revolution. This unity of orientation concealed, however, a profound difference in the understanding of the tasks of the Social-Democracy with respect to the uprising. The Menshevik approach to the problem was emphatically 'political', the Bolshevik emphatically 'military-technical'. There was also a profound difference in the assessment of the very significance of the uprising.

The Bolshevik Congress in May 1905 proclaimed the task of organizing the proletariat for the 'armed uprising' to be 'one of the principal tasks of the Party at the present revolutionary moment'. It could with perfect justice have said not 'one of the principal' but *the* 'principal', since it was just this task that turned out to be paramount in all its resolutions without exception. It was in the light of this that every single point on the agenda was debated and decided. Even the 'mass political strikes' were regarded as a mere auxiliary means 'that might have some importance in the beginning and in the course of the uprising'. It goes without saying that the Congress charged all Party organizations to 'take the most energetic steps to arm the proletariat, as well as to work out a plan for the armed uprising and its direct leadership, creating as many special groups of Party functionaries as needed for this purpose'.

The Menshevik Conference, on the contrary, having mentioned the Provisional Government that had emerged from the uprising as one of the possible forms of 'decisive victory of the revolution', never returned to the question of the uprising again. For the Mensheviks the 'armed uprising' was not an all-defining occasion in the development of the revolution, as it was for the Bolsheviks, but merely one of the transient episodes of that development. It is true that a special commission of the Conference worked out drafts of resolutions about 'arming' and about 'agitation among the troops'. But, as a description of the real place occupied by problems of this kind in the ideas of Menshevism, nothing is more indicative than the fact that in this commission not one of the *Iskra* editors took part. Not only that, but the Conference left without reviewing the drafts worked out by the commission, 'because of lack of time'.

In spite of the expectations, it may be said of all trends in the Russian Social-Democracy without exception, the mass revolutionary movement unleashed on 9 January did not 'slip' into an uprising. The victory over the autocracy – which was, to be sure, very far from decisive, in the sense given this expression by the resolution of the Bolshevik Congress – was won by that movement by methods of political strike without 'transforming' it into an uprising. To be sure a third strike, in December, was apparently 'transformed' into a number of uprisings (Moscow, Latvia, and a few other districts and cities). But this strike itself was not an act of political advance on the part of the working-class, but an act of self-defence, forced on it as a protest against the arrest of the general assembly of the Petersburg Soviet. Thus the December uprisings proved to be rearguard and moreover local skirmishes of the revolution, which was stopped half-way by hostile forces, and far from the first step in its upsurge to a 'higher stage' of the organized and 'all-national' armed onslaught on the autocracy with the aim of liquidating it 'decisively' and replacing it by a democratic republic headed by a Provisional Government of a worker-peasant dictatorship.*

* Anticipating ourselves, we must remark here that the path of an 'armed uprising' in the Bolshevik version was not followed by the February-March revolution of 1917 either; this decisively cast the Russian autocracy into its historic grave, set up in its place the Provisional Government, proclaimed a democratic republic, and made Russia, as Lenin himself admitted in his *April Theses*, the 'freest country in the world'. In their classic form, the Bolshevik methods of 'armed uprising', scheduled beforehand, prepared, organized, and led by a 'staff of trained revolutionaries' and so on, were applied only in the October-November revolution of the same year, when the aim of the uprising was no longer the overthrow of an autocracy, but the overthrow of the Provisional Government – not the establishment of a democratic republic but its replacement by a new 'Soviet order', whose direct result was not a democratic dictatorship of the proletariat and peasantry but a Socialist dictatorship of the Communist Party. Thus, in the historic situation of Russia of the first quarter of the twentieth century, 'political democracy' proved to be an indispensable premise for an 'armed uprising' in its Bolshevik version, and far from its eventual goal. It was only this premise that developed the agitational and organizational activity among the masses and troops indispensable for the preparation and realization of such an uprising, and for the utilization of the hundreds of thousands of peasants, refractory to military discipline but well armed and concentrated in the country's political centres, without which the uprising could scarcely have been feasible.

The December defeats proved to be no transient fiasco, but the historic epilogue of a whole period in the revolutionary workers' movement that was unleashed by 9 January. But it was not until much later that even the Mensheviks were able to grasp their significance. Assumptions of the possibility and even the likelihood of a renewal of the uprising in the most immediate future – of an uprising, of course, that would be far broader, 'all-national' in its dimensions and thus successful – entered into their tactical constructions throughout almost the whole of 1906. It was only towards the London Congress (spring 1907) that Menshevism firmly made up its mind that 'after December 1905 the Mensheviks had underestimated the extent of the defeat', and that it was impossible to expect ' "mass pressure" [i.e. a new upsurge of the mass revolutionary movement – T.D.] which, in the final analysis, was inevitable . . . so quickly as the Menshevik resolutions of the Stockholm Congress had assumed'.[172]

The Bolsheviks even clung substantially longer to the viewpoint that Lenin formulated immediately after 'December' and that he repeated in February 1906. This was to the effect that 'the crushing of the Moscow and other uprisings' was 'merely the preparation of the terrain for a new, more decisive armed struggle' and hence that 'now was just the time for the question of an uprising to be placed on the agenda, on the basis of the practical experience that had been gained proving the possibility of a struggle against troops and outlining the immediate tasks of a more tenacious and patient preparation of the subsequent advance'.[173]

It was not only the general problems of this 'subsequent advance' but also the concrete details of its 'preparation' that Lenin's thought was intensively at work on during the next few years. At the end of July 1906 he reacted to the dispersal of the first Duma by a pamphlet (*The Dispersal of the Duma and the Tasks of the Proletariat*)[174] in which he categorically declared that 'in the given state of affairs . . . on the occasion of the Duma's dispersal, there can be no doubt that an active struggle leads directly to an uprising', and that 'because of this to call for an all-Russian strike without calling for an uprising . . . would be outright lightmindedness bordering on the criminal. . . . Now particularly we must explain in our agitation the necessity . . . of a military organization together with an organization of the Soviets for their defence, for the execution of the uprising. . . .' Such 'military organizations' in their turn, 'must have as their nucleus very small, voluntary unions, tens, fives, perhaps even threes'. Foreseeing the possibility that the 'new struggle' would not 'flare up so unexpectedly or so spontaneously as the preceding one', and that 'the events will demand from us leadership and the designation of a time for the advance', Lenin gave detailed instructions for such a case: 'If it were to turn out this way, then we would advise that an all-Russian strike and uprising be designated towards the beginning or end of August.' However, the 'agreement of *all* [Lenin's italics] influential revolutionary organizations and unions on the timing . . . is indispensable'.

We see how immediately imminent at that time the 'armed uprising' seemed to Lenin. But even after the Bolsheviks too had to set back dates to the indefinite future, the orientation towards the coming 'armed uprising' continued to colour the entire political tactics of Bolshevism; it became the most fundamental of the elements defining both its relationship to all current problems and the evolution in its political thought that found its definitive consummation in the revolution of 1917, that brought it to a definitive rupture with the Social-Democracy, and that made Soviet Communism its ideological banner.

However, independently of the role played in the political ideology of either fraction by the orientation towards the 'armed uprising', in fact they both had to busy themselves more and more not so much with the problems of the uprising, which remained a prospect of a future that grew more and more indefinite, as with the political and organizational problems that were uniformly suggested by the 'revolutionary background' outlined above. But these happened to be problems of the organization of the general revolutionary 'movement of emancipation', especially the organization and consolidation of the positions of the proletariat as a class. It was these problems that in Menshevik strategy and tactics were shelved completely in favour of the problems of the 'uprising' that Menshevik thought was preoccupied by. This explains why it was the lot of Menshevism to play the role of a pioneer, an initiator, a trail-blazer – not only in the pre-revolutionary months and during the 'days of liberty', but also throughout the succeeding period of semi-constitutionalism down to the revolution of 1917, the political organizer, spokesman, and leader of whose first stage was also Menshevism.

We have seen how the Russian 'movement of emancipation' developed, how it spontaneously, by a series of 'partial advances' that became more and more frequent, more and more 'combative', broke the framework of the autocratic law and 'physically' 'seized' for itself the rights of free speech, assembly, strike, street demonstrations, congresses and unions. In contrast to the Bolsheviks, who were afraid that the 'movement of emancipation' would flare up and die down in these 'partial' advances before the occasion could arrive for a decisive 'all-national' tussle with the autocracy, and who consequently insisted on the necessity of 'husbanding forces' until that occasion (as we have seen these fears were partly shared at the time by Parvus and Trotsky) it was precisely in these 'partial' advances that the Mensheviks saw a powerful stimulus of revolutionary forces and the decomposition of the Tsarist 'apparatus'. Hence they made their slogan not the 'husbanding of forces' but the 'unloosing' of the revolution. But, going further, they sought to strengthen these partial and episodic break-throughs into the domain of political liberty, by creating for the defence and exploitation of the rights that were 'physically' obtained just as many 'physical' organizations of every possible type. The slogan of 'revolutionary self-government', which gave this idea a generalized expression, became, together with the slogan of 'unloosing' the revolution, the banner of Menshevism.

In the last analysis the manifest success of this tactic overcame the resistance of Bolshevism. A decisive role in this connexion was played by the idea of exploiting the 'autonomy' that was granted higher institutions of learning (27 August 1905). This idea had been advanced by *Iskra* and at first had also been met by Bolshevik hostility. *Iskra* proposed utilizing this autonomy, contrived as a way of conciliating the students and stopping the hopelessly protracted student strike, not, however, so much in order to resume academic pursuits as to open university auditoriums for popular meetings and mass-meetings. The *Iskra* slogan was taken up by an immense majority of the students, who had already begun being oppressed by the fragmentation, and hence passivity, they had been condemned to in the tempestuous whirlpool of events by the protracted strike. The Petersburg, Moscow and other universities and institutes of higher learning became, in the pre-October and October days, genuine centres of mass agitation for all revolutionary parties. A torrent of people passed through their auditoriums from morning to night. Their role in the organization of the October victory also proved quite exceptional. They had a special significance for the revolutionized petty-bourgeois strata of the cities; it was at these 'university' mass-meetings that for the first time they came into close contact with both the labouring masses and the revolutionary parties. All doubts were stilled by the obviousness of this role.

But for the Mensheviks, as is known, all this activity of unloosing and organizing a general revolutionary movement was focused on the task of exploiting the movement for the organization and reinforcement of the class positions of the proletariat. 'In the present revolutionary upsurge . . . all social classes are entering the arena of a broad and open political struggle; the various elements of bourgeois society are seeking support among the masses of the people,' said the Menshevik Conference of May 1905 in an explanation of the resolutions it had passed. 'Among the masses of the proletariat an effort, characteristic of this occasion and stronger than in any other class, is being made to organize on the terrain of the defence of its political and professional interests. It is vital for the Social-Democracy to take possession of this powerful movement.'

By way of concretizing this general disposition, a resolution, passed by the same Conference, 'On the Economic Struggle', emphasized that 'the Social-Democracy had to exploit' a situation that was 'especially favourable for the working-class', which it had won by its 'heroic struggle' against Tsarism, 'in order for the proletariat to win for itself, in the course of the bourgeois revolution, the most important positions, which in its further struggle for social emancipation would be able to ensure its success'. Hence 'the Conference considers it indispensable for the Party, in its agitation during the revolutionary period, to lead with special energy the struggle for the establishment of a maximum working-day of eight hours, with unrestricted freedom of strikes and unions'. In its turn, the resolution 'On Trade unions', taking as its starting-point that 'the revolution . . . not only would not eliminate capitalist relations of production, but would give a new and powerful impetus of their development', and that 'against the background of revolutionary ferment the conquest of' the rights of free organization and strikes, indispensable for the working-class, 'was substantially facilitated', it recommended to all Party organizations: '(1) The furthering of all efforts of the workers to create unions for the defence of their professional interests, and an appeal for the organization of such unions in spite of the prohibitory laws still in existence; (2) The arrangement for regular meetings of representatives of individual trade unions or plenipotentiaries of industrial institutions (foremen, deputies, etc.) with the aim of setting up permanent liaison between them; (3) The support of a permanent liaison between the Party organizations and the trade unions and constant assistance to them by whatever forces and technical means are at the disposition of the Party.' Finally, passing to a domain where the socio-economic struggle of the proletariat coincided with its political struggle, the Conference passed a resolution on the 'shapeless organizations' that in the next few months were going to play a decisive role in the tactic of the Social-Democracy and create the possibility of close contact between it and the revolutionary movement. The resolution reads:

> In the present atmosphere of revolutionary ferment among the broad masses all kinds of shapeless mergers are arising among the workers. In uniting the workers, without distinction of trades, on the ground of socio-economic and political needs common to the whole working-class, these mergers, by virtue of the historic background, will become the starting-points of the political fusion of the proletariat. . . . The Conference recommends:
> 1. The furthering of such mergers, and
> 2. That they be turned into permanent revolutionary organizations of the proletariat led by the Social-Democracy (revolutionary workers' clubs), which have set themselves the goal of direct intervention in socio-political life in the interests of the working-class.

But in setting the Social-Democracy such broad tasks as the sponsorship of all kinds of 'non-party' workers' organizations, both trade-union and political, Menshevism saw in the fulfilment of such tasks not only the sole reliable path towards the broadening of class conquests and the strengthening of the class positions of the proletariat in the bourgeois revolution, but also a means of radically reforming the Social-Democratic Party itself. In the words of the Conference: 'The necessity of a basic reform of the organization of Party activity has become especially urgent during the present revolutionary upsurge.' And in conditions of that upsurge it was the 'taking possession' of the 'powerful movement' of the proletarian masses and the involvement in the ranks of the Social-Democracy of all the 'thinking elements generated by the proletariat' in the course of that movement that had to serve as the instrument of the reformation of the Party. It had to be converted from an organization leading the labouring masses 'from the side' and in its turn being led by the revolutionarily-inclined intellectuals from a bourgeois *milieu*, into a self-governing organization of the labouring masses themselves, no longer headed by a bourgeois but by a workers' 'intelligentsia', to help in whose political and Socialist education constituted, in fact, the historic obligation of the Social-Democrats. It was Akselrod who paid special attention to the problems of re-forming the Party; it was he who just at this time put forward the ideas of an all-Russian 'workers' congress' of all trade-union, political, cultural and other workers' organizations, as the decisive stage on the path to the creation of a completely new mass medium for the Social-Democratic organization in Russia and for completely new methods and forms of activity.

The ideas and trends of the just-quoted resolutions were milestones of the future activity of the Social-Democracy during the 'days of liberty' and the following years of semi-constitutionalism. This created extremely complicated and contradictory conditions of 'semi-legality'. But these ideas and trends themselves generalized the expression of the activity actually begun by Menshevism even before 9 January, but developed with special energy afterwards. As has already been remarked, 9 January jolted forward the broad advance of the workers' movement. It very soon assumed a predominantly economic character, accompanied by attempts to create non-party workers' organizations for the conduct of a professional trade-union struggle and for the consolidation of its gains. How broad the dimensions were that this movement assumed may be seen if only from the fact that as many as 200,000 registered members were in the trade organizations that came out in the open during the October 'days of liberty'.

Menshevik organizations too had been very energetic beforehand in giving every possible kind of help in the economic struggle of the proletariat and in the origination of 'self-appointed' trade unions that later on was laid upon them as an obligation by the May Conference. But they applied themselves to the creation and consolidation of those 'shapeless organizations' that precisely by virtue of their 'general-worker' and not craft character, could not help but become organs of working-class mobilization. We shall see what role was played by the idea of this type of organization in the definition of the attitude of Menshevism towards the elections to the consultative 'Bulygin' Duma that the government, by announcing its convocation in the middle of August, had hoped would break off any further development of the 'movement of emancipation', but that was broken off by this movement itself even before the drafts outlined had begun to be realized.

But the Mensheviks succeeded in carrying out this work practically too – in direct connexion with 9 January, when the government enjoined the Senator Shidlovsky to convoke a special commission of the elected representatives of the Petersburg workers to discuss their claims and needs.

The Mensheviks responded to the announcement of the Shidlovsky Commission by calling on the workers of all factories and workshops in the capital to hold general meetings to elect electors. These were afterwards supposed to appoint deputies from their midst as members of the Commission, but above all were to enter into negotiations with Shidlovsky about the guarantees of freedom of speech and assembly and the inviolability of the workers' electors and future deputies, without which both further elections and the activity of the Commission itself were impossible. When the government refused to give these guarantees the workers' electors refused to collaborate with the Commission, which accordingly never met. But aside from the immense agitational activity performed in connexion with the elections, they served as a sort of rehearsal for the far more broad-gauge elections of the plenipotentiaries of the Petersburg factories and workshops that in the October days gave rise to the Petersburg Soviet of Workers' Deputies. Historically this was the most massive political and organizational achievement of the proletariat in the revolution of 1905, and it gave impetus to the creation of similar Soviets in all the industrial centres of Russia and became the prototype of the Soviets of Workers' (later Workers' and Soldiers') Deputies of 1917, which were imitated in the international workers' movement and later became the foundation of the Bolshevik state. The workers' plenipotentiaries elected at the summons of the Petersburg Menshevik Group came together on the night of 13 October, in one of the auditoriums of the Technological Institute, under the chairmanship of a member of the Group, L. Zborovsky (Kuzma). It was at this historic session that the first Soviet of Workers' Deputies was founded.

It was not, of course, easy for the Bolsheviks to reconcile these innovational methods of 'unloosing' the revolution and its 'organizations' with their own general ideas. It was still more difficult for them to place these methods within the framework of their own organizational traditions, whose foundations had been laid by Lenin's *What Is to Be Done?* It was only natural that Bolshevism's initial reaction to these methods was a definite hostility to the very idea of a struggle of the workers' movement for 'legality' while still in the preparatory stage of the revolution. It sharply opposed a tactic that strove to turn the broad and non-party forms of political and professional rallying of the workers, which had arisen precisely in a 'physical' sense and in direct connexion with the mass movement, into a fundamental bulwark of the revolution, a fundamental lever for working-class influence on it, and a fundamental arena for the application of the ideological activity of the Social-Democracy.

What the Bolsheviks did was to counterpose the slogan of boycott to the Menshevik appeal for the election of plenipotentiary workers to the Shidlovsky Commission. Nor did the struggle for the semi-legal trade unions meet with their sympathy. We have seen how Lenin (in *Two Tactics*) reproached the Mensheviks especially because 'now', when the struggle for 'political democracy' was on the order of the day, they were 'giving first priority to the trade unions'. *Vperyod* even expressed the idea that in the revolutionary epoch being lived through the organization of workers' trade unions could tranquilly be left 'to the liberals'. The Bolsheviks had to revise their views of the trade union movement radically to make possible the unanimous acceptance, at the Stockholm Congress in the spring of 1906, of a resolution obliging the Party to further in every way the organization of trade unions and Party members to take an active part in them.

At first the Bolsheviks also behaved with hostile wariness with respect to the formation of a 'non-party' Soviet of Workers' Deputies. They saw in this a possible political rival of the Social-Democratic Party and in any case a hindrance to the authoritarian Party leadership of the workers' movement that was one of the fundamental mainstays of their political and organizational programme. An agitational campaign was conducted at the Petersburg factories and workshops by the Petersburg Bolshevik Committee that went on almost until the end of November. Its slogans vacillated between a demand for the passage by the Soviet of the Social-Democratic programme or its official submission to the leadership of the Social-Democratic Party, and a demand for its conversion into a purely trade union organization that would defend the economic interests of the workers but decline any political functions. It was only when the Soviets of 1905 were already beginning to leave the stage *de facto* that the Bolshevik attitude towards them was subjected to the same principled revision as the Bolshevik attitude towards the trade unions and every variety of 'non-party' workers' organizations had been subjected to in general.

It goes without saying that this revision was not applied all at once. For a long time each new upsurge of hope for the imminence of a new flight of the revolution was accompanied by lapses into the old purely negative attitude towards the struggle for legal and semi-legal forms of economic and political organization of the working-class until a 'decisive victory' over the autocracy was won. But the 'revolutionary background' more and more insistently 'suggested' another approach to these organizations, and the 'boycottist' attitude towards them was gradually replaced by their 'acceptance' and by the attempt to find methods of 'exploiting' them that would make participation in them useful from the point of view of the general conception of Bolshevism.

Questions of this order had already cropped up for the Bolshevik Congress of May 1905 to cope with. A resolution it passed 'on the attitude towards the government's tactics on the eve of the "overturn" ', states that 'the government, with the aim of self-preservation . . . in intensifying the customary repression . . . (1) is trying by way of concessions and promises of reform to corrupt the working-class politically, and thus draw it away from the revolutionary struggle; (2) with the same aim it is masking its hypocritical policy of concessions in pseudo-democratic forms, beginning with the invitation to the workers to elect their own representatives to commissions and councils [the Shidlovsky Commission T.D.] and ending with the creation of caricatural forms of popular representation [the Bulygin Duma T.D.] . . . . (3) it is organizing the so-called Black Hundreds'.

In response to this governmental tactic the Congress proposed '(1) to unmask the reactionary aims of the governmental concessions . . . (2) by exploiting the pre-electoral agitation . . . to prove the necessity to the proletariat of convoking in a revolutionary manner a constituent assembly on the basis of a universal, equal, and direct electoral law with a secret ballot; (3) to organize the proletariat for the immediate realization by revolutionary methods of the eight-hour working day and of other working-class demands . . . (4) to organize armed resistance to the actions of the Black Hundreds and in general to all forms of reactionary elements led by the government.'

The difference between the Bolshevik and Menshevik approaches to the problem is plain. For the Mensheviks every 'concession', whatever might have been the actual intentions of the government, was a surrender of one position or another imposed by the revolution on the autocracy. It was the task of the revolution to occupy this position without delay and turn it into a new support point for a further onslaught on the autocratic régime. For the Bolsheviks a 'concession' was merely a manœuvre aimed at 'politically corrupting' the labouring masses and 'drawing them away from the revolutionary struggle'. There could be no 'concessions' to be exploited directly for the objectives of the revolution. The few favourable circumstances they created, such as, for instance, the elections, could be exploited only in order to 'unmask' the reactionary character of the concessions and to counterpose 'revolutionary paths' to methods of exploiting them. But the difference of the Bolshevik from the Menshevik attitude of that period was even more characteristically expressed in a resolution of the third Congress that bore directly on the 'legal or semi-legal' workers' organizations.

The resolution states that, (1) under the pressure of the revolutionary movement 'the autocratic government . . . finds itself forced to allow some liberty of political action to classes hostile to it', and that (2) 'this freedom of political action is made use of now primarily by the bourgeois classes'. This exaggerates 'the danger of turning the working-class into a mere appendage of bourgeois democracy'. But 'among the labouring masses the striving towards an independent and open emergence into the political arena, even without any participation of the Social-Democracy, is also become more and more widely eveident'. Bolshevism did not see, in this 'striving', the historically novel factor that was going to create completely new possibilities both for the Russian revolution as a whole and the class movement of the proletariat in it, and for the Russian Social-Democracy itself, and that had to have a revolutionary significance from now on, accordingly, for all Social-Democratic tactics. Bolshevism approached 'the legal and semi-legal' workers' organizations for the most part from the point of view of their danger for the existing Party organization, if they were to develop 'without the participation of the Social-Democracy', and hence it sought a chance to convert them, on the contrary, into a source of strength for the Party. The sole directive given by the resolution reads as follows: 'To exploit all legal or semi-legal workers' societies, unions, and other organizations in order to ensure the Social-Democracy a predominant influence over them, and to turn them as far as possible into points of support for a future Social-Democratic workers' party in Russia.'

There was a purely 'Party' approach to the problem expressed in the very heading of the resolution, dedicated not to the 'open and independent emergence' of the labouring masses, but to the 'open political emergence of the R.S.D.W.P.' But this approach far from signified an orientation towards those party-reform plans that were linked by Menshevism to an open emergence of the labouring masses into the political arena. The final directive point of the resolution shows that it had in mind merely the episodic, primarily combat 'open actions' of the Party, or of those of its organs specially designed for such actions.

In contradistinction to the resolution on 'concessions', the resolution on open and semi-open forms of the workers' movement already outlines the possibilities and objectives of their 'exploitation' that had come to replace pure 'boycottism' and that, even though after some delay, was in the last analysis applied to the government's 'concessions', too.

According to the resolution, the task of exploiting the legal and semi-legal workers' organizations must consist of their conversion into props for the Social-Democratic Party. But to implement this task by impelling them to accept the programme of the Social-Democratic Party or place themselves under its leadership, that is, renounce their own 'non-partisanship', proved impossible. All attempts in this direction led to nothing but acute conflicts between the Bolshevik Party committees and the ubiquitously emerging workers' mass organizations, including the Soviet of Workers' Deputies, and threatened to isolate Bolshevism from the workers' movement. Hence, largely under the influence of Bolshevik local and lower-echelon functionaries, the tactic of 'conquering' these organizations for the Party as it were 'from outside' began to give way to the tactic of 'exploiting' them 'from within'. This was done by forming cells within them of 'self-restrained and trained revolutionaries', who without attacking their 'non-party' character and while collaborating with them in the execution of their specific tasks – trade union, educational, etc., down to and including political – at the same time tried to exploit the positions won by them in the socio-political arena, their technical-organizational apparatus, and their human personnel, for those special goals the Bolshevik Party was setting itself quite independently of them. Thus there arose the embryos of those 'cells' that were later to play an enormous role in the successes not only of Russian Bolshevism but of international Communism.

For Bolshevism, in the conditions of 1905–6, the guiding idea behind this 'exploitation' of course had to be the preparation of the 'all-national armed uprising' that seemed at the time to be very close and in which it saw the sole path towards the 'decisive victory' over the autocracy and its replacement by a 'democratic dictatorship of the proletariat and peasantry'. It was from this point of view that the Bolshevik 'theory' of the Soviets took shape, in a form, of course, that took some time to be perfected.

In November 1905 Lenin, polemicizing against the Menshevik view of the Soviets, wrote as follows: 'The Soviet of Workers' Deputies is not a workers' parliament, not an organ of proletarian self-government, and not an organ of self-government altogether, but a combat organization for the attainment of definite goals. . . . Hence it is entirely natural to include in its Executive Committee the representatives of the revolutionary peasantry as well. The essence of the matter is that the Soviet of Workers' Deputies is a shapeless, broad combat union of Socialists and revolutionary democrats. . . . In such a union it is plainly necessary to carry on political strikes and other more active forms of struggle for the basic democratic demands acknowledged and approved by the gigantic majority of the populace.'[175] Thus the first explanation of the 'necessity' of such broad organizations with no partisan shape, like the Soviets, boils down to their identification with the 'combat unions of the Socialists and revolutionary democrats', which the resolution of the third Congress on the S.R.s had already declared to be organs for the preparation and execution of the armed uprising in its Bolshevik interpretation. (The article speaks allegorically of 'more active forms of struggle' in order to avoid pouring water into the mill of the conservative and reactionary circles that had more and more insistently begun demanding anti-Soviet repressions.)

A further step towards the reconciling of the assessment of the Soviets with the general ideas of Bolshevism was taken by a draft resolution Lenin wrote for the Stockholm Congress in January–February 1906.

After saying that the Soviets 'arise spontaneously on the terrain of mass political strikes as the non-party organizations of the labouring masses at large', the draft maintained that in the course of struggle they changed both their composition, drawing into their ranks 'the most revolutionary forces of the petty-bourgeoisie', and their activity. They were transformed 'from purely strike organizations into embryos of revolutionary power'. And in so far as this was so 'their strength and significance depended on the strength and success of the uprising'. This led to the conclusion that not only a positive attitude towards the spontaneously emerging Soviets, but also the 'creation of such organizations . . . might in certain conditions be the objective of the local organizations of our Party', and that it was important to draw into the Soviets 'the broadest possible strata of workers, and also the representatives of the revolutionary democracy, especially the peasants, soldiers, and sailors'. But at the same time

> it was indispensable, with the enlarging of the activity and sphere of influence of the Soviets, to point out that such institutions, in not being supported by a revolutionary army and in not overthrowing the government (that is, in not being transformed into provisional revolutionary governments) were inevitably destined to collapse; hence the arming of the people and the strengthening of the military organization of the proletariat had to be regarded as one of the principal tasks of such institutions in every revolutionary situation.

Finally, the last systematic exposition of his own views of the Soviets was given by Lenin at the end of July 1906 in an already-mentioned pamphlet (*Dispersal of the Duma*). 'The Soviets of Workers' Deputies are organs of direct mass struggle,' he wrote.

> They arose as organs of a strike struggle. Very rapidly, under the pressure of necessity, they became the organ of a general-revolutionary struggle against the government. Irresistibly, by virtue of the development of events and the transition from a strike to an uprising, they were transformed into organs of an uprising. . . . But for the organization of an uprising 'Soviets' and similar mass institutions are still insufficient. . . . They are insufficient for the direct organization of combat forces, for the organization of an uprising in the narrowest sense of the word.

Having laid down in this article his (already cited) reflections on the necessity, both for the defence of the Soviets themselves and for the carrying out of the uprising, of special 'military organizations'* that in their turn were supported by combat 'tens, fives and even perhaps threes', Lenin formulated his own definitive judgement of the Soviets in connexion with the question of the Provisional Government:

> The question of the Provisional Government has been adequately explained on the theoretical side. The possibility for the Social-Democracy to take part in it has been proven. But what is more interesting now is

* During the Bolshevik uprising in October to November 1917 these 'military organizations' assumed the form, as is well known, of 'military-revolutionary committees'.

> another practical formulation of this question given by October-December. In fact, after all, the Soviets of Workers' Deputies and so on were embryos of a provisional government; if the uprising had been successful they would inevitably have secured power. We must transfer the centre of gravity to a study of these historically given embryonic organs of the new power. This is more vital . . . at the given moment than surmises 'in general' concerning the provisional revolutionary government.

When Lenin wrote these lines the 'practical formulation of the question' was of purely academic significance. At that time the Soviets had already left the scene, not for a short time, as Lenin thought, but as it turned out for a full eleven years. But these ideas of his about the meaning and possible role of the Soviet of Workers' Deputies received an unusual significance in the general process of the Russian revolution when these Soviets were revived in the very first days of the February-March revolution of 1917. It was 1917 that showed how much Lenin's general conception, oriented towards a struggle for power against the bourgeoisie, allowed him to draw far more penetrating and realistic conclusions from the brief experience of the Soviets' activity during the 'days of liberty' of 1905 than could the actual originators of the Soviets themselves – the Mensheviks.

As noted above, the whole evolution of the Soviets in the conditions of the 1905 revolution irresistibly made them tend towards a transformation into 'embryos of government'; the 'revolutionary background' insistently 'suggested' this conclusion not only to the Bolsheviks but to the Mensheviks too. Yet Menshevik thinking, bound as it was by its basic conception of the bourgeoisie as the historically foreordained heir of the autocracy, was unable either to anchor itself firmly in this conclusion or to think it through consistently. After a relatively short-lived zigzag Menshevism returned to this conception in its most orthodox version, and from this point of view retroactively subjected its whole political conduct in 1905–6 to a merciless critique. In particular it strengthened its theoretical understanding of the Soviets as organizations of 'workers' self-government'. These were called upon to defend the class interests of the proletariat during the bourgeois revolution and to 'push' the bourgeoisie towards the maximum of socio-political radicalism, but not at all to enter into a struggle for power against it, or to strive to maintain a position of 'extreme opposition' throughout the revolution.

The dogmatic and historically illusory attitude towards the Soviets bound up with the whole conception of Menshevism played a fateful role in its own destiny during the 1917 revolution and in the destiny of the February-March period of this revolution itself. For at each stage of that revolution the tendency inherent in the Soviets towards their transformation into organs of power made its presence felt even more irresistibly than in its 'historical rehearsal' – the revolution of 1905. But as it took shape historically, Menshevism, which led the Soviets in 1917 also, proved to be in uninterrupted conflict with all the manifestations of this tendency. It was incapable of conquering it, but the upshot of the situation was the 'dual power', the simultaneous presence of two authorities – the power of the Soviet headed by the Mensheviks and the power of the democratic coalition of the Provisional Government they were members of. Formally these supported each other, but in fact they disorganized, emasculated and paralysed each other. It was this that prepared the destruction of the whole February-March republican-democratic system, and Menshevism, which during the first weeks and months of the revolution had been placed at its head by the workers' vanguard, had the ground cut away from under it with every day that passed. Nevertheless it was only two or three years later that Menshevism, having overcome in its 'Martov' tendency its own sociological conception of the Russian revolution, was also able to overcome its own dogmatic attitude towards the Soviets, out of whose matrix a power really did appear in September-October 1917. It was not, to be sure, the power that had been visualized by Lenin in 1905–6; it was not a democratic dictatorship of the proletariat and peasantry, but a Socialist dictatorship of the Bolshevik Party itself.

It has been shown above how the 'revolutionary background' of 1905 demonstrated the illusoriness in fact of the general-political schemata of Menshevism and Bolshevism alike. In the political actuality of the time there was no such thing as a 'bourgeoisie' that the working-class was able to 'push' into power, but neither was there that 'revolutionary-republican' peasantry that constituted the cornerstone of the Bolshevik idea. In so far as the 1905 Soviets succeeded in drawing into their ranks 'the most revolutionary elements of the petty-bourgeoisie', these were not so much elements of the 'revolutionary peasantry' (as we have seen, Lenin himself speaks of the inclusion of its representatives only as a task still confronting the Soviets) as elements of the radical, 'emancipationist' intelligentsia, which the above-cited letter on the *Attitude towards the Liberals* and the resolution of the Bolshevik May Congress both listed as part of the 'bourgeois-liberal', 'anti-revolutionary and counter-proletarian' sector of the opposition.*

It is true that in the 1905 Soviets of Workers' Deputies the S.R. Party was also represented. But while 'peasant' in its programme this party was unable to represent the peasantry *politically*, in the sense in which the Social-Democracy represented the working-class. The preponderant mass of the Russian peasantry, especially of the former serfs, was unified by the attempt to aggrandize its own land-ownership and land-exploitation at the expense of the land-owners', ecclesiastical, noblemen's, and even merchants' land. It was also unified by the demand for the elimination of all civil restrictions of rights that placed the peasantry in the position of the 'lowest estate'. But purely political tendencies remained extremely feeble in the peasantry. Not only its well-to-do 'kulak' stratum, but its 'intermediate' mass and even the 'rural paupers' also proved incapable of creating a revolutionary-political movement similar in any degree to that which had drawn almost the entire working-class of Russia to a man into its orbit during the first decade of the twentieth century. As for the organization in any breadth of the masses of the peasantry under the banner of the struggle for a 'republican-democratic' programme, the subject never even arose.

Under these conditions the S.R. Party was destined to remain the 'extreme Left', revolutionary wing of the liberal intelligentsia. This was, to be sure, to a considerable degree a Zemstvo intelligentsia, that is, closely linked to the peasantry, predominantly to its 'middle' strata, not only through its social sympathies but also by its occupations and way of life. Under Russian conditions the S.R.s were unable to become a 'peasant' party in the sense in which the Russian Social-Democracy became a 'workers' ' party. They were unable to, not only in the 1905 but also in the 1917 revolution. This was never expressed with such clarity as in the astonishing fact that a party that had just received more than twenty million votes, mostly peasant votes, at the elections for the Constituent Assembly, proved incapable not only of forestalling its dispersal by the Bolsheviks on the very day of its convocation (5 January 1918), but also of summoning any discernible masses of the peasantry to its defence.

* It was only in the draft resolution for the Stockholm Congress and under the manifest influence of the Soviet experience of 1905 that Lenin listed as a 'revolutionary-democratic party and organization' not only the S.R.s and the

Thus, neither in 1905 nor in 1917 did Lenin succeed in exploiting the Soviets as a base for the formation of a government that was worker-peasant in its social composition and democratic-republican in its political programme.* Nor did he succeed in exploiting the Duma for this goal either.

The question of the attitude to be adopted towards the Duma arose before the Menshevik Conference and the Bolshevik Congress as early as May 1905, in connexion with the assignment given the new Minister of the Interior Bulygin to work out a draft for a consultative representative institution.

The Menshevik Conference backed participating in the elections for such an institution. The Mensheviks rested on this decision even when the statute on the Duma published on 6 August left no further doubt with respect to the limited scope of its full powers, or with respect to the reactionary intentions that dictated to the authors of the statute a many-staged process of election and the dividing up of the voters according to social 'estates', or, finally, with respect to the extreme limitation on the rights left to the workers. Placing their hopes on the invincible dynamic of the revolutionary process undergone by the country, the Mensheviks in these conditions too saw in the elections primarily a means of absorbing in the political 'movement of emancipation' the broadest masses of the backward urban lower middle-class and especially of the peasantry, which was left an extremely important proportion of the deputies' mandates because of the assumption of its 'loyalty to the throne'. Hence the Mensheviks spoke out in the most decisive way against boycotting the elections, especially against the tactic of the 'active' boycott, that is, the summoning of workers to a systematic breaking up of election meetings. At the time a considerable number of Party people believed in this, but it would have inevitably led to a clash between the workers and the petty-bourgeois and peasant voters, and have thrust the latter into the arms of reaction.

From the Menshevik point of view the elections opened up new

Peasant Union but also, if not all, at least a 'part of the semi-professional and political unions' in which this intelligentsia was grouped at the time.

* The involvement in the first membership of the first Soviet of People's Commissars of the so-called 'Left S.R.s', who split away from the core of the Party, was merely a brief episode; it had no significance from the point of view of the socio-political structure of the new régime, whose monopolistically Bolshevik character was incontestably obvious from the very first days on.

possibilities both for the general struggle for power and strengthening of the democratic liberties by 'physical' action, and for every form of 'revolutionary self-government' that coloured the whole tactic of Menshevism at this period. They created, finally, new support points for the class organization of the proletariat that was the central idea of Menshevism. In the given case *Iskra* supported the exploitation of the elections for the organization of workers' 'agitational committees' whose tasks included the struggle for a 'self-appointed' broadening of the circle of voters, to the point of making the elections 'universal' and presenting the college of electors with the demand that 'self-appointed' elected delegates be allowed to take an equal part in these colleges and that the slogan of the Constituent Assembly be supported. In this way the Mensheviks thought it possible, against the background of the growing mass revolutionary movement, to fight for the conversion of the 'Bulygin' Duma into something like the French *Etats-Généraux* of 1789, from which there emerged, as is well-known, first the Constituent Assembly and then the plenipotentiary Convention.

Akselrod developed these plans, plainly modelled on the great French Revolution, most consistently of all. In a pamphlet, *The People's Duma and the Workers' Congress*, he summoned the workers to a struggle for the creation, together with a 'legal', consultative State Duma based on a property assessment, of a 'self-appointed' elected People's Duma of a revolutionary nature based on a universal ballot, and at the same time for the construction of a 'broad-gauge workers' organization' that would hold both these Dumas under its own control: 'We must try to call into life a broad workers' organization headed by a central club . . . whose task it would be to rally the local proletariat and form a dense revolutionary atmosphere in control of and acting as dictator over both the "State Duma" and the "People's Duma".'[176]

The analogy with the French Jacobin clubs is evident. But the analogy – which reveals the inner defect and illusoriness of the Menshevik position – ends where the question of the revolutionary power begins. The French Jacobin clubs were organs of the Jacobin revolutionary power; in their own way they 'controlled' the Constituent Assembly and Convention and acted as 'dictator' over them. The 'Jacobin' clubs of the Russian workers had to 'control' the revolutionary power of the bourgeoisie while themselves striving to maintain throughout the course of the revolution the position of an 'extreme opposition'. But in such a form, divided from the revolutionary power and even alien to it by class, if not openly hostile, the workers' Jacobin clubs were turned into a utopia. In their duel with the revolutionary power, either that power had to annihilate them, or else they had to annihilate that power and turn themselves into a new power. After the 1905 'rehearsal' the revolution of 1917 proved incontrovertibly that in the socio-economic and political conditions of Russia in the first quarter of the twentieth century, the 'control' and 'dictatorship' of the revolutionary workers' clubs, which in essence is what the Soviets were, over the 'bourgeois' power that had emerged from the revolution, were historically inevitable. But for this same reason it was also historically inevitable that the power they 'controlled' be destroyed and that they themselves be converted into sources of a new power.

It is of course quite vain to speculate in retrospect to what degree the constantly broadening mass revolutionary movement would have succeeded in forcing the Bulygin Duma to serve it and in 'revolutionizing' it. The all-Russian political strike of October 1905 killed the very idea of a consultative Duma, and the Manifesto of 17 October proclaimed its imminent replacement by a legislative Duma. But the whole subsequent development showed how fruitful was the Menshevik initiative for a positive attitude towards a role both in the elections and in the activity in and around the Duma, both from the point of view of 'politicalizing' Russia's backward peasants and lower-middle classes, which had now begun for the first time, and from the point of strengthening the political positions of the working-class itself.

But it was precisely in this question of the Duma that the transition from the tactic of 'boycott' to the tactic of 'exploitation' proved extremely difficult and long-drawn-out for Bolshevism. In this respect the 'ethnic' Social-Democratic organizations also agreed with Bolshevism. In the beginning of September, at a conference of representatives of the Jewish Bund, the Latvian and Polish Social-Democracies, the Revolutionary Ukrainian Party, and of Bolsheviks and Mensheviks, all those taking part, with the exception of the Menshevik representative, supported not only the boycott of the Bulygin Duma, but its 'active' boycott. They spoke out for the desirability of timing the 'all-national uprising' for the beginning of the elections, and, in the interests of husbanding forces for this uprising, they spoke against any further 'partial démarches' by the masses. In this case Menshevism proved to be all the more isolated since both the S.R.s and the Union of Unions (intelligentsia) came out for the boycott, in contrast to Struve, who in his *Osvobozhdenie* insisted on the necessity of taking part in the elections.

After December 1905 the disputes about the attitude towards the Duma took on a new topicality. As it turned out later, the December strike was an exceptional act of the 'days of liberty'. But in both fractions of the Social-Democracy both the intellectual trends and the illusions engendered by these days survived for a long time. And it was in the light of these trends and illusions that the question of the legislative Duma was decided, when on 11 December 1905 a statute about it was published with a new electoral law that conserved the many staged process of election, the division of the voters into social 'estates', and the attempt to put the peasant voters into the relatively most advantageous position, but that also substantially enlarged the rights of the workers' category, too.

For Lenin (in an already quoted article) the 'two tactical lines' laid down in the Party, including the attitude towards the Duma, stood in direct 'connexion with the two estimates' of the December uprising and the situation created by its repression. 'For some' (the Mensheviks) this defeat 'practically wiped the question of the uprising from the agenda, at least until there was a new situation that would force us to review tactics once again. The adapation to a "constitution". . . . flows from this inevitably.' For others (the Bolsheviks)

> who consider the crushing of the Moscow and other uprisings merely the preparation of the terrain for a new, more decisive armed struggle . . . it is precisely now, on the contrary, that the question of the uprising is placed on the agenda . . . hence the slogan: down with constitutional illusions!, and the assignment to the legal trade-union movement of a modest and in any case not a 'principal' role.[173]

In accordance with this, the Bolshevik conference that assembled in Tammerfors (Finland) on 11–17 December also

> counselled all Party organizations to make broad use of the electoral assemblies not in order to bring about, in submitting to the police restrictions, any elections to the Duma, but to broaden the revolutionary organization of the proletariat and to agitate in all strata of the people for an armed uprising. The uprising must be prepared at once, without delay, and organized everywhere, for only its victory will give us the possibility of convoking a genuine popular representation, that is, a freely elected Constituent Assembly on the basis of a universal, direct, equal, and secret ballot.

It was in this same spirit that the question of the Duma was also decided in the draft resolutions composed by the Bolsheviks (almost entirely by Lenin himself) for the Stockholm Congress. The starting-point of these drafts was the conviction that 'at the present time the armed uprising is not only a necessary means of struggle for freedom, but by now an actually achieved stage of the movement . . . in Russia the democratic revolution is not only not waning, on the contrary, it is moving towards a new upsurge', and that because of this 'the chief form of the emancipation movement at present is not the legal struggle on a quasi-constitutional terrain, but the direct openly revolutionary movement of the broad masses of the people, to break the police-laws of serfdom, to create revolutionary justice and to destroy by force the organs of the oppression of the people'. On this basis the draft resolution on the 'attitude towards the Duma' asserts that any 'participation in the elections for the Duma that does nothing for the development of the class-consciousness of the proletariat, for the reinforcement and broadening of its class organization and combat readiness, is more apt to disorganize and debauch the proletariat', since such a participation 'would support constitutional illusions among the people' and remove the 'focus of the proletariat's attention from the revolutionary movement that was bypassing the Duma to the governmental farce'. Hence, the draft concludes, what is necessary is: '(1) . . . a decisive refusal to take part in the Duma; (2) . . . a decisive refusal to take part in the elections to the Duma at any stage; (3) . . . the exploitation . . . of meetings bound up with the elections . . . for a merciless criticism of the Duma . . . and the appeal to a struggle for the revolutionary convocation of the Constituent Assembly.'

In so far as the basic ideas of Menshevism were far more violently shaken up by the 'revolutionary background' of the time, as has been noted, than the ideas of Bolshevism, the Menshevik response to the question of the Duma could not be so straightforward and one-sided as that of the Bolsheviks. In contra-distinction to the Bolsheviks, the Mensheviks at once assessed the December defeat not as a mere military-technical fiasco of the uprising, but as a political failure of the working-class and of the revolution as a whole. But together with the Bolsheviks they regarded this fiasco as merely 'partial' and transient. They were expecting in the immediate future a new upsurge of the revolution, and, moreover, in the form of an armed uprising that this time would really be 'all-national'. It was from this point of view that the Menshevik-Bolshevik *Severny Golos* elucidated the events; it was this that was accurately reflected in the Menshevik draft resolution 'on the present situation' that was scheduled for the Stockholm Congress but was finally taken off the agenda by the Mensheviks themselves. According to this draft,

> the partial defeat of the proletariat in November and December was a consequence of its isolation, its relative weakness, the disorganization of the revolutionary movement of the bourgeois democracy ... and the treachery and connivance of the topmost strata of the bourgeoisie and the local nobility.... It gave the Tsarist government, supported by armed force, an opportunity to establish for a time a régime of military dictatorship in the country.

But 'this dictatorship could not set limits to the development of the revolution; hence a new upsurge was inevitable'.

In this estimate of the immediate political prospects 'there were two nuances among us,' Martov wrote to Akselrod.

> One was for the revival of the old plan, taking as its starting-point the 'legal' elections in order to disrupt them at the first or second stage and go on to the 'People's Duma'; the second ... was more inclined to gamble on the temporary nature of the set-back to the revolution and to cling to the 'legal' elections to the end. In the interests of beating the boycottists everyone agreed on the defence of the first platform as the most popular among the Menshevik workers. [177]

Coming out for taking part in the elections, the Menshevik platform, counting on an imminent upsurge of the revolutionary movement, and in these conditions in complete agreement with Akselrod's above-mentioned ideas, recommended that the electoral procedure not be carried out to the end, that an attempt be made to transform the electors' colleges into organs of local and central revolutionary self-government, and that general elections be carried on through them to a plenipotentiary 'People's Duma'. The Menshevik members of the United Central Committee went even further; they agreed to leave it up to the local Party organizations to choose between the Menshevik plan of participation in all stages of the elections, except the concluding one, and the Bolshevik plan of boycotting them entirely.

Confronted by this choice, the Party organizations, including the Menshevik ones, came out in an overwhelming majority for the tactic of the boycott – not only by virtue of its 'simplicity' but also because it corresponded more to the then mood of the most revolutionary and activist vanguard of the working-class. Nevertheless, not only was the Menshevik platform not introduced at the Congress but the above-quoted draft of the Bolshevik resolution was not either. For in the second half of April and the beginning of May 1906, when the Stockholm Congress assembled, the question of the Duma confronted it on a level that was now completely different. By this time the elections had already taken place in almost all central Russia; there were only elections to take place in the Caucasus, where Menshevism dominated the Party and where the Social-Democratic organization stood for taking part in the 'legal' elections to the very end. It was convinced that thanks to its immense influence over both the local peasantry and the petty urban bourgeoisie it would be able to send to the Duma, from both urban and peasant categories, its own candidates by its own strength, without any blocs or agreements with other parties. It was thus only with respect to the Caucasus that the Congress still had to deal with the question of playing a part in the elections or not. As far as central Russia was concerned it simply had to express its attitude towards the results already at hand.

These results revealed above all a fundamental divergence between the mood of the workers' vanguard and the broad masses of the workers (there was nothing to say about the peasants) especially in the provinces. In future too, this divergence was to make itself felt more than once at the 'critical' moments in the Russian emancipation and working-class movement. Just when the overwhelming majority of the active Party came out for a boycott, the rank-and-file proletarian and peasant masses remained deaf to the Social-Democracy's appeals for a boycott; together with the Kadets they went to the polls. In this way it came about that when the Duma assembled on 28 April 1906, the composition of the more than 100-member peasant Trudovik ('Labourite') group also included deputies from the workers' deputies elected in sixteen provinces.* Thanks primarily to the activity of Martov, who stayed in Petersburg, fourteen of these, headed by M. Mikhailichenko, soon separated from the Trudoviks, and on 18 May they published an appeal, written by Martov, 'To All the Workers of Russia', in which they announced the foundation of a special Workers' Party, and called on the working-class to 'secure the transfer of all power to the Constituent Assembly.' All this evoked a definitely 'anti-boycottist' reaction among a substantial segment of the Party workers

* The first Duma had a total of 478 deputies, of whom 179 were Kadets.

too, even those with Bolshevik leanings. It was to this, in considerable degree, that the Mensheviks not only owed their receiving a majority at the Congress (sixty to sixty-five Menshevik deputies to forty-five to fifty Bolsheviks), but also the fact that in Petersburg too, where the Bolsheviks had always predominated in the Party organization, Menshevik candidates received, for the first time, a majority of both votes and Congress mandates.

The draft resolution on the attitude towards the Duma, presented to the Congress in the names of Plekhanov, Akselrod, and the author of these lines, and adopted by it with minor emendations, started with the fact that in spite of its pseudo-constitutional character, the sharpness of the 'antagonism between the inherent interests of the new bourgeois society in Russia and the old régime shackling it' made inevitable 'conflicts between the Duma and the Tsarist government as well as between the different elements of the Duma itself'; these conflicts would force 'the oppositionist elements of the Duma to seek props in the popular masses . . . and by that very fact transform even such a mock-constitutional institution as the Duma from an instrument of the counter-revolution into an instrument of the revolution'; that 'in the contemporary revolutionary atmosphere clashes between the Duma and the government will, among other things, exercise a disrupting and revolutionizing influence on the army, too'. Starting from this, the Congress made it incumbent on the Party to

> exploit all conflicts methodically . . . in the interests of broadening and deepening the revolutionary movement, and for that; (a) to try to broaden and sharpen these conflicts to a point that would enable them to become the starting-point for broad mass movements aimed at the overthrow of the present political order; (b) to try at any given stage to link the political tasks of the movement to the socio-economic demands of the worker and peasant masses; (c) by a broad agitation among the popular masses for the presentation of revolutionary demands to the Duma, to organize pressure on it from without with the aim of making it revolutionary.

Keeping in mind the forthcoming elections in the Caucasus, the Congress, in the same resolution, acknowledged it to be in principle desirable, in case Social-Democratic Party deputies entered the Duma, for a 'Social-Democratic group to be formed' in it that would act under the 'constant control of the central Party institutions'. Finally, the final version of the resolution made a direct answer to the question put before the Congress by its delegates from the Caucasus: 'Wherever the elections are still forthcoming and wherever the R.S.D.W.P. can place its own candidates without entering into *blocs* with other parties, it must try to send its candidates to the Duma.'

The Bolsheviks voted against both the resolution as a whole and the point about the eventual formation of a Duma Social-Democratic group, which their own draft resolution came out against: 'Attempts to create a parliamentary fraction of the Social-Democracy, in the present conditions and in the absence in the Duma of any Social-Democrats really in the Party and capable of representing the Party, promise no serious success; they rather threaten to compromise the R.S.D.W.P. and place on it the responsibility for a particularly harmful type of parliamentarians midway between the Kadets and Social-Democrats.' But just when the resolution as a whole was passed by sixty-two votes to forty-six, with three absentions, and its final version – about the participation of the Social-Democracy in the elections still forthcoming – was passed by seventy-seven votes to eleven, with sixteen abstentions, Lenin and another sixteen Bolshevik delegates voted for this point.

It is true that they defended their vote by saying that since 'they did not sympathize' with participating in elections 'that had not yet taken place', they 'ascribed no practical importance' to this question, and were voting for this point 'exclusively because they thought it useful and important to condemn in the presence of the Party any blocs with other parties'. In fact, however, this vote, as well as the absentions of so many other Bolshevik delegates, was a symptom of the appearance in the hitherto integral 'boycottist' position of Bolshevism of a first fissure, which to be sure was also attested by the final version of their own just-quoted draft resolution: 'in view of an eventual dissolution of the Duma by the government and of its reconvening with a different composition, the Congress lays it down that no blocs with the Kadet Party or similar non-revolutionary elements are permissible in the course of the new electoral campaign.'*

The break-up of the original 'boycottism' became manifest when the Georgian Social-Democrats succeeded in winning a really brilliant

* The Bolshevik draft resolution 'on the attitude towards the bourgeois parties' admits that, whatever they might be, agreements of any kind were in general 'possible and appropriate at the given time only with elements that acknowledge the armed uprising as a means of struggle and actively work towards it'.

electoral victory and in sending to the Duma five members of the Social-Democratic Party, headed by Noah Zhordania. Lenin remarked on this victory in an article in May recalling that the Bolsheviks 'stood for the boycott of the Duma' and had 'voted at the Congress against the formation of a parliamentary Social-Democratic fraction', though not for 'considerations of principle' but for considerations of 'caution and the practical circumstances of the moment'. At the same time he categorically declared: 'But in and for itself it stands to reason that now, if genuine Party Social-Democrats entered the Duma by a genuinely revolutionary path, all of us, as members of a single Party, would help them perform their difficult task as much as we could.' 'Let us wait for the lessons of experience in order to judge how far it will be possible to rise up against the reactionary designs of the Kadets within the Duma too.'[178] These 'lessons of experience' were summed up a month later by another article of Lenin's in June: 'None of the Social-Democrats will have any doubts now that the emergence of our Party in the Duma might bring, in the given circumstances, more than a little benefit to the cause of the proletariat and of the whole people.'[179]

In this article, as well as in the whole further course of what turned out to be the very protracted process of transition of Bolshevism from a tactic of boycott to a tactic of 'exploitation' with respect to the Duma, Lenin was very far in advance of the majority of his own fraction. But he too of course understood this 'benefit' he mentioned quite differently from the way it was understood in the above-mentioned Stockholm Congress resolution that underlay the activity of the Duma Social-Democratic fraction formed on the orders of the Central Committee. Aside from five Georgian deputies, this fraction included ten members of the former Workers' Group and three other deputies – eighteen members in all. In a statement of 12 June the Social-Democratic fraction alluded to the tasks the Social-Democracy had set itself, and emphasized that the 'present Duma, with no rights, could not realize all these demands, but only a plenipotentiary Constituent Assembly'. 'But the Duma,' the statement went on, 'is capable at this point of being the centre of an all-national movement against the police autocracy, and its victory over the irresponsible hangmen now tearing the country to pieces may be a stage in the people's struggle for a Constituent Assembly and for the transfer of power to the people.'

This statement provoked harsh criticism in the Bolshevik press.

From a Bolshevik point of view, even the 'benefit' of participation in the Duma was supposed to consist primarily in the saving of the masses of the people, especially the workers, from any 'constitutional illusions'. The tactical line of the Social Democratic fraction in the Duma was not supposed to be to indicate a possible positive role of the Duma, but to unmask its fatal helplessness and to demonstrate the 'conciliationist' tendencies of the Kadet Party, which was able to lean first on the Left wing of the Duma (the Trudoviks) then on the Right in order to hold a ruling position in it. In a word, the goal was to transfer the tactic of boycott inside the Duma itself; it was only in this way that it could 'bring more than a little benefit to the cause of the proletariat and the whole people'.

It was only natural that the practical-political activities of the Duma fraction provoked the Bolsheviks to still more hostile opposition than had its tactical statement of principles. Its support – in accordance with the directives of the Central Committeee, which was predominantly Menshevik – of the demand announced by the Duma for the 'subordination of the executive to the legislative power', that is, the formation of a cabinet responsible to the Duma, and the attempt of the Mensheviks, together with the fraction, to mobilize the labouring masses for the support of this demand, called forth in the ranks of the Bolsheviks a storm of indignation that revived an atmosphere of acute split in the Party that formally had just been unified.

This atmosphere was dissipated to some extent when the Manifesto of 8 July 1906 announced that the State Duma was dismissed – to be sure, with a simultaneous statement concerning the immutability of the law founding the Duma and with a commission to the Senate to convoke a new Duma by 20 February 1907. The Social-Democratic fraction took part in a meeting of 200 deputies – Kadets and Trudoviks – that took place the very next day in Vyborg (Finland) and adopted an address, 'To the People from the People's Representatives'. It ended with this appeal: 'Thus, until the convocation of the people's representatives, don't give a penny to the government or a single soldier to the army!' (This was the Vyborg Proclamation.)*

The attempt of the Central Committee to raise the workers for the defence of the Duma, by calling on them to prepare themselves for a political strike under the slogan of 'renewing the Duma session for the convocation of the Constituent Assembly' aroused the protests of the

* The Kadet majority refused to declare itself a 'self-appointed' session of the Duma that did not submit to the Manifesto dismissing it.

Bolsheviks. But it was not supported by the conference it called of the Left-wing parties or organizations either (the Bund, the S.R.s, the Trudoviks, the Peasant Union, and others); nor did it meet with a sympathetic response among the labouring masses; it had to be discarded. But on 12 July the 'unified Committee' of the Social-Democratic fraction and the Trudovik group published a 'Manifesto to the Army and Navy' that declared the government 'illegal' and called on the soldiers to 'stop obeying an illegal government and to come out against it together with us and the whole of the Russian people'. The Manifesto maintained that in the interests of crushing the revolution the 'government had entered into negotiations with the Austrian and German Emperors'; it declared the 'government, as guilty of high treason, to be outside the law'. The Manifesto ended with this appeal: 'Boldly then, for the fatherland and for the people, for the land and for freedom, against the criminal government!' The Committees of these Duma groups, together with its central committees of Social-Democrats and S.R.s, and the Peasant, Railwaymen's and Teachers' Unions, published a 'Manifesto to all the Russian peasantry' with the slogans: 'Freedom and land to all the People! – Down with the People's Enemies, Traitors, Violators, and Evil-doers! – Down with the whole Tsarist Government! – Make Way for the Free Russian People!' Finally, over the signature of these same Social-Democrats, S.R.s, Jewish Bund and Polish Socialist Party, there came out an appeal 'To all the People': 'We summon you to an all-national strike, to the overthrow of the Tsarist government! Long live the all-national strike – the first step in a decisive struggle for a government of the people!'

None of these proclamations called forth any Bolshevik protests at all. Nor did the steps undertaken by the Central Committee of the Party in connexion with the mutiny that flared up in the fleet on 17 July, in Sveaborg (Finland), and on 20 July in Kronstadt, too. That same night the Central Committee called together a conference of the revolutionary parties and organizations with the aim of supporting the mutiny. Aside from the Central Committee itself, representatives of the Duma Social-Democratic fraction, the Bund, the Polish Socialist Party, the S.R.s and the Trudovik Group took part in this conference, which finally decided to proclaim an all-Russian general strike.

To many of the participants in the conference the prospects of the strike seemed doubtful. Nevertheless it was proclaimed unanimously.

But it instantly became apparent that not everyone interpreted it the same way. For the Central Committee it was a demonstrative protest strike. The Bolsheviks, especially their Petersburg Committee (Petersburg had a twofold decisive importance in this case – both as a capital and through being in direct proximity to the mutiny) regarded the strike, on the contrary, as the first step in the involvement of the workers in the mutiny. But the strike was unsuccessful in both ways. For an understanding both of the mood of the Petersburg proletariat at the time, and of the tactic of the Bolsheviks, there is a highly illuminating description of the reasons for the failure given in an official Soviet note made years later (1927) to an edition of Lenin's works.[180] This note says that the Petersburg Committee,

> to a considerable degree under Lenin's influence,[181] decided to announce the strike in order to broaden and deepen the mutiny that had begun 21 July. By the following day the number of strikers had reached 80,000. But from the very first moment elements had joined the strike that had not taken part in the October and December events of 1905, and to some extent were even recent Black Hundred elements. The most backward sections of the Putilov factory were on strike, as were the horse-drawn tram-drivers and even the drozhky-drivers. But the big factories, where the more thoughtful proletariat was concentrated, for instance the Obukhov factory, the Semyannikov and others, refused to strike. The refusal of these workers, by underlining the necessity of preparing for a decisive struggle, determined the outcome of the strike: on 22 July the strike waned.

But whatever the justifications given by the advanced workers themselves of their attitude towards a strike declared to be in support of an army mutiny taking place only a few miles from the capital, their failure to react stormily attested the 'waning' of the whole mass revolutionary movement. The 'revolutionary background' ceased being 'revolutionary'. But at the same time it ceased to 'suggest' to both Bolsheviks and Mensheviks the 'practical slogans' that were frequently in acute contrast with their pre-established theoretical conceptions, that revealed the one-sidedness of those conceptions, their contradictoriness and incompleteness, and for this very reason placed their critical revision on the order of the day. It would of course be absurd now to make surmises about what might have beeen the results of such a revision. The fact is that the Russian Social-Democracy had to work out the experience of the ascendant phase of the 1905 revolution, including the experience of the first Duma, not only in an atmosphere freed from that 'suggestiveness' that as we have seen brought together and unified its two wings, but, on the contrary, under conditions of an increasingly virulent fraction struggle. Because of this the revision itself was transformed not so much into a critical test by each fraction of its specific conceptions as into an apologetic attempt to extract from the experience undergone anything that in one way or another might be exploited for the justification and reinforcement of those conceptions, forgetting or disregarding everything that contradicted it. In this sense the ten- to eleven-year interval between the two revolutions was also, as we have said, a period of stagnation and even of retrogression in the political theorizing of the Social-Democracy.

It is not difficult now, retrospectively, to ascertain that this period had far more pernicious consequences for Menshevism than for Bolshevism. The reason is understandable. The 'revolutionary background' and the lasting changes it engendered in the Russian socio-economic order brilliantly confirmed, as we have already seen and shall see again, the tactical ideas of Menshevism, its methods of 'unloosing' the revolution and 'organizing' it, in particular the organization of the working-class into an independent socio-political force. But it was with all the greater obviousness that the 'revolutionary background' revealed the worthlessness of the general socio-political conceptions of Menshevism, its orientation towards the self-elimination of the working-class from the struggle for power and towards the bourgeoisie being 'revolutionized' under the pressure of the proletariat as the only possible heir to the power wrested from the autocracy.

This conception could scarcely have been able to withstand the pressure of the 'revolutionary background' if that 'background', in the conditions of the time, had been at all protracted. The worthlessness of the conception also seemed to be confirmed by the entire experience of the first Duma: the ten weeks of its activity were completely filled by the struggle first of the Workers' Group, then of the Social-Democratic fraction against the 'opportunism' of the Kadets, that is, the representatives of the most 'liberal' part of the Russian bourgeoisie, and against their decisive rejection of the revolution. After the dismissal of the Duma, the Social-Democracy had to make its summons to a struggle for the 'power of the people' without them, exclusively through collaboration with parties and groups that were in any case bound up with the peasant, petty-bourgeois, and intellectual strata of the populace. Nevertheless, in the atmosphere of the 'waning' revolution, it was this same old conception, in its most classical form and narrowest version, that Menshevism began returning to more and more consistently. It was just this that became its 'article of faith' and in the course of the following decade acquired the stability of a prejudice. The beginning of this retrogression in the political thought of Menshevism (though under its cover Menshevism accomplished, as we shall see, a vast, historically indispensable and fruitful work of mobilization and organization of the Russian working-class) has not, perhaps, found a clearer expression than in a book, written at the time by the author of these lines in collaboration with M. Balabanov, that tried to sum up the results of the first Duma.[182]

In analysing the tasks confronting the first Duma and the reasons for its undoing, the Introduction to this book starts out from the December defeat: 'The proletariat was beaten in the December fight' because 'the peasantry was silent', while 'the bourgeoisie did not support the workers'. Because of the defeat of the proletariat there 'remained the great unresolved question of the revolution – the question of state power'. For just this reason the 'convocation of the Duma meant, in spite of the intentions of the government, not the end of the struggle, but a renewed sharpening of it'. The Duma was confronted by a task – 'of becoming the organ of authority' and of exploiting that authority 'for the convocation of the all-National Constituent Assembly'. However, not only did it not perform this task, it did not even face it, since the 'decisive role in the Duma fell to the Kadets, the party of National Freedom', a party 'that did not grasp even in the remotest degree the tasks of the Duma' and made 'every effort to separate "parliamentary" activity by a whole abyss from the revolutionary movement of the people', and, on the contrary, to convince the people that the 'revolution was over' and that 'the constitution was already won, since a few 'electoral ballots' were enough to 'crush the head of the autocratic serpent'. But the decisive role fell to the Kadets, on the one hand, 'thanks to the auto-elimination of the Social-Democracy and the other revolutionary parties', for after the December defeat the 'proletariat, emasculated and embittered by the betrayal of the bourgeoisie, turned its back on the Duma in considerable numbers and boycotted it', and on the other, 'thanks to the meagre political awareness and the disorganization of the peasantry, which had not had time to create its own revolutionary party and merely sent "good" people to the Duma'.

If the Introduction thus comes to the conclusion that the reason for the failure of the Duma was the 'decisive role' and the political bankruptcy of the Kadets, the Conclusion of the book begins with the formulation of the question concerning the reasons for the rejection of the revolution by this party of the most democratic sector of the Russian bourgeoisie and its incapacity to head a people's movement in settling the problem, fundamental for every revolution, of the state power. Here is the answer it gives to this question:

> In order to break down the wall, the forces of the people had to be depended on. But it was just this that the Duma majority could not make up its mind to do. It was afraid of losing authority over these people's forces once they were awakened; it was afraid that the revolutionary people would go 'too far' in its movement, would lay hands on the interests not only of the reaction but also of the liberal land-owners, merchants and factory-owners; it was afraid it would have to give up too much in favour of the people. Hence the equivocation and irresolution in all the actions of the Duma majority. On the one hand the proper interests of the bourgeoisie peremptorily called for the annihilation of the old autocratic régime and thus thrust it into sharper and sharper clashes with the reaction; on the other hand the fear of the proletariat and of the other 'lower' classes of the people forced it to fall back every time at decisive moments and thus heightened the boldness of the enemy more and more. It was just this contradiction between words and deeds that the weakness of the Duma was rooted in; this was the cause of its failure and of the triumph of the hated régime.

This explanation of the bankruptcy of the bourgeois democracy indicates with complete definiteness that the source of that bankruptcy was Russian life itself. The insoluble contradictoriness of the interests of the classes represented by this bourgeois democracy emasculated these classes politically and of necessity pushed them into compromises with the autocracy and into capitulating to it.* But such an explanation would seem to lead both the author of this book and his readers close to the conclusion that the socio-political conception of Menshevism was bankrupt, since it assigned to the bourgeoisie a role that in the actual historical conditions of Russia it was unable to play,

* The autocracy deserves a 'blessing' because it 'protects us with its bayonets against the fury of the people'. This cynically frank acknowledgement was made by the author of the Manifesto of the Social-Democratic Party and former editor of *Osvobozhdenie*, the Kadet P. B. Struve, in a sensational collection called *Vekhi* (Milestones), which recorded his definitive rupture (and together with his that of a whole constellation of former 'legal Marxists'), both with Socialism and with republican democracy. (Dan seems to be referring to an article by Gershenzon in the same collection. *Translator's Note.*)

and that accordingly a critical revision of this conception was called for.

The final paragraphs of this Conclusion sound all the more unexpected.

> The Duma will only perform the task incumbent on it if its majority says to itself firmly and definitely: the cause of liberty can only conquer when it is democratic liberty, liberty that lightens the conditions of existence and of struggle not only for the secure topmost strata of the people, but also of the broadest labouring and under-privileged masses. Only such a Duma . . . that is not afraid of the 'immoderate' claims of the people . . . will not be afraid to become a revolutionary Duma. Then . . . the Duma . . . will become, in the hands of the people, a mighty instrument for the conquest of a fully empowered, all-national Constituent Assembly. . . . The Social-Democracy will not take this path itself, but it will push all other parties on to it. . . . However timid, cowardly, and blind the bourgeois parties, like the Kadets, are, they are propped up on classes that are thrust by the real historical background, and by real interests, on to a path not of reconciliation with the old order, but of sharp struggle against it. . . . Until the destruction of the autocracy the majority of the bourgeois classes must be fellow-travellers of the proletariat; and hence also the progressive bourgeois parties must also be fellow-travellers of the Social-Democracy.

In retrospect it is now incontestably obvious that it was possible to return to the Menshevik conception of the revolution only after assuming, in contradiction with the entire content of the book and the analysis given in it, that the ultimate source of the bankruptcy of the Duma was the timidity, cowardice and blindness of the 'bourgeois parties', which behaved as though at odds with the 'real interests' of the classes they represented. But it was the 'real interests' of these classes that made them 'timid, cowardly, and blind', and also forced their representatives in the Duma to display the same unlovely qualities. But at that time it was possible to 'salvage' the Menshevik conception only by closing one's eyes to this blatant contradiction. This is shown by the extent to which it was not the laws of formal logic but historical conditions that determined the Party's political thinking, and also by the degree to which as early as 1906–7 the basic conception of Menshevism was undermined by the brief but real experience of an authentic revolution.

This experience shook the foundations of the Bolshevik conception far less. The brief 'days of liberty', to be sure, showed that the Bolshevik assumption of a 'republican-democratic' peasantry as the ally of the working-class in the revolutionary struggle for a consistent 'political democracy' was no less illusory than the Menshevik assumption of a revolutionary bourgeoisie under the influence of the proletariat. But in the first place the demonstrativeness of the experience of the 'days of liberty' was considerably diminished just as much by the brevity of the experience itself as, even more, by the long-lived confidence, not among the Bolsheviks alone, in the imminence of a new upsurge and in its really 'all-national' character this next time – precisely because the vast mass of the peasantry, which had hitherto held back, would pour into it. But the most important thing was this: the peasantry, of course, played the central role in the Bolshevik socio-political constructions, yet the relative stability of the general conception of Bolshevism, which later made it possible for it to perform with practical success such an apparently sharp about-face in 1917, was primarily based on the fact that in one way or another it was oriented towards the most energetic participation of the working-class in the struggle for power. In this sense it calculated the real correlation of the socio-political forces in the Russian revolution far more realistically than Menshevism.

But if the experience of the 'days of liberty' did not exercise a strong influence on the common fund of Bolshevik ideas, still less influence was exercised in this respect by the experience of the first Duma. This was active when the revolutionary wave was subsiding, when in spite of all illusions the very question of the revolutionary régime and its social composition was in fact removed to the future, losing its practical character more and more, and in that sense becoming 'academic'. But in essence, for Bolshevism as well as for Menshevism, the experience of the Duma was a direct continuation of the historical 'critique' of the conceptions of both fractions, however they were tested practically.

The Trudovik group of the first Duma was distinguished by a considerable radicalism in socio-economic questions, above all in the question of the land. This was the question about which it most often and most sharply clashed with the bourgeois majority of the Duma, especially with the Kadets, who in their agrarian programme were unable to meet the peasantry beyond the principle of the 'forcible alienation' of the big estates – but on the absolute condition of purchasing back the alienated lands by 'fair compensation'. Under the pressure of the Trudoviks, energetically supported by the Social-Democrats, the Duma passed a resolution placing the land question on the agenda, which gave the final impetus towards its dismissal.

It was largely on the ground of the agrarian question that the co-operation between the Social-Democrats and the Trudoviks for a joint struggle against the Kadets also took shape.* But such co-operation arose only rarely and sporadically in questions of 'political democracy', since the political radicalism of the Duma peasant representatives lagged substantially behind its socio-economic, and especially its agrarian radicalism, and in any case was a secondary matter for them. It is only by taking into account, on the basis of the Duma experience, the extreme caution of the peasantry in questions of 'pure' politics that the fact can be explained that, in the above-mentioned appeals launched 'by the revolutionary parties and organizations' after the dismissal of the Duma, not only did the slogan of a democratic republic find no place for itself but neither did the slogan of the Constituent Assembly. The political objectives of the struggle to which these proclamations were summoning the soldiers, peasants, the 'whole people', were cloaked in the archaic and hazy formulae of 'land and liberty' and 'power to the people'.

The experience of the first Duma, supported by the experience of all the succeeding Dumas as well, was in its own way a 'forewarning' that the revolutionary co-operation of the working-class and the peasantry, in the actual Russian conditions of the first quarter of the twentieth century, was possible only on the terrain of social, not political radicalism. The real mainstay of such co-operation could not be '*political* democracy' but only what later came to be called '*social* democracy'. In 1917 Bolshevism not only heeded this forewarning, but in October-November also made it its fundamental lever. But in 1906 it remained deaf to it; it was precisely the worker-peasant 'Left

* The Stockholm Congress, which sanctioned the long-standing practice of Social-Democratic agitation, radically altered the *agrarian programme of the Party*. For Mensheviks and Bolsheviks equally the principal demand of the new programme became the confiscation of the big estates. Both fractions also came out uniformly against the distribution of the confiscated land between individual peasant farms, permitting such distribution only in case no other solution proved feasible. But the Mensheviks, oriented towards a bourgeois régime, stood for the *municipalization* of the land, for the transfer of the entire land reserve to the organs of local autonomy, in which they saw a democratic counterweight to the eventual reactionary degeneration of the bourgeois régime. The Bolshevik programme, on the contrary, was nationalization, as an instrument for the strengthening of the revolutionary-democratic dictatorship of the proletariat and peasantry. The Congress adopted the Menshevik programme, of which P. P. Maslov was the author.

bloc' as the standard-bearer of the 'republican-democratic' policy as a counterweight to the 'monarchist-conciliationist' policy of the Kadets that proclaimed as its guiding idea the 'exploitation' of the Duma, which it began going over to more and more definitely as the hopes that the Duma's dismissal would prove merely the direct prologue to an all-national uprising began to fade.

We have seen the unshakable confidence in the imminence of the uprising, and in the necessity of carrying on all Party activities with that in mind, that imbued the article on the *Dismissal of the Duma* written by Lenin during the last third of July 1906. But there was a completely different tone in an article of his that appeared a month later, entitled *On the Boycott.*[183]

> The Social-Democrats of the Left-Wing [run the first few lines of the article] must review the question of boycotting the Duma. It should be recalled that we always posed this question concretely, according to a definite political situation. . . . History has shown that when the Duma assembles the possibility emerges of useful agitation inside and around it – that the tactic of the *rapprochement* with the revolutionary peasantry against the Kadets is possible inside the Duma. This seems paradoxical, but such, undoubtedly, is the irony of history. It is precisely the Kadet Duma that has shown the masses in a particularly graphic way the correctness of this 'anti-Kadet', let us say for the sake of brevity, tactic. . . . The time has now come when the revolutionary Social-Democrats must stop being boycottists. We shall not refuse to enter the second Duma when (or 'if') it convenes. We shall not refuse to exploit this arena of struggle, without in the last exaggerating its modest significance, but on the contrary, totally subordinating it, on the basis of the experience already given by history, to another kind of struggle – strikes, uprisings, and so on. We shall convoke a fifth Congress of the Party; we shall lay it down that in case of elections an electoral agreement with the Trudoviks is necessary for a few weeks (without calling a fifth Congress a concerted electoral campaign is impossible, while '*blocs* with other parties' are unconditionally prohibited by the rules of the fourth Congress).* Then we'll hit the Kadets on the head.

This article of Lenin's marks the beginning of the accelerated decline of Bolshevik 'boycottism' in the last sphere of Social-

* This remark of Lenin's has some historical interest, in view of the fateful role soon to be played in the sharpening of inter-fraction dissension by the statement of 'Thirty-one Mensheviks' that the ruling of the Petersburg Conference (January 1907) on the 'Left *bloc*' in the elections to the second Duma was a 'direct and gross infraction' of Party liberty, and their refusal, backed by the Central Committee, to submit to this ruling.

Democratic activity, the Duma, in which it had maintained itself with special tenacity. 'Boycottism' was also liquidated in those 'ethnic' parties (the Jewish Bund and the Polish and Latvian Social-Democracies) that had been accepted at the Stockholm Congress into the R.S.D.W.P., and that in questions of a general-political nature were still to gravitate towards Bolshevism for a long time.* A new flare-up of boycottism was almost provoked in Bolshevik ranks and in the Polish Social-Democracy (as well as among the S.R.s and the Populist Socialists, a group that split off from the S.R.s to the right) by the dismissal of the second Duma (3 June 1907), which was accompanied – in the breaking of the decree concerning the Duma, that is, something along the lines of a constitutional overturn – by a basic change in the electoral law. But boycottism, which was supported by almost all the eminent Bolshevik leaders, was energetically opposed by Lenin. At a general Party conference devoted to this question he supported, in contrast with the majority of his own fraction, a resolution introduced by the Mensheviks and Bundists. The question of the Party's participation in the elections to the third Duma was decided affirmatively. This decision conclusively liquidated boycottism, and the insignificant little groups with boycottist leanings that later also emerged within Bolshevism, and in one form or another demanded the 'recall' of the Social-Democratic fraction from the Duma, no longer had any practical importance (they were known as 'Recallists').

A general Party conference that took place in Tammerfors (Finland) in the autumn of 1906, before the elections to the second Duma, adopted a resolution about the independent candidacies of the Party for representatives and electors in all the social categories. Joint lists (though not joint political platforms) with other parties were allowed exclusively in cases where a rejection of such lists would have risked sending some reactionary (Black Hundred) candidates into the Duma. In the workers' category electoral agreements were allowed only with non-party workers' organizations (trade unions etc.), but not with any other parties. In other categories preference was supposed to be given to Trudoviks, S.R.s and Populist Socialists over the Kadets.

Thus the existing agreement concerning the participation of the

* The Bund soon became definitely Menshevik; an intermediate position continued to be held by the Latvian Social-Democracy; the Polish Social-Democracy (Rosa Luxemburg, Tyshko, Varsky) remained Bolshevik, except on organizational questions; later it produced the principal cadres of Polish Communism.

Party in the elections for the second Duma was broken in Petersburg by the above-mentioned decision of the local Party conference to conclude at the very outset an electoral agreement with the Populist groups – not for the sake of forestalling the Black Hundred danger, but for the sake of conducting the whole electoral campaign under the aegis of the 'Left *bloc*', and by the refusal of the Mensheviks to submit to that decision. The result of this split in the local organization was the relatively substantial success of the S.R.s in the big metallurgical factories of Petersburg, where their influence had always been minimal. But in general throughout the country the Party's electoral campaign proceeded smoothly on the basis of the Tammerfors resolutions, and gave the Social-Democracy a great victory. In the workers' category eighty per cent of the voters came out for it. But in the other categories too its success proved to be so great that into a Duma of 478 deputies there went sixty-five Social-Democrats, out of which fifty-four, the candidates of the Party organizations, became fully fledged members of the Social-Democratic fraction, while the rest took part in its meetings with a consultative voice. In these elections (as in all subsequent ones) the most substantial electoral victory was won by the Social-Democracy in the Caucasus, so that in the second Duma the Georgian Social-Democrats* were the heads of the fraction, as they also became the heads of the Social-Democratic fraction in the third Duma, too.†

The Duma representatives of the Social-Democracy, most of them Menshevik, also included fifteen to sixteen Bolshevik-minded deputies (mostly from the Volga and the Urals) who acted as a solid fraction group. Thus, the fraction struggle under the banner of the 'Left *bloc*', which the Bolsheviks were conducting outside the Duma more and more insistently, and which provoked the constantly increasing counteractivity of the Mensheviks, was transferred to the interior of the Duma, which became the principal arena of the open political activity of the Social-Democracy. During both the second Duma, and even more the third Duma, this circumstance proved to be a factor that greatly exacerbated intra-Party dissension and hastened its consummation by a formal split, but it introduced nothing novel in principle into the ideology of either fraction. It merely furthered the definitive consolidation of each of them in political positions already adopted by them, a one-sided 'polarization' of those positions, a

* Irakli Tsereteli, Archil Dzhaparadze and others.

† Karl Chkheidze, Akakii Chkenkeli and others.

reciprocal alienation of Bolshevism and Menshevism, and a transformation of that alienation into virulent enmity.

Just as the disappointment evoked among broad Party circles by the boycott tactic was reflected in the results of the elections to the Stockholm Congress, so now the results of the elections to the new 1907 Party Congress, which convened in London from 30 April to 19 May, were signalized by the dissatisfaction with the more than modest successes of the Menshevik tactic, which was trying, as a draft electoral platform composed by the Central Committee said, to convert the Duma into 'the principal military staff of the all-national army, carrying on a struggle for full freedom and all the land, and for the convocation of a plenipotentiary All-National Constituent Assembly'. According to official data there were ninety-seven Menshevik delegates and 106 Bolsheviks. But Bolshevism also exercised a political pull over the four 'extra-fraction' delegates, headed by Trotsky, and the majority of the delegates of the two 'ethnic' organizations – the Polish (forty-four) and the Latvian (twenty-nine). It was only the delegates of the Bund (fifty-seven) whose majority backed the Mensheviks politically.

These figures show that the decisive role at the Congress was played by just those 'ethnic' organizations that to a considerable extent defined their position in terms of the special conditions in which each of them had taken shape and had to operate. They were always discriminating with respect to the source and the sense of those differences of opinion that harrowed the Social-Democracy. Since in addition they had only just been accepted into the Party and for the first time had taken part in its 'parliament' they were often inclined to subordinate all ideological considerations to a desire to maintain at least the formal unity of the Party in the face of the outside world.

The result was that the Congress adopted resolutions, concerning the attitude towards the non-proletarian parties, the Duma, the workers' congress, and so on, that in tendency were definitely Bolshevik, but in formulations that tried to smooth over as far as possible all the 'sharp' edges. The 'furthering of the recognition by the trade unions of the intellectual leadership of the Social-Democratic Party, and also of the establishment of organizational connexions with it', was declared by the Congress to be 'one of the fundamental tasks of Social-Democratic activity' in the trade unions. But the majority of the Congress refused to condemn the activity of the 'Stockholm' Central Committee and of the Social-Democratic fraction in the

Duma. It removed from the agenda the question of the 'armed uprising', so important in principle for the Bolsheviks, while in the resolution adopted on 'partisan actions' it said that 'Party organizations must carry on an energetic struggle against all partisan activities and expropriations'; that 'any participation in partisan activities and expropriations, or any help to them, is forbidden to Party members'; and that 'all special combat groups attached to Party organizations must be dissolved'.* Finally, in the election of members of the Central Committee and of the editorial board of the Central Organ, the 'ethnic' organizations were concerned with retaining for themselves the role of super-arbiters.

Bolshevism won a victory in London, but the victory was far from complete. It was all the less able to be satisfied with it because, while ensuring it certain propagandistic and organizational advantages, it in no way made it possible for it to make the Party the instrument of its policies with that insistence, straightforwardness and absence of compromise that Bolshevism had been distinguished for, as we have seen, ever since its birth. Nor was this all. The compromise resolutions of the London Congress directly forbade it certain well-known forms of activity[184] indissolubly bound up with the orientation towards the 'armed uprising' that continued nourishing all its political and organizational concepts, even when the practical realization of the uprising began receding into the indefinite future.

The consequence of this was that the secret 'Bolshevik centre', which had not gone out of existence after the 'unifying' Stockholm Congress, at which the Bolsheviks had been in a minority, went on existing even after the London Congress gave them the majority. It was maintained, not in order to become the instrument of a more energetic conduct of the policy dictated by the Party authorities, but, on the contrary, in order to make those authorities the executors of a

* The draft resolution that Lenin had written for the Stockholm Congress itself, which retained a guiding significance for the Bolsheviks, said of 'the partisan combat activities' that they 'prepare open and mass armed actions' and 'are also indispensable for the combat training and military instruction of our combat groups'. 'The most important direct task of such actions must be recognized as the destruction of governmental, police and army apparatuses and a merciless struggle against the actively Black Hundred organizations.' But 'combat actions are also permissible for the seizure of funds belonging to the enemy, that is, to the autocratic government, and for the application of these funds to the needs of the uprising.' 'Partisan combat activities must be carried out under the control of the Party.'

policy dictated by the 'Bolshevik centre'. In circumstances where this was impossible, the centre carried out its own policy independently of the ruling of the Party authorities, of their permission, or of the prohibition of the Congress that had just ended. The Party, which was officially Bolshevik in its political line, became for the Bolsheviks the same object of 'exploitation' as any other general political or working-class institution.

The policy of Bolshevism thus became 'conspiratorial' in two directions – with respect to problems of a general political character, and with respect to the Party itself. The activity of the 'Bolshevik centre' that embodied the idea of a closely knit circle of 'trained revolutionaries', was an elaborate conspiracy not only against the state police, but also against the Party and against the other members of the Central Committee that was 'Bolshevik' in its political tendency. Thus it was the logical culmination of that line of political-organizational development whose foundations had been laid by Lenin's *What Is to Be Done?* But it was also the source of the absolute unscrupulousness in the choice of the means of struggle, that in conjunction with the unrestricted devotion to its fraction as a body, its inexhaustible energy in the performance of a task once set it, its extremely strict discipline, its unqualified subordination to all directives 'from above' and the other 'dynamic' qualities that were nourished by the whole history of its origin and development became the constituent element in the political-psychological profile of Bolshevism and was also implanted by it in the leadership of international Communism.

But even before the delegates to the London Congress had had time to return home, the entire political situation changed fundamentally. Under the pretext of the participation of the Social-Democratic fraction in a 'military conspiracy' fabricated by the political police, the government presented the Duma with a demand to deprive its members of the inviolability of deputies. The attempts of the Duma majority to drag out the settlement of this question and arrive at some 'compromise' with the government involved its dismissal and the arrest of the members of the Social-Democratic fraction, and also, as already pointed out, the publication, as a kind of state overturn, of a new electoral law, basically curtailing the electoral rights of the workers and of the ordinary rank-and-file peasants, and on the contrary, substantially strengthening the rights of the affluent classes.*

* In accordance with a fraction decision the majority of its members made no

It was the political task of the author of this *coup d'état*, Prime Minister P. A. Stolypin, to create in the Duma a solid conservative monarchist majority and to make that majority the bulwark of a bourgeois-landowner *bloc* embodied in the Duma by the Party of 17 October (the 'Octobrists') headed by A. Guchkov. The cornerstone of the internal political programme of the *bloc* was the prevention of an agrarian revolution by furthering the formation in the peasant communes of a stratum of intermediate peasant small-holders.* The foreign political programme was expressed in the words Stolypin addressed to the Social-Democratic deputies: 'You need great upheavals, we need a Great Russia.' In essence this programme meant not only the revival of an intensified cult of Great Russian nationalism, but also the return of Russia's foreign policy from the Far East to Europe, the placing of 'Balkan' and 'Slavic' objectives on the order of the day, the stressing of Russia as a 'Great Power' and the attempt to make her a decisive factor in all European and world problems. As is known, Stolypin's October régime did not succeed in preventing 'great upheavals' by means of this domestic and foreign policy. On the contrary, by preparing the active participation of Russia in the approaching world war, this policy also prepared the 1917 revolution unleashed by that war, while in trying to settle the 'agrarian question' by introducing a split into the countryside, it merely contributed to the sharpening of the struggle between different groups within the peasantry itself, which at a certain stage of the revolution of 1917 took on the ferocious forms of 'dekulakization'.

But it was not only the general political background that had changed. The conditions of activity of the Socialist parties and the workers' organizations in general, had also altered radically. While field court-martials sentenced to death hundreds and thousands of the participants in the stormy events of 1905–6, a police terror descended on the party, trade unions, cultural and other organizations of the workers. A multitude of trade unions were shut down, others were refused registration. Social-Democratic papers were prohibited, and party organizations once again had to go deep underground. The

---

attempt to hide or avoid arrest and trial. Almost all of them were convicted: some (Tsereteli and others) were given five years at hard labour, others permanent banishment to Siberia. Three (Dzhaparadze, Dzhugeli, Lomtaridze) died in gaol; the others were not freed until the revolution of 1917. The Petersburg workers marked the trial of the fraction by a one-day protest strike.

* The '*khutor*'.

Party, which according to the data of the London Congress, had numbered as many as 150,000 members (with 25,000 to 26,000 each in the Bund and the Polish Socialist Party, 13,000 in the Latvian party, and up to 85,000 in the Russian section of the Party) in fact crumbled. It abruptly broke up into small illegal groups scattered throughout the country that met with little response even among the labouring masses and whose political activity was paralysed by the industrial stagnation, the police terror, and the general atmosphere of disapproval of Socialism even in those circles of the bourgeois intelligentsia whose sympathy in the past had been such a substantial bulwark for all forms of workers' organizations. By the beginning of 1908 almost all prominent leaders of both fractions of the Social-Democracy were once again in the emigration.

They carried with them into the new emigration all the same old conceptions. And when, four years and a bit later, there assembled in Prague the Bolshevik Conference that definitively split the Russian Social-Democracy,* its fundamental platform was formulated in three slogans: 'A democratic republic, an eight-hour working-day, and the confiscation of all large estates.' It was under these slogans that the Bolsheviks had to conduct their electoral campaign for the fourth Duma.

The Bolsheviks counterposed these 'unabridged' slogans to every attempt of the Mensheviks to mobilize substantial workers' groups around 'partial' slogans such as a struggle for the 'right of coalition'. It was under their aegis that the Bolsheviks criticized the entire Duma and extra-Duma policy of Menshevism as a workers' policy that was not revolutionary-democratic and republican, but 'liberal' and 'conciliationist'.

The split at Prague was consummated by a string of fraction disputes that lasted for four years and in the emigration attained in just these years a bitterness never seen before. The attempts that were made

* This conference, which sat on 5 to 18 January 1912, was not attended by a single one of the 'ethnic' organizations or by any one of the other groups of the Russian section of the Party. The Conference made a split because in spite of its exclusively Bolshevik composition, it claimed to be an all-Party conference, excluded from the Party a series of Menshevik groups and elected a new, purely Bolshevik Central Committee, which in its turn set up the 'Russian Bureau of the Central Committee'.[185] The response of the other section of the Social-Democracy was a conference that assembled in August 1912 in Vienna, and formed the so-called 'August *bloc*', whose mainstay was the Mensheviks but which a number of small groups also entered (Trotsky and others).

from time to time, chiefly under the influence of Russian 'conciliator Bolsheviks', to restore Party unity and to 'heal' the central institutions of the Party – on the basis of the same decisive role of the 'ethnic' organizations in neutralizing both Russian fractions – merely led to a still greater inflammation of fraction passions and to a fragmentation of the Social-Democratic emigration into a growing number of tiny groups. In the foreign segment of the Party an atmosphere was created of stifling and unendurable brawling that often obscured in the eyes of its participants and victims the meaning of the new forms that the old Menshevik-Bolshevik differences assumed in the new conditions created by the June overturn of 1907.

Conserving their own special ideas of the moving forces and the paths of the Russian revolution, both fractions equally were convinced that this overturn had not solved its problems in any way, and consquently that it was bound to have a new upsurge. But they were also equally convinced that this upsurge was not due for tomorrow, and that years would have to go by before it was possible. The author of these lines, in a pamphlet published in 1907,[172] wrote: 'We stand . . . before a more or less extended period of the accumulation of organizational forces,' while Lenin, in a letter dated 16 December 1909, which spoke in extremely careful terms of the conclusions he had drawn from the 'history of the twentieth century in Russia', i.e., from the experience of the revolution of 1905–6, wrote: 'this [history] gives rise to the possibility of *two* kinds of capitalist agrarian development; the historic struggle between these kinds is not yet finished. . . . The nationalization of the land, the peasant smashing of the land-holding system is the economic foundation of the American path. The law of 9 November 1906 [the Stolypin law on 'small holdings' – T.D.], the landowners' smashing of the old land-holding system, is the economic basis of the Prussian road. Our epoch, 1905–???, is an epoch of revolutionary and counter-revolutionary struggle between these two paths.'[186] But each fraction, in basing its orientation in this way on a more or less extended epoch of 'the accumulation of forces' had its own understanding of the methods of that 'accumulation'.

The Menshevik point of view was formulated in the just-quoted pamphlet written by the author of these lines. While emphasizing that the new revolutionary 'mass pressure' was in the last resort inevitable, but not so imminent 'as had been assumed by the Menshevik resolutions of the Stockholm Congress', the pamphlet continued: 'Meanwhile it is just this "pressure" that in the eyes of the Mensheviks served as a necessary condition for the transformation of the Duma into a direct instrument of the revolution . . . into an organ of state power.' Hence the implication of the impossibility of implementing a tactic of revolutionary 'seizure', conceived of merely in conditions of revolutionary 'mass pressure', means 'the growing necessity of working in a timely and opportune way, within the limits of the legal framework, of directing our Duma activity not towards a stepping "over" the laws in a revolutionary way, but towards exploiting the laws for the preparation of conditions that will make it possible to step over them.' It was this idea – of Party work as intensive as possible within the 'legal' framework as a means of 'accumulating organizational forces' for the coming new revolution – that during the next few years became the guiding tactical idea of Menshevism, and not only in the sphere of the Duma.

The Russian Mensheviks, with exceptional energy and a rare self-restraint, submitting to all the police rules and restrictions, set about the restoration and strengthening of the trade-union, cultural, and other workers' organizations that had withstood destruction; the founding of new organizations of the same type; the conquering of new spheres for organized workers' initiative (social insurance, for instance), the creation of a trade-union, co-operative, insurance, general cultural workers' press and of Social-Democratic reviews (*Nasha Zarya* (Our Dawn), *Delo Zhizni* (the Cause of Life), etc.) which to a certain degree replaced the prohibited Social-Democratic daily press, but which in their turn would vanish now and again beneath the blows of the censorship and revive under new names; the establishment of a regular liaison between the workers' organizations and the Social-Democratic fraction of the Duma; the systematic preparation of politically coloured démarches of 'workers' delegations' at the public meetings that were allowed from time to time (artisans', anti-alcoholic, teachers', factory physicians and others); finally, the conduct of as many agitational campaigns as possible, such as the campaign for the transmission to the Duma of petitions for the workers' right to 'freedom of coalition'.

It is clear from all the preceding that during these years Bolshevik thought and action were proceeding in an altogether different direction. The Bolshevik method of 'accumulating forces' consisted of an attempt to preserve at least the fundamental cadres of the Party's 'illegal' apparatus from dissolution, to strengthen them, imbue them with fighting spirit, and preserve them for the leadership of the coming revolution. The ideological foundation of this tactic was the idea of the 'armed uprising' in its Bolshevik interpretation. For the time being this had lost its practical importance, but it had completely retained its importance in principle. The material basis of this tactic was the practice of 'guerrilla warfare', continued and sanctioned by the 'Bolshevik Centre'. It was this that secured those means without which, against the background of the apathy of the broad labouring masses and the intensified hostility of even the liberal intellectual elements of bourgeois society, the existence of any of the numerous 'illegal cells' was quite simply impossible.

In these conditions it was natural that those 'illegal cells' that had survived or that sprang up again were wholly Bolshevik, and that it was with a constantly growing mistrust and hostility that Bolshevism bore itself towards the 'legal' activity of the Russian Mensheviks. Accordingly, the Prague Conference gave top priority on the one hand 'to the necessity for intensified activity for the restoration of the illegal organizations of the R.S.D.W.P., exploiting even more broadly than before each and every legal possibility suited to the leadership of the economic struggle of the proletariat and alone capable of guiding its constantly increasing political démarches', and on the other to 'the necessity of creating a systematic political agitation and many-sided support of the incipient mass movement and its broadening under the banner of Party slogans'. The Conference finally declared that the group of *Nasha Zarya* and *Delo Zhizni*, that is, in fact, almost the whole of Russian Menshevism, 'had by its behaviour definitively placed itself outside the Party'.

For over two years, the activity of the Mensheviks in the 'legal' arena went on with growing success. It was, in fact, almost the sole 'constructive' form of Social-Democratic activity in Russia. In this activity Menshevism grew intimate with advanced circles of workers and helped to form impressive cadres of highly qualified workers' intelligentsia. Under its influence during these years many prominent Social-Democratic workers were formed.* In the organizations they controlled tens if not hundreds of thousands of Russian workers were given a political and organizational schooling.

This activity was carried on with no help or even any contact with the Bolshevik 'illegal cells' and the Party authorities, any intervention

* Such as the printers Kammermacher(Kefali), Devyatkin, Kubikov (Dementyev), and the metalworkers Gvozdyov, Philip Yudin, Alexander Smirnov, Theodor Bulkin, Vasily Chirkin, Romanov, and a great many others.

by whom was felt to be a pernicious hindrance. The traditionally critical attitude of Menshevism towards the Party organization as it had taken shape historically, and the attempt to reform it, to make it, not only in its mass foundations but also in its apex, genuinely 'worker' (the workers' Congress!) began to take the form, among broad circles of Russian 'legal' Mensheviks, of a special trend, both theoretically and organizationally amorphous, but completely definite in its attempt to break the evolutionary continuity of the Party and re-create it from the ground up, quite independently of its old and still surviving organizations and authorities. The intellectual inspirer of this trend, which the Bolsheviks called the 'liquidation' of the Party (this also gave rise to the polemical epithet 'liquidationism', accepted, as is often the case, by those it had been aimed at) was A. N. Potresov, editor of *Nasha Zarya*, who had stayed on in Russia, while his most outstanding practical assistants were P. A. Garvi (Yurii), K. M. Yermolayev (Roman) and I. Isuf (Michael).

The *Golos Sotsialdemokrata* (Social-Democratic Voice), published in Paris by Martov and Dan, furthered the practical work of the Liquidators in all sorts of ways. They defended them from the attacks of Bolshevism, while actively collaborating in the legal press published by the Liquidators.* But at the same time *Golos Sotsialdemokrata* clearly warned the Mensheviks against any policy of rupture with the old Party. It reminded them that in Russian conditions an illegal party centre was indispensable so that the legal activity of the Social-Democracy itself did not lose its broad-gauge political and Socialist perspectives, but founded its orientation on the new revolutionary upsurge that was inevitably coming in the future. It warned them that once the period of social stagnation had passed the Party, which the Liquidators had called a 'corpse', had every chance of reviving once again. Because of this it called on them to exploit the favourable turn in the temper of the 'ethnic' organizations (during this period the Latvian Social-Democracy also began turning towards Menshevism) in order to make the successors of their legal activity the foundation

* This position of *Golos Sotsialdemokrata* provoked a new split on the part of Plekhanov, who formed a special group of 'Plekhanovites' (or 'Menshevik Party-ites'). These, however, remained an extremely small circle. Akselrod, though he maintained the closest relations with *Golos Sotsialdemokrata*, refused to become part of its editorial board, since his ultra-sceptical attitude towards the possibility of fruitfully exploiting the surviving authorities of the Party drew him closer to the Liquidators.

not for a definite rupture with the 'illegal' party, but for the strengthening of its own position in it, for its conquest and reformation from within.

These appeals of *Golos Sotsialdemokrata* met with little sympathy in the core of the Russian Liquidators. At the end of December 1910 a plenary session of the Central Committee was convoked in Paris. There, through the united efforts of the Mensheviks, the 'ethnic' organizations and the 'conciliationist' Bolshevik members of the Central Committee, who had come from Russia, as well as Chkheidze, the representative of the Duma Social-Democratic fraction, succeeded by a united effort in carrying a resolution for the introduction of two Mensheviks, Martov and Dan, into the editorial board of the Central Organ, the transfer to the Central Committee of a considerable portion of the financial funds of the 'Bolshevik Centre', and the thoroughgoing reorganization of the Central Committee itself. Three Russian Liquidators were made members, and the focal activity of the Central Committee was transferred to Russia. This decision was in fact broken by the refusal of the above-mentioned Yurii, Roman, and Michael to accept the posts offered them. The furious campaign of the Bolsheviks against Liquidationism, which had almost subsided, revived with even greater ferocity.

But it was just at this time that the whole political situation began changing, and together with it the conditions of the Liquidators' activity. Towards the end of 1910 the economic stagnation began yielding to a new revival. This immediately provoked a new upsurge of activity, almost extinct, of the labouring masses, who now tried by means of economic strikes to improve their situation, which had deteriorated immensely during the years of stagnation. During a period when, for 1909, statistics recorded only 56,000 striking workers, by 1911 there were already 137,000 on strike, while in 1912 the figures came to 1,238,000. This jump is explained by the fact that purely economic strikes began to be added to by strikes of a political nature as well. These indicated the growth of political excitement among the masses too, the clearest manifestation of which was the gigantic protest strike against the shooting of the strikers at the Lena goldfields (April 1912). The revival of the workers' movement was immediately reflected in an upsurge of sentiment among the democratic and liberal intelligentsia, by the sharpening of contradictions between the land-owning and bourgeois wings of the 'October' *bloc* and between the *bloc* as a whole and the government, the growth of conflicts in the

Duma, and the general rise in the country's political temperature. The government was forced to slacken the police repressions and, in particular, with respect to the Social-Democracy, to permit the revival of legal newspapers, to liquidate in part the still unfinished political trials and thus make it possible by 1913 for several prominent Party leaders to return from the emigration.*

The Party's illegal apparatus also began reviving in the atmosphere of the incipient social upsurge. 'Illegal cells' began emerging from a state of political nonentity and finding a response not only in the strata of the intelligentsia that were being revolutionized anew, but also in certain circles of the radically inclined big bourgeoisie, which was more impressed by the sharply anti-government political agitation of Bolshevism than by the watchful and politically more and more 'reformist' activity of the Liquidators in constructing workers' organizations.† But to the Liquidators' astonishment, the 'unabridged slogans' began finding a more and more sympathetic response in the restive labouring masses too. To be sure, this was not so much because of their democratic-republican content, which in the given conditions was becoming for the Bolsheviks themselves merely a means of unmasking the 'treachery' of the liberal Kadet bourgeoisie and the 'conciliationism' of the Mensheviks, as an expression of their readiness to support in an 'unabridged' form all the socio-economic demands of the masses. The Liquidators had tried to introduce the struggle for these demands into a framework of methods that the

* The opportunity was immediately taken advantage of by Martov and Dan among the Mensheviks, and Kamenev among the Bolsheviks. This 'liberal' policy, however, was also based on the calculations of the political police aimed at the inflammation of inter-fraction dissension and its transfer from the emigration to Russia, as a means of demoralizing and disorganizing the Social-Democracy and disorienting the working-class on the very threshold of its regeneration. The principal channel for this policy of Beletsky's, the director of the Police Department, was the above-mentioned *provocateur*, the worker-delegate from Moscow to the fourth Duma, Roman Malinovsky, chairman of the Duma Bolshevik fraction, member of the 'Prague' Central Committee and editor of the newly founded legal Bolshevik newspaper *Pravda* (The Truth).

† These representatives of the radical bourgeoisie – one of them, Sabbas Morozov, was mentioned at the very beginning of the book – became a source of funds for the illegal organization that made its 'guerrilla warfare' unnecessary. The chief intermediaries between the Bolshevik centre and these circles of the bourgeoisie were Maxim Gorky and the engineer Leonid Krasin, an old Bolshevik who had occupied important positions in industry and was later Soviet ambassador to London and Paris.

trade union movement of Western Europe had struggled its way towards by lengthy experience in completely different conditions. In this the Liquidators imperceptibly shifted from a Marxist 'europeanization' *theory* of Russian Socialism to an attempt to 'europeanize' its *tactics* as well, an attempt that contradicted the theory and that in the then conditions of Russia was unrealizable.

In these circumstances the negative attitude of the Liquidators towards the old Party and towards the illegal organization of the Social-Democracy in general was somewhat shaken. The same Liquidators who at the beginning of 1911 had refused to take part in the attempts to heal and unify the Party now agreed, together with the 'Trotskyites' and the 'Plekhanovites', to organize the so-called 'August *bloc*' of 1912. But it was already too late. The split within the Party had already taken definitive shape, and the activity of the new *bloc* was distorted in advance by its having to carry on a more and more ferocious fraction struggle against Bolshevism. But what was especially important was that between the labouring masses and, above all, between the spirit of these masses and the spirit of their own vanguard, trained by the Liquidators, a disharmony came about that began making itself felt more and more at each crisis in the further growth of the workers' movement.

This disharmony was smoothed over and may even be said to have been liquidated during the first few years of the 1914–18 war. Then all the possibilities of open Social-Democratic activity once again shrank to a minimum, while the threat of being sent to the front held in check the discontented. On the other hand, the patriotic spirit inevitable in the first phase of a war brought the rank-and-file workers closer emotionally to the Menshevik Liquidators, who in an overwhelming majority had taken up a patriotic-defensist position, and drove them away from Bolshevik 'defeatism'. A skilful exploitation by the 'defensists' of the so-called Military Industrial Committees (created in 1916 by the liberal Zemstvo and city government bourgeoise for the purpose of servicing the army and establishing a political *rapprochement* with it) in order to form within these committees autonomous local Workers' Groups and a central group, which were to acquire extremely broad opportunities for public action, made Menshevism the central organizer of every variety of workers' movement, aroused anew by the fiascos of the war. In the first period of the revolution of 1917 they ensured it a dominant position in the Petersburg Soviet, in the majority of the provincial Soviets, and in the central Soviets of Workers' Deputies. It was with all the more violence that this discord revived in the subsequent course of the revolution. We have already noted what a role was played in its exacerbation by the Menshevik 'reformist' policy, and what fateful importance this had for the fate of Menshevism.

All this time the strike movement kept broadening, overflowing from the capital into the provinces; it suddenly seized entire branches of industry (the Baku oil industry in June 1914) and gradually assumed a revolutionary hue. At the same time, as is known, the international situation was growing more complicated; by now feverish preparations for war were taking place backstage. In these circumstances the government tried, at the end of June 1914, to put an end with one blow to both the reviving Social-Democracy and the growing workers' movement. In the course of a single day the whole Social-Democratic press was shut down; hundreds of Social-Democrats were arrested; dozens of legal workers' organizations were dissolved. The response of the Petersburg proletariat was a general protest strike, which thanks to the arrests lacked any organized political leadership, but which all the more rapidly began passing over into armed clashes with the police and attempts to set up barricades. A witness of these events was Poincaré, the president of the future war ally France, who happened to be in Petersburg at this time as the head of a squadron. The declaration of war put an abrupt halt to this movement and even called forth, as has been noted, a certain upsurge of patriotic spirit in the masses that only just before had been mutinying. But it had been a rather impressive forewarning on the very threshold of war: through the still just beginning rumble of weapons on the front there could already be heard the iron tread of the revolution ripening in the rear.

However paradoxical it sounds, the extreme reactionaries in the Tsarist bureaucracy grasped the movement of forces and the social content of this coming revolution far sooner and better than all the Russian 'professional revolutionaries', and particularly the Russian Marxist Social-Democrats, who in all fractions and tendencies, as we have seen, were oriented almost down to the last moment towards the foreordained fixity of the 'capitalist' and 'bourgeois' boundaries set for it by history.

Thus, as early as 1884 Count Dmitri Tolstoy, one of Alexander III's most reactionary Ministers of the Interior, said to Prince Bülow, the future Chancellor of the German Empire: 'Every attempt to introduce into Russia Western European, parliamentary forms of government is doomed to failure. If the Tsarist régime . . . is overthrown its place will be taken by Communism, by the pure, unveiled Communism of Mr Karl Marx, who died recently in London and whose theories I've studied with attention.'[187] But still more astonishing for the accuracy of its foresight is the picture of the coming Russian revolution drawn by P. N. Durnovo, an even greater reactionary than D. Tolstoy, who was also one of Alexander III's Ministers of the Interior. He handed Nicholas II a secret memo in February 1914, just as the prospects of an eventual war against Germany began to be outlined; the memo was not made known at the time even to all the members of the government.[188]

Starting out from the 'profound conviction' that in contemporary conditions the war would provoke revolutionary upheavals in the conquered countries that could not help but overflow into the victorious countries as well, Durnovo wrote:

> These upheavals will bear a social, not a political character, there can be no doubt of that. . . . Russia will, of course, represent a particularly favourable terrain for social upheavals. Here the masses of the people unquestionably believe in the principles of unconscious Socialism. In spite of the oppositionist spirit of Russian society . . . a political revolution in Russia is impossible, and every revolutionary movement will inevitably degenerate into a Socialist movement. For behind our opposition there is no one; it has no support in the people. . . . The average Russian, both peasant and worker, is not seeking political rights . . . The peasant is dreaming of the gratuitous sharing of other people's land, the worker about the transfer to him of all the capital and profits of the factory-owner. . . . The Russian opposition is wholly that of the intelligentsia, and that is its weakness, since between our intelligentsia and the people there is a profound abyss of mutual mistrust and lack of understanding.

Durnovo ended his note with the following forecast:

> If the war ends with a victory, the pacification of the Socialist movement will not, in the last resort, present any difficulties. . . . But in case of a defeat . . . the social revolution in its most extreme manifestations will be inevitable. . . . It will begin with the blaming of the government for all failures. A furious campaign against it will begin in the legislative institutions, as the result of which revolutionary acts will begin in the country. These latter will at once put forth Socialist slogans, the only ones that have any hope of grouping together the broad masses of the populace. First there will be total reapportionment, followed by general redistribution of all possessions. The conquered army, deprived during just this period of war-time of its most reliable section, the officers, and

seized in most of its sections by the general spontaneous peasant desire for land, will be too demoralized to serve as a bulwark of law and order. The legislative institutions and the oppositionist intelligentsia parties, deprived of any real authority in the eyes of the people, will be incapable of curbing the same unbridled masses they were the ones to raise up; Russia will be hurled into black anarchy whose outcome does not even submit to the imagination.

Durnovo, did not of course foresee, any more than anyone else of the time, nor could he have foreseen, that the 'outcome' of the 'black anarchy' of 1918–19 he had foreseen would be a new 'Soviet' state order. His note, intended to forewarn the government against taking part in the war, did not achieve its aim. A war broke out, and at that a war against Germany, which Russian reactionaries had been so afraid of ever since Alexander III; it was just because of this that they had always preferred a 'Far Eastern' line in Russian foreign policy to a 'Western European' line, or in Martov's words preferred a 'Tsushima policy to a Sebastopol policy'.[189]

The 1914–18 war proved to be a historic landmark in the history not only of Russia and Europe, but of the whole world. It also proved to be a landmark in the ideological development of both fractions of of the Russian Social-Democracy. The metamorphoses their ideology had undergone within the envelope of petrified fraction formulae, dogmas and slogans, and whose symptoms have been noted more than once in these pages, were slashed out into the open by the Caesarean operation of the war. Unexpectedly, what resulted was the change of role between the fractions that has also been referred to more than once. In the final analysis it transformed the fraction known for its emphasis on 'republican democracy' into the exponent of the idea of an authoritarian and initially definitely anti-democratic Socialism, while the fraction that emphasized the priority of 'class-Socialist' objectives became the standard-bearer of the most simplified 'democratic reformism'.

This 'democratic reformist' metamorphosis of Menshevism was prepared during the period between the two revolutions by its principled refusal to struggle for power against the bourgeoisie, and hence also by its inner reconciliation with the 'abridged' formulae of democracy, in so far as it was these formulae that ensured what Menshevism regarded as its basic task in the revolution – the building of a class-workers' organization and the development of the workers' class-consciousness. Menshevism's programmatic slogan remained, of course, the 'democratic republic', but this became a theoretically binding but more or less remote goal, rather than a slogan capable of inspiring a passionate struggle of the moment. As for the practice of the Liquidators, it furthered even more the degeneration of Menshevism into an ideology of 'democratic reformism' that slowly ripened in broad Menshevik circles and took on more definite forms in the conditions of war and revolution. But it has only been in the emigration, by now* a quarter of a century old, that it has attained a finished quality that definitively liquidated the class and Socialist character of the so-called 'Menshevik' groups that are encompassed by it and that in fact share only the name with historic Menshevism.

It was in this same period between the two revolutions that the authoritarian Socialist, anti-democratic metamorphosis of Bolshevism was also being prepared. This metamorphosis was due to the fact that neither in the course of the 1905 revolution nor in all the succeeding years did the 'revolutionary-republican' peasant democracy, which had been the cornerstone of the whole conception of the 'democratic dictatorship of the proletariat and peasantry', assume any tangible form. Because of this the formula not only dropped out of use for all practical purposes, but, as we have said, the very slogan of the 'democratic republic' took on the character of a charge of 'treachery' aimed at the Kadets, and of 'conciliationism' aimed at the Mensheviks, rather than a summons to struggle addressed to the masses of the people. It was not around the slogans of political democracy that the Bolsheviks succeeded in mobilizing the agitated labouring masses against the government and in wrenching them away from the Mensheviks, but around the 'unabridged' socio-economic slogans. It was not on the terrain of general political programmes but on the terrain of a struggle for land and for the abolition of the deprivation of rights of the peasantry as a caste that a certain contact was established between Bolshevism and the 'peasant' groups inside and outside the Duma, just as it was on the terrain of this same struggle that a contact arose between the worker and peasant movements during the periods of their upsurge. All it needed was a push from the outside for the Bolsheviks to decide openly to consign to the archives the thoroughly threadbare banner of 'republican democracy'. And this time, as indeed in all preceding moments in the crises of Bolshevik ideology, it was Lenin who slashed through the Gordian knot.

At the beginning of the war not only was Lenin, who had been in

* I.e. 1945. (*Translator's Note.*)

the emigration since 1908, abroad, but also Martov, whose return to Russia had been blocked by the war. As is known, both of them had taken up an 'internationalist' position with respect to the war and were carrying on a determined struggle against both European 'social-patriotism' and Russian 'defensism'. Both had become participants in the unification of the 'internationalist' groups that had emerged at the conferences at Zimmerwald and Kienthal (Switzerland). For the majority of 'Zimmerwaldians', which included Martov, the objective of the 'Socialist-internationalists' was the rallying of the proletariat and the labouring masses in general under the banner of a struggle for the soonest possible liquidation of the 'imperialist' war and the conclusion of a general peace 'without annexations or indemnities, on the basis of the self-determination of nations'. But for Lenin, who headed the small 'Left' wing of the Zimmerwaldians, this objective was the 'transformation of the imperialist war into a civil war', with the recognition of the 'defeat of one's own government' as the shortest path to the unloosing of such a civil war in each individual country.

As far as internal Russian policy was concerned, this 'war' position of Lenin's had the advantage of allowing him to make his central agitational slogan an immediate, though 'separate' exit of Russia from the war. This was a slogan that met with a response among the masses of the soldiery, who were becoming more and more sympathetic as Russia suffered a series of disastrous defeats that began to decompose and demoralize the army. But what was even more important for the internal policy of both fractions was the general conviction, arrived at by both Martov and Lenin, together with all the Zimmerwaldians, that the war engendered by imperialism would deal European capitalism a blow it would never recover from, and that an epoch of social revolution for Europe was in the offing.

In this case too, of course, Martov, in accordance with the common ideological traditions of Menshevism and of the international Social-Democracy generally, imagined this epoch to be a more or less long-drawn-out period of constantly sharpening organized struggle, taking in broader and broader layers of the labouring masses of the cities and countryside, and in its very course making the Socialist proletariat the natural and desirable political leader – in Marx's phrase a 'class-emancipator'. For Lenin, on the other hand, once again in accordance with the general ideology of Bolshevism, the 'world social revolution' was imagined to be a relatively brief 'civil war' in a number of countries, led by the international staff of 'self-restrained and trained' revolutionary Socialists. It was to be just these, as representatives of the working-class, that the revolution would hand over power to.

The 'social revolution' in Europe did not, of course, materialize after the First World War either in one variant or another. Having made an accurate estimate of the general trends of the epoch, both Martov and Lenin overestimated the speed and straightforwardness of the social development unloosed by the war. A quarter of a century, filled with the catastrophes of Fascism and a new world war, had to go by for a situation to be created in which the radical transformation of the social structure of Europe and the whole world was really put on the order of the day. But the very orientation towards a European 'social revolution' provided that 'international' way out in which, as we have noted in its place, both Menshevism and Bolshevism, since their very emergence, had sought a solution of the contradictions of the Russian revolution. For Russia, too, the international social revolution created the perspective of a shattering of the 'capitalist' and 'bourgeois' framework that had made these contradictions insoluble.

In this perspective, 'a bourgeois régime' ceased being historically inevitable. It became not only useless, but also pernicious – pernicious from the point of view of wartime 'internationalism' and still more pernicious from the point of view of an involvement of backward Russia in the expected process of the social-revolutionary transformation of Europe. Martov made a sharp break with Menshevik political traditions, which had almost begun petrifying, when he made this proposition the mainstay of his policy, though all the conclusions drawn from it were not formulated by him until his 'April' Theses of 1920, which became the platform of the 'Martov' trend in the Russian Social-Democracy. This trend shifted from an orientation towards a 'bourgeois régime' to an orientation towards a 'labourers' régime', towards a political alliance of the proletariat, the peasantry, and the urban petty-bourgeoisie – in sociological terms, towards the orientation that, as we have seen, underlay the Bolshevik conception. It was simply that now the ultimate objective of that alliance was no longer supposed to be the conquest and consolidation of the 'democratic republic', 'bourgeois' in its socio-economic foundations, but the gradual transformation of the socio-economic relations of backward Russia in a direction that would enable it to be drawn into the process of the social revolution that had begun in the advanced

West, and a concerted participation in such a transformation of the non-proletarian labouring classes as well, above all of the peasantry.

The 'international' perspective now opening up also gave an impetus to Lenin's thought in what was essentially the same direction. In a *Farewell Letter to the Swiss Workers* dated 26 March 1917, written before he left for Russia soon after the beginning of the revolution, he declared the task of the coming European revolutions to be 'the transfer of power in all civilized countries into the hands of the revolutionary proletariat, for the realization of the Socialist overturn'. He wrote:

> To the Russian proletariat has fallen the honour of launching a series of revolutions, engendered by the imperialist war with objective inevitability. . . . We know very well that the proletariat of Russia is less organized, prepared and conscious than the workers of other countries. It is not special qualities but merely historical conditions that have developed in a special way that have made the Russian proletariat *for a certain and perhaps very brief time* the pioneer of the revolutionary proletariat of the whole world. Russia is a peasant country, one of the most backward countries in Europe. Socialism cannot conquer there directly and immediately. But the peasant character of the country, with the enormous land reserve of the aristocratic land-owners, on the basis of the experience of 1905, *can* give enormous dimensions to the bourgeois-democratic revolution in Russia and turn our revolution into the *prologue* of the world-wide Socialist revolution, a step towards it.

Further:

> In Russia Socialism cannot conquer directly. . . . But the peasant masses can carry the inevitable and mature agrarian overturn to the point of confiscation of all the boundless landowners' estates. . . . In and for itself such an overturn would still be far from Socialist. But it would strengthen extraordinarily the positions of the Socialist proletariat in Russia and its influence over the agricultural workers and the poorest peasants. . . . The Russian proletariat cannot by its own forces alone *consummate* the Socialist revolution victoriously. But it can give the Russian revolution dimensions that will create the best conditions for it, and that in a certain sense would *start* it. It can ease the circumstances so that its *principal*, its most faithful, its most reliable collaborator, the *European* and American *Socialist proletariat* can enter into the decisive battle.

The same ideas were also expressed in the *Theses* Lenin came out with in the Petersburg Soviet directly he arrived in Russia:

The peculiarity of the present time in Russia consists of the transition from the first stage of the revolution, which gave the power to the bourgeoisie because of the inadequate awareness and organization of the proletariat, to its second stage, which must give the power to the proletariat and the poorest strata of the peasantry. . . . Not a parliamentary republic – a return to that from the Soviet of Workers' Deputies would be a step backward – but a republic of Soviets of Workers', Farm-Hands', and Peasants' Deputies throughout the country, from the bottom to the top. . . . It is not the 'introduction' of Socialism that is our immediate task, but the immediate transition to the control by the Soviets of Workers' Deputies of social production and the distribution of commodities.

But with all the similarity, almost identity, of Martov's and Lenin's general ideas in this period concerning the basic tasks of the Russian revolution, they were divided here, as they were on the question of wartime 'internationalism', by their completely different interpretation of the methods and forms through which those tasks could be successfully performed. Martov conceived of the 'labourers' régime' as a coalition, that is, as a compromise régime of politically conscious and organized social forces on a footing of equality, in which the working-class would win a leading position for itself merely by virtue of its superiority and the breadth of its socio-political horizon. Political liberty, restrictions on which were permissible in times of revolution for the 'exploiting' classes, but not for the labouring masses, seemed to him a direct and indispensable condition for the functioning of such a régime. Democracy, in forms that if not identical with were close to parliamentarianism, was its natural constitutional and juridical bulwark. To use an expression of contemporary political language today, Martov imagined the 'labourers' régime' to be a government of a 'People's Front' type.

But this 'People's Front' democracy could not be realized in the Russia of 1917. The organized and politically educated forces that are an indispensable premise of its realization were not present. Such forces were in the working-class. But in the conditions of the 'freest' country, which was what, according to an expression in Lenin's *Theses*, the revolution had made Russia, the attention of the labouring masses was less taken up than ever by questions of 'politics'. It was consumed more and more by those socio-economic disorders (the disorganization in the provision of supplies, raw materials, and fuel to the factories, the threatening unemployment, the rising prices, the supposed counter-revolutionary sabotage of the entrepreneurs, etc.)

that were brought about by the constantly worsening wartime collapse. But in the peasantry there were no organized political forces at all, least of all in its most combative section, which was concentrated in the cities and key centres of the country, and which against the background of war assumed decisive importance – the mass of soldiery, for whom the revolution meant above all an opportunity to realize a passionate dream: to go home from the front and take part in the anticipated 'total reapportionment'.

With the astonishing revolutionary flair peculiar to him, Lenin assessed this situation immediately when he removed the slogan of the 'democratic republic' completely and made his chief agitational slogan 'workers' control' – among the workers; confiscation of all the big estates – among the peasants; and an immediate peace – among the soldiers. He also made the slogan of his campaign against the Provisional Government 'Down with the Capitalist Ministers!', and when he put forth the demand for 'All Power to the Soviets!', the workers, peasants and soldiers uniformly understood this not as a guarantee of the realization of their *political* rights, but as a guarantee of the 'unabridged' realization of their *socio-economic* hopes and expectations.

In these conditions it was all the easier for Lenin to liquidate his orientation towards the 'democratic dictatorship of the proletariat and peasantry' and to shift openly to an orientation towards a dictatorship of the Bolshevik Party in the form of the 'Soviet régime' since, as we have seen, his original conception had also assumed the presence within the 'democratic dictatorship' of a *de facto* dictatorship of the proletariat in the form of Bolshevism. Under existing circumstances it was not the 'People's Front' conception of Martov, but the 'dictatorial' conception of Lenin – the authoritarian idea the first seeds of which he had sown in *What Is to Be Done?* – that won a complete and decisive victory, and under existing conditions could not help but win it.

But even though Lenin's *Theses* were merely the logical culmination of that idea, we have already mentioned how unexpected they proved even for the leading circles of Bolshevism, and what repugnance they aroused among rank-and-file Bolsheviks. Yet, as had been the case before in moments of sharp intellectual about-faces, it was only two or three weeks before Lenin had all Bolshevism behind him. And when, at the first All-Russian Congress of Soviets, the head of the Provisional Government, Alexander Kerensky, said that in the existing desperately difficult conditions there was no one, of course, who would want to take the power into his own hands, a sharp reply from Lenin rang out in the silence: 'There is!' In this 'There is!' the will to power, not of Lenin alone but of all Bolshevism, rang out.

On 25 October 1917 an armed uprising that was prepared by the Bolsheviks and whose chief force was the Kronstadt fleet overthrew the Provisional Government. And the evening of that same day the writer of these lines himself, in his capacity as Chairman, opened the second All-Russian Congress of Soviets that handed over the power to the Bolsheviks.

A new chapter had opened in the history not only of Russia, which became the Soviet Republic, but also in the social and political evolution of the whole world.

EPILOGUE

Bolshevism – Balance-Sheet and Prospects

The antithesis between Democracy and Socialism, the struggle for whose resolution runs throughout the history of the Russian revolutionary movement and Russian revolutionary thought like a red thread, remained unresolved by the 1917 revolution too. The conception put forward by Martov of its harmonious resolution through a democratic 'labourers' régime' – on the basis, to be sure, of the acknowledgement of the 'Socialist' and not the 'bourgeois' tendencies of the Russian revolution – was incapable of being realized in the 1917 revolution for the same reason that Lenin's conception of a 'democratic dictatorship of the proletariat and peasantry' could not be realized in the 1905 revolution. The organized 'revolutionary republican' peasant partner that both these conceptions counted on, even though in accordance with a different socio-political schema, was missing.

And more than half a century after its emancipation the masses of the Russian peasantry had not shaken off their indifference to purely political questions, an indifference that the hopes of one generation of Russian revolutionaries after another, as we have seen, were shattered on. The war consummated the emancipation of the peasant masses, too, from the Tsarist mystique. The peasantry gladly and extensively utilized the benefits of the republican political liberty proclaimed by the victorious revolution. But neither the war nor the revolution made this liberty a precious thing in its eyes that ought to and had to be fought for; they did not turn the Russian peasantry into a trustworthy bulwark of a free democratic state. Just as in the first, February period of the revolution, so in the second October period it was calculations not of a political but of a socio-economic nature that remained decisive for the peasants. But just as throughout the civil war, so in the years of initial instability and the subsequent gradual consolidation of the Soviet system, shot through by 'crises', the political profile of the régime and forces contending with each other played a minimal role in the peasants' attitude towards them.

The peasantry, or individual strata of it (the 'kulaks', the 'medium peasants', the 'paupers') defined its attitude towards them exclusively from the point of view of its own struggle – in the beginning for land, then for its free use of the products of the land. The 'Constituent Assembly Front' organized by the S.R.s not only condemned itself to defeat in advance, but did a good deal to discredit the very idea of political democracy in its 'European' forms in the eyes of broad masses of the peasantry. This came about just because, having made this idea their banner, the S.R.s went over to the side of the anti-Bolshevik barricade where there were grouped primarily the leading forces of the so-called 'White' movement, that is, forces in which the peasants rightly saw the defenders of the old landed proprietors and the champions of a reversal of the total reapportionment that had just been carried out.

In Russian conditions circumstances so fell out that the 'kolkhoz' system, which definitively shattered the narrow framework of individual peasant farming, also shattered the limited intellectual and political horizon of the peasantry conserved by that framework. For the first time it made tangible and manifest for it the uninterrupted link between its own economic destiny and the destiny of the state. It was only in the school of the Soviets, on the local, district, republican, and all-Union scale, that for the first time the peasantry began to learn the 'state' approach to the problems of its own socio-economic way of life, too. There, in the Soviets, even after the levelling off of the electoral rights of all citizens proclaimed by the 'Stalin' constitution of 1936, remnants of the old privileged classes liquidated by the Soviet revolution were scarcely represented. The monopolists were in fact the 'toilers' – the workers and peasants together with the Soviet bureaucracy and the trade union intelligentsia, who, however, were serving by now not private but state interests. That is why in spite of the 'single candidacy' of Soviet elections and of the 'one-party' regulation of Soviet policy, Soviet 'parliamentarianism' has proved to be far from a 'fiction' but an extremely real factor in the 'democratization' of the Soviet régime. In particular it was precisely in the conditions of this 'parliamentarianism' and later also under its extremely powerful 'ideological' influence, that the 'politicalization' of the Russian peasantry and its formation into a social force capable of becoming one of the stable and reliable mainstays of the 'toilers' democracy' took place for the first time.

This process of the 'politicalization' of the Russian peasantry was greatly advanced during the ordeals and experiences of the anti-Fascist war. It is being consummated before our eyes* under the 'occupation' conditions of contact with the European West and the daily expanding problems of the post-war socio-economic and cultural reconstruction of the country, which are becoming more and more complicated and difficult and demanding, more and more insistently a maximal activization of popular energies. But at that time, during the October-November days of 1917, this process was no more than a distant prospect. In those days all the thoughts, hopes and passions of millions of peasants at the front were totally absorbed by the idea of an immediate return home, while tens of millions of peasants in the rear were taken up by a desire to get on with the 'total reapportionment', also immediately. This 'reapportionment' had begun, to be sure, before October-November, but even the Socialist members of the Provisional Government had held it up in every possible way and even actively worked against it, in the illusory hope of solving the 'agrarian problem' not through the chaotic method of arbitrary seizures, but through the systematic method of the legislation of a future Constituent Assembly. What really bound the peasantry deeply to the new 'Soviet' régime was the sure knowledge that it was 'their own' régime that would set no obstacles either to the immediate liquidation of the war, or to the immediate realization of 'total reapportionment'. It was all the more willingly that they let the completely victorious Bolshevik Party deal with the 'constitutional' formation of the new régime. In such conditions, what with the complete disorganization and substantial destruction of transport that were provoked by the disorderly flight of millions of soldiers from the front and that in their turn threatened the cities with hunger and a stoppage of industry, the 'Soviet régime' – quite apart from the 'dictatorial' ideology of Bolshevism – could not but become a *dictatorship* at its very inception. Met immediately by the sabotage of the bureaucracy and the professional intelligentsia, by the formation of the 'White' armies, the first flare-ups of the approaching civil war, the Soviet régime, in its desperate and nine-tenths hopeless struggle against difficulties of production, economics, and administration, could not help but be transformed into a *terrorist* régime.

The dictatorial, terroristic, and one-party forms in which the Soviet régime immediately began taking shape testified to the fact that after its 'decisive victory' over the Tsarist régime the Russian

* Written in 1946. (*Translator's Note.*)

revolution was leaving unsolved its immemorial, fundamental problem – the fusion of democracy and Socialism. It was just this absence of a solution that was the reason the 'Martov' trend, linked to Bolshevism not only by the unity of the 'ultimate goal' but fundamentally also by their common interpretation of the 'sociology' of the Russian revolution as well as of world evolution in the conditions created by the First World War, was for more than a quarter of a century unable either to fuse with Bolshevism or to dissolve in it. 'Right' Menshevism, which had degenerated in a democratic-reformist way, very soon ceased being a factor in the revolutionary and Socialist development of Russia altogether, and turned into a kind of 'Left' wing of the liberal conservative camp. But the Martov trend played a considerable practical and political role by rallying the non-Bolshevik-minded circles of the proletariat and radical intelligentsia for the defence of the Soviet régime in the civil war, and an even greater role by rallying the international Socialist movement for a struggle against the policy of military intervention, economic blockade, and political non-recognition of the Soviet government. But even after it had stopped being an effective force within the country, the Martov trend continued and still continues existing as a purely ideological group that still exercises some influence on certain Bolshevik circles too.*

But if the existence of the Martov trend is no more than a 'symbolic' testimonial, so to speak, to the unsolved problem of 'democracy and Socialism' in the Soviet revolution, a completely real proof of that unsolved problem is the fact that throughout the existence of the Soviet régime it has been just this problem of 'democracy' that has invariably riveted the attention both of the Soviet government and

* Abroad the Martov tendency was grouped round the review *Sotsialisticheskii Vestnik* (The Socialist Courier) founded by Martov himself in February 1922. But during the quarter-century of emigration the majority of the Martov group abroad underwent the same evolution that, as we have noted at the beginning of this work, the remnants of the former Russian intelligentsia in general had undergone, and that in fact led them to a rupture with their own revolutionary and Socialist past and to their self-dissolution in bourgeois-democratic liberalism. After 1939 the Martov tendency abroad singled itself out of the general Menshevik organizations into a special group whose organ is the review *Novy Put'* (The New Road), published by the writer of these lines in close collaboration with A. Yugov (Jugow), the author of many works on the economics of Soviet Russia, Max Werner (A. Mikhailov), the well-known writer on military and international political questions, and others.

(The *Novy Put'* was dissolved in 1947, after Dan's death. *Translator's Note.*)

of the Bolshevik Party itself, at every stage of the development of the revolution, at every new turn in Soviet policy, and in the course of every new state or Party crisis. This is not only true of the actual formation of the Soviet régime. It was so in the course of the 'trade-unions discussion' that preceded the transition from 'War Communism' to the 'New Economic Policy' (N.E.P.); it was so throughout the whole struggle between fractions and tendencies within the Bolshevik Party that was the prologue to the period of all-out 'collectivization' of agriculture and feverish 'industrialization' of the country, and that was liquidated by the 'purges' and 'trials'; it was so when in the attempt to deflect the military threat of Hitler Fascism the Soviet government proclaimed a policy of 'collective security', and of a 'united' proletarian and 'people's' front outside the country and the Stalin constitution of 1936 as the incarnation of the 'most perfect democracy in the world' inside the country; it was so, finally, when side by side with the 'defence of the fatherland' the Soviet government made the 'defence of democracy' one of the fundamental slogans of the anti-Hitler war. But even now, after the victorious conclusion of that war, the problem of democracy in the domestic political life in the country, in its foreign policy, and in the approach to the international-proletarian question of the mutual relations between the renascent Social-Democracy and renascent Communism, has become a more and more urgent and crucial problem both of Soviet society and of the Soviet government.

But no 'democratization' of the Soviet régime is as yet visible. We shall have occasion to speak of this. But first of all we must clarify in our own minds the factors that allowed a party that at the time of the overturn numbered, by the most optimistic estimates,[190] no more than 250,000 members, most of them recent ones, not only to take power in over a sixth of the earth's surface with a population of almost 200 million, but also to maintain that power for more than a generation, and moreover to make it, in this historically brief period of time, the instrument of a socio-economic and cultural transformation more radical than any preceding revolution had been able to accomplish.

Bolshevism was, of course, prepared for dictatorial methods of rule by its whole preceding history and above all by its unwavering orientation towards the 'armed uprising', which strengthened the hierarchical structure of the Bolshevik Party and all its habits of 'unconditional obedience' to authoritarian directives coming 'from above'. But in order to cope with the tasks of self-defence and administration that instantly confronted the Soviet dictatorship in the chaotic conditions outlined above, and even more – in order to cope with the tasks of restoration, at first, and then of a radical reorganization of the country's economy, shaken to its foundations, what it needed – instantly – was a *new apparatus* that would be capable somehow of replacing the old, which to a considerable degree met the new régime with sabotage or openly shifted to the 'White' counter-revolutionary camp in the civil war. This new apparatus was given the Soviet revolution by all the preceding labours of the Social-Democracy, not only of one, but of *both* its fractions.

The illegal cells, the combat groups, the military-technical organizations, the guerrilla companies, and so on, gave the Bolsheviks the cadres of the organizers for the 'Red Guard', the 'supply detachments', the Cheka, and the other organs of struggle against sabotage and counter-revolution. But it was solely the tens, if not hundreds, of thousands of workers, schooled by Menshevism in the trade unions, co-operative, insurance, cultural and every other kind of organization for workers' autonomy and initiative, who gave it cadres of working-class organizers and administrators for the nationalized economy. It was only relatively few of this 'workers' intelligentsia' who clung to their Menshevik positions to the end, and like other Mensheviks, too, left the stage of practical politics and became victims of repressions. But the overwhelming mass of the 'workers' intelligentsia' trained by the Mensheviks grew up into the Soviet régime and became the most powerful bulwark of its economic system. It sounds paradoxical, but it was only the protracted activity of the Mensheviks, particularly of the Liquidators, that created the workers' vanguard without which the nationalization of industry and commerce and the collectivization of agriculture would have been impossible, and without which the Soviet revolution would have been doomed to failure. Thus the course of events has incontrovertibly proven that in their very dissension *both* fractions of the Russian Social-Democracy were historically indispensable factors in the victory of the Russian revolution. Each of them, in its very 'extremism', served, as Plekhanov said in his time, 'one of the sides' of the dual task that history had set the Russian revolution, but that, for reasons explained more than once, did not permit a straightforward and harmonious solution.

As has already been emphasized, the Russian liberal bourgeoisie and the democratic intelligentsia, in and for themselves, were always politically helpless. By erasing the boundaries between themselves and the 'White' front in the civil war, they conclusively deprived themselves of any possibility of exercising any intellectual and political influence if not over the workers at least over the peasant masses. In these conditions, with the political indifferentism of the peasantry and lower-middle-class already noted in this period, there proved to be enough cadres composed of elements formed by the pre-revolutionary activity of the Social-Democracy to give the Bolshevik régime a chance to consolidate itself and begin to build – of course in the most rough-and-ready form – a new revolutionary apparatus, and to accomplish – once again by the most rough-and-ready methods – at least the most unpostponeable economic tasks, i.e. first of all, the servicing of the Red fronts of the civil war and the supplying of the urban population with food, and transport and industry with raw materials and fuel. The 'Communism' of those days, with its expropriation not only of the bourgeoisie's capital but also of its consumption goods, with its 'levelling' and gratuitous redistribution of available goods among the 'toilers', with its 'supply detachments', which took away the peasants' 'surpluses', and with its 'labour armies' which, by a system of compulsory obedience for the whole able-bodied population of both sexes, tried to organize collective activity in definite districts of the country, primarily for the procurement of fuel – this 'Communism' was not called 'War Communism' by accident. No matter how primitive and essentially ineffective it was, in the conditions of the massive revolutionary shaking up of the agricultural structure of the country, it was just the collapse in industry and transport, bequeathed to the revolution by the 'imperialist' war and monstrously worsened by the civil war, that left the Bolshevik régime no other ways of grappling with these unpostponeable economic tasks. There is no need to explain why, against the background of the civil war, the dictatorial forms of the new régime could not help but become more and more perfected and 'tougher'. And the international background also had an effect along the same lines.

Lenin himself, as is known – entirely in the spirit of his *Farewell Letter to the Swiss Workers* – thought the Bolshevik dictatorship would be no more than a relatively brief episode if the Socialist revolution in the advanced European West did not come to its help, and that the historic importance of the Soviet 'Commune' would in that case be reduced, infinitely more even than the Paris Commune, to a legend, a spiritual banner, a model for coming Socialist revolutions, which would learn from its experience, its victories and defeats. But the meagre tenacity of the German proletariat, morally and politically disoriented by the 'war' policy of the majority of the Social-Democracy and trade unions, and weakened by the dissensions this provided, enabled the capitalist victor countries to nip the Socialist revolution of Europe in the bud and to free their own hands for military intervention and an economic blockade against the Socialist revolution in Russia.

Nevertheless the Bolshevik dictatorship did not perish and was not wiped out. But as the chances vanished for a solution of the socio-economic contradictions of the Soviet revolution via its involvement in the channel of the general Socialist development of Europe (which the Martov tendency also calculated on), these contradictions became sharper and sharper, and the struggle against them kept growing more and more difficult, while at the same time the methods of that struggle grew sterner and tougher, and the state forms of the Soviet régime more and more 'dictatorial'. In the last resort the direct 'surgical' transformation of the socio-economic structure of a backward country, which found its climax and consummation in the policy of 'dekulakization' and 'all-out collectivization', proved to be the high price whose payment was the only way to avoid the destruction of the Soviet revolution and its capitulation to the forces of internal and international capitalist reaction.

What was a most powerful stimulus for the development of the Soviet régime in the same 'dictatorial' direction was the military danger that never ceased to menace the Soviet Union even after the period of blockade and intervention was succeeded by the era of trade relations and diplomatic recognition. The most profound and inexhaustible source of this danger was the instability of continental European capitalist society, especially its vital centre – Germany. This proved to be an inevitable consequence of its 'salvation' through the violent stopping of the European Socialist revolutions, and excluded any possibility of its own peaceful development, without catastrophes, while depriving it at the same time of the moral and political resistance to the onslaught of the anti-capitalist currents that history had made the Soviet revolution the incarnation of. The crushing of this revolution became a question of life or death for tottering continental European capitalism, which in this case had every reason for calculating on the sympathy and collaboration of capitalist reaction and of conservatism throughout the world.

This became completely evident a little after the ruling classes of Europe had begun responding everywhere to the Socialist peril by the support of 'Fascist' movements – in spite of the 'anti-capitalist' banner that enabled these movements to draw into their orbit broad uprooted masses of the lower-middle-class and peasantry that had been the immemorial bulwark of capitalism. It was only natural that after a provincial rehearsal in Italy it was precisely in Germany that Fascism attained its extreme development, and that German National Socialism immediately became the fulcrum for the anti-Soviet policy whose clearest and final pre-war expression was 'Munich'. But Hitler Fascism in Germany meant war. And whatever might have been the preparatory and initial phases of this war it was impossible not to see, as was stated at the time in the so-called *War Theses* of Otto Bauer and the author of these lines, that by forcibly creating a military coalition of the capitalist democracies and the Soviet Union there would be war nevertheless, primarily and above all against Socialism, not only Soviet Socialism but also European and world Socialism, and that in that war the Soviet Union would be fated to become the mightiest Socialist citadel.

But for the Soviet Union from the very outset the war danger meant above all the necessity of surrendering a constantly growing portion of the resources of the impoverished and exhausted country to the creation of an adequately up-to-date military apparatus. Hence it meant the necessity of as massive and rapid an industrialization of the country as possible ('catch up with and outdistance!' 'Five-Year-Plan in four years!', etc.), and the subordination of the very process of industrialization to the demands of defence. Thus it meant the impossibility of any full satisfaction of the needs of the urban and working-class populace. It made more or less compulsory forms of distribution and the pinning down of manpower the sole means of preventing an epidemic flight of the populace into the countryside that would have threatened industry with paralysis and all plans for industrialization with disruption. The extreme impoverishment of the reserve of consumer commodities that the cities and the industrial centres might have disposed of in exchange for food and raw materials of agriculture again and again, with constantly growing acuteness, carried the Bolshevik dictatorship back to the fundamental question of the Soviet revolution – the question of the peasantry.

The 'War Communism' policy of 'supply detachments' that forcibly removed peasants' 'surpluses' led in the last resort to a catastrophic curtailment of peasant sowings. This condemned not only the urban and industrial populace but also a considerable part of the rural populace to a famine that carried off a great many victims. At the tenth Congress of the Soviet Communist Party (March 1921), which convened in conditions of a just finished general protest strike of the Petersburg workers and the still continuing uprising of the Kronstadt sailors, Lenin announced a transition to a 'New Economic Policy' (N.E.P.). This opened up to private capital, both Russian and foreign, a limited access to industry (in the form of 'concessions'), while the peasants were left the right of free use and sale of their own farm products – after the payment of a tax in kind assessed on each farm.

The new policy immediately threw onto the market the reserves the peasants had hidden. This eased the supply situation in the cities, while it later led to a rapid extension of the sowing area and to a considerable expansion in the production of objects of consumption, on which the petty and medium capitalist 'concessionaires' concentrated their attention, at a time when big foreign capital was trying – generally with no success – to lay its hands on the mines (gold) and timber resources. Nevertheless, in spite of the visible successes of the New Economic Policy, Lenin, who in 1921 had announced that the N.E.P. was 'in earnest and for a long time', only a year later, at the eleventh Congress of the Soviet Communist Party (March 1922) was forced to declare that 'the retreat was finished', and to proclaim as slogan 'the preparation of an advance against private capital'.[191] But the brief era of the N.E.P. did not pass by without a trace: it bequeathed the Soviet economy that intermingling of planning and market factors, with dual channels of supply and dual scales of prices, that in various forms and permutations not only became its firm foundation, but also acquired considerable importance on an international scale as well, from the point of view of the theoretical and practical solution of the problems of a planned economy.

The N.E.P. was liquidated first of all in the cities, in industry and commerce. In spite of the negligible amount of capital invested in them, the appearance in the arena of the 'private entrepreneur', who only the day before had been considered a 'parasite' subject to merciless annihilation and today was proclaimed an indispensable and useful, if transitory cog in the Soviet economic machine, proved to be far more dangerous for the Soviet society, incomplete in its structure and still unsettled, than had been imagined beforehand. The 'N.E.P.-man' not only quickly grew rich himself, but in his own way also became a centre of material and ideological attraction for the 'former people', the surviving remnants of the old ruling classes, who felt a rush of new hope. But the N.E.P.-man also impressed the still somewhat unskilful Soviet bureaucracy with his businesslike zeal, especially its economic and administrative sector, which in addition he rather successfully corrupted both by direct bribery and by making individual officials his partners in highly lucrative speculations. But the N.E.P.-man was no less a danger from the point of view of his possible effect on the very socio-economic foundation of the Soviet society still under construction, and at the same time on the new political order created by the revolution, which was only just in the initial phase of formation.

The N.E.P.-man disposed of his own capital, equipment and raw materials, warily brought out from hiding; he disposed of old commercial and technical connexions and could always depend on the support and resources of foreign capital. It was natural that both on the level of productivity and in the quality of products he could not be equalled by a nationalized industry that had only just begun to take form in conditions of an extreme shortage of equipment and raw materials, the technical and commercial inexperience of its leaders, and the lack of sympathy and sometimes even outright sabotage of a considerable part of the service personnel. However few the N.E.P.-man enterprises, against the background of the general ruin, the epidemic poverty, the shortage of literally everything, they sparkled as bright advertisement for 'free enterprise', and sounded a tacit but nonetheless insistent call for a restoration of the régime of 'private capital'.

This call threatened to evoke a response even in the ranks of the workers, all the more since for reasons already indicated the N.E.P.-man had the possibility of creating far better conditions of labour for a circle (in essence extremely limited) of his own workers and employees than were possible for the new Soviet state. Nor was that all. This state itself had to concern itself in every way with the improvement of the conditions of the workers and employees taken up by 'private capital', while in its own enterprises it was, as we have seen, forced just at this time to impose all sorts of restrictions and deprivations on the masses of the Russian proletariat. And it was in this connexion that the question of the trade unions arose once again in an acute form.

The compulsory methods of allocation and fixation of manpower, and the freezing of wages that in existing conditions proved to be an indispensable prerequisite for any approach to the construction of a nationalized and planned economy, at once generated a need for a radical reorganization in the trade-union movement too. Even after this reorganization, which met with stubborn resistance in the ranks of a series of 'free' trade unions inherited from the past (printers, chemists, office-workers, etc.), the Soviet trade unions did not cease being mass, autonomous workers' organizations. But the domain of their democratic initiative narrowed considerably. They were left 'free' in questions of internal organization, cultural-educational activity, workers' labour insurance, caring for the living needs of their own members (security regulations for those at work, allocation of commodities, dining-rooms, gardens, living-quarters, kindergartens, etc.). But it was just in those questions of wages, workers' contracts and so on, which had hitherto been fundamental for them, that their freedom was substantially curtailed; their representatives were members of governmental and economic institutions that elaborated working conditions, but the rates, work norms, rules of hiring, and so on worked out by these institutions became law for these trade unions themselves. The right to strike, which had never been abolished formally, in fact dropped out of the arsenal of the workers' struggle. The working conditions themselves ceased to be an object of collective struggle and became an object of legislation and administration. But this same right to strike remained completely in effect with respect to private businesses. The same questions of wages and workers' contracts remained the focus of attention of the trade unions in so far as they faced not the state enterprises, but just these private businesses. There is no need to enlarge on the corrupting dualism introduced into the spirit of trade-union workers by such a situation.

It was becoming too obvious that any further growth of 'N.E.P.-manism' in industry and commerce threatened the whole system, just being organized, of the economic and working-class policy of the Soviet state with disruption and with the restoration of pre-revolutionary private capitalist relations. But such a restoration would inevitably have had to be paid for by the enslavement of the country by foreign capital – with all its socio-economic, political, and international consequences. Under these conditions the N.E.P. in industry and commerce could not have a long life.

But it was not long-lived in the countryside either. The manifest improvement in the supply and raw material balance of the country, and at the same time of its general economic situation, too, prompted hopes that it would be possible to link 'individual' peasant farming to 'nationalized' industry by means of mutual interaction and of common interests. The growing productivity of peasant farming was supposed to ensure the accelerated growth of industry, whereas this growth of industry, accompanied by the growth of consumption on the part of the urban populace and the workers, was supposed to ensure the peasantry an uninterruptedly expanding outlet for the products of its labour and constantly improving supplying of the countryside both with tools of production and the consumer commodities. It seemed that a formula had finally been found allowing the fusion into a single system of Soviet economy of the 'Socialist' cities and the 'private' countryside in an organic and harmonious way that really would be 'in earnest and for a long time'. It was this formula that underlay the policy of the so-called 'Rightist' tendency in Bolshevism, which the majority of Lenin's 'Old Guard' gravitated towards and into whose hands the power did, in fact, pass after his death (January 1924). But two or three years were sufficient for the illusoriness and the practical worthlessness of this policy, in the material conditions of Soviet life at the time, to begin to be revealed, while at the same time the 'Rightist' tendency began turning into a 'Rightist opposition' that was to be completely liquidated by the 1936–38 'Trials'.*

It was assumed that it would be just the 'thrifty' and well-to-do 'big' peasant (the 'kulak') who would be the first to appreciate all the advantages of the economic co-operation with the Soviet cities signalized by the N.E.P., and precisely by virtue of those advantages would gradually almost automatically 'grow up into' Soviet Socialism. It was precisely the kulak that the impulsive Bukharin, leader of the Rightist tendency, flung that same appeal to – 'Get Rich!' that almost

* The 'Leftist', Trotskyite opposition, which made itself sterile by the idea of an historically unthinkable 'return to October', boiled down to a purely ideological mutiny against the actual historical conditions of development of the Soviet revolution; because of this it acquired no practical importance in the internal politics of the Soviet state, though it played something of a role in the struggle over foreign policy (see below).

a hundred years before the government of the 'plebeian' July monarchy had addressed to the French bourgeoisie. And it was just at this time that an acute critique was applied to the ideas, the psychological habits, and the political slogans of the epoch of the civil war: the 'poor peasant deviations' in the countryside, the tendencies towards the egalitarian distribution of goods in the cities, which now received the mocking nickname of 'levelling', the 'guerrilla' methods of slashing difficulties in half instead of having them solved by competent persons in a patient and 'businesslike' way. It seemed that the whole specific spiritual, psychological, and emotional heritage of 'War Communism' was being liquidated, and that Soviet society was taking a path of serene and methodical development. But this liquidation proved to be premature, since the 'big muzhik' failed to justify the hopes that had been set on him.

He had been unable to justify them because a fundamental and decisive link had at the very outset dropped out of the chain of the logical constructions of the 'formula'. No matter how relatively rapid the tempo of industrialization, neither the quantity nor the quality of the industrial production gave any grounds for assuming that nationalized industry (which, moreover, as we have already said, was for the most part concentrated on the production of equipment for future factories and armaments) would be able within the next few years to establish an exchange of goods with the countryside on the basis of any parity; such an exchange could only be something for the indefinite future. For the time being the 'big muzhik' had to produce more and more and sell cheaply, and buy only a little and that expensively. But that was just what he did not want. He made extensive use of the rights given him by the 'neo-N.E.P.', in order to enlarge his own farm, renting land from impoverished peasants and using it to hire labour, but he did everything he could to sell his produce on the 'black market', and not give it up to the state at regulated prices. His 'self-enrichment' did not lead him into 'growing up into' the system of Soviet economy. On the contrary: it made him resist that system more and more tenaciously.

The Soviet state found itself more and more urgently compelled to apply compulsory measures of a pre-N.E.P. type to the 'big muzhik' too: 'new restrictions on the right to sell products on the free market, the raising of the norms of the compulsory surrender of agricultural products to the government at low prices . . . limitation of the right to rent land and to exploit hired labour', etc.[192] The kulak responded to these measures just as the countryside had responded to the policy of 'War Communism'. He concealed production, curtailed his sowing and dairy farming, auctioned off and slaughtered his cattle, liquidated truck-farms – in a word, he sabotaged all branches of agriculture required by the Soviet cities and industry. The 'betting on the kulak', the final form of the betting on individual peasant farming, was to shift to a new 'general line' in domestic economic policy. This, together with the still more accelerated industrialization, set itself the task of 'dekulakizing' the countryside and 'collectivizing' it 'all-out', that is, of liquidating individual peasant farms as the basic form of agricultural production. And the critical economic situation forced it to carry out the 'dekulakizing collectivization' (as well as the 'industrialization') at a far more stepped up pace than had been envisaged by the 'general line'. It was carried out with a mercilessness and cruelty that were possible only thanks to the presence of two factors.

The first of these was that the state apparatus on hand, which during these tempestuous years had lost a substantial portion of its old former revolutionary energy and was exhausted and drained by the 'purges', was replaced by cadres of the new apparatus. These were the youth trained in the Communist Youth League (Komsomol), elevated by it from the lowest strata of the workers, peasants, and petty-bourgeoisie, and provided with an access to education and to professions that previously had been altogether inaccessible. Growing up into the Soviet régime, with its ideological and political singularity, the youthful Soviet generation acquired not only its political ideas but also its political psychology, which as we have seen was the fruit and result of the whole long history of Bolshevism and the Soviet régime. The boundless devotion to the ideas of the 'Soviet revolution' and an extreme heroism in serving it were combined in this youth with an unwavering austerity, indifferent to 'sentimentality', in the struggle to put them into effect. It self-sacrificingly burnt out its energies in the fire of 'industrialization', which without it would have been impossible. And without the guiding role of the new Komsomol apparatus it would also have been impossible to carry out the painful operation of 'dekulakization' quickly and completely.

But its execution would also have been impossible without a second factor – the energetic support it was given within the peasantry itself, among the rural 'paupers'. While increasing the amount of land at the peasantry's disposal, the revolution was unable to provide it with livestock and tools, and the 'paupers' were forced to rent out their own land to the 'kulak', almost on the same terms of bondage as they had done with their pygmy allotments before the revolution. Treated with condescension by the ideologues of the 'neo-N.E.P.', the 'pauper' part of the peasantry became once again a prime channel of Soviet policy in the countryside: the 'dekulakization' was transformed from a government operation into an act of social conflict within the restratified peasantry itself. The liquidation 'as a class' of the rural, 'kulak' bourgeoisie that had been on the verge of growing stronger, was accompanied by the same expropriation not only of its productive but also of its consumer property, as had taken place in its time at the liquidation 'as a class' first of the landowners, then of the old, pre-revolutionary bourgeoisie, and finally of the 'N.E.P.-man' bourgeoisie. The ideology of War Communism, which had been on the point of being laid away in the archives, with all its passions, excesses, and even its much derided 'levelling' tendencies, had to be resurrected for a time so that the operation of 'dekulakization' could be carried through to a successful conclusion.

But the real problem set the Soviet régime by all the above-mentioned political and economic difficulties, was not whether it would succeed in liquidating the kulak class in the countryside, but whether the liquidation of the kulaks might prove a prologue to the liquidation of the whole system of fragmented individual peasant farming that had no place in the Soviet framework. The 'dekulakization' was merely a means; the end was 'all-out collectivization'. But the successful attainment of this end depended entirely on whether the basic 'medium' mass of the peasantry could be involved in the collectivizing process and whether its alliance with the 'paupers' against the 'kulaks' could be made a lever of that process. And the 'dizziness from success', which more than a few inordinately zealous executors of government policy paid for, did not lie in their attempt to make the collectivization 'all-out', and to accelerate its pace, but in the fact that in this attempt they broke the vacillations and the mute resistance of the 'medium' mass of the peasants by the same 'ruthless' methods that had been applied to the kulaks. They strengthened the solidarity of that mass not with the 'paupers' but with the 'kulaks' and thus threatened to destroy the very possibility of success.

The Soviet régime of course succeeded in solving the task it was set. It isolated the kulaks morally and politically and drew the 'medium' mass of peasants into the kolkhoz system, reinforcing its bonds with this system by the advantages that enable large-scale collectivized farming to utilize the most finished agricultural machines and to apply the most finished methods of agricultural cultivation and animal husbandry. To be sure the process of transition from the immemorial customs of individual farming to the methods, structure and psychology of collectivized farming could not proceed without friction, conflicts and partial upsets. But it moved forward so far and so successfully, and justified itself economically to such a degree that no return to the past was possible any longer. Russia ceased to be a country of individually fragmented peasant farming and became the first country of all-out agricultural collectivization in the world.* It is difficult to overestimate the enormous importance this radical change in the socio-economic structure of the country has and will go on having for its whole political and cultural future!

Such was the internal political development of the country. In its basic tendencies it was rooted, of course, in the socio-economic, political and cultural order established by its history, and in the struggle between its own inner forces, but it proceeded, as has been indicated, under the most powerful pressure of the war danger, which never ceased overhanging it. It was under the most direct influence of this danger that not only its foreign policy evolved, but also its ethnic policy, which in such a many-peopled country, especially along its borders, as Soviet Russia, inevitably became a point of convergence for domestic and foreign policy.

The experience of the intervention and of the civil war disclosed the danger for Soviet Russia of the relative vacillation, in the resistance to the interventionists and the 'White' counter-revolutionaries, of the ethnic conglomerates disposed along its Far Eastern and South-eastern borderlands. These included the Caucasus, which in view of the rich oil deposits had a special strategic importance. The creation of a 'buffer' People's Republic in Mongolia, the consolidation of the assimilation of Turkestan with the abolition of the archaic Khanate of Khiva and the Emirate of Bokhara, the liquidation of the short-lived independent existence of the Caucasian national republics

* The small plots left each kolkhoz peasant for his individual use are merely a supplementary stimulus to his interest in the successes of the kolkhoz. From the point of view of the actual structure of agriculture these plots are of no importance at all, no more than, let us say, the garden-plots sometimes assigned to workers have from the point of view of the structure of capitalist society.

(Georgia, Armenia, Azerbaijan and others) were all designed to eliminate that danger.

In the accomplishment of these tasks the Red Army of course played a prominent role. But the fundamental and characteristic distinction between this borderland policy of the Soviet state in the first years of its formation and the policy of 'imperialism' was that its primary and basic lever was not armed force, but the revolutionary mobilization of the lowest-scale labouring strata of the populace even in the most backward East Asiatic society. It was only by leaning on these lowly popular forces, and in close contact and alliance with them, that the Red Army implemented and consolidated the tasks set for it by Soviet policy. It is important to grasp this in order to understand present-day Soviet policy too.

It is understandable that the execution of this kind of policy proved most difficult and complicated. The resistance to it, even though not tempestuous, was most tenacious and protracted in an ethnic region of such relatively high and stabilized social culture as Georgia, where the Menshevik Social-Democracy, depending on its traditional influence over the peasantry, which had already been expressed in all the elections to the pre-revolutionary Duma, had been able to organize a democratic republic with relative speed and stability. But the general result of this ethnic policy, in the course of which all the patriarchal despotic ruling strata of the backward borderlands in the east and south-east were 'liquidated as a class', was the annihilation of all the remnants of servile exploitation and feudal relations in them and a radical transformation of their whole socio-economic order.

In its subsequent development the ethnic policy established during the first years of the Soviet revolution and executed to a large extent by Stalin, led to the considerable economic progress of the ethnic borderlands of the country, with the introduction of the 'collective' principle into all its branches, to their growing industrialization, and to the rapid upsurge of the general culture of the most backward nationalities. Many of these were given access for the first time to the grammar and literature of their own language, at the same time being introduced to general Russian culture. Such an ethnic policy made the Soviet Union stronger if only because it made it more homogeneous in socio-economic and cultural respects than had been pre-revolutionary Russia. The ultimate result of this policy was the construction of a Soviet state as a union of nationalities with equal rights,* whose cohesiveness not only endured the immense tension and the colossal ordeal of the anti-Hitler war, but was also an indispensable condition for the successful conduct of the war and the final dearly bought victory.

The determining factor in the foreign policy of the Soviet revolution in its initial phase was the profound conviction of the immediate imminence of the European social revolution and of the decisive importance of Russia's example. The first act of that policy was, as is well known, an appeal to all the warring powers and the proposal for 'the immediate initiation of negotiations for a just and democratic peace'. The Germans and Austrians utilized the negative reaction of Great Britain and France (the Entente) for a new attack on Russian territory and a rapid advance as far as Petrograd, which forced the Soviet government to move to Moscow, which ever since has been its permanent location. Powerless to hold back this advance, by the beginning of December it had already decided to enter into 'separate' peace talks with Germany and Austria; on 23 February 1918 (N.S.) it accepted the conditions dictated by the German High Command. The Treaty of Brest-Litovsk not only forced the Soviet state to agree to pay a substantial indemnity and to the occupation by Austro-German troops of a substantial part of its western and eastern territories, but it included among other things the splitting off from Russia of the Baltic republics and the Ukraine, after the Caucasian republics had become 'independent', while Turkey was given the territory of Kars and Ardahan, not very large but strategically important.

In order to carry out the decision to sign such a treaty, Lenin had to overcome considerable resistance within the Bolshevik Party itself. A substantial part of this, grouped around Trotsky and the so-called 'Left' Communists (including at that time Bukharin) saw in this decision the conclusive undoing of the Soviet republic. Believing in the immediate imminence of the European revolution, the 'Left' Communists regarded the proclamation of a 'revolutionary war' against the Austro-German imperialists as the only real way of finally provoking an explosion of the social revolution, which to their minds was altogether ripe – primarily in Germany. However, the complete collapse of the old army and the embryonic condition of the new, on the one hand, and the horrifying general chaos in economics

* The Union of Socialist Soviet Republics (U.S.S.R.) was formally constituted at the First All-Russian Congress of Soviets in December 1922.

and transport, on the other, excluded any possibility of carrying on any kind of war against such a powerful military force as Imperial Germany still was at that time. The stubborn and passionate struggle around the Brest-Litovsk peace treaty* lasted a relatively short time; in the last resort the whole Bolshevik Party took up the position Lenin had held from the very beginning. Taking into account the country's military helplessness at the moment, even the most oppressive peace conditions had to be accepted in order to get a 'breathing-spell' in order to struggle for the improvement of the economic situation, the strengthening of the Soviet revolution, and the creation of a sufficiently powerful 'Red' armed force – in the anticipation of the moment when the European revolution would begin being transformed from a hope to a fact.

This anticipation, though passive, did not remain so for long. The blockade and the military intervention of the Entente and its open support of the 'White' camp in the civil war, made it necessary to look for ways to strike a blow at Entente imperialism by the active 'unloosing' of the belated social revolution. The foreign policy of the revolutionary Soviet state entered into a period that can be characterized as *aggressive*, in the course of which, overlaying the old 'Brest-Litovsk' disputes, there took place a new *rapprochement* of Lenin's line in foreign policy with the line of the 'Left, Trotskyite' line.

The first blows of this revolutionarily aggressive policy were directed against Great Britain as the protagonist of the struggle against the Soviet revolution.† The delivery of a crushing blow against Great Britain, while making the Soviet republic a support point and an organizing centre for the national liberation uprisings and revolutions of the colonial and semi-colonial peoples of Asia, the Middle East and the Far East – such was the then eastern policy of the Soviet government. Its most demonstrative act was the rejection by the Soviet

* In the course of this there took place, among other things, the swiftly liquidated uprising of the 'Left S.R.s' (July 1918), for which the assassination of the German consul by an S.R., the prominent 'Chekist' Blumkin, served as signal.

† This struggle was begun and organized, of course, by Churchill, whom the irony of history later turned, together with Roosevelt and Stalin, into a leader of the anti-Hitler Anglo-American-Soviet alliance. At that time the principal adversary of Churchill's interventionist policy was the Secretary of the Transport Union, Ernest Bevin, who after the war became Minister of Foreign Affairs in the British Labour Government.

government of any imperialist privileges in Persia and China, and the convocation in Baku of the Congress of Peoples of the East. It was just at this time that the 'social revolution', in Bolshevik ideology, was beginning to take on more and more definitely the outlines of a 'world social revolution', not merely European, as in fact it had been before.

But in Soviet western policy, too, elements of revolutionary aggressiveness began to become more and more noticeable at this time. These were based on the firm conviction that in the West, too, the still comparatively weak Red Army would be met everywhere by the upsurge of the same invincible revolutionary movement of the toiling masses as had taken place in the backward borderlands of Russia itself. This conviction, however, proved erroneous, and the attempt to 'feel one's way through Poland with a bayonet', as well as through Estonia and Latvia, in order to remove the barrier separating the Soviet republic from Germany, regarded as the chief hearth of a revolution ready to explode, was unsuccessful. The Riga peace treaty (October 1920) that ended the war with Poland, with its harsh conditions for the Soviet Union, was in essence the 'beginning of the end' of the brief period of aggressive activity in the West European policy of the Soviet government.

Lapses into aggression still went on making themselves felt, of course, in individual acts of that policy, introducing into it features of a zigzag, contradictory, and even adventurous nature. But in general aggressiveness became more and more of a dream about the final victorious 'battle on the Rhine', to be waged by the Red Army allied with central European revolutions against Entente imperialism, rather than a factor of practical politics. Nor was that all. In so far as elements of aggressiveness were preserved in the foreign policy of Bolshevism they became more and more a function not of the Soviet government's organs of foreign policy, but of the Communist Parties of individual countries, and of the Communist International that united them. It was just at this time that 'Comintern policy' began to separate itself from the 'policy of the People's Commissariat for Foreign Affairs'. On occasion it even found itself in contradictions with it that were ultimately settled by the Soviet government. But even the People's Commissariat shifted more and more definitely, from a revolutionary aggressive policy, which even in the east at that time had not produced the anticipated results, to a revolutionary defensist policy.

It was just this shift that finally congealed as the slogan of 'Socialism in one country'. For practical purposes the passionate struggle of the 'Left Trotskyite' opposition against the slogan did not have so much importance in theory or in domestic policy as it did in foreign policy. 'Socialism in one country' meant that Soviet foreign policy no longer aimed at actively bursting through 'capitalist encirclement', but at a 'peaceful co-existence' with it, in the expectation of a time when it would be disrupted by inner forces, even if they ripened more slowly than had originally seemed the case. But this is, at the same time, an explanation and a moral justification of the fact that the defence of the 'one country' where for the time being Socialism was 'being built' became the paramount interest and the paramount principle of policy. It provided in advance a moral and political sanction of any means regarded as necessary, or even helpful, for that defence at any given moment. Soviet Socialism began to become 'patriotic' and 'national'. But in contrast to the aggressive and chauvinist nationalism of imperialist capitalism, Soviet patriotism has remained basically Socialist and defensive.

Soviet foreign policy later on, of course, made broad use of the moral and political freedom of the choice of means we have just mentioned. But it is impossible not to see that even the most risky and 'violent' means invariably served not imperialist or even revolutionary aggression, but always these same tasks of revolutionary defence. This is not the place, to be sure, to mention, however fleetingly, the stages and zigzags in Soviet foreign policy during the years that preceded the Second World War. But it must be noted that the most powerful impetus was given to this revolutionary defensist policy by Hitler's rise to power in Germany. This led the Soviet government to enter the League of Nations (end of 1934), and made it the leader in the struggle for 'collective security', willing to conclude a military alliance with the Western European democracies for joint resistance to Hitler Fascist aggression.

However, the sabotage of the 'sanctions' policy vis-à-vis Mussolini, the policy of 'non-intervention' against Spanish Fascism, openly supported by Italian and German Fascism; the attempts to come to an agreement with Hitler – all gave the Soviet government more and more reason to suspect that the real goal of British and French policy was not so much a joint struggle with the Soviet Union against German National Socialism, as a compromise with Hitler Fascism at the price of leaving it a 'free hand' in the east. This suspicion became all the more alarming as it became clear that both on the question of sanctions and on the question of non-intervention, even on the question of a compromise with Hitler, the policy of the bourgeoisie, in both France and Great Britain, met with the support of influential segments of the Social-Democratic Parties. In other countries (Scandinavia) these parties were inclining more and more towards a policy of 'neutrality', and the Socialist International as a whole was displaying in all these questions very little ability for any energetic action that in any way corresponded with the energetic language of its individual resolutions. 'Munich' turned this suspicion into a certainty: the policy of a military alliance with the Western democracies was shattered.

'Munich' was not merely a political compromise with Hitler. In Munich the governments of Great Britain and France sanctioned his destruction of Czechoslovakia and its *de facto* occupation. After the fusion with Austria, with the then closeness to the Nazi Government of Germany not only of the governments of Hungary and Rumania, but also of the 'Colonels' ' government of Poland, which had taken part in the division of Czechoslovakia and had previously refused to give the Red Army the right to pass through Polish territory in case of a war with Fascist Germany, this meant the definitive military-strategic exposure of the Western border of the Soviet Union, the annihilation of the last obstacle to the invasion of its borders by the Hitler armies.

The Soviet reaction to this policy of Great Britain and France permits the surmise that the prospect of this invasion, suddenly confronting a Soviet Union still completely unprepared for an immediate single duel with the gigantic military machine of Hitlerism, evoked a feeling of fear bordering on panic. The Soviet-German Pact, which was the Soviet response to 'Munich', was in its turn not a mere political agreement, but also a military-strategic one. Its task was to turn Hitler's hand, suspended over the Soviet Union, against those who, according to the conviction of the Soviet government, were egging him on against the Soviet Union. This aim, as is well known, was achieved. Hitler utilized the departure of the Soviet Union from the anti-German front in order to settle once and for all the Polish problem, the most important and 'painful' for him. But through this he moved Great Britain and France into a declaration of war, not because the British and French bourgeoisie considered its obligations towards Poland more 'sacred' than the obligations it had just broken towards Czechoslovakia, but because the occupation of Poland, by securing the German rear with respect to the Soviet Union, was too obviously a prologue to the immediate advance of Hitler Fascism against Great Britain and Western Europe.

It is futile to speculate after the event how the further history of Europe and the whole world would have turned out if the invasion prepared by 'Munich' had succeeded and led the Soviet Union and the Soviet revolution to destruction. But the intentionally vociferous clamour of both sides concerning German-Soviet 'friendship' could not hide the fact even at that time that the real goal of the Soviet-German Pact was not, for the Soviet government, the preparation of an alliance of Soviet Socialism with Hitler-Fascist 'Socialism' for a joint advance against the 'capitalist democracies', but the securing of a 'breathing-spell' to prepare for the future war between Fascist Germany and the Soviet Union, whose inevitability the signatories of the Pact themselves had no doubt of. It is enough to glance at the map to see that in the seizure of the land and sea bases in Finland, in the occupation of the Baltic Republics, and in the participation in the division of Poland, the Soviet Union was not building a spring-board for a joint 'imperialist' advance together with German Nazism against the capitalist west, but a defence line against the coming advance of Hitler-Fascism towards the east. In June 1941 this line justified itself strategically. It held off the Hitler advance long enough to prepare its undoing before Leningrad and Moscow. This was the beginning of Hitler's defeat and of the ultimate victory of the Soviet Union, and at the same time of the victory of the whole anti-Hitler coalition.

But whatever the reasons for the conclusion of the Soviet-German Pact and its ultimate military-strategic consequences, its immediate result within the international working-class movement was the introduction of considerable intellectual and political confusion into the ranks of the labouring masses and an extreme sharpening of the split between the Social-Democracy and Communism that even before this had emasculated that movement in its resistance to the advancing tornado of Hitler Fascism.

International Communism was not, of course, created by Russian Bolshevism. Martov, in his splendid articles on 'World Bolshevism'[193] showed that the bloody harvest of the war also gave rise to elements of 'Bolshevik' psychology in the European working-class movement. The very conditions of the socio-economic and political development of post-war Europe ensured the creation of a mass base for Communism in the European proletariat, too. Having forestalled the destruction of continental European capitalism the Anglo-French conquerors were unable to make that capitalism viable. Increasingly frequent crises and growing unemployment were its lot. This ricocheted more and more painfully off both the peasantry and the urban petty-bourgeoisie, and achieved a particular acuteness in the most advanced country of European continental capitalism – Germany. There the doors 'to a life in the sun' seemed closed forever to millions of young people in the cities and countryside. In these conditions the attempts of democratic Socialism to transform the socio-economic foundations of society by democratic methods were doomed to failure. They led only to the discrediting both of this Socialism and of the very idea of political democracy in the eyes of millions, thus creating mass cadres – extremely 'combative' and 'dynamic' cadres at that – ready for Hitler Fascism in the petty-bourgeois sector of German society, and for Communism in its proletarian sector. Kindred socio-political processes, in a weakened form that was, of course, adapted to national conditions, also took place in all the other countries of the European continent.

But though not created by Russian Bolshevism, international Communism developed under its extremely powerful influence, it might be called pressure, and often became one of the levers of Soviet foreign policy. Soviet Russian pressure was added to the influence of the complex socio-political situation in Western Europe and the influence of that ideological 'polarization' that was an inevitable consequence of the antagonism to and competition with the Social-Democracy, which did not leave the stage, as it had in Russia, but on the contrary preserved its majority in the working-class. This pressure made the history of international Communism even more contradictory, still more imbued with internal crises, unexpected political zigzags and abrupt political about-faces.

The utterly unexpected situations created for international Communism – at first by the Soviet-German Pact, which it interpreted as the definitive departure of the Soviet Union from the anti-Hitler war front, then by the Soviet-German war, which made the Soviet Union, on the contrary, the principal force on that front – undermined still further the ideological stability and theoretical consistency of the policy of the Communist Parties. In each country it thrust them into pure empiricism, paying attention both in their choice of slogans and the means of struggle for these slogans only to the immediate demands of the given moment and the national conditions in a given country.

The disharmony in the policy of the Communist Parties of individual countries became so obvious that the unified and, according to Bolshevik principles, centralized authoritarian international direction of that policy became impossible. The Comintern (the 'Third International'), founded in March 1919 as the organ of that direction, cut short its own existence in May 1943, some time after the Socialist International – for the kindred reason of the constantly intensifying 'nationalist' policy of individual Social-Democratic Parties, which shattered their ideological framework – had also dissolved.

Nevertheless, in spite of all ideological vacillations, and political reversals and collapses, the Communist Parties of individual countries not only conserved their moral and physical links and their mutual solidarity, but in every single place they also became centres of attraction for the most revolutionary strata of the working-class. This was because with all their zigzags the paramount criterion of policy for all of them remained the idea of defending the security of the sole country where the 'construction of Socialism' had already been begun. In conditions of warfare this became the idea of the unconditional defence of the Soviet Union and a ramified promotion of its victory. The correlation between this idea and the real direction of evolution, the real role of the Soviet Union in that evolution and the real interests of the proletariat of all countries without exception in the transitional age of the struggle between two social orders – dying capitalism and nascent Socialism – is the source of the magnetic power that has enabled Communism to be the channel of revolution in the contemporary working-class movement.

It is not, of course, part of our intention to give the history of that movement. But it must be clear that the Hitler Fascist counter-revolution and the war unleashed by it radically altered the conditions of that movement in Europe, and could not help but alter them throughout the world as well. Hitler Fascism and the war dealt European capitalism a mortal blow, and made the socio-economic and political renaissance of Europe possible only as a Socialist renaissance. This means that in Europe, after the Second World War, there could be no renaissance of those socio-economic conditions that after the First World War had split and emasculated its workers' movement, and immobilized and hypertrophied the ideology of democratic reformism at one of its poles, and centralized authoritarianism at the other. In both its wings this movement from now on moved close to the objective of taking power as an indispensable instrument of the Socialist transformation of the social order.

But in the conditions of post-war Europe this gigantic task, which in a revolutionary way slashed into the interests of so many powerful social forces generated by the past, cannot be accomplished by mere parliamentary balloting or by an 'armed uprising' similar to the one by which in 1917 the Bolsheviks had slashed the Gordian knot of the contradictions of the Russian revolution. Nor can it be accomplished by the split working-class. It requires not only the complete mobilization of all its own forces, but also its being able to rally behind itself both the intellectual workers and the non-proletarian toiling masses of the cities and countryside if it is to become for them, in Marx's phrase, 'class-emancipating'. Neither this mobilization nor this rallying round is possible without taking into account the extreme limitedness of purely parliamentarian methods in such a pivotal epoch. But it is also impossible without taking into account those habits of free democratic initiative that have not only been bred into the bone of European intellectual circles, but have been inculcated by the age-old history of Europe into the broadest toiling masses of both the cities and the countryside. It is what distinguishes them from those popular masses that the Soviet revolution of 1917 leaned on, and that in fact made that revolution. Thus the overcoming of the split in the workers' movement has become not merely indispensable, but possible as well. One cannot fail to see how, in the very course of the manifest struggle of the European workers' movement for power, elements are gradually springing forth, in both its wings, of a political and ideological 'synthesis' that is unifying it, trying organically to combine Communist revolutionary dynamism with the freely organized Socialist self-government of the masses.

It goes without saying that the road to the overcoming of a split that has more than thirty years of existence behind it cannot be straight and easy. The petrified ideological, psychological and emotional traditions of both wings of the split workers' movement have made their presence felt before and will again, slowing down and disrupting the process of the restoration of working-class unity. But in the last resort iron historical necessity always bursts through and conquers the ideological and psychological inertia of parties, groups, and leaders. Iron historical necessity is forcing post-war Europe to become Socialist. Iron historical necessity will also lead to the workers' unity without which no Socialist Europe is possible.

But a Socialist Europe will not only create completely new conditions in the evolution of Europe itself and of the whole world. It will also create completely new conditions for the future development of the Soviet revolution. It will make it possible to solve on an international scale the contradictions of Russian Socialism and democracy that are insoluble within a national framework. As we have seen, the theoreticians of both wings of the Russian Social-Democracy always thought this the only way out of these contradictions. But it will also create completely new conditions for the future of the Bolshevik leadership of the Soviet revolution. But this is a theme outside the sphere of the history this book has been devoted to. It is part of current politics. Hence only a few concluding lines can be devoted to it here.

* * *

We have been following the gradual formation of the ideological, political, and moral-psychological profile of contemporary Bolshevism. In many respects that profile is, of course, alien to the individualistic humanitarian and democratic juridical ideas that, having thrown out roots in millennial European civilization, took final shape in the nineteenth century on the basis of the 'organic' development of progressive and self-confident capitalism. They remain the official ideological banner of capitalist society wherever that society still feels in any way stable. They have also become a fixed feature of the spiritual make-up of the toiling strata of that society as well, including the working-class, for which history has predestined the role of its 'grave-digger'.

But whatever the profile of contemporary Bolshevism, that profile is the direct child of the revolutionary struggle of the Russian Social-Democracy out of whose depths Bolshevism emerged. Moreover, it emerged from that struggle with a contradiction that was immanent in it – the belatedness that made it impossible to realize democracy without Socialism, and the backwardness that made it impossible to realize Socialism in freely democratic forms. But what is even more important is that whatever the profile of contemporary Bolshevism is like, history has made it the bearer of the 'key' idea of our age – the idea of Socialism. It has placed it at the head of a gigantic state, and simultaneously made it a factor of gigantic power in the complex and catastrophic process of the practical implementation of this idea.

It is impossible to assess the prospects either of Socialism, in Europe and the world, or of Bolshevism itself without taking into account these two factors as the historical and irreplaceable data. The only question that can arise is whether the process of the historical realization of Socialism will also be the process of the evolution of the Soviet régime (together with that of Bolshevism itself) – not in the sense of an historically inconceivable return to a régime of parliamentary democracy, of course, but in the sense of its 'humanization' and 'democratization' in the direction of that ideological 'synthesis' that is maturing in the European Socialist-Communist movement.

We have said that the question of the democratization of the Soviet régime has been raised among the Bolsheviks themselves at every new stage in the development of the Soviet state. It may be said that the internal 'organic' democratization of the Soviet system never ceased from the very day of its genesis: it has become more and more its inalienable and characteristic hallmark. The 'politicalization' of the Russian peasantry was part of the democratization of the Soviet régime, as was the emergence throughout the country, down to its most obscure crevices, of cultural, educational, theatrical, athletic, etc. groups, societies, and clubs, in quantities that pre-revolutionary Russia could never even have dreamt of, especially not its impoverished and cultureless peasant countryside. The most powerful lever of this democratization is the involvement of tens of millions of workers, peasants, and recent urban petty-bourgeois into collective and organized activity, down to the activity of administration and government, in the public organizations of the country (trade unions, co-operatives, etc.) as well as in its economic system (nationalized industry and commerce, the kolkhozes) and in its organs of local and central government (the Soviets).

One of the solid achievements of the Stalin constitution of 1936 was indubitably a long stride towards this internal organic democratization of the régime – the annihilation of the 'disenfranchized' category, the proclamation of the juridical equality in principle of all citizens without exception, independently of their 'social origins'. One must assume that what will be even more important in this direction, in the country of party dictatorship, will be the democratic idea of the primacy of the 'nation' over the 'Party', of 'civic virtue' over the 'Party card'. This was insistently stressed in the patriotic propaganda of wartime and prompted the entry into the Bolshevik Party itself of millions of soldiers, white-collar workers, labourers and peasants, who had grown up together with the Soviet order but had no specific Bolshevik ideology.

Nevertheless, at no single stage of this uninterrupted democratization of the Soviet régime was democracy ever given a political structure. Nothing has ever ensured the citizens freedom of speech, debate, criticism, assembly, or of organized activity not only in 'practical' corporate economic questions or questions of 'applied' politics, but in 'higher' politics either, in the sphere of constitutional principle, the construction of the government, the fundamental lines of domestic and foreign policy. Inevitably, this was due to the fear that this kind of freedom would be exploited by social forces that might become the channels for a capitalist restoration, or even more – a bulwark and internal agent of the hostile foreign 'capitalist encirclement' that was still a military menace to the Soviet Union. Thus, while trying to exploit these non-proletarian social forces the Soviet authorities at the same time refused to allow them the formal, juridical conditions outside of which they were unable to operate successfully. In the last resort, as we have seen, they inevitably cut the knot of the contradictions flowing from this by the 'liquidation as a class' of one such social force after another: of the Tsarist bureaucracy and the generals, of the big landowners, of the financial, commercial, and industrial bourgeoisie, of the N.E.P.-man, of the kulak.

The cruel operations of this 'liquidation' conserved and consolidated, as we have seen, the grimly dictatorial character of the Soviet régime. But they forestalled the possibility of its 'bonapartization', which for a number of years had been forecast by its Socialist critics and which its capitalist enemies had been hoping for. The country lacked those new bourgeois strata grown up out of the revolutionary destruction of feudalism from which historical 'bonapartism' had always drawn its political and material forces. And with the liquidation of the kulak there also vanished any possibility of the revival of the broad stratum of big peasants grown rich in the revolution that gives every kind of 'bonapartism' its mass support. During the process of liquidation Soviet society was levelled off socially. The boundaries between its governing 'summits' and the governed 'lower depths' ceased to be discernible; between these summits and the lower depths there took place an uninterrupted 'exchange of social goods'. Constantly replaced popular layers kept rising up the social ladder.

The 'dekulakization' and the 'all-out collectivization' of the countryside are making Soviet society 'classless' – in the sense that its material inequality remains not a socially fixed inequality, but the transitory inequality of a way of life that does not enable anyone to make this inequality a springboard for taking over the economy of the country, or an instrument of exploitation of other strata of the populace. Least of all is it a source for the formation of a new 'ruling class'. This 'classlessness' of the country in its turn excludes the possibility of a Fascist degeneration of the Soviet régime, which even its capitalist and democratic critics never cease predicting and even 'acknowledging'. This same classlessness also excludes the revival of those internal dangers that used to be bound up for the Soviet régime with the political shaping-up of its organic democratization.

It was the disappearance of this internal danger that allowed the Soviet government not only to proclaim 'democracy', and the 'most perfect' democracy at that, to be the fundamental principle of the Soviet system, but also to take democratic steps towards its political formulation. In its internal policy there was the Stalin constitution of 1936, which for the first time proclaimed the equality of all citizens and replaced the traditionally open Soviet balloting practice with the secret vote. In international proletarian policy there was the 'united working-class' and the 'people's fronts'. In foreign policy there was the tack of *rapprochement* with the democratic powers in the name of resistance to Fascism. This line in Soviet policy, as we have seen, was shattered by 'Munich', while the war curtailed its further development.

But the same war likewise created, as has been indicated above, all the premises for the Socialist reconstruction of Europe, and for the restoration of working-class unity as the indispensable lever of that reconstruction. A Socialist Europe means the elimination of all the external dangers that, as we have seen, ever since the very first days of the Soviet revolution were one of the basic factors that made the régime tend towards dictatorship, and one of the basic obstacles to the political democratization of that régime. At the same time they were one of the principal reasons for the 'self-isolation' of the Soviet Union, its attempt to hedge itself in against the influence of the external world by as impenetrable a wall as possible.

With the disappearance of the internal and external dangers, completely new conditions will come about for the further evolution of the Soviet régime and for its political democratization. That democratization will become historically feasible. The vital interest of the Soviet Union in the swiftest possible construction of a Socialist Europe, hence too in the successes of Socialist-Communist unity, will make this democratization historically more and more *real* for it. The gigantic labour confronting the Soviet Union in the raising of the general standard of living, destroyed by the war and fallen still further in the course of it, and in the satisfaction of popular self-consciousness, elevated by the war, and the people's intellectual and moral demands, sharpened by the war, are reason to believe that this democratization will become historically more and more necessary.

Of course the process of the political democratization of the Soviet régime will scarcely be able to proceed smoothly, without halts and jolts. The inertia of parochial, collective, and personal interests, and even more the inertia of decades of congealed ideological, political, and psychological habits and aversions, will increase the thousands of obstacles in its path. And, of course, the result of this democratization will hardly be able to be a simple transformation of the Soviet régime into the régime of parliamentary democracy now so customary.

Underlying this régime is a system of political parties representing the socio-economic interests of antagonistic classes or individual sections of these classes, and contending with each for the voters' ballots. Its symbol and crown is the parliament, of one kind or another, which is the arena in which the rhetorical contest of the parties takes place. It is the highest authority whose vote decides disputed questions. But in a society where there are no antagonistic classes there will scarcely be room for the political parties of the type that has taken shape in the course of the development and functioning of capitalism. This bears not only on Soviet society. Marx used to predict that in a Socialist society the 'manipulation of people', that is, 'politics', will have to retreat backstage more and more before the 'manipulation of things', that is, 'economics'. It would seem that this prediction of his has every chance of being confirmed by the actual course of social development. Hence one is entitled to think that freedom of speech, criticism, organization, electoral struggle, etc., which is what gives the Soviet citizens political democratization, will be exploited not so much by political groupings as by groupings of a predominantly professional, corporate, local, national, ideological, etc., nature.

But as for the forms in which that freedom will be moulded, that can only be guessed at today. What is important is that it guarantees a truly free spiritual self-delineation for Soviet society in all strata and in all stages, from the bottom to the top, of its vital processes, not only economic and social, but constitutional as well. That will finally be the solution of that tormenting problem of the fusion of liberty and Socialism that was insoluble for more than a century and that the Russian revolutionary movement, in all its successive and often so bitterly and passionately contending tendencies, self-sacrificingly and heroically beat itself against.

For more than a hundred years Herzen's prophetic vision of Russia has been nearing fulfilment: 'We shall go through Socialism to freedom.' But what Herzen failed to foresee was that 'we' would 'go through Socialism to freedom', not in distinction to Europe, not in contrast with it, not without it, not alone. It can only be together with 'us' that Europe too will be able to go back to the freedom lost by it in the catastrophes of Fascism and war. It is only through Socialism that Asia too, which is beginning its struggle for national and political equality, and the colonial and semi-colonial peoples of Africa and the Pacific Ocean, which stand on the threshold of that struggle, will be able to go on to freedom. It is only through Socialism that Great Britain, Australia and other democratic countries will be able to renew their surviving freedom and give it stability. And doubtless only through Socialism will the democracy of the United States too preserve its own freedom, whose foundations are beginning to be undermined by the social dissensions that are engendered by obsolescent capitalism and that within its framework are insoluble.

'Through Socialism to freedom' – this, the former banner of Russian 'peculiarity' has every chance of becoming the universal banner of the development of all countries and peoples of the earth. The premonition of the prophets of the 'Russian idea' – its 'pan-humanity' as proclaimed by Dostoevsky, an extreme Russian nationalist but also a great Russian seer – is being transformed into an historical reality. The 'Russian idea' is becoming a 'pan-human' idea because in the course of a century, in all its questing, in all its soaring and falling, it has been the idea of a supreme struggle for the resolution of the task that is becoming the true task of our epoch: the task of realizing freedom through Socialism and Socialism through freedom.

19 March 1946 (N.S.)

Bibliographical References

(Very few of the references below, except Lenin's works, have been translated into English. Lenin's collected works have, of course, been translated into many languages, and the articles cited can easily be found in the index to any of them. TRANSLATOR'S NOTE.)

1. *Obshchestvennoye Dvizhenie v Rossii v Nachale XX Veka*, an anthology of articles edited by J. Martov, P. Maslov, and A. Potresov: St Petersburg 1909–1914, Vol. I, p. 57.
2. M. Tugan-Baranovsky, *Russkaya Fabrika v Proshlom i Nastoyashchem*, St Petersburg, 1898, Vol. I, p. 278.
3. In an essay, *Peterburg i Moskva*.
4. A. Kornilov, *Kurs Istorii Rossii XIX Veka*, Moscow 1912. Part II, p. 76.
5. M. Tugan-Baranovsky, *Intelligentsia i Sotsializm*, in the anthology *Intelligentsia v Rossii*, St Petersburg 1910.
6. P. Sakulin, *Russkaya Literatura i Sotsializm*, Part I, p. 167. Moscow 1924.
7. N. K. Mikhailovsky, *Literaturnye Vospominaniya i Sovremennaya Smuta*. Also, Vol. VII of the Collected Works of D. N. Ovsyaniko-Kulikovsky, Moscow, State Publishing House.
8. P. A. Berlin, *Russkaya Burzhuaziya v Staroye i Novoye Vremya*, Moscow 1922.
9. S. Y. Yelpatyevsky, *Vospominaniya za 50 Let*, Leningrad 1929.
10. Potresov's essay, *Evolutsiya Obshchestvenno-politicheskoy Mysli v Predrevolyutsionnuyu Epokhu*, in 1 above.
11. I. I. Panayev, *Literaturnye Vospominaniya*, Leningrad 1928.
12. Ibid., pp. 144, 214, 484, and others.
13. Plekhanov, *V. G. Belinsky*, in a collection of articles, Moscow and Petrograd 1923.
14. Koshelev, *Zapiski*, Berlin 1884.
15. A. A. Kornilov, *Obshchestvennoye Dvizhenie pri Alexandre II: 1855–1881*. Published by *Osvobozhdenie*, Paris 1905.
16. *Dnevnik*, 18 June 1843.

17. *Kolokol*, No. 210. 15 December 1865.
18. In an article on Eugene Sue's *Secrets of Paris*.
19. *Bor'ba Partii vo Frantsii pri Lyudovike XVIII i Karle X*.
20. *Kolokol*, No. 191, 15 November 1864.
21. Ibid. No. 107, 15 September 1861.
22. Plekhanov, *N. G. Chernyshevsky*, St Petersburg, 1910, p. 305.
23. *Sovremennik*, No. 6.
24. In an 'open letter' to Alexander II, *Polyarnaya Zvezda*, No. 1.
25. *Kolokol*, No. 101, 15 July 1861.
26. Ibid., Ogaryov's article in No. 134, 22 May 1862.
27. M. Lemke, *Ocherki Osvoboditel'nogo Dvizheniya '60 Godov*, St Petersburg 1908.
28. *Kolokol*, No. 107, 15 September 1861.
29. J. Martov, *Obshchestvennye i Umstvennye Techeniya v Rossii 1870–1905 Gg.*, Leningrad-Moscow, 1921.
30. G. Dzhanshiyev, *Epokha Velikikh Reform*, 10th edition, St Petersburg 1907.
31. For greater detail concerning the evolution of the Russian monarchy after the 'great reforms' see my work on 'The General Politics of the Government' in Vol. I of the anthology *Obshchestvennoye Dvizhenie* (Note 1 above).
32. A. Kornilov, *Kurs Istorii*, loc. cit., Part III, p. 137.
33. The article on Pisaryov and Dobrolyubov in *Sbornik Statei* of V. I. Zasulich, St Petersburg 1907.
34. O. V. Aptekman, *Moi Pervye Shagi na Puti Propagandy*, Moscow 1926.
35. D. N. Ovsyaniko-Kulikovsky, Collected Works, Moscow, State Publishing House, Vol. VII, Chap. 14.
36. Lavrov, *Ocherki Voprosov Prakticheskoy Filosofii. Lichnost'*. This book, published in 1860, laid down an 'anthropological principle' that evoked a sharp response from Chernyshevsky.
37. *Vperyod* anthology, Vol. IV.
38. Ibid.
39. Letter to Herzen dated 28 October 1869.
40. P. B. Akselrod, *Perezhitoye i Peredumannoye*, Z. I. Grschebin Verlag, Berlin 1923. Only the first book of reminiscences came out, stopping in 1883. Extracts from the projected second volume were later printed in the *Leninskiye Sborniki* (Leninist Anthologies).
41. N. F. Annensky, *Entsiklopedichesky Slovar'*, Br. Granat.

42. Friedrich Engels, *Soziales aus Russland.*
43. V. Figner, *Zapechatlenny Trud*, p. 108.
44. Quoted in I. Teodorovich's Foreword to M. R. Popov, *Zapiski Zemlevol'tsa*, Moscow 1933.
45. Popov, ibid.
46. Aptekman, loc. cit., p. 53.
47. Figner, loc. cit., p. 94–95.
48. Popov, loc. cit., p. 60.
49. Ibid., p. 61.
50. Figner, loc. cit., pp. 108, 113.
51. Popov, loc. cit., p. 162.
52. Figner, loc. cit., p. 107–108.
53. Ibid., p. 120.
54. Popov, loc. cit., p. 73.
55. Popov, loc. cit., p. 102–3.
56. Ibid., p. 107–8.
57. Figner, loc. cit., p. 149–50.
58. Ibid., p. 152–3.
59. Ibid., pp. 154–66.
60. Akselrod, loc. cit., p. 339 et seq.
61. Popov, loc. cit., p. 214.
62. Figner, loc. cit., p. 171–2.
63. Ibid., p. 179–80.
64. Ibid., p. 176.
65. Ibid., p. 181–2.
66. Ibid., p. 287.
67. Ibid., p. 248.
68. Martov, loc. cit., p. 50–51.
69. B. Chicherin, *Zadachi Novogo Tsarstvovaniya*, in Vol. I of the anthology, *K. Pobedonostev i ego Korrespondenty. Pis'ma i Zapiski.* Published by the State Publishing House. Moscow-Petrograd, 1923. p. 104 et seq.
70. Professor K. A. Pazhitnov, *Razvitie Sotsialisticheskikh Idei v Rossii ot Pestelya do Gruppy Osvobozhdeniya Truda*, Vol. I, p. 256. *Byloye* Publishing House, Petrograd 1924.
71. A. S. Suvorin, *Dnevnik*, edited and with a foreword and notes by Michael Krichevsky. Published by L. D. Frenkel, Moscow and Petrograd 1923., p. 15–16.
72. Shchedrin borrowed this phrase, which he put into the mouth of a character in his *Dnevnik Provintsiala* ('Diary of a

Provincial') (1872–3), from the *Peterburgskiye Vedomosti* (Petersburg News), V. Korsh's newspaper.

73. Named after Y. V. Abramov (1858–1906), a contributor to *Otechestvennye Zapiski*, who went over to the *Nedel'* in the middle of the '80s and made it the chief organ of the new tendency.
74. Martov, loc. cit., p. 47.
75. V. P. Vorontsov, *Nashi Napravlyeniya*, 1893, p. 7.
76. Martov, loc. cit., p. 48.
77. Mikhailovsky, *Pis'ma Postoronnego*, in *Otechestvennye Zapiski* of April 1883.
78. Vorontsov, *Sud'by Kapitalizma v Rossii*, 1882.
79. An article, *Ekonomicheskii Upadok Rossii*, in No. 9 of *Otechestvennye Zapiski*, 1881.
80. An immediate forerunner of V. V.'s was G. Z. Yeliseyev, the author of *Vnutrenniye Obozreniya* in the *Sovremennik* and the *Otechestvennye Zapiski*. As early as the very beginning of the '60s he expressed the ideas that V.V. rounded off later. See *Russkaya Zhurnalistika. I. Shestidesyatye Gody*. Edited and with a foreword by Valerian Polyansky. Published by *Akademia*, Moscow and Leningrad 1930.
81. Potresov, loc. cit., p. 544.
82. N. F. Danielson, *Ocherki Po-Reformennogo Khozyaistva*. The book appeared in 1893, but its first part – 'On the Capitalization of Agricultural Revenues' – had been printed in 1880 in the review *Slovo*.
83. Ibid., p. 346.
84. Potresov, loc. cit., p. 539.
85. Mikhailovsky, *Chto Takoye Progress?*, 1869.
86. See Martov, loc. cit., p. 46.
87. G. A. Kuklin, *Severny Soyuz Russkikh Rabochikh i Stepan Khalturin* (*1878–1882*); Geneva 1904. Also, L. Martov, *Razvitie Krupnoy Promyshlennosti i Rabocheye Dvizhenie do 1892 Goda*, in the 26th number of *Istorii Rossii V XIX Veke*, published by Br. Granat.
88. Institut Akademii Nauk SSSR. *Istoriya SSSR*, Vol. II. *Rossiya v XIX Veke*, Edited by Professor M. V. Nechkina, Moscow 1940, p. 597.
89. Plekhanov, *Russky Rabochii v Revolyutsionnom Dvizhenii*.
90. Plekhanov, *Sotsializm i Politicheskaya Bor'ba*.

91. Plekhanov, *Nashi Raznoglasiya.*
92. *Perepiska G. V. Plekhanova i P. B. Aksel'roda.* Edited and annotated by P. A. Berlin, V. S. Voitinsky and B. I. Nikolayevsky. Published by R. M. Plekhanova, Vols. I and II, Moscow 1925.
93. P. B. Akselrod, *Sotsializm i Melkaya Burzhuaziya.*
94. V. Ilyin (Lenin), *Razvitie Kapitalizma v Rossii.*
95. J. Martow (Martov), *Geschichte der russischen Sozial-demokratie.* Mit einem Nachtrag von Th. Dan: *Die Sozialdemokratie Russlands nach dem Jahre 1908.* Autorisierte Uebersetzung von Alexander Stein. Berlin 1926, J. H. W. Dietz Nachfolger, p. 14.
96. Plekhanov, *Vsyerossiickoye Rozorenie.*
97. Martov, *Zapiski Sotsialdemokrata.* Publisher Z. I. Grschebin, Berlin 1922, p. 86.
98. *Russkoye Bogatstvo* for 1894; Mikhailovsky's article *Literatura i Zhizn* in Nos. 1 and 2.
99. P. Struve, *Kriticheskiye Zametki.*
100. *Materialy k Voprosu ob Ekonomicheskom Polozhenii Rossii,* 1895.
101. N. Beltov (Plekhanov), *K Voprosu o Razvitii Monisticheskogo Vzglyada Na Istorii.* An English translation: 'In Defence of Materialism: the Development of the Monist View of History' (1947).
102. Plekhanov, *Obosnovanie Narodnichestva v Trudakh G-na Vorontsova.*
103. Martov, loc. cit.
104. Kremer, Arkady (Alexander), *Ob Agitatsii.*
105. *Novy Put'*, Russian Social-Democratic organ published in New York City, No. 14, 3 January 1942 (N.S.).
106. Akselrod, *K Voprosu o Sovremennykh Zadachakh i Taktike Russkikh Sotsialdemokratov.* Geneva, 1898, pp. 4 and 9.
107. Lenin himself noted this reference with satisfaction in an article, *Popyatnoye Napravlyenie v Russkoy Sotsialdemokratii.* This article, written in 1899, as well as the 'Draft Programme' written in gaol, was printed for the first time in 1924.
108. Martov, ibid., p. 264–5.
109. Martov, ibid., p. 316–17.
110. K. M. Takhtaryov, *Ocherk Peterburgskogo Rabochego Dvizheniya 90-kh Godov.* Petrograd, State Publishing House, 1921.
111. Plekhanov, *Eshcho Raz Sotsializm i Politicheskaya Bor'ba.*

112. Martov, ibid., p. 235.
113. *Rabocheye Delo*, No. 7, August 1900.
114. Original title, *Die Voraussetzungen des Sozialismus und die Aufgaben der Sozial-Demokratie*; English translation *Evolutionary Socialism*, by Edith C. Harvey, New York 1912.
115. Akselrod, ibid.
116. Lenin, *Zadachi Russkikh Sotsialdemokratov.*
117. Akselrod, ibid.
118. *Iskra*, No. 4, May 1901, *S Chego Nachat'?*
119. Lenin, *Pis'mo k Tovarishchu o Nashikh Organizatsionnykh Zadachakh.*
120. Martov, a pamphlet, *Bor'ba s Osadnym Polozheniyem v RSDRP*, Geneva 1904.
121. Lenin, *Druzya Naroda*, 3rd edition.
122. Lenin, *Rapport* to the *Zagranichnaya Liga* (Foreign League) Congress, which met in October 1903.
123. Plekhanov, an article, *Tsentralizm ili Bonapartizm?*, in No. 65, 1 May 1904 (N.S.), *Iskra.*
124. Lenin, *Shag Vperyod, Dva Nazad.*
125. *Iskra*, No. 53, 25 November 1903 (N.S.).
126. *Iskra*, No. 55, 15 December 1903 (N.S.).
127. *Iskra*, No. 63, 1 April 1904 (N.S.).
128. Ibid., p. 100.
129. Akselrod, *Ob'yedinenie Rossiickoy Sotsialdemokratii i yeyo Zadachi*, No. 55, *Iskra*, 15 December 1903 and No. 57, 15 January 1904.
130. First draft of the programme of the Emancipation of Labour Group, 1884.
131. A. Yegorov (Martov), *Zarozhdenie Politicheskikh Partii i ikh Deyatel'nost'*. Vol. I, *Obshchestvennoye Dvizhenie . . .* (see 1 above).
132. In a pamphlet, *Nasushchny Vopros.*
133. *Revolyutsionnaya Rossiya*, No. 7.
134. Ibid., No. 8.
135. Ibid, No. 32, an article by P. Novobrantsev.
136. Ibid, No. 46.
137. *Osvobozhdenie*, No. 25.
138. Martov, *Obshchestvennoye Dvizhenie . . .* (see 1 above).
139. *Voina i Byurokratiya*, in the review *Pravo* for 26 September 1904.
140. *Osvobozhdenie*, No. 15.

141. Ibid., No. 17.
142. Ibid., No. 33.
143. Ibid., No. 43.
144. *Listok Osvobozhdeniya*, No. 1.
145. *Osvobozhdenie*, No. 57.
146. In a pamphlet, *Istoricheskoye Polozhenie i Vzaimnoye Otnoshenie Liberal'noy i Sotsialisticheskoy Demokratii v Rossii.*
147. In the *Sbornik*, a Marxist anthology that appeared in the spring of 1895, sub-titled 'Materials for a description of our economic development'. It contained articles by Plekhanov, Lenin, Struve and others. After the anthology was published it was, in spite of having been authorized in advance, confiscated by a special decision of the Council of Ministers and burnt. The few copies that survived had great influence.
148. Martov, *Zapiski*, p. 310.
149. Ibid., p. 328.
150. Lenin, *Ot Kakogo Nasledstva My Otkazyvayemsya?*
151. In a foreword to the 1902 second edition of *Zadachi Russkikh Sotsialdemokratov.*
152. Akselrod, *K Voprosu. . . .*
153. *Vperyod*, 22 December 1904.
154. Cf., for instance, the notes of A. A. Shilov (pp. 167, 171 and others) to the book *Istoriya Moey Zhizn* ('Story of My Life'), by G. Gapon, published in 1925 by the Leningrad Workers' Publishing House *Priboy.*
155. *Iskra*, No. 62, 2 March 1904, *Tak li My Gotovimsya?*
156. *Devyatoye Yanvarya, Iskra*, No. 85, 14 January 1905.
157. Dan, *Iskra*, No. 86, 21 January 1905, *v Vodovorote Revolyutsii.*
158. Lenin, *Vperyod*, No. 7, 1 February 1905, *Dolzhny li My Organisovat' Revolyutsiyu?*
159. The leading article, *Tvyordy Kurs, Vperyod*, No. 5, 25 January 1905.
160. Lenin, *Vperyod*, No. 4, 18 January 1905, *Nachalo Revolyutsii v Rossii.*
161. Lenin, *Vperyod*, No. 8, 8 February 1905, *Otnoshenie RSDRP k Liberalam.*
162. Lenin, an article: *Goniteli Zemstva i Gannibaly Liberalizma.*
163. Martov, *Zapiski* . . . p. 331.
164. *Za 12 Let*, 1908.
165. A pamphlet, *Dve Taktiki Sotsialdemokratii v Demokraticheskoy*

Revolyutsii. It was written in June-July 1905 and printed in Geneva in August.

166. A leading article, *Vperyod*, No. 14, 30 March 1905.
167. Lenin, *Otnoshenie Sotsialdemokratii k Krestyianskomu Dvizheniyu*, quoted in the *Kratkii Kurs Istorii V.K.P.*, 1938 edition, p. 71.
168. *Proletarii*, No. 11, 27 July 1905.
169. *Ko Vsyem Partiinym Organizatsiyam i ko Vsyem Rabochim Sotsialdemokratam*, *Novaya Zhizn'*, No. 9, 10 November 1905.
170. Lenin, *Pobeda Kadetov i Zadachi Rabochey Partii*, a pamphlet written in March-April 1906.
171. P. A. Garvi, *Vospominaniya Sotsialdemokrata.* New York, 1946, p. 584.
172. Th. Dan, *Sotsialdemokratiya v Resolyutsiyakh Londonskogo Syezda.* Published by Gudok, 1907.
173. Lenin, *Sovremennoye Polozhenie Rossii i Taktika Rabochey Partii*, No. 1 (the united), *Partiinye Izvestiya*, 7 February 1906.
174. Lenin, *Rospusk Dumy i Zadachi Proletariata*, a pamphlet, July 1906.
175. Lenin, *Novaya Zhizn'*, 25 November 1905.
176. Akselrod, *Narodnaya Duma i Rabochii Syezd.*
177. Dan was the author of this 'First Platform'. The leaflet and pamphlet published by the United Central Committee contained as an official expression of the Menshevik position, his article *Pochemu My Protiv Boykota Vyborov?* and *Gosudarstvennaya Duma i Proletariat*, together with articles by Lenin explaining the Bolshevik position, e.g., *Boykotirovat' li Gosudarstvennuyu Dumu?* and *Gosudarstvennaya Duma i Sotsialdemokraticheskaya Taktika.*
178. Lenin, *Volna*, 14 May 1906.
179. Lenin, *Ekho*, No. 1, 22 June 1906.
180. Lenin, Vol. X, Collected Works, 1927 edition.
181. Cf. *Proletarskaya Revolyutsia*, No. 7, 1924, p. 175.
182. M. Balabanov and Th. Dan, *Rabochiye Deputaty v Pervoy Gosudarstvennoy Dume.* St Petersburg, 1906. Published by N. Glagolev. Balabanov was responsible for all the purely 'factual' pages, while the quotations used here are taken from chapters written by Dan.
183. Lenin, *O Boykote*, *Proletarii*, No. 1, 21 August 1906.

184. Euphemism for the 'expropriations', or armed hold-ups then being carried on by the Bolsheviks.
185. *Istoriya Kommunisticheskoy Partii. Kratkii Kurs*, 1936. Published by State Publishing House, Moscow and Leningrad, p. 137–8.
186. Lenin, quoted in a foreword to the third (1926) edition of his Collected Works, containing a reproduction of his work, 'The Development of Capitalism in Russia'.
187. Bernhard Fürst von Bülow, *Denkwürdigkeiten*. Vierter Band, p. 573. Published by Ullstein Verlag, Berlin.
188. Cf. an article by E. Tarlé, *Germanskaya Orientatsiya i P. N. Durnovo v 1914 Godu*, in No. 19 of the review *Byloye*, published in Moscow under the editorship of P. E Shchegolyov.
189. In an article in *Golos Sotsialdemokrata*.
190. *Kratkii Kurs Istorii VKP*, p. 188.
191. Ibid., p. 245.
192. A. Jugow, Russia's Economic Front for War and Peace. Harper & Bros. New York, 1942, p. 44.
193. These articles formed part of an anthology, *Mirovoy Bol'shevizm* (World Bolshevism), published in 1924 in Berlin under the editorship of Dan.

INDEX